W9-BBQ-007

Women's Issues

Ready Reference

Volume III

Psychiatry and women – Young Women's Christian Association

Indexes

A Magill Book

from the **Editors of Salem Press**

Consulting Editor
Margaret McFadden
Appalachian State University

Salem Press, Inc.
Pasadena, California   Englewood Cliffs, New Jersey

∞ The paper used in these volumes conforms to the American National Standard for Permanence of Paper for Printed Library Materials, Z39.48-1984.

Library of Congress Cataloging-in-Publication Data

Women's issues / consulting editor, Margaret McFadden
p. cm. — (Ready reference)
"A Magill book"
Includes bibliographical references and index.
ISBN 0-89356-765-5 (set : alk. paper) — ISBN 0-89356-768-x (vol 3 : alk. paper)
1. Women—Encyclopedias. 2. Feminism—Encyclopedias. 3. Women—United States—Encyclopedias.
I. McFadden, Margaret. II. Series.
HQ1115.W6425 1997
305.4'03—dc21 96-48989
CIP

First Printing

PRINTED IN THE UNITED STATES OF AMERICA

CONTENTS

ALPHABETICAL LIST OF ENTRIES

Volume I

Volume II

Volume III

Women's Issues

Psychiatry and women

RELEVANT ISSUES: Psychology, sex and gender

SIGNIFICANCE: From the start, women made substantial contributions to psychiatry, in terms of both theory and research; their accomplishments have been made despite their being viewed as having inferior personalities and weak moral development compared with men

Psychiatry is the branch of medicine that deals with mental, emotional, or behavioral disorders. Psychiatry has different theories of how personality develops, which in turn suggest different treatment modalities for personality disorders. Psychiatry developed with a bias against women, as evidenced in early views of personality development, initial theories of moral development, and the treatment of women.

Personality Development. Views on personality development, and early bias, began with Sigmund Freud (1856-1939), who proposed that women are masochistic (deriving pleasure from being mistreated) and inferior to men to the extent that they envy male genitalia. His writing is liberally sprinkled with passing references to the inferiority of women.

Freud believed that gender identity is formed for boys and girls in the phallic stage of development (ages three to six). During this normal developmental phase, a boy directs his sexual desires to the primary love object in his life, his mother. He develops the Oedipus complex, unconscious sexual desire for his mother combined with jealousy of and hatred toward his father, whom he considers a rival for her affections. Because of these feelings, the boy becomes fearful that his father will retaliate in the ultimate punishment, castration. Freud said that only boys have this fateful combination of love for the one parent and simultaneous hatred for the other as a rival. A boy copes with these threatening feelings, said Freud, by repressing them and identifying with the rival, his father. Through this identification process, boys resolve the Oedipus complex, develop a superego (conscience), and form a sense of their own gender identity.

Freud theorized less about girls than about boys, and some say that his ideas about how girls and women develop are less organized and coherent. He believed that a girl in the phallic stage of normal development goes through a parallel Electra complex, in which she develops unconscious sexual desires for her father combined with jealousy of and hatred toward her mother, whom she considers to be a rival for her father's affections.

At some point during the phallic phase, girls discover the anatomical differences between the sexes and develop penis envy because of (in Freud's terms) their insufficiency. Like boys, girls resolve their complex by identifying with their mothers. So, both boys and girls resolve the phallic stage by identifying with the same-sex parent.

Girls' fears of punishment, however, are less than those of boys, according to Freud, because they have less to lose (they have no penis). Thus, according to many early psychiatrists, girls have a superego that is weaker than that of boys. The view of Freud and early psychiatry is that girls' sense of their own physical inadequacy is the beginning of their long slide into inferiority. Freud's biologically determined view is that there is no other alternative in terms of girls' personality development.

Freud's theories about women's inferiority sparked much interest and considerable disagreement. Other early psychiatrists, such as Karen Horney (1885-1952), challenged Freud's ideas about penis envy and weak superegos for women, stating that his views on women were the result of the historical era in which he lived, in which society was prejudiced against women. Horney asserted that it is both insulting philosophy and bad science to claim, as Freud did, that half the human race is dissatisfied with the gender into which it was born. She argued that women are more likely to envy men's status in society than their genitals, and she proposed the concept of womb envy, the envy men have of women's ability to bear and nurse children. Men glorify their own genitals, Horney said, because they are unable to give birth themselves.

Horney softened the biological emphasis that Freud had placed on personality development, focusing on social and interpersonal drives and instincts. She, and other early psychiatrists, emphasized conflicts between people that foster feelings of helplessness. Her theory revolved around basic anxiety, which develops because the child feels isolated and helpless in a potentially hostile world, and basic hostility, which arises from the child's resentment over the parents'

Psychiatrist Karen Horney, who disputed Sigmund Freud's theories about childhood development. (Culver Pictures, Inc.)

indifference, inconsistency, and interference. Young children, according to Horney, discover that they are weak and small in a land of giants and soon learn that they are utterly dependent on parents for all their needs and safety. Parents who are warm, loving, and dependable create a sense of security that reassures the child and produces normal development. Children cannot express their hostility directly because they need and fear their parents, but repressing the hostility increases feelings of unworthiness and anxiety. So, in Horney's view, all children are torn between hostility toward parents and dependence on them. Neither gender is superior.

Research has produced no evidence for penis envy. In fact, most young girls are unconcerned about genital differences or relieved that they lack this (in their view) unattractive anatomical structure. Furthermore, research has failed to support Freud's assumption that young children acquire a sexual identity in one fell swoop. So Freud's ideas about the inferiority of women developed out of not only the historical bias against women which characterized his culture at that time but also his personal egocentrism in assuming that women want to be like men. Despite many who disagree with him, Freud's views are widely held and have contributed to psychiatry's prejudice against women.

A contemporary psychoanalytic therapist, Nancy Chodorow, parted company with Freud over the issue of biological determinism. She pointed out several areas of Freud's bias against women, including his beliefs that women had lesser orgasms than men; that women were all vain, jealous, and full of shame; and that women made no contribution to civilization except for weaving. Chodorow's modifications of Freudian theory included the acknowledgment that cultural socialization plays a large part in psychosexual stages of development. Furthermore, she noted that women play a larger role in socializing children than do men; thus, it is only natural that both boys and girls develop a primary dependency on their mothers.

Chodorow's feminist revision of psychoanalysis contains suggestions for changes in society's socialization practices that might lessen psychological conflict in men and women. First, she argued that both boys and girls should grow up in an environment that allows them to identify with more than one adult. Second, she recommended that boys should have masculine role models who take an active part in child care and nurturing and that girls should see feminine role models who are involved in areas of power and control.

Newer theories of personality development see neither gender as superior. Many see these changes in how psychiatry views men and women as improvements. Newer personality theorists also make suggestions for changes in child-rearing practices that would contribute to healthier personality development for both boys and girls.

Moral Development. Another area of bias in psychiatry against women is in views of moral development. Lawrence Kohlberg identified three distinct stages of moral development, stages that parallel Piaget's stages of intellectual development. In preconventional morality (stage 1), decisions are based on rules made by others. In conventional morality (stage 2), decisions are based on internalized standards derived from interactions with others. In postconventional morality (stage 3), decisions are based on one's own abstract principles about right and wrong. In Kohlberg's view of moral development, individuals mature in their moral beliefs as their thinking becomes less concrete and more focused on abstract principles, particularly the principle of justice.

In some early research testing this theory of moral development, boys tended to score at a higher level of morality than girls. Does this mean that boys have higher levels of moral development than girls? Most experts say no. Carol Gilligan pointed out that Kohlberg's theory narrowly concerns justice, a traditionally masculine focus. Also problematic is the fact that his theory was developed on an all-male sample. Thus, this initial theory of moral development was biased against women by emphasizing traditional masculine concerns with justice and by excluding women from the samples of those being evaluated.

Gilligan proposed an alternative set of three distinct periods of moral development. In preconventional morality (stage 1), decisions are based on what is helpful or harmful to oneself. In conventional morality (stage 2), decisions are based on what is helpful or harmful to others. In postconventional morality (stage 3), decisions are based on what is helpful or harmful to oneself as well as others. Gilligan's levels of morality were concerned with caring and responsibility toward others. She contended that a comprehensive theory of moral development should emphasize not only traditionally masculine concerns such as justice but also traditionally feminine concerns such as caring, compassion, and social relationships.

Notably, researchers usually find that men may be a little more likely to talk about justice and women a little more likely to talk about caring, but both sexes actually respond similarly on tests of moral reasoning. Boys and girls, men and women often use both the morality of justice and the morality of care in responding to moral dilemmas. Thus, in terms of moral reasoning, the similarities between women and men are more noteworthy than are the differences.

Furthermore, level of moral reasoning is only one way to look at moral development—and may be a poor way at that. Levels of reasoning have little or nothing to do with actual behavior. People may reason poorly yet do the right thing, or reason well yet do the wrong thing. Thus, behavior is another, perhaps better, way of looking at moral development; boys and girls and men and women show about the same levels of moral behavior.

Newer theories of moral development emphasize concern for others in addition to a concern for justice and, thus, stress both traditionally masculine and traditionally feminine concerns. In these theories, neither gender is viewed as superior to the other. Also, both sexes use both types of moral reasoning: justice and concern for others. Finally, moral reasoning has little to do with actual moral behavior.

The Treatment of Women. In addition to viewing women as personally deficient and morally inferior, early psychiatry was biased in how women were actually treated. Despite notable exceptions, such as Karen Horney and Anna Freud (1895-1982), for a long time, psychiatry as a discipline was populated almost entirely by men. Women were denied admission to prestigious schools, discouraged from seeking terminal degrees, barred from laboratories and professional societies, rejected from publication in prestigious journals for nonscientific reasons, and offered employment at levels inferior to those held by their equally qualified male counterparts. For example, Horney's career was delayed until a German university was willing to admit women to study. This early bias was part of the historical era in which psychiatry developed.

Indeed, the entire *Zeitgeist* of the Western world in the late nineteenth and early twentieth centuries was biased against women. For example, in the beginning of the twentieth century, Harvard University refused to grant a Ph.D. degree to Mary Whiton Calkins, who had completed all degree requirements. Her appeal of this decision was denied by Harvard trustees even though the famous philosopher William James described her as his brightest student. Even as recently as the 1970's, female faculty members were rare and research on gender was scarce. Thus, bias against women in early psychiatry was pervasive and pronounced.

This bias, however, is diminishing. By the 1990's, many women were active researchers, and hundreds of studies on gender and sex discrimination had been done. Women were attending medical schools in record numbers, though their professors were still predominantly men. The historical era in Western society is evolving such that women have more opportunities than in the past, and psychiatry is evolving in reflection of these changes. —*Lillian M. Range*

See also Electra and Oedipus complexes; Mental health; Psychological theories on women; Socialization of girls and young women

Bibliography

Fisher, S., and R. P. Greenberg. *The Scientific Credibility of Freud's Theories and Therapy*. New York: Basic Books, 1977. A review of research on psychoanalytic theory.

Freud, Sigmund. *A General Introduction to Psychoanalysis*. Garden City, N.J.: Garden City, 1953. This brilliantly written single volume gives a survey of the central ideas of psychoanalysis.

Gilligan, Carol. *In a Different Voice: Psychological Theory and Women's Development*. Cambridge, Mass.: Harvard University Press, 1982. Presents an interesting and controversial discussion of Gilligan's theory of moral development in women. She points out the shortcomings and bias against women in Kohlberg's theory, arguing that it was developed by and about men.

Horney, Karen. *Feminine Psychology*. Edited by Harold Kelman. New York: W. W. Norton, 1973. The paperback edition of the classic discussion of the forces that influence the development and expression of personality in women.

Intons-Peterson, M. J. *Children's Concepts of Gender*. Norwood, N.J.: Ablex, 1988. It is difficult to summarize the wealth of information on the development of gender roles, but this book is among the best available resources.

Jones, Ernest. *The Life and Work of Sigmund Freud*. New York: Basic Books, 1981. The best resource on Freud's general theories of personality is Freud himself. Jones provides, however, an interesting discussion of Freud's life as well as his lengthy writings.

Kohlberg, Lawrence. *The Psychology of Moral Development: The Nature and Validity of Moral Stages*. San Francisco: Harper & Row, 1984. This book brings together many of Kohlberg's papers on moral development.

Psychological theories on women

Relevant issues: Psychology, sex and gender

Significance: The "soft" science of psychology, born in the mid-nineteenth century, sought in various ways to deal with the highly complex study of women's roles, personalities, and responsibilities in society and culture

Gender and Psychology. Before the middle of the nineteenth century, much of the argument supporting women's "difference" and inferiority was supported by appeals to religion, philosophy, theology, and nonempirical theories of such writers as Aristotle. Woman was the imperfect human, created after man and from man. Woman was the source of the Fall; woman, said Aristotle was the lesser and imperfect being. Juvenal, a Roman satirist, declared that a virtuous woman is as rare as a white crow.

In the centuries before a science sought to explain human behavior, humans created or inherited myths to help them come to terms with other humans, to understand and attempt to control the inexplicable. Myths about the powers, motives, and special qualities of women appear in every known culture. Certain themes are dominant in cultures everywhere: the Mother Earth figure (Gaia, source of life); the enchantress or witch (Circe, the Strange Woman, Hecate); and a necessary evil, lacking reason and untrustworthy but needed for the propagation of the race (Eve or Pandora). Unless controlled by man, woman was destined to cause trouble, to go astray, or to be helpless.

Psychology, born as a science in the nineteenth century, sought to explain human behavior, including that of women. Sigmund Freud, who pioneered the formal study of human personality, spoke, as late as 1933, of femininity as being a riddle to him. One concept that had persisted to Freud's time and continued after his death was that of the virtuous woman, whose personality needs were fulfilled best by being a loving wife, a dedicated mother, a diligent homemaker, upholder of the moral and religious values of her society. Such a person had been praised by St. Augustine, who took his mother, Monnica, as an ideal; by Geoffrey Chaucer in the tale of Patient Griselda; and in the literature and ideals of courtly love, which presented the woman as ennobling her knight- errant and inspiring him to courage, honor, and courtesy. In fact, the ideal plantation mistress of the nineteenth century South hymned as pure, good, angelic, and selfless continued the tradition, which culminated in public life as the Cult of True Womanhood in middle-class America, Canada, and Great Britain.

Physicians, early in the century, taught that such a woman had little or no sex drive, responding to her husband's ardor primarily to produce heirs. Her religious piety protected the home and led wayward men to repent and fallen women to be saved. She deferred to her man in all things, never seeking to question male authority or to compete with men in higher education, in public life, or employment. For the home, she was consort, mother, nurse, comforter, and much more. Physicians and psychologists warned that a woman—frail, weak, and smaller-brained—would succumb to mania, sterility, "brain fever," and hysteria should she step from her established roles. In 1902, a study of women admitted to insane asylums showed that 40 percent (compared to 10 percent of men) were products of higher education. The conclusion was that higher education was driving women to insanity. The woman who sought to vote, study for a profession, or otherwise trespass beyond the bounds of domesticity was castigated as harridan, lesbian, or mentally unbalanced.

When psychology began to study women apart from men, most of its practitioners focused on differences in brain size, contributions to arts and other studies, and nurturing behavior—all long accepted as causes for female inferiority and now, through the theory of functionalism, seen as the natural order of things. Data showed that men were achievers, producers, inventors, leaders, and builders. The hypothesis that resulted was that men (basically Western European men) would always be found at the superior end of intelligence scales; the many exceptions, those with severe mental handicaps, were used to support another hypothesis: that of the greater power of the male brain to show either genius or madness, with the female brain capable mainly of mediocrity. Certainly, the researchers agreed, a woman could opt for brain over nature, but such a woman was unnatural, not really feminine; she would tend to be angular, muscular, abrupt in motion and strident in speech.

In these years, women were doing research in psychology, some whose studies are still major works in the field: Mary Whiton Calkins, Helen Wolley, and Mary P. Jacobi, for example. These women and others protested the sex role stereotypes presented by research in clinical and experimental psychology, the high status areas of the still-new science. Because these fields functioned in laboratories, using rats and other creatures in controlled situations, and published "objective" tables of data, they were given some of the high status accorded the hard sciences. Social psychology, the field in which studies of humans in human situations were the focus of attention, was looked upon as inferior, "soft," humanistic, and not rigidly scientific. The women and men who directed their research to social psychology had low prestige; graduate students were not encouraged to carry out research in studies of human relations.

A further hypothesis of the functionalist school was that of maternal instinct, shared with females of the mammalian species, innate and biologically determined. It naturally followed that a human female's reproductive physiology was causally related to her behavior. Because of her small sexual drive, the female also lacked self-confidence and self-esteem. Over and over again, researchers reported, women scoring high on "femininity" in written psychological tests had fewer full orgasms than women scoring high in "masculinity," in whom there was said to be a greater concentration of androgens (the male sex hormones). There was debate concerning this finding. In the 1960's, numerous books encouraged women to enjoy sex, seek sex frequently, and play assertive roles with husbands and lovers. Other popular pundits advised submissiveness and femininity. In a conference of female leaders in 1967, Richard Farson declared that "women really want to be dominated . . . they're not happier for enjoying frequent sexual relations. The trouble with educated women, sexually aggressive, is weak males."

Another school of research, behaviorism, disputed functionalist theories, proposing that behavior is a learned, not an innate quality in humans. Reaching its best known forms in the work of B. F. Skinner and Erik Erikson between the 1940's and 1970's, this area of study devoted much research to play construction among boys and girls, not only in mainstream American society but also, for Erikson, among Sioux and Athabascan tribes. Choice of toys and games was a social development, research concluded, noting that girls seem to direct their play to cooperative functions (playing house, dressing dolls), while boys choose competitive play (war games, work with pointed objects and tools). Erikson dealt particularly with the boy growing up in American society particularly in relation to his mother, who had to be not only the parent who directed the child's religious, social, and cultural life but, with increasingly long hours for many fathers in the workplace, a paternal figure as well.

A central problem with behaviorism was its concentration intensively on males, with little specific research on females, who seemed to be seen as deviant. "Women wish first and foremost to be womanly companions of men and to be mothers," remarked psychologist Bruno Bettelheim. In other words, the behaviorist hypothesis in many ways supported the earlier biological view. In fact, interest in specifically female behavior declined with most major researchers until the early 1970's—when both male and female researchers sought to move away from stereotypes and the view that woman was a deviant from the male norm—to develop, on the basis of study in social psychology, theories about the determinants of female behavior. More recent writing on psychology focusing specifically on women continues the controversy between experimentalists, who think that behavior is a physiological-biological heritage in humans (although not with the intensity once shown) and social psychologists, who emphasize the sociocultural component in the development of human behavior, with neither sex seen as deviating from a norm set by the other.

Major Figures. Sigmund Freud, most noted for his work in psychoanalysis, a form of applied psychology, grew up in a

Famed psychoanalyst Sigmund Freud with his daughter, Anna, who was a psychiatrist in her own right. (Library of Congress)

patriarchal society that clearly distinguished male and female roles: The male was destined to deal with the outer world of business, politics, professions; the female, to concentrate on the inner world of husband, children, and home. The ideal of society was male dominance; a woman, in turn, was entitled to a man's love, protection, and support.

Helene Deutsch, a student of Freud, presented modifications of his views. In 1944, she theorized that penis envy is not peculiar to women: The girl's detachment from her mother is never fully achieved, but forms the basis of feminine identification. Unlike Freud, who perceived sex differentiation as occurring toward the sixth to eighth years, Deutsch proposed that sex differentiation begins at birth. She attributed frigidity in women to several causes: failure to move from clitoral to vaginal stimulation, neurotic repression of some early sexual trauma, and social restrictions placed on feminine sexuality. Central to her theories were the personality qualities, already outlined by Freud, of narcissism, passivity, and masochism.

When directed in a healthy way, narcissism—focus on oneself—could enrich a woman's life through self-preservation and self-respect, but it could impoverish her life if it became a selfish demand for constant affirmation based on intense feelings of insecurity and inferiority. Passivity—receptive waiting and expectancy—could play a positive role in developing mature female personality in a social environment offering love and tenderness. The negative aspect would be lack of self- assurance and self-respect, leading to self-hatred and guilt complexes. Finally, masochism (not necessarily the enjoyment of cruel treatment) could in healthy development be the suffering-pleasure of such experiences of female life as menstruation, intercourse, and childbirth. The pathological masochist would seek injury, brutality from males, even death.

These three qualities, Deutsch theorized, were in delicate balance in the feminine personality. She idealized the integration of feminine personality and the mother role as model for motherhood and a satisfactory sexual and personal life. She also reinforced the theory of dual sex roles: the male predominantly intellectual and nondomestic, the world his domain; the female filling the domestic and nurturing needs of society.

In his studies of neurasthenia and hysteria, Freud wrote extensively about the unconscious motivation of behavior and the role of sexuality in human development. He hypothesized that suppressed memories, if they had a sexual basis, could produce symptoms of hysteria. His best-known thesis was the Oedipus complex, a stage of development in which children of both sexes fixate on the mother as love object and see the father as a rival. Furthermore, he theorized that the young boy, observing a girl's lack of a penis, assumed that she had been castrated for some misdeed, perhaps for seeking to challenge the father. Freud ascribed "penis envy" to the female, who assumed that she had indeed been castrated and was somehow imperfect. If she developed normally into maturity, she would transfer her love to her father, thence to a husband. If her sexual impulses were repressed, neurosis and hysteria could result. She might also develop a masculinity complex, becoming a dominant matriarch or a lesbian. The normal woman, Freud believed, would be delighted with the birth of a son, through whom she could realize the ambitions denied her as a woman. Also, since she was not under the duress exerted on male peers during growing years to compete, excel, and take risks, she would not develop a superego, the source of conscience and other traits of civilized men. She would have little sense of justice, a weak social conscience, and a weak commitment to ethical behavior; this would incline her to nurture the weak, the failures, and the immature.

These and many other theories Freud treated as theories, not proven facts or truths. For him, they needed continual testing and modification. Late in his life, realizing that superficial social changes would not overcome the unconscious power of the Oedipus complex, he recognized that a politicocultural revolution would be needed to end the patriarchal ideology. Yet, psychoanalysis continues to be an analysis of the human condition in a patriarchal society.

In their hypotheses, Deutsch and Freud (along with Erik Erikson) have two major characteristics in common: First, they give predominance to a woman's body as the determinant of her personality and behavior. Second, they evolve a double standard to explain behavior, with the male as the prototype and norm; women are assigned social roles essentially as wives and mothers and are seen as variants from the male norm.

This view of the model as male correlates with Simone de Beauvoir's observations of women's history in *Le Deuxième Sexe* (1949; *The Second Sex*, 1953) as well as with observations in other classic works on feminism and women's roles, such as Betty Friedan's *The Feminine Mystique* (1963), Kate Millett's *Sexual Politics* (1970), and Germaine Greer's *The Female Eunuch* (1971). It also plays a central role in such controversial writings as those of Camille Paglia and Susan Faludi.

In a collection of essays edited by Ellen Burman, a British-Canadian psychologist and therapist, a number of women in the field report on the problems faced by women in research on the psychology of women. Social psychology, even in the mid-1990's, lacked the prestige in the academic field held by experimental and applied psychology. Women in doctoral programs were discouraged from focusing their work on humanistic topics that are essential to understanding gender and sex roles perceived and directed by society. A few men and women have, however, been accepted as reputable scholars.

Karen Horney, as early as 1933, was highly critical of Freud's hypotheses, seriously questioning whether submissiveness, masochism, and narcissism were biologically caused. Cultural factors (environment) could reinforce such traits, which would appear in any culture. For women, these factors include the blocking of outlets for sexuality; the estimation of women as inferior; the economic dependence of women on men; the restriction of women to roles built on such emotional bonds as family and religious and charitable works; and the limiting of women's progress in business and the professions. Horney also proposed that a surplus of marriageable women could be socially directed to feel themselves threatened by lack of male partners, prey to pressures to make themselves desirable to men in wife-mother roles. In her last book, *Neurosis and Human Growth* (1950), Horney broke completely with Freudian views of the male as born to conflict and presented, instead, theories that humans could best use their energies in striving toward knowledge, the development of spiritual powers, achievement in all areas for both sexes, and full use of intellect and imagination. Social roles would be those of the individual human, not of the sex or gender.

In 1964, following closely on Horney's work, Clara Thompson presented extensive evidence that characteristics which Freud considered specifically female and biologically determined were rather to be explained as developments arising in and growing out of "Western women's historic situation of underprivilege, restriction of development, insincere attitude toward sexual nature, and social and economic dependency." Assumption of biological determinants, in other words, had reinforced social myths well in place when psychology was recognized as a reputable academic area.

Alfred Adler also broke sharply with Freudian views of women's roles. His hypothesis was that the maturing girl loses self-confidence as she experiences prejudice against women and is continually thwarted in acting out basic drives for superiority that are common to all human beings. His research noted that families in which the mother was the sole support produced daughters who were more capable and talented than those in which the mother was subordinate to the father and economically dependent on him most or all of the time. The traits that society valued, he added, were "masculine" (powerful, capable, inventive, assertive), while the "feminine" traits of obedience, subordination, nurturance, and service were less valued.

Between 1976 and the 1990's, both men and women in psychology used their research to describe women's qualities as being able to encompass the experiences and well-being of others. It was important to begin a description of women's strengths and to account for the reasons that such strengths were still going unrecognized. Furthermore, since it seemed that women were being encouraged to become like men (as if man were the only model for the psychologically mature person), researchers in the United States, Great Britain, and Canada began to look for new images and visions and to explain why women should break from traditional male limitations and make use of their particular values and qualities.

The attempt to build a new image of the full personality—male and female—means building a new way of living, on global economic, social, and political levels as well as in intimate personal relationships. Women have made great progress, but much is left to be done, as Susan Faludi's *Backlash: The Undeclared War Against American Women* (1991) so clearly argues. Women have entered and succeeded in professions in large numbers, but the glass ceiling still remains in a work setting that often seems to value conflict rather than collaboration. The majority of working women worldwide still hold the lowest-paying jobs and are often in serious economic straits.

Women's outlook has changed as a group, however, thanks to the work of recent psychological research; they are learning to value themselves and other women, not to accept the hypothesis that men are the norm and the model of human behavior.

Yet, the problem of backlash remains, as women are accused, especially in popular writings, of destroying family ties, depriving men of jobs, and being a cause of juvenile crime, drug addiction, and teen pregnancy among their children. There are still those in the scholarly community who consider the study of women's psychology to be less than serious research. Teaching often does not include reference to the large amount of new scholarship on women, and the training of mental health professionals is still seriously deficient in specific knowledge of women's personalities and problems. Nevertheless, the study of women's specific psychological development has opened up paths to better understanding of all psychological development. A study of women's personality development has begun to offer greater understanding of how interaction and support of others can enhance human growth, whether in the working world or in other areas of daily life. Problems of men's development can be seen in a new way as the close study of women's experience leads to a better description of all human experience. According to Naomi Weisstein, "Despite backlash, no longer does psychology view the female as frivolous, childlike, unable to handle male concerns, intended by providence—or biopsychology—to be a "be-ing" person unlike the male "do-ing person." *—Anne K. LeCroy*

See also *Backlash*; Electra and Oedipus complexes; *Feminine Mystique, The*; Gender differences; Insanity and women; Mental health; Psychiatry and women; *Second Sex, The*; *Sexual Politics*; Sexual stereotypes; Sexuality, women's; Stereotypes of women

BIBLIOGRAPHY

Ballou, Mary. *A Feminist Position on Mental Health*. Springfield, Ill.: 1985. Offers an overview of work by feminist researchers between 1900 and 1983.

Bird, Caroline. *Born Female*. New York: Pocket Books, 1971. A classic study of the stereotypes applied to women.

Chodorow, Nancy. *Feminism and Psychoanalytic Theory*. New Haven, Conn.: Yale University Press, 1989. Discusses in detail the work of Freud, Deutsch, and Erikson.

Ehreneich, Barbara, and Deirdre English. *For Her Own Good*. Garden City, N.Y.: Anchor Press, 1978. A detailed and interesting study of "experts'" advice to women over one hundred years.

Faludi, Susan. *Backlash: The Undeclared War Against American Women*. New York: Anchor Books, 1991. The controversial work that advised women not to take for granted the accomplishments of the women's movement.

Miller, Jean B. *Toward a New Psychology of Women*. 2d ed. Boston: Beacon Press, 1986. A readable textbook that provides background on varieties of psychological research.

Reeves, Nancy. *Womankind: Beyond the Stereotypes*. 2d ed. New York: Aldine, 1982. Although somewhat dated in its information, this text provides a good foundation for study.

Westkott, Marcia. *The Feminist Legacy of Karen Horney*. New Haven, Conn.: Yale University Press, 1986. Offers a detailed account of the life and work of one of the major scholars whose research focused on women as humans, not deviants from the male norm.

Publishing houses, women's

RELEVANT ISSUES: Literature and communications

SIGNIFICANCE: Publishing houses that specialize in feminist and/or lesbian works emerged during the women's movement of the 1960's and 1970's and shortly after the Stonewall Riot in 1969 marked the beginning of the gay rights movement

In the 1950's and early 1960's, lesbian pulp novels were published by major publishing houses. When the books stopped selling, the houses quit printing them, eliminating the outlets for such works. There had never been outlets for serious and literary feminist and lesbian works. With the women's movement of the 1960's and the gay rights movement of the 1970's, women became aware of the need for feminist and lesbian presses. Several were established to serve more than one purpose: Selling books supported not only the publishers and authors but also women's centers and bookstores, and it provided a means for social and political commentary. Women's publishing houses succeeded because they grew from a need to fight homophobia, challenge sexism, and raise people's consciousness about lesbian and feminist issues.

Of the early publishing houses, only Naiad Press, started in 1973 by Barbara Grier, still exists, but others have taken their place. Lesbian and feminist publishing has found its niche, and each company has found a niche within the niche. Naiad Press is the oldest and largest lesbian publishing company in the world and publishes every genre of fiction by, for, and about lesbians. It also has reprinted much of the pulp fiction from the 1950's, as well as the novels of Canadian writer Jane Rule. From 1973 to 1995, the company had an average growth of 17 percent per year. Other important publishing houses include Barbara Wilson's Seal Press, started in 1976 to emphasize the feminist perspective; the publishing of lesbian books evolved from its original purpose. Firebrand Books, created in 1984 by Nancy Bereano, publishes poetry as well as feminist and lesbian fiction and nonfiction. Cleis Press specializes in political books for lesbians and feminists but also publishes high-quality novels. Crossing Press, while not strictly feminist or lesbian, has a feminist series and was one of the first companies to publish lesbian and gay literature.

Approximately three dozen women's publishing houses now distribute books to women's bookstores nationwide. While many mainstream publishing houses have returned to or have started publishing feminist or lesbian books, it is the smaller houses, specializing in these books, that can give their audiences what they want.

See also Feminism; Feminism, lesbian; Feminist literary criticism; Fiction writers; Lesbian rights movement; Lesbianism; Periodicals, feminist

Quinceañeras

Queer

Relevant issues: Civil rights, politics, sex and gender

Significance: This term is used by lesbian and gay activists to suggest new ways of thinking about gender and sexuality and of acting politically in the face of increasing heterosexism and homophobia

Traditionally used as a homophobic epithet against lesbians and gay men to evoke shame and fear, the term "queer" has been transformed by gay and lesbian activists and theorists into an empowering symbol of social rebellion and political dissidence. Queer suggests whatever is at odds with the sanctioned forms of human sexuality and celebrates the full range of diverse sexualities often rejected by a heterosexist culture. The term was first used in this way in the 1980's by members of AIDS Coalition to Unleash Power (ACT-UP) and Queer Nation, whose direct-action politics attracted a younger generation of lesbian and gay activists. Although many lesbians participate in queer activism, some lesbian feminists debate the merit of using the term. Some say that it represents a false unity of women and men and collapses the experiences of women into the experiences of men. Others question whether queer activism can connect its constituents to broader demands for justice and freedom, especially in terms of racism, sexism, and classism. Although the importance of the queer concept in feminism has been debated, feminist theorists such as literary theorist Eve Sedgwick and philosopher Judith Butler have begun to utilize queer as a primary category in their exploration of gender issues.

See also Feminism, lesbian; Heterosexism; Homophobia; Lesbian and gay studies programs; Lesbian rights movement; Lesbianism

Quilting bees

Relevant issues: Arts and entertainment

Significance: First begun in the 1750's, quilting bees became an important means of socialization among women

Because space at home was limited, women often pieced their quilts individually and then gathered outside in social groups, or "bees," during the summer months, when the large quilt frames could be set up. Several women could mark a quilt, converse, teach girls quilt-making techniques, and finish the quilt in time for dinner with the men. Girls who had already learned to stitch often held their own quilting bees, a practice continued into the late nineteenth century. Quilting involved marking intricate designs on the quilt tops, placing these tops on cotton batting, and then placing a bottom sheet or fabric piece underneath. This "sandwich" was then basted, placed in a frame, and quilted by stitching along the previously marked lines. Appliqued quilts required intricate designs to be sewn or embroidered to a whole-cloth background before quilting. After dinner, the group listened to music, danced, conversed, and planned the next quilting bee. In the early nineteenth century, quilt makers used a greater variety of fabrics and techniques. The sewing machine, invented in 1845, speeded block piecing or patchwork but did not curtail the quilting bees. Among the Amish, whose quilts date from 1860, both boys and girls received dowry quilts.

In a patriarchal society with women unable to vote until 1920, quilters often displayed their political, religious, and personal beliefs in their patches. Historical names of blocks included "54-40 or Fight," "Whig's Defeat," "Martha Washington's Rose," "Dolly Madison's Workbox," "Lincoln's Platform," and "Burgoyne Surrounded." Religious blocks included "Jacob's Ladder," "Rose of Sharon," "Tree of Life," "Star of Bethlehem," and "Children of Israel." The "Road to California" block, recorded in 1890, and "Prairie Queen" commemorated the western migration. Many Civil War quilts conveyed important messages. Slave quilts preserved oral and folk traditions as well as animal and Christian symbols. The blocks of Lorraine Mills Niehus' "Oklahoma Sampler," commissioned for Representative James Inhoff's office, depict Oklahoma property seekers, the Trail of Tears, the 1893 Cherokee Strip Land Run, American Indians, and the state's lakes and flowers.

In 1933, Sears Roebuck sponsored the Sears Century of Progress in Quilt Making Contest, offering $1,200 in prize money. This contest encouraged the entry of 24,878 quilts, the largest number of entries in quilt contest history. Margaret Rogers Caden of Lexington, Kentucky, submitted the winning entry, known as the "Unknown Star Quilt." The original quilt was presented to Eleanor Roosevelt but has since been lost.

In the early 1990's, the Smithsonian Institution authorized importers to reproduce four of its nineteenth century quilts. To protest this action, quilters collected more than five hundred petitions and twenty-five thousand signatures and appeared before congressional committees. In a compromise, the quilters donated $25,000 to the Smithsonian and the National Museum of American History for quilt exhibits. One American company reproducing fabric from the collection agreed to donate part of its proceeds to support and preserve the Smithsonian's quilt collection. It has reproduced fabrics from Mary Betsy Totten's "Rising Sun Quilt" (c. 1830; 72″ × 72″), a combination eight-pointed star (with 648 diamond-shaped pieces) and appliqued quilt, and Susan Theresa Holbert's "Little Sisters Quilt" (c. m-1800's; 92″ × 95″), a diamond-shaped centerpiece surrounded by appliqued blossoms and four partridges.

See also Crafts and home arts; History of women

Quinceañeras

Relevant issues: Family, race and ethnicity

Significance: A girl celebrating her quinceañeras recognizes and assumes the responsibilities of womanhood in Latina culture

Quinceañeras, a Spanish word that can be translated as "fifteen years" or "fifteenth birthday," is a traditional rite of passage for Latina girls that can be traced to the ancient cultures of Latin America, in particular to the Aztec culture of Mexico and its forced embrace with Catholicism. The ceremony that developed and is practiced today is a combination of the passage from childhood to adulthood and an affirmation of religious faith.

The quinceañeras celebration consists of two parts, a special Mass and a party following the religious ceremony. The expense can be considerable, and some families are assisted by extended family members and friends. Because some of these relatives and friends may live far away, the quinceañeras may be postponed past the girl's actual fifteenth birthday so that the guests can attend. Months of planning are needed for the preparations. The special dress worn by the girl, usually white and resembling an ornate wedding dress, must be ordered, sometimes from a specialty store in Mexico.

The quinceañeras traditionally involves an escort for the girl and a group of peers, paired boys and girls, making up a court of honor (*corte de honor*) of attendants. The boys, or *chambelánes* (lords), wear rented tuxedos, but the girls, or *damas* (ladies), must fashion matching dresses much like bridesmaids in traditional weddings. The total number of couples may equal fifteen, one for each year celebrated. Invitations must be ordered, and food and music must be chosen for the party afterward.

Friends and relatives gather at the Catholic church where the ceremony will be performed, and the girl arrives like a bride. Final instructions and flowers are given to all in the *corte de honor*, and they enter the church, followed by the girl and her parents. Gifts may be presented to the girl by her parents, such as a necklace, rosary, and prayer book, to symbolize the continuity between the church and her family. A special Mass is said, accompanied by songs of praise and thanksgiving. At the conclusion of the Mass, the participants and onlookers may travel to the party, or the celebration may occur later in the evening. The girl may dance a special dance with her father before her escort claims her and the traditional first dance, a waltz, begins. The party may continue into the night as people dance, eat, and enjoy the celebration.

The quinceañeras has become a major social event, a coming out party for many Latina girls. One criticism of the quinceañeras ceremony is its expense for the girl's family members, who may feel pressured to provide her with a lavish ceremony and party. This concern has led in some instances to group quinceañeras, sometimes sponsored by professional Latino groups to alleviate the cost.

Some priests have refused to perform the quinceañeras Mass when confronted with candidates who lacked awareness of the religious significance of the ceremony. A requirement has been instituted in some parishes that girls desiring a quinceañeras must take special classes in Bible study, Hispanic history, quinceañeras history, and modern morals. In addition, they may be required to attend a church-sponsored retreat with their parents. Other priests believe the value of the quinceañeras ceremony in affirming cultural bonds is important enough that they will overlook deficiencies in religious preparation. For many girls undergoing the ceremony, however, it is first a social event, a recognition of their coming-of-age.

See also Christianity and women; Girlhood; Latinas; Religion; Socialization of girls and young women

Adrienne
Rich

Rabbis, women as

Relevant issues: Religious beliefs and practices

Significance: In 1983, the faculty at the Jewish Theological Seminary of America (JTSA), the seminary for Conservative Jews, voted to admit women to the rabbinical program

Reform Judaism regards the Halakah, the body of Jewish law, as a source of guidance rather than something to be followed literally, and therefore decided that the ordination of women as rabbis was permissible, given the changing status of women in general. Orthodox Judaism, on the other hand, maintains that since women have not been rabbis in the past, they will not be so in the future. For Conservative Judaism, however, the problem has been how to remain faithful to the tradition and still adapt to modern times.

The first modern female rabbi was a German-Jewish woman, Regina Jones. In 1940, she was seized by the Nazis and sent to a concentration camp, where she died. A few years later, Helen Levinthal Lyons decided to seek ordination and enrolled at the Jewish Institute of Religion in New York. In 1939, she received a master's degree in Hebrew literature but was denied ordination.

Sally J. Priesand, the first woman to be ordained as a rabbi in the United States. (UPI/Corbis-Bettman)

In the 1960's, the Jewish Institute of Religion in Cincinnati began to admit women, and, on June 2, 1972, Sally J. Priesand became the first woman ordained in the United States. Since then, the number of female students in the Reform and Reconstructionist schools constitutes about one-third of the student bodies.

Pressure soon began to mount within Conservative Judaism. In 1981, a young female rabbi, Beverly Magidson, who had been ordained by the Hebrew Union College Jewish Institute of Religion, applied for membership in the Rabbinical Assembly. After long discussion and debate, her admission was denied by four votes. In 1983, however, the faculty at JTSA voted to admit women to the rabbinical program, which meant that at the end of their studies, they would be ordained. In 1985, Amy Eilberg became the first female rabbi to be ordained in Conservative Judaism.

There are three major reasons for resistance to the ordination of women as rabbis. First, women are not obligated to observe many of the commandments in Judaism, which are required for ordination. Second, there is a question about women as witnesses in Jewish law. Traditionally, women were restricted to their homes and were not part of the world of the court or of commerce. The third reason involves the question of whether women, who were thought to have inferior intelligence, are able to fulfil the classical functions of the rabbinate, such as teaching the law and judging. In modern times, these obstacles have been overcome by all but the orthodox tradition.

See also Clergy, women as; Jewish women; Judaism and women; Religion

Racism

Relevant issues: Civil rights, race and ethnicity

Significance: As both an evaluation of human beings utilizing pseudoscientific criterion and as a constructed system of social oppression, racism has been an external and an internal influence on the history of women and women's issues

The issue of racism is derivative of the concept of race as a valid, biologically based distinction among human beings. As this belief developed as a fundamental characteristic of western expansion and was applied to the Americas, the indigenous peoples of the continent were designated by the invaders as they were expected to be: inferior human beings as compared to normal (and superior) Europeans. While this evaluation of non-European peoples included religious, cultural, and other differences, it was the nineteenth century science of Western

Europe and the United States that articulated and reified physical distinctions as synonymous with intellect and morality.

As Stephen Jay Gould chronicled in *The Mismeasurement of Man* (1976), a number of theories appeared that began with the already accepted Western belief in the superiority of European, white elite men. Consequently, the study of other human groups by race and gender proceeded to explain this qualitative difference, not to determine its accuracy. Biological determinism as expressed in observed and then quantified racial (physical) properties defined non-European peoples by such standards as brain or cranium measurement, origin of evolution, or arm and leg lengths, with all comparisons rooted in the superior-inferior dualism. When questioned about selection of subjects for investigation, one of the major practitioners of the mid-nineteenth century answered: "We surmount the problem easily by choosing, for our comparison of brains, races whose intellectual inequalities are completely clear. Thus the superiority of Europeans compared with African Negroes, American Indians, Hottentots, Australians and the Negroes of Oceania, is sufficiently certain to serve as a point of departure for the comparison of brains." (In a similar vein, Gustave Le Bon, a founder of social psychology and one of the most respected European social scientists, wrote about women in 1879 as the "most inferior forms of human evaluation . . . without doubt there exist some distinguished women, very superior to average man, but they are as exceptional as the birth of any monstrosity, as, for example, of a gorilla with two heads," and that, "consequently, we may neglect them entirely.")

At the beginning of the twentieth century, a measurement of intelligence was developed and then concentrated on what came to be labeled intelligence quotient (IQ) testing. It was not until the aftermath of World War II that this "evidence" of racial gradation and its basis were seriously challenged by a majority of those involved in such inquiry, and serious reform or attention to the use of such devices was not altered until the early 1980's. Even as the concept of race as a physical and biological reality is being repudiated by the vast majority of official scientific inquiry, racism as a social system that empowers white, European-origin people over non-European is firmly embedded and only minutely affected by the rejection of most of the scientific community. The primary groups affected by racism or white racism were (and are) African Americans, American Indians, Latinos, and Asian Americans, also referred to as people of color. (These terms, which were developed in the 1980's by non-European origin peoples in the Americas, express self-defined identity rather than relying on dominant group designations such as "minority group.")

Racism and Women. By the beginning of the European colonization of North America, the white supremacist, patriarchal, and Christian ideologies predicated what a superior, civilized, Christian nation should be and the character and roles of the women in such a society. The peoples of the Americas did not fit this configuration.

European men encountered quite different societies from Europe in the Americas. Women participated in most tribes as political leaders, religious leaders, warriors, agricultural and horticultural practitioners, and in other roles associated or designated by European patriarchy as male. Many American Indian nations were matrilineal; for example, in the League of the Iroquois, final political decisions rested with female consent. Throughout North America, the many tribes differed in their degree of female authority, but comparison of American Indian society with European society as the basis of gender would designate American Indian culture as nonpatriarchal. It is most significant that indigenous peoples included women in the center of religious and supernatural authority, unlike male-centered Christianity. These contrasts produced immediate and sustaining conflicts. Europeans, and especially European men, observed American Indian women as "beasts of burden" and "slaves" to lazy men who, except for hunting and warring ventures, were indolent, nonproductive (read "unintelligent") creatures. As Sara Evans points out in *Born for Liberty: A History of Women in America*, (1989), European missionaries were determined to convert heathens to Christianity, particularly establishing the primacy of male deity Christian and male supremacy in heaven or Christian earth, replacing female authority by patriarchy in all aspects of American Indian culture. A significant theme of the European-American Indian conflict and confrontations of the eighteenth and nineteenth centuries was the battle by Europeans for racial and patriarchal supremacy. American Indians resisted this imposition fiercely but with limited success. In the late twentieth century, however, American Indian nations began reclaiming their traditional nonpatriarchy.

The experience of African American women initially was framed and defined by the institution of slavery. The brutality and death inflicted on millions of Africans in the slave trade was exacerbated for African and then African American women by the sexual control and violence enacted by Europeans and white American slave owners. Many scholars have described the conditions of life for African American women in slavery with the labor requirements essentially no different than those for African American men, the punishments and sanctions exacted just as severe, and the family responsibilities within the controls established by slave owners. Slave women were also subjected to intense, volatile, and negative attitudes and acts by white women in slave-owning families. While clearly aware of the sexual violation by white male slave owners, these Southern white women were also distinctly privileged by their racial identity.

In the post-emancipation nineteenth century and well into the twentieth century, a dual location in the family/community and labor force produced two results. Jacqueline Jones demonstrates in *Labor of Love, Labor of Sorrow: Black Women, Work, and the Family, from Slavery to the Present* (1985) that the activities of African American women in the home and community centered around a positive locus of family feeling, which is a refuge from external white racism, whereas their presence in the labor market reinforced the subordinate racial and gender status in the United States. Again, as in the era of slavery, the link between racial and economic positions of white females depended upon control by white women over African American women. While it is clear that white men provided the economic resources for such economic leverage, it is also significant to note that racism precluded any effective bonding or formation of a biracial sisterhood. The image and stereotype of the domestic servant as an African American woman became common among women in both the South and the North.

The history of racism and Latinos poses a similar but a distinct experience. As indigenous people, Latinas also experienced a comprehensive imposition of Spanish-European religion and culture; as with other European nations, racial consciousness (although not so labeled) dominated social classification. Incorporating a foreign religion with indigenous spirituality and coping with European patriarchy and racial stratification posed several dilemmas that were severely exacerbated by what some have called the invasion and theft of Mexican land by the United States in 1848. The subsequent dispossession of Mexican land, which affected all classes in remaining support systems, forced Mexican Latinos into agricultural work while also maintaining traditional familial roles. United States immigration policies, unofficial or official from the late nineteenth century, eventually encouraged Mexican women to join their spouses in the United States, with many becoming part of the domestic workforce in the Southwest. By the mid-twentieth century, they had expanded into other areas of the marketplace, but Latinas remained in the lowest economic strata and subject to essentially unchanged ethnic or racial discrimination. Puerto Rican women experienced the historical invasion of their island, severe population reduction (as suffered by most indigenous peoples throughout the hemisphere), colonization by the United States, and, for many, subsequent migration to the mainland. The ethnic origins (African, indigenous, and Spanish) of Puerto Rican people engendered a severe racism from Eurocentric or European origin people on the mainland.

Asian American women were a limited part of the nineteenth century Asian immigration by both Chinese and Japanese design and United States immigration policy. Although control broke down in the late nineteenth and early twentieth century, the racial antipathy remained. The Asian female experience was characterized by particularly intense oppression by white labor opposition, the patriarchy of Eurocentric American society, and "normal" racial antagonism. The racially based concentration camp internment of Japanese Americans by the United States government during World War II was a particularly onerous (and distinctive) event for this group, especially for Japanese American women. Ironically, this event was also one of the first comprehensive opportunities for Asian American women of Japanese origin to be outside of their traditional Japanese family context.

This brief examination of the issues and history of racism—particularly racism directed toward women of color and structured by European invaders, colonizers, and immigrants—demonstrates the different applications of racism as governed by the origins of contact, confrontation, and subsequent racial conflict with each non-European, nonwhite community. It should be noted that the issues and status of class, religion, and sexual orientation also intersected with race and gender. The obsessive nature of racial classification and control by European Americans significantly exacerbated these other factors.

Racism and Feminism. The issue of racism within the women's movement and as a component of feminist theory was and is quite problematic. Although the participation of white women in the abolitionist movement was instrumental in developing a comprehensive perception and analysis of women's rights, and then organized action on its behalf, the content and context of its meaning was exclusive of women of color. As Angela Davis describes in *Women, Race, and Class* (1981), the racism underlying the woman suffrage movement became evident in the outcome of the struggle for the Fifteenth Amendment, which granted black male suffrage. The response by major leaders such as Elizabeth Cady Stanton and Susan B. Anthony indicated their naïveté about white racism as a system of control; some critics have called their language vehemently racist. This reaction characterizes the overall tendency of the women's movement to define the universal struggle of women in Eurocentric, middle-class terms with both conscious and unself-conscious marginalization of women of color. White middle-and upper-class women often employed women of color as domestic servants, undermining the concept of sisterhood. In the context of white supremacist patriarchy, racial location (that is, being white) established the dominant societal authority of white women over nonwhite men and women. The acceptance of the European racial value system prevailed among white women.

Elizabeth Spelman, the author of *Inessential Woman Problems of Exclusion in Feminist Thought* (1985) is one of the few important feminist scholars to depict and analyze the marginalization of women of color, which had been, until recently, a virtual exclusion. Spelman's indictment is particularly eloquent as it calls upon the work of feminists of color. As most feminists of color concluded quite early in the second wave of the women's movement in the 1960's, the centering of gender was not adequate to explain the influence of race and racism; that approach or perspective ignored the complicity by white women in sustaining racism. Bell Hooks insists that the "location" of women of color cannot be understood by a singular concept of gender; she is also quite emphatic that neither can the concept of race by a privileged explanation. Paula Giddings, the author of *When and Where I Enter . . . : The Impact of Black Women on Race and Sex in America* (1984), underscores the intersection of race and gender that separates the experience of women of color from white women and men of color. White feminist Nancie Caraway, in *Segregated Sisterhood: Racism and Politics of American Feminism* (1991), is very critical of the consistent exclusion by white feminist scholars in working with or incorporating the critique by feminists of color. She also convincingly examines the complex process required of white female feminists to listen to their female colleagues of color. Caraway and Christine Sleeter suggest that appreciating difference within women's lives is to be more concerned with political solidarity than the historical search for sisterhood.

Feminists of color describe this goal of political solidarity as bridging the chasm in the women's movement created by racism. It is a chasm initially constructed by European racism and white supremacy as imposed by male white supremacy. Hooks and Sleeter, however, further locate a strength of racism in the blindness of most white women and feminists to the rewards granted them through complicity in white racism, whether it is unconscious or not. They and others have concluded that feminism rooted in the singular presentation of gender in regard to women's history and contemporary condition is quite problematic. A more inclusive evolution must be the recognition of a matrix or intersection of race with gender as fundamental to a comprehensive feminism. *—Carl Allsup*

See also Abolitionist movement and women; African American women; American Indian women; Asian American women; Black feminism; Ethnic identity; Intelligence and achievement tests, bias in; Latinas; Multiculturism; Reverse discrimination

BIBLIOGRAPHY

Allen, Paula Gunn. *The Sacred Hoop: Recovering the Feminine in American Indian Traditions*. Boston: Beacon Press, 1986. Presents a general analysis of traditional American Indian society as nonpatriarchal and a model for European-origin feminist development.

Caraway, Nancie. *Segregated Sisterhood: Racism and Politics of American Feminism*. Knoxville: University of Tennessee Press, 1991. A comprehensive overview of the disregard and/or exclusion by white women feminists of the experience of women of color and the theoretical analysis of feminists of color.

Davis, Angela. *Women, Race, and Class*. New York: Vintage Books, 1981. Offers a concise analysis of racism and class division within the historical women's movement; includes an especially valuable examination of the post-Civil War period.

Hooks, Bell. *Feminist Theory: From Margin to Center*. Boston: South End Press, 1984. Analyzes the complex relationship of the oppressor and the oppressed by examining race, gender, and class in feminist theory.

McIntosh, Peggy. "White Privilege and Male Privilege: A Personal Account of Coming to See Correspondences Through Work in Women's Studies." In *Race, Gender, and Class: An Anthology*, edited by Margaret Anderson and Patricia Hill-Collins. Belmont, Calif.: Wadsworth, 1992. An essay on understanding white female privilege through identification of racial exclusion and dominance.

Spelman, Elizabeth. *Inessential Woman: Problems of Exclusion in Feminist Thought*. Boston: Beacon Press, 1988. One of the most incisive presentations of exclusionary practices in the development of feminist theory.

Radcliffe College

ALSO KNOWN AS: The Society for the Collegiate Instruction of Women

DATE: Founded in 1879

PLACE: Cambridge, Mass.

RELEVANT ISSUES: Education, sex and gender

SIGNIFICANCE: Founded to open Harvard University instruction to women, the college from the start provided advanced instruction at the highest level

The forerunner of Radcliffe College was the Society for the Collegiate Instruction of Women, organized in 1879 by a committee of Cambridge and Boston women. Unable to secure admittance to Harvard College for their daughters and unwilling to send them to coeducational institutions in the West, the committee resorted to indirect tactics to achieve their goal. Led by Elizabeth Cary Cabot Agassiz, widow of renowned scientist and Harvard professor Louis Agassiz, the committee arranged for members of the Harvard faculty to duplicate their courses for women able to pass the Harvard entrance examinations; the instructors would then issue certificates testifying to the successful completion of the courses.

The Society (popularly called the "Harvard Annex") slowly expanded. Formally incorporated in 1882, it purchased buildings in Cambridge for the women. In 1894, Agassiz succeeded, over bitter opposition from opponents, in convincing the Massachusetts legislature to issue a charter empowering the college to grant degrees to its students; she became the college's first president. The Harvard governing boards agreed to oversee the college; the president of Harvard would countersign the diplomas, testifying that they were equivalent to Harvard degrees. At the suggestion of President Charles Eliot of Harvard, the college was named for Lady Ann Radcliffe, the first woman to contribute funds to Harvard. The pattern of coordinate men's and women's colleges pioneered by Radcliffe College as a way of integrating women into elite male academic institutions would be emulated at Columbia University and other men's colleges.

Progress toward the full equality with Harvard men that ardent feminists wanted was slow. Although graduate level courses at Harvard were open to women after 1894, diplomas were issued by Radcliffe, and undergraduate courses were taught separately in Radcliffe buildings north of the Harvard Yard. Not until 1943, faced with empty classrooms as men went off to war, did Harvard admit women to undergraduate classes, a temporary expedient that proved permanent. It took until 1963 for Harvard to take the final step of agreeing to award Harvard degrees to women.

In the 1920's, Radcliffe joined the Seven College Conference of private women's colleges referred to colloquially as the Seven Sisters. Although it continued to maintain the reputation for academic rigor that had been one of the aims of its original organizers, the college evolved into a national institution drawing women of high social status from across the country.

The college supports a number of programs dealing with women's issues. In 1960, the Radcliffe Institute for Independent Study opened, providing women with children the opportunity to return to an academic setting to work on independent projects. No longer a teaching institution, the college sponsors many research projects dealing with women's issues. The Arthur and Elizabeth Schlesinger Library on the History of Women in America contains papers of outstanding women and provides major research facilities for the study of the role of women in American life.

See also Barnard College; Bryn Mawr College; Coeducation; Colleges, women's; Education of women; Higher education, women in; Mills College; Mount Holyoke College; Smith College; Vassar College; Wellesley College

Rand, Ayn (Feb. 2, 1905, St. Petersburg, Russia—Mar. 6, 1982, New York, N.Y.)

AREA OF ACHIEVEMENT: Literature and communications

SIGNIFICANCE: A popular novelist and militant individualist, Rand pioneered a philosophy of self-interest called objectivism

Ayn Rand was graduated from the University of Leningrad in 1924 but, unable to adjust to Communism, emigrated to the United States in 1926, becoming a naturalized citizen. She became an outspoken opponent of all forms of collectivism, touted capitalism, and believed in the victory of individualism over all forms of totalitarian government. Her philosophy is outlined in *The Virtue of Selfishness: A New Concept of Egoism* (1964). A screenwriter in Hollywood until 1949, Rand became a best-selling novelist with *The Fountainhead* (1943) and *Atlas Shrugged* (1957).

See also Academia and scholarship, women in; Fiction writers

Rankin, Jeannette (June 11, 1880, Missoula, Mont.—May 18, 1973, Carmel, Calif.)

AREAS OF ACHIEVEMENT: Peace advocacy, politics, women's history

SIGNIFICANCE: Rankin, the first woman elected to the U.S. Congress, was a lifelong peace and women's rights activist

Jeannette Rankin began working with the National American Woman Suffrage Association (NAWSA) in the West. After leading the successful fight for enfranchisement in Montana, in 1916 she became the first woman to win a seat in Congress. A progressive and a pacifist, Rankin served on the committee charged with drafting what later became the Nineteenth Amendment. In 1917, Rankin voted against U.S. entry into World War I and as a result lost the 1918 Senate race in Montana. She also faced condemnation from NAWSA leader Carrie Chapman Catt, who had urged her to support the declaration of war so that she would seem to conform to gender stereotypes.

Over the next twenty years, Rankin worked as a lobbyist and a social worker. She was active in the Women's International League for Peace and Freedom (WILPF), the National Council for the Prevention of War, and the Second International Congress of Women. In 1928, she established the Georgia Peace Society in Athens, Georgia. In 1940, Rankin again ran for Congress as a pacifist and won a seat representing Montana. Within a year, however, as the sole voice against declaring war on Japan, she once more saw political ruin.

Pacifist and politician Jeannette Rankin, c. 1918 (Culver Pictures, Inc.)

From 1942 until her death, Rankin continued lecturing and working for social issues in the United States and in Third World countries. She established a women's cooperative in Georgia and, at the age of eighty-seven, led the five thousand-woman Jeannette Rankin Brigade march on Capitol Hill protesting the Vietnam War. In 1972, she became the first woman elected to the Susan B. Anthony Hall of Fame established by the National Organization for Women (NOW).

See also Candidacy and political campaigns, women's; Catt, Carrie Chapman; Jeannette Rankin Brigade; Nineteenth Amendment; Pacifism and nonviolence; Peace movement and women; Politics; Suffrage movement and suffragists; War and women; Women's International League for Peace and Freedom (WILPF)

Rape

RELEVANT ISSUES: Crime, law, psychology, sex and gender, women's history

SIGNIFICANCE: For centuries, rape has been used to keep women afraid and dependent on men for protection; feminists have broken the silence surrounding rape and have instigated significant legal and social reforms

In 1992, the Federal Bureau of Investigation (FBI) defined forcible rape as "the carnal knowledge of a female forcibly and against her will. Assaults or attempts to commit rape by force or threat of force are also included; however, statutory rape (without force) and other sex offenses are excluded." The complexity of this definition mirrors the complexity of rape as a subject; it received significant scholarly attention only in the latter part of the twentieth century. Yet, rape has been a part of world history for thousands of years and can be found in ancient Greek myths, such as that involving Zeus and Leda. The constant presence of rape over many millennia and in diverse cultures has led many twentieth century feminists to speak of a "rape culture." They argue that modern society has been built on rape, that rape—a powerful tool for the oppression of women—has become normalized as acceptable sexual behavior.

Definitions. The word "rape" usually means sexual intercourse that occurs without the consent of the victim through force or the threat of force. What constitutes "force" is a controversial issue: Some believe that using a weapon such as a knife or a gun is the only thing that constitutes force; others argue that simply using one's size and weight advantage also constitutes force. When there is more than one assailant, the crime is called "gang rape." "Sexual assault" is a broader term covering a range of coerced behavior that includes, but is not limited to, forcible vaginal intercourse. Anal intercourse, oral sex, penetration with an object, and sexual touching and kissing that do not result in intercourse all constitute sexual assault when they occur without the consent of the victim through force or the threat of force. In many American states, having sexual relations with a person who is unable to consent because he or she is unconscious or intoxicated is also considered sexual assault. Alcohol appears as a major factor in sexual assault, but recent legal reforms forbid the use of alcohol or drugs as an excuse for rape. The aggressor bears responsibility despite alcohol or drug use.

The term "sexual abuse" usually refers to the sexual victimization of children who are not sexually mature and who participate because they are forced or manipulated. When the abuser is a parent, sibling, or other blood relative, the sexual abuse is classified as incest. Like sexual assault, sexual abuse covers a spectrum of behavior including anal sex, oral sex, sexual touching, penetration with an object, and vaginal intercourse. The definition of "force" in sexual abuse situations tends to be broader than in adult sexual assault because children lack the knowledge to make informed decisions and often lack the power to resist an adult. Therefore, the child's nonconsent is assumed even if he or she does not tell anyone about the behavior or physically resist.

Demographics and Reporting. Statistics on rape and sexual assault are difficult to compile. Because these crimes have traditionally carried a stigma for the victim that other crimes do not, only a small fraction are ever reported to the police. Victims who report sexual assaults against them often have to endure unsympathetic police and courtrooms where their behavior, rather than the behavior of the alleged perpetrator, is scrutinized. The assumption is that the victim somehow "asked for it" through her behavior or her dress. Many victims begin to believe the mistaken notion that women bring rape on themselves and therefore never tell anyone, certainly not the police. Instead, they suffer guilt, fear, and anger silently, and the scope of the problem continues to be underestimated.

In *Rape in America: A Report to the Nation* (1992), the Crime Victims Research and Treatment Center concluded that only 16 percent of rape victims file police reports. Other studies have placed the reporting percentage at 10 percent or less. These low reporting percentages cast doubt on the accuracy of the official FBI statistics on forcible rape in America. The *FBI Uniform Crime Report for the United States* (1992) reported 109,062 rapes against female victims; this translates to 90 victims per 100,000 females, an increase of 15 percent since 1988. The rape rate has also been on the rise in Canada. Thirty-seven percent of U.S. rapes occurred in the most populous Southern states, 25 percent in the Midwestern states, 24 percent in the Western states, and 14 percent in the Northeastern states. These are reported rapes; the number of unreported rapes cannot be officially tabulated.

Scholars have tried to use anonymous surveys to obtain a more accurate count of unreported sexual assaults. According to these surveys, rape occurs much more frequently than the FBI reports. Multiple studies of various sizes have concurred

The Age of Rape Victims When the Crime Occurred

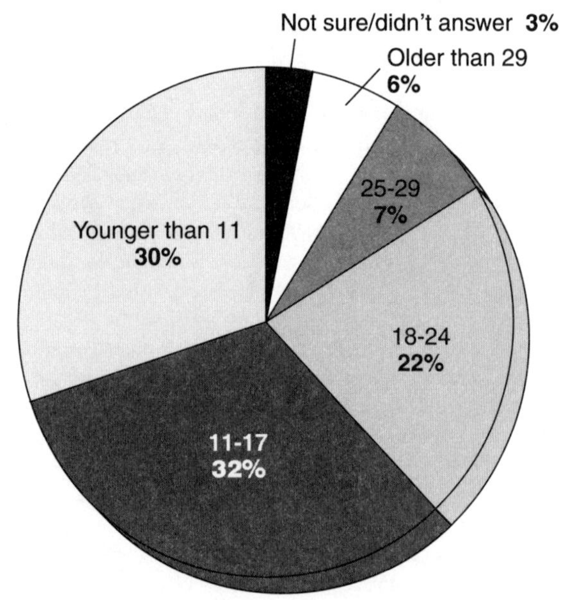

Source: National Victim Center

PERPETRATORS OF REPORTED RAPES

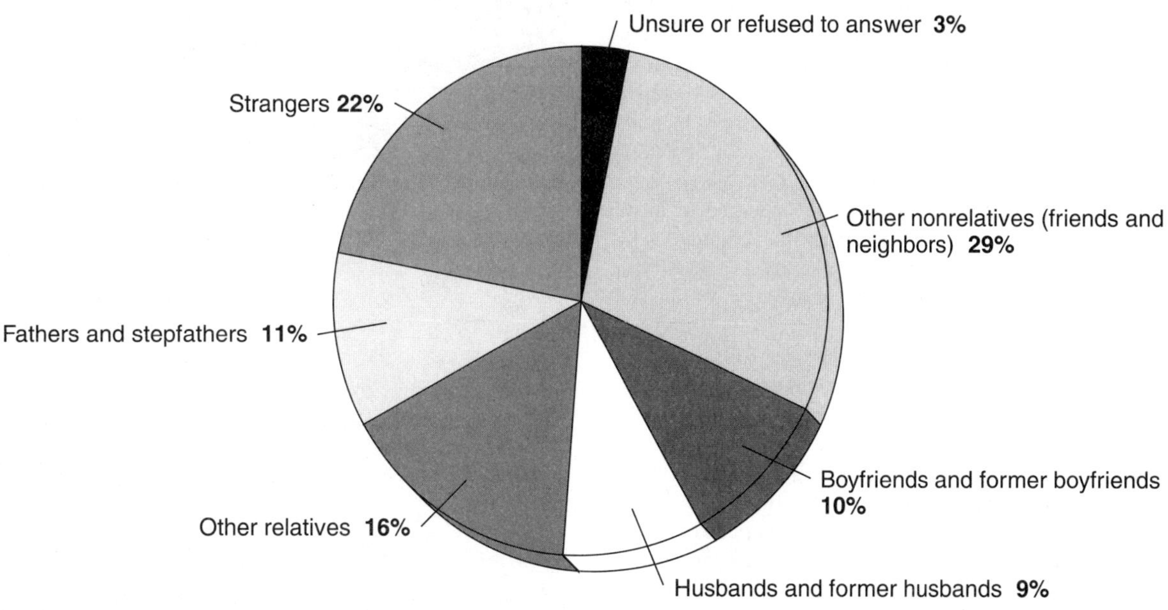

Source: National Victim Center

that a more precise representation of the actual sexual assault rate is 25 percent, or one in four women. The estimated sexual assault rate among men is high as well, ranging from 10 percent to 16 percent. Men commit an overwhelming percentage of the rapes against both male and female victims. Men who are raped report at an even lower percentage than do women, perhaps because of societal beliefs that men should be able to fight off attackers and because of serious stigmas associated with homosexuality.

Contrary to popular belief, most rapes occur between people who know each other. A woman is much more likely to be raped by someone she knows than by a stranger. Stranger rape, which constitutes about 20 percent of all rapes, tends to draw the most media attention because it plays on public fears of crime and vulnerability. Women are advised not to go out alone at night, always to lock their doors, and to avoid secluded and poorly lit places. Although these are sensible precautions, they do not speak to the 80 percent of rapes that occur between people who know each other. The victim and perpetrator may be family members, spouses, or lovers, or they may be acquainted as neighbors, colleagues, friends, or classmates. According to the statistics, women have more to fear from men they know and perhaps trust than they do from strangers.

The FBI reports that 30 percent of arrested rapists are between the ages of eighteen and twenty-four. In "Hidden Rape" (1988), Mary Koss cited Bureau of Justice statistics to show that women from the same age group—eighteen to twenty-four—are at four times the risk of being raped than are women in other age cohorts. The rate of victimization peaks between the ages of sixteen and nineteen for females. Only one in one hundred rapists is sentenced to more than one year in jail. Given that the reporting rate for rape and sexual assault is so low, many rapists never enter the criminal justice system.

Rape Culture. Given the alarming statistics on the prevalence of rape, many feminist and human rights organizations have sought to understand its causes in an effort to reduce sexual assault. Although people think of rapists as criminal social deviants, Ilsa Lottes argued that most rapists are not very different from other men. Rape, Lottes claimed, is a logical extension of patriarchal ideology that degrades women and legitimizes sexual assault. Her argument suggests that men have internalized a societal message that violence against women is acceptable because women matter less than men and should be submissive to men's authority and will. This message is conveyed in multiple ways: the socialization of young children according to gender roles; media depictions of male sexuality, female sexuality, and rape; and the myths that circulate about sexual assault, its victims, and its perpetrators. Because almost all perpetrators of sexual assault are male, feminists wonder if society gives young boys the message that violence, and specifically violence against women, is acceptable. Similarly, they question whether women receive a message encouraging them to think of sexual assault as unimportant and not worth reporting despite the emotional and physical trauma it causes. The concern is that boys and girls are taught to value different emotions and behaviors. Boys learn that rough play is acceptable, that men should not display emotion readily, and that aggressive behavior qualifies them for leadership—a good quality. Girls learn that they should be well mannered and subdued, that they should think of others and sympathize with them, and that aggressive behavior is unladylike and inappropriate. These different socializations facilitate sexual assault in that some males (the overwhelming percentage of perpetrators) feel they have the right to force themselves sexually on women, and some women (the overwhelming majority of victims) feel that they cannot resist physically or call attention to what has happened to them. Many rape activists try to resist or reverse this conditioning by calling women who have been raped "survivors" rather than "victims," in tribute to their strength and endurance during and after the rape.

Popular depictions of male and female sexuality aggravate the problem. Films and television are full of images of violence, particularly violence against women. Some scholars speculate that viewers, male and female alike, become desensitized to violence against women and begin to see it as "normal." More subtly, romance as depicted in films or on television often has an undercurrent of violence that serves, presumably, to heighten the passion. On-screen lovers may begin their romance by bickering and fighting, the assumption being that love and hate are closely connected and that eventually the combatants will realize their love and desire for one another. Scarlett O'Hara and Rhett Butler from the 1939 film version of Margaret Mitchell's novel *Gone with the Wind* are one famous example. Although these on-screen romances usually end happily, viewers can come away with the message that if a woman resists sexual activity, she only needs to be persuaded with a little more force. In the simplest terms, men may grow up believing that "no" does not mean "no" where sexual activity is concerned, that women who resist them do so out of modesty but deep down want to have sexual intercourse. Such men may falsely interpret a woman's resistance as sexual foreplay.

Several myths about rape support the faulty logic of this belief. Because rape is a crime of sexual violence, many assume that it arises from overwhelming, uncontrollable sexual desire. The rapist, proponents of this myth argue, seeing an attractive woman, feels that he must have intercourse with her and therefore rapes her. In fact, rape does not primarily spring from sexual desire but from the desire for power and control. Rapists use forced sexual intercourse as a means to assert power over individual women and sometimes over women as a group. In "The Art of Interrogating Rapists" (1995), William F. Merrill asserts that rapists tend to have traditional and conservative views of women and that they feel threatened by the gains that women made in the late twentieth century. Rapists, writes Merrill, "view rape as a way to remain dominant over women."

The myth that rape springs from sexual desire leads directly to the myth that women can bring rape on themselves by dressing or acting provocatively. In the wake of a reported rape that receives any publicity, people will often comment on

A young woman proclaims her status as a rape survivor—not a victim—in a Take Back the Night march. (Mikki Ferrill)

what the victim was wearing or doing at the time of the attack. This approach assigns blame to both parties rather than to the rapist alone. Until the 1970's and 1980's, when all American states passed rape shield laws to protect the victim, which disallowed the victim's sexual history or personal behavior from being used against her, this sort of evidence could be used against the victim in a court of law. Even though the victim was not on trial, the defense lawyer could attempt to cast doubt on the accuracy of her testimony by damaging her reputation and implying that she was sexually promiscuous and therefore could not have been raped. Although this kind of strategy is no longer allowed in courtrooms, it continues informally at all levels. Women who do report rapes, whether to the police or to family and friends, often have to endure blaming statements and tend to internalize this blame and feel responsible for the crime. In truth, a woman's behavior or clothing does not cause her to be raped, and rape victims bear no responsibility for the violence committed against them.

Legal History. Although rape law in North America has undergone significant changes since the 1970's, the legal history of rape is as ancient as rape itself. Susan Brownmiller cited ancient Hebrew laws that differentiated between rape occurring inside and outside the city gates. If it occurred outside, only the rapist was executed because, presumably, no one could have heard the victim's cries for help. Inside the city gates, however, the lawmakers assumed that cries for help could have been heard and answered, and therefore both the rapist and the victim were stoned to death. Rape has also existed in the context of war as long as wars have been waged, argues Brownmiller. The rape of a conquered people's women has been and continues to be among the victor's spoils, despite human rights laws of the late twentieth century.

Until the twentieth century, women were considered the property of their fathers until marriage and of their husbands after that. Fathers received a bride price for their daughters, and their virginity was exceedingly important. Rape, therefore, was a crime against another man's property rather than a violation of a woman's human rights; a rapist might have to pay restitution to the victim's family for diminishing her value on the marriage market. For married women, the distinction between forcible sexual assault and consensual adultery was often not made, so that a victim of rape might be punished as an adulterer. The rape of white women, when reported, almost certainly resulted in shame and a diminished reputation, at the very least, for the victim. Like their twentieth century counterparts, many rape victims probably kept this information to themselves.

For black slave women in the United States before the Emancipation Proclamation, the situation was even worse. Slave women lacked even the right to marry; they were the property of their masters, as were any children they might produce. It was therefore in their master's best interest for them to reproduce, and the white masters often resorted to rape both to exercise their power and to impregnate the slave women. Slave women had no legal recourse in these situations because they belonged to their masters and the masters could dispose of their "property" as they chose. Many slave women devised methods of resistance, however, including running away, hiding, or threatening to tell the master's wife. Any resistance could lead to whipping, sale, or death. Slave women also experienced rape at the hands of slave men who believed that they had no other avenue to power. After the Civil War, when whites could no longer "own" black people, whites still used rape as a weapon of control against black men and women. Well into the twentieth century, racist white men would claim that a black man had raped a white woman as an excuse to lynch him. These claims were rarely true, but the murder of a black man was not likely to lead to the conviction of a white man. Similarly, the rape of a black woman by a white man would not be taken nearly as seriously by the legal system as the reverse situation; many argue that this double standard still exists.

When the United States began writing its laws in the eighteenth century, the young country relied heavily on British common law, which defined rape as carnal knowledge of a woman by force and against her will. Given the nature of rape—the fact that there are seldom witnesses, that it is one person's word against the other's—early lawmakers worried that women might make false reports of rape in high numbers. This fear continued into the mid-1990's even though FBI statistics show that less than 2 percent of reported rapes are fabricated, and even though rape is widely underreported rather than overreported. In order to ensure against false reports, eighteenth century jurists introduced several safeguards: They required corroborating evidence besides the victim's testimony, required evidence of overt physical resistance by the victim to prove her nonconsent, and allowed the victim's sexual conduct prior to the rape to be admitted as evidence. These safeguards arose from the myth that rape was a sexual situation that had gotten out of hand rather than a violent crime, and jurists placed an unfair burden on the victim in the courtroom. The laws written in the eighteenth century remained on the books, virtually unchanged, into the second half of the twentieth century. Canadian law differed little from American law, except that it showed slightly greater latitude about nonconsent, allowing that a victim might consent in order to avoid bodily harm. Both Canadian and American law assumed that a husband could not rape his wife.

The second wave of the feminist movement (particularly its radical wing) was instrumental in demanding and enacting legal reform in the United States and Canada beginning in the 1970's. These activists argued that the standards of proof were extreme and discouraged victims from reporting rapes. They also understood that merely because a woman does not resist rape to the fullest extent does not mean that she consents. Instead, a woman may submit to a rapist because she believes he will kill her if she fights back, or she may submit to protect the lives of others or because the rapist has economic power over her. Feminist activists sought changes in the law, including the abolition of special jury instructions in rape cases and an end to the admissibility of victim conduct. They also sought a shift from the term "rape" to the broader "sexual assault" or "criminal sexual conduct" because these terms would allow for crimes other than forced vaginal intercourse and would also enable male victims to prosecute their attackers. These activists hoped to rewrite the law so that fewer cases would be disqualified and more could be successfully prosecuted. At the same time, feminists were opening rape crisis centers across the United States and Canada to provide better services to victims.

According to Mary Ann Largen, feminist activists had the most success in enacting rape shield laws. Although this provision met vigorous opposition, it was eventually adopted by every state. More gradually, reform advocates had prompt reporting requirements repealed as well as the requirements for independent corroboration of the victim's statement. Cautionary jury instructions slowly disappeared. The efforts to lower standards of resistance the victim must display have met with mixed success; many states have lowered these standards, but few have abolished them altogether. It is a crime for a husband to rape his wife in most, but not all, states. As Largen put it, most states grappled with the conceptual leap required to view rape as violent crime rather than "illicit sex." Rape law reformers still have work to do; even when better laws are on the books, law enforcement officials, judges, and juries sometimes still revert to the old, victim-blaming ways.

The 103d U.S. Congress enacted the Violence Against Women Act of 1994 as part of a broader crime bill. This act recognizes the shortcomings of the justice system in combating violence against women and makes a commitment to change. The act appropriates increasingly large amounts of money to improving criminal justice response to sexual assault and domestic violence. It particularly targets improved training for law enforcement officers, improved prosecution policies, better services for victims, more comprehensive stalking laws, and a higher level of service to American Indian women. The Canadian province of British Columbia has a Ministry of Women's Equality, a free-standing ministry that cooperates with other ministries in policy initiatives, including stopping the violence against Canadian women.

Prominent Figures. Women have always led the fight to end rape, sometimes in response to their own experiences. Ida B. Wells-Barnett provided leadership in the fight against the lynching of black men in the South in the first decades of the twentieth century. These lynchings were usually "justified" by claiming that the victim had raped a white woman. Many of the other heroines of the rape crisis movement came from the second wave of feminism, particularly from the radical wing. Susan Brownmiller published *Against Our Will: Men, Women, and Rape*, a definitive history and analysis of rape, in 1976, as the feminist movement was creating community-based rape crisis centers throughout the United States and Canada. These centers, located in communities of all sizes, have done a remarkable job of changing public attitudes about rape in less than three decades. Rape crisis centers typically offer counseling, emotional support, legal advocacy, support groups, twenty-four-hour hot lines, medical assistance, and referral at little or no cost to the rape victims. Many also train volunteers as speakers to educate the community about rape and offer self-defense classes. The founders and staffers of these centers, whose names go largely unrecognized, have themselves been leaders and have provided help and support to countless women throughout the years.

Several other feminist scholars have also brought national attention to sexual assault. Bell Hooks's book *Ain't I a Woman* (1981) brought detailed attention to the plight of enslaved black women in America who endured rape at their masters' hands. Diana Russell has written several volumes on sexual assault, including a book-length study of marital rape. Her work has been notable for its extensive interviews with victims. Mary Koss conducted a survey of rape on college campuses for *Ms.* magazine that was written up in *I Never Called It Rape* (1988), by Robin Warshaw. The survey and the book present compelling evidence about the prevalence of sexual assault on college campuses and the magnitude of the problem. Ellen Bass and Laura Davis, coauthors of *The Courage to Heal* (1988), deserve special recognition for the impact their book has had on adult survivors of childhood sexual abuse. It has been the virtual bible of the recovery movement.

Impact on Women. Rape affects all women—not only its direct victims—because the fear of rape is so pervasive that women alter their behavior in response. It has proven an effective tool throughout history for keeping women submissive. Victims of rape and sexual assault experience problems, including overwhelming anger, depression, difficulty with sexual relations, and post-traumatic stress disorder. Because so few of those women speak out about their experiences, however, people continue to treat rape as an individual rather than a societal problem. Although the outlook for helping rape victims has improved significantly in the late twentieth century, much remains to be done to eliminate rape altogether.

—*Donna Eileen Lisker*

See also *Against Our Will*; Brownmiller, Susan; Date rape; Domestic violence; Hate crimes against women; Incest; Marital rape; Rape crisis centers; Rape trauma syndrome; Rape victims, treatment of; Sexual harassment; Violence against women; Violence Against Women Act of 1994

Bibliography

Brownmiller, Susan. *Against Our Will: Men, Women, and Rape*. New York: Bantam Books, 1976. The landmark book in the history of rape scholarship.

Buchwald, Emilie, Pamela Fletcher, and Martha Roth. *Transforming a Rape Culture*. Minneapolis: Milkweed Editions, 1993. A diverse guide to activism and strategies for change.

Burgess, Ann Wolber, ed. *Rape and Sexual Assault II*. New York: Garland, 1988. A useful overview containing articles by Mary Koss on "Hidden Rape," Mary Ann Largen on legal reform, and Ilsa Lottes on sexual socialization.

Merrill, William F. "The Art of Interrogating Rapists." *FBI Law Enforcement Bulletin* 64, no. 1 (January, 1995): 8-12. An article from the law officer's point of view that distinguishes between different types of rapists.

Russell, Diana E. H. *The Politics of Rape*. New York: Stein & Day, 1975. A powerful book that lets rape victims speak out about their experiences at length.

Warshaw, Robin. *I Never Called It Rape*. New York: Harper & Row, 1988. A thorough and convincing study of acquaintance rape.

Rape crisis centers

Relevant issues: Crime, health and medicine, law

Significance: Rape crisis centers provide advocacy and counseling services to the victims of rape and to their family and friends

Rape crisis centers originated during the resurgence of feminist activism in the 1970's. Women began to share openly the previously hidden reality of sexual violence in consciousness-raising groups and were angered by the horrendous treatment of rape victims by legal and medical personnel. Starting in 1971, women across the United States began to create organizations to address these problems. Today, rape crisis centers or similar organizations are found in most cities and many rural areas of the United States and many other countries. In the United States, services typically include telephone crisis lines that offer immediate confidential counseling to victims, information and referrals to other services, and support to people close to victims. Additionally, an advocate will accompany the victim to the hospital emergency room and to the police station if she chooses to make a report. If a rape case goes to trial, many rape crisis centers will provide an advocate for the victim, who often has little say in how a case is handled. Rape crisis centers also provide community education about rape prevention.

Some rape crisis centers are independent, nonprofit organizations, while others are programs within larger institutions, such as Young Women's Christian Association (YWCA) centers, hospitals, community organizations, and victim-witness programs. Many rely on trained volunteers for peer counseling, following the feminist ideal of women helping one another. Others use professional staffs not only for managing the work but also for such direct services as counseling.

See also Date rape; Incest; Marital rape; Rape; Rape trauma syndrome; Rape victims, treatment of; Violence against women; Young Women's Christian Association (YWCA)

Rape trauma syndrome

Relevant issues: Crime, psychology, sex and gender

Significance: This syndrome describes the various mental, physical, and emotional aftereffects experienced by rape victims, thus legitimizing the depth and severity of rape trauma

Rape trauma syndrome is a form of post-traumatic stress disorder, which was identified as a psychological disorder in 1980. Rape trauma syndrome, which is recognized as common among rape survivors, is characterized by depression, loss of self-esteem, self-loathing, sleep and eating disturbances, and suicidal ideations. Ironically, this syndrome is more prevalent and more pronounced in women who fail to identify their experience as rape, especially young women. Sexual violence is seen as normal, acceptable, and expected by many women, as well as by men who believe that a woman is always responsible for a man's physical arousal. In such a rape-supportive environment, the fear of being blamed for their own victimization leaves many women unwilling to file crime reports against their attackers. This inaction furthers the victim's sense of guilt and shame and often enhances her feelings of defilement, isolation, and helplessness. The recognition of rape as a violent crime that carries with it the same trauma as other violent assaults has led to the establishment of rape crisis centers. The aim of these centers is to provide the rape survivor with psychological, legal, and medical attention in a sympathetic, women-oriented atmosphere. This attention is seen as vital in helping to lessen the aftereffects of rape and to allow rape victims to make a full emotional recovery from their trauma.

See also Date rape; Depression and women; Eating disorders; Incest; Marital rape; Rape; Rape crisis centers; Rape victims, treatment of; Self-esteem, women's; Sexual stereotypes; Violence against women

The Psychological Effects of Rape: Mental Health Problems Among Victims

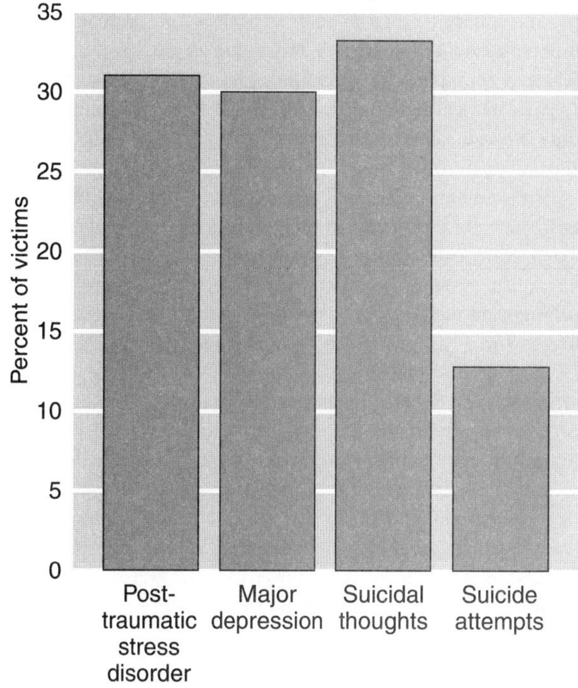

Source: National Victim Center

Rape victims, treatment of

Relevant issues: Crime, health and medicine, law

Significance: Improvements have been achieved in the treatment of rape victims since the 1970's, but women are still often treated with suspicion and blamed for being assaulted

Feminists argue that rape is a violent and traumatic crime whose victims deserve treatment designed to turn them into survivors. Although this perspective has gained acceptance, notions of the "worthy victim" still permeate society. Persistent sexist stereotypes about women, men, and rape, as well as racism and classism, lead to vulnerable women (particularly the poor, women of color, and prostitutes) being treated badly by some law enforcement and medical personnel.

Two mainstream institutions handle rape victims: hospitals and the criminal justice system. In the past, rape victims often sat in emergency rooms for hours before being examined and treated, and many feminists characterized the medical examination as a "second rape." Consequently, one of the first services offered by rape crisis centers was accompaniment to the hospital. Now, many emergency rooms in the United States have trained staff to treat rape victims respectfully and with sensitivity to the trauma that they have experienced. Standardized medical examinations in some states facilitate good evidence collection of semen, hair, skin, and fiber, as well as the documentation of injuries such as bruises. Unfortunately, the process of collecting these items is psychologically invasive (for example, plucking pubic hairs for comparison), and the specific evidence is often not used because so few cases go to trial. Nevertheless, law enforcement officials consider the results of the examination as central to their decision to prosecute.

Beginning in the 1970's, legal reforms have attempted to mitigate some of the traditional unfairness to rape victims. For example, rape shield laws are intended to protect victims from having their sexual history used in a rape case. Many police officers and prosecutors receive sensitivity training that challenges the myth that women often make false accusations. Despite these reforms, research has shown little change in how sexual assault cases are handled. For example, recognition of acquaintance rape has not translated into increased prosecution and conviction. In the criminal justice system, the rape victim is simply a witness to the crime who has little power to determine whether a prosecution takes place. Police are the front line in deciding how seriously to take a rape report. Some groups of women are not believed if they report a sexual assault. For example, women of color are often suspected of being prostitutes or drug users. Even if police and prosecutors believe the victim, they are often reluctant to prosecute if they think that the defense could discredit the victim. Most cases are closed before they come to trial, through either rejection or plea bargaining.

Public debate has arisen about revealing the names of rape victims in the mass media. Because rape still carries a stigma, many argue that victims' names should remain confidential. Others argue that publicity will help to remove the stigma by treating rape victims like other crime victims. Those who see confidentiality as an important protection for a rape victim believe that publishing that woman's name, even with consent, puts pressure on other victims to reveal their names. These critics question whether the rape victim realizes the nature of the scrutiny that public disclosure may precipitate.

See also Date rape; Incest; Marital rape; Rape; Rape crisis centers; Rape trauma syndrome; Violence against women

Red Cross and women

Relevant issues: Health and medicine, war and the military

Significance: Women in the Red Cross have established themselves in careers as nurses and leaders in community organizations to aid minorities, disabled persons, and youth

A nonprofit, volunteer organization, the American Red Cross had its origins in the International Red Cross and the League of Red Cross Societies, which operated under the Geneva Treaty of 1864. Its purpose was to aid wounded soldiers during wartime. This tradition was continued when the American Red Cross was founded by Clara Barton (1821-1912).

Although lacking in professional training, Barton volunteered to tend to the wounded in the U.S. Sanitary Commission during the Civil War. She bandaged soldiers on the battlefield amid shelling and was named superintendent of the Department of Nurses for the Union Army in 1865. A year later, she assisted in locating missing soldiers, identifying the dead, and marking graves. She earned the names of "Angel of the Battlefield" and "American Nightingale."

After the Civil War, Barton persuaded the American government to ratify the Geneva Treaty, and the American Association for the Red Cross was founded on May 21, 1881, with Barton as president. Under a flag of neutrality, the association brought relief at home and overseas to victims of forest fires, hurricanes, and floods by setting up shelters and food distribution centers.

After 1898, the Red Cross split into two factions between Barton and socialite Mabel Thorp Boardman. Boardman wanted reorganization, and the dispute brought about Barton's resignation from the Red Cross. Boardman opened an office in Washington, D.C. After the San Francisco earthquake of 1906, the Red Cross became more aggressive in its approach to aid.

The workings of a true nursing service began with Jane Delano, superintendent of the Army Nurse Corps. Delano started a program for nursing in 1909; her programs were instrumental in fighting communicable diseases and also enabled many women to enroll in nursing programs. By World War I, eight thousand nurses had become members of the Red Cross. The organization gained significance as President Woodrow Wilson formed a war council to run the organization. About eighteen hundred black nurses were certified by the American Red Cross for duty with the military. Because of racism, however, their services were not utilized until the influenza epidemic of 1918-1919. After the war, American Red Cross workers aided European refugees. By 1941, a blood services program was begun. Volunteer services increased again during World War II; there was a marked increase in first-aid course enrollment and blood donor centers doubled and tripled their output.

Women have become an integral part of the Red Cross expansion, which has opened up many careers and opportunities for them all over the world. Canadian women have also been active in the Red Cross and as registered nurse volunteers have taught basic nursing skills by calling on homes in remote areas. The establishment of the Sickroom Equipment Loan Service provided free use of sickroom supplies. The American Red Cross has filled the gaps in communication and gone where emergency help is needed. In the 1990's, an educational program was in effect to educate the public about the dangers of acquired immunodeficiency syndrome (AIDS).

See also Barton, Clara; Benevolent organizations; Health and medicine; Nurses, women as; War and women

Reed v. Reed

Date: Decided on November 22, 1971

Relevant issues: Family, law, sex and gender

Significance: States can use this decision to support the contention that the U.S. Supreme Court has accepted sex-based discrimination as long as it is reasonably related to a legitimate state interest

The case of *Reed v. Reed* began when the separated parents of a deceased minor each sought to be appointed administrator of his estate. The probate court ruled that because of an applicable state statute, a man must be given mandatory preference over an equally qualified woman. The decedent's mother appealed to the district court, which treated the case as a constitutional attack on the state statute. The district court concluded that the applicable state statute violated the equal protection clause of the Fourteenth Amendment and was therefore invalid.

The father appealed the district court decision, and the case subsequently went to the Supreme Court. The Court held that the preference favoring men violated the Fourteenth Amendment prohibiting a state from denying the equal protection of the law to any individual within the state's jurisdiction. Nevertheless, the Court noted that the equal protection clause does not prohibit states from treating different classes of people in different ways, as long as that different treatment is reasonable and not arbitrary. By condoning this passive standard of equal protection review, the Supreme Court granted the states broad discretion as to the treatment of women's rights. Thus, the Court refused to expand the scope of the equal protection clause to prohibit gender-based discrimination.

See also Antidiscrimination laws; Fourteenth and Fifteenth Amendments; Gender-neutral legislation and gender-based laws; Supreme Court rulings on discrimination against women

Religion

Relevant issues: Religious beliefs and practices, women's history

Significance: Many feminists argue that human lives are religious, whether or not they are bound to institutions, and that religious lives are gendered, whether or not one is aware of the relationship between gender and the sacred

Religion defines women; it is the matrix in which women have been described, challenged, or celebrated. Religious language and practice inform other aspects of culture; thus, as women are perceived, controlled, or extolled religiously, so they will be affected in other cultural arenas, and so they will derive their understanding of themselves. Conversely, women define religion. That is, the ways in which women are described by a tradition indicate the very contours of that religion. (Gender defines religion, but gender language is dominated by the "problematic" terms for women rather than the normative terms for men.) Woman is a learned concept rather than a biological given; thus, the ways in which woman is described, or the ways women act out their lives, expose the primary elements of a religion or worldview. This reciprocal relationship between gender and religion, however, has been largely unacknowledged in mainstream culture except for various movements in women's action and human rights and, until the 1970's forward, when the discipline of women's studies began to mature and influence other academic fields.

Categories for Analysis. Religion is a notoriously troublesome word to define. Does the term "religion" refer to historically, politically, and generationally sustained groups? Does it refer to private impulses that are philosophical or psychological? Is religion primarily in social relationships and organization or in the encounter with the divine? Does religion focus on human responses to birth and death as well as on dramatic changes in consciousness? Does it encompass attitudes toward preparing and receiving food as much as attitudes toward the uncanny? Religion defies definition because it is not necessarily a separate category of experience but, rather, a quality that pervades any category of experience. The term "worldview" may be more useful than the term "religion" because worldview reminds one that religion enhances and interprets everyday life as well as special phenomena. The term "worldview" may also be more suitable when studying various cultures or individual lives. Indeed, when religion is defined inclusively, as worldview, rather than exclusively, as, for instance, a particular historical institution, then women are immediately more visible in the patterns of religion. The catch and the key is that the category and characteristics of woman are defined by a worldview.

Defining women may be as elusive as defining religion. Typically, religions or worldviews present a concept of women that they hold to be universal—that is, naturally or even supernaturally designed. This universalizing concept is called essentialism, which claims that cultural phenomena are (or are not) natural, or that gender habits and customs are destined, or that they are rational, or that society is bound to reflect divine order. The essentialisms, or assumptions about the nature of things, are crucial to explore in order to understand any tradition but treacherous for the scholar who might unwittingly apply his or her own essentialism to the subject. For example, a tradition may claim "woman's place is in the home," but a scholar claiming "women's greater roles have been as mothers" will be exercising his or her own biases. Traditions express their values in essentialist language; investigators of those traditions must avoid imposing their own essentialist values or assumptions about the way things are.

When one uses the terms "women" and "religion," does one mean the participation of women within religious institutions; female leaders, innovators, or reformers in the history of religions; or feminine metaphors and images in sacred traditions? All three of these categories—female participants, female leaders, and feminine metaphors—are necessary elements of investigation, and each overlaps and influences one's understanding of woman as "the other."

Innovators and Reformers. Religion in the Americas has been most noteworthy for its pluralism and innovations. The national histories of the United States and Canada are profoundly interwoven in the histories of religious movements, shifting institutions, and reform convictions. Women appear more frequently as leaders in new religions in contrast to culturally secure traditions that, until generally late in the twentieth century, tend to reflect the patriarchal standards of the dominant culture by denying women priestly or pastoral roles. The Roman Catholic church, although denying women the rights and responsibilities of priesthood, is thoroughly supported by female leadership in monastic, social reform, educational, and worship groups. The governing hierarchy is exclusively male, whereas local parishes are likely to be sustained by often unrecognized female efforts. The Episcopal church, deriving from the Church of England in the sixteenth century, ordained its first female priest in 1976; Judaism acknowledged its first female rabbi in 1972.

Numerous sects that have sprung up on the Western continent were originated by female founders, such as Ellen White (1827-1915) of Seventh-day Adventism or Mary Baker Eddy (1821-1910) of the Church of Christ, Scientist (Christian Science) and system.

Given the gender asymmetry of the dominant culture, women were much more likely to have been influential as social reformers, critiquing rather than representing mainstream values. Elizabeth Cady Stanton (1815-1902), along with Susan B. Anthony (1820-1906), worked for woman's suffrage as a key to her larger agenda for social reform. She, along with Matilda Joslyn Gage and a committee of feminist scholars, published *The Woman's Bible* in 1895, asserting that the degradation of women she read in the biblical heritage was the primary cause of women's oppression. *The Woman's Bible* is a compilation of all the biblical texts having to do with

Milestones in the History of Women and Religion

1637	Anne Hutchinson is tried for heresy in Massachusetts Bay Colony and expelled from the community.
1774	"Mother" Ann Lee, the founder of Shakerism, emigrates from England to the American colonies.
1809	Elizabeth Ann "Mother" Seton forms what becomes the Sisters of Charity, a Roman Catholic religious order for women.
1853	Antoinette Brown Blackwell is ordained by the Congregational Church in South Butler, New York, as the first female minister in the United States.
1855	Ellen White organizes the Seventh-day Adventist church, which will become a worldwide religious organization within a few decades.
1859	Revivalist Phoebe Palmer publishes *The Promise of the Father*, which defends a woman's right to preach.
1879	Mary Baker Eddy founds the Church of Christ, Scientist, in Boston.
1880	The Women's Auxiliary Conference of the Unitarian Church begins, based on ideas of Fanny Baker Ames.
1893	The National Council of Jewish Women is founded by Hannah Greenbaum Solomon.
1895	Elizabeth Cady Stanton publishes *The Woman's Bible* to argue the role of religion in the oppression of women.
1903	The Catholic Daughters of the Americas is launched.
1915	Aimee Semple McPherson begins her career as a Pentecostal revivalist preacher.
1920	The National Council of Catholic Women is organized.
1933	The Catholic Worker movement is founded by Dorothy Day.
1955-1956	Presbyterian and Methodist churches approve the ordination of women.
1968	Mary Daly criticizes the Roman Catholic church's attitude toward women in *The Church and the Second Sex*.
late 1960's	The Womanchurch movement addresses the issue of discrimination in institutional religions.
1972	Sally J. Priesand becomes the first woman to be ordained as a rabbi in the United States.
1974	Catholic Women for the ERA is established.
1975	Mother Seton is canonized as the first American saint.
1983	Rosemary Radford Ruether's *Sexism and God-Talk: Toward a Feminist Theology* explores the topics of God, Creation, Christology, Mariology, evil, redemption, and life after death.
1985	Amy Eilberg is ordained as the first female rabbi in Conservative Judaism.
1989	An African American woman, Barbara C. Harris, is confirmed as the first female Episcopal bishop in the United States.

women, translations and commentary. The commentary is historical, comparative, political, and philosophical; deeply controversial as it was, it was widely read and went through several printings and translations. Stanton's own noninstitutional religious sensibility of moral justice and human equality was influenced by Quaker, Unitarian, and Transcendentalist thought. She brought to light the then-radical subject of women and religion—particularly women's subjugation by religious bigotry and generations of gender inequality—in order to demonstrate what she saw as the ideological and traditional barriers to women's rights. Religion itself, she argued, was the major cause of the oppression and degradation of women. Moreover, she worked for religiously enlightened thought and women's rights that would usher in liberty and dignity in government and domestic realms.

Participation. It is tempting to focus on the iconoclasts—such as Mary Daly's creative rejection of what she perceived as Christian hierarchial and dualistic values—or to look at the reformers—such as Frances Willard, temperance leader and advocate for women in the pulpit. One might then, however, overlook those generations of women who have sought to live within the inherited values of their traditions. Their stories, too, are part of the history of gender and religion, nearly impossible to retrieve, as their sacred values include women's silence or modesty. How can a history be made out of silence? How can stories be told about those whose narratives demand anonymity?

The reason that generations of historians of religion passed over the roles women have played in religious traditions is that society has been slow to recognize women's participation in and contribution to religion, for three main reasons. First, patriarchal systems exalt metaphors or images of masculinity and suppress or degrade images of femininity. Second, historically, women have been relegated to the domestic sphere and men to the public realm. Third, religious institutions have prevailed in the control of women—their politics, arts, family structure, bodies, and procreation. In considering the history of women and religion, however, it is well to remember that for all the courageous female reformers or outstanding religious female thinkers, most women are part of their dominant patriarchal culture, living out and expressing its values, and do not see themselves in tension with their institutions or the primary descriptions of reality.

Often, living through their domestic concerns, women have worshipped amid their work and their children, without books, officiating clergy, hierarchial governance, or territorial conflict. Thus, when histories are written, women's devotional lives are invisible. Until recently, few historical records have detailed the preservation or analysis of lullabies or the steps in purifying the kitchen. Commonly, women's religious lives have been made more of ritual and devotion than of doctrine; religious histories have emphasized belief over practice, text over experience. Religious participation can be overlooked in historical surveys as well because the ideologies of secularism fail to note the consistent role that religion has played in describing American realities. Religion is the root of all the rest of culture. Even a culture that claims separation of church and state is permeated with values and images derived from sacred traditions.

American religion is a paradoxical history of social movements that ennoble both individual and internalized experience. For example, in the Second Great Awakening (1795-1830), the traditional stereotype that held that women were more naturally virtuous led to women's taking moral responsibility for their families and for the larger community; the cultural expectation that they were more naturally prayerful led to revivalist fervor spurred by women's participation. By claiming the genderizing of piety (that women are, by nature, pious), one might expect greater social control: that women would act out their femininity by acting out religiousity. By genderizing piety, however, the result was also, paradoxically, that women took on more of what had been considered masculine-gendered church leadership and responsibility for social issues. Women responded to supernatural authority (the infusion of the Holy Spirit) rather than social authority (ministerial, marital, or civil).

Underestimated Influences. When Europeans arrived on the Western continents, they were perplexed by the people they encountered. European invaders were subtly influenced by the indigenous peoples they were intent on defining and eradicating. The various nations of indigenous peoples raised metaphysical, moral, and practical problems for the invaders because the misnamed "Indians" displayed worldviews, gendered living, and styles of worship that seemed not only strange but challenging to the invading settlers' most deeply held ideas about themselves. The newcomers asked whether these Indians were lost tribes of Israel, innocents who did not suffer the Fall, beings without souls, or hosts of the Devil. Each question they asked was formed from the invading worldview and sought to fit Indians into the invaders' religion rather than from consideration of the variety of American Indian cultures and the natives' own visions of reality. European (or newly arrived American) claims about indigenous women—for example, reporting that they gave birth without pain, or accusing them of lasciviousness, or claiming that they did not know the art of cooking—often indicated as much about the reporters' gender anxieties and questions about the sacred as they supplied information and misinformation about the various American Indian groups observed.

One of the most significant aspects of religion in America is bound up in the history of Africans in the Western hemisphere; however, because of the patterns of investigation and analysis, this history often was overlooked until social movements of the 1960's and forward affected the very questions asked in scholarly pursuit. Africans, forced to leave behind land, community, and coherent sacred systems, preserved religion within the confines of slavery by means of ritual and storied memory; the rest was actively suppressed by those who held them in slavery. Their oppressors then inflicted European religion on African slaves. The resulting synthesis was so fertile and powerful that, following emancipation, African American Christianity has had an ongoing influence on mainstream American Christian forms of worship and popular culture.

In the nineteenth century, a number of African American women, such as Sojourner Truth, Maria Stewart, Jarena Lee, and Julia Foote, had religious or mystical experiences. Despite the constrictions placed on them because of race and gender, these women felt divinely called to speak out publicly. Narratives of their lives were printed and sold at the gatherings. They became itinerant revivalists or preachers, proclaiming their theological differences with mainstream ideas about women, family, race, and God. They answered their call in the face of what the writer of the introduction to Julia Foote's "A Brand Plucked from the Fire" ironically called "three great crimes": color, womanhood, and evangelism—taking on a fervent pastoral or missionary role. One of the most-quoted proclamations in America's abolitionist, gender, and sacred history is from Sojourner Truth; she received that name from her supernatural voices, having been born Isabella Van Wagener. Truth refuted with imposing dignity the stereotype that women needed help into carriages and over ditches with

> And a'n't I a woman? Look at me! Look at my arm! I have ploughed, and planted, and gathered into barns, and no man could head me! And a'n't' I a woman? I could work as much and eat as much as a man—when I could get it—and bear de lash as well! And a'n't I a woman? I have borne thirteen chilern, and seen 'em mos' all sold off to slavery, and when I cried out with my mother's grief, none but Jesus heard me! And a'n't I a woman?

Reformer Frances Gage, who recorded the event in 1881, said that Truth refuted the charge that women deserved fewer rights because Christ was not a woman with the statement "Whar did your Christ come from? From God and a woman! Man had nothin' to do wid Him."

Another form of religious participation that has been barely noticeable because of problems of categorizing scholarship is the tremendous contribution women have made to religion in literary forms. Canadian novelists Margaret Lawrence and Margaret Atwood, U.S. poets Emily Dickinson and Adrienne Rich, and novelists Harriet Beecher Stowe, Flannery O'Connor, Toni Morrison, Maxine Hong Kingston, and Leslie Marmon Silko are but a handful of examples of literary artists who have interpreted culture that has had an impact on religious dialogue in both institutional and private spheres. Another of the most affecting literary figures is Annie Dillard, whose essays have helped to revitalize interest in and legitimate mystical experience, nature writing, and the honor of women's independent experiences. In some sense, profound artists such as Morrison participate in the creation of American religious experience, especially in women's communities. As Silko said in *Ceremony*, "You don't have anything if you don't have the stories."

Metaphor and Image. Western culture is patriarchal, which means rule by fathers; fatherhood is not a literal condition, but a position of authority and/or the symbols or tokens of fatherhood. (For example, the prime metaphorical descriptor in ancient Israelite religion is that the god is called father to indicate his special love for his people; the priest in Roman Catholicism is called father as a signifier of his authority and care.) Thus, images that are considered masculine are related to the sacred, and images that are considered feminine are volatile, ranging from invisible, to inferior, to wicked, to esteemed as mother and wife of a patriarch. Because the history of religion is also the history of gender, it is told most frequently by exalting the metaphors of one gender and denigrating or ignoring the other. One effect of the most recent wave of feminism has been to change liturgical language for gender-inclusiveness (for example, instead of "God the Father" a text might read "God our Father and Mother"). This metaphorical shift reflects changes in secular culture and reinforces changes in other areas.

The study of the sacred stories of religion demands that one distinguish between representations of divine beings and those of mortals; it also demands that one distinguish between allegorical or metaphorical figures and descriptions of social life. Divinities appear in metaphors; thus, divine language utilizes sacralized gender stereotypes. The Abrahamic monotheisms (Judaism, Christianity, and Islam) display throughout their histories a tension with gender, as monotheism itself so privileges masculine metaphors that the resulting gender asymmetry permeates all the rest of social behavior and attitudes.

Preacher, abolitionist, and women's rights advocate Sojourner Truth with President Abraham Lincoln. (Library of Congress)

Both scholars and religious innovators in America have been interested in recovering images of ancient goddesses (particularly Near Eastern divinities in conflict with the patriarchal Yahwism of the early Israelites) and to explore religion—either academically or devotionally—by means of its metaphors or tropes and of its images of the sacred. Although investigation about goddesses in nontextually recorded cultures is controversial, scholarship and speculation have fostered various celebrations of feminine-described divinity in numerous forms among women (as well as men) who are seeking to reimagine their religious heritage both metaphorically and ethically, sometimes associated with informally designated movements called New Age Spirituality. These movements, books, celebrations, and private devotions often include stories and metaphors from American Indian and other non-Western cultures in an attempt to affirm the depth of religious experience with positive images of women and divine images that are feminine. Attention to the complexities of myth (great sacred stories) and the dynamics of metaphor (symbolic expressions) has yielded ways of understanding religion that reveal basic gendered systems of reality.

One of the primary gendered metaphorical complexes in any tradition involves language about the earth. In the context of ecological questions, the examination of gendered sacred language reveals the ways in which the earth has been characterized as feminine, thus both fruitful mother and loathsome female body. The dualistic metaphysics of Western culture glorifies spirit and the masculine while reviling earth and the feminine. Feminist theologians, culture critics, environmental activists, and scholars seek to undo that dualistic split in order to free both persons and planet from a destructive metaphorical system. Rosemary Radford Ruether's work exemplifies the combination of an analysis of history, an examination of metaphor, and a call for change. Joanna Macy, a Buddhist scholar and a peace and environmental activist, represents a syncretistic, noninstitutional approach to religion, whose own mystical core, as well as her world-respected teaching, has made her both an influential reformer and a role model for women-centered religion.

Another primary complex of metaphor is the human body and sexuality. In addition to the environmentalist's quest to examine the metaphor of the body of the earth, studies of women and religion have generated theories of the human body as well. Western culture, from both its Hebraic and Greek sources, is a history of the inferiority of the female body and attempts to answer the great riddles of sexuality. Secular America—democratic, mobile, and inventive—has been in tension with its Western heritage, with much religious discourse focusing on concepts and metaphors of body and sexuality.

Enthusiasts—groups that express spirituality through bodily displays of ecstasy—have a long and prominent history in American religion. "Mother Ann" Lee (1736-1784) was an English religious leader who was imprisoned for her zeal and her claim about the mother element of Christ. Founded in England, a number of Shakers, popularly named for their physical displays of spiritual emotion, along with Ann Lee, emigrated to America and established numerous communities practicing celibacy, fine craftsmanship, and the belief in a dual aspect of divinity wherein the masculine principle is incarnate in Christ and the feminine in Mother Ann. Ann Lee and the Shakers are not the first or the last to change the world they lived in by changing the metaphor they lived by.

Part of the political rhetoric of a religious group is to manipulate metaphors that its culture considers feminine so as to make itself more acceptable to the dominant power structure or to set itself apart from the dominant culture. Metaphors are not easily controlled, however, nor are they used completely mindfully. On examining sacred metaphorical constructs, one finds that they are inextricably embedded in gender language. Much of what religion is, under the surface, is to assert and act out what it is to be female or male, or how the genders interact and to what purpose.

Finally, to examine the question of women and religion, one must begin with these considerations: to ask where feminine imagery resides in the cosmic scheme of a religious tradition; to ask what roles women play in the functioning of a religion tradition; what roles they play in the key moments of origins or reforms within a religious tradition; and how these tropes and roles within a sacred context contribute to the tropes and roles of women in every social and personal context.

—Lynda Sexson

See also Christianity and women; Clergy, women as; Daly, Mary; Eve; Feminism, spiritual; Goddess, concept of the; Inclusive language; Islam and women; Judaism and women; Religious movements founded by women; Spirituality movement, women's; Stanton, Elizabeth Cady; Theologians and women's theology; Truth, Sojourner; *Woman's Bible, The*

Bibliography

Bloom, Harold. *The American Religion: The Emergence of the Post-Christian Nation*. New York: Simon & Schuster, 1992. Original analysis of religion in America—or, rather, religion as it uniquely exists in America. Bloom does not work from a feminist perspective but from perspectives that evoke lively dialogue from feminist thinkers.

Daly, Mary. *Beyond God the Father: Toward a Philosophy of Women's Liberation*. Boston: Beacon Press, 1973. A classic in women's studies. Daly provokes readers to recognize the oppression of the gender system within Western patriarchy. Ultimately, she is a separatist opponent of the historical Western tradition rather than merely a critic or reformer.

Dillard, Annie. *Pilgrim at Tinker Creek*. New York: Harper's Magazine Press, 1974. In the first of her collections of beautifully crafted essays, Dillard observes and reflects on the natural world and a world of reading that has influenced environmentalism, mysticism, and letters.

Lerner, Gerda. *The Creation of Patriarchy*. New York: Oxford University Press, 1986.

________. *The Creation of Feminist Consciousness: From the Middle Ages to Eighteen-seventy*. New York: Oxford University Press, 1993. These two books, collected as *Women and History*, bear the typical flaws of all surveys but are splendid in the development of Lerner's argument and an ideal overview that captures the evidence and implications of the history of patriarchy, as well as the celebration of women who created their own nonpatriarchal worldviews.

Macy, Joanna. *World as Lover, World as Self.* Berkeley, Calif.: Parallax Press, 1991. Reflecting the standard of creativity in women and religion, this book covers Buddhism and environmental and peace issues. It is at the same time a document of Macy's reflective and playful religious sensibilities. Macy is scholar, mystic, and reformer.

Morrison, Toni. *Beloved*. New York: Alfred A. Knopf, 1987. Nobel Prize-winning novelist brilliantly evokes American experience in her work, especially in *Beloved* and *Song of Solomon*. She discovers the sacred in a scrap of cloth, in the terror of memory, in the desperation for freedom.

Ruether, Rosemary Radford. *Gaia and God: An Ecofeminist Theology of Earth Healing*. San Francisco: HarperSan Francisco, 1992. Ruether is one of the most articulate feminist theologians, influencing academia, churches, and social organizations. Her books are both historical and theological, both analyses of patriarchy and calls for new consciousness. She also edited, with Rosemary Skinner Keller, the three-volume documentary history *Women and Religion in America*, which includes *The Nineteenth Century* (1981), *Colonial and Revolutionary Periods* (1983), and *1900-1968* (1986).

Sexson, Lynda. *Ordinarily Sacred*. 2d ed. Charlottesville: University Press of Virginia, 1992. Explores the metaphorical ground of religion in terms of everyday experience and aesthetics. The book concentrates on memory, dream, and play, challenging institutional and dualistic definitions of religion while reaffirming the sacred within what has been called the woman's sphere.

Stanton, Elizabeth Cady. *The Woman's Bible*. 1895. Reprint. Boston: Northeastern University Press, 1993. Characterizes radical social reform in American nineteenth century thought. It is both instructive as a historical document and a still-relevant, sharp-voiced challenge to sexist assumptions and patriarchy in the biblical tradition. Includes a foreword by Maureen Fitzgerald.

Stewart, M. W., J. Lee, J. A. J. Foote, and V. W. Broughton. *Spiritual Narratives*. In *The Schomburg Library of Nineteenth-Century Black Women Writers*, edited by Henry Louis Gates, Jr. 25 vols. New York: Oxford University Press, 1988. The entire *Schomburg Library* makes available significant historical and literary works; the *Spiritual Narratives* volume, with an introduction by Sue E. Houchins, includes autobiographical writings of these evangelicals who explored the meaning of freedom as women, as blacks, as Americans, and as a matter of faith.

Religious movements founded by women

Related issues: Social reform, religious beliefs and practices, women's history

Significance: Women, the majority of church members, play a major, if unrecognized, role in several religious movements

Almost from the arrival of the first Europeans in North America, women have occupied a significant, though not widely recognized, position in organized religion. Even though women outnumbered men in church membership throughout most of North American history, they were generally relegated to the pew; however, there are numerous examples of women who became renowned leaders.

History. Generally, the characteristics that "identify" women—piety, sacrifice, domesticity, servanthood, and altruism—are also basic tenets of Christianity. As a personal influence, religion coexisted with domesticity, both realms closely associated with women, providing them with an opportunity for reform. Dorothea Dix began her campaign for the mentally ill as the result of teaching Sunday school classes in the Cambridge, Massachusetts, jail. Angelina and Sarah Grimké became involved with the abolitionist movement through the church, as did Sojourner Truth and Amanda Berry, two of the more prominent nineteenth century black evangelists. The Seneca Falls Convention, beginning the movement for woman suffrage, met in the Wesleyan Methodist Church.

Women provided the underpinning for North American religious activity. They conducted midweek meetings, organized communities, and built support fellowships. Several women either formed religious societies or held prominent positions in existing movements.

Puritans. Anne Hutchinson (1591-1643) emigrated from England to continue as a parishioner of John Cotton, being especially interested in his doctrine of free grace. In Boston, she invited women to midweek meetings in her home to review Cotton's sermon. Hutchinson believed in salvation by grace freely given by God, a concept that became central to American Protestantism. The Puritan elders, however, had no interest in seeing women preach, and they banished Hutchinson. After spending time in Rhode Island and Long Island, she went to the Hudson River Valley, where she died at the hands of American Indians. Church elders saw her death, along with her earlier birth of a handicapped child, as signs of God's displeasure with Hutchinson's activities.

Shakers. Mother Ann Lee (1734-1784), the founder of Shakerism, emigrated from England to the American colonies in 1774. Jailed for preaching the concept of the Second Pillar—the doctrine that Christ has a feminine counterpart—Lee saw herself as the Bride of the Lamb, or Christ's female counterpart, contending that the Second Coming would be through her. Illiterate and believing in speaking in tongues and her ability to work miracles, she supported celibacy, simplicity, religious perfection, community living, and the imminent return of Christ. The Shakers flourished in the first half of the nineteenth century under the direction of Lucy Wright (1780-1821) and Anna White (1831-1910), after Lee the two most important Shaker leaders. By 1860, there were between 6,000 and 10,000 Shakers in some nineteen communities.

A community of Shakers, a religious sect founded by Mother Ann Lee and composed predominantly of women. (Culver Pictures, Inc.)

Christian Science. After a doctor labeled her as incurable following a serious fall, Mary Baker Eddy (1821-1910) effected her own cure through studying the healing ministry of Jesus. In 1875, she wrote a Bible companion, *Science and Health with Key to the Scriptures*, and she founded the Church of Christ, Scientist, in Boston four years later. Eddy emphasized God's masculine and feminine qualities, arguing that love and nurturing were as much a part of God as strength and protection. To Eddy, the world and humankind, created by God, were good. Evil, sickness, and sin were illusions that humans could overcome through a correct relationship with God.

Revivalism. Concurrent with the American Revolution, the doctrine of democracy, and an adherence to a frontier spirit came revivalism, which moved women to a more prominent place in the many Protestant churches. Many women spread the doctrines of sacrifice, devotion, and spirituality. The last, an outgrowth of the revival movement, focused on the belief of the holiness of life, espousing that those who had received the Holy Spirit were to help spread the word, regardless of gender. Phoebe Palmer (1807-1874) preached this concept in both the United States and Canada. In 1859, she published *The Promise of the Father*, which defended a woman's right to preach.

Seventh-day Adventism. Ellen White (1827-1915) certainly accepted the concept of a woman's right to preach. When William Miller's predictions of the world's end in the early 1840's proved false, White preached that Christ had in fact returned, in a spiritual sense. She saw herself as a messenger; throughout her life, she had as many as two thousand visions, each of which she accepted as spiritual authority next to the Bible. Converted to Adventism in 1842, through prophecy and spiritual gifts she always encouraged communicants to prepare for the Second Coming of Christ. She organized the Seventh-day Adventist church in 1855 in Battle Creek, Michigan, which in a few decades became a worldwide religious organization.

Amana Community. Barbara Heinemann (1795-1887) was considered a prophet by the Amana Inspirationists. She assumed leadership after the death of Christian Metz, who led the group from persecution and forced conscription in Germany to settle near Davenport, Iowa. Under Heinemann, the society, which is pacifist and communal, shunning the modern, secular world and supporting cooperation, reached its zenith with 16,000 members. She led the sect as a vehicle of the Spirit, and as such, her sayings were reserved as coming from God. Since her death, there have been no more prophets.

While the group succumbed to the changes wrought by the automobile and the Great Depression of the 1930's, the Amana Inspiritionists remain the longest surviving communal society in American history.

Roman Catholicism. After she was widowed, Elizabeth Ann Seton (1774-1821) determined to enter religious work, founding the Sisters of Charity in Maryland. By the Civil War, there were a few dozen communities of women, with an additional fifty-nine added by 1900, for a total of 40,000 workers. While they engaged in a variety of charitable activities, most of the sisters devoted their energies to parochial education. Most of the 4,000 parochial schools and 700 female seminaries were staffed by Sisters of Charity. In 1975, Mother Seton became the first American woman to be canonized.

Dorothy Day (1897-1980), another Roman Catholic, took to heart Jesus' commandment to feed the hungry, clothe the naked, visit the imprisoned, and shelter the homeless. As a result, she cofounded and led the radical Catholic Worker Movement, which lived the dictates of Jesus.

Judaism. Of many Jewish women of note, Rebecca Gratz (1781-1869) and Hannah Solomon (1858-1942) deserve mention. Gratz, from a well-established, wealthy Jewish family in Philadelphia, worked in many philanthropic activities. In 1838, she established the first Jewish Sunday school, serving as its superintendent until her death. Solomon organized the Congress of Jewish Women for the World Parliament of Religions, held at the 1893 Chicago World's Fair. She brought together leading Jewish women who went on to establish the first permanent Jewish women's organization in America, the National Council of Jewish Women, with Solomon as its first president.

Foursquare Gospel. Aimee Semple McPherson (1890-1944) after conversion at a revival in 1907, began her own career as a fundamentalist, Pentecostal revivalist in Ontario at the age of twenty-five. She then undertook a transcontinental tour, which ended in Los Angeles, where she established her headquarters. She conducted other transcontinental tours, raising money for her Angelus Temple, incorporated in 1927. When preaching on Ezekiel's vision of the four cherubim with the four faces, she realized she led a four-part ministry—Christ as Savior, Baptizer, Healer, and the Second Coming. She founded the Church of the Foursquare Gospel, using radio to spread her message. —*Duncan R. Jamieson*

See also Christianity and women; Day, Dorothy; Eddy, Mary Baker; Evangelists and faith healers, women as; Grimké, Angelina, and Grimké, Sarah; Judaism and women; Religion; Spirituality, women's; Theologians and women's theology; Truth, Sojourner

Bibliography

Noll, Mark. *A History of Christianity in the United States and Canada*. Grand Rapids, Mich.: Wm. B. Eerdmans, 1992.

Ruether, Rosemary, and Rosemary Keller. *Women and Religion in America*. 3 vols. San Francisco: Harper & Row, 1981-1986.

Shulman, Albert M. *The Religious Heritage of America*. San Diego: A. S. Barnes, 1981.

Religious Right and women

Relevant issues: Family, politics, religious beliefs and practices

Significance: The Religious Right, a loose collection of conservative Christians in the United States, favors the repeal of all abortion rights and opposes feminism

Emerging in the 1970's as a reaction to liberalizations and perceived excesses of the 1960's, the Religious Right is a loose collection of interlocking organizations and individuals who share a belief in a fundamentalist interpretation of the Bible. Beginning its political alliance with the New Right in the early 1980's, it seeks the curtailment of pornography, homosexuality, divorce, feminism, humanism, and related ideas and practices.

Seeking to return the United States to so-called traditional values, members of the Religious Right believe that the heterosexual, monogamous family is a God-given institution in which all humans should live. This family should have a breadwinning husband, a homemaker wife, and children. Changes in American society since the late 1960's, however, seem to point away from this idealized norm. According to the Religious Right, these changes—including freer sexuality for both heterosexuals and homosexuals, easier-to-obtain divorce, the legalization of abortion and increases in abortion rates, a lack of prayer and the teaching of humanism in public schools—have created a declining and decaying America which needs a return to God and biblical values. For women, these values mean the cessation of all or most abortions (some Religious Right adherents accept abortion in cases of rape or incest or to protect the life of the mother); a rollback of the acceptability of women in the working world, especially married women with children; and a strong push for women to marry, have children, and care for them and their husbands on a full-time basis.

While the Religious Right is not a monolithic entity and many followers are not allied with any organized group, a number of such groups do exist, including the Moral Majority, Religious Roundtable, Christian Coalition, and Citizens for Decency. Of special significance for women are the Eagle Forum, founded and run by Phyllis Schlafly, and Concerned Women for America (CWA), founded and run by Beverly LaHaye. These two groups seek the same goals as the groups founded and run by men, but their views are perhaps given greater credence concerning women's issues. Active since the late 1970's, CWA has had many political successes at both local and national levels and claims to be the largest women's organization in the United States. The group petitions cases before state and federal courts and has won battles as diverse as the elimination of pornographic materials from convenience stores and the alteration of public school curricula.

The Religious Right is a backlash movement that calls into question such basic tenets of feminism as women's equality in all spheres and a woman's right to choose when and whether to become a mother and what she does with her body and with whom. The Religious Right has had significant influence on the American political system, especially within the Republican Party.

See also Abortion; Antifeminism; *Backlash*; Breadwinner ethic; Career vs. homemaker debate; Christianity and women; Family life; Homophobia; Motherhood; Politics; Religion; Reproductive rights; Republican Party and women; Schlafly, Phyllis

Reproductive rights

RELEVANT ISSUES: Family, law, health and medicine, science and technology, sex and gender

SIGNIFICANCE: Reproductive rights, including the right to choose procreation, contraception, abortion, and/or sterilization, became among the most hotly debated and politically divisive issues in the late twentieth century

Women's search for autonomy and self-identity has caused the modern family to evolve. The traditional role of women as companions to their husbands and bearers of children changed as women entered the workforce in increasingly large numbers. A marked decrease in fertility and the recognition that women had the absolute right to control their own bodies followed.

Historical Overview. Legal regulation of abortion was virtually nonexistent throughout early history and into the nineteenth century. In preliterate primitive societies, abortion and infanticide were the chief practices limiting population growth; contraception was relatively infrequent. In the Roman Empire, abortion was so frequent and widespread that authors such as Ovid, Juvenal, and Seneca mentioned it in their works, and natural historian Pliny listed prescriptions for drugs to induce abortion. Roman law explicitly held that the "child in the belly of its mother" was not a person, and therefore abortion was not considered murder. The early Christians, however, denounced abortion, contraception, homosexuality, and castration as being the moral equivalent of murder, but those acts were never legally punished and were often ignored in most early Judeo-Christian writings. From the third century A.D. onward, Christian thought concerning early abortion was not unified. In A.D. 1100, Ivo of Chartres, a prominent church scholar, condemned abortion but held that early abortion (that of the "unformed" embryo) was not murder. This position was reiterated by Gratian fifty years later in a work that became the basis of canon law for the next seven hundred years.

In postrevolutionary America, abortion early in pregnancy was neither prohibited nor uncommon. Each state was governed by English common law (judge-made law that evolved over the centuries) and supplemented by legislation. Until 1821, no state had enacted a statute regulating or outlawing abortion. In common law, abortion was permitted until "quickening," when the first movement of the fetus was noticed by the mother, generally between the fourth and sixth months of pregnancy. This distinction was made because abortion before quickening presented little danger to the health of the woman. Because of the limitations of technology at the time, before quickening there was no scientific test to determine with certainty that a woman was pregnant. Abortion undertaken before quickening was generally ignored. Postquickening abortion was considered a crime, but only a misdemeanor. In common law, even when an illegal abortion was performed, the woman was immune from prosecution. At the beginning of the nineteenth century, therefore, first-trimester and many second-trimester abortions faced little legal regulation, presumably because of liberal attitudes toward sexuality. Historian Michael Gordon estimated that three in ten women in late eighteenth century New England were pregnant at the time of marriage. The subsequent decline in the overall birthrate during the period suggests an increased use of both birth control and abortion. In the primarily rural society of eighteenth and nineteenth century America, children were considered a source of economic strength, and abortions were sought primarily by single women and those with the necessary financial means. Abortion was not considered a moral issue but, rather, a subject discussed behind closed doors in terms of illicit behavior condemned by society.

By 1900, however, every state in the Union had passed laws forbidding the use of drugs or instruments to procure abortion at any stage of pregnancy unless necessary to save the life of the woman. Those performing abortions were guilty of a felony, and in many states, the woman herself faced possible criminal prosecution. The earliest laws were primarily concerned with women's health and the use of dangerous poisons to induce abortion. Connecticut was the first state to enact antiabortion legislation in 1821; its law applied only to postquickening abortions. Although surgical abortions carried a high mortality rate, by 1840, only eight states had enacted antiabortion legislation.

It was during the second half of the nineteenth century, therefore, that changes in the social order accompanied by a shift in demographics from rural-agricultural to urban-industrial also changed patterns of fertility as well as social roles and moral values. At the same time, the midnineteenth century estimates of one induced abortion for every four live births presented cause for concern about the safety of abortions. The popular press carried advertisements for abortifacients and remedies to relieve "menstrual blockage" or "obstruction," primarily caused by pregnancy. Advertisements for patent medicines designed to bring on "suppressed menses" were common, as were advertisements for "clinics for ladies" to treat menstrual "irregularities" confidentially. The notices were generally accompanied by the admonition that the medicines were not to be used by married women, as they could cause miscarriages. Other unsafe and ineffective home remedies ranged from strenuous exercise to soap solutions and mild poisons to physical intrusions into the uterus.

Medical practitioners were thrust into the midst of the abortion debate for several reasons: concerns about the safety of abortions as well as the desire to police the boundaries of the profession and eliminate competition in abortion services. Trained physicians vied with homeopaths, apothecaries, and other "healers" who advocated new methods of treatment and claimed the title of "doctor" for themselves. New medical schools, open to all who could pay their tuition, were reluctant to fail a regularly paying student, however incompetent. The medical profession wanted to upgrade its standards of practice and education, but the absence of licensing laws made this difficult.

By midnineteenth century, regular physicians were members of the society committed to defending the value of human life. In 1857, Dr. Horatio Storer, an obstetrician and gynecologist and leading American advocate for the criminalization of abortion, began a drive to end legal abortion. At its convention in 1859, the American Medical Association (AMA) called for a general suppression of abortions, including those performed prior to quickening. The physicians organized a media and lobbying effort that focused on the fetus' right to life. Claiming to be saving lives by refusing to perform abortions, but in reality only removing a lucrative source of income from their competitors, the educated and trained physicians attempted to distinguish themselves scientifically and socially by claiming to be following the Hippocratic Oath, which expressly forbids giving a woman "an instrument to produce abortion." That phrase has been interpreted as forbidding the inducement of abortion by any method.

The earliest American Catholic position on abortion belonged to Bishop Francis B. Kendrick of Philadelphia, who in 1841 declared that there were no "therapeutic" indications for abortion, consistent with nineteenth century Catholic theology, which forbade abortions during the entire pregnancy. In 1869, Pope Pius IX declared that anyone procuring an abortion would be excommunicated from the Catholic church. In the late 1800's, following the discovery of fertilization, the debate shifted in favor of the church's position that human life begins at conception. The religious press, however, did not address the issue of abortion until after the Civil War.

From the end of the nineteenth century until 1960, therefore, abortion had become a medical issue. Passage of abortion laws that permitted abortions to "save the life of the woman" were vague, arbitrary, and haphazard in application. There was an absence of criteria against which to measure how that "life" was to be defined: physically, socially, emotionally, or intellectually. Consequently, other bases also became acceptable reasons for providing therapeutic abortions: poverty in the 1930's and psychiatric reasons in the 1940's and 1950's. Although debated in the literature, there was little effort to overturn the antiabortion legislation. The situation became even more tenuous when abortion decisions became more difficult to justify as life-threatening and when hospitals established review boards to decide whether abortion was necessary in each case. The number of therapeutic abortions dropped dramatically. Public discussion of abortion was rare because of the "delicate" nature of public sensibilities, but privately, an underground network for sharing names of abortionists and illegal abortion techniques existed. Until 1960, therefore, medicine's control of abortion was basically not challenged, in part because the procedure was still available to the upper class to control fertility and also because women lacked the knowledge or expertise to challenge medical decisions. At that time, women were excluded from decision making, giving doctors unquestioned authority.

Reform. As improved and advancing technology of the 1960's brought increased public scrutiny to medical procedures, the social climate also favored mobilization in many causes such as civil rights, the women's movement, the antiwar movement, and gay liberation. Changing sexual mores evidenced by frequent premarital sex and a certain degree of freedom provided by the birth control pill and the intrauterine device (IUD) caused the traditional family structure to erode. "Pro-choice" was another option among many. Women entered the workforce in increasing numbers; the marriage rate declined and the divorce rate increased; single women had to work to support themselves and their families. Women who valued childbearing, but in their chosen time frame, began to make the claim that abortion was a woman's right, and one that was integrated into their right of equality, the right to be treated as individuals rather than potential mothers. Because they felt it was their right to control their own bodies, they believed it was their individual decision to determine when to bear children, if at all, and, conversely, whether an abortion was appropriate. Some called for a redefinition of the laws governing abortion; others wanted repeal of the laws governing abortion. In California, the Society for Humane Abortions was formed in 1961 and aimed to change public opinion about abortion by distributing leaflets, conducting teach-ins, and circulating petitions to repeal abortion laws.

Legislative reform of abortion laws that began in the 1950's became active between 1967 and 1973. The thrust of the legislation was to create exceptions to strict prohibitions on abortion, making it legal when the fetus had a serious physical or mental defect or when the physician considered it necessary to protect the mental or physical health of the woman, and also in cases of rape or incest. The turning point for reproductive choice as an issue took place at the 1967 national conference of the National Organization for Women (NOW) led by Betty Friedan, who succeeded in having the "Right of Women to Control Their Reproductive Lives" included in NOW's Women's Bill of Rights. The National Association for the Repeal of Abortion Laws (NARAL) was created in 1969. After 1973, it became the National Abortion Rights Action League, the principal national lobbying group for grassroots pro-choice organizations in the United States.

Other reform efforts followed. The Presidential Advisory Council on the Status of Women, appointed by President Lyndon Johnson, released a report in 1968 calling for the repeal of all abortion laws. Planned Parenthood supported the repeal of criminal abortion statutes in 1969, and the Commission on Population Growth in 1972 issued a report favoring abortion reform. Between 1967 and 1973, nineteen states had reformed their abortion laws. The climate was ripe for *Roe v. Wade*.

In a 7-2 decision on January 22, 1973, the U.S. Supreme Court ruled that a woman had a constitutional right to choose

Activists on both sides of the debate over abortion often point to the death toll involved: the deaths of aborted fetuses, for pro-life groups, and the deaths of pregnant women who seek out unsafe abortions, for pro-choice groups. (Sally Ann Rogers)

to terminate her pregnancy based on two principles: the woman's fundamental right of privacy and the status of the fetus. Elaborating on its reasoning, the Court wrote that because the right to privacy is fundamental, only a compelling reason will allow the government to interfere with the exercise of that right. The Court also answered the claim that abortion destroyed life when it explained that the unborn was not a person entitled to the guarantees of life and liberty of the Fourteenth Amendment; as set out in that amendment, "person" is used in the postnatal sense only.

For ease of reference, the Court divided the term of the pregnancy into trimesters. During the first trimester, the woman herself, in consultation with her physician, can decide to terminate her pregnancy without government interference; during the second, the government can regulate abortion only to preserve and protect the woman's health; during the third trimester, after "viability," when the fetus is capable of living outside the womb, the government's interest in the protection of fetal life becomes compelling. Only then can the government prohibit abortion.

In 1973, Congress passed a "conscience clause" bill that permitted any individual or hospital opposed to abortion to refuse to perform the procedure. Similar bills were enacted in many states. The progeny of *Roe v. Wade* attempted to erode the sweeping reform that ensued. States enacted restrictions on abortion in the nature of waiting periods, bans on Medicaid funding, record-keeping requirements, restrictions on facilities, medical testing requirements, and consent requirements from the male partner or parents of a minor. In each case, the constraints were tested in the courts, but *Roe* was not overturned.

Emotionally charged marches followed in which some pro-life advocates carried posters of macerated fetuses and some pro-choice advocates carried placards of bloody coat hangers symbolizing the era before the legalization of abortion. Pro-lifers used aggressive methods to stop legal abortion, such as picketing clinics and homes of clinic staffpersons, shouting at women entering abortion clinics, throwing plastic models of fetuses, harassing clinic employees, chaining themselves to doors, and lying prostrate in streets and driveways. Sham counseling centers were set up that showed films of aborted fetuses; abortion clinics were vandalized and bombed. Operation Rescue, a national group based in Binghamton, New York, attracted national attention when its members blocked a clinic in Atlanta during the 1988 Democratic National Convention. Similar disruptions were staged nationwide.

Canada and Abortion Reform. The reform movement was slower to develop in Canada than in the United States. Canada inherited Great Britain's 1861 Offenses Against the Person Act, which provided that anyone procuring an "unlawful" abortion, including the woman herself, could be sentenced to life imprisonment; an aider or abettor could be imprisoned for three years. As in the American statute, the language was ambiguous and did not specify which abortions are "unlawful." In 1892, the Canadian legislature made possession of all "obscene" materials, including all contraceptives and abortifacients, a criminal offense.

In 1969, following a gradual liberalization of Canadian abortion law, Canada adopted a statute permitting abortions in hospitals with three-physician appointed committees to review abortion decisions and decide whether continuation of a pregnancy would endanger the life or health of the woman. Access to therapeutic abortion, however, was dependent on regional location and economic status.

On January 28, 1988, invoking *Roe v. Wade*, the Supreme Court of Canada, in *Morganthaler, Smoling, and Scott v. Attorney General of Canada*, held that the provisions of the Criminal Code of Canada that allowed restricted access to abortion were unconstitutional. The Court reasoned that the 1969 statute was an impermissible restriction of a woman's right to abortion, an aspect of the "right to security of the person" guaranteed by the 1982 Canadian Charter of Rights and Freedoms. Abortions performed in hospitals or clinics in Ontario were thereafter funded under the provincial health insurance plan. Other provinces limited access to and payment for abortion services. The Ontario Law Reform Commission (OLRC) issued the only government report in the world recommending the legalization of surrogacy. In the mid-1990's, there was also a movement in Ontario to legalize midwifery.

Right of Contraception. The controversy over birth control was not as vocal and emotionally charged as that over abortion. The birth control movement reflected the changing social environment and growing emancipation and independence of women. Birth control technology and capability have expanded rapidly, with the introduction of methods ranging from the IUD and the birth control pill to injectable contraceptives (Depo-Provera), reversible subdermal (under the skin) implants (Norplant), morning-after pills, medicated vaginal rings containing steroids absorbed into the bloodstream, and biodegradable systems. The birth control pill, first approved for use in June, 1960, revolutionized contemporary birth control methods as a result of its simplicity, accessibility, and effectiveness. Within twenty years of its advent, an estimated ten to fifteen million American women and eight to one hundred million women worldwide were using oral contraceptives for birth control.

The birth control movement was not without its opposition. While programs were under way to educate the public about birth control methods and access, a countermovement condemning contraceptive practice became active. Led by Anthony Comstock, director and organizer of the New York Society for the Suppression of Vice, a relentless and vigorous campaign ensued initially against birth control advocates and later against gamblers. In 1873, the U.S. Congress passed the Comstock Act, which prohibited interstate transport of contraceptive information and devices.

Comstock used the power of his position as special agent of the U.S. Post Office to travel around the country arresting those acting in violation of the law. Fear of prosecution inhibited the development, dissemination, and discussion of birth control information. Sections of medical treatises containing information on birth control methods had to be excised. In 1926, twenty-four states had anticontraception laws modeled on the Comstock Act; twenty-two other states' obscenity laws were interpreted to include a ban on contraception. The act was not challenged as a constitutional issue, and its clause on contraception was not specifically repealed until 1971.

On June 7, 1965, in a seven to two decision, the U.S. Supreme Court in *Griswold v. Connecticut* declared unconstitutional a Connecticut statute that outlawed contraceptives and made their use a criminal offense. (In the same case, the Court first recognized a constitutional right of privacy and gave it legal protection.) The immediate consequence of the decision was the repeal of birth control statutes in Connecticut and thirteen other states and a dramatic increase in the number of women who gained access to birth control devices and counseling. The decision was confined to traditional notions of contraception by married persons. The privacy guarantee was extended to contraception for single persons in 1972 and to minors in 1977.

The Crusaders. Several women assumed major roles in reproductive reform. Frances Wright (1795-1852) was a Scottish reformer associated with a socialist group in New Harmony, Indiana, experimenting in cooperative living to show that poverty could be abolished through shared labor and collective ownership. She advocated equality for women, free love, liberal divorce laws, and birth control to contribute to equality between the sexes.

Emma Goldman (1869-1940), a Lithuanian immigrant, devoted her adult life to the promotion of anarchism (a theory that the state should be abolished and replaced by free agreements between individuals as a means of bringing about equality and justice). She stressed the rights of the individual and was arrested in 1916 because of her stance on birth control. Goldman worked as a midwife but did not perform abortions because she felt incompetent to do so. The Emma Goldman Clinic for Women opened in 1973 in Iowa City, Iowa.

Margaret Sanger (1879-1966) was born in the United States. A public health nurse in New York City who campaigned for female emancipation and birth control, she was devoted to making contraception available to all who wanted it and to everyone she could persuade to use it. In 1912, she began her campaign against "comstockery." Although she did not persuade Congress to repeal the Comstock Act, she began to change public attitudes about birth control and the right of women to control their reproductive lives. She opened her first birth control clinic in 1916 in a Brooklyn tenement, where she distributed handbills that provided information in English, Yiddish, and Italian. Sanger's clinics also served as educational centers where private physicians were instructed in contraceptive technique, a subject not taught in medical schools at that time.

Mary Dennett (1872-1947), also born in America, was a leader in a voluntary parenthood league focusing on sex education. She was convicted for using the mail to distribute such literature.

Voluntary Sterilization. Voluntary sterilization for purposes of fertility control is a development that occurred during the second half of the twentieth century. Sterilization for eugenic reasons, however, has existed since the early part of the twentieth century. Voluntary sterilization is legal in all fifty states despite some restrictions, such as age, spousal or parental consent, and waiting periods. In the mid-1990's, the federal government funded approximately 10 percent of all voluntary sterilizations for the poor annually.

Impact on Women's Issues. The right to reproduce also includes the right not to reproduce through abortion, contraception, or sterilization. Pro-choice advocates support women's right to control their own bodies and decide whether to bear children. Right-to-life advocates argue that abortion is murder and a threat to the foundations of the traditional roles of motherhood, the American family, and religious and moral precepts. The biological partner has also raised the issue of his right to have a voice in the abortion decision.

Although the decision whether to become pregnant or to abort is private, it must be made within a social context. Legalization of abortion, contraception, and sterilization has expanded the procreative choices of the affluent and middle class. Groups such as the poor, the uneducated, and the unemployed, many of whom make up the ethnic subcultures, who may be dependent on the state for financial support, remain disadvantaged. Demographics and insufficient dissemination of health care information have restricted access to the reproductive options available to women. *—Marcia J. Weiss*

See also Abortion; Antiabortion protests and women; Birth control and family planning; Civil rights and civil liberties for American women; Civil rights and civil liberties for Canadian women; Fertility and infertility; Goldman, Emma; Health and medicine; History of women; Motherhood; National Abortion and Reproductive Rights Action League (NARAL); Pregnancy and childbirth; Pro-choice; Pro-life; Right to privacy; *Roe v. Wade*; Sanger, Margaret; Sexuality, women's; Social reform movements and women; Sterilization of women

Bibliography

Blank, Robert, and Janna C. Merrick. *Human Reproduction, Emerging Technologies, and Conflicting Rights*. Washington, D.C.: CQ Press, 1995. Examines the controversial and complex issues surrounding late twentieth century reproduction (for example, abortion, surrogacy, assisted reproduction, sterilization, prenatal intervention, fetal research, and neonatal care) from a public policy perspective, focusing on the degree to which emerging technology has reshaped the debate.

Brodie, Janet Farrell. *Contraception and Abortion in Nineteenth-Century America*. Ithaca, N.Y.: Cornell University Press, 1994. A carefully detailed historical chronology of nineteenth century information on reproductive control based on primary sources such as pamphlets, newspapers, and letters. Excellent notes and bibliography.

Degler, Carl N. *At Odds: Women and the Family in America from the Revolution to the Present*. New York: Oxford University Press, 1980. A major source synthesizing the history of women and the history of the family with emphasis on the eighteenth and nineteenth centuries in an effort to resolve the conflict between women's search for individuality and equality and their family responsibilities.

Dienes, C. Thomas. *Law, Politics, and Birth Control.* Urbana: University of Illinois Press, 1972. Excellent and scholarly coverage of the latter part of the eighteenth century to the 1970's. Detailed research on Comstock and Sanger, and much information about legal cases. Contains copious primary and secondary source material, including cross-references, appendices, and extensive bibliography.

Luker, Kristin. *Abortion and the Politics of Motherhood.* Berkeley: University of California Press, 1984. A major detailed sociological and historical study; copious notes and extensive bibliography.

Mohr, James C. *Abortion in America: The Origins and Evolution of National Policy, 1800-1900.* New York: Oxford University Press, 1978. Classic overview discussing the shift in social policy that brought about the criminalization of abortion.

Overall, Christine, ed. *The Future of Human Reproduction.* Toronto: Women's Press, 1989. Multidisciplinary collection of papers which examines a broad range of issues in reproduction and reproductive technology within the Canadian context. Focuses on contraception, abortion, prenatal diagnosis and treatment, and donor insemination.

Reynolds, Moira Davison. *Women Advocates of Reproductive Rights: Eleven Who Led the Struggle in the United States and Great Britain.* Jefferson, N.C.: McFarland, 1994. Biographical sketches of major nineteenth and twentieth century reformers advocating contraception, abortion, and equality for women.

Tribe, Laurence H. *Abortion: The Clash of Absolutes.* New York: W. W. Norton, 1990. In a scholarly yet readable work, this noted constitutional scholar discusses the historical and cultural aspects of abortion and the clash between the "absolutes" of life and liberty guaranteed in the Constitution.

Republican Party and women

Relevant issues: Politics, social reform

Significance: Although many women in the Republican Party have been cast in a variety of supporting roles over the years and have been active in traditional party activities, only more recently have they been center stage political candidates or elected officials

In the 1990's, the upsurge in the number of women running for office in the United States contributed to an enlargement of the pool of Republican candidates; today, the pool includes more women than ever before. These women are actively recruited, advised, and supported. The National Federation of Republican Women, an affiliate of the Republican National Committee composed of dues-paying grassroots activists, works toward these ends.

The issue of reproductive choice is the most divisive women's issue within the Republican Party. It has overtaken the discussion of the Equal Rights Amendment (ERA), which for many years was an object of intense discussion. For years, a contingent of stalwart party members have been supportive of choice because this position can be seen as consistent with the philosophy of the Republican Party: Individuals are best able to control their own lives, without government interference. For a number of years, many Republicans hoped that the issue of abortion would go away. With the ascendancy of the Religious Right in the party, however, these hopes have been dashed. The responses have varied; some Republicans have argued the "big tent" philosophy espoused by former party chair Lee Atwater, while others have more actively responded by creating national groups, pro-choice political action committees such as Republicans for Choice and Pro-Choice America, in an effort to push the party to adopt a pro-choice position. Members of these organizations fear, perhaps rightly so, that the issue of choice has the potential to drain female support from Republican Party candidates; their efforts are intended to head off this event. This contingent argues that taken in combination with the gender gap, which has severely disadvantaged the Republicans in a number of elections since 1980, the electoral future of the party may be dire, especially if the Democrats find ways to capitalize on the pro-choice and pro-feminist sentiments that are held by a majority of the electorate (as is regularly reported by the media).

The division over abortion is often apparent when female party activists confront one another. Many no longer share the same mind-set or goals, which stems partially from the lack of social homogeneity in the party, something that was not an issue in the past. Upper-class, suburban, liberal Republican women have increasingly come face to face with working-class, rural, conservative Republican women who may belong to the Religious Right. The disparate positions that members of these two groups espouse contribute to the escalation of conflict within the party as a whole.

Women and the Party-in-the-Electorate. Numerically and substantively, the gender gap has disadvantaged the Republican Party. In terms of sheer numbers, women are less likely to support Republican presidential candidates. In 1992, this preference was not manifested as obviously as in the past. Female voters preferred the Democratic candidate, Bill Clinton, by a margin of only 4 percent, while men preferred George Bush, the Republican, by one percentage point. Women are also less likely, overall, to support Republican congressional candidates; in 1994, 46 percent of female voters voted Republican, while 54 percent voted Democrat. (The numbers for men were exactly opposite.)

Women are less likely to support the Republican Party for a number of reasons. First, it is less liberal on issues about which women evidence greater concern than do men. Second, many Republican women characterize themselves as feminists. Finally, most Republican Party candidates have not been committed themselves to the issues that Republican women identify as high priorities.

Women and the Party Organization. Republicans have been later off the starting block than Democrats when it comes to moving women into leadership positions and encouraging their political candidacies, in part because the Republican Party is more centrally controlled than the Democratic Party. Thus, the Republican Party has fewer access points for women. In addition, the different party cultures affect the manner in which each party deals with the presence of women. The Democratic Party was initially more responsive to the demands of women to be let into its inner circles because Democratic women banded together outside the party, under the rubric of women's and feminist organizations. They developed skills and expertise that the party, given the aggressive manner in which political power is pursued, had little choice but to become inclusive. Somewhat differently, male Republican elite first needed to rethink what was in the best interests of the party prior to making a place for women in the party; only then did powerful Republican men carefully select, invite, sponsor, and mentor female candidates. Many of the most influential women in the party today are connected to male Republican leaders. Although these women have not aggressively pursued power, they have assumed important leadership roles within the party. The Republicans pride themselves on a number of "firsts"—for example, the Republican Party appointed a woman as director of the National Republican Congressional Committee.

The Republican Party has been less directly concerned with the issue of delegate representation at national nominating conventions. Unlike with the Democratic Party, it is not mandated by Republican Party rules that state delegations be evenly divided between men and women. Even so, the Democrats' efforts to diversify state delegations as a result of the McGovern-Fraser Commission has led to an increase in the number of women serving in delegate slots at Republican conventions. The average percentage of female delegates at the five nominating conventions prior to 1972 was 15 percent. This percentage jumped to 30 percent in 1972 and was somewhere between 35 percent to 45 percent at the Republican conventions in the 1980's and 1990's.

Women and the Party-in-Government. A party-in-government includes all elected and appointed individuals affiliated with a party. Republican women have made significant

Christine Todd Whitman was elected governor of New Jersey in 1993 and became a prominent member of the Republican Party. (AP/Wide World Photos)

gains at both the state and federal levels. In 1995, of the fifty-eight women serving in the 104th Congress, twenty were Republicans. In the 1994 congressional election, female Republicans gained five seats in the House (bringing their number from twelve to seventeen) and one seat in the Senate (doubling, from one to two, the number of seats held there). Many of these politicians were more conservative, as evidenced by their pro-life positions.

Leadership opportunities for Republican women increased dramatically with the Republican takeover of the Congress in 1994. Senator Nancy Kassebaum of Kansas became the first woman to head a major Senate committee, Labor and Human Resources. Representative Jan Meyers of Kansas became the first female chair of a standing committee, the Small Business Committee, since 1976. Two Republican women served on the powerful Rules Committee. Within the party structure itself (the Republican Conference) in the House, two women served in important leadership positions, one as vice chair and another as secretary.

Republican women gained ground in the state legislatures, where women overall held 21 percent of the total seats; they gained six percentage points, from 38 percent to 44 percent, on Democratic women from 1994 to 1995. Republican women hold a number of statewide elected offices. In 1994, the only female governor, Christine Todd Whitman of New Jersey, was Republican. Of the nineteen women who served as lieutenant governors, twelve were Republican. Four of the nine female attorney generals, five of the thirteen female treasurers, and seven of the ten female secretaries of state were Republican.

The Republican Party is in the difficult position of having to confront head-on the needs of its female constituency. Until it does this, it still runs the risk of alienating female voters. It is likely that the ability of women to make a difference both inside and outside the Republican party will continue to expand.

—*Sharon A. Sykora*

See also Abortion; Candidacy and political campaigns, women's; Democratic Party and women; Gender gap; Politics; Pro-choice; Pro-life; Religious Right and women; Reproductive rights; Voting patterns among women; Women in the House and Senate (WISH List)

BIBLIOGRAPHY

Fact Sheet on Women's Political Progress. Washington, D.C.: National Women's Political Caucus, 1995.

Freeman, Jo. "Feminism vs. Family Values." In *Different Roles, Different Voices*, edited by Marianne Githens, Pippa Norris, and Joni Lovenduski. New York: HarperCollins, 1994.

Mandel, Ruth, Kathy Kleeman, and Lucy Baruch. "No Year of the Woman, Then or Now." In *Extensions*. Norman: Carl Albert Center, University of Oklahoma, 1995.

Retail sales, women in

RELEVANT ISSUES: Business and economics, employment

SIGNIFICANCE: In the United States, the shift to an industrialized economy following the Civil War gave many women employment opportunities in sales, especially in department stores

As early as the Colonial period, women worked as clerks in small stores. Most proprietors soon decided that the female shoppers preferred to be waited on by men, however, and changed their hiring policies. Although there were some exceptions—such as in Macy's in New York City, which employed women as salespersons, cashiers, and bookkeepers—women did not become truly integrated into sales in the United States until the revolution of department stores and ready-to-wear clothes. Catering to a clientele of mainly middle-class and upper-class women, store owners once again hired women.

Women were paid less than male workers, as was the case in most other professions. Unable to afford entrance into a business school to learn the skills needed for coveted, higher-paying clerical jobs, many women settled for sales positions, which earned better salaries and more prestige than unskilled factory work. Since sales jobs were plentiful, owners could keep wages low and fire those employees who did not perform up to standard. The number of saleswomen employed dramatically increased between 1880 and 1900, rising some 1,800 percent.

After World War II, the typical profile of the female employee changed. More women who worked were married, middle-class, and older. By 1981, women had almost half of the sales jobs in the United States but were by no means representative in management. Although women gained access to jobs as buyers and in certain male-dominated sales areas such as appliances, the primary income-earning jobs in retail sales still belonged to men in the 1990's.

History. The rise of women in the sales industry followed the Civil War as corporate and industrial expansion provided more opportunities. The shop mentality of more customized service gave way to an impersonal structure of routine. Many men found their talents wasted on such menial labor and were told that clerking was emasculating. Most male salespeople moved into management or sought more challenging employment. The women who were hired to fill their positions received lower wages. The preferred female employee was young, single, native-born, white, and of the working class but properly dressed and mannered. Excluded from the sales floor were African Americans and immigrants.

Different position levels existed for women. At the bottom was the young worker, normally under fourteen years old, who was a "cash girl" or "runner." She hurried to a central cashier with the customer's money and returned with the change. The saleswoman would then complete the transaction. During idle times, runners were responsible for sweeping and dusting. A girl often moved up from runner to the position of wrapper, who packaged the item, or stock girl, who put new merchandise on the shelves. These positions paid less than unskilled factory work, but after two years of service an employee would be eligible for a promotion to salesclerk, earning up to seven dollars per week, a higher wage than that of a factory worker. The highest paying job for a woman was that of cashier, whose salary was as much as ten dollars per week. Cashier skills required intelligence and a knowledge of basic arithmetic. Male floorwalkers or floor managers supervised all employees, ensuring that everyone conformed to the rules.

The normal working week was about 60 to 80 hours long but sometimes went as high as 112 hours. Stores often opened on Sunday for individual customers and kept their employees to do inventory work on Sunday evenings. The conditions for women were poor—some workers stood for twelve or more hours a day and were not provided with adequate toilet facilities—and several states passed legislation to aid women.

The employment of saleswomen continued to grow at a fast rate. Consumer interest enlarged the female workforce after World War II, when many wives sought to supplement income with part-time work. Retail sales allowed women to maintain their homes while working in seasonal or temporary sales work. After the Civil Rights movement of the 1960's, many African American women left domestic occupations to join the sales force. Between 1960 and 1970, the number of African American women increased from 17 to 33 percent in northern states and from 3 to 11 percent in the South.

While women in the 1980's and 1990's continued to work part-time, many women sought full-time employment in the retail industry. The highest-paying and most prestigious sales jobs, however, were still retained by men.

Saleswomen and Unions. In 1867, many saleswomen began to fight against the long hours by becoming members alongside men in the Clerks' Early Closing Association. In 1890, Mary Burke, a charter member and the first vice president of the Retail Clerks International Association, became the first female delegate to attend an American Federation of Labor (AFL) convention. Although a resolution that she introduced to bring female organizers and members into the union passed at the convention, it took years to implement and enforcement was unsuccessful. By the end of the 1920's, less than 1 percent of the total number of America's saleswomen were a part of the union. For the most part, women were placed in separate locals.

Efforts to aid female workers in general helped saleswomen in some respects. In 1886, Josephine Shaw Lowell and Leonora O'Reilly formed the Working Women's Society to give assistance to strikers and to further legislative efforts for better conditions and shorter hours for workers in the garment industry. After studies revealed that women working in New York's retail stores endured the same poor working environment, Lowell dedicated her time to the plight of saleswomen. Involving reformers, settlement workers, and wealthy women in her cause, she founded the Consumers' League of New York in 1890. Their "White List" educated buyers on what to purchase and advocated the boycott of department stores that did not provide good working conditions for employees.

The Consumers' League of New York and the Retail Clerks International Association began a drive in 1913 to unionize women in New York's department stores. Seeking publicity, the groups used socially prominent women to distribute leaflets. After their arrest, these women gave interviews to newspaper reporters in order to draw attention to the cause, but their efforts largely failed to arouse interest.

Women have made little headway in unionizing efforts to secure equity in pay. Retail sales has often been regarded as transitional work with high turnover rates. The lack of training programs and the unspecialized skills needed in sales make it difficult for workers to become active leaders in unionization. By the mid-1980's, fewer than one in twenty women in the industry had become union members.

Division of Labor. As technology entered the department store, sales became less skilled. Women were less involved in selling, and division into specific sales areas by sex was common. A majority of women sold apparel, while the sales of televisions, appliances, and automobiles were generally male-dominated. Such large items are often commission-based sales and produce higher earnings. By the late twentieth century, most women were still unable to achieve equity in specialized sales departments and remained primarily cashiers for low-ticket items. *—Marilyn Elizabeth Perry*

See also Clerical work; Employment of women; Labor movement and women; Wages, women's

Bibliography

Benson, Susan Porter. *Counter Cultures: Saleswomen, Managers, and Customers in American Department Stores, 1890-1940.* Urbana: University of Illinois Press, 1986.

Bergmann, Barbara R. *The Economic Emergence of Women.* New York: Basic Books, 1986.

Hower, Ralph M. *History of Macy's of New York, 1858-1919: Chapters in the Evolution of the Department Store.* Cambridge, Mass.: Harvard University Press, 1943.

Stromberg, Ann Helton, and Shirley Harkess, eds. *Women Working: Theories and Facts in Perspective.* 2d ed. Mountain View, Calif.: Mayfield, 1988.

Wertheimer, Barbara Mayer. *We Were There: The Story of Working Women in America.* New York: Pantheon Books, 1977.

Retirement Equity Act of 1984

Relevant issues: Business and economics, employment, law

Significance: This act has made it easier for women to participate in pension plans and to receive benefits

Pension plans were developed to provide income for workers after retirement. The Employee Retirement Income Security Act of 1974 (ERISA) set up certain rules about qualifying for a pension and methods of payment. Because some of these rules discriminated against women, the Retirement Equity Act of 1984 was passed.

The act helped women qualify, or become vested, in pension programs by changing the guidelines for years of service. All workers are required to be vested after ten years with a company. Interruptions in those ten years cause loss of pension.

The Retirement Equity Act stated that one-year maternity or paternity leaves could no longer be considered interruptions. It also allowed workers with less than five years of experience to take a five-year break (or less) without loss of credit. This allowance gave women the opportunity to pause in their careers to have time with their children.

The new law also ensured that a woman would receive her husband's benefits even if he died before the age of fifty-five. It protected spouses by requiring written permission before a worker could have a method of pension payment that would cease with his death. (Such payments usually gave a higher monthly income during the spouse's life, but left the survivor with nothing.) Pension benefits also became a required portion of divorce settlements.

See also Antidiscrimination laws; Maternity leave; Wages, women's; Widowhood

Reverse discrimination

Relevant issues: Civil rights, law, race and ethnicity

Significance: This type of preferential treatment by employers and educational institutions to undo the effects of discrimination has been particularly beneficial to white women in increasing their representation in occupations historically dominated by white men

Reverse discrimination can be defined as preferential treatment in the hiring, promotion, or admission of specific underrepresented social groups, particularly women and ethnic minorities, for the purpose of achieving a more equitable representation. Title VII of the Civil Rights Act of 1964 explicitly states that preferential treatment is not required to undo the effects of past discrimination. By the end of the 1970's, however, efforts to implement President Lyndon Johnson's executive orders calling for affirmative action had led to the practices of reverse discrimination. As opposed to "weak" forms of affirmative action to equalize opportunities, such as engaging in wider recruitment efforts to increase minority applicants or hiring a woman over a man with equal qualifications, these practices represent "strong" affirmative action. Included among these practices are the creation of "diversity" faculty positions in universities and the hiring, promotion, or university admission of a lesser-qualified woman over a better-qualified man.

Many white women were better able than members of racial minority groups to take advantage of the initial expansion of educational opportunities brought about by affirmative action, including gaining increased representation in law, medical, and graduate schools. White women were often better economically situated than members of minority groups, and they arguably suffered less from prejudice. For similar reasons, white women became the first group to benefit from reverse discrimination practices in hiring. As a result, white women made quicker inroads into numerous male-dominated professions than minority women and have tended to reach higher levels of leadership within these professions at a faster pace than other intended beneficiaries of affirmative action. White women, for example, now comprise a significant number of university professorial positions of all ranks, while members of racial minorities, both men and women, tend to be fewer in numbers and concentrated at the lower ranks.

An important issue connected to the practice of reverse discrimination is the question of whether it is just. From the beginning, reverse discrimination was criticized for unfairly disadvantaging white men and therefore being as wrong as the discrimination that it was designed to counter. By the 1990's, another debate arose over reverse discrimination concerning that gains of white women as a group. Critics of reverse discrimination argue that giving preferential treatment to individuals with minority status independent of their socioeconomic background goes against one of the purposes of affirmative action: providing greater equality of opportunity to those who are genuinely disadvantaged. Its supporters argue that preferential treatment leads to more positive effects than negative ones and is necessary if workplaces and educational institutions are to reflect the larger diversity of society as a whole. Whether gender-based preferential treatment will continue as a means of affirmative action remains to be seen.

See also Affirmative action; Antidiscrimination laws; Civil Rights Act of 1964; Employment of women; Executive Orders 11246 and 11375; Hiring quotas; Racism; Sexism; Title VII of the Civil Rights Act of 1964

Rich, Adrienne (b. May 16, 1929, Baltimore, Md.)

Area of achievement: Literature and communications

Significance: Rich, one of the most respected poets in America, explores women's lives and personal growth in feminist poetry and essays

Adrienne Rich's poetry and essays reflect her experiences as a fairly traditional 1950's wife and mother through her growing consciousness as a "woman-identified" feminist and lesbian. In her poems, Rich voices the conflicts, confusion, anger, and desire for wholeness felt by millions of women. In the title poem of *Diving into the Wreck* (1973), she describes American culture's "book of myths/ in which/ our names do not appear." The collection received a National Book Award; Rich declined the award personally but accepted in the name of all women. Her other books of poetry include *The Will to Change* (1971), *The Dream of a Common Language* (1978), and *An Atlas of the Difficult World* (1991).

In her essay "When We Dead Awaken: Writing as Re-Vision," from *On Lies, Secrets, and Silence* (1979), Rich urges women to practice feminist "re-visioning" of literature, history, and myth to find the silenced experiences and voices of women. She sees the "act of looking back, of seeing with fresh eyes" as "an act of survival" for women. In *Of Woman Born: Motherhood as Experience and Institution* (1976), Rich ties this re-visioning to women reclaiming ownership of their bodies. By thus learning to "think through the body, . . . [s]exuality, politics, intelligence, power, work, motherhood, community, intimacy will develop new meanings; thinking itself will be transformed."

Another key essay, "Compulsory Heterosexuality and Lesbian Existence" (1980), suggests that women who have strong relationships with other women apply a wider definition of the term "lesbian" to themselves as a challenge to the patriarchal mandate of "compulsory heterosexuality."

See also Feminist literary criticism; Heterosexism; Lesbian continuum; Lesbianism; Literature, images of women in; Poetry and poets; Sexuality, women's; Women-identified women

Ride, Sally (b. May 26, 1951, Encino, Calif.)

AREA OF ACHIEVEMENT: Science and technology

SIGNIFICANCE: Ride became the first American woman in space

Educated at Westlake High School in Los Angeles and at Stanford University, Sally Ride studied physics and English, earning a Ph.D. in physics; she also achieved a national ranking as a tennis player. In 1978, Ride was selected as an astronaut candidate by the National Aeronautics and Space Administration (NASA) and became a mission specialist for Space Shuttle crews. She served on the six-day flight of the orbiter *Challenger* in June, 1983. In August, 1987, she wrote a report for NASA entitled "Leadership—and America's Future in Space."

See also Astronauts, women as; Pilots, women as; Science, women in

Right to privacy

RELEVANT ISSUES: Family, law, reproductive rights

SIGNIFICANCE: The right to privacy was formally recognized by the U.S. Supreme Court in *Griswold v. Connecticut* (1965), a case concerning the use of contraceptives by married couples

Although the right to privacy per se is not set out in the Constitution, the word "private" does appear in the Fifth Amendment, which states that "private property [shall not] be taken for public use, without just compensation." Accordingly, the U.S. Supreme Court's initial approach to the right to privacy occurred in the context of the debate about substantive due process around the beginning of the twentieth century. Substantive due process, as developed by the Supreme Court, was a Fourteenth Amendment concept meant to protect private property and free enterprise.

Astronaut Sally Ride, who in 1983 became the first American woman in space. (AP/Wide World Photos)

The modern concept of the right to privacy, growing out of "penumbras and emanations" of the Bill of Rights and emphasizing civil rights, developed from Justice William O. Douglas' majority opinion in *Griswold v. Connecticut*, in which the Court declared unconstitutional a state law prohibiting the use of contraceptives and the distribution to married couples of information about family planning. By this time, the Supreme Court had undergone a revolution of sorts, deferring to legislation for protection of private property and discarding its prior allegiance to substantive due process. Instead, the modern Court came to see its role as the defender of individual liberties from state interference. Privacy—particularly as it related to sexuality—was counted as one of the rights guaranteed by the first ten amendments to the Constitution, the Bill of Rights.

A number of subsequent Supreme Court cases concerning contraception followed the precedent set by *Griswold v. Connecticut*, but in 1973, the right to privacy took on a whole new significance when it was used to uphold a woman's right to abortion in *Roe v. Wade*. Adherents of *Roe v. Wade*, emphasizing the civil liberties aspect of the decision, called themselves "pro-choice," while opponents went by the rubric "pro-life." *Roe v. Wade* has since been significantly narrowed, and reaction to it arguably led to the defeat not only of the Equal Rights Amendment (ERA) but of numerous pro-choice Democratic legislators as well. During the Reagan and Bush administrations, commitment to overturning *Roe v. Wade* also became a litmus test for potential Supreme Court appointees.

Perhaps inevitably, *Roe v. Wade* led to another, more starkly delineated test of sexual autonomy. By a one-vote margin, the Court upheld a state statute outlawing sodomy in *Bowers v. Hardwick* (1986). While declining to address the constitutionality of the statute with regard to certain apparently prohibited heterosexual acts, Justice Byron White's majority opinion stated unequivocally that the Constitution does not protect the right of individuals to engage in homosexual activity. *Bowers v. Hardwick* thus set boundaries to the right to privacy and at the same time impeded integration of gay men and lesbians into mainstream American society.

See also Abortion; Birth control and family planning; *Griswold v. Connecticut*; Reproductive rights; *Roe v. Wade*

Roe v. Wade

Date: Decided on December 13, 1973

Relevant issues: Law, reproductive rights

Significance: Undoubtedly the most controversial Supreme Court opinion of its time, *Roe v. Wade* reinforced a constitutional right to privacy and established a woman's right to abortion

Using the name Jane Roe to protect her privacy, Norma McCorvey, a pregnant Texas woman, challenged her state's prohibition of all abortions save those necessary to save the mother's life. Responsibility for writing the Supreme Court's opinion was given to Justice Harry Blackmun, who initially drafted an opinion that struck the Texas statute down because of its vagueness. When it became apparent that his opinion did not have the support of a majority of the justices, the case was reargued, and Blackmun wrote a second opinion based on the right of privacy. The Court upheld a woman's right to abortion by a vote of seven to two. The opinion of the Court did not rule out state regulation of abortion altogether: While government interference of any sort was prohibited during the first trimester of a pregnancy, during the next three months states were permitted to enforce reasonable regulations regarding the mother's health, and they could ban abortion outright during the final trimester.

Laypersons responded by making *Roe v. Wade* a cause célèbre. Among conservatives, the pro-life movement gained strong support, and when Ronald Reagan was elected president in 1980, his administration made federal judicial appointments—including those to the Supreme Court—contingent on opposition to *Roe v. Wade*. Because the Court left some room for state regulation, the pro-life movement also succeeded in pressuring some state legislatures to pass laws restricting abortion as much as possible. A number of these statutes passed constitutional muster, and supporters of *Roe v. Wade*, faced with the prospect that the Court might overrule the decision, rallied to help defeat President Reagan's 1987 nomination of Robert Bork, an abortion opponent, as the replacement for retiring Justice Lewis Powell. Subsequent Court appointments, as well as state and federal elections, have been colored by an ongoing public debate over the mother's right to privacy versus the fetus' right to life.

The right to privacy was a relatively recent innovation in constitutional jurisprudence and, based on *Griswold v. Connecticut* (1965), its clearest explication prior to *Roe v. Wade*, its primary application was in the area of sexuality. In *Griswold v. Connecticut*, the Supreme Court had decriminalized the dissemination of contraception, but this decision did not ensure reproductive freedom. In the 1960's and 1970's, the burgeoning women's movement made the attainment of abortion rights one of its primary goals. With the defeat of the proposed Equal Rights Amendment (ERA) in 1982, however, the movement lost some of its momentum. With such decisions as *Webster v. Reproductive Health Services* (1989), which did away with the tripartite regulatory framework fashioned in *Roe v. Wade*, the Court retreated from its earlier endorsement of a woman's right to abortion, leaving its future very much in doubt.

See also Abortion; Antiabortion protests and women; Birth control and family planning; *Griswold v. Connecticut*; National Abortion and Reproductive Rights Action League (NARAL); Pro-choice; Pro-life; Reproductive rights; Right to privacy; *Silent Scream, The*

Room of One's Own, A

Author: Virginia Woolf (1882-1941)

Date: 1929

Relevant issues: Literature and communications

Significance: This key feminist text explores the personal and economic circumstances required for women to create great literature

A Room of One's Own is an expansion of two papers that British writer Virginia Woolf read in 1928 to literary societies at Newnham and Girton, the women's colleges of Oxford and Cambridge universities. The book and its title have become a reference point for feminists who have carried on Woolf's argument that in order for women to create great works of literature, they must have both economic independence and a private space for their writing.

Woolf was addressing an audience of women less than ten years after women had won the right to vote in England. Securing the vote had been an arduous and sometimes violent fight, with militant suffragists imprisoned and sometimes force-fed when they refused to take nourishment. Woolf alludes to these events and to the publications of male antisuffragists who questioned women's capabilities and referred to them as the second and inferior sex. She speculates that resistance to women's rights has led some men to assert their superiority in ways that they might not have thought of had women not launched their protests.

Woolf distinguishes herself from strident feminists (most notably in her allusions to Rebecca West), admitting that women still have much to prove. Rather than squarely attacking the male domination of literature and literary arguments, she opts for an indirect approach—questioning why, for example, there is no female William Shakespeare. To answer, she takes a novelist's approach, inventing the character of Shakespeare's sister Judith and showing how neither family nor society would have tolerated a female playwright. Women were not even allowed on the stage as actors, Woolf emphasizes. Indeed, women were still considered men's property, had few rights of their own, and were often subject to beatings and other humiliations that they were powerless to prevent. Women were both a protected and a subjugated class.

To her audience at Newnham and Girton, Woolf suggests that intelligence and even education are not enough. The most brilliant woman without an independent income and a room of her own would soon find herself bogged down in family responsibilities and beholden to a father and husband. Leisure and income are not luxuries for female writers; they are necessities—as they are for men, who rely on women to provide them with the comforts of home and family so that they have the time and space in which to write.

Woolf's arguments have not been superseded. They remain a bedrock of feminist belief and have been filtered through every aspect of feminism—applicable not only to female writers but to all women wishing to have careers and independent lives. Woolf's historical approach, which shows how culture shapes women's perceptions of themselves and their roles, still pervades discussions of women's issues. Woolf shows that women should not be viewed merely in biological terms—that is, defined solely in terms of their sex and childbearing capacity—but in terms of the idea of woman as a social construct.

See also Drama and dramatists; Feminism; Fiction writers; Literature, images of women in

Roosevelt, Eleanor (Oct. 11, 1884, New York, N.Y.—Nov. 7, 1962, New York, N.Y.)

Areas of achievement: Civil rights, politics, social reform

Significance: Roosevelt reinvented the position of First Lady, building on her earlier years of political and social activism to become one of the most influential and admired women of the twentieth century

After polio limited her husband's political activity in the 1920's, Anna Eleanor Roosevelt began her involvement in politics, at first to help his career but quickly with her own agenda. She became active in the Consumers' League, the Women's Trade Union League, the League of Women Voters, and the Democratic Women's Clubs. Working for labor, minority, and women's rights, she made lifelong friendships with progressive, radical women.

After Franklin Delano Roosevelt (FDR) became president in 1932, Eleanor Roosevelt held the first press conference by a First Lady, as well as women-only press conferences to help female journalists. She wrote syndicated columns for newspapers and magazines, broadcast radio talks, and traveled throughout the United States and the world as an official representative of the president.

Roosevelt gathered information on her travels to support her calls within FDR's administration for greater economic and educational opportunities for women, people of color, and the poor. She also raised public awareness of these issues by such symbolic acts as flying with black pilots when the Army questioned their capabilities and sitting in the middle of the aisle when confronted with a segregated meeting hall in Birmingham, Alabama.

A delegate to the newly formed United Nations, Roosevelt chaired the Human Rights Commission and guided through the adoption of the Universal Declaration of Human Rights in 1948. In later years, she spoke out against McCarthyism. During the Kennedy Administration, she chaired the President's Commission on the Status of Women and worked for passage of the Equal Pay Act of 1963.

See also Civil Rights movement and women; Equal Pay Act of 1963; Journalism, women in; National Women's Trade Union League (NWTUL); New Deal and women; Politics; President's Commission on the Status of Women

Rosenfeld v. Southern Pacific

Date: Rendered on June 1, 1971

Relevant issues: Civil rights, employment, sex and gender

Significance: This U.S. Court of Appeals Ninth Circuit opinion strictly interpreted the Civil Rights Act of 1964 with regard to the prohibition of discrimination in employment based on sex, thus striking down a California law permitting sex discrimination in employment

In 1966, Leah Rosenfeld applied for the job of sole agent-telegrapher in Thermal, California. Her employer refused to consider her application, stating that the decision had been made that women would not be employed in such a position. Rosenfeld responded by filing a complaint with the Equal

Employment Opportunity Commission (EEOC) claiming that the refusal to hire women as agent-telegraphers violated the Civil Rights Act of 1964.

Southern Pacific argued that it could not hire women for the sole agent-telegrapher position under a California law that prohibited the employment of women in jobs involving lifting more than a certain amount of weight. The job, as defined by Southern Pacific, required the lifting of objects weighing as much as fifty pounds and extraordinarily long workdays during the harvest season. The Court responded by striking down the California law, ruling that prospective employees should be considered regardless of sex and "on the basis of individual capacity."

See also Civil Rights Act of 1964; Equal Employment Opportunity Commission (EEOC); Supreme Court rulings on discrimination against women; Title VII of the Civil Rights Act of 1964

RU-486

Relevant issues: Health and medicine, law, reproductive rights

Significance: RU-486 is a drug that can be used to induce miscarriage; debate over its use and legalization is thus part of the ongoing debate over legal abortion

RU-486 is a synthetic hormone, given in pill form, that causes the resorption or shedding of the uterine lining, thus inducing menstruation or (if the woman is pregnant) a miscarriage. Taken at an early stage of pregnancy, in the first or second month, RU-486 can be used by itself as a method for causing an elective abortion of the embryo. In later stages of pregnancy, in the third or fourth month, an abortion can be achieved by using RU-486 followed by one or more doses of prostaglandin, a hormone that causes the uterine contractions necessary to expel a fetus.

While RU-486 seems to hold promise for other medical purposes, it was originally tested and marketed in France for its contragestive properties (properties contrary to those needed for normal gestation). Once RU-486 was approved and made available to the French public, Roussel-Uclaf, the company that produced it, was threatened with a boycott by several pro-life consumer groups in the United States. Roussel-Uclaf tried to remove the drug from the market in order to avoid the U.S. boycott of its other products but was ordered by the French government, which had paid for the drug's development and testing, to keep it available as an option for French women.

In the United States, the availability of RU-486 is embroiled in the ongoing debate over abortion. Pro-choice groups argue

The controversy over RU-486, the so-called French abortion pill, caused bitterness on both sides of the abortion issue. (AP/Wide World Photos)

that since abortion is legal, the U.S. government has no basis from which to prevent this drug from receiving Food and Drug Administration (FDA) approval. They believe that availability of RU-486 is a consumer right that would benefit those women who find it too difficult or too expensive to go to a hospital or clinic to procure a surgical abortion. Pro-life groups, on the other hand, fear that even if RU-486 were made available only by prescription, the option of simply taking a pill to induce abortion chemically, rather than undergoing a surgical procedure, will result in more women choosing to have an abortion rather than to continue their pregnancies.

Whether the availability of RU-486 would actually make abortion easier or more common is not really known. While its use would not require going to a hospital or clinic, the pregnant woman would have to take an action herself (take the pill) rather than have a procedure performed on her by somebody else; this shift may increase feelings of personal responsibility and second thoughts. In addition, a woman who uses RU-486 as an abortifacient must undergo the physical and psychological experience of expelling the fetus—an experience not part of a surgical abortion.

See also Abortion; Birth control and family planning; Gynecology and obstetrics; Health and medicine; Morning-after pill; Pro-choice; Pro-life; Reproductive rights

Rubella

Relevant issues: Health and medicine

Significance: Rubella may cause birth defects when a woman is exposed to the virus during the first three months of her pregnancy

Rubella, also known as German measles, is a viral infection that typically has little impact on infected children and adults beyond a rash and swollen lymph glands. If the infected individual is a woman in her first three months of pregnancy, however, this virus may have dramatic effects on the developing fetus: There is an approximately 50 percent chance that her infant will be born with birth defects. Birth defects occur because the rubella virus affects specific structures that are developing at a rapid pace during this time, including the central nervous system structures of the eyes and ears. Thus, exposure during the first three months may lead to the birth of an infant who has cataracts or who is deaf. Rubella may also cause brain damage and mental retardation. Prenatal exposure to rubella has also been linked to the development of autism, a psychological disorder. The high probability of birth defects may cause a pregnant woman who has been exposed to rubella to consider having a therapeutic abortion. The use of abortions to prevent birth defects, however, has moral, legal, and ethical ramifications. It is possible to prevent birth defects caused by exposure to the rubella virus through immunization of women before they become pregnant.

See also Abortion; Family planning services; Gynecology and obstetrics; Health and medicine; Pregnancy and childbirth; Prenatal care

Rubyfruit Jungle

Author: Rita Mae Brown (1944-)

Date: 1973

Relevant issues: Literature and communications, sex and gender

Significance: Brown's book bridged the gap between the women's movement of the 1960's and the lesbian rights movement of the 1970's

Only Radclyffe Hall's *The Well of Loneliness* (1928) surpasses *Rubyfruit Jungle* in fame as a lesbian coming-of-age story. The titles of both books have become code words for homosexuality; a reader in a strange city, seeing a sign that read "Rubyfruit Books," could expect to find a good selection of gay and lesbian literature. Rita Mae Brown was a member of several groups in both the gay rights and women's movements in New York City. Mainstream women's groups such as the National Organization for Women (NOW) considered her too radical, while many lesbian groups thought her not radical enough. Brown has since written several mysteries and historical novels, as well as other books with lesbian heroines.

Critics often compare *Rubyfruit Jungle* to Mark Twain's juvenile heroes. Molly Bolt has the same uncertain parentage, colorful lifestyle, enterprise, cheerful self-regard, and ability to get into scrapes as Huck Finn and Tom Sawyer. The character of Molly, however, differs in important respects. Unlike Huck or Tom, she must confront gender issues in each of her escapades. Brown handles these problems as wittily as Twain, but with more of a ribald twist. Molly's growing awareness of her sexual orientation is but one way in which she differs from other people in the small town of Coffee Hollow. None of these differences shakes her appealing innocence or her firm belief that society's ideas are wrong, not her own.

See also Brown, Rita Mae; Fiction writers; Lesbian and gay studies programs; Lesbian rights movement; Lesbianism; Literature, images of women in

Rust v. Sullivan

Date: Decided on May 23, 1991

Relevant issues: Family, health and medicine, reproductive rights

Significance: In this case, the Supreme Court upheld the constitutionality of guidelines forbidding government-funded family planning agencies from providing counseling, information, or referrals related to abortion

In 1988, Louis Sullivan, Secretary of Health and Human Services, issued guidelines under Title X of the Public Health Service Act of 1970. These guidelines—constituting the so-called gag rule—forbade employees from counseling, providing information, or making referrals concerning abortion. Irving Rust, who represented Title X grantees and doctors, filed a lawsuit. Losing in a lower court, Rust filed with the Supreme Court. By a vote of five to four, the Court upheld the guidelines, noting that because family planning clinics provide no postconception services, discussion of abortion is unnecessary. The majority ruled that the ban did not violate freedom of speech since employees could express their views outside of work. Additionally, it denied that the guidelines restricted the doctor-patient relationship since these doctors were employed to provide only family planning information. The Court's majority opinion in *Rust v. Sullivan* reaffirmed the government's interest in promoting childbirth.

The minority opinion described the guidelines as "viewpoint-based suppression of speech" that prevented physicians from fulfilling their professional duties. The four dissenting justices noted that Title X limited funds for the practice of abortion but permitted abortion counseling as a family planning alternative. The decision highlighted the power of presidential appointment to shape abortion policy, especially since the guidelines were rescinded by the Clinton Administration. Such cases have mobilized women and women's groups at the national political level as a means of having an impact on abortion policy and debate.

See also Abortion; Birth control and family planning; Family planning services; Pro-choice; Pro-life; Reproductive rights

Margaret Sanger

Sanger, Margaret (Sept. 14, 1879, Corning, N.Y.—Sept. 6, 1966, Tucson, Ariz.)

Areas of achievement: Health and medicine, reproductive rights

Significance: Planned Parenthood founder Sanger spent her life crusading for women's reproductive rights

As one of eleven children and later as a nurse among poor women, Margaret Sanger became convinced that "no woman can call herself free who does not own and control her own body." From 1913 until 1936, Sanger wrote and challenged the Comstock Law, which equated information about sexual diseases and contraception with obscenity. In 1914, under indictment for breaking the law in her journal *Woman Rebel*, she fled to Europe and spent a year studying under Dutch midwives.

In 1916, after her return, Sanger and her sister Ethel Byrne opened a birth control clinic in Brooklyn, the first one in the United States. In the ten days before the clinic was closed, five hundred women sought information and the diaphragms that Sanger had smuggled into the country. In 1921, she established the American Birth Control League and opened the Birth Control Clinical Research Bureau in 1923; the two organizations merged in 1942 to become the Planned Parenthood Federation of America. Sanger traveled the country to educate the public and physicians about contraception and to raise money for research, including the development of a birth control pill. She was active internationally as well, founding the International Planned Parenthood Federation in 1953.

Sanger's writings include *What Every Girl Should Know* (1916), *Happiness in Marriage* (1926), *Motherhood in Bondage* (1928), *My Fight for Birth Control* (1931) and *Margaret Sanger: An Autobiography* (1938). In addition, she edited and wrote for such journals as *Birth Control Review*, *Journal of Conception*, and *Human Fertility*.

See also Birth control and family planning; Clinics, women's; Condoms, male and female; Family planning services; Intrauterine device (IUD); Planned Parenthood; Reproductive rights

Sauvé, Jeanne (Apr. 26, 1922, Prud'Homme, Saskatchewan, Canada—Jan. 26, 1993, Montreal, Quebec, Canada)

Areas of achievement: Literature and communications, politics

Significance: Sauvé was the first woman to serve as governor-general of Canada

Educated at universities in Ottawa and Paris, Jeanne Sauvé had distinguished careers as both a journalist and a politician. She worked for the British Broadcasting Corporation (BBC), served as president of the Canadian Institute of Public Affairs, and was elected to Parliament in 1972. She served as secretary of state for science and technology, minister of environment, and minister of communications. After a term as speaker of the House of Commons from 1980 to 1984, Sauvé was named governor-general of Canada. While in office, she maintained her position as an outspoken advocate of women's rights.

See also French Canadian women; Journalism, women in; Politics

Schlafly, Phyllis (b. Aug. 15, 1924, St. Louis, Mo.)

Areas of achievement: Politics, women's history

Significance: Schlafly organized an influential antifeminist movement and has been an effective proponent of ultraconservative political causes

Ultraconservative Phyllis Schlafly is one of the most effective activists against the women's movement. With postgraduate degrees from Radcliffe College and Washington University Law School, she has been an articulate, persuasive voice against liberal politics, the National Organization for Women (NOW), the Equal Rights Amendment (ERA), and "women's libbers."

Schlafly began her political activity working for the Republican Party in the late 1940's and ran unsuccessfully for Congress in 1952, 1960, and 1970. Despite these defeats, Schlafly's rhetorical skill and strong anticommunist views, coupled with her devout religious and social conservatism, made her an important writer and campaigner for other Republicans. She wrote the best-selling book *A Choice Not an Echo* (1964) in support of Barry Goldwater's presidential bid.

In addition to serving in such groups as the National Federation of Republican Women and the Cardinal Mindszenty Foundation, Schlafly has founded organizations to promote the ultraconservative agenda, including the Eagle Trust Fund, Stop ERA, and the highly influential Eagle Forum. Schlafly's strongly stated belief that "God intends the husband to be the head of the family" finds strong support from a wide variety of conservative constituencies, both male and female.

In addition to her public writings and lectures, Schlafly has hosted a nationally syndicated radio show and authored such books as *The Phyllis Schlafly Report* (1967), *Kissinger on the Couch* (1975), and *The Power of the Positive Woman* (1977), a Conservative Book Club selection and best-seller.

See also Antifeminism; *Backlash*; Equal Rights Amendment (ERA); National Organization for Women (NOW); Religious Right and women; Republican Party and women

Science, women in

Relevant issues: Science and technology

Significance: The mid- to late 1900's have brought widespread recognition of some women's scientific abilities and questioned the reason for the relatively small number of female scientists

A brief survey of scientific achievements by women dispels the notion that women inherently cannot "do" science. The specific examples presented below demonstrate the variety of eras and social contexts in which women have made noteworthy scientific contributions.

Early History. In the fourth century B.C., upon the death of her father, Aristippus, Arete of Cyrene took over leadership of the academy of natural philosophy (what is now called "science") that he had founded. In her thirty-five years of teaching, she instructed more than one hundred students and wrote forty books. After her death, the academy was led by her son, Aristippus II, called "Metrodidactos" ("taught by his mother").

Hypatia (A.D. 370-415), daughter of the mathematician and astronomer Theon, lectured on science and philosophy in Alexandria during the golden age of that city. Her inventions included the astrolabe. Accused of pagan beliefs, she was stoned to death by a Christian mob.

Hildegard of Bingen (1098-1179), abbess of a Benedictine convent in twelfth century Germany, is regarded as a cosmologist. Her writings were a blend of science, mysticism, and theology—she saw the universe as the handiwork of God. She was also skilled in medicine and enjoyed considerable prestige in political and ecclesiastical circles.

Emilie de Breteuil, Madame du Chatelet (1706-1749), was a close associate, intellectually and sexually, of the philosopher Voltaire. During the years of their alliance, she conducted experiments, had a paper on the nature of fire published by the French Academy, and wrote a summary of the physics of her age, ostensibly for her son, the future Marquise du Chatelet. Her translation into French with her own commentary of Sir Isaac Newton's *Principia Mathematica* remains the standard in France.

Two eighteenth century female scientists were Italian, both from well-to-do, academic families that provided their daughters with a complete education. Laura Bassi (1711-1778) was admitted to study at the University of Bologna and received her doctorate in 1733. Soon after, she joined the faculty there, the first woman ever to occupy a faculty chair at any university. She published treatises on mechanics and hydrodynamics and became well known in scholarly circles throughout Europe. During her marriage to Jean-Joseph Veratti, she gave birth to twelve children. A devoted mother and pious woman, after her death her remains were interred in the Church of Corpus Domini. Maria Agnesi (1718-1799), whose father was a professor of mathematics, the eldest of his twenty-one children, was recognized early by him as a prodigy. After receiving tutoring in philosophy and mathematics, she displayed her knowledge in the Agnesi salon to local and visiting intellectuals. After the death of her mother, she assumed the responsibility for the Agnesi household and the education of her younger brothers. She wrote and had published some ninety essays, primarily on mathematical topics including Newton's theory of gravity, but she also wrote an essay pleading for the education of women. In 1750, the pope appointed her to replace her father as the chair of mathematics and natural philosophy at the University of Bologna.

The entry of Caroline Herschel (1750-1848) into the annals of famous female scientists is a curious one. She was born in Hanover into a family that was largely musical but was also interested in astronomy. She received no formal education before going to England in 1772 to train as a singer under the guidance of her brothers, who were already established musicians there. She became a successful soprano, but when her brother William's primary interest shifted to astronomy, she elected to train to become his assistant, a role she admirably fulfilled. William prospered as a telescope builder and observer, relying on his sister for domestic as well as scientific help. By 1786, she had her own small observatory where she discovered her first comet and reported it to the Royal Society; news of it was published in *Philosophical Transactions*. By 1797, she had discovered seven more comets while continuing to assist William in his nebular observations. In 1828, when she was seventy-five years old, she was awarded a Gold Medal by the Royal Society for her completion of the cataloging of the nebulae that her brother had discovered in his lifetime.

It is noteworthy that the science activity of all the women discussed above, with the exception of Hildegard, occurred in relation to a strong male figure—father, brother, or lover.

History Since 1800. The nineteenth century brought increasing numbers of women to scientific study. One circumstance was the growth in the popularization of science in books and lectures. These provided women with access to scientific information and, in many cases, sparked their interest and led to their involvement. Lectures for the general public at the Royal Institution in London and those delivered in several American cities by John Tyndall during his visit in 1871-1872 attracted numerous female attendees. Some women subsequently pursued further scientific study, either on their own or with the encouragement of male relatives or friends.

Mary (née Fairfax) Somerville (1780-1872), an outspoken feminist and largely self-taught, was especially successful in writing expository books in physics and mathematics. She was elected to membership in several scientific societies and had a supportive husband who edited and copied her manuscripts. Mrs. Jane (née Haldimand) Marcet (1769-1858), born in London of Swiss parents, also enjoyed the encouragement of her husband, a Swiss physician. She wrote "Conversations in Chemistry Intended More Especially for the Female Sex," which was hugely successful, reprinted in sixteen editions in England, fifteen in America, and two French translations. Boys as well as girls were among her readers. Michael Faraday credited her with sparking his interest in chemistry.

Ada Lovelace (1815-1852), the daughter of Lord Byron, was associated with the early computer designer and builder Charles Babbage, for whom she provided valuable assistance. A computer language, "ADA," was named in her honor.

With the founding of women's colleges, scientific study was opened to young women, such as these students in a physics class in 1900. (Corbis-Bettman)

In the United States, astronomer Maria Mitchell (1818-1889) became the first internationally recognized female American scientist. Initially introduced to astronomy by her father and later self-taught, she received a gold medal from the king of Denmark for her 1847 discovery of a new comet. In 1849, she began making mathematical computations for the *American Ephemeris and Nautical Almanac* at an annual salary of $300—one of the first recorded incomes from the U.S. government to a female scientist. With little formal education, she was nevertheless invited to become a professor of astronomy at Vassar College when it opened in 1865.

The opening of women's colleges in the latter part of the nineteenth century in the United States, Canada, and England provided hitherto unheard-of opportunities for women to enter scientific fields. Some graduates pursued doctoral study at home or abroad and went on to faculty positions primarily at women's colleges. Many others, however, found life-long employment in auxiliary roles. One such opportunity was found at the Harvard College Observatory, where the director, Edward Pickering, for many years hired women as "computers" to examine and catalog photographs of stars. Annie Jump Cannon (1863-1941), a graduate of Wellesley College, where she had majored in astronomy, was one such worker from 1896 to 1940; in her lifetime, she cataloged more than 300,000 stars. Valuable though her services were as curator of astronomical photographs, she was denied real status by Harvard University but was awarded an honorary doctorate by Groningen University in 1921 and by Oxford University in 1925. Only in 1938 did Harvard University give her a formal appointment as astronomer, a singular distinction for a woman at that time. She conformed to the expectation that a female scientist would remain unmarried.

Harriet Brooks studied physics as an undergraduate at McGill University in Montreal with Ernest Rutherford near the turn of the century, at the time when he was doing research in radioactivity. For a brief time, she was associated with the newly opened women's college there, Royal Victoria College, where she did important research on radioactive decay. She then took a position as assistant at Bryn Mawr College in Pennsylvania while continuing her contacts with Rutherford, who recognized her talent and experimental skill. Rutherford encouraged her to go to the Cavendish Laboratory, then directed by Sir J. J. Thomson, who was receptive to female students, having married one himself. (Mrs. Thomson, however, discontinued her studies in favor of serving as the director's wife.) Brooks later worked in the laboratory of Marie Curie in Paris. In 1911, she accepted a marriage proposal from a former Rutherford assistant and returned to Montreal, ending her scientific activity but enjoying a satisfactory marriage.

A compatriot of Brooks, Elizabeth Laird (1874-1969) obtained her bachelor's degree in physics at the University of Toronto, came to the United States for graduate study at Bryn Mawr College, where she obtained Ph.D.'s in mathematics and physics, and saw her research published in the newly founded *Physical Review*. On four occasions, she studied in Europe prior to World War I. From 1901 to her retirement in 1940, she taught physics at Mount Holyoke College, a women's college in Massachusetts that had a strong emphasis on science. She always kept abreast of new scientific developments. On retirement, she returned to Canada and worked on a radar project for the Canadian Research Council during World War II. After the war, she taught herself enough biophysics to be able to contribute to the work of the Ontario Cancer Research Foundation in the medical use of radar wavelength radiation.

Maria Goeppert Mayer (1906-1972), a theoretical physicist with a Ph.D. from the University of Gottingen, arrived in the United States in 1930 as the bride of Joseph Mayer, an American chemist who had gone to Gottingen for postdoctoral study. In three different academic settings where Joseph was employed, no position was ever offered to Maria. She did some teaching and mentoring on a voluntary basis while rearing two children. Well respected professionally, especially among the European scientists, such as Enrico Fermi and Edward Teller, who had immigrated to the United States in the 1930's, she managed to keep abreast of new developments and did the important work for which she was awarded the Nobel Prize in 1963. She was, by that time, professor of physics at the University of California at San Diego, where both she and her husband were offered positions in 1960. Her health was declining by that time, and she died in 1972 at the age of sixty-five, never having been able to enjoy the full potential of her long-awaited professorship. The Depression years, 1929 to 1941, when the United States entered World War II, were particularly precarious for a married woman seeking employment. It was generally assumed that first call on openings would be given to men with wives and families to support. It also should be recognized that Mayer's employment prospects would not have been good had she stayed in Europe, where women were even less likely to obtain positions on university faculties.

In the years between the two world wars, women's colleges and coeducational state universities in America were training more young women to be scientists than could be employed in academic institutions. Civil service positions with the federal government and employment in industry seemed to offer alternative opportunities. For the most part, aspirants to such positions were underemployed, frequently being urged, if hired at all, to accept "womanly" positions, such as science secretaries or science librarians. Conversely, Katherine Blodgett (1898-1979), educated in physics at Bryn Mawr College and at the University of Chicago, had a satisfactory experience at the General Electric Company in Schenectady, New York, where she worked from 1918 to her retirement in 1963. As a member of the research staff at General Electric, she became closely associated with the chemist Irving Langmuir who, impressed by her ability, encouraged her to pursue further graduate study at the Cavendish Laboratory, then directed by Ernest Rutherford. By taking a two-year leave of absence from General Electric, Blodgett was able to obtain her Ph.D. from Cambridge University in 1926, the first to be awarded to a woman by that institution. At General Electric, she resumed working with Langmuir but later gained fame on her own as the inventor of a thin-film technique that rendered glass "invisible." Both Blodgett and Laird conformed to the image of successful, unmarried female scientists.

Employment with the federal government was sought and found by some female scientists, especially after the passage of the Nineteenth Amendment granting woman suffrage in 1919. Margaret Rossiter's detailed account of their successes and difficulties can be found in *Women Scientists in America* (1982). Under pressure from women, civil service tests were opened to women, but the route to employment was not straightforward. Male veterans were automatically placed at the head of all lists for jobs. Even after reaching the top of the list, a woman had to be "accepted" by the supervisor under whom she would work.

Honors Received and Denied. A system of recognition and honors is an integral part of contemporary science. Some women have received their due share. Mention has already been made of the gold medals awarded to astronomers Caroline Herschel and Maria Mitchell. Such awards, however, must be in addition to the more fundamental prerequisites of suitable employment and opportunity to pursue one's individual scientific interests and research.

Each scientific discipline has its own internal cast of awards. Some, such as the Nobel Prizes, restricted to the areas of physics, chemistry, physiology, or medicine, are especially famous and lucrative. Others, such as election to membership in the National Academy of Sciences and to the presidency of a particular scientific society, are purely honorary but do carry considerable prestige. A brief look at how women have fared in these categories shows actual achievement but frequent underrepresentation or even denial of credit due.

Since the inauguration of the Nobel Prizes in 1901, nine women have been so honored. Marie Curie was the first, and she won two: the first in physics in 1903, jointly with husband Pierre and with Henri Becquerel; the second in chemistry in 1911 entirely on her own. The women who have won Nobel Prizes in science since then include Gerty Radnitz Cori (1947, in biochemistry, jointly with her husband); Irene Joliot-Curie, Marie's daughter (1935, in physics, jointly with her husband); Barbara McClintock (1983 in physiology); Maria Goeppert Mayer (1963 in physics); Rita Levi-Montalcini (1986 in physiology); Dorothy Crowfoot Hodgkin (1964 in chemistry); Gertrude Elion (1968 in biochemistry); and Rosalind Yalow (1977 in medicine and physiology).

Not all deserving female scientists have won awards, however. Lise Meitner's contribution to nuclear fission research was ignored when her coworker, Otto Hahn, was given the Nobel Prize in 1946 for that work. China-born and American-educated Chien-Shiung Wu, professor of physics at Columbia University, was not included when Tsung-Dao Lee and Chen Ning Yang were awarded the 1957 Nobel Prize in Physics for the violation of the law of parity. They had theoretically predicted the violation, but it was Wu who showed it in an experiment that stunned the physics community. She received many other awards, some never having been previously awarded to a woman.

Similarly, Rosalind Franklin's crystallographic studies, used without her knowledge and permission by James Watson and Francis Crick, were ignored when the Nobel Prize for unraveling the structure of deoxyribonucleic acid (DNA) was given to Watson and Crick in 1962, four years after Franklin's death at age thirty-seven. Jocelyn Bell Burnell was a graduate student working under Anthony Hewish in radio astronomy when she discovered pulsars, but he alone was awarded the Nobel Prize for their discovery. In each of these four cases, the injustices involved were recognized within the scientific community, but little could be done to redress the damage to the woman's prestige or to her monetary advantage.

A look at the membership in the prestigious National Academy of Sciences shows how few women have thus far been elected, although their number has increased in recent decades. The academy was founded in 1863 to provide the U.S. government with access to scientific advice and information. Between then and 1994, more than three thousand men and fewer than one hundred women had been so honored. Prior to the end of World War II, only three women were elected: medical doctor and anatomist Florence Sabin in 1925, psychologist Margaret Washburn in 1931, and cytogeneticist Barbara McClintock in 1944. In each case, the woman became a member only after having her candidacy delayed well beyond those of men with lesser accomplishments. In 1994, there were about eighty women among the more than eighteen hundred members.

Female presidents of professional scientific societies are rare but not unheard of. The American Physical Society has twice elected a woman as president: Mildred Dresselhaus, a professor at the Massachusetts Institute of Technology (MIT) and Chien-Shiung Wu.

Why So Few? Despite the disappearance of many of the barriers that had kept women of past generations from greater participation in science, at the end of the twentieth century, relatively few women were entering the scientific professions. Several reasons have been advanced to explain this situation—some more obviously valid than others but all taken seriously by contemporary authors and lecturers. Social expectations influence and reinforce self-doubts among young women who are considering scientific careers. There are not many role models or mentors to encourage them. Families, teachers, and publications often convey the impression that female scientists must be virtual geniuses who lead lonely lives. In coeducational schools and colleges, girls are frequently discouraged from taking the courses that will be prerequisites for advanced scientific study, in contrast to the encouragement previously found at all-female institutions. A typical example is the lack of confidence fostered with regard to mathematics, leading to "math anxiety" and a self-fulfilling prophecy. Girls so hampered then fail even to register for courses in the physical and biological sciences in which they might find immediate intellectual stimulation and that might lead to successful scientific careers.

A real and more serious dilemma occurs with regard to the accepted early career schedules for young scientists, male or female. For example, young persons are usually in their late twenties by the time they arrive at the assistant professor level of the academic ladder. Promotion to the next, tenured, level requires another six to seven years, by which time the young female scientist may feel that her opportunity to have children is passing. Even at an academic or research institution that permits an interruption for family duties, a hiatus of a year or more can cause a woman to fall behind her colleagues in a rapidly moving scientific field. Compromises between spouses and availability of child day care can alleviate some difficulty but never completely remove the attendant pressures.

Finally, under the influence of feminist authors and spokeswomen since the late twentieth century, questions have been raised about the nature of Western science as it has developed for centuries in the hands and minds of male practitioners. How valid is the observation that the natural sciences require objective, impersonal rationality, popularly regarded as male attributes, whereas women are regarded as being by nature subjective, emotional, personal, or even possibly irrational? Such considerations have even led some authors to suggest the abandonment of present-day, male-dominated science, considered to be so androcentric and faulty that it needs replacement by one with a more "natural," feminine perspective. Much has been and continues to be written about what is termed the "gender and science" question.

Recent Progress. During and after World War II, women gained entry into many areas previously closed to them. Nepotism regulations, however, precluding the employment of a husband and wife remained in effect at many state universities until well into the 1970's. Since the rise of feminism in the 1960's and the adoption of the Equal Employment Opportunity Act in 1972, women have become a more visible component of the scientific community. Some of the increase in visibility has occurred by virtue of women's own activity and

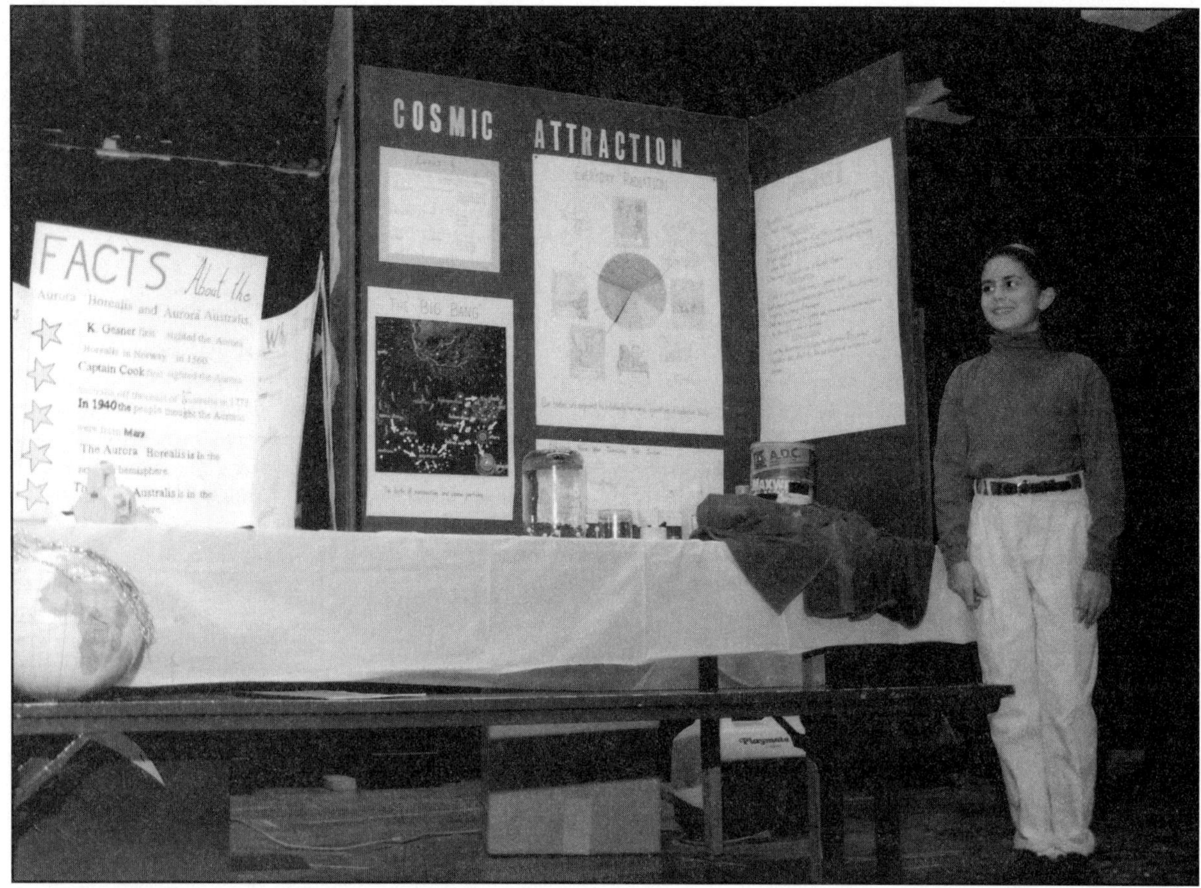

Major strides have been made in encouraging girls to pursue their interest in science, such as this student taking part in a junior high school science fair. (BmPorter/Don Franklin)

some by virtue of society's recognition of the inequities visited on female scientists in the past. Employment announcements routinely append a statement that the organization "is an equal opportunity/affirmative action employer; women . . . are strongly encouraged to apply."

Women themselves have initiated their formation into subgroups within professional scientific societies such as the American Association of Physics Teachers, the American Chemical Society, the History of Science Society, the American Mathematical Society, and the American Physical Society (APS). The Committee on the Status of Women in Physics, part of the APS, is a particularly active group, consisting of representatives from industry, government, and academic institutions. The committee publishes a newsletter to keep its readers—both men and women—informed about developments and issues of particular interest and importance to women, such as employment opportunities, congressional bills, and available prizes. It sponsors gatherings at national meetings of the APS, where networking is fostered and female students find support and encouragement. It also circulates a list of female physicists who are competent to present lectures, colloquia, and seminars in their areas of expertise at universities, colleges, and high schools, with financial support provided for travel.

Many more female scientists than previously are employed in research and administrative capacities in government and industry. In addition, they are increasingly being called to Washington, D.C., to serve on committees. One highly visible female holder of a Ph.D. in physics is Sally Ride, a former astronaut who became a professor of physics and the director of the California Space Institute at the University of California at San Diego. She served on the President's Committee of Advisors on Science and Technology in the Clinton Administration and received a science writing award from the American Institute of Physics for *The Third Planet: Exploring the Earth from Space* (1994), which she coauthored with Tam O'Shaughnessy.

Another woman, Grace Murray Hopper (1906-1992), became well known in the field of computing. A mathematician by training at Vassar College and Yale University, she joined the Navy during World War II and was assigned to Harvard University, where the first working computer was being built for military use. Hopper remained in the Navy after the war, rising to the rank of admiral, the first woman to do so. She was instrumental in developing COBOL, one of the first computer languages to allow communication with the computer using the English language.

Yet, the number of women overall in scientific professions, though varying considerably among the sciences, has remained relatively small. Whether future decades and centuries will see any marked change toward equal male-female representation remains to be seen. It can be hoped that talented young women who love science and contribute to its advance will not be deterred from its study and will find a congenial atmosphere in which to work if they decide to enter one of the scientific professions. —*Katherine R. Sopka*

See also Astronauts, women as; Colleges, women's; Education of women; Inventors, women as; Math anxiety; Psychological theories on women; Ride, Sally; Stereotypes of women; Technology

Bibliography

Alic, Margaret. *Hypatia's Heritage: A History of Women in Science from Antiquity Through the Nineteenth Century*. Boston: Beacon Press, 1986. Detailed compendium of the lives and accomplishments of female scientists in several fields.

Harding, Sandra. *The Science Question in Feminism*. Ithaca, N.Y.: Cornell University Press, 1986. According to Harding, from the mid-1970's to 1986, "feminist criticisms of science have evolved from a reformist to a revolutionary position."

Kass-Simon, G., Patricia Farnes, and Deborah Nash, eds. *Women of Science: Righting the Record*. Bloomington: Indiana University Press, 1990. A series of essays on individual women's scientific accomplishments in ten fields in the twentieth century.

Keller, Evelyn Fox. *Reflections on Gender and Science*. New Haven, Conn.: Yale University Press, 1985. By a former mathematical biologist, one of the earliest and most vocal critics of male-dominated science.

McGrayne, Sharon Bertsch. *Nobel Prize Women in Science: Their Lives, Struggles, and Momentous Discoveries*. Secaucus, N.J.: Carol, 1993. Fourteen biographical sketches, with good notes on sources, for each of the women who have won Nobel Prizes, plus information on overlooked women of comparable caliber.

Mozans, H. J. *Woman in Science*. New York: D. Appleton, 1913. Reprint. Cambridge, Mass.: MIT Press, 1974. The earliest collection of sketches of women outstanding for scientific achievement published in the United States.

Phillips, Patricia. *The Scientific Lady: A Social History of Women's Scientific Interests, 1520-1918*. New York: St. Martin's Press, 1990. A study of the ways in which society defined the relationship between women and science.

Rossiter, Margaret W. *Women Scientists in America: Before Affirmative Action, 1940-1972*. Baltimore: The Johns Hopkins University Press, 1995.

________. *Women Scientists in America: Struggles and Strategies to 1940*. Baltimore: The Johns Hopkins University Press, 1982. These two works by Rossiter examine the contexts within which individual American women achieved their place in science.

Schiebinger, Londa. *The Mind Has No Sex?: Women in the Origins of Modern Science*. Cambridge, Mass.: Harvard University Press, 1989. Scholarly investigation of the history of women in science prior to the twentieth century, with extensive bibliography.

Sonnert, Gerhard, with Gerald Holton. *Gender Differences in Science Careers: The Project Access Study*. New Brunswick, N.J.: Rutgers University Press, 1995. Results of a comparative study on the career trajectories of two hundred matched male and female mathematicians, scientists, and engineers, beginning with their status as postdoctoral fellows.

Science fiction, feminist

Relevant issues: Literature and communications, politics, sex and gender

Significance: Feminist science fiction, as Joanna Russ noted, has grown as a major field of writing for women because it has been considered marginal writing

Beginning with the nineteenth century writers of utopian novels, feminists have explored the possibilities of life outside a patriarchy and have considered the worst possible scenarios if certain patriarchal practices were to be magnified into a dystopian world. Ursula Le Guin, considered by many as one of the most significant female science-fiction writers in the late twentieth century, offers a broad definition of science fiction: The writer asks "what if" and then explores the imaginary results.

This definition may seem too broad for many. Octavia Butler, for example, does not consider her book *Kindred* (1979) to be science fiction, although its premise is that a twentieth century African American woman is repeatedly transported back into the time of slavery. As a working definition, however, Le Guin's allows for a variety of novels with the common ground of speculation. In her own work, such as *The Left Hand of Darkness* (1969), winner of Hugo and Nebula awards from the Science Fiction Writers of America, and *Always Coming Home* (1985), a collage of different genres, she emphasizes the imaginative in creating societies. For many, the genesis of science-fiction writing was Charlotte Perkins Gilman's *Herland* (1915), which was concerned with a society of women who, isolated from men, had evolved their own culture; Inez Haynes Gillmore's *Angel Island* (1988) explores similar themes. The earliest science-fiction text, certainly representing feminist values of a healthy respect and fear of the results of science and a concern for all living creatures, is Mary Shelley's *Frankenstein* (1818). Written by a nineteen-year-old, it remains in print and has been considered a classic by the standards of the most traditional canon.

Writers of feminist science fiction face two problems, one common to all writers of utopian communities, the other a dilemma for feminists in particular. For all science fiction, exposition can be unwieldy and boring, and many writers solve the problem by having an outsider approach the utopia or dystopia in need of explanation. This character is often a man who does not understand how women could develop self-sustaining communities (Gilman's *Herland* and Joan Slonczewski's *A Door into Ocean*). In both these novels, female characters who have lived in a women's society choose to enter into relationships with men from the outside. Although many male science-fiction writers, both in characterization and marketing, have used women's bodies to sell books, women rarely have posed a problem to the creation of their imaginative societies. For the feminist author writing a utopian novel, men as they represent the patriarchy must often be killed or left behind if women are to bond and have the opportunity to create a sisterhood. Suzette Haden Elgin, in the dystopian *Native Tongue* (1984), created a utopian women's community in the Barren Houses, where older women have been abandoned as useless to an extraterrestrial trading society in which linguists have power. In Sally Miller Gearhart's *The Wanderground* (1979), a group of women fled a barbaric patriarchal society in which women were hunted, raped, and killed and formed a separatist colony in which each person is respected. In Gearhart's book, the problem of men is more complex, as it is in most feminist science fiction, because an unusual group of men, the gentles, have also separated and hope to learn how to be self-sustaining separate from the women's community. Although separation is often necessary for women to form these worlds, many deal with the reality of men by permitting men to return, introducing men who are not patriarchal, or by having the women give birth to sons, who must be accepted or rejected. In some books, interaction is allowed but carefully controlled, as in Sheri S. Tepper's *The Gate to Women's Country* (1988) and Leona Gom's *The Y Chromosome* (1990), in which men have been trained to see themselves as inferior.

Many feminist science-fiction writers explore lesbian themes through separatist communities or through women's relationships within a dystopian society. In Joanna Russ's "When It Changed" (1972), which won the Nebula Award, a women's society is structured with strong roles and is on the verge of threat by men. In both *A Door into Ocean* and *The Wanderground*, women alone are responsible for reproduction, and the relationships between female characters are as compelling as the novelty of the society.

For some feminists, possible utopian worlds would emphasize what they see as abilities or characteristics special to women. Examples are Octavia Butler's empath in *Parable of the Sower* (1993) and Elgin's trilogy of Arkansans transplanted to another planet and ruled by grannies, magicians, and a fourteen-year-old girl: *Twelve Fair Kingdoms*, *The Grand Jubilee*, and *And Then There'll Be Fireworks* (1981). Others revise the past to ask how a traditional story might be different if women were seen positively, such as Marion Zimmer Bradley's *The Mists of Avalon* (1982) and Persia Woolley's *Child of the Northern Spring* (1987). Some give women special powers or privileges to survive such horrors as the Inquisition, as in Gael Baudino's *Strands of Starlight* (1989). In Carol Hill's *The Eleven Million High Dancer* (1985), an astronaut finds being a woman to be an incredible advantage to her work.

Acknowledging the patriarchy's obsession with controlling women's reproductive powers, feminist science fiction has explored horrific possibilities in Margaret Atwood's *The Handmaid's Tale* (1985), in which fundamentalist Christians divide women into categories by function and execute feminists. In Sybil Claiborne's *In the Garden of Dead Cars* (1993), the mutation of the AIDS virus has made all sex taboo. In Marge Piercy's *Woman on the Edge of Time* (1976), a birth is allowed, but only if someone has died. In this society, as in many others in feminist science fiction, child care has been redefined, and all children are wanted. In feminist utopias, women are not domestic slaves, and the tradition of "women's work" is shared in most cases.

Feminist science fiction has allowed writers to explore a variety of women's issues by revealing the absurdity of patriarchal fears of reproduction, women's bodies, lesbianism, and sisterhood. In some cases, as in the dystopias, an element of repression is explored in the extreme; in other cases, the patriarchy has robbed women of the rights to work and vote and to make decisions about their bodies. In the utopias, women often explore the possibilities of women's values, language, and the redefinition of women's nature. In some, women gain power and resist efforts from outside the community to gain control; in others, the community operates from a set of traditions that are arrived at by consent. Even in the utopias, conflict arises, and this conflict is usually caused by outsiders or by the individual whose values do not correspond with those of the rest of the community. —*Georgia Rhoades*

See also Fiction writers; Gender differences; Gilman, Charlotte Perkins; Literature, images of women in; Patriarchy; Separatism

Bibliography

Barr, Marleen, and Nicholas Smith, eds. *Women and Utopia*. Lanham, Md.: University Press of America, 1983.

Le Guin, Ursula K. Introduction to *Angel Island*, by Inez Haynes Gillmore. New York: New American Library, 1988.

Russ, Joanna. *The Female Man*. New York: Bantam Books, 1975.

Starhawk. *The Fifth Sacred Thing*. New York: Bantam Books, 1993.

Webber, Jeannette L., and Joan Grumman, eds. *Woman as Writer*. Boston: Houghton Mifflin, 1978.

Sculpting and sculptors

Relevant issues: Arts and entertainment

Significance: Few women sculptors seem to have existed prior to the late nineteenth century because of societal restrictions, lack of access to education and training, and a disinclination on the part of many women to compete with men for large art commissions

Where Were the Female Sculptors? The legend of Sabine von Steinbach illustrates the role of women in sculpting before modern times. Sabine was a young sculptor whose father, Erwin, was the architect and sculptor of the Strasbourg Cathedral during the fourteenth century. When he died while construction was underway, Sabine was given the job of completing the sculptures. A statue of St. John holds a scroll on which is carved, "Thanks be to the holy piety of this woman, Sabine, who from this hard stone gave me form." The legend also speaks of jealous male sculptors who destroyed her work during the night, only to find it restored by angels in the morning.

Sculpture has traditionally been the domain of men, because of the heavy, dirty materials and physically demanding techniques, and because of the time and cost associated with sculptural commissions. Large amounts of money were needed at the beginnings of commissions to pay for materials, assistants, and a studio. The few female artists who attempted to compete with men on this scale often encountered resistance. In addition, marriage, bearing children, and caring for a household were often the only careers allowed women, and few women had time for other things. Wealthy women were allowed to pursue "womanly" arts such as needlework and lace making, but they were not encouraged to pursue sculpture. Until the late nineteenth century, Western culture generally forbade women to study the male nude. Since much of sculpture since Greek and Roman times took as its subject the male figure, this restriction was disastrous for any girl who might consider sculpture as a career. Women were rarely allowed to attend art schools or belong to academies, and guild membership was often restricted or forbidden to them.

The Nineteenth Century. The number of important female painters increased steadily following the Renaissance, but the same could not be said for female sculptors. By the end of the nineteenth century, however, there were a remarkable amount of noteworthy women who sculpted. These artists came form France, America, and Germany, and, in spite of continuing unequal access to anatomical studies, they sculpted not only portrait busts but also large, dramatic, multifigure compositions, tomb and fountain sculptures, and historical scenes.

The tastes of the time were toward the neoclassical, and the most compelling group of female sculptors were several from the United States who studied in Rome and were devoted to neoclassical ideals. Among this closely knit group, Harriet Hosmer (1830-1908) was the most famous. Writer Henry James referred to Hosmer as "the most eminent member of that strange sisterhood of lady sculptors." She was a wealthy tomboy from Massachusetts who, after studying in Rome with the famed sculptor John Gibson, was so enamored with neoclassical art that she refused to drape any figures in modern garb. The group also included Emma Stebbins, who was born in New York and who created the fountain sculpture *Angel of the Waters* in Central Park; Edmonia Lewis, who was born to a Chippewa mother and black father and who created many sculptures with a neoclassical look that celebrated her dual heritage; and Vinnie Ream Hoxie, who sculpted the standing statue of Abraham Lincoln that can be found in the Capitol Building, having received the first U.S. government commission ever given a female artist. These women were known as freethinking nonconformists; most of them never married, choosing art as their only career.

The Twentieth Century. The trickle of female sculptors that became a stream in the nineteenth century became a river in the twentieth century. Many more opportunities for the education of female artists existed, and materials began to emerge that made sculpting more approachable for women. In the beginning of the century, bronze casting became popular, nearly replacing the more rigorous stone carving. Small sculptures for the home also became the vogue. This broadening of the market and the smaller scale of the pieces created new possibilities for women who wished to sculpt. Malvina Hoffman (1887-1977), an American, was one of the artists who benefited from this new atmosphere. She studied in Paris, where she was a friend of Auguste Rodin, who was known as the father of modern sculpture. Her most complicated commission was for the Field Museum of Natural History in Chicago.

Sculpting has become an accepted form of artistic expression for women; Jacquelyn Smith finishes her piece "The Womb of Time" in Eugene, Oregon. (Susan DeTroy)

Called *The Living Races of Man*, it was composed of more than one hundred statues and required that she travel the globe to research her subjects.

Female sculptors were included among the artists who created an environment of constant change in the world of art, with artists such as Barbara Hepworth exploring biomorphism, Germain Richier working in surrealism, Marisol working primarily in the pop art mode, Dorothy Dehner and Louise Bourgeois influenced by cubist abstraction, and Louise Nevelson and Lee Bontecou embracing assemblage.

The investigation and experimentation involved in working through the various "isms" of modern art led to the use of myriad new materials for sculpting, many of which, like cloth, had been used by women in domestic art for centuries and had a female feel to them. Other materials, such as fiberglass, polyethylene, and polyurethane, worked well for the kind of abstraction that emerged after the women's movement made its mark on the art world in the 1960's and 1970's. The female body and its processes became part of the vocabulary of abstraction, as illustrated by the unsettling, biological-feeling, powerful sculpture of Eve Hesse. Other female sculptors celebrate the female body in representational ways; Niki de Saint Phalle does so with her large, rounded, polyester females she calls Nanas. The list of contemporary women working in the arena of sculpture seems endless. The expansion of the traditional definition of sculpture to include performance and large-scale, environmental pieces has offered an even greater variety of ways for women to express themselves through sculpture.

The possibilities for success and the kind of impact that one female sculptor can make is illustrated by Judy Chicago and her piece entitled *The Dinner Party* (1979), which consists of a life-size, triangular-shaped table on which sit thirty-nine porcelain place settings placed on embroidered fabric runners. Each place is set for a woman who was important to history. The craftsmanship and needlework is exquisite, and many of the images resemble women's sexual organs. The sculpture was very controversial: Some viewed it with awe, while others rejected it as pornographic. It has traveled all over the United States and has been well attended everywhere. The impact of this one sculpture by a woman suggests what is possible in the future for female sculptors. —*Christine Waters*

See also Art, images of women in; Chicago, Judy; Crafts and home arts; *Dinner Party, The*; Feminist art movement; Painting and painters; Visual art

BIBLIOGRAPHY

Chadwick, Whitney. *Women, Art, and Society.* New York: Thames and Hudson, 1990.

Heller, Nancy G. *Women Artists: An Illustrated History.* Rev. ed. New York: Abbeville Press, 1987.

Rosen, Randy, and Catherine C. Brawer, comps. *Making Their Mark: Women Artists Move into the Mainstream, 1970-85.* New York: Abbeville Press, 1989.

Rubinstein, Charlotte Streifer. *American Women Artists from Early Indian Times to the Present.* New York: Avon, 1982.

Slatkin, Wendy. *Women Artists in History: From Antiquity to the Twentieth Century.* 2d ed. Englewood Cliffs, N.J.: Prentice Hall, 1990.

Second Sex, The

AUTHOR: Simone de Beauvoir (1908-1986)

DATE: *Le Deuxième Sexe*, 1949 (English translation, 1953)

RELEVANT ISSUES: Literature and communications, psychology, sex and gender, women's history

SIGNIFICANCE: This classic feminist text is credited by some for having begun the worldwide resurgence of feminism, including the second wave of the women's movement in the United States

French author Simone de Beauvoir completed the research and writing for *The Second Sex* over two years. The book was begun in October, 1946, while Beauvoir toured colleges and universities in the United States and interviewed American women about their lives; it was finished in June, 1949. Beauvoir credits the idea for *The Second Sex* to writer and friend Colette Audry, who always wanted to write a book about women's inequality. Beauvoir admits that as an unmarried writer, teacher, and intellectual with no children, she enjoyed an egalitarian relationship with men. Yet, while wanting to write an autobiographical book about herself as a French existentialist—Beauvoir was the lifelong friend of Jean-Paul Sartre, the founder of French existentialism—Beauvoir first began to think seriously about the "lot of women" and about herself as a woman. Though much of her other writings contain strong feminist underpinnings, Beauvoir became well known as a feminist because of *The Second Sex*, especially toward the end of her life: From 1970 until her death in 1986, she actively and publicly committed herself to women's issues.

The Second Sex, which contains more than eight hundred pages, is an examination of the condition of women in Western culture. The work looks at the plight of women from biological, psychological, sociological, and historical perspectives, analyzing the condition of women through the philosophical context of existentialism, a philosophy concerned with freedom, responsibility, conscious choice, and active engagement in living. It is essentially a series of analytical essays divided into two volumes: *Les Faits et Les Mythes* (*Facts and Myths*) and *L'Expérience Vécue* (*Woman's Life Today*). *The Second Sex* analyzes the ways in which women's freedom has been curtailed or annihilated. Beauvoir explains how, in a patriarchy, women—as the "second sex," as "the other," as "objects"—are negatively defined through men and how women then in turn define themselves. Whether daughter, wife, mother, or lover, a woman's life, according to Beauvoir, is prescribed and confined; she dwells in what Beauvoir calls immanence, a vicious cycle of uncreative and repetitious duties and ways of being in the world that creates unhappiness and despair. Roads to what she calls transcendence—actively creating, confronting, and engaging oneself in the world (the opposite of immanence)—are closed to her, and so she waits passively and is literally, Beauvoir says, "bored to death."

In her analysis, Beauvoir examines broad issues such as women's exploitation in work and in love and shows how a capitalistic economy as well as the patriarchy benefit from women's subservient role. She talks specifically about such issues as reproductive rights, religion, motherhood, and marriage. She disputes the idea of an Eternal Feminine, the idea that all members of womankind are biologically predetermined to act out their lives in a peculiarly passive and stereotypically feminine mode. Her thesis throughout the book is the emphatic statement that she makes at the beginning of part II of *The Second Sex*: "One is not born, but rather becomes a woman." Her book examines in detail how the various forces of culture and civilization work to create this figure of the human female, a "creature intermediate between male and eunuch, which is described as feminine." Beauvoir sees meaningful work and economic independence as the keys to women's liberation.

The Second Sex, first published in France in 1949, was immediately translated into many languages. Considered controversial and even scandalous by some when it was first published, *The Second Sex* was widely debated in France. It received more superficial attention in the United States, although it was admired by intellectuals such as anthropologist and writer Ashley Montagu, who said that it was one of three outstanding books on women, along with Mary Wollstonecraft's *A Vindication of the Rights of Woman* (1792) and John Stuart Mill's *The Subjection of Women* (1869). The impact of *The Second Sex* on the American feminist movement continues to be debated. Though sometimes called the bible of American feminism, *The Second Sex* has received less attention in the United States by American second-wave feminists than Betty Friedan's *The Feminine Mystique* (1963), even though the latter book is a much less radical, scholarly, and original work.

Decades after the first English translation of *The Second Sex*, it remains a controversial text. Beauvoir is often called the mother of second-wave feminism, yet some feminists see her book as dated and some of her ideas as misogynistic and Sartrean. As psychological and philosophical approaches to gender and culture became more popular in the 1980's and 1990's, however, Beauvoir's ideas on gender, sex, and culture enjoyed a renaissance. Ever popular with Canadian and British socialist feminists, Beauvoir's ideas in *The Second Sex* were also debated by such influential French thinkers as Luce Irigaray and Julia Kristeva. Between 1981 and 1990, at least ten books on Beauvoir's life and work appeared in North America, many by British authors, reaffirming Beauvoir's cross-continental influence. The focus for essays and articles spanning the disciplines of politics, philosophy, and literature, *The Second Sex* is acknowledged for its framing of the field of feminist scholarly inquiry.

—Candace E. Andrews

See also Feminism; History of women; Patriarchy; Second wave of the women's movement; Socialization of girls and young women; Women's movement

Second shift

Relevant issues: Business and economics, employment, family

Significance: The concept of who is responsible for homemaking is crucial to women's range of choices

Although women as a group have become integrated into the workforce in the United States, the idea that the home is the woman's responsibility lingers. Studies in the 1980's and 1990's showed that employed wives spend roughly half of the time spent by full-time homemaking wives on household work and responsibilities and that husbands spend a little less than half of the time spent on housework than wives employed full-time. Additionally, the work usually done by men is occasional work, while that done by women usually must be done on a daily basis. Studies have also shown that generally it is the wife who is responsible for child care and for seeing that tasks are done. The husbands of employed wives have increased the social time that they spend with their children but not the time spent in their physical care. Thus, in general, women have a daily "second shift" of work and responsibilities to do after their regular outside workday is done. Unless the household can afford full-time child care or at least part-time household help, the wife's career choices are often circumscribed by these responsibilities. In response, wives may cut back their hours at work, eliminate tasks at home, or try to be "supermoms" who do everything. While some women complain about this situation, many do not seem to have a sense of entitlement to equal sharing and therefore do not continue to press for change in the face of resistance by their husbands.

Percentage of Time Spent on Various Activities by Married Women in the U.S. (1980's)

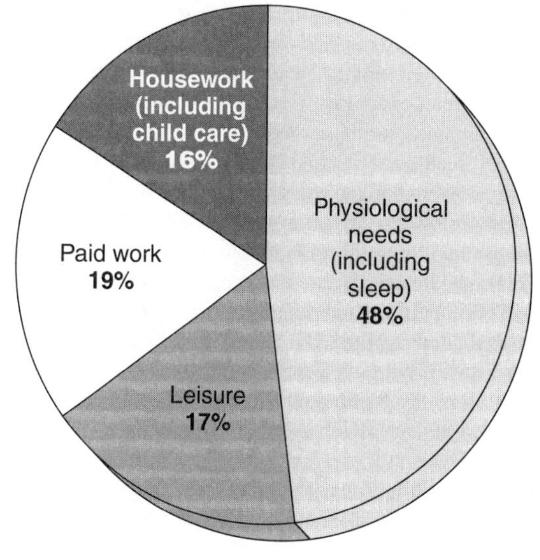

See also Breadwinner ethic; Career vs. homemaker debate; Child care; Child rearing; Employment of women; Homemakers and homemaking; Housework technologies; Marriage and marital status; Mommy track; Superwoman

Second wave of the women's movement

Also known as: Feminist movement; women's liberation movement

Relevant issues: Politics, social reform

Significance: Second-wave feminism placed issues of sexuality and discrimination on the public agenda; this mass movement raised consciousness, created and sustained institutions, generated organized interest groups, and developed a women's culture

Historians divide the North American feminist movement into two parts: The first wave focused on the campaign for suffrage, which ended in 1920 in the United States with the passage of the Nineteenth Amendment, and the second wave was a broader social movement that began in the 1960's. Unlike interest groups or political parties that have members, dues, and officers, such social movements are informally organized, connected by informal networks, and geographically dispersed. Women came together to form discussion groups, plan a protest, or campaign on an issue and then dispersed or joined again for other purposes. Social movements, which often leave few written records, are more difficult to study than interest groups, whose members are easier to identify. Many of the accounts of second-wave feminism are written by its participants and reflect their interests, activities, and geographic locations.

The Origins of the Movement. Second-wave feminism emerged from the convergence of women with two very different kinds of experiences. The first group had been active in other social movements of the 1950's and 1960's, such as the Civil Rights movement, the antiwar movement, and the radical student movement. It is more accurate to note that feminists were active in many social movements rather than to see those movements as causing or generating second-wave feminism. The challenge to authority, the emphasis on participation and direct action, the critique of oppression, the use of protest strategies such as sit-ins and boycotts, the emphasis on personal empowerment and grassroots organizing all were mutually reinforcing. Civil rights organizers such as Ella Baker, the organizer for the Southern Christian Leadership Conference (SCLC) who helped nurture and create the Student Non-Violent Coordinating Committee (SNCC), and Fannie Lou Hamer, a member of the SNCC and the Mississippi Freedom Democratic Party, impressed and influenced college-age women from the North and Midwest who joined the Civil Rights movement. Members of this group were often called radical feminists.

The second strand consisted of those women who had been active within political parties, government, interest groups, and labor unions—sometimes called liberal feminists, other times characterized as older feminists. If one carefully examines the activists who participated in the National Organization for Women (NOW) in New York or campaigned for abortion rights, for example, it is harder to identify two separate camps. Many women from this second strand were active in the President's Commission on the Status of Women created by John F. Kennedy in 1961. State commissions formed in forty-nine states, met at an annual conference, and shared information. These women documented women's oppression and proposed legislation to eliminate the most egregious forms of legal discrimination. At the Third National Conference in June, 1966, delegates formed NOW. Bella Abzug, Shirley Chisholm, Betty Friedan, and Gloria Steinem (editor of the soon-to-be-launched feminist magazine *Ms.*) founded the National Women's Political Caucus in 1971 in an effort to elect more women to office from both parties.

Second-wave feminism in Canada similarly coalesced around the 1970 Report of the Royal Commission on the Status of Women, leading to the formation of the Canadian Advisory Council on the Status of Women in 1973. Cleavages over party, nationalism, and language bisect Canadian feminists in addition to the divisions over race, sexuality, and class found among feminists in the United States.

Methods of Social Action. Perhaps one of the most distinctive features of second-wave feminism was the consciousness-raising group. Brandishing the slogan "the personal is the political," women came together in small groups to talk. Through intimate sharing, they came to discover and name common experiences that had been seen as individual and shameful: rape, incest, sexual harassment, illegal abortions, domestic abuse, or anorexia nervosa. Out of these groups emerged women-run institutions: abortion clinics, women's health clinics, women's centers, women's studies programs, battered women shelters, and women's bookstores and coffeehouses. Many such organizations tended to organize themselves in ways reminiscent of the consciousness-raising group. They eschewed leaders, made decisions by consensus, and favored minimizing if not eliminating hierarchy, rotating tasks so that inexperienced women became empowered by developing new skills.

Controversial books burst on the scene. Friedan published *The Feminine Mystique* (1963), which argued that educated suburban women were dissatisfied with domesticity, coining the phrase "the problem that has no name." Simone de Beauvoir's *Le Deuxième Sexe* (1949; *The Second Sex*, 1953) was rediscovered and widely read, as were Germaine Greer's *The Female Eunuch* (1971), Kate Millett's *Sexual Politics* (1969), and Marilyn French's novel *The Women's Room* (1977). Susan Faludi's *Backlash: The Undeclared War Against American Women* (1991) and Naomi Wolf's *The Beauty Myth* (1991) became best-sellers in the 1990's.

Women also became active in the struggle to change patriarchal institutions. The passage of the Equal Pay Act of 1963 and Title VII of the Civil Rights Act of 1964 (prohibiting sex discrimination in employment) was a catalyst for formation of the women's movement in the United States rather than a result of its lobbying. NOW originally focused on pressuring the newly created Equal Employment Opportunity Commission (EEOC) to enforce the sexual discrimination provisions as vigorously as racial ones. Working-class women filed many employment discrimination cases in the 1960's and 1970's against both employers and unions. They formed organizations such as the Coalition of Labor Union Women.

While feminists on the Left debated the merits of working within or outside of left-wing (and male-dominated) groups, feminists within NOW quickly differed over central issues such as the importance of issues of sexuality (especially abortion and lesbianism) and over tactics. The Women's Equity Action Group, New York Radical Feminists (which included Shulamith Firestone and later became the Redstockings), Radicalesbians (including Rita Mae Brown), and The Feminists (including Ti-Grace Atkinson) were only a few of the breakaway groups from early chapters of NOW.

As NOW grew from a membership of 35,000 in the mid-1970's to 250,000 in 1982, culminating in Eleanor Smeal's assumption of the presidency in 1982, the women's movement became increasingly identified with the campaign to ratify the Equal Rights Amendment (ERA) to the Constitution. In the mid-1970's, women on the Right, such as Phyllis Schlafly, began to organize aggressively against feminism and particularly against the ERA. They successfully fought ratification of the amendment in several states, and some states rescinded their approval.

Impact. By the mid-1990's, despite the backlash against the women's movement, despite media announcements that the decade was a postfeminist era because women were no longer oppressed, despite best-sellers thrashing feminism, the women's movement was alive and well. The vast majority of women reported to pollsters that they had a long way to go to achieve equality and that the women's movement had improved their lives. Membership in feminist organizations was high, and women's institutions were holding strong, many celebrating anniversaries of twenty or twenty-five years. Often characterized as immobilized by divisions over sexuality, race, class, and even personality, the feminist movement has now firmly begun the process of embracing and representing the diversity of women. *—Sally J. Kenney*

See also Abzug, Bella; Atkinson, Ti-Grace; Brown, Rita Mae; Civil Rights movement and women; Consciousness-raising; Equal Rights Amendment (ERA); *Feminine Mystique, The*; Feminism; Feminism, lesbian; Feminism, liberal; Feminism, radical; Firestone, Shulamith; Friedan, Betty; National Organization for Women (NOW); New Left and women; "Personal is the political, the"; President's Commission on the Status of Women; Problem that has no name; Steinem, Gloria; Women's movement

BIBLIOGRAPHY

Adamson, Nancy, Linda Briskin, and Margaret McPhail. *Feminist Organizing for Change: The Contemporary Women's Movement in Canada*. Toronto: Oxford University Press, 1988.

Echols, Alice. *Daring to Be Bad: Radical Feminism in America, 1967-1975*. Minneapolis: University of Minnesota Press, 1989.

Evans, Sara. *Personal Politics: The Roots of Women's Liberation in the Civil Rights Movement and the New Left*. New York: Alfred A. Knopf, 1979.

Freeman, Jo. *The Politics of Women's Liberation: A Case Study of an Emerging Social Movement and Its Relation to the Policy Process*. New York: McKay, 1975.

Morgan, Robin. *Sisterhood Is Powerful: An Anthology of Writings from the Women's Liberation Movement*. New York: Random House, 1970.

Noun, Louise R. *More Strong-Minded Women: Iowa Feminists Tell Their Stories*. Ames: Iowa State University Press, 1992.

Ryan, Barbara. *Feminism and the Women's Movement: Dynamics of Change in Social Movement Ideology and Activism*. New York: Routledge, 1992.

Willis, Ellen. *No More Nice Girls: Countercultural Essays*. Hanover, N.H.: University Press of New England/Wesleyan University Press, 1992.

Self-esteem, women's

RELEVANT ISSUES: Psychology, sex and gender

SIGNIFICANCE: Affirming self-esteem gives women the strength and confidence to become full and participating members of society

Self-esteem has been extensively explored in traditional psychological theories and encompasses such concepts as self-respect, self-acceptance, and a sense of competence. Its antonym includes self-doubt, self-effacement, and self-hatred. Stanley Coopersmith defined self-esteem mainly as a self-appraisal process. He said that people constantly judge themselves on whether they are "capable, significant, successful, and worthy." Self-esteem, in short, is a personal evaluation of one's worthiness based on those qualities.

Using a similar framework, Nathaniel Branden delineated the concept in terms of self-confidence and self-respect. Self-confidence refers to a sense of personal efficacy based on one's ability in rational thinking; self-respect is a sense of worth that people have about themselves in relation to the goals they are pursuing. Branden also placed rational thinking above emotions, stressing that the latter cannot be used as "guides for actions" or "criteria for judgment."

In Morris Rosenberg's terms, people with high self-esteem have self-respect, appreciate their own merits, and recognize their own shortcomings. They do not consider themselves superior to other people, nor do they see themselves as inferior. People with low self-esteem, however, lack self-respect and consider themselves inadequate and seriously deficient.

Feminist Response. Traditional psychological theories explaining self-esteem have been dominated by an androcentric approach, whereby authors draw examples from men, formulate their thinking on studies conducted with men, and use "he" as a generic reference in their discussions. Based on their study of 320 women, Linda Tschirhart Sanford and Mary Ellen

Noted feminist Gloria Steinem has analyzed the reasons for women's lack of self-esteem and promoted ways of regaining confidence in such works as Revolution from Within. (AP/ Wide World Photos)

Donovan recast the discussion of self-esteem with reference to women. First and foremost, they pointed out that the concept is a social and cultural construct that traditionally applies more to men than to women. Although it is the norm for men to demonstrate high self-esteem, women are considered arrogant and conceited if they do the same. Sanford and Donovan claimed that as women internalize what society expects of them, they tend to berate themselves, giving minimal attention to their own development. Low self-esteem is the result of a wide discrepancy between how women see themselves (a perceived self) and how they think they ought to be (an ideal self), and it is the root of many other problems for women. To help women to be more analytical about the issue, Sanford and Donovan introduced a center/periphery schema that examines how people weigh their attributes. In general, people place the attributes that identify themselves (for example, "I am a teacher" or "I am a mother") in the center and the less important ones (for example, "I like snacking" or "I know nothing about cars") in the periphery. If women put one devastating attribute, such as obesity, in the center, it is possible that they may still have low self-esteem despite their other positive qualities.

Feminist Contributions. Various prominent women have addressed the concept. Betty Friedan brought the nation's attention to the issue in her book *The Feminine Mystique* (1963). She pointed out that although women have the desire to achieve, the lack of self-esteem produces feelings of inferiority and helplessness, limiting their ability to succeed outside marriage and motherhood. Carol Gilligan agreed that women are often drawn into the role of caretaker and nurturer in society and are psychologically conditioned to feel guilty if they put their own needs before those of their family members.

Gloria Steinem described self-esteem as an internal center of power that can enhance every aspect of women's lives. Unlike men, who are taught to find power within themselves, however, women are not encouraged to locate this internal power. Therefore, women need to develop and nurture themselves in order to tap into an unlimited source of internal power. Steinem also introduced the concept of "core self-esteem," which women derive from the unconditional love they receive from parents and loved ones. Core self-esteem is the basis for the development of self-worth that sustains women through hardships and disappointments in life. On this point, Steinem has expanded and refined Branden's construct of self-respect.

Robin Dillon joined the discussion with reference to self-respect as defined in terms of two kinds of self-worth: intrinsic worth that women possess simply by being human, and extrinsic worth that women earn through their accomplishment at work. Dillon called the former "recognition self-respect" and the latter "appraisal self-respect." Women with recognition self-respect see themselves as having the same intrinsic value as other members in the community, protect their rights, and resist humiliating treatment. Appraisal self-respect involves women's positive evaluation of their performance and ability in their jobs.

Dillon has primarily been interested in exploring the aspect of recognition self-respect. She contended that the traditional concept of self-respect incorporates androcentric elements, which makes it hard for women to come to terms with themselves. A feminist interpretation of recognition self-respect takes in all aspects of a woman's life, including inadequacy, despair, and "shining moments of achievement." This total acceptance of oneself is similar to Steinem's concept of core self-esteem, but whereas in Steinem's framework, the acceptance comes from outside (parents and loved ones), in Dillon's terms, the acceptance comes from within.

Dillon's expansion on Rosenberg's idea that all people should respect themselves as equal and legitimate members of a community marks a point of departure in the discussion of self-esteem. It greatly empowers women who have internalized the traditional concept that they are of lesser value than men. Dillon's proposal of a total acceptance of oneself may sound uncritical; however, it is important for women first to come to terms with themselves before they take steps for improvement.

For Ann Ferguson, self-respect is vital to women's political empowerment. It serves as the "source of strength and confidence" for women "to effectively challenge and change" unfair practices. Joining other women, as suggested by Steinem, is also essential in recovering women's sense of self-respect. The growth of consciousness-raising groups in which women share their experiences and concerns with others has been instrumental in raising their self-esteem. Through connecting with others, many women have transformed themselves into leaders and activists in the women's movement. Without the networking and their newly gained self-esteem, many of those women may still be confined in their traditional, submissive roles.

In contemporary America, more and more women enter the workforce, head households, and attend college. Although research shows that it is easier for working women to gain high self-esteem than those who do not work outside the home, it is also documented that many working women do not have much of a sense of themselves. An awareness of the importance of self-esteem is therefore vital in enabling women, both working and nonworking, to find their places and voices at home, in school, and at work. Self-esteem is an important issue for women; however, it does not imply that all women lack self-esteem, nor does it mean that factors such as race and class can be ignored in exploring women's self-esteem. *—Clara Lam*

See also Career vs. homemaker debate; Depression and women; Empowerment; *Feminine Mystique, The*; Feminism; Friedan, Betty; Psychological theories on women; Steinem, Gloria

BIBLIOGRAPHY

Branden, Nathaniel. *The Psychology of Self-Esteem: A New Concept of Man's Psychological Nature.* Los Angeles: Nash, 1969.

Coopersmith, Stanley. *The Antecedents of Self-Esteem.* San Francisco: W. H. Freeman, 1967.

Dillon, Robin S. "Toward a Feminist Conception of Self-Respect." *Hypatia* 7, no. 1 (Winter, 1992): 52-69.

Evans, Sara. *Personal Politics: The Roots of Women's Liberation in the Civil Rights Movement and the New Left.* New York: Alfred A. Knopf, 1979.

Ferguson, Ann. "A Feminist Aspect Theory of the Self." In *Science, Morality, and Feminist Theory*, edited by Marsha Hanen and Kai Nielsen. Calgary, British Columbia: University of Calgary Press, 1987.

Rosenberg, Morris. *Conceiving the Self.* New York: Basic Books, 1979.

Sanford, Linda Tschirhart, and Mary Ellen Donovan. *Women and Self-Esteem: Understanding and Improving the Way We Think and Feel About Ourselves.* Garden City, N.Y.: Anchor Press/Doubleday, 1984.

Steinem, Gloria. *Revolution from Within: A Book of Self-Esteem.* Boston: Little, Brown, 1992.

Seneca Falls Women's Rights Convention

DATE: July 19-20, 1848

PLACE: Seneca Falls, N.Y.

RELEVANT ISSUES: Civil rights, politics, women's history

SIGNIFICANCE: This convention launched the woman suffrage movement and anticipated major issues of twentieth century feminism

The Seneca Falls Women's Rights Convention was to be a local gathering of reformers, mostly women. Lucretia Mott, Elizabeth Cady Stanton, and other women, many of whom had been entirely involved in the abolitionist movement and other social reform movements, met to share mutual concerns and insights. What they did not know was that concern for women's rights in the United States, when linked to other human rights movements, was becoming a powerful magnet attracting people to their organizations.

The convention was called to "discuss the social, civil, and religious condition and rights of women." The Declaration of Sentiments developed by the participants was cast in the words of the Declaration of Independence substituting "Men" for "King George." The declaration met with unanimous approval except for its ninth proposition, which argued for the right of women to vote. Frederick Douglass, the former slave and fiery abolitionist speaker, was the only man who argued strongly for this resolution, which passed with a slim majority.

Issues critical to the twentieth century women's movement—gender and wage equality, race relations, woman suffrage, and women in leadership positions in organizations demanding social and political equality—had a first rehearsal at the Seneca Falls convention.

See also Abolitionist movement and women; Declaration of Sentiments; Feminism; History of women; Mott, Lucretia; Slavery; Stanton, Elizabeth Cady; Suffrage movement and suffragists

Separatism

RELEVANT ISSUES: Sex and gender, women's history

SIGNIFICANCE: It was necessary at the beginning of the women's movement in the 1960's for many women to organize and act entirely apart from men, a practice that is still advocated by some women's groups

In the 1960's, many women were beginning to accept the notion that they could oppose and change a sexually discriminatory society. Much planning and organization were required to get such an effort off the ground. Because women could not organize to take power away from men if half of their organizers were men, women had to set up their own structures to bring about change. Separatism was thus a necessary instrument of the early women's movement of the 1960's and 1970's. The idea was to rejoin men after they had begun to recognize the necessity and inevitability of change. Some groups, however, by temperament or conviction, continue in the belief that women should maintain a society entirely separate from that of men. In this way, they hope to avoid male domination, to associate with others congenial to them, and to accomplish certain goals in politics or business that men still do not regard as important. Some extremism can be found: Lesbian separatists, for example, will have nothing to do with men (even male children) or with women who have anything to do with men. Now that the women's movement is well underway, however, most women are willing to work side by side with men on other societal problems, such as racism and discrimination against handicapped individuals.

See also Feminism; Feminism, lesbian; Feminism, radical; Matriarchy; Sisterhood; Women's movement

Settlement houses

RELEVANT ISSUES: Community affairs, education, employment, health and medicine, poverty, race and ethnicity, social reform

SIGNIFICANCE: The settlement house movement provided social services and cultural programs to immigrant and poor urban women and their families and professional opportunities to college-educated women who desired to work on behalf of social reform

The settlement house movement began among Christian Socialists and university-affiliated reformers in England and spread to major cities in North America in the 1890's. The houses, which were established primarily in the urban centers of the Midwest and Northeast, multiplied from six in 1891 to more than four hundred in 1910. They became principal agencies of social reform during the Progressive era.

Philosophy and Ideals. A reaction to growing urbanization, immigration, and changes in labor patterns, settlement houses emphasized social action to improve impoverished living conditions and exploitative labor practices. Influenced by the Social Gospel movement, they emphasized character building and an organic vision of society based on cultural mediation and mutual reciprocity between native-born citizens and immigrants and between the middle class and the poor. They simultaneously advocated social assimilation to middle-class norms and cultural pluralism or diversity. These positions often came into conflict. The original settlement houses were also experiments in collective living. Located in poor ethnic neighborhoods, they attracted resident workers who were mainly young, idealistic, college-educated men and women from well-to-do households.

Programs and Services. Early programs focused on providing services for children, including day care nurseries for the children of working mothers, kindergartens, boys' and girls' clubs, recreation programs, nature outings, playgrounds, and gymnasiums. Citizenship classes, emphasizing literacy and the English language, were held for adults, as well as practical training courses in home economics, dressmaking, cooking, sanitation, and nutrition. Medical and nursing services were provided by some houses, most notably by the extensive visiting nurse service of the Henry Street Settlement House in New York. Family counseling and job referral bureaus were offered to working women. Exhibitions, art history, and the performing arts, including music and drama, also played an important part in settlement house programming. Resident workers and teachers such as Ellen Gates Starr of Hull-House believed in the uplifting value of fine art appreciation.

Efforts were made to attract Italian, Greek, and East European women to the houses by appealing to nationalist loyalties, including the planning of ethnic festivals, receptions, and celebrations of folk dancing and crafts. At Hull-House, a labor museum was established in which immigrant women demonstrated the history of textile arts. The museum program sought to bridge cultural gaps that had developed between first-generation immigrants, who were highly skilled in handicrafts and traditional manufactures, and their children, who were more familiar with factory work and mechanization, many having lost respect for older ways.

Institutionalization and Reform. Many of the programs that existed on a trial basis in the settlement houses were adopted by public school systems, park and urban planning agencies, and the developing juvenile justice system and social work institutions. In addition to providing services and stimulating appreciation of diverse cultural heritages, settlement workers were also in the forefront of the formation of social policy. They gathered data to educate the population at large as to the needs of the urban poor, and they lobbied for municipal reform and state and federal legislation that addressed the issues of housing, labor, women's rights, and prostitution. Many of the reforms that they advocated became central tenets of the Progressive Party platform during Theodore Roosevelt's presidential bid in 1912.

Ethnicity and Race. While settlement workers saw themselves as advocates for the lower classes, their application of middle-class values was sometimes at odds with immigrant women's perspectives. Conflicts existed, for example, over economic issues involved in child labor. While settlement workers sought to abolish the practice, many immigrant families relied on the income that children earned. Settlement workers also stressed white slavery aspects of prostitution, portraying the prostitute as a victim and emphasizing the sexual double standard and the curbing of male behavior while avoiding the idea of sex work as a chosen occupation. Few immigrant women ascended to positions of leadership in the protective leagues that emerged from the houses or in the resident work itself. While most settlements were run by native-born whites on behalf of white ethnic immigrants, some offered separate branches for black residents, and a few, such as the Phillis Wheatley Settlement in Minneapolis, were founded specifically as residence facilities for African Americans.

Women's Opportunities and the Legacy of Reform. Although settlement houses served both men and women, women such as Lillian Wald of the Henry Street Settlement House and Jane Addams of Hull-House were among the earliest founders of houses and the most prominent leaders of the movement. The settlement houses in general provided outlets of usefulness for educated women, aid to working women with families, and models of effective female leadership, networking, and authority.

Many women who initially were involved in settlement work went on to positions of influence in organizations, unions, and government agencies, broadening the impact of the

Settlement houses such as Hull-House in Chicago offered immigrants and poor families social and cultural opportunities, such as this girls' club. (University of Illinois at Chicago, The University Library, Jane Addams Memorial Collection)

settlement houses on the wider sphere of reform. Florence Kelley went from settlement experience to founding the National Consumers' League in 1899, which worked to improve labor conditions for women and children. Julia Lathrop and Grace Abbott both became directors of the Children's Bureau. Alice Hamilton became a leading expert on industrial medicine and a professor at Harvard Medical School. The National Women's Trade Union League (NWTUL), a labor organization, and the National Association for the Advancement of Colored People (NAACP), a civil rights group, were formed with support from settlement workers. Alice Gannett of the Henry Street Settlement House led the lobbying efforts that resulted in the passage of the Mothers' Aid Law of 1913, which provided pensions to needy mothers of dependent children, and Sophonisba Breckinridge and Edith Abbott were leaders in the new field of social work. Both Addams and Wald became central figures in the war-era pacifist movement, with Addams chair of the Women's Peace Party and head of the Women's International League for Peace and Freedom (WILPF), and Wald president of the American Union Against Militarism.

The settlement movement bridged the gap between older Victorian concepts of charity and philanthropy and modern social work. Over time, the unique nature of the houses was eclipsed by the professionalization of social services, which changed the cooperative volunteer staffing of the settlements to salaried and specialized positions. Post-World War I conservatism and changes in fund-raising methods also diminished the operations of the houses. *—Barbara Bair*

See also Abbott, Edith and Abbott, Grace; Addams, Jane; Crafts and home arts; Education; Ethnic identity; Health and medicine; Henry Street Settlement House; Home economics; Hull-House; Immigrant women; Mentoring and networking by women; National Women's Trade Union League (NWTUL); Social reform movements and women

BIBLIOGRAPHY

Addams, Jane. *Twenty Years at Hull-House*. New York: Macmillan, 1910.

Bryan, Mary L., and Allen F. Davis, eds. *One Hundred Years at Hull-House*. Bloomington: Indiana University Press, 1990.

Carson, Mina. *Settlement Folk: Social Thought and the American Settlement Movement, 1885-1930*. Chicago: University of Chicago Press, 1990.

Davis, Allen F. *Spearheads for Reform: The Social Settlements and the Progressive Movement, 1890-1914*. New Brunswick, N.J.: Rutgers University Press, 1984.

Hayden, Dolores. "Public Kitchens, Social Settlements, and the Cooperative Ideal." In *The Grand Domestic Revolution*. Cambridge, Mass.: MIT Press, 1981.

Lissak, Rivka Shpak. *Pluralism and Progressives: Hull House and the New Immigrants, 1890-1919*. Chicago: University of Chicago Press, 1989.

Trolander, Judith Ann. *Settlement Houses and the Great Depression*. Detroit: Wayne State University Press, 1975.

Woods, Robert A., and Albert J. Kennedy. *The Settlement Horizon*. 1922. Reprint. New Brunswick, N.J.: Transaction, 1990.

Sex change operation

RELEVANT ISSUES: Health and medicine, psychology, sex and gender

SIGNIFICANCE: A small number of people, for unknown reasons, believe that they are trapped in a body of the wrong sex; some undergo surgery to alter their genitalia and legally change their sex

Transsexuality describes the rare condition when an individual feels that his or her gender identity—that is, psychological sense of gender—does not match the body with which he or she was born. In some cases, it is found that the person is hermaphroditic, having internal body structures that are partially male and partially female, but in most cases, there is no obvious explanation for the conflict. It is much more common for someone with a male body to have a female gender identity than for someone with a female body to have a male gender identity; the reasons for this pattern are a matter of debate.

Transsexuals have an intense desire to relieve the perceived mismatch of their psyche and body. Historically, they have had few options: cross-dressing (transvestism); finding a homosexual partner and taking the role of the opposite sex; and/or remaining in psychological distress. In the last half of the twentieth century, however, physicians have been able to develop medical and surgical procedures to allow people to change the sex-related features of their bodies sufficiently to allow them to change their social role and legal standing to match their psychological gender.

Male-to-female surgery involves the removal of the testes, penis, and internal genitalia and the creation of an artificial vagina from the remaining tissue. Male-to-female transsexuals also have their facial hair removed and undergo hormone treatments to enlarge their breasts and soften their skin. Male-to-female transsexuals have fully functioning vaginas and can even reach orgasm through coitus; because they have no ovaries and incomplete uteruses, however, they cannot bear children. The surgical techniques for this operation have been perfected to the point that it is impossible to tell a male-to-female transsexual from someone born female without performing a gynecological examination to reveal the absence of ovaries and Fallopian tubes.

Female-to-male surgery involves the removal of the internal genitalia and the addition of an artificial scrotum and penis. Female-to-male transsexuals take hormones to increase growth of facial hair. Breasts do not shrink from hormone treatment, and each individual must decide whether to have the breasts surgically removed, leaving scar tissue. Female-to-male surgery is much more difficult than male-to-female surgery: The skin which is used to create the artificial penis is taken from the thighs or the abdomen and is not as sensitive as the sexual skin. It is impossible to create artificial erectile tissue or to reroute the urinary opening; thus, the artificial penis is present but nonfunctioning.

Many transsexuals adjust well to their new social roles, but some do not. Psychotherapy is recommended as an accompaniment to the hormone treatments that each transsexual must continue throughout life.

See also Bisexuality; Cross-dressing; Gender differences; Gynecology and obstetrics; Mental health; Plastic surgery

Sex object

RELEVANT ISSUES: Literature and communications, politics, psychology, sex and gender

SIGNIFICANCE: This term is used to describe the way in which a woman is valued, whereby her worth is measured primarily by her sexual attractiveness

The objectification of women as sexual things to be looked at and evaluated is a pervasive view that is culturally accepted and reinforced. Typical female sexual images are reductive and stereotyped, promoting a specific physical ideal that is usually unattainable. In the media especially, where the line between advertising and pornography has been blurred, sexuality is conflated with beauty, and beauty is synonymous with worth. Men are consistently discouraged from viewing a woman as anything more than a vehicle for their physical and voyeuristic pleasure. The women's movement of the 1960's and 1970's, with all its legal and material gains, seems to have brought about an increase in the sexual objectification of women. Some feminists believe that this situation is a direct result of female empowerment, sexually and otherwise, which some men find emasculating. Imagery that focuses exclusively on the female body and its desirability preoccupies many women so completely that their own desires are neglected. In severe cases, this critical sexual comparison has led to female self-hatred, deep sexual shame, eating disorders, risky cosmetic surgery, and fears of aging and losing control over one's body. Whether it be Greta Garbo, Marilyn Monroe, or Madonna, each generation adopts an ideal sexual icon to which women aspire in order to be seen as adequately female.

See also Advertising; Beauty pageants; Breast implants; Cosmetics and beauty industry; Date rape; Eating disorders; Machismo; Magazines, men's; Magazines, women's; Misogyny; Plastic surgery; Pornography; Self-esteem, women's; Sexism; Sexual stereotypes; Sexuality, women's; Stereotypes of women

Sexism

RELEVANT ISSUES: Civil rights, sex and gender, social reform

SIGNIFICANCE: The lives of all women are shaped by the sexism that they encounter in society

The simplest definition of sexism is that it is the belief that males are superior to females. Like all beliefs, it entails certain behaviors: Sexism gives rise to sexual discrimination—that is, the negative treatment of women in society simply because they are women. While sexual discrimination is a phenomenon whose pervasive existence is officially acknowledged by many governments, the same cannot be said of sexism. (It is not considered the business of governments to analyze behaviors, only to regulate them.) To understand why sexual discrimination occurs, and therefore to combat it effectively, it is necessary to understand sexism. The reality of sexism is considerably more complicated than the above definition may suggest. For example, it may be that the totality of human culture presupposes sexism, so that to call sexism into question must involve a willingness to call into question one's most fundamental beliefs and assumptions. Moreover, sexism is a difficult concept to grasp because unlike racism, with which it otherwise has much in common, sexism often expresses itself as love. Indeed, male heterosexual love for women is by no means incompatible with sexist contempt for them.

In order to show how various culturally approved and even mandated attitudes and behaviors in Western society can be considered expressions of contempt for women, one of the more controversial aspects of the topic of sexism, one can begin with incontrovertible statements. For example, in many places women cannot go out alone at night without running the risk of being physically attacked. (In fact, a "good" neighborhood is often defined as one in which a man, or a woman accompanied by a man, can go out at night without running a risk of being attacked.) An analysis can be made of this fact in the light of another, similar one from American history: It was once the case, especially in the South, that African Americans could not travel outside their neighborhoods without running the risk of being physically attacked simply because of their race. While most people would regard this phenomenon as a reflection of racism, many would not come to the same conclusion in the case of the physical lack of safety of women—namely, that it is a reflection of sexism. Instead, they are likely to regard the limitations placed upon women as a "fact of life" that may be regrettable but must simply be endured. It is important to recall that the miserable socioeconomic condition of minority groups such as African Americans has been similarly regarded by some people as an unalterable fact of life. Where human agency has been introduced to try to explain these facts, the actions of the victims were often isolated as the causal factor: for example, the "laziness" of blacks. In similar fashion, sexual assaults against women have traditionally been explained in terms of women's seductiveness.

Thus, the meaning of women's physical lack of safety can be interpreted in accordance with the history of the physical lack of safety of African Americans—that is, as a reflection of a socially institutionalized contempt. The example of physical lack of safety can be used because it is relatively incontrovertible and because it shows that sexism is often a matter of life and death. The question that can then be raised is "How can one describe the way in which society is organized in order to make the phenomenon of the physical lack of safety of women understandable as a consequence of that organization?"

Sexism and Socialization of the Young. In present-day social science, the word "sex" is used to refer to the biological aspects of maleness and femaleness, while "gender" refers to their social aspects. Thus, "male" and "female" describe a sexual difference; "masculine" and "feminine" describe a difference in gender. From the moment that they are born, humans inhabit a gendered world in which many socially constructed meanings are ascribed to the anatomical facts of maleness and femaleness. Thus, while persons are born male or female, they must become "normal" males and females: They must learn to think and act in the ways that society deems appropriate for males and females. In infancy and childhood, the three principal agents of socialization are the family, the school, and the media (especially television). These three major social institutions introduce children into the world of normal maleness and femaleness in which a basic message, transmitted to both sexes alike, is that males are more important than females.

Parents treat sons and daughters differently from the earliest stages of infancy. For example, parents typically talk more to baby girls than baby boys and are more solicitous of them when they injure themselves. In these and other ways, parents communicate their perception that boys are more self-sufficient, and stronger, than are girls. In the past, this message was reinforced quite concretely through the use of different dress codes: for example, blue for boys and pink for girls, jeans for boys and dresses for girls. Such codes often functioned as self-fulfilling prophecies: Girls were defined as more delicate creatures than boys and therefore were given dresses rather than jeans to wear; therefore, they could not play as roughly at the playground as boys and grew up to be more delicate. Dress codes for children have broken down: Girls and boys both typically wear jeans or overalls and can meet more as equals at the playground than they did in the past. Yet the breakdown of the dress code is incomplete: Girls can wear what used to be considered strictly boys' clothes, but boys cannot yet wear what are considered girls' clothes. A boy in a dress or a pink outfit is as subject to ridicule today as he would have been in the past. (If the ridicule is justified, why is similar treatment not justified in the case of girls who have the nerve to wear overalls or the color blue?)

Parents further influence their children's self-concepts through the toys that they buy for them, which traditionally have been as gender-specific as clothing. Girls are given dolls to prepare them for the domestic tasks to which they will later be assigned; playing with dolls means playing at the caregiving, nurturing role. Boys, on the other hand, are given action figures, soldiers and other dynamic characters whom the boys send off into battle or some other challenging activity calling for physical fortitude and courage. The boys' role is not to change the figures' clothes or dress their wounds—buying action figures, unlike buying Barbie dolls, does not

Sexism often begins with the reenforcement of traditional gender roles in childhood, such as buying dolls for girls and action figures for boys. (BmPorter/Don Franklin)

entail buying endless outfits and accessories—but to identify with the figures. Boys vicariously participate in the action—they "become" the soldiers—while girls merely "relate to" their dolls.

Schools teach children by example as well as by explicit instruction. For example, the disproportionate number of male to female principals communicates to students that the "real world"—of which the school is the first sustained example to which most children are exposed—is run by men. Unless the question of why this is so is raised in the classroom (or somewhere else, such as in the home), children are likely to assume what all people assume about unquestioned phenomena: They are to be treated as natural, as the way that things are supposed to be. As for explicit content, recent studies of elementary school texts reveal that gender stereotyping is not yet a thing of the past: Male leading characters outnumber female leading characters; heroic, adventuresome activities are more often performed by males than by females; and females are still disproportionately cast in domestic roles. It can be argued that because most primary school teachers tend to be women, and teachers are significant authority figures for children, the effects of textbook stereotyping and the presence of a male principal are offset. An analogy can be made, however, in the home. Throughout early childhood, mothers are in most cases more significant authority figures than fathers, but traditionally their subordinate status in the household (and the outside world) has had a much greater impact on shaping the attitudes of children toward sex roles—convincing many girls that they are destined to take care of a husband and children, and many boys that they should expect to be waited on by their wives.

The most pernicious school experiences for girls, however, typically occur later on, in junior high or high school: the experience of being discouraged from pursuing subjects (such as mathematics and science) that are supposed to be for males only, or even from becoming too serious about academic pursuits in general, and the overwhelming likelihood of being the victim of sexual harassment at some point or another during their high school years.

Developing the capacity for normal peer relations is an important element in effecting a successful transition from childhood to adulthood—a transition in which the child learns to give up a dependency on the comforting, all-consuming love represented by parents and the home. Both academic and social skills are necessary for adult survival. It is most important to note that peers, notorious for enforcing group conformity, do so in the area of gender. They exert tremendous pressure on peer group members to live up to the group's definition of appropriate male or female behavior. This pressure becomes more pronounced as children approach adolescence and become increasingly self-conscious about their sexuality, but it is present earlier as well. The presence of pressure to follow the rules, as well as the existence of the rules themselves, becomes evident when violations occur and the violator is punished for them. Violations of group definitions of appropriate behavior typically lead to ridicule, if not ostracism from the group. Girls are routinely disparaged as "ugly" by girls as well as boys, both groups having accepted the wider culture's idea that girls are valuable to the extent that they are "pretty" (just as "real boys" are "tough").

Even in the early grades, sex stereotyping occurs among peer groups; these are the same children who, at home, were already playing with either dolls or action figures, according to their sex. It is interesting to note, however, that while girls who deliberately forsake the girl role to imitate boys are not considered serious rule violators, boys who forsake the boy role most definitely are. This double standard is clear from playground taunts: Girls are "tomboys," but boys are "sissies." Logically, the violators should be treated equally, since the violations are equivalent. Instead, this situation resembles that of the "girl in blue versus the boy in pink." A girl who wants to be a boy is considered cute; a boy who wants to be a girl is considered sick. This difference is attributable to the fact that society considers the boy role superior or more desirable than the girl role. Although a tomboy is subject to ridicule if she persists in the boy role, refraining from diagnosing her as sick in the initial stages is a way of acknowledging that her aspirations are understandable.

Peers are important in this respect not only because they come increasingly to dominate the child's social scene, as parents increasingly recede into the background, but also because their insistence on conformity is actually much greater than that of typical parents. Most parents do not, or do not consistently, convey the message that nonconformity is absolutely unacceptable. They generally do not call their effeminate son a "faggot" or ridicule him because he has acne; that job is left to his friends. When parents do exhort their children to conform, more often than not they justify it on practical grounds: One must conform in order to survive, not because nonconformity is pathological.

Throughout this entire period during which parents, teachers, and peers in one form or another are teaching children what is expected of boys and girls, the television is on: Between the ages of six and eighteen, the average American child spends more time in front of the television than in school. What impact does this have on gender socialization? First of all, children's toys, and their accompanying gender stereotypes, are advertised principally by means of television. Second, the shows themselves are filled with gender stereotypes. Even shows that are usually regarded as good influences contain such messages. For example, all the leading *Sesame Street* characters—Big Bird, Oscar, Grover, Cookie Monster, Telly, Elmo, Bert, and Ernie—are male. The same is true of the Muppets with the exception of Miss Piggy, who is mainly an object of ridicule. She is ridiculed in sex-stereotyped ways: as a lovelorn female who must get her clutches on her beloved Kermit (who considers her a pest); as a vain female, obsessed with her beauty (which is illusory) and with material things in general rather than principles (which are Kermit's domain); as a bossy female, who must always have the last word and have her way. As with life in the peer group, however, sex stereotyping in children's television is more obvious and more intense on shows designed for preadolescent and adolescent viewers. Here girls are typically treated as being more interested in relationships than boys are, while boys are depicted as typically obsessed with girls' looks; in this context, "liberation" for girls often consists of their ability to be as obsessed with boys' looks as boys are with theirs. With regard to such gendered behavior, the world "is" this or that way largely because boys and girls see certain behaviors as the only realistic option, the only one to which they have been exposed.

The medium through which all this learning and communicating takes place—language—is itself sexist. This is a vast topic in its own right, but two examples are the generic masculine and "hyphenization." When people in general are being discussed, they are referred to as men (for example, "mankind," "man-made," "man's inhumanity to man"). In descriptions of individuals where gender is not specified, the pronoun "he" is similarly employed as the generic. Women are thus invited to regard themselves as part of "man." It is clear, however, that man is the measure. This standard becomes obvious when one imagines the use of a female generic: How would men feel to hear themselves referred to constantly as instances of "womankind"? In "hyphenization," when women occupy certain social roles in which gender is supposedly irrelevant, their gender is nevertheless noted, such as a "woman doctor." The effect (if not the purpose) of such usage is to reinforce the idea that medicine is a profession that is normal for men, but not for women, to enter. One can consider how unsettling the expression "female prostitute" would be. Perhaps the pinnacle of this linguistic arrogance is found in the language of religion. The biblical God—creator, judge, and redeemer of the human race—is conceptualized as male; God is not "our Mother" but "our Father." (This led Sigmund Freud and his followers to speculate that religion originates in the individual's projection onto the universe of the absolute power of the father experienced as a child within the family.)

Sexism and Sexuality. Perhaps the most fundamental way in which Western culture is sexist is that it tends to promote the belief that the purpose of women's existence is to serve and please men. Traditionally, this meant that women's purpose in life was to bear and rear children for men, to cook their meals, to do their laundry, and so on. It also meant that women are to serve as objects of sexual gratification for men. Thus, women are required to be physically attractive and accessible to men. The amount of time and money that women devote to their appearance is so clear that in order to distract attention from its real meaning—that women must try to conform to male standards of beauty in order to be accepted in society—the culture encourages both men and women to regard it as a consequence of women's supposed natural vanity. That women are supposed to be at all times physically accessible to men is shown by society's continued resistance to the concept of marital rape, by the fact that the terms "date rape" or "acquaintance rape" have only recently become accepted usage (implying that the behaviors they describe have only recently been reconceived as unacceptable), and that the traditional judgment of society that rape victims must have done something to provoke (and so to deserve) being attacked has only recently begun to be called into question.

From a feminist point of view, sexual violence against women is not qualitatively different from more accepted modes of heterosexual male sexual behavior. Cultural norms enjoin men to play the role of sexual aggressor: The man pursues and the woman is pursued; men evaluate themselves and each other in terms of their competence as sexual conquerors. "Having sex" is defined not in terms of emotion or passion but erection, penetration, and (male) orgasm: When all these have occurred, "sex" is said to have taken place. Society defines the normal means by which men are supposed to pursue the goal of sexual conquest; these means may include verbal and financial pressure—that is, aggressive beseeching with words and gifts—but not physical force. Yet, if the only goal for the man is indeed sexual conquest, he may be tempted to cross the line from persuasion to coercion if he feels that otherwise the object of his attentions is unwilling to submit. Coercion can take many forms, but they are all variations on the same theme of interpreting a "no" as a "yes." Men decide what women want; many convicted rapists describe their perception that their victims "wanted it."

Sexual Discrimination. Given the sexist nature of the social environment described, it should come as no surprise that discrimination against women—that is, the denial of equal opportunity on the basis of sex—is a pervasive feature of society. Women are regularly subject to discrimination in education and employment, to name the two areas that have become the principal focus of antidiscrimination laws. While the existence of antidiscrimination laws indicates substantial social progress, it should not be taken to mean that discrimination has been eliminated—any more than the existence of an elaborate and continually expanding criminal justice system means that crime is not a problem. Indeed, it means exactly the opposite.

It cannot be denied that, in terms of numbers of degrees earned and professional positions held, women are doing better than they ever have. Consequently, the analysis of sexual discrimination has undergone a shift in focus. Instead of analyzing how women are kept out of educational institutions and the workplace, sociologists and others are interested in how they are systematically ill-treated within them. Of the following forms of discrimination, only the first has yet to be recognized as discrimination in the legal sense, and that only since the 1980's. First, women at school and at work are routinely subjected to sexual harassment. Second, female students at all levels of the school system tend to be ignored in favor of male students. Third, the workplace—professional and blue-collar alike—tends to be characterized by occupational segregation: Within the same field, the more desirable positions tend to be reserved for men and the less desirable ones for women (for example, female elementary school teachers and male Ivy League professors, male waiters in exclusive restaurants and female waitresses in diners). There is also an unspoken assumption that mothers, but not fathers, are primarily responsible for the care of their children, which means that parental obligations often keep women from pursuing educational and career opportunities that would otherwise be available to them.

The last point especially illustrates the limits necessarily placed on social progress when only half a revolution takes place. Since the late 1960's, the lives of most Western women—because of the women's movement and the social and legal changes that it instigated—have been radically transformed. Despite sexism and sexual discrimination, problems that the women's movement is responsible for forcing into the open, most girls in American, Canadian, and Western European society in particular grow up expecting and demanding a range of choices for themselves that only a generation ago was scarcely conceivable: for example, whether and when to marry, whether and when to have children, what type of education and career to pursue, and how much emphasis to place on these things in the overall context of one's life. Unfortunately, no corresponding radical change has occurred in the consciousness and the lives of most men. To women's demand for freedom to enter the professions, there has been no corresponding demand by men to be allowed to share child care and other household obligations with women. In general, the most that women have been able to expect from men is that they will not forcibly obstruct women's efforts at emancipation; the day when men will actively aid such efforts by changing their demands and expectations as women have changed theirs has not yet arrived. In other words, as long as society tolerates tomboys but persecutes sissies, it cannot be said that a revolution has occurred in the understanding of gender. To move in such a direction, it is necessary to recognize that it is men who enforce traditional "macho" expectations on themselves; men often terrorize each other in this process. Most women would not ridicule the father of their children for wanting to change diapers or to help prepare meals, but the man's friends might do so. One can claim that the next stage in the liberation of women must take place among men. —*Jay Mullin*

See also Antifeminism; Feminism; Language and sexism; Patriarchy; Phallocentrism; Pornography; Sexual harassment; Socialization of girls and young women; Stereotypes of women; Violence against women; Women's movement

BIBLIOGRAPHY

Dworkin, Andrea. *Intercourse*. New York: Free Press, 1987. Offers a painfully vivid analysis of the misogynist foundations and connotations of the institution of heterosexual genital intercourse.

Frye, Marilyn. *The Politics of Reality: Essays in Feminist Theory*. Trumansburg, N.Y.: Crossing Press, 1983. A clear, closely reasoned presentation of the radical feminist perspective by a philosophy professor and lesbian. Especially interesting for its analysis of the nature of sexism and oppression and for its critique of the male supremacist premises of gay culture.

Hite, Shere. *The Hite Report: A Nationwide Study of Female Sexuality*. New York: Dell, 1976. This landmark investigation of women's sexual lives is fascinating in its own right but is especially illuminating when read in conjunction with Dworkin's *Intercourse* (above).

Leidholdt, Dorchen, and Janice G. Raymond, eds. *The Sexual Liberals and the Attack on Feminism*. Elmsford, N.Y.: Pergamon Press, 1990. This collection of talks, originally presented at a conference at New York University Law School in 1987, focuses on life-and-death matters involving the intersection of sexism and sexuality: pornography, incest, rape, and domestic violence. The contributors include leading feminist scholars, authors, and activists.

Lindsey, Linda L. *Gender Roles: A Sociological Perspective*. 2d ed. Englewood Cliffs, N.J.: Prentice Hall, 1994. A representative contemporary sociological introduction to the subject. Discusses sexism in the media, law, religion, politics, and the workplace; the gender socialization process; sexism in language; the history of gender roles; and many other fundamental issues.

Sadker, Myra, and David Sadker. *Failing at Fairness*. New York: Charles Scribner's Sons, 1994. The most comprehensive survey available of discrimination against girls in the school system. An eminently readable, and disturbing, treatment of a critically important issue.

Sexual harassment

RELEVANT ISSUES: Business and economics, politics, sex and gender

SIGNIFICANCE: Since Anita Hill accused Supreme Court nominee Clarence Thomas of sexual harassment in 1991, other women have been prompted to come forward; both cases and reports of sexual harassment have been steadily on the rise

Definition. According to Joel Friedman, author of *The Complete Handbook* (1992), "sexual harassment is by its very definition, offensive and unwelcome. More specifically, it is conduct or behavior characterized by unwanted sexual advances made in the context of a relationship of unequal power or authority." Sexual harassment can often start as an off-color comment or joke. Soon the comments turn menacing when the person they are addressing is made to feel uncomfortable, or in cases in which the person is made to fear job loss. The Equal Employment Opportunity Commission (EEOC) uses the following guidelines to define what constitutes abuse: first, unwelcome sexual advances and, second, requests for sexual favors and/or other verbal or physical conduct of a sexual nature when submission to such conduct is made either explicitly or implicitly a term or condition of an individual's employment, when submission to or rejection of such conduct by an individual is used as the basis for employment decisions affecting the individual, or when such conduct has the purpose or effect of reasonably interfering with an individual's work performance or creating an intimidating, hostile, or offensive working environment.

Sexual harassment cannot be traced back to a specific time. It is an act that can take many forms and often goes unreported. According to one writer, "For decades, many victims felt the only way to cope with sexual harassment at work was to quit their job or suffer in silence." Traditionally, the victims of sexual harassment have been women, though in some cases the victims are men. It became an issue in the workplace after World War II, when women began working outside the home. Many anecdotes and cartoons have depicted women being chased around their desks by lecherous bosses. Sexual harassment was not taken seriously by companies and the government until the Civil Rights Act of 1964 was passed.

The Civil Rights Act of 1964 prohibited discrimination based on gender, race, or religion. Not until 1977, however, was sexual harassment first recognized by the courts with the introduction of Title VII. Title VII states that the employer must make an employment decision guided by the following factors: the necessary qualifications for the job, a "business necessity," or bona fide occupational qualification. Under these guidelines, sexual harassment violates Title VII because it is considered a form of discrimination.

Even Title VII did not lead to changes in the attitudes surrounding sexual harassment. Before 1977, the courts and corporate America excused men's behavior; because of this attitude, many women were too intimidated to take legal action against their aggressors. Although Title VII prohibited sexual harassment, it still occurred in some companies. In 1977, a federal court ruled that sexual harassment is a form of discrimination based on sex. Despite that ruling, however, women still remained silent because they were afraid of what a legal case would do to their careers.

In order to prove a case of sexual harassment, a woman had to show that the harassment had been taking place over a long period. She also had to demonstrate that there was a pattern to the abuse. In many cases, if a woman refused to grant sexual favors in exchange for a raise or promotion, she was "constructively fired." In addition to the difficulty of proving that there was a pattern to the harassment, the woman had to deal with a legal system that blamed her for the abuse. Often it was the complainant who was put on trial and not the aggressor. In most cases, it became her word against that of her boss or coworker.

In 1986, the U.S. Supreme Court heard *Meritor Savings Bank v. Vinson*, the first major case addressing sexual harassment in the workplace. Mechelle Vinson, a bank teller, filed suit against her employer, Meritor Savings Bank, FSB. The Court declared that no court or legislation could create a law that denies that sexual harassment is against the law and upheld the EEOC guidelines in the workplace. Vinson was able to sue for punitive damages, thus making her case quid pro quo. In 1991, Anita Hill put Title VII to the test in her case against Clarence Thomas. Hill did not win her suit, but as a result of the case, President George Bush signed a law amending Title VII to allow victims of sexual harassment to seek compensatory damages. In their handbooks on policies and procedures, companies now must include a section on sexual harassment, and a company can be held accountable for an employee's violation of the sexual harassment policy. Many companies conduct workshops on sexual harassment. The U.S. military, particularly after the Tailhook case in which a group of petty officers assaulted and harassed several women (one of whom was a seventeen-year-old girl), has adopted policies on sexual harassment. Even with the government-mandated workshops, however, state legislatures have neglected to comply. Many of them believe that attending a workshop on sexual harassment is unnecessary because they acknowledge its existence. Senator Bob Packwood apparently believed this until he was forced to step down after ten women came forward with allegations that he had sexually harassed them, prompting a preliminary hearing by the Senate Ethics Committee.

Sexual Harassment in Schools and Universities. A taunt in the schoolyard, a sexually suggestive gesture, or continuing patterns of threats that are sexual in nature can be considered sexual harassment. A 1993 survey of 1,632 students found that "most girls and many boys can expect to be poked, pinched, grabbed, and put down in sexually explicit ways." The students surveyed ranged from grades eight to eleven in seventy-nine schools across the United States. According to the survey, "more than 75 percent of the girls and 42 percent of boys have been touched, grabbed, or pinched. 80 percent of these unwanted sexual behaviors are by students and directed at other students with the remaining 20 percent by teachers or administrators."

Students at this age are reluctant to come forward. Often they are unaware or unsure that they were sexually harassed. When these students do complain, parents or teachers cite children's tendency toward cruelty. As in the case with a woman in the workplace, a student complaining of sexual harassment must be able to prove that the harassment had taken place on several occasions and caused the student emotional suffering. This may be easier to prove against another student, but it can be difficult if the complaint is made against a teacher. The student may fear retaliation and take steps to avoid the teacher. In 1978, Title IX applied the same set of guidelines that Title VII placed on sexual harassment in the workplace. Schools and universities are required to treat all complaints with due process or they can be held accountable for the actions of the aggressor.

Sexual harassment at the university is as common as it is in the workplace, the difference being that most cases in universities go unreported. Many women who are harassed by a professor fail to report it out of concern for the male ego. Other women think that somehow they invited advances. Traditionally, institutions have taken the side of the faculty member, valuing his or her career over the student's career aspirations. Because female students are usually far from their families and lack the financial resources necessary to pursue a solution, they avoid the harasser. Women who do report the sexual harassment often lose financial support from teaching assistantships or face career obstacles.

In 1991, the issue of sexual harassment was brought into the open by the testimony of Anita Hill against Supreme Court justice nominee Clarence Thomas; the Senate committee's treatment of Hill and Thomas' confirmation sparked angry protests among some feminists, who vowed that "Women Will Remember" at the next election. (Bettye Lane)

The laws governing suing for punitive damages are clear regarding sexual harassment in the workplace, but not so in educational institutions. Under Title IX, the university is considered the employer and the faculty member, the employee. The student, then becomes the third party. Cases such as *Alexander v. Yale University* (1977), *Cannon v. the University of Chicago* (1979), *Grove City College v. Bell* (1984), and *Brown City College v. California State Personnel Board* (1985) have challenged this view. The passage of the Civil Rights Act of

1991 enabled complainants to receive compensatory and punitive damages ranging from $50,000 to $300,000.

Types of Sexual Harassment. Sexual harassment can be placed in general categories. One type of harassment is known as quid pro quo, in which the work environment is altered so that an employee who refuses the sexual advances of a supervisor is either dismissed or forced to resign. The victim of quid pro quo harassment can file a lawsuit against the former employer as well as the company for allowing the harassment to take place and can expect to recover $30,000 to $50,000 in compensatory damages depending on the size of the company. In 1991, the Equal Remedies Act attempted to lift the cap on compensatory damages, but the matter failed to come to a vote in the Senate.

Third-party sexual harassment is a type of harassment in which a spouse is targeted. For example, a husband who is fired for refusing to grant his employer sexual access to his wife can seek compensatory damages, as in quid pro quo harassment, against his boss.

Another form of sexual harassment involves the creation of a hostile environment. A group of people set out (either deliberately or accidentally) to make someone feel uncomfortable or threatened. Traditionally, hostile environment has been harder to prove than quid pro quo harassment because there is a fine line between what constitutes a hostile environment and what does not. Displaying offensive pictures that degrade men or women can be clearly labeled as hostile; sexual innuendoes and off-color jokes meant to humiliate and hurt also contribute to a hostile environment. Congress defined an environment to be hostile if a "reasonable person" would be made to feel uncomfortable. The question arises, however, of what constitutes a reasonable person, and what might make one person uncomfortable may not have the same effect on another person. By using Congress' guidelines governing hostile environment, many college courses dealing in human sexuality through the use of suggestive films and printed matter would be considered hostile environments. These courses set out to challenge the preconceived notions of sexuality, and this often makes many people uncomfortable. The same could be said in regard to nude models in an art class. Many institutions have taken steps to narrow the guidelines regarding sexual harassment in an attempt to protect students and faculty. The following elements were added to policies on ethics: Sexual harassment statements should address three specific topics: the differentiation of sexual and physical contact, the sexual content of certain curricula for educational purposes, and the importance of context when determining sexual harassment.

Sexual Harassment by Proxy. A type of harassment that is similar to third party and quid pro quo harassment occurs when the victim is not necessarily the subject of the harassment. For example, a woman who is up for promotion has the qualifications and the seniority, but her supervisor is having a sexual relationship with his secretary. The secretary is not qualified for the position, nor has she been with the company long enough to earn the promotion, but she is promoted for the position anyway because of her relationship with the supervisor. The qualified woman can file a lawsuit against the supervisor for deliberately promoting someone who was willing to provide sexual favors in return for the position. Her coworkers can also file a lawsuit if they were affected as well.

Psychological Effects of Sexual Harassment. The psychological effects of sexual harassment are similar to those suffered by rape victims. Sexual harassment is a violation of trust and a misuse of power. Some of the symptoms that harassment victims experience include heightened anxiety, depression, flashbacks, disturbed relationships, changed routines, reclusiveness, and difficulties with eating, sleeping, and sex. Many women are forced to hold lower-paying jobs because they have been blacklisted from their field. Seldom will a company hire a woman who has filed a sexual harassment suit against her previous employer. These reasons, coupled with the shame and humiliation brought about by a lengthy trial, make many women reluctant to come forward. Despite the strengthening of the laws governing sexual harassment since the Civil Rights Act of 1964, this reluctance continues. —*Randi A. Drubin*

See also Civil Rights Act of 1964; Date rape; Employment of women; Equal Employment Opportunity Commission (EEOC); Equal Rights Amendment (ERA); *Meritor Savings Bank v. Vinson*; Sexism; Title VII of the Civil Rights Act of 1964

Bibliography

Clark, Charles S. "The Issues (Sexual Harassment)." *Congressional Quarterly Researcher* 1, no. 13 (August 9, 1991): 539-559. An overview of sexual harassment in the workplace: a brief working definition, the issues surrounding it, and steps the government is taking to stop it.

Clark, Jeffrey K. "Complications in Academia: Sexual Harassment and the Law." *SIECUS Report* 21, no. 6 (August/September, 1993): 6-10. A complete explanation of sexual harassment and the law in academia. Defines the problems faced by victims.

Friedman, Joel, et al. *The Complete Handbook, Including a Directory of Regional Offices of the Equal Employment Opportunity Commission on Sexual Harassment*. Lexington, Mass.: Health Communications, 1992. An informative discussion on sexual harassment using anecdotal examples to illustrate the different kinds of harassment. Also offers help to victims by providing a list of EEOC branches.

Gordon, Dianna. "It's Not About Sex—It's About Power." *State Legislature* 19, no. 7 (July, 1993): 51-54. Insight into the politics at work in the workplace. The author makes the important distinction that sexual harassment is not sexual but a misuse of power.

Sexual Politics

Author: Kate Millett (1934-   )

Date: 1970

Relevant issues: Literature and communications, sex and gender

Significance: Millett's book is one of the crucial works in the establishment of feminist literary criticism, a major reevaluation of the canon of modern and contemporary male writers, revealing their often degrading portrayal of female characters

Sexual Politics remains one of the founding works of contemporary feminist criticism. Even as feminist critics have dissented from some of Millett's conclusions and acknowledged the polemical nature of her book and its skewed readings of literary history, they have championed its bold staking out of the female critic's right to assess literature from a woman's perspective. There has been such an explosion of feminist criticism since 1970 that Millett's importance can easily be forgotten. Few women's studies departments or programs existed when her book was published, relatively few female critics, and a still smaller number of female academics who were assessing literature's treatment of women. Moreover, Millett's argument that the male ego in literature (especially in the novel) had steadily devalued women proved to be a shocking and controversial position attacked by writers such as Norman Mailer in his counterargument, *The Prisoner of Sex* (1971).

Although Mailer shows instances in which Millett simplifies the characters and situations created by male authors, his attack has not done much to deflect the force of her argument. There might be legitimate reasons that authors such as Mailer have shown women in debased roles, but Millett prevails in her assertion that it is always women who must be given such subordinate roles. Women read the characters created by Mailer, D. H. Lawrence, Henry Miller, and other men differently from the way those authors and male critics do, Millett contends. Mailer's reputation among feminist readers and critics has never recovered from Millett's critique, and the other male authors discussed in *Sexual Politics* have been subject to major reevaluations in large part because of Millett's penetrating and skeptical treatment of them.

Sexual Politics stimulated or perhaps released a torrent of feminist criticism because it demonstrated that the canon of modern literature was subject to revision. The canon was dominated by male writers, and their maleness had rarely been made an issue before Millett's book. The structure of *Sexual Politics* and its very title heralded many of the developments in women's studies programs and in feminist criticism. Part 1 of her book, "Sexual Politics," establishes the term as a diagnostic tool in chapters titled "Instances of Sexual Politics" and "Theory of Sexual Politics." In "Instances of Sexual Politics," Millett uses Mailer's novel, *An American Dream*, to show how a female character, Ruta, is depersonalized in terms of her class, sex, and nature, whereas the narrator, Rojack, a Harvard graduate who is a college professor and politician, is given the role of lording it over her and other women. The essential relationship of men and women in Mailer's fiction is that of master and servant, Millett concludes. Women are repeatedly at men's service; they are, in short, the obscene projections of men's imaginations. Millett couples this analysis of Mailer with her statement in "Theory of Sexual Politics" that the "term 'politics' shall refer to power-structured relationships, arrangements whereby one group of persons is controlled by another." The creative decisions made by an author such as Mailer are thus attached to an overarching reading of how society works; the suppression of women in fiction has its roots in society itself, as she attempts to demonstrate in part 2 of her book, "Historical Background."

Part 2 ranges from 1830 to 1930, showing the political, polemical, and literary phases of the sexual revolution. Millett traces the rise of a women's movement, the call for political rights, and the recognition of women as authors. Then she describes the "counterrevolution" that occurred between 1930 and 1960, linking the reactionary policies of fascism in the 1930's with the growth of Freudianism and its emphasis on the individual's adjustment to the status quo to a society that is male-dominated. In this respect, Millett anticipates much of later feminist criticism that has often been hostile to Freud's view of women and to the therapeutic and intellectual views of his followers.

Sexual Politics argues, then, that the male writer's creation of female characters cannot be considered in isolation but must be seen as part of a historical process. It is the historical process of the steady erosion of women's rights and the value of the female imagination that she pursues in the third and last

Kate Millett, the author of Sexual Politics, *in 1971.* (Bettye Lane)

part of her book, "The Literary Reflection." Here she shows that writers such as Miller and Lawrence should not be heralded as heroes of the sexual revolution, freely dealing with issues that their societies try to censor, but rather as males determined to use women as mere projections of their own sexual fantasies. For example, Millett does not regard Jean Genet as a revolutionary who liberates literature, allowing it to treat all forms of sexuality. On the contrary, she observes that Genet equates strength and intelligence with masculinity.

Sexual Politics is a relentless work. It presents a powerful thesis and excludes all evidence that contradicts that thesis. Millett's reading of modern history is tailored to support her interpretation of individual works, and so those individual works seem to support her reading of history. Critics of all persuasions have admitted as much. Yet the principle of her book has survived: There is a value to examining the historical milieu that influences the author's imagination in ways that that author may not recognize; there is a danger in treating works of art as autonomous products of the imagination ungrounded in history.

Feminist criticism has continued to follow Millett's lead in the sense that it continues to explore the cultural conditions out of which art is created. *Sexual Politics* remains a challenge to literary study and a model that feminist critics consult while elaborating more sophisticated approaches to art and politics.

—*Carl Rollyson*

See also Academia and scholarship, women in; *Female Eunuch, The*; Feminism; Feminist literary criticism; History of women; Language and sexism; Literature, images of women in; *Madwoman in the Attic, The*; Politics; Psychological theories on women; *Second Sex, The*; Second wave of the women's movement; Stereotypes of women; Women's studies programs

Sexual revolution

RELEVANT ISSUES: Reproductive rights, sex and gender, social reform

SIGNIFICANCE: This 1960's social movement in the United States led to major changes in sexual attitudes and behavior, with important consequences for women's sexuality

The sexual revolution was a consequence of a number of earlier social changes and was also strongly related to other societal changes occurring in the 1960's. A higher level of education, greater ethnic and ideological heterogeneity, some modernization of religious beliefs, and a generally less negative attitude toward sexuality had been occurring for decades in the United States. Significant changes had begun in the nineteenth century and continued early in the twentieth century, especially after the end of World War I. A sexual revolution occurred in the 1920's, but its visibility decreased with concern about the Great Depression in the 1930's, World War II in the 1940's, and the "yearning for stability after so much turmoil" in the 1950's. Despite these three decades, however, many attitudes and expectations continued to change, and a number of forces came together in a period of tremendous social activism in the 1960's.

Feminism and Sexuality. The second wave of the women's movement (also called the feminist movement), often said to have begun in 1963 with Betty Friedan's book *The Feminine Mystique*, and the sexual revolution, which was given impetus by approval of the birth control pill in 1960, were two of the strongest interacting forces. Women increasingly had worked outside the home in the 1940's and 1950's, and many women were no longer content to be only homemakers. "The Pill" did not cause the sexual revolution, but it and the legalization of abortion in the United States with *Roe v. Wade* (1973) removed the technological obstacles to sex for pleasure (instead of only procreation). These factors encouraged change and allowed changed attitudes to be put into practice.

Not only had many women left the homemaker-only role, but many younger women (especially in colleges) had been activists in the Civil Rights movement, the anti-Vietnam War movement, the gay rights movement, and the drug culture. Unsatisfied with the way in which they were treated socially and sexually by some men in these movements, many women transferred the skills that they had learned to the women's movement, with female sexuality being one issue of major concern. A medical cure for most sexual diseases, the youth culture's emphasis on pleasure, the media's greatly increased openness on sexuality, and the social acceptance of divorce (and the drastic increase in divorce rates) were all additional, intertwined aspects of rapid social change. The interaction of all these changes, but especially the interaction of the sexual movement and feminism, led to profound changes in sexual attitudes and behavior for both women and men.

Changes in Female Sexuality. Because women started from a more passive position than men did, and because feminism put much attention on female sexuality with little attention on male sexuality (and most of that very negative), female sexuality was affected much more than male sexuality by the sexual revolution. This was especially true for teenage girls. Precise comparative data on sexuality is difficult because definitions and research methods vary by studies. Some writers also suggest that both men and women provide false answers concerning some sexual issues—that men tend to exaggerate and women tend to deny some things that they have done. Nevertheless, most data suggest major changes in sexual attitudes and behavior beginning in the 1960's, reflected by people who grew up in different time periods. For example, *The Janus Report on Sexual Behavior* (1993), by Samuel S. and Cynthia L. Janus, concluded that, for people aged fifty-one to sixty-four, 19 percent of men but only 3 percent of women had experienced their "first full sexual relations" by age fourteen. For people aged eighteen to twenty-six, however, the comparable figures were 21 percent for men and 15 percent for women. *Sex in America* (1994), by Robert T. Michael and colleagues, concluded that, for people aged fifty to fifty-nine, 59 percent of men and 44 percent of women had engaged in active oral sex by age fourteen. For people aged twenty-five to twenty-nine, the comparable figures were 85 percent for men and 76 percent for women. These findings and others show that the changes generally were greater for women than for men. In the 1940's and 1950's, Alfred C. Kinsey had estimated that by the age of forty, 50 percent of husbands and 30 percent of wives had taken part in an extramarital affair. By the early 1990's, the comparable figures were estimated to be 60 percent for husbands and 40 percent for wives. The divorce rate more than doubled from 1963 to 1979. The number of births to unwed mothers also increased greatly from the 1960's to the 1990's.

Continuing Change. The sexual revolution generally is considered to have ended by the late 1970's, but its impact continues to be felt. The changed attitudes toward sexuality have had significant consequences, positive and negative, for both women and men. Although women still are more likely than men to be criticized (by both genders) for being "too sexual," women are much more free to have premarital sex and extramarital sex, to use different sexual positions, and to leave unsatisfying marriages. More openness, combined with sex therapy and increased sexual knowledge, have helped women emphasize such practices as passive oral sex, women-on-top positions, and clitoral orgasms as major ways of increasing female pleasure. Nonsexual changes also have been important. Women are likely to be working outside the house at either jobs or careers, to have more available income (with a gap still existing between average incomes for men and women but having narrowed significantly, especially for younger women), and, like men, to marry at a later age and have fewer children than they did at the beginning of the twentieth century. Factors such as these also have given women more flexibility in expressing themselves sexually.

Negative consequences, and intense social and political controversies, have resulted from the rapid changes in sexuality-related issues. Sexuality is more accepted, but safeguards frequently are not followed by either women or men, resulting in major increases in sexually transmitted diseases and out-of-wedlock births; some of these births are to career women, but most are to poor, unemployed teenagers, which has led to a major increase in female poverty, especially among female-headed households. Major conflicts remain and are increasingly reflected in the political arena: Are rape, sexual harassment, and the sexual molestation of children underreported, or are there many false accusations? Should the right to have an abortion be protected or curtailed? What are the rights of unmarried birth parents versus those of adoptive parents? What are the responsibilities of birth fathers for out-of-wedlock children, and what is the government's responsibility regarding welfare for children and for unwed mothers? There is every indication that such conflicts will continue and, in some cases, escalate. —*Abraham D. Lavender*

See also Abortion; Birth control and family planning; Reproductive rights; *Roe v. Wade*; Sex object; Sexual harassment; Sexual stereotypes; Sexuality, women's; Social reform movements and women; Teen pregnancy; Women's movement

Bibliography

Friday, Nancy. *Women on Top: How Real Life Has Changed Women's Sexual Fantasies*. New York: Simon & Schuster, 1991.

Janus, Samuel S., and Cynthia L. Janus. *The Janus Report on Sexual Behavior*. New York: John Wiley & Sons, 1993.

Kinsey, Alfred, et al. *Sexual Behavior in the Human Female*. Philadelphia: W. B. Saunders, 1953.

Michael, Robert T., et al. *Sex in America: A Definitive Survey*. Boston: Little, Brown, 1994.

Reiss, Ira. *An End to Shame: Shaping Our Next Sexual Revolution*. Buffalo, N.Y.: Prometheus Books, 1990.

Rubin, Lillian B. *Erotic Wars: What Happened to the Sexual Revolution?* New York: Farrar, Straus, & Giroux, 1990.

Sexual stereotypes

Relevant issues: Psychology, sex and gender

Significance: Although sexual stereotypes are becoming more flexible in Western society, they continue to impose second-class status on women

Sexual stereotypes are beliefs that an individual should behave in certain ways or show certain characteristics because that person is male or female. Despite the current trend toward equality of the sexes, sexual stereotypes are prevalent in American culture.

In learning sexual stereotypes, children learn the preferences, abilities, interests, personality traits, actions, and self-concepts that their culture says are appropriate for males and females. For example, in the United States, children have traditionally learned that boys are supposed to like carpentry and girls are supposed to like cooking. Boys are supposed to be good with gadgets; girls, with babies. Boys are supposed to be aggressive and mathematical; girls, nurturing and verbal. Sexual stereotyping starts early, with blue for boys and pink for girls. By age three or four, most children prefer games and activities that are traditional for their gender and predominantly have same-sex friends.

Sexual stereotypes persist even in the absence of any basis in reality. For example, newborn boys are undistinguishable from newborn girls when both are wearing diapers. Adults, however, viewing infants through the window of a hospital nursery, describe boys as robust, strong, and large-featured and girls as delicate, fine-featured, and "soft." In general, male infants are perceived by both parents as hardier and less in need of nurturance than female infants.

In the landmark study *The Psychology of Sex Differences* (1974), Eleanor E. Maccoby and Carol N. Jacklin analyzed more than two thousand articles and books for evidence on gender differences in children. There was no evidence that girls were more social than boys and no differences in self-esteem throughout childhood and adolescence. Both sexes were equally skilled at simple repetitive tasks. Boys were as analytical as girls, and girls were as likely as boys to be persuaded by others and to imitate the behavior of others. The researchers concluded that boys and girls are more alike than different, and they found insufficient evidence for a number of longstanding biases about sex differences.

Among all these similarities, they found only four gender differences. Boys were more aggressive, perhaps because of a biologically higher activity level that is socialized into aggression. Also, after age eleven or twelve, boys were better in mathematical and visual-spatial skills and girls were better at verbal skills. These differences were small and occurred when average scores of large groups of boys and girls were compared.

Sexual stereotypes overlook the fact that the variation within each sex is almost always greater than the average difference between the sexes. Thus, sexual stereotypes are broad overgeneralizations that ignore the diversity within groups of women and men and foster inaccurate perceptions.

See also Child rearing; Gender differences; Sexism; Socialization of girls and young women; Stereotypes of women

Sexuality, women's

RELEVANT ISSUES: Psychology, sex and gender, religious beliefs and practices, reproductive rights, women's history

SIGNIFICANCE: Sexuality is not merely erotic physical activity and reproduction; it is also implicit in many activities and thoughts

All of human culture is concerned with gender, including the human beings who inhabit a culture and the culture that they create—their religious, social, artistic, technological, political, and personal expressions. Both work and play are gendered; that is, they carry gender implications or metaphorical resonances, which are more often hidden than apparent. Perhaps gender is a primary texture of human language, and thus sexuality is implicit in the warp and woof of culture.

Categories for Analysis. Any or all of these three categories for analysis illuminate the complexity of women and sexuality: first, attitudes, habits, and theories of the body, including practices and beliefs concerning procreation; second, the politics of patriarchal power and control; and, third, pleasure and the erotic. An initial analytical step necessary to discuss women and sexuality is to determine whether woman is subject or object; most of art, literature, law, and custom in patriarchal cultures place women not as the subjects of their own lives, but as the objects of male sexuality. Analysis then demands that one distinguish among several groups: females as a biological category (sex must be distinguished from gender); an individual person who might be female (who may or may not be subject to the implications of gender assumptions); women as a social group (often stereotyped by way of androcentric or patriarchal values); women as artistic or religious representations (imagery and metaphors that carry feminine connotations or qualities in a given culture); and, finally, divine figures (or sacred metaphors that are designated as feminine). These categories overlap and implicate one another in cultural discourses and systems of meaning.

Gender. Recently, the English language has accommodated a shift in understanding of sex-based categories. "Sex" now refers to the biological, while "gender" refers to social and cultural identities. The question, then, is not whether someone is a woman biologically (sex), but rather how persons (or texts and phenomena) are gendered as feminine, how "woman" is understood in a culture (gender). This question is reflected in the famous aphorism by feminist philosopher Simone de Beauvoir (1908-1986) that "One is not born a woman, but rather becomes one." The American writer Ursula Le Guin gave the thought another turn when she made the provocative statement, "I am a man. . . . Women are a very recent invention." To begin to discuss gender, one must set aside biological imperatives for clues about cultural traditions. Gender is a set of conventions that is specific to its particular culture. Gender serves to establish social interactions and power relationships; all human cultures use gender language to control individual behavior. When children are very young, their families and the larger world inform them, and will continue to inform them throughout their lives, about their gender status and relationships, about how they will exist in the world, in their bodies, in their professions, and in their relationships. Gender is less about postpuberty body designations than it is about theories of reality.

Body. Given that human sexuality involves a culturally learned language rather than being solely conferred biologically, recent feminist studies have emphasized investigations of "body" in order to reveal cultural meaning. "Body" is a paradoxical term that is both an abstraction, a collective term, as well as a term that refers to concrete matter. The abstract body is indecipherable except by way of emotions and intellectual ideas.

In a phallocentric culture (a system or tradition that values masculine metaphors over metaphors designated to be feminine), the woman's body is a contradictory object of desire, derision, shame, and/or value, often at the same time. The "body" might be said to be a map of a culture more than it is a biological realm of a person. For example, until recently in prevailing American culture, the clitoris was undesignated in conventional, popular anatomical maps of human females. At the same time, women throughout the world (including in the United States) still undergo genital mutilations, specifically clitoridectomies (removal of the clitoris).

A culture that is dominated by phallocentric mapping or describing of the female body includes women's views of their own bodies that are phallocentrically influenced as well. Naomi Wolf's investigations and reflections in *The Beauty Myth: How Images of Beauty Are Used Against Women* (1991) have revealed women's emotional perceptions of body: "When they discuss [their bodies], women lean forward, their voices lower. They tell their terrible secret. It's my breasts, they say. My hips. It's my thighs. I hate my stomach. This is not aesthetic distaste, but deep sexual shame. The parts of the body vary. But what each woman who describes it shares is the conviction that that is what the pornography of beauty most fetishizes." Body parts and body dimensions go in and out of fashion; what remains constant is that what one understands as the body is a collection of projections and fantasies just as much as it is a concert of bones, blood, and flesh. The body, which at a glance would seem to be a biological given, also has

Milestones in the History of Women's Sexuality

1926 Mae West is brought to court on charges of obscenity for her Broadway play *Sex*.

1939 Margaret Mead publishes *From the South Seas: Studies of Adolescence and Sex in Primitive Societies*.

1953 Alfred C. Kinsey's report *Sexual Behavior in the Human Female* is published.

1953 *Playboy* magazine begins publication with a nude centerfold of Marilyn Monroe.

1960 The introduction of "the Pill" encourages greater sexual activity.

1962 Helen Gurley Brown's *Sex and the Single Girl* champions the sexual liberation of single women.

1963 Journalist Gloria Steinem publishes an exposé based on her one-month undercover assignment as a Playboy "bunny."

1966 William Masters and Virginia Johnson's study *Human Sexual Response* brings new attention to the issue of female sexuality.

1969 *Penthouse*, a more explicit magazine than *Playboy*, begins publication.

1970 Anne Koedt's article "The Myth of the Vaginal Orgasm" influences how the women's movement views sexual responses and female needs.

1976 Shere D. Hite publishes *The Hite Report: A Nationwide Study of Female Sexuality*, which becomes controversial because of its methodology and interpretation of women's ambivalence toward the sexual revolution.

1983 The Coalition Against Media Pornography is created in Canada to protest cable television showings of soft-core pornography.

1984 The Feminist Anti-Censorship Task Force (FACT) is founded to challenge an antipornography statute developed by Andrea Dworkin and Catharine A. MacKinnon.

1987 Andrea Dworkin's *Intercourse* argues that this fundamental sexual act is the means by which men exert dominance over women.

1992 Antioch College develops a sexual consent code requiring that students secure clear verbal consent before any romantic gestures or actions are initiated.

1993 Husband-and-wife team Samuel S. and Cynthia L. Janus publish *The Janus Report on Sexual Behavior*.

1993 In *The Morning After*, Katie Roiphe discusses date rapes on college campuses, arguing that women need to start taking responsibility for their sexuality.

1994 The study *Sex in America: A Definitive Survey* appears, edited by Robert T. Michael and colleagues.

a history—geographical and chronological versions of understanding of what the human body is, what it does, and, especially consequential for women, how it is perceived. Women in Western culture long have been defined as "not-men" or "imperfect men": As Aristotle (384-322 B.C.) said in *The Generation of Animals*, "The male and the female are distinguished by a certain ability and inability. Male is that which is able to concoct, to cause to take shape, and to discharge, semen possessing the 'principle' of the 'form.' . . . Female is that which receives the semen, but is unable to cause semen to take shape or to discharge it." Western culture is deeply ingrained with both Greek philosophy and with Hebraic thought. It is just as relevant to look at the more ancient narrative of Creation in Genesis 2-3, where God (Yahweh) creates a man, then the animals from the same earth as the man, and then puts the man to sleep and takes a woman from "his rib," performing what some anthropologists call *couvade*, or "male hatching." These representative texts became intertwined paradigms, Greek and Hebrew, forming the basis of gender ideas in the West. They became part of the mainstream dialogue and concern, underscoring that what was male was normative and what was female was "other" or inferior.

As women, historically and mythologically, have been defined primarily by body, they have been further limited by a definition of their bodies as primarily functioning as procreative. The designation of women as mothers has several political and psychological effects: It marginalizes independent, celibate, childless, lesbian, or postmenopausal women; it creates the fallacy of essentialism (which claims universal qualities for specific cultural values); and, it contributes to a given subculture's control of women and children. As Jessie Bernard, among other scholars, has pointed out, "Motherhood as we know it today is a surprisingly new institution. It is also a unique one, the product of an affluent society. In most of human history and in most parts of the world even today, adult, able-bodied women have been, and still are, too valuable in their productive capacity to be spared for the exclusive care of children."

The female body has been the object of the patriarchal gaze, by which is meant that culturally women are perceived as body before personality and considered an object in relation to a (male) subject. Even women themselves have considered females as objects to be observed, as bodies more than persons. Much of popular and consumerist culture is based upon the woman as the object of culture's gaze. Popular culture relies on images that exaggerate perceived feminine attributes to sell products, which may simultaneously idealize and degrade. In the early years of television, giant dancing cigarette packages had beautiful, womanly legs. More recently, an ingenue declared provocatively that nothing came between her and her Calvins (jeans). Advertisements in all media consistently use feminine sexual imagery to enhance and sell products unrelated to sexuality. Numerous studies suggest that visual representations of women featuring generic faces and highlighted hair, breasts, and thighs affect attitudes about women's sexuality and social roles. Pathologies such as eating disorders are exacerbated by the commercial use of sexually charged, impersonal images of women.

Patriarchy. Patriarchy means simply "rule by fathers." The "fathers" in a culture have value or authority over women, children, weaker men, and the anomalous—which might include such disparate categories as the elderly, the sick, the intellectual, or the artistic. This gender system is a reflection of patriarchal worldviews that claim rule by phallic power and use women's sexuality as tokens of that power or exchanges of meaning between patriarchs.

Marriage customs, vows, and laws indicate patriarchal and gender assumptions. For example, when a bride is "given" to the groom by the bride's father, it may be a touching, sentimental ceremony but nevertheless one that also has its roots in a property-exchange ritual. A groom may make the gesture of placing his fingerprint on the forehead of the bride (as in the Philippines) or placing a bracelet on her arm (as in the Book of Genesis) or a diamond ring on her finger (as in the United States). As Emma Goldman (1869-1940), an American reformer and social radical, noted

> The popular notion about marriage and love is that they are synonymous, that they spring from the same motives, and cover the same human needs. Like most popular notions this also rests not on actual facts, but on superstition. Marriage and love have nothing in common: they are as far apart as the poles; are, in fact, antagonistic to each other. No doubt some marriages have been the result of love. Not, however, because love could assert itself only in marriage; much rather is it because few people can completely outgrow a convention.

The recent changes in Western marriage customs, including the prevalence of divorce, same-sex relationships, and cohabitation, have raised questions not only about values but also about the very structure and dynamics of human sexuality.

Although the concepts of virginity and chastity in contemporary culture may be grounded in personal integrity and faithfulness, these concepts historically are largely attempts to ensure the exclusive ownership of a woman's procreative potential by patriarchal authorities. Margaret Sanger (1883-1966) introduced the term "birth control," opened the first birth control clinic in the United States, lobbied for birth control laws, established clinics around the world, generated international conferences, and founded the Planned Parenthood Federation. For her efforts, she was arrested, her clinic was raided by the police, and she exiled herself to England to escape prosecution for publishing and mailing birth control information. Women's freedom, she contended, was dependent upon the freedom to choose motherhood.

The assumptions underlying patriarchy often lead to sexual violence against women. Susan Brownmiller's key study *Against Our Will: Men, Women, and Rape* (1975) demonstrated that rape is used to display power or rage rather than to communicate an overwhelming sexual urge. The history of rape is emblematic of the history of the control and disgrace of women or the powerless; it is an expression of warfare. Brownmiller attempted to relieve popular culture of two of its cherished clichés: that women (such as the biblical Potiphar's

Susan Brownmiller, whose groundbreaking study Against Our Will *emphasized that rape is about power and violence, not sex.* (Bettye Lane)

wife) falsely cry rape and that rape is about sex rather than violence. Many activist groups are working to offer assistance to battered women and to help prevent violence against women, children, and subjugated men.

Eros. Women's images have epitomized fertility, asceticism (purity and celibacy), techniques for spiritual discipline, the object of pleasure, and an expression of the ineffable. Even to question these gender and sexuality assumptions is a creative act that profoundly affects attitudes about work and love. To study sexuality from the perspective of the erotic is to let go of issues of procreation and virginity and to concentrate instead on the affirmation of sensory, intellectual, and spiritual life. From that perspective, bisexual and lesbian experiences are as relevant as heterosexual experiences. Although ancient literatures sometimes celebrate female desire apart from reproduction or ownership, nevertheless, nonreproductive and "unowned" sex has been set apart by taboos within Western culture.

Courtship customs reveal the nature of their cultures: Courtship may include displays of singing, dancing, or wealth. Engagements, or formal intentions for marriage, range from economic contracts drawn up between families to the setting up of housekeeping together as a preliminary stage to a formal and legal marriage. The decline in American culture of conventional courtship obligations and rituals imply cultural change and cultural pluralism. Even more recently, sites on the Internet provide both formal and informal dating alternatives in cyberspace—and with them, a new set of risks and opportunities regarding courtship.

In the nineteenth and twentieth centuries, biologists, physicians, psychologists, sociologists, and anthropologists began to conduct research on sexuality. In the late nineteenth century, the first survey of elite women's sexual behavior was conducted by Clelia Mosher (1863-1940), an American physician. In the 1940's, Alfred C. Kinsey and a group of colleagues studied values and surveyed sexual behavior. The study itself was controversial, both in terms of the methods and the propriety of such research, but sexual attitudes became part of the public discourse. In the 1960's and 1970's, William Masters and Virginia Johnson studied sexual techniques, eventually including gay and lesbian participants; they used direct observation and the measurement of physiological responses. These studies have been as influential as they have been descriptive, but neither can address sexuality as a substratum of a culture.

Sigmund Freud (1856-1939), the most influential twentieth century thinker on sexuality, attempted to correlate biological sexual development to the development and pathologies of the individual personality. His famous statement that "anatomy is destiny" places the source of a female's psychological sexuality in the discovery of anatomical difference between male and female children. Freud is often oversimplified and maligned for his views on women's psychology and sexuality in general; what is more important is that he took up the issue of women's sexuality and emotional lives, not the ways in which he answered (or failed to answer) the questions of biological determinism and freedom of the personality. Freud's followers and critics, however, have taken psychoanalytic theories into numerous accounts of personality.

Despite these biological studies and attempts to dissociate sex from culture, desire is as socialized as table manners. Ideas about and expressions of love vary by time, geography, ethnicity, and class. Anyone and anything can be sexualized or eroticized in human culture. Eros can be positively or negatively charged. It is not only the expression of sexual affection between individuals; it is also expressed in entire communities. In the late seventeenth century, a group of girls aged thirteen to nineteen seized the power of the sexually charged language of Puritan theology and helped to touch off a phenomenon known as the Salem witch hunt that eventually took the lives of almost thirty persons and imprisoned a hundred.

Scholars have noted a historical correlation between Western cultural attitudes regarding women's sexuality and nature. The metaphorical femininity of nature—as mother, siren, or virgin—parallels dominant metaphors of women as more akin to earth or the unconscious. The dualistic system that links these ideas also denigrates earthly and feminine images as inferior. Some contemporary ecologists and culture critics are committed to addressing the asymmetry, as well as the politics, of both sides of the equation of nature/woman.

Romantic love, although culture-specific, is characterized by declarations of its universality and eternal values. The largest book sales in the United States are found in the genre of romance fiction. In these novels, generally a lonely, spirited young woman encounters a mysterious, somewhat threatening, but attractive man with whom, after an emotional adventure, she settles into a marriage bond. These works loosely follow the model of the European fairy tale, in which a maiden in distress finally is united with her "Prince Charming." These fictional models continue to influence women's expectations regarding heterosexual love and marriage.

Today, there are options for women that are not defined by their relationships to family or religious institutions. These options threaten generations of patriarchal comfort afforded by gender stereotypes, for women as well as for men. Perhaps the cultural habit in the United States of valuing individualism, pioneers and innovators, has affected gender restrictions, making culture more vulnerable to changes in attitudes about gender and sexual behavior.

Two general perceptions have guided views of women's sexuality: myth and analogy. Both are metaphorical, and they are intertwined. The first view assumes that society understands women and controls their sexuality by authority of the great sacred stories. For example, the story of the Garden of Eden from the Book of Genesis has been used for three millennia to link knowledge, sexuality, work, fear, and death and to make generally negative claims regarding women's minds and bodies. The second view assumes that women's sexuality can be known by drawing an analogy from nature (although scientific descriptions of nature are derived from and seen through cultural lenses). For example, partial and selective information about animal behavior is extrapolated to make claims about human propriety.

Gender as a Social Construct. Sexuality is coded by gender constructs; thus one might say that sexuality, rather than identification or behavior, is a language. In other words, sexuality is communicated metaphorically and understood culturally. In the nineteenth century, romantic and intimate relationships between women began to be redefined, and, by the twentieth century, lesbianism and bisexuality were being described as pathological, as psychological or social problems. More recently, social theorists and political activists have been seeking to address issues of stereotyping, sexual choice, and personal freedoms. The vocal and visible movements for human freedoms also raise basic questions about sexuality and erotic relationships.

As gender is redefined, patriarchy is threatened and eros is reimagined. Whether a strategy for species survival or an aspect of personality, whether described by biologists or by poets, human sexuality is a prime element in the lives of individuals and societies. —*Lynda Sexson*

See also *Against Our Will*; Antioch College Sexual Consent Code; *Behind the Sex of God*; Bisexuality; Brownmiller, Susan; Clitoridectomy; Coming out; Dating and courtship; Dworkin, Andrea; Electra and Oedipus complexes; Essentialism; Feminism, lesbian; Gender differences; Genital mutilation; Heterosexism; *Hite Report, The*; Homophobia; Hysterectomy; Lesbian continuum; Lesbianism; *Male and Female*; Marginalization of women; Marriage and marital status; Motherhood; "Myth of the Vaginal Orgasm, The"; Patriarchy; Phallocentrism; Plastic surgery; Pregnancy and childbirth; Prince Charming syndrome; Prostitution; Psychological theories on women; Rape; Religion; Reproductive rights; Rich, Adrienne; Sanger, Margaret; *Second Sex, The*; Sex change operation; Sex object; Sexism; *Sexual Politics*; Sexual revolution; Sexual stereotypes; Stereotypes of women; Sterilization of women; Teen pregnancy; Turner's syndrome

BIBLIOGRAPHY

Armstrong, Karen. *The Gospel According to Woman: Christianity's Creation of the Sex War in the West.* New York: Doubleday, 1987. The author of the acclaimed book *The History of God* (1993) issues a provocative challenge to look at the relationship of gender stereotypes through the history of Christianity. Armstrong begins the book with the assertion, "Women's main problem in the Western world has always been sex."

Beauvoir, Simone de. *The Second Sex.* Translated by H. M. Parshley. New York: Alfred A. Knopf, 1953. This book is the foundation of contemporary feminism. It combines insights and speculations from the social sciences and philosophy.

Bernard, Jessie. "The Mother Role." In *Women: A Feminist Perspective*, edited by Jo Freeman. 3d ed. Palo Alto, Calif.: Mayfield, 1984. This well-selected collection takes up social conditions and feminist issues in the United States.

Brownmiller, Susan. *Against Our Will: Men, Women, and Rape.* New York: Simon & Schuster, 1975. This book has made an impact in the social sciences and, perhaps even more important, in the media and in community action and dialogue.

Chodorow, Nancy. *The Reproduction of Mothering: Psychoanalysis and the Sociology of Gender.* Berkeley: University of California Press, 1978. Chodorow's psychoanalytic and feminist social theories use the experience of motherhood as the source of both gendered personality and gendered labor divisions in society.

Dworkin, Andrea. *Intercourse.* New York: Free Press, 1987. Dworkin analyzes heterosexual assumptions and behavior in terms of the history of patriarchal oppression, calling for women's freedom from heterosexist institutions and habits of thought.

Fausto-Sterling, Anne. *Myths of Gender: Biological Theories About Women and Men.* New York: Basic Books, 1985. This study demonstrates how social ideas create biological theories. For example, when Western scientists considered variability to be a liability, women were the variable sex; however, when variability became a biological asset for human populations, then it became a male property.

Gilligan, Carol. *In a Different Voice: Psychological Theory and Women's Development.* Cambridge, Mass.: Harvard University Press, 1982. A classic in the social sciences and humanities, having an enormous influence across disciplines. Remains controversial in its claims about gender difference in moral development. Gilligan claims that "The disparity between women's experience and the representation of human development, noted throughout the psychological literature, has generally been seen to signify a problem in women's development. Instead, the failure of women to fit existing models of human growth may point to a problem in the representation, a limitation in the conception of human condition, an omission of certain truths about life."

Goldman, Emma. *Anarchism and Other Essays.* 1917. Reprint. New York: Dover, 1969. This collection contains the essay "Marriage and Love."

Hooks, Bell. *Ain't I a Woman: black women and feminism.* Boston: South End Press, 1981. Hooks's analysis takes up the complexities of two stereotyping factors, race and gender, from slavery to contemporary feminism.

Laqueur, Thomas. *Making Sex: Body and Gender from the Greeks to Freud.* Cambridge, Mass.: Harvard University Press, 1990. An important book for delineating Western history's two models of sexual reality: that women are inferior men and that women and men are opposites. As significant for its study of metaphor, rhetoric, and image as for its history of the conceptualization of anatomy and procreation.

Merchant, Carolyn. *The Death of Nature: Women, Ecology, and the Scientific Revolution.* New York: Harper & Row, 1980. Merchant is one of the most influential contemporary feminists who addresses the correspondent issues of ecology and women's sexuality.

Rich, Adrienne. *Of Woman Born: Motherhood as Experience and Institution.* New York: W. W. Norton, 1976. Rich discusses motherhood in the context of patriarchy; this book has become a classic as a result of the poet's moving and provocative personal voice.

Shaw, Evelyn, and Joan Darling. *Female Strategies: Animal Patterns, Human Choices.* New York: Walker, 1985. One of the most accessible books on biology and culture, particularly the mistaken analogies drawn between animals and humans, as well as the cultural assumptions that have misdirected scientific observation and conclusions. The authors claim, "Words—not our hormones, and not some neurological gestalt etched into our brains—teach us how to find a mate, who is appropriate as a mate and who isn't, when to have babies, how to give birth to them, and how to take care of them."

Snitow, Ann, Christine Stansell, and Sharon Thompson, eds. *Powers of Desire: The Politics of Sexuality.* New York: Monthly Review Press, 1983. A range of essays that place the seemingly personal aspects of sexuality into their social contexts.

Stimpson, Catharine R., and Ethel Spector Person. *Women—Sex and Sexuality.* Chicago: University of Illinois Press, 1980. Calls into question the habit of defining women in relation to, or as a variation of, men.

Wolf, Naomi. *The Beauty Myth: How Images of Beauty Are Used Against Women.* New York: William Morrow, 1991. Examines aesthetic issues, social science studies, and psychology to assert that idealizations of beauty have political and psychological implications. The book has been effective in bringing the discussion into popular culture, into the arena that Wolf is critiquing.

Sexually transmitted diseases

Relevant issues: Health and medicine

Significance: Sexually transmitted diseases are increasing in incidence and prevalence, carry different social meanings for women than for men, and have serious repercussions for women and their unborn or newborn children

The rise in sexually transmitted diseases (STDs) to near epidemic proportions that began in the mid-1950's has accompanied significant social changes, which include changing moral views of sexuality, greater personal freedom, the advent of oral contraception, and increasing prosperity. More than twenty-five diseases are now classified as sexually transmitted. In addition to acquired immunodeficiency syndrome (AIDS), the most common STDs in the United States are gonorrhea, syphilis, genital herpes, genital warts (condylomata acuminata), chlamydia, and hepatitis B. Symptoms in a woman may be nonexistent, vague, or similar to other diseases and are typically insufficient to cause her to seek medical evaluation. A woman may also delay seeking medical care for more noticeable symptoms because of dread of a pelvic examination. When women do seek care, laboratory tests to confirm a suspected diagnosis of an STD frequently take longer or are less accurate for them than for men and are often more expensive. Furthermore, the typical female STD patient is likely to be young, a member of an ethnic or racial minority, and poorly educated, while the typical medical provider is more likely to be male, older, white, and highly educated, raising issues of race and class in addition to gender in the care offered to, and the education of, patients.

The long-term health consequences of STDs are more serious for women than for men. Untreated gonorrhea or chlamydia in women can lead to pelvic inflammatory disease (PID), in turn leading to peritonitis, ectopic pregnancy, infertility, or Fallopian tube abscess and sometimes to the need for hysterectomy. Genital warts and genital herpes are associated with precancerous and cancerous changes of the cervix. STDs hold special problems for pregnant women. Undetected STDs can lead to miscarriage, premature labor, and infection of the fetus or newborn. These infections can result in mental retardation, blindness, pneumonia, or stillbirth. The presence of genital herpes or genital warts may require delivery by cesarean section, subjecting women to the risks of surgery and more complicated recovery from childbirth.

STDs also hold more severe psychological and social consequences for women than for men. Despite changing social mores, STDs are often associated with promiscuity, a concept that society still finds more objectionable in women than in men. Women are also held accountable for the health of their

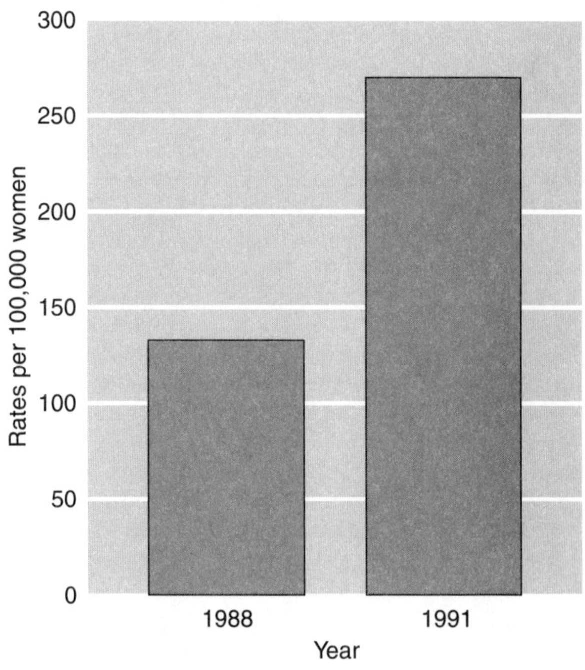

Source: Centers for Disease Control

Rates of Gonorrhea Among American Women, by Age (1990-1992)

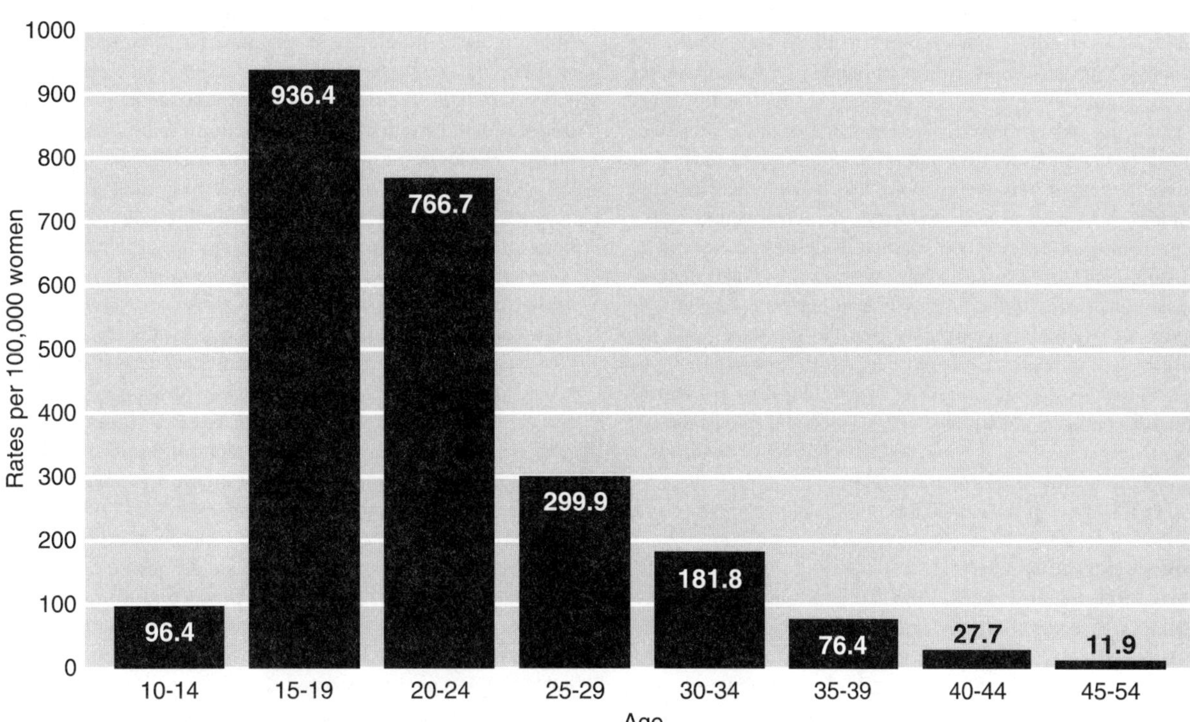

Source: National Institute of Allergy and Infectious Diseases

unborn children. A woman not only may feel guilt over infecting her child but also may be blamed by health care providers, while the person who infected her is generally not held to be socially responsible.

See also AIDS epidemic and women; Birth control and family planning; Condoms, male and female; Fertility and infertility; Gynecology and obstetrics; Health and medicine; Health equity for women; Health movement, women's; Pregnancy and childbirth; Prenatal care; Sexual revolution; Sexual stereotypes

Sheppard-Towner Act

Also known as: Sheppard-Towner Maternity and Infancy Act

Date: Passed on November 23, 1921

Relevant issues: Family, health and medicine, social reform

Significance: This legislation was the first federally funded health care act in the United States

The Children's Bureau, established in 1912, reported an increase in the mortality rate of infants and mothers exacerbated by the influenza epidemic of 1918. These conditions led social feminists to advocate national action. The Sheppard-Towner Maternity and Infancy Act of 1921 provided states with matching funds to establish prenatal and child health care centers. These centers established in forty-five of the states were staffed by physicians, primarily women, and public health nurses. The measure was enacted by an overwhelming majority of senators and congressional representatives. It was signed into law by newly elected President Warren Harding, who was anxious to curry favor with female constituents who had recently gained the right of suffrage. Although generally supported by women's groups, the act was initially opposed by the National Woman's Party, led by Alice Paul, and by birth control advocate Margaret Sanger, who held that it was a program that encouraged women to have larger families, not smaller ones. Funding for the legislation ended in 1929 amid continued opposition by the American Medical Association (AMA). Nevertheless, the Sheppard-Towner Act did encourage a continuing emphasis on preventive health care by physicians and provided thousands of infants and mothers with needed medical services during its nine years of existence.

See also Health and medicine; Prenatal care

Shoes

Relevant issues: Business and economics

Significance: Although shoes were first devised by and for men, women are most identified with footwear because of the nearly unlimited styles, colors, and designs that are available in women's shoes

Fashion counselors warn modern women that regardless of ability, career advancement comes to those who "dress for success." Shoes have taken on such importance to some career women and teenage girls that comfort and foot health often become secondary to style. The great challenge for shoemakers is to combine comfort and style. Some women wish to have the best of both worlds: One joke advises that the only solution is to wear a sturdy oxford on the left foot and a sexy high-heel on the right foot. Lightweight, well-padded, fashionable shoes are available, but many styles remain dangerously constricting to the foot. Women themselves take greater notice of whether other women wear the proper shoe in the proper setting. Fashionable women select appropriate shoes for all occasions, whether at the beach, the office, or downtown shopping. Some people believe that an outdated shoe is a social disaster unless a woman's self-confidence is stronger than her concern with her public image.

See also Dress for success; Fashion, women's

Silent Scream, The

Date: Released in January, 1985

Relevant issues: Reproductive rights, science and technology

Significance: This antiabortion film has attempted to shift the focus of the abortion debate from the arena of women's reproductive rights to the capacity of the fetus to experience pain during abortion procedures

The Silent Scream is a twenty-eight minute documentary film of the dilation and curettage (D & C) abortion of a twelve-week-old fetus recorded by means of real-time ultrasound technology. The film's producer, Dr. Bernard N. Nathanson, a founder of the National Abortion and Reproductive Rights Action League (NARAL) and director of its New York clinic in the mid-1970's, claims to have changed his position on abortion after advances in the field of ultrasound imaging allowed him to view the fetus in motion. He decided to make the film as a response to critics who berated President Ronald Reagan for asserting that fetuses feel "long and agonizing pain" during abortion. The film, which Nathanson claims depicts abortion "from the victim's vantage point," relies on sound waves to provide a computer with enough information to project a detailed image on a television screen. The grainy black-and-white images are accompanied by a narration by Nathanson, who points out each step in the abortion process—including the "pathetic attempt of the fetus to escape" (as evidenced by the increased heart rate) when the suction instrument is introduced into the womb and the fetus' open mouth, which Nathanson refers to as a "chilling silent scream."

Critics of the film attacked it on many different levels. Allegations were made that sections of the film were speeded up to simulate the fetus struggling. Some proposed that the "silent scream" was nothing more than a fetal yawn. Most of the criticism was directed at Nathanson's primary assertion that the fetus can feel pain. Following the statement issued by the American College of Obstetricians and Gynecologists in 1984 that the fetus does not feel pain during an abortion, experts in fetal development assembled by Planned Parenthood argued that the cerebral cortex was not sufficiently developed for pain stimuli to occur. They argued that the convulsions exhibited by the fetus were nothing more than animal reflexes. Biologist Patricia Jaworski defined this debate as one involving the "personhood" of the fetus in her half-hour audio presentation "Thinking About *The Silent Scream*," in which she interviewed five scientists who agreed that there is no biological basis for personhood until the thirty-first week of gestation.

On January 22, 1985, President Reagan said that if this film were made available to every member of Congress, they "would move quickly to end the tragedy of abortion." Every member of Congress and the Supreme Court was, in fact, sent a copy of the film, and pro-life organizations financed its distribution to state legislators. The response was not nearly as dramatic as Reagan had predicted, and, by the mid-1990's, the question of the ability of the fetus to experience pain had not reemerged as a focal point in the debate.

See also Abortion; Antiabortion protests and women; Dilation and curettage (D & C); Gynecology and obstetrics; National Abortion and Reproductive Rights Action League (NARAL); Planned Parenthood; Pro-choice; Pro-life; Reproductive rights; Ultrasound

Single mothers

Relevant issues: Family, reproductive rights, sex and gender, women's history

Significance: Single mothers make up a diverse group, and their life experiences and the issues they face have been a significant part of the women's movement

Single mothers are women who rear children without the assistance and support of a father. They include widows and women who are divorced or separated. They also include a growing number of single women who make a deliberate choice to become pregnant with a lover or through artificial insemination. Another group of single women opt to keep the baby in the case of accidental conception. Still others choose to adopt a child to rear alone.

History. Historically, the single mother's experience has been a difficult one. A woman's connection to a man was often a critical factor in her eligibility for assistance. In the past, the vast majority of single mothers were widows, and the next largest group consisted of divorced women. From the early twentieth century to the 1940's, only about 4 to 6 percent of women heading households with children had never been married.

After World War II, the number of families with a single mother as the head of household grew dramatically in nearly every major industrialized country except Japan. In Canada in 1966, single-parent families headed by women made up 8 percent of all families; by 1986, they constituted 13 percent of all families. In the United States in 1970, single-parent families headed by women represented 13 percent of all families with children under the age of eighteen years; by 1986, this figure had risen to 22 percent.

Social Attitudes. More than a quarter of all babies born in the United States in 1988 were born to single mothers, and the typical age of the unmarried mother has increased. Several factors have influenced this phenomenon. During the 1970's and 1980's, women began to postpone marriage as they pursued educational and career goals. The societal acceptance of single mothers has grown, especially in the middle class. Increasing numbers of intelligent and educated women are setting higher standards for their spouses and finding that not enough men measure up to them. They have grown weary of waiting for "Mr. Right" or have no interest in finding him at all, and yet they realize that their biological clock is approaching midnight. These women have made an intentional decision to rear a child alone. They may become pregnant through artificial insemination or with a chosen lover. Other single women become mothers through adoption.

Challenges for the Single Mother. Maintaining financial stability and security is a major problem faced by single mothers. Many single-mother households tend to live at, or near, the poverty level. According to one study in Franklin County, where the Center for New Directions is established, only 9 percent of female-headed households with no children lived below the poverty level, as compared to 40 percent of female-head households with children. In general, the financial dilemma experienced by single mothers is not because they are not working. According to the findings of the U.S. Department of Commerce Bureau of the Census, a growing majority of single mothers with one or more children are in the labor force. In the twelve-month period ending June, 1992, 54 percent were in the labor force, as compared to 44 percent in June, 1982.

Adequate and low-income housing is another major challenge for single mothers. In 1988, it was estimated that 40,000 "garage families" lived in the area in and around Los Angeles, California. Most of these families are single mothers who live in substandard housing and are minimum-wage earners, and a significant portion of their income is used for housing costs.

Single mothers experience "role overload" as they attempt to provide discipline, financial stability, and emotional support to their children. They feel the pinch when a child is ill, school holidays conflict with work, or overtime demands cut into family time. Single mothers must provide child care when they work outside the home. Only a small percentage of these women can afford live-in care for their children, and some women have family members who will provide care at minimal or no expense. The vast majority of single mothers, however, struggle to find adequate child care out of an income already stretched to the limit.

Many divorced or separated mothers have difficulties with former husbands and lovers over the custodial care of the

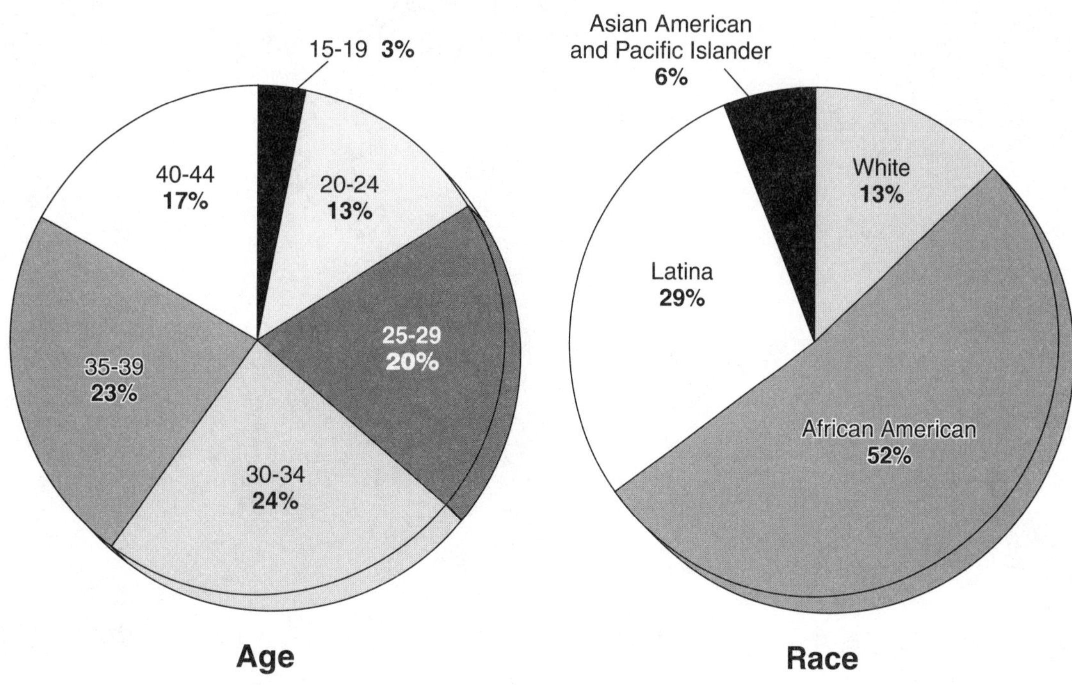

children and do not receive child support on a regular basis. According to a study in 1992, less than half of the women who are supposed to receive child support from the fathers of their children actually do.

For most of history, unwed mothers have been viewed from a moral and legal perspective, with society more interested in punishing the unwed mother and her illegitimate children than in understanding her plight. Before the 1930's, illegitimate children were seen as the result of an unwed mother's immorality and mental deficiency. Both in the United States and Canada, single-mother households have been blamed for all manner of social problems with children and society, including delinquency, academic failure, poverty, and crime.

Traditionally, the income of unwed mothers has been much lower than other groups of single mothers. According to U.S. Department of Labor statistics for 1992, families maintained by widows averaged $22,790 before taxes; those maintained by divorced and separated women, $18,580; and those by never-married mothers, $9,820.

One study indicated that there were somewhere between one to five million lesbian mothers in the United States in the mid-1990's. Of this number, approximately 10,000 lesbian mothers were rearing children who had been conceived through artificial insemination. Lesbian mothers are particularly vulnerable to custody suits. The judicial system often views them as less desirable custodial parents because of their sexual orientation. This attitude prevails even when there is no direct evidence of improper or inappropriate parental behavior. Studies have found overwhelming similarities between lesbian mothers and heterosexual mothers in nurturing and parenting behavior toward their children.

Impact of the Women's Movement. The women's movement has had a significant influence on the lives of single mothers. Child care concerns and the poverty of single mothers and their children continue to be major issues among feminists.

Certain groups in society continue to blame unwed mothers for all kinds of social problems, but the educated public ex-

Financial, social, and emotional challenges come with single motherhood, but many women find the experience rewarding and create close bonds with their children. (Jim King/Photo Agora)

tends greater acceptance toward unwed teenagers and greater tolerance toward unmarried women who choose to have a child either through adoption or through other means.

Feminists have focused on the difficulties of lesbian mothers and the prejudice that they face in custody battles. There is more understanding of the difficulties that many divorced mothers have in obtaining child support from former husbands. The voice of single mothers, whatever their situation, has been heard through the women's movement.

—Marleen Ramsey

See also Child care; Child custody and visitation rights; Divorce; Family life; Lesbianism; Mother-child relationships; Motherhood; Single women; Teen pregnancy; Widowhood

Bibliography

Burns, Ailsa, and Cath Scott. *Mother-Headed Families and Why They Have Increased.* Hillsdale, N.J.: Lawrence Erlbaum, 1994.

Gordon, Linda. *Pitied but Not Entitled: Single Mothers and the History of Welfare, 1890-1935.* New York: Free Press, 1994.

Laabs, Jennifer. "Unmarried with Children: Living in Poverty." *Personnel Journal* 73, no. 10 (October, 1994): 53.

Lewin, Ellen. *Lesbian Mothers: Accounts of Gender in American Culture.* Ithaca, N.Y.: Cornell University Press, 1993.

Lino, Mark. "Income and Spending Patterns of Single-Mother Families." *Monthly Labor Review* 117, no. 5 (May, 1994): 29-37.

Morton, Marian. *And Sin No More: Social Policy and Unwed Mothers in Cleveland, 1855-1990.* Columbus: Ohio State University Press, 1993.

Seligmann, Jean. "Husbands No, Babies Yes." *Newsweek* 122, no. 4 (July 26, 1993): 53.

Vincent, Clark. *Unmarried Mothers.* New York: Free Press of Glencoe, 1961.

Single women

Relevant issues: Aging, employment, family, poverty, sex and gender

Significance: As a result of the rising number of women who chose not to marry, viewpoints regarding single women have changed, enabling them to gain independence and to have greater career opportunities

In preindustrial society, single women headed large convents (during the Middle Ages), were in charge of estates (during the Renaissance), and ran shops and businesses (in Colonial America). By the middle of the nineteenth century, however, the life of a middle-class single woman no longer held such options. Unmarried women were practically social outcasts and often had to depend on family members for support. Those women who earned wages took menial and low-paying jobs. Their one advantage was that they had femme sol rights and could own property or make contracts.

Following rapid industrialization and urbanization, the roles of middle-class and upper-class single women began to change. Women's educational opportunities increased, and they opened settlement houses and became activists in labor unions and in the woman suffrage movement. Nevertheless, narrow attitudes about "spinsters" prevailed. Married women were traditionally held in esteem, while single women were often shunned. Single motherhood was frowned upon, and these women were thought of as wicked and ignorant. In the 1960's and 1970's, the women's and lesbian rights movements, both in the United States and Canada, defended a woman's right to remain single. Many feminists encouraged women to give up traditional male surnames and to avoid having children. Liberation also freed women to make new sexual choices. Helen Gurley Brown's book *Sex and the Single Girl* (1962) gave rise to the image of the economically independent woman. As editor of *Cosmopolitan* magazine, Brown popularized the upwardly mobile working woman.

The 1960's saw a rise in the number of American women who remained single. As the women's movement gained momentum, "singlehood" included feminists, lesbians, unmarried mothers, and those women who were in relationships but who chose not to marry. The average age for women to marry increased, and the divorce rate rose dramatically. Women left unsatisfactory and unhappy marriages to become independent wage earners and to concentrate on their careers. Although divorce laws changed to make settlements more egalitarian, men retained the advantage as women's alimony rates were reduced. After divorcing, many single women experienced discrimination when they sought to establish credit or to apply for loans. Many single mothers, unable to keep up with rising costs, joined the ranks of the poor in the 1980's. As women increasingly outlive men, widowed women have added to the number of single women living in poverty. Some widows have seen their situations improve as more old-age benefits become available to them.

Single women of all sexual orientations have had to deal with rumors and innuendoes about why they have not married and with the discrimination that sometimes results. Nevertheless, many single women have successfully entered the political arena and the corporate world. While they still face hurdles in some areas, single women as a group have gained wider acceptance in society.

See also Alimony; Credit discrimination against women; Divorce; Heads of household, female; Lesbian mothers; Lesbianism; Marriage and marital status; Property rights, women's; Single mothers; Spinster; Stereotypes of women; Widowhood

Sisterhood

Relevant issues: Civil rights, politics, women's history

Significance: The concept of sisterhood was often the glue that held together the women's movement against a male establishment that wanted to ignore or halt it

In the United States, the idea that all women are sisters in the struggle against patriarchy goes back at least to the suffrage movement of the nineteenth century. The women of the time were not only disenfranchised but, in marriage, stripped of property and effectively of citizenship. With no help from the law or, for the most part, from men, as a group women had no one but themselves to turn to for comfort, understanding, and organization. Therefore, the fact that they regarded one another as "sisters" in the closest emotional sense is not surprising. Sisterhood was also promoted at some of the early women's colleges such as Mount Holyoke, where lifelong friendships were encouraged between roommates and fellow students. After the establishment of equal voting rights in 1920 with the passage of the Nineteenth Amendment, the concept of sisterhood lost some of its force. With the resurgence of the women's movement in the 1960's and 1970's, however, it again proved a valuable means of rallying and organizing, as well as an emotionally satisfying way of relating to other women in a man's world.

See also Benevolent organizations; Colleges, women's; Communes and collectives, women's; Feminism; Nineteenth Amendment; Social reform movements and women; Suffrage movement and suffragists; Women's movement

Slavery

Relevant issues: Family, race and ethnicity, women's history

Significance: Although black and white women frequently found themselves at odds regarding slavery, women from both races transcended prevailing stereotypes and played an important role in the demise of this "peculiar institution"

History. The first known African slaves to arrive in North America were brought to Jamestown, Virginia, in 1619. Initially, British colonists were reluctant to embrace slavery, choosing rather to use white indentured servants. As late as 1680, only about seven thousand black people could be found in all the colonies combined. In time, however, labor demands, as well as the profitability of tobacco and cotton, made slave labor an increasingly attractive economic investment for white landowners.

Not everyone, however, was happy with slavery. By the mid-eighteenth century, Pennsylvania's Quakers were denouncing slavery as immoral. By the nineteenth century, the sentiment to free the slave population was growing nationwide. The American Colonization Society was organized in 1817 with the aim of recolonizing freed slaves in Africa. Their efforts, however, were largely unsuccessful: Most freed slaves considered North America to be their home and were unwilling to go to Africa. Additionally, most masters were unwilling to free their slaves without financial compensation, and no adequate plan was ever formulated to that end.

In 1831, a Virginia slave named Nat Turner led an uprising that left some sixty white people dead. Fear of massive uprisings had been prevalent (although largely unsubstantiated) since the late eighteenth century, and Turner fulfilled the worst nightmare of slaveholders. Subsequently, many white people became more determined to control the South's slave population. To free the slaves would cost a fortune, and most white Southerners feared reprisal from the black community. As a group, white women in the South were as determined as their male counterparts to keep African Americans legally subjugated.

It is important to note, however, that most Southerners did not own slaves. In 1860, only about 25 percent of all Southerners owned slaves. About one-half of this group owned five or fewer slaves. These figures were partially the result of the high cost of purchasing them; in the 1850's, field hands were usually sold for at least $1,500. Consequently, slave ownership served as both a gauge of personal wealth and as a social status symbol. The more slaves one possessed, the more wealth one commanded. Even those white Southerners who did not own slaves had a vested interest in the South's upper class. Poorer white people could always look to the slaveholding gentry for inspiration to gain more wealth.

Gender and Plantation Society. Throughout the early nineteenth century, American society, particularly in the South, was typically patriarchal. Most men and women lived their lives under the assumption that each gender had a distinctive "sphere." Men assumed roles of leadership and power, while women were expected to live according to the tenets of what scholars call the Cult of True Womanhood. As such, women were to be sexually chaste and pure. They were to be religiously pious, guarding society's morality by keeping their households in good order. Likewise, they were to be keepers of the home for their husbands. Finally, they were to be submissive to established authority structures.

These expectations bore especially heavy on Southern women. Contrary to prevalent mythology, Southern women rarely conformed to the "Southern belle" stereotype, and the plantation did not shield them from a hard life. Since plantations emphasized large-scale agriculture, plantation women usually suffered from social and cultural isolation. In order to compensate for their loneliness, some wealthy women hosted extravagant social functions for which guests sometimes stayed for days. Despite their loneliness, however, plantation wives did not seek friendship from their female slaves.

In addition to rural isolation, Southern women also had specific jobs to perform. Plantation wives usually supervised the slaves who worked in "the great house." Moreover, the nature of plantation agriculture demanded frequent business trips, and, in their husbands' absence, plantation wives were responsible for maintaining the entire plantation, including supervising field labor and managing the financial ledgers.

Middle-class and lower-class Southern white women left few detailed accounts of their lives. Nevertheless, several things are clear. Most poor white women lived a much harder life than their plantation sisters. In addition to their family duties, such as cooking, cleaning, making clothes, and rearing children, most women worked in the fields with their husbands whenever possible. These women tended to be fiercely independent and generally refused to do certain menial tasks they deemed "servant work."

Naturally, life for slave women in the antebellum South was substantially different from life for white women. In slavery's earliest phases, black men outnumbered black women by an overwhelming margin. Sex ratios stabilized over time, however, and black women were expected to labor in the fields side by side with black men. Those who did not perform fieldwork had other chores. For example, if they were too old to perform manual labor or were specifically chosen for the task, some women supervised the young children of other slaves. In some cases, they might even watch their masters' children. Thus, unlike white women, many slave mothers were frequently denied the opportunity to rear their own children. Still others worked in the plantation home as a house servant. Such opportunities were a mixed blessing. On the one hand, house servants had a higher status on the plantation than field hands. Some house servants, especially on large plantations, considered themselves to have a higher social status than poor white people. On the other hand, they generally labored under closer supervision than the other slaves, and the slightest offense could invite harsh discipline.

Despite the hardships of slave life, many women were able to forge family and kinship ties that proved valuable when freedom finally came. (Library of Congress)

Most masters realized that they had an interest in promoting slave marriages, believing that married slaves were less likely to run away. The masters also valued female slaves for their ability to bear children. Slave children were likewise valuable both as part of the plantation's labor force and as a measure of control over their parents. Among slaves, it was understood that those who seemed loyal and docile were less likely to be sold, and few slaves would cause dissention on the plantation if they thought their children would be punished as a result of their actions.

Family life also added a measure of stability to the slave quarters, from the slaves' perspective. However bad plantation conditions might be, family members could always look to one another for solace. The family was one of the few places where slaves were free to be themselves, and mothers and fathers taught their children how to survive the rigors of plantation life.

Unfortunately, slave marriages had no official legal standing in white courts. Even so, both men and women sought companionship. Sometimes, men tried to marry women from neighboring plantations to avoid seeing their wives and children mistreated. The masters had the final say in such matters, however, and they generally encouraged male slaves to marry on the plantation; otherwise, determining who owned the resulting children might be problematic. Yet, it does appear that a female slave had some role in choosing who would become her husband.

Despite the benefits that marriage and family life afforded, slaves lived in constant fear. Women lived in a special kind of fear that is difficult to describe. In addition to the fear of seeing their husbands and children sold, female slaves had no protection from their masters' unwanted sexual advances. White men sometimes fathered children by their female slaves, thus creating tension between black and white women. As Mary Boykin Chesnut, a plantation mistress in South Carolina, wryly observed, "Any lady is ready to tell you who is the father of all the mulatto children in everybody's household but her own."

Women and Abolition. As slavery became more ensconced in the social and economic fabric of early nineteenth century America, critics, many of whom were women, began calling for its demise. Among white women, Angelina and Sarah Grimké were particularly outspoken critics of "the peculiar institution." Reared in a slaveholding household in Charleston, South Carolina, the Grimké sisters came to abhor slavery in their early adulthood because of their belief that slavery was in moral opposition to God's purposes. Angelina published two forceful indictments against slavery entitled *An Appeal to the Christian Women of the South* (1836) and *An Appeal to the Women of the Nominally Free States* (1837). Both sisters earned a reputation for their public lectures against slavery.

In addition to lecturing, some female abolitionists committed their sentiments to verse. Julia Ward Howe was an American poet who coedited *Commonwealth*, an abolitionist newspaper in Boston, with her husband, Samuel Gridley Howe. In 1861, she visited military camps near Washington, D.C., and received the inspiration for her most famous work, "The Battle Hymn of the Republic." It was an instant success, and Union forces soon whistled and sang the tune as they marched into battle. This song so pointedly expressed the abolitionists' righteous indignation against slavery that it was widely published in church hymnals.

Among the white women who championed abolition, however, Harriet Beecher Stowe is without peer. Her novel *Uncle Tom's Cabin* (1852) has been hailed by some as the most influential fictional work in American literary history. Stowe depicted slavery, at its worst, as a monstrous institution that would victimize even the best, most loyal slaves such as Uncle Tom by allowing them to fall into the clutches of sadistic ogres such as Simon Legree. She infuriated many Southerners by implying that their form of Christianity had sinned in failing to respond to slavery's cruelty. Stowe also struck a chord with many Northerners who had never considered the many negative aspects of slavery.

White women were not alone in the campaign against slavery. Several black women gained notoriety as abolitionists, particularly Harriet Tubman and Sojourner Truth. Tubman became famous as a "conductor" in the Underground Railroad, a system of individuals who helped fugitive slaves flee the South prior to the Civil War. Tubman herself had escaped from slavery in 1849, and she returned to the South nineteen times to help an estimated three hundred slaves, including her parents, secure safe passage to the North.

Likewise, Sojourner Truth became a popular antislavery lecturer in the North. Born in Hurley, New York, in 1797 as Isabella Baumtree, she ran away from her master when he refused to acknowledge New York's emancipation law of 1827. In 1843, after a series of visions, she adopted the name "Sojourner Truth" because she believed that it reflected her divine mission. Truth believed that God had ordained her to speak out against slavery. While she may not have convinced every person in her audiences of slavery's evils, few could listen to her and not be impressed by her resonant voice and oratorical skills.

Legacy of the Abolitionist Movement. Assessing the antislavery movement can be difficult, partly because many reform efforts had overlapping objectives. Such is the case with women and abolition. Many women who favored abolition also favored equal rights for women, creating one reform movement within another. These white women tended to see the plight of black slave women in the light of their own social and political powerlessness. Consequently, they sincerely wanted to see slavery abolished, but they also wanted to better their own state. Some male critics, notably William Lloyd Garrison, editor of the abolitionist newspaper *The Liberator*, agreed that women should have full social and political equality with men. Garrison also called for the immediate freedom of all slaves without compensation to their masters, as well as full social and political equality for freed African Americans. Many people saw Garrison as a radical, but it was his attitude toward women's rights that separated him from some of his earliest backers, particularly Arthur and Lewis Tappan. Quite simply, equality for women was an issue some abolitionists refused to address.

Ironically, as women called for equality and slave liberation, they may have been stifled most by a feminine influence. Abolitionists constituted a minority in nineteenth century America, and most women tended to stay within their own sphere. Catharine Beecher was perhaps the most outspoken proponent of distinct spheres for men and women. As she saw it, women had considerable power to shape society's morality by shaping the home. Many women chose to remain keepers of their homes rather than to fight for either abolition or women's rights.

By the end of the nineteenth century, the idea of dual spheres had assumed a new cast. Many women demanded the right to vote precisely because society needed their perceived moral influence. The experience and organizational skills learned by an earlier generation of female abolitionists, both black and white, was without doubt extremely useful to subsequent reformers.

—*Keith Harper*

See also Abolitionist movement and women; African American women; Cult of True Womanhood; Female supremacy; Grimké, Angelina, and Grimké, Sarah; Howe, Julia Ward; Indentured servitude; Plantation life and women; Racism; Truth, Sojourner; Tubman, Harriet

Bibliography

Abzug, Robert H. *Cosmos Crumbling: American Reform and the Religious Imagination*. New York: Oxford University Press, 1994. Abzug argues that reformers, particularly abolitionists, were motivated by religious conviction.

Clinton, Catherine. *The Plantation Mistress: Woman's World in the Old South*. New York: Pantheon Books, 1982. This work focuses on plantation women. Excellent statistical data can be found in an appendix.

Fox-Genovese, Elizabeth. *Within the Plantation Household: Black and White Women of the Old South*. Chapel Hill: University of North Carolina Press, 1988. Perhaps the most comprehensive treatment of the interconnectedness between black and white women in the antebellum South.

Friedman, Jean E. *The Enclosed Garden: Women and Community in the Evangelical South, 1830-1900*. Chapel Hill: University of North Carolina Press, 1985. This multidisciplinary study argues that community, not gender, shaped the sociocultural roles of both black and white women in the South.

Genovese, Eugene D. *Roll, Jordan, Roll: The World the Slaves Made*. New York: Pantheon Books, 1974. A classic Marxist study of slavery. This work explores the extent of self-determination by African Americans while they were in bondage.

Scott, Anne Firor. *The Southern Lady: From Pedestal to Politics, 1830-1930*. Chicago: University of Chicago Press, 1970. Scott's classic work demythologizes white Southern women.

Smith, Theophus H. *Conjuring Culture: Biblical Formations of Black America*. New York: Oxford University Press, 1994. The author explores the formation of a distinct, African American "conjure culture," with close attention to the particular role that women played in its creation.

Walters, Ronald G. *American Reformers, 1815-1860*. New York: Hill and Wang, 1978. The author explores reform as an adjustment or accommodation to nineteenth century social, economic, and political forces.

White, Deborah G. *Ar'n't I a Woman?: Female Slaves in the Plantation South*. New York: W. W. Norton, 1987. White's work is one of the most thorough treatments of female slaves.

Smith College

Date: Founded in 1875

Place: Northampton, Mass.

Relevant issues: Education, sex and gender

Significance: When Smith College opened in 1875 it was the first women's college that did not offer secondary-level courses

Smith College is a privately endowed liberal arts college located in Northampton, Massachusetts, among the foothills of the Berkshire mountains. In 1871, Sophia Smith left the fortune of $300,000 that she had inherited from her brother to be used to establish a college for women. It would differ from existing female academies and seminaries by insisting that candidates be able to meet the same standards set in men's colleges; the women would live in small cottages that would be more homelike than barren dormitories. The trustees purchased land and buildings and were finally able to open the college with a class of fourteen in 1875.

Smith College struggled to attract students in the nineteenth century as it slowly accumulated the funds needed to sustain the founder's vision of a women's college equal to the best for men. Few young women were prepared to meet the mathematics and language requirements then common. Not until secondary education for women began to catch up with that for men, and the college eased the requirement in ancient languages for nonclassical students, did the school expand.

In the nineteenth century, the majority of the students were from middle-class homes and intent on preparing for careers in teaching or other professions. In the twentieth century, as the college succeeded and as the nation became more affluent, the student body began to change. The college began to attract upper-class young women from across the nation, women more interested in the "college experience" than in preparing for a profession. In 1915, Smith became a founding member of the Seven College Conference (better known as the Seven Sisters) that would unite the socially elite women's colleges in the 1920's, drawing in Mount Holyoke, Vassar, Wellesley, Bryn Mawr, Barnard, and Radcliffe.

Coeducation became a major issue in the 1960's, but despite the defection of Vassar College, which admitted men in 1970, Smith refused to change. After long and vigorous discussions, the faculty and students voted overwhelmingly to continue as before. Men are not absent from the campus, yet it remains a woman's world. Exchange agreements permit students at any of five Connecticut River colleges—Amherst, Hampton, Mount Holyoke, and the University of Massachusetts at Amherst—all within easy shuttle bus distance from one another, to take courses for credit on any campus. The college's renowned School of Social Work has opened its master's and doctoral degree programs to both men and women since its founding in 1917. Undergraduate degree programs are open only to women, and the faculty remains predominantly female. The "house system" that replaced Sophia Smith's cottages with dormitories that average sixty-five residents, continues to provide small group living and dining experiences to students. The college is especially proud of its art collection and library, which contains an extensive collection of books and manuscripts dealing with the social and intellectual history of women.

See also Academies, female; Barnard College; Bryn Mawr College; Coeducation; Colleges, women's; Education of women; Higher education, women in; Mills College; Mount Holyoke College; Radcliffe College; Vassar College; Wellesley College

Social reform movements and women

RELEVANT ISSUES: Civil rights, social reform

SIGNIFICANCE: Reform movements in education, temperance, treatment of the mentally ill, religion, peace, suffrage, and, in the United States, abolition of slavery and civil rights for African Americans are central to New World society

From the inception of European settlement, North America has been interested in and receptive to reform. Historians have turned to the Bible to describe America as "the city upon the hill" and its people as "chosen." The Pilgrims came to the New World with the intent of escaping the perceived evils of the Anglican church, and they were followed within the decade by the Puritans, who, by name, were interested in "purifying" (that is, reforming) the Anglican church. Among those Puritans, Anne Hutchinson gave women a greater opportunity in the church and expanded the concept of salvation by grace. When the faithful began to fall away after a few generations, the Halfway Covenant reformed church doctrine to allow more members. Still later, the Great Awakening again "reformed" the church.

In secular society, the interest of the colonists had always been social reform, a process that culminated in the American Revolution and the Constitutional Convention. The American Revolution stood as a beacon for other nations to emulate, and the Constitution has been widely copied for use by other emerging nations. For its part, Canada's dominion status set the example for the creation of the British Commonwealth.

In the nineteenth century, American interests focused on reforms of every conceivable kind. At various times, the emphasis was on virtually every disadvantaged group. The antislavery and abolitionist movements worked diligently to end slavery. Canadians participated by refusing to return escaped slaves who crossed their border. The Washingtonian Society, an early type of Alcoholics Anonymous, began in midcentury Baltimore. Later, the Women's Christian Temperance Union (WCTU) warned North Americans of the evils of strong drink. Yet another group involved were the incarcerated, who suffered, despite the constitutional admonition to the contrary, the most barbarous, cruel, and unusual punishments.

As firearms became more lethal, an increasing interest in world peace spread throughout North America. As the population count rose and the immigrants concentrated in newly formed cities, social, political, and economic reforms rose to prominence, reaching, in the late nineteenth century, a national audience with the Populist Party and the settlement house movement. For those immigrants and natives who chose to live on the land, a variety of farmer organizations provided a means for them to improve their quality of life.

Perhaps the most visible image of nineteenth century social reform, after the antislavery campaign, was the continent's interest in perfectionism. Following the Enlightenment, which emphasized humankind's ability to understand its physical surroundings through unlocking the laws of the universe, came the Age of Romanticism. Accepting the place of science in human existence, the Romanticists believed that humankind could be improved. Taken to its extreme, Romanticism argued that people could achieve perfection. Many different types of communities came into existence in the second quarter of the nineteenth century to speed the human race along this path. Both religious and secular communities accepted a belief in the ultimate perfection of human society. Scattered from the Atlantic Coast to the Great Plains, they thrived until the bloodshed of the American Civil War undermined any belief that humans were improving, let alone perfectible.

In the twentieth century, both the United States and Canada contributed millions of men and women to the two world wars. Although war is not generally considered in discussions of social reform, the goals of these conflicts closely matched the reform ideals that led to the settlement of North America. Despite the fact that World War I was clearly limited to Europe, the United States and Canada willingly contributed men, women, money, and matériel to "make the world safe for democracy." Again, in World War II, both nations played a significant part in defeating the totalitarian regimes to guarantee access to the four freedoms by the world's population. A few years later, it was the men and women of the United States and Canada who helped turn back the threat of communism in Korea in the early 1950's.

Education. One of the areas of reform in which women had a significant early impact was education. Women changed the nature of education at the primary level for both boys and girls, as well as creating higher educational opportunities for women. Prior to reform, young women rarely went to school, and those who did were mostly taught "ornamentals"—for example, embroidery, harpsichord, painting, and French—which were designed to improve their marriageability.

Among the early female pioneers creating equal educational opportunities for women was Emma Willard, who believed that women had the same capacity for mathematics and sciences as did men. To prove this, she first taught herself these subjects, and then opened a school for girls. This enterprise culminated in the Troy Female Seminary (still in existence as the Emma Willard Academy). Although no teacher education courses were given, hundreds of Willard's students spread throughout North America to advance the cause of women's education. After relinquishing the reigns of the Troy Female Seminary, Willard sought directly to improve education for children in general. Combining forces with Henry Barnard, and using Connecticut as a model, she advocated higher salaries for teachers, better facilities for students, and more teaching opportunities for women. As a result of Willard's activity, many people took an interest in educational reform. Her own interest in educational reform for women was highly utilitarian; along with Mary Lyon, Catharine Beecher, and Zilpah Grant, she wanted to establish schools that would improve a woman's ability to be a homemaker and mother, as well as a teacher.

The rise in educational opportunities indicates the expanding opportunities for women in the 1820's and 1830's. In many ways, education formed the basis for other reforms. Even though Willard was not interested in temperance, abolition, or women's rights (she was interested in international peace), these became major nineteenth century reform movements, and their success was attributable in large measure to the work of women.

Abolition. The antislavery movement began with the Society of Friends. The revolutionary era, and especially the Declaration of Independence, made it philosophically impossible to defend slavery. For American colonists to wage war for independence at the same time they held African Americans in chattel slavery was difficult for many to justify. One of these people was Frances Wright, who, in 1825, proposed a plan for gradual emancipation. Citing the concept of natural rights, Wright opposed slavery on Enlightenment terms—that is, it was wrong for one human being to hold another human being in bondage. Early in the nineteenth century, the abolitionist movement divided, with the western center located in Oberlin, Ohio. Among the leaders was Theodore Weld, who met Angelina and Sarah Grimké, among the most active of the female abolitionists. Sharing a belief in the equality of all human beings, Theodore and Angelina married with vows, written by the couple, that spoke of both as equals, thus contravening the accepted standards of the day.

Angelina was the younger sister of Sarah, also an abolitionist. Both were active in the abolitionist movement, writing and lecturing to bring an end to the peculiar institution. Their involvement began in the mid-1830's, when the sisters heard different abolitionist leaders. In 1835, Angelina joined the Philadelphia Anti-Slavery Society, thus making official her reformist position. Frances Wright, Sarah and Angelina Grimké, along with many other women attacked slavery from a different philosophical basis: As nineteenth century women, they bore a sense of moral responsibility for those who suffered. Female abolitionists were especially concerned with the slave family and protecting the moral purity of the slave women. That concern is evident in Harriet Beecher Stowe's *Uncle Tom's Cabin: Or, Life Among the Lowly* (1852), which vividly described the abuses of slavery. A decade later, on meeting Stowe, President Abraham Lincoln remarked, "So this is the little lady who made this big war."

Laws protected neither the sanctity of the family nor the virtue of slave women. Not only were slaves denied basic human rights, but slave women were denied the inviolable rights of women. Sojourner Truth's powerful refrain, "and ain't I a woman," clearly brought home this extra burden of the slave woman.

Although the North's victory in the Civil War and the subsequent Reconstruction amendments ended slavery and guaranteed African Americans equal rights before the law, racists soon developed other techniques to keep African American women and men in subservient positions. Early in the twentieth century, social worker Mary White Ovington found their position to be so limited that the only title she could use for her study was *Half a Man*. Ovington continued her work in civil rights, joining with others (for example, Ida B. Wells) to found the National Association for the Advancement of Colored People (NAACP).

Voluntary Association. Abolitionism stemmed from two interrelated areas. First, women, along with men, benefited from the expanding middle class. Second, sex stereotyping kept women from gainful employment in most instances, which forced them to direct their energies toward reform, something that "naturally" fell within their realm. Women founded voluntary associations and channeled their energies first toward religious goals, then toward more secular concerns.

Within the church, the voluntary association provided material assistance (food and clothing) at the same time it worked to convert the heathen. Visiting the poor became a part of the volunteer's duties, which ultimately led to the development of the social work profession. Undoubtedly the most famous of these visitors was Dorothea Dix, who entered the public spotlight while teaching a Sunday school class in the jail in East Cambridge, Massachusetts. Finding the mentally ill incarcerated with the morally deficient and the criminal, she spent the next two decades working for the establishment of state insane asylums.

Women were active throughout the United States, but they were especially successful in the urban Northeast, where they assisted the needy, saved the deviant, and found work for the unemployed and shelter for the homeless. Beyond the church, several charitable associations were established from this work. The Boston Seaman's Aid Society, New York's Society for the Relief of Poor Widows with Small Children, and the Providence Employment Society are only a few of many.

Moral Reform. Nineteenth century women rebelled against the historical reality of one code of sexual conduct for men and a different one for women. Through moral reform and the establishment of a single code of sexual conduct, women intended to end prostitution and adultery, reform fallen women, and redirect the interests of men away from licentiousness and vice.

Temperance. Despite the fact that people living in the seventeenth and eighteenth centuries consumed large quantities of alcohol, by the early nineteenth century, drinking was taking on a different appearance. The call for temperance, which could be clearly heard in the 1840's, was quickly followed by an appeal for abstinence. Women and men both "signed the pledge" and called on others to renounce the evils of drink. After the Civil War, women became leaders in the temperance movement, which began in earnest in Ohio, where women lobbied to close saloons. Their two main devices were prayer and civil disobedience, often used together.

Though not an Ohioan, one of the most famous female temperance campaigners was Carry Nation, who, with her hatchet, closed several saloons and struck fear in the hearts of countless other saloon keepers. In the late nineteenth century, Carry Nation showed people the power of direct action, especially on a moral issue. Employing both nonviolent techniques and brickbats, depending on the situation, Nation brought tremendous attention to the cause.

The radical approach of such reformers as Carry Nation prompted both snickers and genuine admiration. (Culver Pictures, Inc.)

Women's Christian Temperance Union. Carry Nation organized a chapter of the Women's Christian Temperance Union (WCTU), which had been founded in Chicago in 1873. Led first by Annie Wittenmyer, the WCTU quickly became a major force in the temperance crusade. Furthermore, it was important in social reform because the WCTU emphasized general societal improvement, including more protection for women. By the time of America's entry into World War I, the WCTU was the largest woman's organization in the world, boasting nearly 250,000 members.

The real driving force behind the success of the WCTU was Frances Willard, who became its leader in 1879. An organizational genius, Willard transformed a local organization with a narrow focus into a national one with a broad agenda for social reform. She established an organization with local, state, and national offices and involved everyone at one or more of these levels. Wearing their white ribbons, a symbol of both WCTU membership and the purity of the home, the women advocated temperance, international peace, labor reform, urban improvement, education, and women's rights. The WCTU was a strong advocate of woman suffrage, which was seen as another way to achieve the desired social reforms. Considering that women were naturally disposed to reform, granting them the vote would increase government activity in that area.

As with any social reform organized and led by women before 1920, the WCTU targeted men for conversion. As long as women were denied the franchise, it was mandatory to convert men to the cause, as they were the ones who would be making the final decision through their voting right.

Women's Clubs. The WCTU, though the largest and most famous, was not the only nineteenth century women's organization. When it rose to prominence, women's clubs were a major issue for women. Whereas the WCTU had a specific agenda for reform and admitted virtually all women, women's clubs began with a more exclusive membership and focused first on issues of cultural significance. Organized to read and discuss literary works, for example, clubs invited women with similar interests to join. The New England Woman's Club attracted women interested in social reform; in New York, journalists (for example, the muckraker Ida Tarbell) and other professional women came together. Soon, in addition to their interest in art, music, and literature, most women's clubs took on the mantle of social advancement. Women expressed their interest in organization through the formation of local women's clubs; those clubs further expressed women's interest in organization through the creation of the General Federation of Women's Clubs, established in 1892 when approximately 100,000 women belonged to some 500 affiliated clubs. By 1914, the number of female members had increased to one million, providing middle-class women a chance to participate in public life at the same time they maintained their position as guardians of morality and the home.

Women's Rights. Another area of reform that stemmed from the new world interest in improvement was the women's rights movement. The nineteenth century woman existed in a state only slightly removed from slavery. She had little opportunity to enter higher education or work for a living; she could not hold property; she was denied custody of her children; and she suffered from the widespread acceptance of the double standard. From their base in the abolition movement, women began to question the relationship between their position and that of the slaves. In part, as a result of that analysis came the Seneca Falls Convention of 1848, during which the delegates approved the Declaration of Sentiments. Through the abolitionist movement, women had gained considerable organizational experience, which they used to their advantage in the drive for equality.

At the same time that it helped, the association with abolitionism also hindered the women's rights campaign. Many in America opposed the antislavery campaign and anything associated with it, however remote the connection. Nevertheless, women continued their drive for equal rights, including the right to vote, until they succeeded in forcing the passage of the Nineteenth Amendment in time for the 1920 presidential election.

American Civil War. Abolitionism, along with other, related crises, brought on the Civil War. From 1861 until 1865, while the men went off to fight, women found new opportunities at home and on the battlefield. At home, more women moved into teaching, a profession in which they had already made inroads. They also established a foothold both in the office and in the store as clerks.

As with any war, casualties from battlefield wounds and disease mounted and, with them, the demand for physicians and nurses. Despite the advances in the practice of medicine made by the Blackwell sisters, Emily and Elizabeth, women were not welcomed as doctors. As nurses, however, they found a niche to occupy, even if the male medical community did not welcome them with open arms. Combining both medicine and domestic service, women revolutionized the field of nursing. Despite the doctors' complaints that women were too delicate for the work, they successfully used their skills as caregivers. Much of their work consisted of housekeeping—making beds, cooking, and cleaning—but after the war, nursing veterans ran hospitals, wrote nursing textbooks, and opened training schools. There were only a thousand nurses at the war's end, but by 1900, there were twelve thousand, 90 percent of whom were women.

Only the fortunate few were paid; the majority of Civil War nurses were volunteers, many simply appearing at battlefield aid stations or in hospitals. The Sanitary Commission, also composed of volunteers, though with quasi-official status, along with the surgeon general's office oversaw the nursing function. Working for the surgeon general was Dorothea Dix, the only woman to win a significant federal position during that time.

The war produced another, albeit questionable, change for women. Hundreds of thousands of men died, both Union and Confederate, and several times that number suffered disabilities that kept them from working. Despite the nineteenth century Cult of True Womanhood, which saw the place of the woman to be in the home, conditions forced many women into the workplace. This was a somewhat unfamiliar position for white women of some means, but poor immigrant women and African American women had worked for generations. With the end of slavery, African American women entered the free labor market, competing with white women for jobs.

If the Civil War met the abolitionists' goal of ending slavery, it also showed women their place in American society. At the war's conclusion, the Reconstruction amendments abolished slavery, extended civil rights to the freed slaves, and offered African American men the right to vote. All women, however, would have to wait an additional fifty-five years for the vote.

Settlement House Movement. While the Civil War raged in the United States, the Booth family in England created a different kind of army to fight another type of war. William Booth and his family established the Salvation Army to fight the problems of poverty through adopting a relatively simple lifestyle while living among the poor. Later in the nineteenth century, young idealistic, reform-minded American women and men came face to face with a new type of poverty. They were familiar with the abject conditions in America's tenements, where immigrants from southeastern Europe struggled against overwhelming odds to survive. In London's South

End, however, American women and men came in contact with people who were in similarly dire straits but who resembled themselves both ethnically and religiously. This revelation spurred the young Americans to return home to open "settlement houses," places where the poor could improve their lot and preserve their identity.

Settlement houses abounded in American cities; on the eve of World War I, there were more than four hundred. They provided an outlet for reform-minded, middle-class, college-educated women such as Jane Addams and Ellen Gates Starr. As more and more women graduated from college, settlement houses provided many of them with an opportunity to use their newly developed skills and talents. As in so many reform movements, women dominated the effort; here, they also represented the majority of recipients. Whereas poor and immigrant men were more likely to turn to the ward boss for assistance, women and children came to the settlement house to learn English, improved housekeeping skills, and new methods of child care.

The Great Depression. In the years after passage of the woman suffrage amendment, increasing numbers of women went to college and entered the professions. Within a decade, however, the stock market crashed, and the nation, as well as the industrialized world, found itself in the worst depression since the Industrial Revolution. In North America, the unemployment rate reached 25 percent. Following the adage of "last hired, first fired," as well as the idea that women's place was in the home, countless women lost their jobs.

World War II and Beyond. Following the Depression, World War II created an enormous demand for women in the workforce. Millions of women joined "Rosie the Riveter"; others entered the military. When the war ended and the men came home, women were expected to leave the office and the factory to return to their "proper" place. African Americans who had migrated to the North to fill jobs vacated by white men going off to war were also expected to disappear. Neither group cooperated.

First, African Americans began lobbying for their rights. The initial shots fired in the revolution of the Civil Rights movement involved women. Rosa Parks refused to surrender her bus seat, touching off a year-long boycott against the Montgomery Bus Company. A few miles away and a few years later, Autherine Lucy risked her life in an attempt to integrate the all-white University of Alabama. In Kansas, Oliver Brown sued the school board, protesting that his daughter was being bused several miles when an appropriate, albeit all-white, elementary school was only a few blocks from her home. Finally, several of the first African American students to attend the all-white Central High School in Little Rock, Arkansas, were female.

Over the next fourteen years, countless women joined the struggle for civil rights. They belonged to all the major civil rights organizations, undertaking all manner of tasks to end segregation. All of them gave willingly of their time and talent, and some, including Viola Liuzzo, gave their lives.

Women's Liberation. During this work, as so often in the past, women found themselves relegated to subservient positions. Although not all men were as crude as Stokely Carmichael of the Student Nonviolent Coordinating Committee (SNCC), who was quoted as saying that "the only position for women is prone," women found their ideas and their work demeaned. This realization, along with a general sense of ill ease—Betty Friedan, in *The Feminine Mystique* (1963), referred to it as "the problem with no name"—brought on the women's movement of the 1960's. In keeping with the efforts of past reformers, women's objective remained the same: equal rights for women.

Conclusion. Throughout their involvement in the history of social reform, women have employed a variety of techniques to achieve their goals. They used everything from one-on-one persuasion and quiet letter-writing campaigns to marches and public demonstrations of civil disobedience. Throughout, despite social impressions to the contrary, women were urged to "raise less corn and more hell," to borrow the late nineteenth century rallying cry of Populist activist Mary Elizabeth Lease. Because of their subordinate status (that is, lacking access to power), women had to convince the men who had the power to institute the necessary reform.

One should not infer that women represented a unified force for social reform. Not all women participated, nor were all women invited to participate. Reform-minded women historically have been of the middle class—they had the time, the talent, and the connections to instigate change. Although some working women participated in different movements—labor reform, for example—they were definitely in the minority. Furthermore, some women were not welcome; at first lesbians found themselves excluded from the post-World War II women's rights movement. Some women—Phyllis Schlafly, for example—organized women who were opposed to the women's movement. Overall, however, women have exerted a tremendous force for significant social reform.

—Duncan R. Jamieson

See also Abolitionist movement and women; Civil rights and civil liberties for American women; Civil rights and civil liberties for Canadian women; Civil Rights movement and women; Civil War and women; Environmental movement and women; General Federation of Women's Clubs; Grimké, Angelina, and Grimké, Sarah; History of women; Labor movement and women; Nurses, women as; Settlement houses; Temperance movement and women; Willard, Frances; Women's Christian Temperance Union (WCTU); Women's movement

BIBLIOGRAPHY

Berkin, Carol Ruth, and Mary Beth Norton. *Women of America: A History*. Boston: Houghton Mifflin, 1979. A good combination of historical analysis through secondary documents.

Hofstadter, Richard. *The Age of Reform: From Bryan to F.D.R.* New York: Alfred A. Knopf, 1955. A classic study of the reform impulse from the late nineteenth century to the 1930's.

Tyler, Alice Felt. *Freedom's Ferment*. Freeport, N.Y.: Books for Libraries Press, 1970. A basic analysis of Antebellum reform.

Woloch, Nancy. *Women and the American Experience*. 2d ed. New York: McGraw-Hill, 1994. A readable history of women in the United States.

Socialization of girls and young women

Relevant issues: Education, employment, sex and gender, women's history

Significance: Socialization is the process by which human beings learn to live in their cultures; gender-role socialization is the process by which human beings learn behaviors and attributes deemed by their cultures as appropriate for their genders

History. Although there are obvious physical and biological differences between males and females, these differences do not explain all the differences between males and females. They do not explain why girls should play with dolls and boys with trucks. They do not explain why women are better suited for housekeeping than men when most men are physically stronger than most women. They do not explain why men make more money at jobs for which it has not been shown that men are inherently more capable, such as law and college teaching. Despite the fact that nothing truly explains these differences, various theories have tried.

Sigmund Freud's psychoanalytic theory posits that women are devalued because they lack essential equipment, a penis. It is not only men and boys who devalue them; as soon as the girls are old enough to know what they do not have, they devalue themselves. They blame their mothers, who gave birth to them this way, and turn their attention to their fathers. Boys compete with their fathers for their mothers' attention while fearing their fathers' power of punishment and of castration. Men's gender identity, therefore, is considered stronger than women's because the fear of castration is stronger than penis envy. Because of her anatomical deficiency, a woman's self-esteem suffers and her interests turn to home and family, whereas a man's interests are not so limited.

Lawrence Kohlberg's cognitive-developmental theory focused on the stages children go through to learn gender roles. Children first learn that there are different genders, then learn gender roles. They also learn to value their genders and their roles, often rigidly conforming to stereotyped roles while very young. They seek out and identify with same-sex models and adopt same-sex behaviors. Boys tend to be more rigid than girls in conforming to gender norms. Kohlberg explains that this is because both genders recognize the power and prestige that goes along with being male. Girls do tend to follow gender norms, but not as strictly as do boys.

According to social learning theory, children learn gender roles through observation and imitation. Because parents treat boys and girls differently, the children learn that they are supposed to act differently. "Boys will be boys" and "act like a lady" may or may not be phrases spoken aloud, but children hear them nonetheless. Girls who are taught to play quietly with dolls while their brothers run and yell while playing football learn to be passive rather than active, quiet rather than loud. Girls who watch their mothers in the kitchen and boys who help their fathers in the shop learn that there are female activities and male activities. Social learning theory includes rewards and punishments: The boy who is rewarded for being strong, active, and independent and the girl who is rewarded for being weak, passive, and dependent will learn those roles even more quickly than they would merely by observing.

Gender-schema theory attempts to integrate various theories and cultural factors by suggesting that a child's perceptions of the world are organized by a network of associations. Those who see the world in sex-specific terms are considered sex-typed, whereas those who do not see the world that way are non-sex-typed or androgynous. There are degrees to which people organize their thoughts and lives around gender issues in order to understand the world. The more sex-typed an individual is, the more likely he or she is to remember sex-typed words, to mix up members of the opposite sex, and to categorize people and things according to gender. Gender-schema theory uses cognitive developmental theory to show the relationship between identity and gender meanings and social learning theory to show how social interaction creates rules and meanings. It emphasizes individual participation in the socialization process, both in learning social roles and in maintaining or rejecting those roles.

Socialization Forces. If people and institutions do not provide sex-typed models, children are not as likely to learn sex-typed roles and attributes or create gender schemas. Although there are alternatives, however, sex-typed modeling—or traditional socialization—still predominates. Parents begin the process at birth. A baby girl is wrapped in a pink blanket and her brother in a blue one. She is given a doll to play with, and he is given a toy truck. She is talked to more (because girls are verbal) and he is handled more (because boys are physical). She is soft, gentle, and fragile. He is tough, strong, and hardy. Parental modeling includes behaviors toward their children, activities with them, and their own behaviors, attributes, and activities. If children see parents who divide chores by gender, who work in stereotypical occupations (such as nurse for mother and doctor for father), who encourage their children to take part in stereotyped activities, they will come to believe that the world is divided into male and female pursuits.

When the children are old enough to have friends, they will also adhere to their proper roles, especially if their friends have also been socialized to create gender schemas. Part of the traditional socialization process includes learning that males are more highly valued in society, so young boys will not play with dolls for fear of being called "sissy," but the girls may engage in male activities without fear of ridicule. In the second half of the twentieth century, girls as well as boys have been encouraged to participate in physical activities, but girls are not encouraged and rewarded as often as are boys.

When the children begin school, they find a whole new set

Efforts have been made to correct misperceptions in the classroom about women's history and the roles that women can play in society. (Bettye Lane)

of rules and social patterns. Because boys have been taught that they are important and that being loud is part of being a boy, they carry that behavior into the classroom. The girls who have been taught to be calm, quiet, and undemanding are not given as much attention as are the boys. Though much of the attention toward boys is negative, it is, nevertheless, attention. Peggy Orenstein, for her book *Schoolgirls* (1994), spent a year observing and talking with middle school girls, their teachers, and their parents. She discussed the "hidden curriculum" in schools, the running subtext through which teachers communicate behavioral norms and status in the school—in particular, norms and status according to gender. In one of the schools she visited, she found that the ratio of boys to girls in interaction with teachers was five to one. This, she said, leads to a lesson in self-importance for boys and a lesson in self-abnegation for girls. In addition, it leads to an ever-widening gap in achievement between boys and girls, with boys' test scores increasing and girls' decreasing from elementary school to high school. This is especially true in math and science courses.

It is not only student-teacher interactions or student behaviors that play a part in the hidden curriculum; the materials used in teaching convey the same message. Despite years of attempting to combat sexism, both sexes are still stereotyped. Males are the doers and females the observers. Males understand math; females do not. Women's achievements are also underrepresented in classroom materials, which promoted Dale Spender to ask in her introduction to *Women of Ideas and What Men Have Done to Them* (1982): "Why didn't I know (about the women of the past)? How is it that women have been made to disappear?" She answers herself, saying that the patriarchy does not like it. Women and their ideas constitute a political threat, so they are censored. Those in power can and do keep those without it from getting it, according to Spender.

Gender stereotypes are reinforced in the media. Television, a pervasive force in society, contributes significantly but is not the only medium. As in textbooks, television content underrepresents women, emphasizes youth and beauty in women but not in men, and shows women in primarily stereotypical roles. Although more exceptions occurred in the 1990's than in past decades, strong, feminist women are the exceptions and not the norm. Even child characters are stereotyped: The boys play loudly and aggressively outside while the girls play quietly with dolls or help in the kitchen. Teenage girls' and women's magazines emphasize fashion and beauty in both advertising and editorial content and devote much editorial space to getting and/or keeping a boy or man. In fiction stories in those magazines, the heroine tends to let someone else solve the conflict and is more likely to be concerned with "guy" problems than with any other type of problem. The effects of such media content can be seen in the results of many studies: High school students, as recently as the late 1980's, still stereotyped occupations. Both children and adults who watch a lot of television are more stereotyped in their views than are those who do not watch as much. Children who watch roles that are not gender-typed learn that those roles are not the sole property of one gender. Women viewing nontraditional commercials score higher in self-esteem and independent judgment than do women who view traditional commercials.

When a woman leaves school, she faces decisions and choices that her male counterpart does not. She wrestles with the question of family versus career or whether she can have both. Whatever her choice, she encounters disagreement. Should she choose a career, she will likely face economic discrimination; women typically earn seventy-two cents to a man's dollar. If she is in a gender-typed job, such as clerical work or teaching, she will automatically earn less than those in typically male occupations, such as engineering or medicine. In a typically male environment, she may face resentment, hostility, or sexual harassment. Sometimes the treatment of women is deliberate and sometimes it is inadvertent. So-called old boys clubs still abound, though men do not always "mean" to exclude women. Men still hold the majority of the top positions in organizations.

Bringing About Social Change. For these problems to be overcome, changes in society have to take place and nontraditional socialization must replace traditional. Women have tried to bring about such changes for centuries through various feminist movements, but as Spender said, women's ideas have been so successfully downplayed through the ages that each new feminist movement requires reinventing the wheel. Despite such pessimism, gains have been made with each movement.

Because of such women as Emma Willard (1787-1870), who opened a school for young women similar to men's colleges, women now attend college. Because of the efforts in the late nineteenth century of a group—including Elizabeth Cady Stanton, Susan B. Anthony, and Sojourner Truth—women won the right to vote. Because of Betty Friedan and others in the 1960's, attention was given to the woman-as-housewife malaise, and many women's lives were radically changed when they realized they did not have to stay home. In 1966, Friedan and friends started the National Organization for Women (NOW), which has worked for various aspects of women's rights. A few years later, through the efforts of Sarah Weddington, women won the right to reproductive freedom.

Women are no longer restricted to the homemaker role or to teaching, secretarial, or nursing careers, and compensation for women and men is equalizing. Although men do not do their share of the housework, they are doing more than they used to. Television is showing more women in less stereotypical roles than used to be the case. The first step in solving a problem is recognizing that there is a problem.

The most recent feminist movement, in the late 1960's and early 1970's, pointed out many of the aforementioned problems, and recent research points out that some still exist. Individuals and organizations are working to correct the problems. Orenstein talked of teachers in the schools she visited who devised their own methods for handling aggressive boys and timid girls; women's groups are monitoring the media; and the Ms. Foundation for Women created Take Our Daughters to Work Day in 1992. The ideas behind this event were to make girls feel important, to raise their self-esteem, and to give them a positive outlook on the future. Not surprisingly, boys have protested from the beginning about being left out. Yet companies that let boys come with the girls report that the boys take over, which tends to reinforce what girls already experience and defeats the purpose of Take Our Daughters to Work Day. Despite improvements in women's lives over the years and throughout the centuries, there is still much to do. —*Kate L. Peirce*

See also Biased classrooms; Child rearing; Education of women; Gender differences; Mother-child relationships; Psychological theories on women

BIBLIOGRAPHY

Basow, Susan. *Gender Stereotypes*. 2d ed. Monterey, Calif.: Brooks/Cole, 1986. A detailed overview of socialization theories, forces, origins of sex roles and stereotypes, and the consequences of stereotypes.

Butler, Matilda, and William Paisley. *Women and the Mass Media*. New York: Human Sciences Press, 1980. Somewhat dated but one of the best discussions of the images of women in various media.

Lont, Cynthia M. *Women and Media: Content, Careers, Criticism*. Belmont, Calif.: Wadsworth, 1995. Covers the images of women in the media, women working in various aspects of the media, and profiles of outstanding women in each area.

Orenstein, Peggy. *Schoolgirls*. New York: Doubleday, 1994. A case study of how the media and the educational system are shortchanging girls.

Sapiro, Virginia. *Women in American Society*. 3d ed. Mountain View, Calif.: Mayfield, 1994. Discusses theories of sex-role development, socialization forces, and the effects of sex-role differentiation. Designed to be an introductory text in women's studies courses.

Spender, Dale. *Women of Ideas and What Men Have Done to Them*. London: Routledge and Kegan Paul, 1982. A history of women's ideas, what happened to them, and how it happened.

Weitzman, Lenore J. *Sex Role Socialization*. Palo Alto, Calif.: Mayfield, 1979. Short but information-filled book about the socialization process at various stages of a child's growth.

Wood, Julia T. *Gendered Lives*. Belmont, Calif.: Wadsworth, 1994. More about gendered communication than other topics but also includes chapters on theoretical issues, education, and the media.

Softball, women in

Relevant issue: Sports

Significance: Long a popular sport with women, softball affords female athletes an opportunity to showcase their talents in a male-dominated sports world

Originally an indoor form of baseball called kittenball, softball moved outdoors in 1900 and became an official outdoor game in 1933 when a tournament was held during the Century of Progress World's Fair. Fifteen women's teams competed in the tournament, which included church and industrial teams as well as the Canadian national team. Renamed softball for the tournament, the sport gained popularity during the Great Depression years as the unemployed sought recreational diversion.

Many women participated in softball at recreational facilities. The sport was considered suitable for women because a soft ball was used, and one observer claimed softball had become the "most common female game." It became so popular that with the founding of the Amateur Softball Association in 1934, rules and a separate seasonal world series were established for women, making the sport more competitive. By decade's end, women's softball teams were sponsored by banks, bakeries, restaurants, ice cream shops, truck lines, and many other businesses.

The slow pitch and a national softball hall of fame for women encouraged more female athletes to join the growing sport in the 1950's. One notable softball player was Connecticut's "Blazin'" Bertha Tickey, a pitcher who threw a thirteen-inning perfect game in 1968. In a career spanning twenty-three years, Tickey won 757 games and lost only 88, and she pitched 162 no-hitters. An eighteen-time All-American, she was voted the most valuable player in the national tournament eight times, and she played for eleven championship teams. In the 1960's, softball grew internationally to more than thirty countries after a women's team from Connecticut, the Raybestos Breakettes, traveled on a world tour promoting the sport.

Softball became important to many women, and, during the 1950's and 1960's, it provided a needed social outlet for lesbians. Softball teams enabled lesbians to make contact with one another and offered them a safe place where they would not be subjected to overt homophobia. Sharing the common experience of sports, gay women's softball leagues formed the core of many lesbian communities.

By 1969, more than two million women were participating in softball. The implementation of Title IX of the Education Amendments of 1972 stated that female athletes must have the same opportunities in sports as male athletes in interscholastic, club, and intramural athletics; if they did not, the schools would be denied federal support. This legislation prompted the beginning of Women's College World Series tournaments. An official Women's Professional Softball League was established in 1975. The women in the league averaged 140 games per year, traveling the country by bus. The league folded in 1979, however, not only because of poor-quality fields and large inequities in pay levels between baseball and softball players but also because of baseball's popularity with spectators and the media. Although softball remained popular, golf and tennis received the greatest commercial television coverage among women's sports during the 1980's and 1990's. It was hoped that the introduction of softball as an Olympic sport in the Atlanta Games in 1996 would boost interest. The much-publicized gold medal victory of the U.S. team, led by veteran Dot Richardson, seemed to deliver on this promise, but the future of both baseball and softball in Olympic competition was in doubt.

See also Baseball, women in; Lesbianism; Professional sports, women in; Sports, women in; Title IX of the Education Amendments of 1972

Son preference

Relevant issues: Family, sex and gender

Significance: Son preference refers to the positive bias that many couples have toward producing male offspring

Adults in the United States show an overwhelming preference for having sons, with fathers having a stronger preference than mothers. (If it is a boy, however, mothers are much more satisfied with the gender of their newborn child.) This preference for sons influences the use of contraception and the size of families. Families with firstborn sons tend to be smaller than families with firstborn girls because parents with daughters tend to keep having children, with fewer years between children, presumably in the hope of having a son. Religious and economic factors also affect the level of son preference. Strong religious traditions lead many parents to prefer sons. In some cultures, economic factors increase the value of sons over daughters. Emotional factors, such as a desire to continue the family name, also influence the level of son preference.

Although techniques have been developed for selecting the sex of a child at the time of conception, generally in order to help parents deliver a son, many of these techniques are not effective. In rare cases, parents use extreme measures to ensure the birth of a male child. For example, in some countries, genetic screening and ultrasound scanning, which can determine the sex of the fetus, may lead to the abortion of female fetuses. In China, with its one-child-only policy, many instances of the murder of female infants have been reported.

See also Abortion; Birth control and family planning; Infanticide; Patronymy; Pregnancy and childbirth; Sexism; Ultrasound

Sontag, Susan (b. Jan. 16, 1933, New York, N.Y.)

Areas of achievement: Literature and communications

Significance: Sontag is an influential essayist and cultural critic

Susan Sontag's essay collections have earned her a place as one of the most important nonfiction writers in the United States. While only a few of her essays are explicitly feminist, her outspoken criticism of the political establishment in *Trip to Hanoi* (1969) and of modern medicine in *Illness as Metaphor* (1978) seems to spring from a feminist and contrary nature.

She is less admired as a novelist, although her romantic historical novel *The Volcano Lover* (1992) was a surprise bestseller. Sontag remains a touchstone figure for contemporary thinking on radical politics.

See also Fiction writers; Politics

Sororities

Relevant issues: Education, race and ethnicity, sex and gender

Significance: Social, professional, and honorary societies exclusively for women have both provided much-needed support and perpetuated stereotypes

A sorority (from the Latin *sororitas*, meaning "sisterhood") is a college organization composed exclusively of women, often joined for social interaction and housing. Gender may be the sole determinant for admission to such a society; a common race, religion, or ethnicity may also play a role. The first Greek-letter sorority, Kappa Alpha Theta, was founded in 1870 at Indiana Asbury University, which later became De Pauw University. Sororities for African American women have been an important touchstone for many students, especially at prestigious Howard University; the first Greek-letter sorority on campus was Alpha Kappa Alpha, in 1908, followed by Delta Sigma Theta in 1913 and Zeta Phi Beta in 1920.

A sorority can be a source of mentoring and networking for women during and after college, creating lifelong career opportunities that can aid women in the business world. Some feminists support the concept of sororities as crucial woman-identified places, where women can share bonding experiences and help one another achieve empowerment without pressure from or intimidation by men.

Other feminists have objected, however, to the exclusively social tone of some societies. The traditional "rush week," in which hundreds of prospective pledges may be granted interviews with the sororities on a campus, can seem demeaning and superficial. In the past, this ritual was used as a way of screening out "undesirable" women, either for racial or ethnic reasons or for social ones (such as appearance). Some sororities continue to categorize women by interests, value systems, or reputations. The tradition of hazing, in which pledges are given tasks to perform to test their loyalty to the society, is not as prevalent or controversial among sororities as it is among many fraternities. A sorority is much more likely to choose activities that involve bonding and cooperation rather than fear and humiliation.

The sorority was created as a counterpoint to the fraternity (from the Latin *fraternitas*, meaning "brotherhood"), a college organization for men that may be a hallmark of academic distinction (such as Phi Beta Kappa), a means of networking, a sports-related club, or a group joined for social interaction and housing. The latter type of fraternity has often been criticized for its separatism from women and, in some cases, for demeaning attitudes and even violence against women (such as date rape). As a result, many college campuses have wrestled with the issue of coeducation for fraternities, either forced or voluntary. Several fraternities have lost their national charters by admitting women to local chapters. Some women believe that achieving coeducation within fraternities would lessen sexual harassment on college campuses and is preferable to the continuation of existing sororities or the founding of new ones.

See also African American women; Colleges, women's; Date rape; Education of women; Mentoring and networking by women; Sexual harassment; Sisterhood; Socialization of girls and young women; Stereotypes of women; Violence against women

SPAR

Date: Founded in November, 1942

Relevant issues: War and the military

Significance: SPAR was organized as a women's auxiliary to perform clerical and other duties previously done by men, thus freeing them for sea duty during World War II

In November of 1942, the U.S. Coast Guard organized a reserve auxiliary for women in order to free men for sea duty manning invasion craft, supply ships, and transport ships. The Coast Guard, normally operating under the Treasury Department, was assigned to the Navy during World War II. The Coast Guard had seen heavy action in the North Atlantic, South Pacific, and Aleutians and had suffered heavy casualties.

Shortly after the law creating SPAR (taken from the motto of the Coast Guard, *Semper Paratus*) was signed, twelve female officers from the Navy Women Accepted for Voluntary Emergency Service (WAVES) resigned from the Navy to accept commissions in the Coast Guard. One of these, Dorothy C. Stratton, was appointed as director with the rank of lieutenant commander. Later, thirty-four enlisted WAVES transferred to the SPARs.

Original SPAR training was conducted at the Biltmore resort hotel in Palm Beach, Florida. Later, training for enlisted personnel was moved to the station at Manhattan Beach, California, and officer training was moved to the U.S. Coast Guard Academy in New London, Connecticut. Thus, the Coast Guard became the first branch of the armed forces to train women officers at its academy. It would not be until the 1970's that women would be allowed to become cadets at the service academies.

SPAR was to include one thousand officers and ten thousand enlisted personnel. More than 70 percent of these recruits were to serve in yeoman, or clerical, positions, releasing office-bound men for duty at sea. Other occupations were available to SPARs, such as storekeepers, radio technicians, truck drivers, cooks, bakers, and pharmacist mates. African Americans were not allowed to join the SPARs until 1945.

When World War II ended, there was a full complement of SPARs. All were discharged or placed on inactive duty by June of 1946, and the SPAR program was dissolved. The SPAR program was reactivated in November of 1949, shortly before the Korean War broke out. It was disbanded again in 1974, when women gained equality in the military and were allowed to become part of the regular Coast Guard.

The SPAR program placed women in jobs traditionally performed by men in military service. It moved women from the traditional homemaker role to wage earner status. It helped prove that women could perform equally with men or replace them in many of the combat support fields. The SPARs set a precedent in training at the Coast Guard Academy, a right that would not otherwise be extended to women for thirty more years. In the 1990's, women serve alongside men with equal pay and status in the military because of the dedication and devotion to duty that the SPARs shared with their female colleagues in other branches of the armed forces during World War II.

See also Army Nurse Corps; Military, women in the; Military academies, integration of; Military officers, women as; Women Accepted for Voluntary Emergency Service (WAVES); Women's Airforce Service Pilots (WASPs); Women's Army Corps (WAC); Women's Reserve in the Marine Corps; World War II, women's military roles in

Speculum

RELEVANT ISSUES: Health and medicine, literature and communications, sex and gender

SIGNIFICANCE: "Speculum" has become a multilayered term signifying penetration, objectification, and domination of women and their bodies by men

In ancient times, the term "speculum" referred to a primitive mirror, usually made of bronze or silver. With the rise of neoclassicism in medieval and Renaissance literature, the term was expanded to define the concept of reflection and portraiture for the sake of mimesis and also for the purpose of instruction. A speculum is also a medical instrument for dilating cavities of the human body for inspection—most notably, the vagina. As such, it is a term of particular importance to feminist concerns, as it comes to represent a patriarchal discipline of science ignorant of women's sexual biology and sexuality. It was an instrument frequently used by mid-nineteenth century physicians to perform clitoridectomies, then an accepted method of managing a host of "women's" disorders such as uterine or nervous maladies. It eventually became symbolic of both the oppression of women and the suppression of knowledge of their own sexuality. French feminist and philosopher Luce Irigaray uses the term as a controlling metaphor in *Speculum de l'autre femme* (1974; *Speculum of the Other Woman*, 1985). Conflating both aspects of the speculum as a mirror that reflects and as an instrument with which to see, Irigaray critiques Western (male) philosophy as phallocentric—an ideology that, like the speculum, reflects women's "lack" while objectifying them through control of "the gaze." In this regard, feminist film critics have likened the speculum to the camera lens.

See also Clitoridectomy; Feminist film theory; Feminist literary theory; Gynecology and obstetrics; Health and medicine; Marginalization of women; Phallocentrism

Spinster

RELEVANT ISSUES: Sex and gender, women's history

SIGNIFICANCE: This term for an unmarried woman has carried many negative connotations

Originally, the word "spinster" meant only "one who spins," and it has always been used almost exclusively for women. The first usage of the word, attributed to William Langland in 1365 by the Oxford English Dictionary, was clearly a synonym for "spinner." The term was also appended to the names of women, originally to denote their occupation. From the eighteenth century, it was the legal designation for unmarried women, especially those beyond the usual age for marriage, and became synonymous with "old maid." The image of the spinster is laden with cultural stereotyping: She is the unchosen woman who is unattractive to men, incapable of finding a husband or respectable work, and a potential threat to society in her freedom. Unlike the wife, mother, or prostitute, the spinster was less clearly defined and confined by societal convention; therefore, she was denigrated. Many times, the harsh shrew or local gossip was unmarried, reinforcing the stereotype of the old crone envious of the success and happiness of family life. Often, however, the spinster defined a useful role for herself in society—not as the safe, married woman as mother but as the nurturing aunt, the stand-in mother for someone else's children; as the caregiver to elderly or ill parents or other relatives; or as the governess or schoolteacher who devoted her life to the children of others. Some feminists, such as Mary Daly in *Gyn/Ecology* (1978), have tried to reclaim the image of the spinster as a spinner in order to emphasize the ability of women to weave connections, to spin webs of unity in consciousness, and to whirl in motion rather than remaining static.

See also Daly, Mary; Marriage and marital status; Misogyny; Single women; Stereotypes of women

Spirituality movement, women's

RELEVANT ISSUE: Religious beliefs and practices

SIGNIFICANCE: This multifaceted religious phenomenon initiated by women seeks the transformation of self, society, and the natural world through artistic creativity, ritual, and activism

The women's spirituality movement characterizes the myriad ways in which women experience the sacred and construct new rituals in the search for wholeness and health. Rejecting the prescriptive mandates of organized religion, women's spirituality conjoins organic ways of being in the world with a growing concern for the mental and emotional health of women and all sentient beings. In healing rituals and seasonal gatherings, in groves of trees and under the stars, women (and a few men—depending on the context) gather to shape a new reality and to evoke hope for the life of the planet and future generations. Upholding the feminist adage that "the personal is the political," practitioners of women's spirituality advocate the rights of marginalized groups, address the world's ecological crisis, and seek world peace and other forms of social justice. Utilizing the rich resources found in women's art and story, music, ritual, and community, women's spirituality envisions a new set of social relations for all women, men, and children.

History. In the 1970's, small groups of women throughout North America gathered together with the common purpose of restoring hope and health to their lives as they witnessed military and ecological crises and experienced spiritual malaise. With the advent of the modern women's movement, they heeded Mary Daly's recommendation to women to retreat into their own cultural space and envision alternative values and actions that would be women-centered. Daly's historical and political critique of male-centered religion in *Beyond God the Father* (1973) spurred interest in women-centered religiosity. Other writings of the 1980's helped to expand the parameters of women's spirituality. Based on archaeological and anthropological research, Merlin Stone's essay "When God Was a Woman," discussed the power of ancient feminine symbolism for contemporary women. Carol P. Christ's essay "Why Women Need the Goddess" continued this theme and spoke of the psychological, existential, and political benefits of using feminine imagery for the divine. These and other groundbreaking essays focusing on women's ritual, experiences, and historical past were collected in *Womanspirit Rising* (1979), a classic text in feminist spirituality. The diverse themes found in the women's spirituality movement are featured in other prominent writings of the 1980's. Christ's *Diving Deep and Surfacing* (1980) affirms the many ways of women's knowing and chartered the awakening stages of the feminist spiritual quest. In *Dreaming the Dark* (1982), Starhawk, a self-proclaimed witch, fuses paganism, feminism, and politics to aid in the healing of self and society. Canadian writer Anne Cameron celebrates the religious aspects of erotic love between women in *Earth Witch* (1985), and Luisha Tesh's *Jambalaya* (1985) describes positive female imagery in black women's spiritual experience.

Concurrent with the proliferation of literature on women's spirituality was the growth of major women's conferences and festivals, where women share experiences and information and attend assorted workshops on topics ranging from drumming to building altars. One of the earliest gatherings took place in Boston in 1975, where approximately 1,800 women came together to celebrate and share information about spirituality. In 1978, the Great Goddess Re-emerging Conference in Santa Cruz, California, helped to signal the women's spirituality movement as a national phenomenon. In the 1990's, many regional, national, and international festivals and conferences on women's spirituality occurred throughout North America and other parts of the world. In the United States and Canada, these popular gatherings are attended in general by young, college-educated, middle-class women, mostly in their twenties or thirties, who have formal religious training. Although

A ceremony at the Earth Women Spirituality Festival held in New York City in 1980. (Bettye Lane)

there is often a lack of racial pluralism at major conferences and celebrations, many women of color organize their own festivals and conferences, which combine cultural and historical and religious elements.

Key Features. Women's spirituality transforms women's lack of political, psychological, and social well-being into a creative sense of empowerment. There is an insistence on valuing women's experiences, revering nature, reconstructing Western history, and employing the feminine as the primary mode of analysis and celebration. The term "spirituality" is preferred by many women who associate "religion" with restrictive or prescriptive dogma, doctrine, and rituals that oppress women and stifle their creativity.

One distinguishable feature of the women's spirituality movement is its use of ritual as a form of self-empowerment. Through ritual, these women claim that they can name and encounter the divine, achieve personal transformation, and enjoy ecstatic experiences. Engaging in ritual also provides social identity and community for the participants. The women commemorate events in daily living (such as a job promotion), perform rites of passage for various stages of life (such as the start of menstruation), and explore and celebrate various forms of sexuality. Within the various communities, women engage in meditation, dream quests, and goddess worship and make use of sweat lodges, tarot cards, herbal healing, astrology, and crystals.

The eclecticism of the movement resists any orthodox interpretations of ultimate reality. The symbolism and images celebrated in women's spirituality derive from Christian, Jewish, American Indian, African, Caribbean, ecofeminist, goddess, and pagan traditions. In addition, women's spirituality places emphasis on and celebrates different types and practices of sexuality. Although lesbianism is the norm in the various organized festivals and gatherings, the women who participate in this phenomenon represent various sexualities.

Feminist Issues. In the 1980's, many political feminists were suspicious of women's spirituality, which was considered to be the luxury of middle-class women who were indifferent to concrete, structural problems addressing women as a class. In *The Politics of Women's Spirituality* (1982), Charlene Spretnak wrote of the political ramifications of challenging patriarchy, wasteful technology, and androcentric values through women's spirituality. Since the 1980's, the women's spirituality movement has evolved to include diverse forms of political activism and concerns, including issues of environmentalism and cultural misogyny. In the United States and Canada, certain segments of women continue to debate whether the movement should be inclusive or exclusive of men, how to eradicate the world of the denigrating effects of patriarchy, and how best to ensure a future for all beings. The larger women's spirituality movement of the 1990's grew to include New Age thinkers, Protestant ministers, male allies, Catholic nuns, biblical feminists, lesbians, and Jewish, Buddhist, Christian, African American, and American Indian women. Despite particular differences, all would insist that their lives are linked through a faith in the sacredness of life and an active love that seeks to bring forth the feminine spirit in themselves and their cultures. —*Carol Wayne White*

See also Ecofeminism; Feminism, lesbian; Feminism, spiritual; Goddess, concept of the; Lesbianism; New Age movement and women; Religion; Sexuality, women's; Theologians and women's theology; Wicca; Witchcraft

BIBLIOGRAPHY

Adams, Carol, ed. *Ecofeminism and the Sacred.* New York: Continuum, 1993.

Carson, Anne. *Goddesses and Wise Women: The Literature of Feminist Spirituality, 1980-1992.* Freedom, Calif.: Crossing Press, 1992.

Christ, Carol P., and Judith Plaskow, eds. *Weaving the Visions: New Patterns in Feminist Spirituality.* San Francisco: Harper & Row, 1989.

Eller, Cynthia. *Living in the Lap of the Goddess: The Feminist Spirituality Movement in America.* New York: Crossroad, 1993.

King, Ursula. *Women and Spirituality: Voices of Protest and Promise.* 2d ed. University Park: Pennsylvania State University Press, 1993.

Sports, women in

RELEVANT ISSUE: Sports

SIGNIFICANCE: Women have participated in sports to varying degrees, depending on prevailing attitudes toward exercise and recreation for women

The participation of American women in sports has included various activities and levels of competition since Colonial days. Recreational pastimes have been enjoyed alongside intense competition, giving way to professionalization during certain time periods. The few original leisure activities acceptable for women have expanded to include almost all modern-day sports. Sport as an organized phenomenon for women started in the nineteenth century and has continued to expand through the glory days of the 1920's and 1930's to the large number of women entering sports after the passage of Title IX of the Education Amendments of 1972.

Although society has dictated the restrictions around women's lives, there have always been women willing to take risks to expand those boundaries. Their efforts have gained greater freedom for others to enjoy sports, and women have come down from the bleachers and onto the playing fields. The achievements of such women as Mildred "Babe" Didrikson Zaharias, Gertrude Ederle, Wilma Rudolph, Toni Stone, Helen Wills, and Jackie Mitchell have made it possible for today's female athletes to enjoy their respective sports.

Early Sports. Early recreational activities for women were restricted to those that allowed ladies to meet socially but not exercise strenuously, including dancing, walking, card playing, and horseback riding. Early horse races did not include women as participants, but, as spectators, they went to be seen. The goal seemed to be to ensure that women remained ladylike and in line with the ideals of "true womanhood," domesticity,

Milestones in the History of Women's Sports

1891 The Women's Athletic Association is established by students at Bryn Mawr College to formalize sports competition among college women.

1896 Stanford University and University of California play the first women's intercollegiate basketball game.

1923 The Women's Division of the National Amateur Athletic Federation is formed to promote sports for women at high school and college levels.

1926 Gertrude Ederle becomes the first woman to swim the English Channel.

1932 Track and field star Mildred "Babe" Didrikson wins one silver and two gold medals at the Olympic Games in Los Angeles.

1943 The All American Girls Professional Baseball League is founded by Philip K. Wrigley.

1946 The first U.S. Women's Open Golf Tournament is played in Spokane, Washington.

1953 Maureen "Little Mo" Connolly wins the first women's Grand Slam of tennis: Wimbledon, the French Open, the U.S. Open, and the Australian Open.

1957 Althea Gibson becomes the first African American to win the Wimbledon and U.S. Open tennis tournaments.

1968 Figure skater Peggy Fleming wins a gold medal at the Olympic Games in Albertville, France.

1970 The first Virginia Slims tournament is held in Houston, beginning the long and sometimes controversial relationship between the Philip Morris tobacco company and professional women's tennis.

1970 Gymnast Cathy Rigby becomes the first American woman to win a medal in international competition, inspiring Americans to take a greater interest in gymnastics on local, national, and international levels.

1971 The Association for Intercollegiate Athletics for Women is launched to replace the dormant Woman's Division of the National Collegiate Athletics Association.

1972 Title IX of the Educational Amendments Act prohibits sexual discrimination in institutions of higher education that receive public funds; it produces a large expansion in women's athletics.

1973 Billie Jean King defeats Bobby Riggs in the Battle of the Sexes, a tennis match in the Houston Astrodome.

1973 Billie Jean King and other female tennis players found the Women's Tennis Association to pursue more equitable policies toward women in their sport.

1974 The Women's Sports Foundation is created to expand opportunities for women in athletic pursuits.

1974 Little League Baseball is opened to girls by an act of Congress.

1976 Janet Guthrie becomes the first woman to compete in the Indy 500 auto race.

1978 Latina Nancy Lopez becomes the first professional golfer to win five consecutive tournaments.

1983 Basketball player Cheryl Miller leads her USC team to a national championship.

1984 In *Grove City v. Bell*, the U.S. Supreme Court rules that Title IX of Education Act of 1972 applies only to college programs getting direct federal support.

1984 Gymnast Mary Lou Retton earns three perfect scores and five medals at the Olympic Games in Los Angeles.

1984 Volleyball player Flo Hyman leads the U.S. team to a silver medal at the Olympic Games in Los Angeles.

1985 Tennis champion Martina Navratilova wins her fourth consecutive Grand Slam tournament.

1988 African American women dominate the track-and-field events at the Olympic Games in Seoul, South Korea, including Jackie Joyner-Kersee (two gold medals) and Florence Griffith-Joyner (three gold medals and one silver medal).

1992 Swimmer Janet Evans wins three gold medals at the Olympic Games in Barcelona, Spain.

1993 Julie Krone becomes the first female jockey to win a Triple Crown race.

1993	Tennis player Monica Seles is stabbed in the back by a fan of rival Steffi Graf during a changeover; Seles will not return to the court for years.
1994	Figure skater Nancy Kerrigan is attacked and injured during a practice session; rival skater Tonya Harding is implicated and is later banned from professional skating.
1996	In Florida high schools, a debate ensues concerning whether female students can wear tight uniforms in track and field events.
1996	U.S. women capture gold medals in gymnastics, basketball, swimming, track and field, soccer, and softball at the Olympic Games in Atlanta.

submissiveness, piety, and virtue. Dancing stood out as the most socially acceptable activity for women. Balls, barn dances, and outdoor picnics created dance opportunities for women of all classes. Dancing also created a chance for mixing with the opposite sex in a socially accepted arena.

A sport's popularity depended on its social and health aspects, which for women, meant moderation. With the establishment of seminaries for girls and young women, however, gymnastics became a part of the curriculum. These exercises were introduced by German educators and usually were modified from those performed by men and boys. As time passed, many physicians and others stressed the physical benefits enjoyed by women involved in physical activities. Early American doctor Benjamin Rush believed that dancing was a healthy activity for young ladies, as were walking and riding. Most of the early activities were geared toward outdoor recreation, except dancing. Many sports were restricted to the upper classes, who had both time and money to participate in individual contests.

Amelia Bloomer, Catharine Beecher, and Emma Willard all advocated sports for women to improve their health and academic performance. Inactivity, they believed, resulted in the weakening of female constitutions and accounted for many health problems. Bloomer thought that the only thing keeping women from greater activity was the fear that they would be labeled unfeminine. She created a new costume of loose-fitting pantaloons, soon dubbed "bloomers," to make it easier for women to play sports.

Questions were raised regarding women's participation during menstruation and pregnancy. The general belief in the nineteenth century was that women should exercise common sense during these periods, which meant that they should stay away from most sports. Sports were considered dangerous, especially when women were at their most vulnerable. Allowing women to participate in competitive sports took much convincing, since many educators believed that such activity would be harmful to women and their reproductive abilities. As a result, most women's sports prior to the Industrial Revolution were recreational and noncompetitive.

Croquet developed as a sport enjoyed by both sexes in the 1830's. It allowed people to socialize and flirt without being improper. It was not a strenuous or dangerous sport. Archery also developed as a nineteenth century sport for women because it took place outdoors but allowed women to stand still. The bow could be adjusted in size and weight to the individual without changing the essential nature of the sport.

The sport that seemed to encourage women's participation the most was golf. By 1895, the first national tournament was held at Meadowbrook, Long Island. Golf became popular because strength was not the sole factor in hitting the ball; speed and accuracy also counted. It was also not overly strenuous, was not dangerous, and allowed for a feminine costume. There were even country clubs such as the one in Morris County, New Jersey, that were run by women for women. The second national tournament took place there in 1896.

Lawn tennis was introduced to the United States in 1874 by Mary Ewing Outerbridge after she returned from a vacation in Bermuda, where she had observed British army officers playing it. A national women's tournament took place in 1877, and by 1889 the U.S. Lawn Tennis Association allowed women to join. Tennis worked well for ladies because the early rules placed extra women on the courts so that no one had to run after the ball.

Women's Colleges and Competitive Sports. Team sports began to develop as women's colleges created physical education programs, mainly after the Civil War. Vassar College led the way with baseball clubs and boating teams. With the invention of basketball, women's colleges had a sport on which they could focus their attention in developing rules, uniforms, and leagues. Senda Berenson introduced the sport at Smith College in 1892, and it spread quickly because of the rules that Berenson developed to cut down on the amount of running that the players had to do. She divided the court into sections, with players assigned specific places that they could not leave, and limited the number of times that an individual player could dribble before passing or shooting. Basketball began a trend toward more strenuous activities such as field hockey and rollerskating, as well as greater variety among participants. These games were no longer restricted to the upper classes and began to be played indoors. These sports also raised questions about what was proper for women, as they went against the image of women as weak and fragile.

Questions about women in sports stemmed from the views that American society held about women's roles, about what was acceptable and what was not. The reverse also held true when issues were addressed about competitive sports and how they would affect women who participated, as well as all other women: Success in such sports might encourage other young women to abandon family and marriage in favor of more "manly" pursuits. This thought scared parents who wanted their daughters to follow traditional, accepted paths, not step out on their own, risking ridicule and censure.

By the beginning of the twentieth century, the first true sportswoman emerged in the form of Eleanora Randolph Sears from Boston. Sears was an expert horsewoman, rode astride rather than sidesaddle, and played polo. She became one of the first women to drive a car and to fly in a plane. She won a number of tennis tournaments and became an accomplished long distance walker and a champion in squash. Such outrageous actions were accepted because of her wealth and family position. Her sporting activity opened the way for other women in the century.

By the 1920's, women's sports developed tournaments, international competitions, and interleague collegiate play, coinciding with the growth of sports as a whole during what is sometimes referred to as the Golden Age of Sports. Sports benefited from increased leisure time and spending habits. Ederle, Didrikson, and pilot Amelia Earhart gave women role models to emulate in competitive sports. Women's sports organizations were created to oversee these developments. These groups elevated limited contests to the highest level of competition, leaving most women to participate in noncompetitive sports.

One of the first sports to create an organization for women was bowling, with the Women's National Bowling Association. The following year, the Women's Swimming Association of New York formed to promote swimming meets for women in preparation for their Olympic participation. The Amateur Athletic Union (AAU) worked to sponsor women's competitions in almost all major sports by the mid-1920's. The U.S. Field Hockey Association was created in 1921 to oversee the growth of this sport at women's colleges. A women's division of the National Amateur Athletic Federation was created in 1923 to encourage participation and growth in women's sports. The group created a sixteen-point creed that advocated play for the sake of play, which meant that sports were for all women and not only a talented few. One of the strongest voices in this new organization was Mabel Lee of the University of Nebraska. Lee led the movement against the growth of intercollegiate competitions in the belief that they exploited women, causing physical and psychological damage because of the added stresses placed on women to win at all costs. Leading physical educators also worried about sacrificing sports for lesser players in favor of only the most skilled in competitive games. Classes were developed to teach team sports to encourage participation by as many women as possible.

With the onset of the Great Depression in the 1930's, many people lost interest in leisure activities. The need to create jobs, lift morale, and escape from the dreariness of the slowed economy, however, led to the growth of women's sports such as softball, volleyball, and bowling. A number of famous female athletes toured the country, offering free classes teaching the basics of bowling and tennis to women from all walks of life.

During World War II, women moved into the war industries in large numbers, leaving the comfort of home for the workplace and independence. Not coincidentally, at this time young female athletes joined Philip Wrigley's All American Girls Professional Baseball League (AAGPBL), which lasted from 1943 to 1954. The publicity generated by these teams helped other women's sports grow in the succeeding decades. These were not the first women's baseball teams—"bloomer teams" had existed since the nineteenth century—but it was the first women's league. The owners and the media tried to emphasize the players' femininity. They were accompanied by chaperones, and charm schools and other lessons were used to teach the players to behave like ladies in public.

As modern sports have developed, certain competitive sports have become associated with women, such as softball and field hockey. Endurance events such as marathons and triathlons have also become popular among women. Aerobics and walking are popular noncompetitive activities for women who want to become, or remain, physically fit.

As sports grew and changed for women in the nineteenth century, so did their fashions and uniforms. The more strenuous the activity, the greater the need was to simplify and loosen the style of dress. Gradually, women shortened their exercise clothes, exposing legs and arms. Amelia Bloomer helped this trend, as did the advent of the bicycle, swimming, basketball, tennis, softball, and field hockey. The bicycle, which was developed in the 1890's, became popular with women and forced the adoption of new fashions so that their dresses would not get caught in the spokes or pedals. Even as costumes became more sensible, they still tended to focus on femininity. For example, the short skirts that professional baseball players of the 1940's and 1950's were required to wear emphasized their femininity but were not practical for sliding on the basepaths.

As women's sports have become more competitive, the need has grown for increased funding and sponsorship. Women have worked hard to raise their sports from obscurity to national television and international competitions such as the Olympic Games. Many people helped in the push for such recognition, but one of the key figures was tennis player Billie Jean King. After winning a few tennis tournaments, she learned that female champions made considerably less money than men. King organized a boycott to end the discrimination. When she ran into resistance from the existing women's tennis organization, she generated private sponsorship for the Virginia Slims Tournament and other tennis tournaments, raising the women's purse to comparable levels with men's. King's greatest publicity stunt to generate interest in women's sports was her match against Bobby Riggs in September, 1973. Riggs had boasted that he could defeat any woman in professional tennis, and King rose to the challenge. She beat Riggs soundly in an event billed as the Battle of the Sexes. Later, King helped found the Women's Tennis Association, the Women's Sports Foundation, and a magazine called *womenSports*.

Lesbian Athletes. Billie Jean King made one other contribution to women's sports: In 1981, she acknowledged her bisexuality, which cost her some sponsorship but made it easier for others to follow her example, such as Martina Navratilova. Nevertheless, the stigma attached to lesbian athletes has remained. The general treatment of female athletes who have announced they are lesbians has not been positive and has portrayed them as manly. Some critics have even suggested that competitive sports can "turn" women into lesbians. When the AAGPBL existed, players were warned they would be released if they paired off as couples. Two players were sent home out of fear that they would negatively influence the other players.

This lack of understanding has raised many issues with regard to female athletes, in addition to those concerning homophobia. The general assumption by the media is that female athletes must be lesbians if they are not married, especially since they travel on tour together in close-knit groups. Some feminists argue that those men who feel threatened by women try to demean them, making them less "feminine" and "womanly" so that they will have a harder time being accepted. This reaction has kept many female athletes silent on the subject of their sexual orientation because of the fear of public backlash. Such speculation also highlights a larger problem: Media attention tends to focus more on a female athlete's love life or family life than on her achievements.

Notable Women in Sports. Looking back at the history of women's sports reveals many stars, but a few stand out for the changes that they helped bring about because of their achievements. Babe Didrikson Zaharias was named the female athlete of the century by the Associated Press in 1949 to honor her accomplishments in basketball, track and field, and golf. She played for the Golden Cyclones in basketball and won five events in the AAU track and field championships. She participated in the 1932 Olympics, setting three world records, and she won twenty-two tournaments as a professional golfer. From 1932 until 1934, Zaharias toured the country, giving demonstrations in basketball, baseball, billiards, and swimming.

Gertrude Ederle pushed swimming into the limelight after her successful crossing of the English Channel in 1926, breaking the existing male record by more than two and a half hours. She received much public acclaim and many questions about how a woman, with her "natural physical frailties," was able to accomplish something that only five men had been able to do. Ederle had proved her critics wrong and gave many women a role model, a success story to emulate.

Wilma Rudolph encouraged women's participation in sports, particularly African American women. As a child, Rudolph overcame a bout with polio that required her to wear a brace until she was a teenager. In 1956, she took part in the junior division of the AAU track and field championships. She also represented the United States in the 1956 Olympics, winning a bronze medal in the relay. After attending Tennessee State University, Rudolph again went to the Olympics in 1960.

Track and field champion Wilma Rudolph, who won three gold medals in the Olympic Games in Rome in 1960, was an inspiration to many female athletes. (AP/Wide World Photos)

Her dominance was complete, with gold medals in the 100 and 200 meters as well as in the relay. Thousands were able to see her victories because the competition was televised. As a result, the number of women's sports receiving television coverage increased. In 1960, Rudolph was named Female Athlete of the Year.

The 1970's and Beyond. The passage of Title IX of the Education Amendments of 1972 affected the number of scholarships available in the United States for female athletes, money for equipment and coaches, the number of varsity sports offered, and playing facilities. In 1971, about 295,000 women played high school and college sports. By 1991, that number had risen to nearly two million. Budgets for women's sports rose from about 1 percent of the total to 20 percent. Nevertheless, many issues remain unresolved. Congress held a subcommittee hearing on the issue of gender discrimination in sports, and the National Collegiate Athletic Association (NCAA) placed the question first on its agenda in 1994.

Since the early 1970's, women have established and participated in numerous new tournaments and organizations. Nancy Lopez's early victories on the Ladies Professional Golf Association (LPGA) tour in 1978 set a record for winnings by a male or female golfer. A professional track and field tour was set up in 1973, and the International Women's Professional Softball Association and the International Volleyball Associa-

Popular Sports Among Working Women in the U.S.

Athletic Activities	*Percentage of Women Who Participate*
Bowling	33
Tennis/racket sports	20
Golf	17
Volleyball	17
Softball/baseball	16

Source: Women's Sports Foundation

tion, with both men's and women's teams, were formed in 1975. A number of women broke barriers in previously all-male sports. Basketball player Ann Meyers signed a one-year contract with the Indiana Pacers, and auto racer Janet Guthrie competed in the Indianapolis 500 in 1976. The Boston and New York Marathons gradually opened their races to female runners in the mid-1970's.

Leading female sports figures such as Billie Jean King and Wyomia Tyus founded the Women's Sports Foundation (WSF) in 1974. The goal of the organization was to promote and enhance sports experiences for all women. The WSF maintains a resource library and a speaker's bureau, provides camp scholarships, and sponsors the International Women's Hall of Fame. The organization also helped to pass the Amateur Sports Act of 1978. This act promotes and aids the development of sports for girls and women and assists elite athletes in finding the necessary training and competitions.

Women in sports have come a long way since the Colonial days, but there is still a long path ahead. The number of professional women's sports is limited in the United States, so that female athletes in college have little hope of making careers for themselves in sports unless they look elsewhere; for example, some women go to Europe to play professional basketball. (Tennis, bowling, and golf are major exceptions to this general rule.) In Olympic Games, men make up more than 60 percent of the entrants. Media coverage is slowly increasing to include the NCAA Women's Basketball Championships and figure skating. Skating, a "feminine" sport, receives prime-time coverage, whereas the basketball contests are only televised during less competitive time slots. The number of women in leadership positions within athletic departments has been slow to increase at all levels of competition, from local schools to college and professional ranks. As long as society continues to struggle with the position of women in the larger culture, female athletes will struggle as well.

—Leslie A. Heaphy

See also All American Girls Professional Baseball League; Association for Intercollegiate Athletics for Women; Auto racing, women in; Baseball, women in; Basketball, women in; Battle of the Sexes; Dance; Dress reform; Golf, women in; Ice skating, women in; Lesbianism; Little League Baseball; Navratilova, Martina; Olympic Games, women in the; Physical fitness for women; Professional sports, women in; Softball, women in; Swimming, women in; Tennis, women in; Title IX of the Education Amendments of 1972; Track and field, women in; Volleyball, women in; Women's Sports Foundation

Bibliography

Birrell, Susan, and Cheryl L. Cole, eds. *Women, Sport, and Culture*. Champaign, Ill.: Human Kinetics, 1994. Twenty-four articles examine the relationship between sports and gender. Examines where feminist sport studies have been and where they are headed.

Cahn, Susan. *Coming on Strong: Gender and Sexuality in Twentieth Century Women's Sport*. New York: Free Press, 1994. Cahn focuses on sexual discrimination and gender identity in twentieth century women's sports. Discusses issues regarding lesbian athletes, women in baseball, competitive sports, and African American women in track and field.

Geadelmann, Patricia. *Equality in Sport for Women*. Washington, D.C.: American Alliance for Health, Physical Education, and Recreation, 1977. Focuses on sexual discrimination as defined by law and legislation. Discusses the effect of various legislative measures, such as Title IX, on the growth of competitive women's sports.

Gerber, Ellen W. *The American Woman in Sport*. Reading, Mass.: Addison-Wesley, 1974. A discussion of the development of women's sports from recreational to competitive, spectator to participant. Considerable attention is paid to societal attitudes toward women's athletics and how those attitudes have affected women's participation. A specific focus involves the physiological, psychological, and social concerns of female athletes.

Guttmann, Allen. *Women's Sports: A History*. New York: Columbia University Press, 1991. A look at women in sports from antiquity to the present. The author examines sports within a social and cultural context. Focuses on general trends and specific individuals, such as Babe Didrikson Zaharias and Gertrude Ederle. Guttmann also looks at modern sports in Europe, Australia, and New Zealand. His final analysis involves the question of exploitation of women because of their gender.

Howell, Reet, ed. *Her Story in Sport: A Historical Anthology of Women in Sports*. West Point, N.Y.: Leisure Press, 1982. A series of articles touching on various aspects of women's sports in the United States and beyond.

Lenskyj, Helen. *Out of Bounds: Women, Sport, and Sexuality*. Toronto, Ontario: Women's Press, 1986. Deals with history, femininity, and sexuality. Social attitudes and practices that have kept women out of sports are studied, as is the link between women's participation in sports and their control of their own reproduction and sexuality.

Nelson, Mariah B. *The Stronger Women Get, the More Men Love Football: Sexism and the American Culture of Sports*.

New York: Harcourt Brace, 1994. Deals with psychological and social aspects of women's participation in sports in the United States. The role of sexuality is examined in a variety of ways.

Sparhawk, Ruth M., et al. *American Women in Sport, 1887-1987: A 100-year Chronology*. Metuchen, N.J.: Scarecrow Press, 1989. An important source for looking up the facts and important events related to women's participation in American sports since the late nineteenth century.

Twin, Stephanie L., ed. *Out of the Bleachers: Writings on Women and Sport*. Old Westbury, N.Y.: Feminist Press, 1979. This book is divided into sections dealing with physiology and social attitudes, specific individuals, the structure of women's sports, and sexual discrimination.

Stanton, Elizabeth Cady (Nov. 12, 1815, Johnstown, N.Y.—Oct. 26, 1902, New York, N.Y.)

Areas of achievement: Civil rights, religious beliefs and practices, women's history

Significance: Stanton, the primary organizer for the first women's conference at Seneca Falls in 1848, was a leader in the early women's rights movement

Elizabeth Cady Stanton, like most abolitionist and women's rights activists of the nineteenth century, spent her adult life juggling family demands and activism. She wrote close friend Susan B. Anthony that "my whole soul is in the work, but my hands belong to my family." She lectured audiences that "radical reform must start in our homes, in our nurseries, in ourselves."

Stanton helped organized the Seneca Falls Women's Rights Convention in New York in 1848, the first of its kind. In the convention's Declaration of Sentiments, Stanton wrote, "The history of mankind is a history of repeated injuries and usurpations on the part of man toward woman, having in direct object the establishment of absolute tyranny over her." Such rhetorical flair characterized her speeches and writings. In calling for divorce reform, Stanton paralleled the situation of married women to that of slaves, saying that a "man marrying gives up no right, but a woman, every right."

When the women's movement split over the decision to support the Fourteenth and Fifteenth Amendments, which would extend the franchise to all men but not to women, Stanton and Anthony were united in their decision not to support the laws. They formed the National Woman Suffrage Association (NWSA), of which Stanton was president for twenty-one years.

From 1881 to 1886, Stanton, Anthony, and Matilda Joslyn Gage edited the first several volumes of *History of Woman Suffrage*. Stanton also wrote *The Woman's Bible* (1895), a controversial feminist analysis of the Old and New Testaments. Stanton's final work was her autobiography *Eighty Years and More* (1898).

See also Anthony, Susan B.; Declaration of Sentiments; Fourteenth and Fifteenth Amendments; Gage, Matilda Joslyn; National Woman Suffrage Association (NWSA); Seneca Falls Women's Rights Convention; Suffrage movement and suffragists; *Woman's Bible, The*; Women's movement

Starhawk (Miriam Simos; b. June 17, 1951, St. Paul, Minn.)

Areas of achievement: Ecology and the environment, religious beliefs and practices

Significance: Starhawk is a leader in the pre-Christian, Goddess-centered religion known as the Old Religion, the Craft, Paganism, New Paganism, Wicca, or witchcraft

Starhawk (Miriam Simos) practices witchcraft, a religion similar in spirit, form, and practice to American Indian and African religions. She is a sought-after lecturer in California's Bay Area; a faculty member at the Institute on Culture and Creation Spirituality on the campus of Holy Names College in Oakland, California; and a codirector of Reclaiming, a center that offers classes, workshops, public rituals, and private counseling in the tradition of Goddess religion. She is the author of *The Spiral Dance: A Rebirth of the Ancient Religion of the Great Goddess* (1979) and *Dreaming in the Dark: Magic, Sex, and Politics* (1982), books that clear up misconceptions about witchcraft and explore its influence on the feminist and ecology movements.

See also Christianity and women; Ecofeminism; Environmental movement and women; Goddess, concept of the; Religion; Spirituality movement, women's; Theologians and women's theology; Wicca; Witchcraft

State government, women in

Relevant issue: Politics

Significance: In the United States, the role of women in state government has increased dramatically, resulting in an emphasis on issues of interest to women

Women have historically, although not formally, been involved in state politics and government in the United States since its founding. Until the late 1860's, however, their activity in politics was limited by a male-dominated power structure that prevented women from voting in state elections and excluded them from holding public office. Only on a few rare occasions, such as local referendums, were women allowed to participate formally in the democratic process. The politically active woman was relegated to crusading on behalf of social reforms such as emancipation, suffrage, or temperance, or to working with her husband to further his political views and endeavors.

Suffrage. The role of women in state government changed dramatically in 1869, when Wyoming became the first territory or state to grant women the rights to vote and hold public office; it soon became known as the "Equality State." Two months after Wyoming set this precedent, Utah also granted suffrage to women. Other western territories and states began to follow suit. With the path to public service open to them for the first time, women came forward to serve their states and communities. The first women to hold office in Wyoming were justices of the peace. Ester Morris, the most notable of these women, served only eight months but managed to prove that her gender is worthy of public service. Nearly one hundred years later, in 1955, she was recognized for her contribution to the suffrage movement with statues placed in Washington, D.C., and in front of the Wyoming state capital.

The Nineteenth Amendment. The enfranchisement of women in a few western territories did not ensure the eventual spread of suffrage to women in all states. In 1871, less than two years after granting woman suffrage, members of the Wyoming legislature nearly succeeded in rescinding the vote to women in the territory. It was not until the passage of the Nineteenth Amendment to the Constitution in 1920 that woman suffrage was guaranteed throughout the United States. After suffrage was finally realized, however, a women's voting bloc did not emerge as many had hoped. Most women continued to support traditional gender roles in society. Ironically, despite all their gains, women rarely supported female candidates. For example, the first two women to run for the Wyoming territorial legislature received a total combined vote of thirteen. Politics was considered a man's role. As a result, few women prior to the 1960's held public office, and those few who did were often appointed to fill the unexpired term of their husbands or other male relatives. Nellie Tayloe Ross, the first woman inaugurated as a state governor, was elected in Wyoming in 1924 to complete her husband's term.

Whether by choice or by necessity, the first successful female candidates for state offices typically disassociated themselves with suffrage activists and other women's rights advocates. By the early twentieth century, some women were gaining election to seats in state legislatures on a limited scale. For example, Gladys Pyle won election as the first female member of the South Dakota legislature in 1922. Following four successful years in the house of representatives, she moved on to serve as South Dakota's secretary of state. Pyle later served in the Congress and made an unsuccessful bid to become governor of South Dakota. Like most of her contemporaries in other states, Pyle tended to focus on issues of interest to women and children. Education and child labor laws were common concerns of these female state officials. Despite common goals, they often preferred to be considered foes of the League of Women Voters and the National Woman's Party in order to improve their chances of election and reelection. The articulation of the women's movement during the 1960's, however, awakened the female electorate. Women in large numbers began to pursue public office while openly advocating a woman-oriented agenda.

The 1960's and Beyond. Ella T. Grasso, a Democrat who served in the Connecticut state legislature, became the epitome of the new woman in state government during the 1960's. Aggressive and outspoken, she condemned U.S. involvement in the Vietnam War and became an advocate for the unemployed as a state legislator and as Connecticut's secretary of state. In 1975, Grasso became the first woman to be elected as a state governor in her own right. Grasso set the stage for the likes of Ann Richards of Texas, who became the first woman to win statewide office as state treasurer in 1982. In 1990, Richards was elected governor of Texas.

More women were elected to statewide administrative and legislative offices in 1990 than in any previous election. Approximately one-fifth of all such offices were held by women. Members of the female electorate, many of whom had been outraged by sexism displayed toward Anita Hill during the confirmation hearings of Supreme Court Justice Clarence Thomas, helped nominate a record number of women for statewide office in 1992. That year became commonly referred to as the "Year of the Woman." The year 1994 was a blow to women in government, however, as every female candidate for governor was defeated, along with many women running for state administrative and legislative offices. Some observers argued that the losses sustained by female candidates were the result of unbelievably high expectations on the part of the electorate and the lack of a catalyst for female interest in the election.

Whatever the reason for the dramatic losses in 1994, women remained a driving force in state government at all levels. The women involved in state government today, like their sisters in previous generations, are still primarily concerned with issues of interest to women and children but with an expanded scope. Victim's rights, women's health issues, child care, the environment, and family leave are the focus of women in state government. —*Donald C. Simmons, Jr.*

See also Candidacy and political campaigns, women's; Equal Rights Amendment (ERA); Federal government, women in; Nineteenth Amendment; Politics; Social reform movements and women; Suffrage movement and suffragists; Women's movement; Year of the Woman

Bibliography

Buhle, Mari Jo, and Paul Buhle, eds. *The Concise History of Woman Suffrage*. Urbana: University of Illinois Press, 1978.

Flexner, Eleanor. *Century of Struggle*. New York: Atheneum, 1972.

Larson, T. A. *History of Wyoming*. Lincoln: University of Nebraska Press, 1965.

U.S. House of Representatives. Office of the Historian. *Women in Congress, 1917-1990*. Washington, D.C.: U.S. Government Printing Office, 1991.

Weiser, Marjorie P. K., and Jean S. Arbeiter. *Womanlist*. New York: Atheneum, 1981.

Stein, Gertrude (Feb. 3, 1874, Allegheny, Pa.—July 27, 1946, Neuilly-sur-Seine, France)

Area of achievement: Literature and communications

Significance: One of the great literary innovators of the twentieth century, Stein was also famous for celebrating her lifelong lesbian relationship with Alice B. Toklas

In 1903, Gertrude Stein moved to France, where she befriended great artists such as Pablo Picasso and inspired writers such as Ernest Hemingway to forge a new American style. Stein wrote the experimental novels *Three Lives* (1909), a three-part work focusing on women, and *The Making of Americans* (1925), a family chronicle, and she told her own story in *The Autobiography of Alice B. Toklas* (1933). Stein's most explicitly feminist work is *The Mother of Us All* (1947), a play about women's rights activist Susan B. Anthony.

See also Anthony, Susan B.; Autobiographies, diaries, and journals by women; Drama and dramatists; Fiction writers; Lesbianism

Steinem, Gloria (b. Mar. 25, 1934, Toledo, Ohio)

Areas of achievement: Literature and communications, politics, women's history

Significance: Steinem, the most widely recognized feminist of the late twentieth century, cofounded *Ms.* magazine in 1972 and has written and spoken widely on all aspects of women's rights

Journalist Gloria Steinem first made her mark in 1963, with an exposé based on her one-month undercover assignment as a Playboy "bunny." She joined Betty Friedan and others in organizing the Women's Strike for Equality in 1970 and the National Women's Political Caucus in 1971. Although her focus has always been women's rights, Steinem's activism extends to work with United Farm Workers, environmental issues, various liberal political campaigns, and antiwar protests.

Repeatedly named one of the twenty-five most influential women in the United States, Steinem defines feminism as "equality for all females—a transformation of society." In the 1970's, Steinem was aligned with the radical wing of the women's movement, supporting strong lesbian rights initiatives. By the late 1980's, however, many feminists criticized her for moving into the mainstream, especially after publication of the best-seller *Revolution from Within* (1992). They charged that Steinem had abandoned feminism with her focus on "self-recovery," while she responded that "self-authority is the single most radical idea there is."

Steinem's strongest impact has been through her speeches, articles, and books and through the publications that she cofounded, especially *Ms.* magazine, whose first press run of 300,000 copies sold out in eight days. Steinem's articles, such as "What If Freud Were Phyllis" and "Sex, Lies, and Advertising," have been widely reprinted. Her best-selling books include *Outrageous Acts and Everyday Rebellions* (1983), *Marilyn: Norma Jean* (1986), and *Moving Beyond Words* (1994).

See also Feminism; Feminism, radical; Friedan, Betty; Journalism, women in; *Ms.* magazine; Self-esteem, women's; Women's movement

Stereotypes of women

Relevant issues: Sex and gender

Significance: Narrow and limiting preconceptions of women's capabilities and women's nature prevent society from recognizing the broad range of talents, interests, physical appearances, and abilities that exist among women

One of the most important contributions of the women's movements in the nineteenth and twentieth centuries has been the expansion of the concept of "woman." At times in the history of the United States and Canada, the prevailing assumptions and images of women's capacities and incapacities have been restrictive and demeaning. Feminism has attacked these stereotypes and has strived to raise public consciousness of the damage they can do. The perpetuation of stereotypes impedes women's progress toward equality by limiting the images of women to a few narrowly defined roles.

Definitions. The term "stereotype" derives from printing and originally referred to a metal plate from which multiple identical copies could be printed. It has come to mean a fixed image or set of images that are taken to define an entire group of people, such as women or African Americans. A stereotype allows assumptions to be made about a person based on his or her sex, race, religion, sexual preference, social class, or other identifying characteristic. These assumptions may or may not be valid, but they never encompass the entirety of a person's character, let alone that of a group of people.

Stereotypes can be positive, negative, or neither and typically have some truth to them, though by definition they fail to describe adequately the diversity of a group of people. They often emerge from common experiences or traits. For example, Asian immigrants to the United States in the late twentieth century were noted for their aptitude in math and science. Mathematical ability is not a biological trait of Asian people; cultural conventions that value study and rigorous education more likely account for their success. Nevertheless, a stereotype that all Asians are gifted mathematicians and scientists has been created. This stereotype may inhibit Asian students from pursuing the humanities, or it may intimidate non-Asian students who take math and science classes with Asian students. The stereotype has a kernel of truth, but it reduces the experiences and skills of a diverse group of people to an oversimplified statement and makes skills that are socially constructed appear to be inborn.

Stereotypes of women are so many and varied that they cannot be easily summarized. Stereotypes vary by culture and by historical period; twentieth century stereotypes of women and their behavior may differ significantly from nineteenth century stereotypes. In fact, many stereotypes of women directly contradict one another, further evidence that stereotypes do not do justice to the diversity of women around the world. Three major stereotypes of women have repeatedly appeared throughout world history: woman as Madonna, the pure exalted mother; woman as illogical and unstable hysteric; and woman as evil, sexualized shrew or witch.

Maternal Purity. This stereotype maintains strong ties to the Christian story of the Virgin Mary. According to that story, Mary was chosen by God to give birth to his son, Jesus Christ, and she was inseminated with the child by immaculate conception. This makes her the Virgin Mother, a sexually pure woman who gave birth to a child. Mary represents the ideal from which the stereotype of maternal purity emerges. Although other women cannot be virgins and still become pregnant, the image lingers that women as mothers are pure, nurturing, spiritually exalted, and selfless. These stereotypical mothers do not have needs of their own (and do not indulge them if

FRANK LESLIE'S ILLUSTRATED NEWSPAPER

No. 1834.—VOL. LXXI.] NEW YORK—FOR THE WEEK ENDING NOVEMBER 8, 1890. [PRICE, 10 CENTS.

NEW YORK CITY.—THE DAY-NURSERY OF GRACE PARISH, ONE OF THE PROPOSED BENEFICIARIES OF THE "FRANK LESLIE'S ILLUSTRATED NEWSPAPER" DOLL CHARITY—A MOTHER'S MORNING GOOD-BYE TO HER BABE.

The stereotype of maternal selflessness was tested by the need for female workers in the Industrial Revolution, as shown in this artist's sentimental portrait of a nursery and "a mother's morning good-bye to her babe." (Library of Congress)

they have them) but think only of their children's best interests. The stereotype is an impossible image of a woman without anger, sin, or vexed emotions, a gentle soul who acts as compassionate mother not only to her own children but to the world.

This stereotype has taken several historical forms. In nineteenth century antebellum America, white women were glorified as devout and passive souls who provided spiritual leadership to their families. This stereotype, which feminist historians have referred to as the Cult of True Womanhood or the Cult of Domesticity, was promulgated by popular women's magazines such as *Godey's Lady's Book*. The Cult of True Womanhood did assign women more moral power than they had enjoyed previously, but it also confined them to the home as their "natural" sphere. These women had spiritual control over their families but still could not vote or own property and therefore lacked control over the material conditions of their lives. A generation later, women in the early twentieth century played off this stereotype of women's moral purity to enact social reforms, such as the prohibition of alcohol. Perhaps not coincidentally, this stereotype of maternal purity began to fall out of favor around the time of Prohibition in the United States.

African American women, who were enslaved in nineteenth century America, were affected by a slightly different version of the maternal purity stereotype. Many white children were reared by "mammies," slave women who were responsible for cooking, cleaning, and child rearing in the masters' houses instead of fieldwork. Mammies were considered moral, religious, and upright, although they never enjoyed the exalted status of white middle-class mothers. White slave owners separated mammies from other black women; they had a higher status by virtue of caring for the white children and cooking for the masters. These women also had their own children to care for, but the masters cared far less about these children than their own. Whereas most slaves were considered ignorant and were forbidden to learn to read, mammies did receive credit for a sort of folk wisdom. Even in late twentieth century America, the image of the mammy continued to appear on food products as a symbol that the food is wholesome and lovingly prepared. African Americans have pointed out the racism of the mammy image; it is a white fantasy of servile black women rather than a realistic representation. As with all stereotypes, this one does not do justice to the strength, intelligence, and diversity of African American women.

The maternal purity stereotype has worked to women's advantage by giving them credit for their mothering and by recognizing their contributions to their communities. During times when women have had very little legal and economic power, it is important that they are at least recognized for the important work of rearing children. The image of woman as mother, however, does not easily mesh with the image of woman as high-powered professional. In late twentieth century United States and Canada, people continued to debate whether women can combine the work of rearing children with challenging careers. Conservative politicians often fall back on the maternal purity stereotype to argue that women's natural calling is motherhood and that a woman who works outside the home is "unnatural."

Such politicians cite popular media images such as June Cleaver from the 1950's television series *Leave It to Beaver*, the perfect stay-at-home mother dispensing maternal wisdom to her sons and husband. More liberal politicians (and feminists) argue that the stereotype traps women in their homes and prevents a proper appreciation of men's parenting skills. Both sexes, they contend, are equally fit to rear children and work outside the home. There are fewer media images of women who successfully combine family and work, and fewer still of men who do an equal share of housework and child rearing. One exception was the 1980's American situation comedy *The Cosby Show*, in which the father worked as a doctor and the mother as a lawyer, and both did an equal share of housework and child rearing. This show presented a positive image of a woman balancing career and home, as well as of a man who did not leave the care of the home to his wife.

Hysterical Women. The root of the word "hysteria" refers to women's wombs, and this reproductive organ has long been associated with the stereotype of women as hysterical. Eighteenth and nineteenth century physicians thought that women had floating wombs that caused hysteria and emotional outbursts. In many other historical periods, women have been considered illogical, irrational, less intelligent than men, and prone to emotional outbursts. Even with the modern anatomical understanding that women's wombs are stationary, men and women alike associate the menstrual cycle with moodiness and irritability. Men assume that an angry woman suffers from premenstrual syndrome (PMS) or that so-called female troubles prevent women from achieving emotional stability.

For many people, this stereotype of hysterical women is understood as biological "fact": They believe women are born with less intellectual capability but more emotional volatility than men. Others recognize that children are socialized differently, that male children are discouraged from expressing emotion while female children are encouraged to do so. Females are then denigrated for being softer and weaker even though they have been reared to be exactly that. The stereotype perpetuates itself in that women who have been reared to be emotionally open then rear their daughters the same way, and both men and women suppress emotional expression in sons.

The stereotype of woman as hysterical has very few positive qualities. It is most typically used to deny women opportunities by supporting the argument that their temperament renders them unfit for great challenges. For example, some have argued that women cannot be surgeons, airline pilots, or astronauts because they will crack under the pressure. Although these arguments are specious, they still denied women the opportunity even to try for these jobs for many years. Trailblazing women such as pilot Amelia Earhart, physician Elizabeth Blackwell, and astronaut Sally Ride demonstrated that women can succeed under great pressure, and they opened doors for other women. The success of Harriet Beecher Stowe, who, in *Uncle Tom's Cabin* (1852), wrote the most popular American novel of the nineteenth century, proved wrong the nineteenth century male writers who dismissed their female counterparts as scribbling bluestockings. Men have used the stereotype of the hysterical woman to protect their own privileged position. As Virginia Woolf wrote in *A Room of One's Own* (1929), "when the professor insisted a little too emphatically upon the inferiority of women, he was concerned not with their inferiority, but with his own superiority."

Woman as Shrew. In 1692 in Salem, Massachusetts, nineteen women were hanged or burned at the stake as witches. Women have frequently been connected with witchcraft, typically because of their menstrual cycle and their ability to bear children. In stark contrast to the stereotype of woman as pure, spiritual mother, this stereotype presents an image of women as evil, shrewish, unclean, highly sexualized beings. (This is a compelling example of how stereotypes of the same group can be so generalized as to contradict one another.) According to this stereotype, women are assigned a certain power, though it is a power for evil rather than for good. They are suspected of corrupting children and men, of working against organized religion, and of being unable to control their sexual urges. The witch is typically depicted as an old and disfigured woman, but shrewishness is associated more with character traits than with physical appearance.

Several variants of this stereotype exist. In Orthodox Judaism, all women are considered unclean because of their menstrual cycle, and they must cleanse themselves at the end of their cycle before rejoining their families. Similarly, Catholicism does not consider women holy enough to enter the priesthood. Outside religion, the stereotype of the shrewish woman haunts women in other ways. Women who are assertive in their speech risk being called "strident" and "shrewish." Women who do not restrict their sexuality to marriage are also regarded with suspicion as "sluts," even though the same behavior in their male counterparts is considered manly and appropriate. The threat of being called a shrew keeps many women from expressing their anger and dissatisfaction with the treatment they receive. Like the hysterical woman stereotype, the shrewish woman stereotype is used as a tool to keep women from rebelling.

Literary and media images of the shrewish woman abound. William Shakespeare's Lady Macbeth is a famous example; she chides her husband for not being sufficiently ambitious and goads him into regicide. The popular film *Fatal Attraction* (1987) presented the image of an ambitious career woman who has an affair with a married man and then stalks him when he refuses to leave his wife. (The character of the virtuous wife, incidentally, provides a perfect example of the maternal purity stereotype.) In this film, two stereotypical women do battle, and the pure and moral mother wins in the end. In the realm of American politics, Hillary Rodham Clinton, the wife of President Bill Clinton, also was accused of shrewishness because she is assertive, powerful, and an equal partner with her husband. Clinton's political opponents attacked his wife as "co-president"—a veiled reminder to keep in her place. Hillary Rodham Clinton's response was to move closer to the maternal purity stereotype by concentrating on her daughter and on issues that affect children.

Impact. Stereotypes can be positive, as in the maternal purity example, or they can be negative, as in the hysterical woman and shrewish woman examples. They affect all women by creating generalized images of what women should or should not be. If a woman fails to live up to an idealized stereotype, she will not feel good about herself. If a woman is accused of fitting a negative stereotype such as "shrew," her self-esteem will also be adversely affected. Stereotypes are powerful political tools and have been used to halt the progress of the movement for women's equality. Different stereotypes can be played against one another to create two extreme positions with almost no middle ground. Women may perceive their options in stark terms: Either they are pure and virtuous mothers or they are shrews. Although a certain amount of stereotyping may be inevitable, it is better to question stereotypes of women or any other group. Women constitute 51 percent of the world's population; no stereotype could ever do justice to so large and complex a group of human beings.

—*Donna Eileen Lisker*

See also Art, images of women in; Cult of True Womanhood; Literature, images of women in; Marginalization of women; Motherhood; Psychological theories on women; Self-esteem, women's; Sexual stereotypes; Socialization of girls and young women

Bibliography

Ellmann, Mary. *Thinking About Women*. New York: Harcourt Brace & World, 1968. A humorous and still timely analysis of stereotypes of women and the damage they do.

Faludi, Susan. *Backlash: The Undeclared War on American Women*. New York: Crown, 1991. An incisive analysis of the 1980's as a period of political backlash against the gains of feminism, including several chapters on media images and stereotypes.

Mann, Judy. *The Difference: Growing Up Female in America*. New York: Warner, 1994. Combines personal accounts with broad scholarship to analyze the socialization of females in late twentieth century America.

Millett, Kate. *Sexual Politics*. New York: Avon, 1971. This comprehensive analysis of gender relations provides an excellent introduction to stereotypes of women.

Woolf, Virginia. *A Room of One's Own*. New York: Harcourt Brace, 1929. One of the most important documents in the history of feminism, a witty and highly readable argument for women's economic, legal, and social equality.

Sterilization of women

Relevant issues: Health and medicine, reproductive rights

Significance: As a voluntary procedure, sterilization enables women to prevent further pregnancies; forced sterilizations, however, have terminated the reproductive rights of many women

Sterilization prevents a woman from becoming pregnant through hysterectomy (in which the uterus and sometimes the ovaries and Fallopian tubes are removed) or through tubal ligation (the cutting and/or sealing of the Fallopian tubes); the latter procedure is much more popular as a means of birth control because it has considerably fewer side effects. Many middle-class white women pursue the course of voluntary sterilization, usually through tubal ligation; most of them fully understand the generally permanent nature of this procedure (although, in a few cases, the ends of the tubes can be reconnected at a later time). In the past, a set of standards formulated by the American College of Obstetricians and Gynecologists was followed in determining whether a woman should undergo sterilization. The formula consisted of multiplying the woman's age by the number of children that she had delivered. If the number exceeded 120, doctors were willing to perform the procedure. Many women, however, were turned down by doctors on an arbitrary basis.

While white women have fought for the right to be sterilized as a method of birth control, women of other racial and ethnic backgrounds and women with physical and mental handicaps have battled to prevent being sterilized against their will. Some women who speak little English have given their consent to the procedure without knowing that the surgery would be permanent. In addition, some employers have required women to be sterilized in order to hold jobs that are considered hazardous to themselves or a fetus they might carry (although the same concerns have seldom been extended to men and the damage that might be inflicted on sperm).

In 1973, the plight of two African American girls who were sterilized after being misinformed received attention. The Southern Poverty Law Center filed a class-action complaint on behalf of the girls and poor women who had been involuntarily sterilized. The suit prompted the Health, Education, and Welfare (HEW) Department to create new guidelines, such as a seventy-two-hour waiting period and the stipulation that a woman be told that the procedure is considered permanent. The case brought the active participation of health activists and both radical and socialist feminist organizations in the effort to eradicate sterilization abuse. In 1977, the Committee for Abortion Rights and Against Sterilization Abuse (CARASA) was founded. CARASA, along with other groups, persuaded New York City to strengthen its guidelines and pressured HEW to revise its 1974 policies. The Mexican American Women's National Association (MANA) worked with HEW officials to require doctors and clinics to explain sterilization to each woman in her primary language. The goals and guidelines of CARASA emphasize that women have the right to be protected against forced sterilizations and abortions. During the 1980's, statistics showed that ethnic and racial biases continued to exist, with 16 percent of sterilizations performed on white women, as opposed to 24 percent on African American women and 25 percent on Latinas.

Attention given to sterilization during the 1970's and 1980's markedly improved techniques and safety. Although the total number of voluntary sterilizations has increased, this rise is attributable to the greater number of male sterilizations through vasectomies that has resulted from the publication of clinical studies demonstrating the safety of this procedure. In the late 1980's, vasectomy was proven to be the safest option of sterilization for a couple, whereas female tubal ligation caused two deaths per every 100,000 operations performed.

See also Abortion; Birth control and family planning; Fertility and infertility; Gynecology and obstetrics; Health and medicine; Hysterectomy; Mexican American Women's National Association (MANA); Protective legislation for women; Reproductive rights; Tubal ligation

Stone, Lucy

Stone, Lucy (Aug. 13, 1818, Coy's Hill, near West Brookfield, Mass.—Oct. 18, 1883, Dorchester, Mass.)

Areas of achievement: Civil rights, women's history

Significance: Stone, a gifted orator and activist for the abolitionist movement, was the first woman to speak out full-time for women's rights

"From the first years to which my memory stretches, I have been a disappointed woman. . . . In education, in marriage, in religion, in everything, disappointment is the lot of woman. It shall be the business of my life to deepen this disappointment in every woman's heart until she bows down to it no longer." When Lucy Stone spoke these words in 1855, she had already been traveling the country and speaking out as a full-time women's rights activist for eight years. Educated at Oberlin College, she was initially sparked to political activism by reading the antislavery writings of Angelina and Sarah Grimké.

In the abolitionist movement, Stone met future husband Henry Blackwell, the brother of pioneer female physicians Elizabeth and Emily Blackwell; she retained her birth name upon marriage. At the wedding, Stone and Blackwell read a "Marriage Protest": "This act on our part implies no sanction of, no promise of voluntary obedience to such . . . laws of marriage, as refuse to recognize the wife as an independent, rational being, while they confer upon the husband an injurious and unnatural superiority."

The women's movement split over the Fourteenth and Fifteenth Amendments, which granted citizenship and suffrage to men only; Stone founded the group that chose to support the amendments, the American Woman Suffrage Association (AWSA). This group focused on grassroots activism in the belief that women can gain rights only by changing individual state laws.

See also Abolitionist movement and women; American Woman Suffrage Association (AWSA); Blackwell, Elizabeth; Fourteenth and Fifteenth Amendments; Lucy Stone League; Marriage and marital status; Nineteenth Amendment; Oberlin College; Suffrage movement and suffragists; Women's movement

Suffrage movement and suffragists

RELEVANT ISSUES: Civil rights, social reform, women's history

SIGNIFICANCE: Women—one half of the adult population—were denied the right to vote in Canada until 1918 and in the United States until 1920

England and its North American colonies denied women most rights. They lived in a subordinate position in which society expected them to bear children, keep house, and work alongside men. Because there were property qualifications to vote and women usually did not own land, they rarely voted. In 1832, the English Reform Act specifically disfranchised women, and in 1849, a Reform government in Canada did the same. The United States, however, never passed similar legislation.

Although several women fought their inferior status, some among the first few generations of colonists made only minimal gains. Abigail Adams, wife of Founding Father and second President John Adams, emerged as one of the first to push for equal rights in the political arena. With the coming of the American Revolution and the Declaration of Independence, women in New Jersey took the initiative; they voted from 1790, when a state law granted them suffrage, until 1807, when that right was revoked.

Rise of Reform. Three reform movements, all relevant to woman suffrage, began in the second quarter of the nineteenth century. First came the abolitionist movement, in which several women made notable contributions. The more involved they became, the more women saw a parallel between their situation and that of the slaves. Abolitionism led, at least indirectly, to the women's movement, begun formally with the 1848 Seneca Falls Women's Rights Convention. There, delegates issued their Declaration of Sentiments, a proposal for equal rights patterned after the Declaration of Independence. Resolution number 9—"that it is the duty of the women of this country to secure to themselves their sacred right to the elective franchise"—would remain unfulfilled for seventy-two years.

The temperance (later Prohibition) movement also had a profound effect on woman suffrage. Specifically, the Women's Christian Temperance Union (WCTU) saw the franchise as an ideal way for women to ban liquor, thereby preserving the sanctity of the home. These reform impulses gave way to the Civil War in 1861. At the war's conclusion, the states adopted, in quick succession, three constitutional amendments: The Thirteenth ended slavery; the Fourteenth defined civil rights more clearly; and the Fifteenth granted to freed slaves the franchise. Because they pursued the ballot as a major rallying point (relating it to the natural rights doctrine of the Enlightenment and the Declaration of Independence), women everywhere were jubilant when Congress and the states ratified the Fifteenth Amendment. Joy quickly turned to sorrow when women realized that because it did not mention gender, they would not be allowed to vote. Elizabeth Cady Stanton, who had read resolution number 9 at Seneca Falls, and who favored equal rights for blacks and whites alike, was especially disappointed.

Political Activism. The post-Civil War period saw women become more active in efforts to achieve the right to vote. In 1869, St. Louis attorney Francis Minor married the president of the Missouri Woman Suffrage Association. Three years after the wedding, Minor sued a St. Louis registrar when he refused to permit Virginia Minor to register to vote. When the Minors lost that case, they appealed to the U.S. Supreme Court. Minor based his argument on two premises: the lack of specific enabling legislation denying women the right to vote, and the fact that the Fourteenth Amendment granted states the right to regulate the franchise but not to deny it to anyone. The Supreme Court decided in *Minor v. Happersett* that the franchise was not coextensive with the civil rights guaranteed in the Fourteenth Amendment and that the states could, therefore, refuse women the right to vote, as it did to certain classes of men.

Other women tried to vote as well and with equally dismal results. The most famous of the court cases involved Susan B. Anthony, who had led a group of Rochester, New York, women through the process of registering and voting in the 1872 presidential election. When the case went to court, Anthony based her defense on the Fourteenth Amendment; again the

MILESTONES IN THE HISTORY OF WOMAN SUFFRAGE

1776 Women gain the right to vote in some parts of New Jersey if they own $250 worth of property.

1777 New York's constitution prevents even women who own property from voting.

1807 New Jersey ends the right of women to vote in elections, which had been granted in the 1776 constitution, because many women have been voting for the political enemies of the legislators.

1848 The Seneca Falls Women's Rights Convention is held in New York. Three hundred delegates, including Elizabeth Cady Stanton and Lucretia Mott, attend and pass a resolution favoring woman suffrage.

1849 The Canadian government passes a law barring women from voting in both Upper and Lower Canada.

1866 Elizabeth Cady Stanton runs for Congress as an independent but is defeated.

1866 The American Equal Rights Association is started; it will be the forerunner of woman suffrage organizations.

1867 Susan B. Anthony and Elizabeth Cady Stanton campaign for the adoption of a suffrage amendment in Kansas, but voters defeat the proposal.

1869 Some female abolitionists oppose the Fifteenth Amendment granting black men the right to vote because it does not include suffrage for white and black women.

1869 The women's movement splits with the founding of two suffrage organizations, the American Woman Suffrage Association (AWSA) and the National Woman Suffrage Association (NWSA).

1869 Woman suffrage is adopted in Wyoming Territory merely as an effort to attract settlers, but it becomes established as part of the political culture of the future state.

1870 Utah Territory institutes woman suffrage.

1872 A group of women that includes Susan B. Anthony is arrested for voting in the presidential election.

1872 Victoria Woodhull runs for president of the United States.

1873 Female property owners in British Columbia receive the right to vote, the first women in Canada to do so.

1875 The U.S. Supreme Court rules in *Minor v. Happersett* that while women are citizens, they do not have the right to vote.

1878 The first woman suffrage amendment to the U.S. Constitution (often called the Anthony Amendment) is introduced in Congress; it is defeated in 1887.

1883 The Canadian Woman Suffrage Association forms.

1886 Susan B. Anthony, Elizabeth Cady Stanton, and Matilda Joslyn Gage complete the first three books in the six-volume study *History of Woman Suffrage*.

1889 The Dominion Women's Enfranchisement Association revitalizes the struggle for woman suffrage in Canada.

1890 Wyoming is admitted into the Union and becomes the first state in which women have the right to vote in all elections.

1890 The schism in the women's movement is healed with the creation of the National American Woman Suffrage Association (NAWSA) out of the NWSA and the AWSA.

1893 Woman suffrage is achieved in Colorado.

1896 Utah and Idaho adopt woman suffrage.

1904 The International Woman Suffrage Alliance is created.

1907 The Dominion Women's Enfranchisement Association changes its name to the Canadian Suffrage Association.

1911 The National Association Opposed to Woman Suffrage is founded.

1913 Alice Paul founds the Congressional Union for Woman Suffrage to pursue a more militant strategy for obtaining the vote; it becomes a radical alternative to the more mainstream NAWSA.

1913	A suffrage parade is held in Washington, D.C., the day before Woodrow Wilson's inauguration as president. Eight thousand marchers are watched by half a million spectators, and police allow rioters to disrupt the march.
1914	Woman suffrage is achieved in Montana.
1914	Suffragists stage a march on Washington, D.C., to demand voting rights.
1915	Carrie Chapman Catt becomes the president of the NAWSA, reenergizing this mainstream suffrage group.
1916	Canadian women in Manitoba, Alberta, and Saskatchewan win the right to vote; several other provinces extend the franchise to women during the next several years.
1917	Voters in New York State adopt woman suffrage in an important referendum signaling national approval of the reform.
1917-1918	Alice Paul and other advocates of woman suffrage picket the White House to advance their cause during World War I; some are jailed amid growing controversy over tactics.
1918	Euro-American women in Canada gain the right to vote when the Women's Franchise Act grants suffrage to all women over the age of twenty-one who are British subjects.
1920	The Nineteenth Amendment, establishing the right of women to vote in the United States, is ratified when the Tennessee legislature votes for its adoption.
1920	Members of the NAWSA form a new organization called the League of Women Voters.
1924	American Indian women gain the right to vote in the United States.
1940	The Canadian province of Quebec grants women the right to vote.
1960	American Indian women gain the right to vote in Canada.

court ruled that the amendment did not include the protection of the right to vote.

In the 1870's and 1880's, women pursued the ballot on three fronts: demonstrative, legal, and political. Within a few years, the political realm took precedence. At both the state and federal levels, women lobbied for the vote. While women lobbied in the United States, their counterparts in Canada did the same.

The question became one of tactics. Should women continue to work for the vote state by state, or should the emphasis be placed on securing the ballot at the federal level? This led to a split in organization: Lucy Stone and Henry Blackwell formed the American Woman Suffrage Association (AWSA), which favored a state-by-state approach; and Stanton and Anthony formed the National Woman Suffrage Association (NWSA), which leaned toward forcing action at the federal level. The NWSA became the dominant organization, working toward a constitutional amendment to grant women the vote. In Canada, meanwhile, the dominant organization was the Canadian National Suffrage Association.

State Approval. Between 1870 and 1910, women waged 480 campaigns to win the right to vote; only four ended successfully when Wyoming (1890), Colorado (1893), Idaho (1896), and Utah (1896) granted women the franchise. In the case of Colorado, neither the political machine nor the liquor interests mounted a serious opposition campaign, assuming that the issue would fail.

The early gains were made in states west of the Mississippi. Perhaps the frontier experiences, which made life seem more fleeting and precious, or the lack of established traditions and precedents made these states more flexible relative to women's issues. In any event, the early states granting women the right to vote were all in the trans-Mississippi West. Because the states were in the West, they had smaller populations and therefore less clout. Furthermore, as frontier states, they were seen to be "on the fringe" and somehow less central to the power structure. Canadians had the same experience, in that women in Manitoba, Alberta, and Saskatchewan won the vote two years earlier than did women in Canada generally.

Opposition. At this time, there was no organized opposition to woman suffrage; there were so many enemies that none were needed. As women became more active, so did those opposed to their voting. In 1872, an anti-woman suffrage association formed in Boston, soon followed by organizations in twenty other locations. Then, in 1911, a National Association Opposed to Woman Suffrage appeared in New York, headed by Mrs. Arthur M. Dodge.

Who represented the opposition? Liquor purveyors who feared the possibility of prohibition and textile manufacturers who opposed reform labor legislation led the list. Two other groups included urban political machines, which opposed any attempts to clean up urban government, and Southern males who thought women would work against white supremacy. Despite these differences, all those opposed to woman suffrage agreed to the basic principle that men were rational beings whereas women were governed by their emotions.

A National Agenda. The two U.S. organizations merged in

1890 to form the National American Woman Suffrage Association (NAWSA). The merger coincided with the appearance of the so-called new woman. She had a greater interest in social issues and was more likely to work outside the home. Throughout the nineteenth century, the declining birth rate, the spread of public education, the lengthening of the school year, and the increase in labor-saving devices made it easier for women to pursue other interests. Although many women could engage in volunteer and charitable work, others had, by choice or necessity, to work for wages. The jobs available to women were often only those with long hours, low wages, and poor working conditions. Increasingly, women saw the ballot as necessary to improve their poor economic situation.

The first two decades of the twentieth century witnessed the Progressive Era, when reform became fashionable. At this time, votes for women became simply one of many reforms and by no means the most radical issue. In the Progressive Era, new tactics were applied to woman suffrage. In Boston, for example, young women formed two new organizations, both intended to reach new audiences. The Boston Equal Suffrage Association sent women door to door through neighborhoods and across the state on the interurban trolley to spread the word; the College Equal Suffrage League attracted young women who previously had not been interested in suffrage.

Opponents to woman suffrage were threatened by the idea of women taking part in public life; an artist in 1909 portrays the unthinkable role reversal that would take place on election day if women could vote and, in the righthand corner, imagines the ticket of the "Hen Party": "Mrs. Henry Peck" for president, "Mrs. Wm. Nagg" for vice president, and "Mrs. Thos Katt" for governor. (Library of Congress)

Between 1910 and the outbreak of World War I, women made major gains. First, in the state of Washington, Emma DeVoe, a protégé of Carrie Chapman Catt, ran a district-by-district campaign for the vote, winning by nearly a two-to-one majority. Suffragists then won a narrow victory in California, which was followed by yet another, when Illinois granted women the right to vote in presidential elections. This represented the first such victory east of the Mississippi.

The Final Push. Two years after the Illinois victory, NAWSA elected Catt president. A competent organizer, she had waged several successful state campaigns, including the one in Illinois. She saw low-key lobbying, ladylike behavior, mass action, and effective organization as the means to achieve the vote.

Competing with Catt and the NAWSA was the more militant Congressional Union for Woman Suffrage, formed by Alice Paul and Lucy Burns. Both had lived in England, where they learned to be more radical and more activist. They saw the need for dramatic events to keep the issue in the headlines.

Woman suffrage was a political issue for both the Democrats and the Republicans. This became abundantly clear in 1916, the year in which the nation elected Woodrow Wilson to his second term as president. The Congressional Union for Woman Suffrage organized the National Woman's Party in the twelve states where women had the right to vote. The women reasoned that through bloc voting, they held the power to swing the election. They intended to use that power to prevent President Wilson's reelection for his failure to support national woman suffrage. Catt and the NAWSA had only slightly more support for Wilson. Disappointed with the Republicans' failure to endorse a strong woman suffrage plank, they were hardly more pleased with the Democrats' state-by-state approach to suffrage. Wilson did address the NAWSA, supporting the states' right to choose, but he was ambiguous on his position relative to a constitutional amendment. Suffrage was important, and the NAWSA was the largest voluntary organization in the nation, but Wilson's interests focused on international affairs as he worked to end the war in Europe.

Wilson was not opposed to woman suffrage; in fact, when New Jersey held a referendum in 1915, he publicly stated his support and traveled to his home in Princeton to vote for its passage. In addition to favoring the philosophy of woman suffrage, Catt saw the need for presidential support for the constitutional amendment. At the same time, she saw the need for a plan to get such an amendment ratified by thirty-six states.

While Catt planned her organization's strategy, the National Woman's Party sent pickets to parade before the White House in an attempt to embarrass the president into supporting a constitutional amendment. By the summer of 1917, with the United States involved in World War I, female pickets were

Suffragists, led by Alice Paul, picketed the White House in 1917; they faced jeers, mob violence, and imprisonment. (Library of Congress)

being arrested and sent to jail for obstructing the sidewalks around the White House. The detainees complained of rough treatment and poor conditions. They demanded to be treated as political prisoners. When they went on a hunger strike, the federal government relented, dropping the charges and releasing the women.

The suffrage amendment was clearly a political issue. Former president Theodore Roosevelt urged the Republican National Committee to persuade congressmen to vote for it. He also supported adding women from suffrage states to the Republican National Committee. This type of support, added to behind-the-scenes lobbying of the NAWSA, plus the embarrassment from the negative publicity generated by the arrests of National Woman's Party activists, won a sufficient number of votes. On January 10, 1918, the House of Representatives passed the constitutional amendment. In the Senate, however, even though both political parties supported the amendment and President Wilson spoke on its behalf, in October, 1918, the amendment failed to achieve the two-thirds majority by two votes.

Later in October, with Armistice near in Europe, Wilson urged voters to help him achieve peace by electing Democrats. The NAWSA had other ideas, targeting four antisuffrage senators for defeat. In two of the campaigns they were successful, thus giving them the needed two-thirds majority.

At the request of President Wilson, the Sixty-sixth Congress convened in a special session in May, 1919. The House quickly passed the suffrage amendment, and, after a "states' rights" debate, the Senate too passed the amendment, first introduced by Senator Aaron Sargent of California some forty years earlier. The wording had not changed: "The right of citizens of the United States to vote shall not be denied or abridged by the United States or by any state on account of sex."

To become law, approval of the amendment required thirty-six states. Eleven did so in the first month, and then another eleven states joined the tide in the next several months. By the middle of 1920, thirty-five states had approved the Nineteenth Amendment. Finally, in August, 1920, Tennessee cast the thirty-sixth affirmative vote, thus constitutionally granting women the right to vote. Legend has it that Tennessee's youngest representative cast the deciding "aye" to please his mother, a supporter of Catt.

Women succeeded because of their well-organized lobbying efforts and their highly publicized demonstrations, and because Congress and the states had recently approved another amendment to the Constitution. With the passage of the Eighteenth Amendment, instituting Prohibition, the liquor opposition to woman suffrage was lost.

In Canada, women had earned the right to vote two years earlier than in the United States and had accomplished it without the need to rely on demonstrations for passage.

—*Duncan R. Jamieson*

See also Abolitionist movement and women; American Woman Suffrage Association (AWSA); Anthony, Susan B.; Catt, Carrie Chapman; Civil rights and civil liberties for American women; Civil rights and civil liberties for Canadian women; Congressional Union for Woman Suffrage; Declaration of Sentiments; Fourteenth and Fifteenth Amendments; History of women; *Minor v. Happersett*; National Woman Suffrage Association (NWSA); National Woman's Party; Nineteenth Amendment; Paul, Alice; Seneca Falls Women's Rights Convention; Social reform movements and women; Stanton, Elizabeth Cady; Temperance movement and women; Women's Christian Temperance Union (WCTU)

Bibliography

Buechler, Steven M. *The Transformation of the Woman Suffrage Movement: The Case of Illinois, 1850-1920.* New Brunswick, N.J.: Rutgers University Press, 1986. A case study for Illinois that shows how the suffrage movement grew and changed.

Buhle, Mari Jo, and Paul Buhle, eds. *The Concise History of Woman Suffrage: Selections from the Classic Work of Stanton, Anthony, Gage, and Harper.* Urbana: University of Illinois Press, 1978. An excellent sourcebook.

Flexner, Eleanor. *Century of Struggle.* Rev. ed. Cambridge, Mass.: The Belknap Press of Harvard University Press, 1975. A general analysis of the woman's rights movement from 1800 to the passage of the Nineteenth Amendment in 1920.

O'Neill, William. *Ideas of the Woman Suffrage Movement, 1890-1920.* New Brunswick, N.J.: Transaction, 1989. An excellent account of women and politics in the Progressive Period.

Prentice, Alison, et al. *Canadian Women: A History.* Toronto: Harcourt Brace Jovanovich, 1988. A history of women in Canada, including the suffrage movement.

Scott, Anne Firor, and Andrew MacKay Scott. *One Half the People.* Philadelphia: J. B. Lippincott, 1975. A brief history of the suffrage movement, along with relevant documents.

Superwoman

Relevant issues: Employment, family

Significance: The term "superwoman" may be defined as a woman who successfully combines a promising career, a good family life, and other demands on her time and energy

This term arose in the 1980's as women became more visible in responsible workplace positions. The superwoman seemed able to do everything: rear children, manage the home, and be a charming wife. Observers enviously stated that the superwoman had it all: financial security, a happy home life, and a challenging job. Envy obscured the price that women paid for these achievements. Exhaustion, limited time with children, and marital and work stress often haunted so-called superwomen. They encountered resentment from coworkers and from spouses who were less successful.

The concept of superwoman has great significance for women's issues. First, it is clear that successful women do not "have it all," and there is usually a heavy price to pay for success. For example, delayed childbirth, with accompanying complications, has been characteristic of successful career women. Others have discovered that some men will not tolerate such rivalry from women, and the superwoman may find herself a single mother, adding further stress to her life. Feminists have argued that the myth of the superwoman makes it possible for society to avoid developing structures to help women cope with their many responsibilities.

Thus, the term "superwoman" may be seen as a compliment or as a myth. It also has derogatory overtones, implying an obsessive overachiever.

See also Career vs. homemaker debate; Child rearing; Employment of women; Second shift

Supreme Court rulings on discrimination against women

Relevant issues: Civil rights, law, politics

Significance: Until the 1970's, many rulings of the most authoritative court in the United States served to sustain the unequal treatment of women

The Supreme Court's rulings on discrimination against women date back to the 1870's, but it was not until the 1970's that the Court began to rule in favor of women's legal equality with men. Rulings have consistently reflected prevailing social attitudes about women, which for most of American history restricted women to their "separate sphere" in the home, taking primary care of children and related domestic duties. Outside the home, women were largely confined to occupations akin to domestic work: nursing, teaching, and sewing. The American political and legal system, dominated by men, served to perpetuate this second-class status of women by enacting discriminatory laws that were consistently upheld in state courts and by the U.S. Supreme Court. It was not until the 1970's that the Supreme Court began to strike down state and federal laws that discriminated against women.

Nineteenth Century Decisions. The Supreme Court's first significant decision on women's legal status occurred in 1873, and it remains a classic example of the influence of social attitudes on Court rulings. The case, *Bradwell v. Illinois*, involved the question of whether a state could prohibit an individual who had passed the state bar examination from practicing law solely because she was a woman. The Supreme Court ruled that Myra Bradwell did not have a constitutionally protected right to engage in this profession. In so ruling, one member of the Court explicitly justified the Illinois practice as being consistent with the dictates of God and nature. In a clear expression of prevailing nineteenth century views, Justice Joseph P. Bradley argued that society's interest in family harmony "is repugnant to the idea of a woman adopting a distinct and independent career from that of her husband." Despite this defeat, Bradwell founded the first law journal printed in the West, and she remained active in the cause of women's rights.

Two years later, the Supreme Court was asked to consider whether a woman's right to vote was included as one of the privileges of citizenship in the Fourteenth Amendment. Women were denied the vote in virtually every state, and the Supreme Court ruled in *Minor v. Happersett* (1875) that women did not enjoy a constitutional right to vote, leaving it to individual states to decide. The prevailing view that politics was "man's work" lasted at least until 1920, with the passage of the Nineteenth Amendment.

Twentieth Century Decisions. In the early years of the twentieth century, the Court regularly struck down state laws that interfered with the liberty of employers to run their businesses as they wished but, acting consistently with the idea of separate spheres, made exceptions for laws regulating women's working conditions. In *Muller v. Oregon* (1908), for example, the Court ruled that a law limiting the number of hours that women could work was not unconstitutional because the state had a justifiable interest to protect women, who were deemed to be especially vulnerable to exploitation. The Court maintained this view into the 1940's, when, in *Goes-sart v. Cleary* (1948), it upheld a Michigan law prohibiting a woman from being a bartender unless she was the wife or daughter of a male owner of the bar. The Court was persuaded by the argument that the presence of a female bartender may cause moral and social problems unless a male protector is present.

The Supreme Court's final direct expression of the separate spheres perspective came in a 1961 decision, *Hoyt v. Florida*. Gwendolyn Hoyt was convicted by an all-male jury of second-degree murder in the killing of her unfaithful husband. Hoyt claimed that the jury-selection process of Florida, in which men were automatically placed in the potential juror pool when they registered to vote and women had to request admittance, was discriminatory and resulted in an unsympathetic and biased jury. In a unanimous ruling, the Court decided that Florida's process did not violate the Fourteenth Amendment's equal protection concept and that it was reasonably related to the state's interest in recognizing that women, being at the "center of home and family life," have "special responsibilities" that may be harmed by mandatory jury service.

Legal Equality Begins. The 1960's was a period of great social change that resulted in the erosion of the separate spheres mentality, and the Supreme Court issued a landmark ruling on behalf of women's equality. For the first time, in *Reed v. Reed* (1971), the Court struck down a state law as a violation of the Fourteenth Amendment's guarantee of equal protection under the law. The law by which the state of Idaho automatically chose men over women to administer estates of deceased relatives was ruled to serve no reasonable purpose and to discriminate arbitrarily against women.

The Supreme Court subsequently continued to expand the Fourteenth Amendment's protection of women against laws that rest on outdated gender stereotypes and that serve no important public purpose. In *Frontiero v. Richardson* (1973), the Court struck down a federal policy that required female, but not male, officers in the Air Force to prove that their spouses were financially dependent on them in order to receive benefits. Only four of the justices in this 8-to-1 decision, however, argued that all laws that involved gender discrimination ought to meet the toughest constitutional standard—that discrimination would only be upheld in the rare event that it served a compelling state interest that could not be achieved in a nondiscriminatory way. As a result, it continues to be the case that the Supreme Court will occasionally uphold a gender discriminatory law against a constitutional challenge. For example, in *Kahn v. Shevin* (1974), the Court allowed Florida to give a property tax exemption to widows, but not to widowers, based on the view that women's lesser earning power in their working years made it reasonable for the state to give them a financial break. Similarly, in *Rostker v. Goldberg* (1981), the Supreme Court ruled that the exclusion of women from the military draft did not violate the Constitution.

More favorable Court decisions have been issued in the area of discrimination against women in employment. In 1991, the Court limited the ability of employers to segregate jobs on the basis of sex in *UAW v. Johnson Controls*; in its 1986 decision in *Meritor Savings Bank v. Vinson*, the Court affirmed that sexual harassment on the job is a form of illegal discrimination against women. The Court has also approved some types of affirmative action programs for women, as in *Johnson v. Transportation Agency, Santa Clara County* (1987). The overall trend of Supreme Court decisions in the latter half of the twentieth century was to erect strong, though not impenetrable, legal barriers to prevent discrimination against women.

—Philip R. Zampini

See also Affirmative action; Antidiscrimination laws; Civil rights and civil liberties for American women; *County of Washington v. Gunther*; Employment of women; *Frontiero v. Richardson*; Gender-neutral legislation and gender-based laws; Jury duty; *Meritor Savings Bank v. Vinson*; *Minor v. Happersett*; *Muller v. Oregon*; Protective legislation for women; *Reed v. Reed*

BIBLIOGRAPHY

Hoff, Joan. *Law, Gender, and Injustice: A Legal History of U.S. Women*. New York: New York University Press, 1991.

Lindgren, J. Ralph, and Nadine Taub. *The Law of Sex Discrimination*. 2d ed. St. Paul, Minn.: West, 1993.

Mezey, Susan Gluck. *In Pursuit of Equality: Women, Public Policy, and the Federal Courts*. New York: St. Martin's Press, 1992.

Stetson, Dorothy McBride. *Women's Rights in the U.S.A.* Pacific Grove, Calif.: Brooks/Cole, 1991.

Thomas, Claire Sherman. *Sex Discrimination in a Nutshell*. 2d ed. St. Paul, Minn.: West, 1991.

Surrogate parenting

RELEVANT ISSUES: Family, reproductive rights, science and technology

SIGNIFICANCE: Reproductive technologies have pitted the concerns of infertile women and surrogate mothers against each other, as surrogacy has altered the meaning of motherhood

Surrogate motherhood involves one woman carrying a fetus to term with the understanding that a second woman will become the child's legal mother at birth. The birth mother is termed a "surrogate," standing in for the pregnancy only. Unlike traditional adoption, this relationship is determined prior to conception and involves a legal contract. Typically, the surrogate is impregnated through artificial insemination by the husband of the contracting mother. Thus, the sperm and half the genetic material come from the parents who plan to rear the child, and the contracting father is also the biological father. This arrangement addresses the concerns of infertile women. In some cases, however, fertility problems do not prohibit the use of the contracting mother's ova. Her eggs can be fertilized by her husband's sperm through in vitro fertilization and implanted to the surrogate's uterus. In the first, more common case, the surrogate is clearly the biological mother. In the second case, there are two biological mothers: the woman who provides the ovum and the woman in whose uterus the fetus develops. In the latter case, all the genetic material comes from the prospective child-rearing parents. The difficulties in labeling parents are reflected in the legal, ethical, and social conflicts that have resulted from the use of this technology.

Individual Cases. The most well known legal battle involving surrogate parenthood pitted the rights of Mary Beth Whitehead, a surrogate mother, against the rights of the contracting parents, Elizabeth and William Stern. In this case, Whitehead was the sole biological mother, and William Stern was the biological father. The child was born on March 27, 1986. Despite the surrogate contract, Whitehead changed her mind about the arrangement while she was still in the hospital. In the ensuing legal battle, the child became known as "Baby M" because the two sets of parents were referring to the child by different names. After a court order to turn the child over to the Sterns, Whitehead fled with the child. The child was eventually forcibly removed from her, in the presence of her other children. The Sterns retained custody through the remainder of the legal fight. On February 3, 1988, the State Supreme Court of New Jersey abrogated the surrogacy contract, ruling that the contract involved the illegal purchase of a human being. While the court affirmed Whitehead's parental status, custody was awarded to William Stern; Elizabeth Stern was allowed to adopt Melissa Stern through traditional legal channels. By April of that year, and against the wishes of the Sterns, Whitehead was granted liberal, unsupervised visitation.

Whitehead's case was unusual in that the media were forced to tackle the legal, ethical, and social issues that have concerned health care professionals and social scientists from the outset of surrogate parenthood. Typical media coverage includes an article from the *St. Paul Pioneer Press* of October 13, 1991, which reports that the first American to bear her own grandchildren gave birth to twins on behalf of her daughter. The article quotes participants on the miraculous nature of the event and cites none of the concerns, not only with surrogacy but with inducing pregnancy (by implantation) in a middle-aged woman. In this case, the surrogate was not postmenopausal, but this case raises that potential issue, also not mentioned in the newspaper account.

A case shedding light on the difference between media reporting and reality is that of the pseudonymous Elizabeth Kane, the first American surrogate, who gave birth on November 9, 1980. She did not fight for custody and at first appeared on television talk shows to promote surrogate parenthood. Later, she wrote *Birth Mother: The Story of America's First Legal Surrogate Mother* (1988), in which she claimed that the experience nearly destroyed her and her marriage and seriously harmed one of her own children. She is the founder of the Coalition Against Surrogacy, which has testified before the United States Congress. Her book testifies to many complex issues, many of which did not affect her immediately. These include the stigma for her and her family (which was physically impossible to hide during the pregnancy) and the pain experienced by her children by losing a half sister, with the insecurity engendered by watching their mother cheerfully give her away. Kane forcefully points out that hers was not the only life affected by her surrogacy.

The Response of the Professional Community. It is important not to lose sight of the original impetus for surrogate parenthood. It seems to provide one more solution for infertile couples. Yet criticisms have been expressed from the beginning. In addition to the issues discussed above, many others have been raised.

The nature of the relationship between the two mothers is critical: Do they have a previous relationship, possibly a familial one, or is surrogacy being negotiated through an agency? If so, is it for profit, and what legal protections are involved for all parties? How well are surrogates screened in terms of their physical and mental health? If pay is involved, is money the surrogate's primary, or even major, motivation? (This question raises concerns with exploitation of the economically desperate.) Does the biological mother have the right to change her mind, as with most adoptions, and for how long and with what legal consequences? What happens if a fetus is deformed, miscarried, or stillborn? Does informed consent fully explain to the surrogate the psychological and physical consequences of all possible procedures, from conception through birth? What right do the contracting parents have to control the diet and lifestyle of the pregnant surrogate or to make medical decisions involving the pregnancy or labor and delivery?

Approaches to these issues vary. In the United States, while there have been sharp critics such as Kane and Phyllis Chesler, who oppose surrogacy contracts, the general emphasis has been on compromise and regulation. Efforts have been made to screen potential surrogates and contracting parents and to protect all parties' legal rights. In Canada, by contrast, the feminist National Action Committee on the Status of Women (NACSOW) demanded a legal review of all surrogacy. As a result, the Royal Commission on New Reproductive Technologies conducted a four-year study, begun in 1989, after which it proposed banning all surrogate parenthood and the compulsory licensing of all sperm banks and all clinics using in vitro fertilization or artificial insemination. There were reports, however, of intense infighting among commission members. As Chesler has noted in *Sacred Bond: The Legacy of Baby M* (1988), the emotionality of the issue results from the larger question of what it means to be a mother. —*Nancy E. Macdonald*

See also Adoption; Child custody and visitation rights; Fertility and infertility; In vitro fertilization; Lesbian mothers; Mother-child relationships; Motherhood; Pregnancy and childbirth; Reproductive rights; Single mothers

BIBLIOGRAPHY

Baruch, Elaine Hoffman, Amadeo F. D'Adamo, Jr., and Joni Seager, eds. *Embryos, Ethics, and Women's Rights: Exploring the New Reproductive Technologies*. New York: Harrington Park Press, 1988.

Chesler, Phyllis. *Sacred Bond: The Legacy of Baby M*. New York: Times Books, 1988.

Kane, Elizabeth. *Birth Mother: The Story of America's First Legal Surrogate Mother*. San Diego: Harcourt Brace Jovanovich, 1988.

Rae, Scott B. *The Ethics of Commercial Surrogate Motherhood: Brave New Families?* Westport, Conn.: Praeger, 1994.

Whitehead, Mary Beth, with Loretta Schwartz-Nobel. *A Mother's Story: The Truth About the Baby M Case*. New York: St. Martin's Press, 1989.

Swimming, women in

RELEVANT ISSUE: Sports

SIGNIFICANCE: The continuous struggle of women to gain recognition in international swimming competition has resulted in parity with male swimmers in terms of recognition and participation

Women compete in swimming and diving events in the Amateur Athletic Union (AAU) and its successor, The Athletic Congress (TAC); the National Collegiate Athletic Association (NCAA); the Pan American Games, World, European, and Pacific championships; and the Summer Olympic Games. Until women's sports were assumed by the NCAA in 1981, the principal avenues for female swimmers were local swimming clubs and entrance into the AAU. For example, Tracy Caulkins starred with the Nashville Aquatic Club before capturing forty-eight national AAU titles from 1975 to 1984.

By 1924, more than a hundred NCAA swimming teams had been formed, and national meets were held as tryouts for the Olympic Games. After 1937, these contests were for national titles. Female athletes had no intercollegiate organization to represent them until the Association for Intercollegiate Athletics for Women (AIAW) began to hold national aquatic contests in the 1970's. The first NCAA national championships were held in 1982; the Division I winner was the University of Florida, led by Caulkins, a later Hall of Fame swimmer. NCAA championships for female swimmers have been held annually for Divisions I, II, and III.

No women participated in the first modern Olympic Games at Athens in 1896, but sixteen—ten in golf and six in tennis—competed at Paris in 1900. A milestone for women's sports in general was the acceptance of three women's swimming events at the Olympic Games at Stockholm in 1912. More contests were added in the 1920 Games in Antwerp.

Achievements. An early heroine of North American swimming was Ethelda M. Bleibtrey, who overcame childhood polio to take three Olympic titles in the freestyle races. Another was fourteen-year-old Aileen M. Riggin, a winner in women's platform diving; her victory marked the first of eight straight Olympiads that Americans won this award.

American women demonstrated their dominance in swimming by winning the gold medal in the 400-meter relay for four Olympiads in a row, from 1920 to 1932 at Antwerp, Paris, Amsterdam, and Los Angeles. After the Associated Press (AP) chose American swimmer Helene Madison as Female Athlete of the Year in 1931, she won three gold medals at the Olympic Games the following year. At Berlin, the American team finished third in 1936, as celebrated champion Eleanor Holm was dropped from the team for her heavy drinking on the eve of the Games. After the Olympic Games resumed in 1948 after World War II, American women continued to excel. Diver Pat McCormick won four medals (in 1952 and 1956). American women, led by record-setter Ann Cuneo, won the 400-meter relay race in London (1948); Americans won this event again at Rome (1960), Tokyo (1964), Mexico City (1968), Munich (1972), Montreal (1976), Los Angeles (1984), Barcelona (1992), and Atlanta (1996).

Australian swimmers such as Dawn Fraser and Shane Gould challenged Americans in the 1950's and 1960's, but American Donna de Varona so dominated this sport that she was named by AP and United Press International (UPI) as the World's Outstanding Female Athlete in 1964. She set six world records in the 40-meter individual medley at the Olympics in Rome and Tokyo. Four years later in Mexico City, American swimmers Claudia Kolb and Debbie Meyer won the headlines by winning two and three gold medals, respectively. In the next decade, East German women emerged as champions in women's swimming. At the 1973 World Aquatic championships in Belgrade, Yugoslavia, they shocked the spectators by wearing spandex, nearly see-through swimsuits. When they won ten of fourteen gold medals, other national teams adopted the same apparel. Led by Kornelia Ender, the East Germans won eleven of thirteen titles at the Olympic Games in 1976, as they did four years later at Moscow, where Americans and most other Western nations did not compete.

American Nancy Hogshead won the most medals in swimming at the Los Angeles Games in 1984, although most East European swimmers were absent. Other stars in the 1980's were Caulkins, the winner of numerous Pan American, NCAA, and Olympic titles; and Mary T. Meagher, a master of the butterfly stroke and the winner of three gold medals in Los Angeles and the gold medal in the butterfly at the 1986 World Championships in Madrid. With the political collapse of East Germany in 1989, and more stringent examination of athletes for steroids and other physically enhancing drugs, the German swimmers fell back in international competition.

In the 1990's, Chinese women, led by divers Gao Min and Fu Mingxia, rose to challenge for the world titles in swimming and diving, although Americans continued to be major competitors. At the 1992 Summer Games in Barcelona, Chinese women won six gold medals, Hungarian Krisztina Egerszegi won three, and Americans, led by Janet Evans, won five. The 1996 games in Atlanta proved to be a bit of a surprise. While Fu Mingxia won both diving competitions, the U.S. team dominated the swimming contests, winning gold medals in the relay races. In addition, such team members as Amy Van Dyken, Amanda Beard, and Angel Martino earned several medals in individual competitions.

Americans introduced a new women's event at the Olympic Games in 1984: synchronized swimming. As with gymnastics, swimming was given a contest that emphasized the artistic elements of the sport. American Tracie Ruiz won the solo event in 1994, and Kristen Babb-Sprague (solo) and Karen and Sarah Josephson (duet) won the two contests in 1992, while Canadian women Carolyn Waldo (solo) and Michelle Cameron (duet with Waldo) captured both titles in 1988.

Gertrude Ederle, who in 1926 became the first woman to swim the English Channel. (AP/Wide World Photos)

Another modern American swimming star was Shirley F. Babashoff, who won two Olympic gold and six silver medals (in 1972 and 1976). Her total medals place her second only to Australian swimmer Dawn Fraser, the first swimmer of either sex to win an Olympic gold medal three times for the same event (100-meter freestyle). American Janet Evans won four Olympic titles in freestyle contests (in 1988 and 1992). In 1988 and 1989, she set world records for the 400-, 800-, and 1500-meter races. Chinese swimmer Le Jingyi set astounding world records for both the 50-and 100-meter races at the Swimming World Championships in Rome in 1994. So many Chinese women set world records at this meet that officials questioned whether the use of drugs was a factor. Random drug tests disqualified several Chinese women in 1995, and, perhaps as a result, the Chinese team did not perform up to expectations in the Atlanta Games. The door was opened for such American swimmers as Amy Van Dyken, who took home four gold medals in 1996.

Impact of Women. Perhaps the most astonishing feat in women's swimming came on August 6, 1926, when young Gertrude Ederle of New York City succeeded against all odds to be the first woman to swim the English Channel. This feat surprised the world and, more than any other event, convinced people that women possessed the endurance and strength for many athletic contests. Her record time was surpassed by another American distance champion, Florence Chadwick, the first to swim the channel both ways (in 1950 and 1951). The continued success of American, Australian, East German, Hungarian, and Chinese women in world swimming and diving competitions has enabled women to enjoy a reputation in this sport that is the near equal of male athletes; for example, twelve American swimmers and divers have won the Sullivan trophy for the leading amateur athlete of the year, five of whom were women. Among the world athletes chosen for inclusion in the "Sports Who's Who" for the *1995 Information Please Sports Almanac*, fourteen of the twenty-four swimmers were women.

—John D. Windhausen

See also Association for Intercollegiate Athletics for Women (AIAW); Olympic Games, women in the; Sports, women in

Bibliography

Falla, Jack. *NCAA, the Voice of College Sports: A Diamond Anniversary History, 1906-1981.* Mission, Kans.: National Collegiate Athletic Association, 1981.

Meserole, Mike, ed. *The 1995 Information Please Sports Almanac.* Boston: Houghton Mifflin, 1995.

Porter, David L., ed. *Biographical Dictionary of American Sports: Basketball and Other Indoor Sports.* New York: Greenwood Press, 1989.

Wallechinsky, David. *The Complete Book of the Olympics.* New York: Viking Press, 1984.

Harriet
Tubman

Tailhook scandal

Date: September, 1991

Place: Las Vegas, Nev.

Relevant issues: Sex and gender, war and the military

Significance: One of the largest and most infamous incidents of sexual harassment in the U.S. Navy, this scandal provided a major impetus for a review of the treatment of women in the military

The Tailhook Association was founded in 1956 for reunions of naval aviators. It expanded in 1963 to include lectures and programs dealing with topics in aviation. Although the association was a private organization, these programs were supported directly and indirectly by the Navy. In 1991, the annual three-day symposium of the association was held in the Las Vegas Hilton Hotel and was accompanied by rowdy partying, as was the norm at these meetings. This behavior reflected what has been referred to as a "flyboy culture" as well as the macho self-image of naval aviators. Activities included performances by strippers, explicit exhibitions and films, heavy drinking, and bawdy revelry, including the shaving of women's legs and the gauntlet, a hallway lined with men groping and fondling women who were herded into the corridor.

Lieutenant Paula Coughlin, a helicopter pilot and admiral's aide, was one of the many women subjected to the gauntlet and other abuses. Fearing gang rape, she escaped and fled the party floor. She complained to her superior, Rear Admiral John Snyder, who dismissed her complaint; he was later removed from command. Coughlin persisted, and, after much stonewalling and closing of ranks, several investigations were held. Eventually, the Pentagon's inspector-general identified eighty-three women who complained of being molested, but the investigation was frustrated by a "wall of silence." Hundreds of naval and marine officers were involved in or were aware of the assaults. Some received reprimands and other administrative punishments, but none was convicted of legal wrongdoing.

The publicity generated by these investigations led to the resignation of several senior officers, as well as of Navy Secretary H. Lawrence Garrett in June, 1992. Coughlin successfully sued both the Tailhook Association and the Hilton Hotel. After appeals, she was finally awarded nearly six million dollars in punitive and compensatory damages in 1995. She resigned from the Navy in April, 1994, because of the retaliation that she endured from male colleagues for going public with her story.

This scandal led to congressional inquiries on the roles and problems of women in the military. Increased penalties for sexual harassment as well as changes in military training and increased sensitivity to women's concerns were the direct results of the Tailhook scandal. The Navy acknowledged that the conditions that produced the incident were attributable to a failure in leadership and to a military culture that treated women as second-class citizens. Thus, the scandal was a factor in such changes as increased Navy recruitment of women, their integration on combat ships, and an order allowing women to fly combat aircraft.

See also Military, women in the; Military officers, women as; Sex object; Sexism; Sexual harassment

Take Back the Night

Date: First organized in 1976

Relevant issues: Crime, social reform

Significance: This tradition of marches and meetings spreads the awareness of rape and other violence against women to a wide audience

Take Back the Night is a feminist tradition comprising marches and rallies to protest violence against women. Take Back the Night grew out of a meeting of the International Tribunal on Crimes Against Women (ITCAW) held in Brussels, Belgium, in 1976. Women from all over the world came together at ITCAW to give testimonials about incidents in which they had been victimized. They realized that they were being victimized simply because they were female. After the meeting, the women marched through a small town with candles, symbolically united to stop sexual assault. Since then, Take Back the Night marches have been organized worldwide and are usually held once a year. The goal is to raise the consciousness of the public about the atrocities being committed daily against women. Take Back the Night attempts to fight the fear of sexual violence, especially rape, and the marches are used to promote rape prevention and male responsibility. Take Back the Night supports those who have survived such violence. The march is an assertive commitment to ending further violence against women and a safe forum where the collective outrage of women can be expressed. A major part of the rally occurs when the microphone is left open to allow participants to give testimonials about their own experiences.

See also Consciousness-raising; Empowerment; Rape; Rape victims, treatment of; Self-esteem, women's; Sexism; Sexual harassment; Violence against women

Talk shows

Relevant issues: Arts and entertainment, psychology

Significance: In a frantic scramble for ratings points and financial success, television and radio talk shows seize on women's issues

Hosts on television and radio talk shows present a wide variety of topical issues. Daytime talk hosts, in particular, emphasize women's issues, ranging from obscene phone calls to genital mutilation, hoping that these stimulating topics will boost ratings.

Early Days. Long before television, talk was a staple during the early years of radio, the 1930's. Besides the news, male commentators interpreted news events while females provided health, beauty, and domestic advice. Talk personalities, such as Walter Winchell from New York and Louella Parsons from Hollywood, featured "fluff" talk with film stars and popular entertainers.

When television eclipsed radio during the early 1950's, it logically borrowed the commentary and fluff traditions of radio because they fit any time slot and were economical. Writers, actors, and promoters willingly appeared for minimum union wages to publicize their new films, books, or songs. The National Broadcasting Company (NBC) offered the first successful nationwide talk shows, both daytime and nighttime.

Television Talk. Male hosts dominated the talk-circuit during the 1950's and 1960's. Mike Wallace introduced the now-familiar aggressive style of grilling guests; satirists Henry Morgan and David Frost entertained; and David Susskind and William F. Buckley, Jr., held the high ground by exploring controversial politics. Female hosts were few, used primarily as decor or relegated to the kitchen to discuss needlepoint or household chores. One cut above such fare was Virginia Graham's show *Girl Talk*, which often featured journalists and politicians.

Donahue, hosted by Phil Donahue, developed a different spin for the talk format during the 1970's, focusing on women's issues and asking a studio audience to make moral judgments about his guests. Using issues such as women's insecurities, abuse, inadequacy, sexuality, and self-improvement, Donahue artfully wrung out the dramatic possibilities as he revealed his guest's most intimate relationships with others.

The 1970's saw more female hosts on talk shows. Barbara Walters not only appeared on *The Today Show* but first hosted *Not for Women Only* (1971-1979), centering on wide-ranging issues, from counterculture beliefs to the effects of divorce on children. Dr. Joyce Brothers and Dr. Ruth Westheimer dispensed advice on morals and sex. Two sharp journalists, Joyce Davidson and Barbara Howar, showcased governmental and health care problems on *For Adults Only*.

Of all the new talk host personalities of the 1980's, Oprah Winfrey—overweight by television standards, unpretentious, and African American—seemed the least likely to succeed. Nevertheless, Winfrey's show posted top ratings. Critics extolled her outspokenness, her no-nonsense approach to controversy, and her irreverent humor. They recognized Winfrey's ability to commiserate with the heartbreaking stories told primarily by her female guests, while including at the same time her own tearful confessions of abuse and abandonment during her earlier life. A contender for Winfrey's throne at the time was Sally Jesse Raphael, a former therapist who explored such issues as working women, welfare queens, and single mothers.

Cynics labeled the talk shows of the 1990's as "ambush television," in which hosts humiliated their guests in front of millions of people and deliberately set off confrontations, encouraging guests to fight and curse to overheat their audiences. Both male hosts (for example, Jerry Springer and Maury Povich) and female hosts (for example, Ricki Lake and Rolanda Watts) engaged in shock, titillation, and the weird, hoping viewers would stay tuned with the prospect of violence. *The Jenny Jones Show* was a case book of how a talk show's desperate search for ratings produced dire consequences. The first year of Jones's show was sweet and light, leading to dismal ratings. When she changed her format to exploitation and embarrassment, her ratings increased. Her efforts backfired in 1995, however, when a former male guest was charged with murdering another, allegedly in part because he had been humiliated on the show.

Not all talk shows of the 1990's offered trash. Female commentators contributed to the political and social debates on the Sunday morning shows *Face the Nation*, *Meet the Press*, and *This Week with David Brinkley*. Cable television provided a public forum for women's issues as well, including the all-female *To the Contrary*. *The McLaughlin Group*, a news analysis program, intertwined conservative issues and values with humor. A media report in 1993, however, reported that male hosts dominated these prestigious shows; of the 137 political talk show hosts, 113 were men (about 83 percent). Women's groups strongly urged equal gender representation.

Political candidates of both genders during the 1990's recognized the value of talk shows. On the traditional networks, they could only get their messages across in thirty-second sound bites. On talk shows, however, candidates—such as Bill Clinton, George Bush, and Ross Perot during the 1992 presidential campaign—could engage in dialogue with potential voters.

Talk Radio. Music, the dominant format of the 1950's and 1960's, gave way in the 1970's to "topless radio," a sort of radio-as-therapy. As a first, Bill Ballance hosted "Feminine Forum," a call-in show about marital discord, unwanted pregnancies, and autoerotic fixations. Because the program featured taboo subjects, federal regulators cited stations carrying the program for indecency. "Psychological radio" took its place, with Dr. Toni Grant dispensing general diagnoses rather than providing individual counseling. During the 1980's, approving audiences listened to "shock jocks" (such as Don Imus and Howard Stern), who provided abusive humor and raw language. Larry King's liberal bent and soft-style interviews were offset by Rush Limbaugh's put-downs of liberals and feminists. Such shows had estimated audiences of more than twenty million per day on more than six hundred radio stations nationwide.

As with television talk shows, male hosts dominated the radio air waves. Only a few women managed to break through, such as Leslie Marshall, who was recognized as the first female host of a nationally syndicated issue-focused radio talk show (1992). A year later, the first all-female radio talk team,

"The Brooks Daniels and Roberta Gale Show," introduced a high-energy, raucous, but intellectual discussion of substantive issues. Nanci Donnellan, known as the "Fabulous Sports Babe," became the female sports host on national radio in 1993, after having proven her extensive knowledge of sports to callers and managers of radio stations.

Critics and radio insiders agreed that talk radio became more professional during the 1990's as its influence with the general public increased. For example, Ann Lewis, an activist for Planned Parenthood, extolled talk radio because it empowered ordinary women with a political voice during the 1994 elections, providing information and encouraging active participation.

Impact. Detractors point out the defects of talk shows: the mixing of important issues with mere entertainment, the simplistic handling of complex topics, and talk shows' appeal of voyeurism, titillation, and melodrama to increase ratings. The defenders, however, believe that talk shows provide interactive or participatory experiences for their audiences, information, and a greater concern about social and political issues.

Feminists in particular make an important point about talk shows: Women's issues are significant not only to the women in the audiences but also in sensitizing men to these issues. If women are to succeed in achieving parity with men in the workplace, more discussions of these issues are needed.

—Richard Whitworth

See also Advertising; National Association of Media Women; Stereotypes of women; Television, women in

BIBLIOGRAPHY

Brown, Mary, Ellen, ed. *Television and Women's Culture*. London: Sage Publications, 1990.

Levin, Murray. *Talk Radio and the American Dream*. Lexington, Mass.: Lexington Books, 1987.

Livingstone, Sonia, and Peter Lunt. *Talk on Television: Audience Participation and Public Debate*. London: Routledge, 1994.

Munson, Wayne. *All Talk: The Talkshow in Media Culture*. Philadelphia: Temple University Press, 1993.

Sather, Edgar, and Catherine Sadow. *Talk Radio*. Redding, Mass.: Addison-Wesley, 1987.

Teaching and teachers

RELEVANT ISSUES: Education, employment

SIGNIFICANCE: This occupation has traditionally been open to women, although with certain expectations and restrictions involving personal life and conduct

History. During America's beginnings, women were to have one goal in life—to marry. Those unfortunate enough to remain single had to find some way of supporting themselves. Many single women, whether unmarried or widowed, turned to a career in teaching.

Dame schools were run by older, respected women of the community. They were especially common during the Revolutionary War, when it would have been dangerous to keep other schools open. Pupils recited and read from the Bible while the dame completed her household chores. Both boys and girls were taught to sew and knit. Wealthy families and plantation owners recruited young women to serve as governesses. These governesses were expected to take care of the children, teach them manners, and ensure that the young girls acquired the skills necessary to run a home.

Women constitute the majority of kindergarten and elementary school teachers. (BmPorter/Don Franklin)

As settlers moved west, towns were created, and more teachers were needed. Since teaching skill was measured by the ability to keep order (through physical force, if necessary), strong men were preferred. Women were allowed to teach the younger children but were not given responsibility in academic areas. Where populations were widely dispersed, an itinerant teacher might be hired. A woman in this job would be required to ride from three to twenty miles a day to her schools.

In later years, single women were boarded by families who "subscribed" to specific schools. The teacher served as groundskeeper, janitor, and cook, receiving four dollars a month for her efforts. Taxes were not available to support a school, so families with children provided the building, housing for the teacher, and firewood. It was considered dangerous for a woman to live alone, so female teachers had to make do with attic rooms and poor food.

Teachers had to adhere to strict community expectations if they wished to keep their jobs. Female teachers were to be unmarried, uninterested in becoming married, and plain in dress and adornment. They were to use no alcohol, tobacco, or foul language. They had to be active church members and keep the schoolhouse in good repair. There was little time for or tolerance of frivolous behavior under these rules.

Women Who Changed Education. In 1897, Margaret Haley decided that certain teaching conditions needed to be improved. She and a group of primary school teachers formed the Chicago Teachers Federation. They brought suit against public utilities to force payment of taxes. Next, they lobbied the board of education to use the added tax income to raise teacher's salaries. When the pension plan was shown to be unsound, Haley tackled that problem as well.

Other women, seeing the needs of the children around them, championed "child-centered" causes. Susan Blow worked to provide kindergarten as a part of the public school system in St. Louis, Missouri. She wanted young children to have a successful, cheerful start to their school careers. Instead of a gloomy, grim classroom, she provided a colorful environment filled with sunshine and plants.

Mary McLeod Bethune had no proper schooling available for her son, so she opened her own school for black children. She convinced the white community leaders of Daytona, Florida, to support her program, paving the way for equal education for all races.

Martha McChesney Berry was concerned about the underprivileged children of the Georgia mountains. Her actions led to a vocational boarding school for children too poor to attend anywhere else. She was a pioneer in the effort to ensure opportunities for all economic groups.

Women have also shaped the curriculum presented within the classroom. Helen Parkhurst wanted children to take responsibility for their learning. Rather than using recitation and rote memorization, she reorganized elementary school lessons into "units" or "contracts." Children selected the areas that interested them and "contracted" to complete their lessons.

Secondary curriculum received a new perspective when Alice Keliher and the Commission on Human Relationships began looking at adolescent needs and interests during the 1930's. Keliher helped in the movement to develop a "core curriculum" to provide the skills that high school graduates would need and appreciate in their adult lives.

Modern women continue to make changes in education by working locally, in state leadership, or in national positions. On the local level, teachers work within their buildings, school districts, and communities to improve the quality of education and teaching conditions. They serve on salary committees and as curriculum chairs, and they work as liaisons with community agencies that oversee disadvantaged children. On the state level, teachers may serve in a position of leadership affecting the education of thousands of students. Dr. Grace McReynolds, a Missouri educator for forty-seven years, worked as State Director of Curriculum. She and her colleagues formed a list of key skills and competencies that shaped the state's education for elementary and secondary students.

On the national front, Mary Hatwood Futrell worked for improvements in education during her six years as the first African American woman to be named president of the National Education Association (NEA). Futrell, a high school business teacher, led her organization to the two million-member mark, exposed political leadership's lack of funding for drug education, and brought attention to the dropout frequency of linguistic minorities. Her efforts helped achieve her vision of national security—a well-educated public.

The Characteristics of Teaching. Teachers spend an estimated ten to thirty-one hours a week on unpaid school-related activities. They are expected to oversee lunchrooms, playgrounds, and bathrooms. They must be well-instructed in the use of telephones, televisions, computers, and copy machines. They must satisfy the demands of parents, principals, and school boards while being sensitive to the needs and abilities of their students. They must be skilled mediators capable of stopping fights and maintaining order in the classroom.

As families have changed, so have the students inhabiting the classrooms. Some are desperately ill with acquired immunodeficiency syndrome (AIDS) or cancer. Others have suffered physical or sexual abuse at the hands of a family member. Some students are pregnant, and others are involved in alcohol and drug use. Young children may exhibit learning difficulties because of the drugs that their mothers took during

BASE SALARIES OF TEACHERS IN ELEMENTARY AND SECONDARY SCHOOLS, PUBLIC AND PRIVATE (1988)

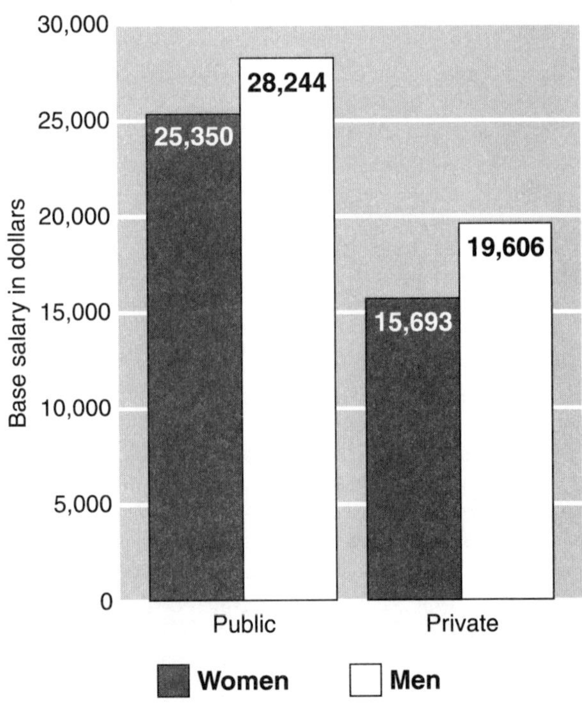

Source: Bureau of the Census

pregnancy or the drugs that saved their lives as premature babies. Some are homeless, and some do not speak English. Several may be mentally challenged, and others are emotionally disturbed.

In elementary schools, the majority of these challenges occur in classrooms staffed by women. In 1987, there were 2,250,000 teachers in the United States. The one million secondary teachers were evenly split between men and women. The remaining elementary staff was 70 percent female.

Although salaries in teaching have lagged behind those in other professions, salary schedules have been adopted to guarantee equal pay for equal work regardless of gender or teaching assignment. Extra-duty pay remains more accessible to secondary teachers, with coaches of boys' sports receiving the highest compensation. Teachers receive other benefits that may include pensions, paid sick leave, personal leave, and various types of insurance. Many school districts provide reimbursement for college tuition to encourage continuing education. Other teachers participate in "career ladder" opportunities, which enable them to earn a lump sum for completing an agreed upon program of activities or study.

—Suzanne Riffle Boyce

See also Education of women; Employment of women; Pioneer women; Single women

BIBLIOGRAPHY

Casey, Kathleen. *I Answer with My Life: Life Histories of Women Teachers Working for Social Change*. New York: Routledge, 1993.

Fleming, Alice Mulcahey. *Great Women Teachers*. Philadelphia: J. B. Lippincott, 1965.

Harris, Sherwood, and Lorna B. Harris. *The Teacher's Almanac*. New York: Facts on File, 1988.

Raven, Susan, and Alison Weir. *Women of Achievement: Thirty-five Centuries of History*. New York: Harmony Books, 1981.

Smith, Carney Jessie. *Epic Lives: One Hundred Black Women Who Made a Difference*. Detroit: Visible Ink Press, 1993.

Technology

RELEVANT ISSUES: Education, employment, science and technology

SIGNIFICANCE: Technology has played an important role in women's lives, in the contributions of female scientists and in the impact of innovation on women's issues

The word "technology" has had many meanings since its earliest use in the seventeenth century. Based on a Greek word signifying art, skill, or craft, it came to mean the tools, machines, expertise, and procedures people use to manipulate the materials of their environment to achieve practical goals. Unfortunately, the term is seldom used with precision, and definitions of technology in the literature range from its popular meaning as synonymous with machines to its scholarly use, by Charles Singer and others in the monumental work *A History of Technology* (1954-1984), as "how things are commonly done or made and what things are done or made."

All these definitions have weaknesses. The identification of technology with inventions restricts its meaning too narrowly, since it neglects skills and processes, and the view that technology is all humans do and learn is too broad, since most scholars would not want to include the making of laws, for example, as part of technology. Many dictionaries define technology as "applied science," but this description has serious flaws because it ignores technology's long history when inventors without any scientific understanding developed numerous and sophisticated tools, machines, and processes.

Redefining Technology. In the twentieth century, feminists shifted this traditional discussion about the meaning of technology to new ground. They pointed out that these classic definitions are rooted in male experiences of various crafts, industries, and technical professions. Critics of technology, such as Jacques Ellul and many feminists, have explained that all societies differ in the quantity and quality of their technologies, the access that various individuals have to these technologies, and the purposes of various people in using them. Social, political, religious, and economic forces often foster some types of technology in a particular culture while inhibiting others. Modern feminists have been concerned with the ways in which a society's pattern of development and use of technology may reinforce a patriarchal ideology. Using their experience of sexual oppression, these feminists have criticized the male understanding of technology as the mastery of nature, since this view has led to the exclusion of women from many technical fields and to the excessive depletion of natural resources and the massive production of pollution and hazardous waste.

The early writings of women about technology sought to justify their participation in scientific and technical fields by asserting that they could be the equal of men in these traditional male pursuits. Because these early feminists had to combat biological determinism (the view that biology predetermines differences between human beings), they sharply distinguished sex from gender. A person is born male or female (sex), but he or she becomes masculine or feminine (gender). Certain sexual differences are programmed into each person's genes, but society basically determines gender roles. The meaning of masculinity and femininity may vary in different societies and in different historical periods, whereas the biological categories of male and female are generally regarded as fixed. Feminists could therefore use gender to contest the misuse of sexual differences in technology, which many in the area saw as a masculine world that women rarely entered.

Since the seventeenth century, women interested in increasing the participation of their sex in technical fields have had to contend with great differences between male and female levels of achievement in invention and engineering. For example, both in the United States and Canada, patents have been dominated by men, with women's share varying from a tiny fraction of 1 percent to about 3 percent. Male engineers have generally outnumbered their female counterparts by about a hundred to one. While these statistics make it clear that men have dominated patents and technological fields, the reasons for this state of affairs have been ardently debated. Those scholars strongly espousing biological determinism claim that anatomy is destiny, and so society is essentially unable to eradicate these inequalities. They explain the paucity of female inventors through an inherited inability to invent that is genetically built into the female sex. Some nineteenth century scientists even argued that educating women in science and technology would impair their fertility. As recently as 1982, I. I. Rabi, a Nobel laureate in physics, maintained that women are "unsuited to science" and technology because they have the "wrong" brain and nervous system.

Feminists unanimously reject this crude biological determinism. Furthermore, they assert that, given equal education and equal opportunity, as well as a revision of the masculinist understanding of technology, women will succeed at technology in the same numbers as men. These feminists believe that inventive ability is a human, not a sex-linked, trait and that the historical disparity in inventiveness between men and women has been the result of a sexual division of labor that hindered women's opportunities to invent and participate in various technical fields. When technology comes to be understood as something that people (rather than men alone) do, then technology's face will become both feminine and masculine.

While feminists generally reject biological determinism, they are divided about the degree and depth of gender differences. Some argue that genetic and social factors influencing male and female development are so inextricably intertwined that it is extremely difficult to discover what patterns of male and female behavior are determined by nature (genes) or by nurture (the environment and culture). Others hold that emphasizing certain differences between the sexes can lead to valuing women above men or to gaining special protection for women in particular jobs or situations. Still others declare that gender is an arbitrary social construct mainly used in the past to keep women subordinate and powerless. Evelyn Fox Keller has pointed out the pitfalls of these extreme views. Those who glorify difference to the denigration of men are prone to romanticize women; for example, they may believe that women's sensitivity to the interrelatedness of all life will humanize technology and save the planet from decline. On the other hand, those who believe deeply in a woman's ability to occupy any social role that she might desire are prone to ignore the ineradicable connections between biology and the brain's and body's functions in both men and women.

Some scholars think that the way to resolve these differences between groups of feminists and between feminists and biological determinists is through science. For example, sociobiologists claim that observations of human ancestors among lower animals reveal that males are rewarded for being aggressive, whereas it is profitable for females to be discriminating. In the nature-nurture debate, sociobiologists tend to emphasize the nature of men and women as determined by their genetic inheritance and to defend the sexual division of labor in technical fields.

A different interpretation of sex roles in technology is found in the work of such social scientists as Bruno Bettelheim and Erik Erikson. Bettelheim believed that engineering problems had no characteristically male or female solutions. For example, dams built by male and female engineers will show no differences attributable to the sex of their creators, though these engineers will experience distinctively male and female emotions about their work. Erikson, on the other hand, used observations on how young children played at building various structures to corroborate the traditional view that men and women are innately drawn to different areas of work. Specifically, he discovered that given blocks, more than two-thirds of the girls had built "peaceful interiors," whereas more than two-thirds of the boys had built bold structures (for example, towers) that they liked to destroy. Erikson interpreted these results as showing that women are skilled in solving problems that unfold within "inner space," whereas men are adept in exploring "external space."

Feminists, however, have criticized Erikson's views as vague and confused. Inner and external space are demonstrably ambiguous terms as they relate to women's roles in science and technology. For example, it is certainly ridiculous (and contrary to fact) to state that women will tend to study particles in an atom's interior (nuclear physics) whereas men will concentrate their efforts on particles that exit the atom (radioactivity). Furthermore, feminists question whether observations of the constructions of little boys and girls actually tell anything about the nature of men and women; more likely, they are probably revealing something about the nature of society.

In defending his espousal of a complementarity of roles for men and women, Erikson emphasized that he did not intend these differences as prejudicial to women's advancement; they were simply expressions of what it means to be fully human in two equipotent ways. Yet feminists might counter: What technological roles are suitable to the special genius of women, and who defines them? In their long history on this planet, women have found that declarations of difference have often been converted into conditions of inequality. These experiences explain why many feminists have battled mightily to invalidate what they see as the myth of the feminine mind and to affirm the radical equality of men and women in all areas of life, but especially in cognitive abilities.

Some scientists have attempted to resolve this debate through testing boys and girls at various stages of their development. For feminists, even these tests have not been able to escape the normative conventions of white middle-class men. Men in positions of power have been influenced by these test results in their assessments of the behavior and performance of boys and girls. For example, tests for aptitude in mathematics, science, and technology have generally shown that males score higher on these tests than females, and these results have been used to justify the small numbers of women in scientific and technical fields. Yet, when the results of mathematical aptitude tests are controlled for the number of mathematics courses taken in high school, most, if not all, of these differences disappear. Furthermore, social scientists have not observed differences in the mathematical interest or performance of very young boys and girls. Other studies show that timely encouragement during adolescence was extremely important in creating and sustaining mathematical, scientific, and technological interest in girls, but girls are far less likely than boys to receive this encouragement.

Although this debate continues, it has become clear that neither the assertion nor the denial of differences between the sexes can obtain equity for women in scientific and technical fields. The denial of differences would mean the repudiation of an immense body of well-established scientific research in evolutionary biology, brain chemistry, twin studies, and many other fields. On the other hand, the affirmation of differences has problems. Difference emphasizes duality, and, traditionally, technology and "the feminine" have been socially constructed in opposition to each other. Technology's traits have been generally seen to mean the objective, logical, dispassionate, mechanistic, and powerful, whereas the feminine has been seen to mean the subjective, emotional, passionate, organicist, and passive. This radical dualism implies that women as a class will create a different (or "feminine") kind of technology, whereas in fact female engineers have not performed significantly different types of technological work than men, when they have been given the chance. This radical dualism also ignores the modern view that technology, in its laws and evaluation, is subject to social forces. The norms of society inevitably influence the problems that engineers choose to solve, the methods that they use to solve them, even the answer that they find satisfying.

Evelyn Fox Keller has argued that the exclusion of women from technology has been rooted in an interpretation of technology as objective, universal, mechanical, and impersonal, and thus as incontrovertibly masculine, but such a definition sustains and is sustained by a historical and modern division of technical work along the lines of sex. This deeply ingrained division has led to the denigration of an excluded set of values dismissively labeled "feminine." The only way to transcend this dilemma, Keller believes, is through a recognition of the enormous variability, both individual and cultural, that exists among actual men and women. An openness to this variability between different men and women and between different interpretations of masculinity and femininity, which goes far beyond the biological, will undoubtedly change technology. These changes, drawing on the talents of a previously neglected multitude, will certainly be for the betterment of all people.

Women in Technology. Despite real gains, exclusion of women from scientific and technical training remains a problem both in the United States and in Canada. To resolve these difficulties, many women have pursued a policy of integration (rather than separation). Female engineers tend to put their faith in the claims that science and technology are genuinely objective and neutral. Therefore ability and hard work should lead to success, for just as racial, religious, and political discrimination should have no place in scientific and technological fields, neither should sexual discrimination. Women with the appropriate technical ability and training should have access to technological jobs in the same way that men do.

A good example of this integrative policy is Dr. Lillian Gilbreth, who has been called "America's first lady of engineering" and "the best known woman engineer in history." One of her major contributions was the use of time-and-motion studies to show companies how to budget time, human energy, and money to increase industrial efficiency and production. With her husband, Frank Gilbreth, another pioneer in scientific management, she founded a company, Gilbreth, Inc., to advance their ideas and discoveries, but his untimely death in 1924 left her to manage this company by herself for nearly fifty years. Her book *The Psychology of Management* (1914) has been called "the most important in the history of engineering thought."

During the interwar period, Canada had no female engineers of the stature of Gilbreth and no inventors of the productivity of Beulah Louise Henry ("the lady Edison"). Nevertheless, changes came to Canada, for with the increase of American investment in Canadian companies after World War I came advanced technology and some of the advanced ideas and attitudes of American women. For example, some Canadian women in technical work began to insist that qualified women should be promoted under the same standards as men. World War II continued the stimulation of Canada's technology, and, by 1945, farms, mines, shipyards, and factories were highly mechanized. During World War II, Canadian women, like their American counterparts, took over many technical jobs that had previously been almost solely the domain of men, though at lower wages. At war's end, the incentives attracting women into technical work were withdrawn, and married women were encouraged to leave the labor force. Many women remained, however, and their numbers continued to grow. By 1951, Canadian women made up 22 percent of the total labor force, and, by 1981, this number was 41 percent. Despite these increases, serious inequalities in pay and the relative position of women remained. In 1967, the Canadian government set up the Royal Commission on the Status of Women to examine the concerns that the new women's movement in Canada was bringing to public attention. In its 1970 report, the commission made 167 recommendations relating to the just treatment of women in the workplace, and some of these applied to gaining equity for women in technical enterprises and invention. In the late 1970's, Canadian women formed various national groups, including Women in Science and Engineering. These groups, which consisted mainly of women from the English-speaking provinces, encountered problems with French Canadian women, who tended to align themselves on linguistic rather than national grounds. Nevertheless, both the French and the English groups had the same goal—to eliminate sexism in all areas of science and engineering, including education and the workplace.

By the 1990's, women were beginning to make inroads into such predominantly male fields as chemical engineering. (BmPorter/Don Franklin)

In the United States, the Society of Women Engineers had been founded in 1949, considerably earlier than its kindred group in Canada. Because many people perceived engineering as a highly masculine field, female engineers faced far higher hurdles than those faced by women in other professions. A growing number of women did succeed in becoming engineers, but they had to be particularly persistent, intelligent, determined, and shrewd. This persistence characterized such women as Grace Murray Hopper, who was one of the most important pioneers of the modern computer. During World War II, the Navy introduced her to the computer via the Mark I and Mark II digital machines. After the war she became a research fellow in engineering science and applied physics at the Computation Laboratory of Harvard University, where she created the first operating programs for the Mark I. Later, at Eckert-Mauchly Computer Corporation, Hopper helped develop a group of programs on tape for the UNIVAC I. To satisfy UNIVAC's customers who wanted data processing, she invented the first computer language consisting of words. This and other early computer languages evolved into COBOL, the Common Business-Oriented Language, which was used on numerous government and business computers.

Hopper is an appropriate symbol for the relatively unbiased openness of a new technical field to women. By the 1980's, women made up about a quarter of all computer professionals in the workforce. Despite these numbers (much greater than the small percentage of female chemical engineers, for example), women still pursue careers in computer science far less frequently than men. In 1990, only 13 percent of doctorates in computer science went to women, and only 7.8 percent of computer-science professors were female. Nevertheless, for many women the computer industry has been one of the few technical fields that appears to be slowly evolving into a true meritocracy.

Much of the success of women in such technological fields as computer science can be traced to the women's movement of the 1960's. This was also the period when, in response to the Soviet satellite Sputnik, the U.S. government encouraged young people to enter science and engineering. Consequently, more women than ever before were educated in science and engineering, and more began to seek and gain employment in scientific and technical jobs. The 1970's witnessed an unprecedented increase in the number of women entering engineering fields. This decade was also the first in which the percentage of doctorates granted to women matched or exceeded the levels achieved in the 1920's. This increase was attributable to many factors, including public and private programs that encouraged women to enter engineering. Because this increase in female engineering doctorates continued into the 1980's, people expected that the movement of women into engineering would continue into the 1990's and beyond, but in the late 1980's the increase in women's share of technical degrees slowed. By 1989, it had leveled off at 15 percent of the degrees awarded to all persons. The early data in the 1990's indicated that the surge of women into engineering had peaked and that the increases seen in the 1970's and early 1980's probably would not continue.

The Impact of Technology on Women's Lives. For most of history, mainstream scholars have largely ignored gender issues in their studies of technology. Male supremacy in these fields was taken for granted, and issues on women and technology were consequently neglected. Fortunately, this neglect has begun to be remedied. For example, American scholars have studied sex segregation, wage discrimination, and limited employment opportunities for women in the workplace.

Although women played at most a minor role in bringing about the Industrial Revolution, they became important users of several of the technologies that grew out of that revolution. The impact of these technological changes in the United States and Canada varied according to women's class, race, educational level, and job. New technologies produced by the Industrial Revolution transformed the workplace, and this transformation drew women into low-status jobs, freeing men for reassignment to high-status jobs. Certain types of routine technical work thus became "feminized" through the ghettoization of women in the workplace. Just as the teaching of elementary school students changed from a male-dominated profession in Colonial America to a female-dominated profession in the nineteenth century, so too did certain industries such as textile manufacturing become feminized during the American Industrial Revolution. For example, the Lowell mills in Massachusetts, which produced cotton goods, became a major employer of young women. Initially, this situation seemed an ideal way for New England farm girls to raise some capital before marriage, but it also created the perception that women were merely transitory members of the labor force. Low wages and unsatisfactory job conditions led to strikes by the female workers, but the men, who held all the supervisory positions, had a poor understanding of the issues of exploitation that were troubling the female workers. Industrial technologies had certainly changed the workplace, but these advanced technologies had done little to advance the status of the women who were operating them.

In the early days of the American Industrial Revolution, entrepreneurs gave women the opportunity to labor at repetitive, detailed tasks in association with a machine. They even admitted that women were better at this sort of technical work than men were, but this attitude reveals an underlying prejudice that women were inferior to men in technical tasks that required creativity and highly developed skills. This prejudice also contributed to women's exclusion from scientific and technical education for many years. Even after women began to be admitted to technical schools, their numbers increased only slowly.

During the twentieth century, technology became an even more dominant force in women's work than it had been in the nineteenth century. As before, certain professions created by new technologies became feminized—for example, the airline industry's workforce became predominantly female—and, as before, women were forced to organize in order to battle for better wages and working conditions through largely female unions. Despite these efforts, it remained difficult for women to advance from routine jobs such as flight attendants to positions of power and influence.

New technologies affected some occupations more than others, but the sexual division of labor continued to be a structural feature of most modern advanced industrial societies. In many instances, the fusion of modern technology with an ancient patriarchy worked to reaffirm sexual divisions of labor rather than to reduce them, and women's situation in technical work remained disadvantaged. On the other hand, the women's movement and other social forces brought about changes in the way that work was organized. The twentieth century witnessed shifting lines between what was considered appropriate men's and women's work. As advanced industrial societies created new workplaces, women's roles in these workplaces were constantly renegotiated.

Despite these modern technologies and modern plumbing, automobiles, electricity, and computers, and despite growing numbers of women in technical jobs, many American and Canadian women have not risen above their traditional proletarian status. Women continue to battle for equitable participation in various technological professions. Research in the 1970's revealed that one of the major reasons that women earn less than men is because women do not work in the same occupations as men. This occupational segregation forced women into a narrow range of relatively low-paid, low-status jobs. Some gains have been made: The percentage of women employed as scientists and engineers increased by more than 10 percent a year to 868,000 between 1978 and 1988. Nevertheless, scientific and technical female workers continue to constitute a much smaller percentage of the technical workforce than they do of either the entire American workforce (45 percent) or the total professional workforce (50 percent). The conclusion that many feminist scholars draw from these and other data is that skilled and creative technical work is still not gender-neutral.

The Impact of Women on Technology. Traditional historians of technology have generally passed off women's inventions as "domestic" and therefore negligible, but feminist scholars have pointed out that domestic inventions, since they involve the daily lives of most people, have been more important than most traditional scholars realize. Although no invention by a woman has been as central to a technological revolution as James Watt's improved steam engine was to the Industrial Revolution, inventions by women have nevertheless been influential and economically successful. If technology means more than machines—and most scholars believe that it does—then such social innovations as Christel Kammerer's idea of flextime in work and Frances Perkins' welfare plan of the 1930's (which influenced the Social Security system that was eventually adopted) stand as symbolic examples of how women's ideas have transformed society.

Some feminist scholars believe that women's impact on technology has been more through their critique of how technology has been corrupted by certain masculine values than through any specific inventions. Many people have been made aware that, in addition to their well-publicized advantages, modern technologies have negative consequences. For example, Rachel Carson was instrumental in calling attention to the deleterious effect on wildlife (especially birds) of such chemical technologies as the massive spraying of DDT for insect control. Carson's work played a pivotal role in the modern environmental movement, whose major theme has been the need of an enlightened respect for the natural environment within which modern technologies operate. As several feminist scholars have pointed out, men, with their characteristic will to dominate and control, have favored massive building projects and permitted environmental neglect. What women can and have brought to technology is an approach that seeks to nurture, rather than dominate, life. Following interactive models, female engineers have been at the forefront in developing technologies that are respectful of entire systems of life—that is, technologies appropriate to the needs of humans that complement nature rather than exploit it. This approach is also economically viable, since it minimizes the extensive damage control necessary when entrepreneurs ignore the environmental impact of the technologies that they develop.

Women have also transformed the context of technology in the period since the Industrial Revolution. Traditionally, engineering was seen as masculine, but many scholars now believe that there is nothing intrinsically masculine in engineering techniques. Engineers of either sex can develop and apply technologies equally well to achieve a variety of goals. In the past, men tended to see only the dominative characteristics of technology and were blind to its integrative nature. That technology means only machinery is a myth, and that technology fulfills men only, and not women, is also a myth. Women's participation in technology has shown that women can do most work that men can do, and essentially male and essentially female technical professions seem to be vanishing. The hope is that all technical professions will become simply human professions.

Evidence exists that women are helping to transform the social environment of technological work. Some women even believe that a specifically feminine contribution is possible in certain technological disciplines. According to these feminists, women tend to emphasize the social context of technological work more than men do. Women seek to learn and respect the interests not only of the business for which they work but also of those consumers who will be affected by the technological tasks that they perform. By developing the capacity for genuine interacting with humans and nature, by studying the natural and social environment within which certain technologies are embedded, some women believe that a radical transformation of modern technology could be effected for the betterment of all.

The Impact of Technology on Women's Issues. For some feminists, technology, as a way of using scientific knowledge about the world, must be made to reflect women's ways of knowing in order to be complete. Because of their highly objective conception of nature, science and technology have posed a particularly profound problem for those feminists advocating a special feminist approach. What these feminists call the male model of technology, which treats inventions as subject to impersonal laws and as independent of humanity, presents a challenge to these same feminists who emphasize interdependence between inventions and their social, cultural, and personal contexts. Some modern research supports this feminist approach: Inventions cannot be fully understood when they are isolated from their inventor and his or her historical situation, community, and natural environment.

The advantages of the feminist approach to technology become clear when issues involving technology and human values are analyzed. Many women tend to see technology as something that evolves in the context of various relationships, not as an autonomous entity cut off from human beings. Researchers have found that men and women tend to resolve conflicts between technology and human values differently. Women view an ethic of care and responsibility as more authentic than the ethic of rights based on a logical hierarchy of universal principles that men find most amenable. Feminists therefore try to understand technological problems in the context of each person's perspective, needs, and goals, and they interpret the male model of technology as a prison from which humanity should be freed. For example, these feminists see the surrogate industry, which often treats women as reproductive commodities, as violating women's autonomy and dignity. By emphasizing interdependence over separation, understanding over assessment, and collaboration over confrontation, feminists want to put technology back into the web of interconnections from which it has been unnaturally sundered.

In another attack on the male interpretation of technology, some female inventors and engineers have challenged the traditional belief that emotions have no place in technology, that technology is value-free. In reality, technology is an inescapably human enterprise, and, as such, it is a product of everything constituting the human being, heart as well as mind. This feminist view of technology has been quite controversial, however, since the defenders of the traditional view have a deeply held conviction that feelings have no place in technology because they lead easily to bias. Centuries of experience in science and technology provide many examples where passions have blurred perceptions. The intense desire to see what one wants to see can lead one to see what is not really there. Scientists and engineers should base their analyses of the world on hard evidence and logical thinking, not emotional persuasion and "feminine" intuition. Feminists have responded to these attacks by insisting that they are not advocating a purely emotional approach to technology. Instead, they want an exploration of how, for example, a feeling for the interconnections in nature might prevent humans from treating natural products in a cavalier fashion. Furthermore, humans do not create their inventions in a void; these inventions are intimately related to humanity and to nature, and it is natural and good for human beings with deep moral feelings to evaluate their technologies through an enlightened set of values. An inventor may be inspired by passionately held values, and her invention may well express these values. Rather than banish feelings from science and technology, feminists would use them as instruments of understanding and creativity. In this way, technology can become a beneficent part of the human community. Without knowledge of and compassion for the needs of others, men and women cannot create a genuinely good technology.

In this way, feminists have become allies of those seeking to deepen the knowledge of technology by interpreting it as a socially constructed field. Psychological, cultural, religious, political, and economic values have shaped inventions and the formation of engineers. Adversarial procedures often play a role in how inventors and engineers gain and develop technical knowledge. Like lawyers zealously representing their clients, inventors fight for their inventions and engineers are advocates for their constructions. This is not to say that bridge builders need pay no attention to the law of gravity, but it is to say that social factors inevitably influence how technologies are created and developed. Objectivity remains an ideal worth striving for, but feminists believe that an awareness of these social factors will actually make the practice of technology more objective, since consciousness of the marvelous complexity of invention will improve the understanding of how technology works in the real world.

Although feminists have certainly broadened and deepened the modern understanding of technology, the idea of a "feminist technology" still rankles critics who point out that many men have been as critical of excessive competition (and as passionate in advocating compassion and cooperation) as have feminists. For example, R. Buckminster Fuller dedicated his life to bringing humanity and nature into harmony through technology. He believed that technological success is based on cooperation, since no event can be isolated from the rest of the universe. As he put it, "integrity can no longer tolerate selfishness." True human happiness can only develop through an awareness that efforts in technology must always be in the direction of progressively improving the condition of humankind.

Conclusions. The problem in assessing women and technology is that the fields of women's studies and the history of technology are in a state of flux, with a plethora of competing viewpoints. Against this pluralist background, however, some things have become clear. Since the seventeenth century, women have definitely made progress in the fields of invention and engineering. Similarly, while granting that the status of technology in today's world is far from ideal, few would deny that technological knowledge has been increasing exponentially, thereby giving humanity great powers over nature. What feminists have questioned is whether this expansion of technological knowledge is genuinely progressive or whether it needs to be reevaluated in terms of the ideologies hidden behind these developments. This questioning has led to a more complex but profound depiction of the many meanings of technology in modern society.

Historians have shown that the meaning and practice of technology have shifted over time in various societies. Even in twentieth century North America, technology's meaning was rethought and reevaluated several times. For example, in the 1960's and 1970's, the Civil Rights, women's, and environmental movements had as one of their goals to deprivilege scientific and technological knowledge wielded by experts and authorities. The work of Thomas S. Kuhn in *The Structure of Scientific Revolutions* (2d ed., 1970) contributed to dissipating the image of scientific and technological knowledge as autonomous, objective, impersonal, and value-free. While the barriers separating science and technology from other ways of knowing and doing things were being pulled down, feminists were recasting these disciplines as ideologies of power and control. This depiction of science and technology as instruments of repression rather than symbols of progress was enormously appealing to women who were trying to gain entrance into what had been forbidden territory.

Despite these barriers, increasing numbers of female inventors and engineers have succeeded in many technical professions. These women have helped to alter the image of engineering as inherently masculine, and thus engineering in the twentieth century has become a much more diverse profession than its nineteenth century male-dominated counterpart. Nevertheless, much needs to be done to increase the number of women in technological fields, because these very real gains are considerably less than those of women in such professions as law and medicine. The paucity of female inventors and engineers is also a reprehensible waste of potential talent.

At various conferences, successful women inventors and engineers have stated that the traditional roles of wife and mother and the modern role of the dedicated inventor or engineer can be successfully combined. Surveys show that most women want to be good parents and good professionals, and they feel that they can be both if the work of the home is equally shared by men. In terms of the great problems facing humanity, women realize that they share equally with men the task of responsibly transforming the world through science and technology. Human beings and the planet they inhabit can be improved by the judicious use of old and new technologies. If women are fully integrated into this task, the energies of significant human resources—women—will be liberated and the chances of the improvement of nature and humanity will be vastly enhanced. *—Robert J. Paradowski*

See also Crafts and home arts; Employment of women; History of women; Household technologies; Intelligence and achievement tests, bias in; Inventors, women as; Science, women in

BIBLIOGRAPHY

Ainley, Marianne G. *Despite the Odds: Essays on Canadian Women and Science*. Montreal: Vehicule Press, 1990. An account of how some Canadian women overcame their marginality and made important contributions in scientific and technical fields.

Cowan, Ruth Schwartz. *More Work for Mother: The Ironies of Household Technology from the Open Hearth to the Microwave*. New York: Basic Books, 1983. This book, which won the 1984 Dexter Prize of the Society for the History of Technology, shows how the transformation of the American household by modern technology left women in the position of devoting as much time to housework as their Colonial ancestors.

Hynes, H. Patricia, ed. *Reconstructing Babylon: Essays on Women and Technology*. Bloomington: Indiana University Press, 1991. An analysis of the nature and direction of modern technology as it affects women.

Jenson, Jane, Elisabeth Hagen, and Ceallaigh Reddy, eds. *Feminization of the Labor Force: Paradoxes and Promises*. New York: Oxford University Press, 1988. Focuses on how new technologies influenced the kind of work women have done, especially as industries tried to cope with rapidly changing marketplaces.

McIlwee, Judith S., and J. Gregg Robinson. *Women in Engineering: Gender, Power, and Workplace Culture*. Albany: State University of New York Press, 1992. An analysis of how the occupational segregation of women away from highly paid engineering jobs is maintained, despite efforts to dismantle it.

Mattfeld, Jacquelyn A., and Carol G. Van Aken, eds. *Women and the Scientific Professions*. Cambridge, Mass.: MIT Press, 1965. An exploration of the practical problems faced by American women in the scientific and engineering professions.

Stanley, Autumn. *Mothers and Daughters of Invention: Notes for a Revised History of Technology*. Metuchen, N.J.: Scarecrow Press, 1993. A massive collection of information about female inventors from prehistory to the present in five major areas: agriculture, medicine, reproductive technologies, machines, and computers. This exhaustively researched reference work has an extensive bibliography and a detailed index.

Weisbard, Phyllis Holman, ed. *The History of Women and Science, Health, and Technology: A Bibliographic Guide to the Professions and the Disciplines*. 2d ed. Madison: University of Wisconsin System, Women's Studies Librarian, 1993. This updated bibliography grew out of the work of the Committee on Women of the History of Science Society. Its purpose is to aid colleagues in designing gender-centered courses and integrating new feminist scholarship into survey courses.

Wright, Barbara Drygulski, ed. *Women, Work, and Technology: Transformations*. Ann Arbor: University of Michigan Press, 1987. An analysis of the impact and consequences of new technologies on working women through an examination of the ideological, social, and economic forces that have shaped these technologies.

Teen pregnancy

RELEVANT ISSUES: Health and medicine, poverty, sex and gender

SIGNIFICANCE: Teen pregnancy is an issue of major concern in the United States because of the health risks to both mother and infant, its adverse effects on educational achievement levels, and the intergenerational poverty that can result

The rate of pregnancy for teenage girls between the ages of fifteen and nineteen in the United States increased from 95 per 1,000 women in 1972 to 110 per 1,000 women in 1989. Approximately one million teenagers become pregnant every year in the United States. There was also an increase in births to teenagers outside of marriage in the United States between 1960 and 1995. In 1960, 15 percent of births to teenagers occurred outside marriage, compared to 66 percent of births to unwed teenagers in 1988.

Social Attitudes. Throughout the history of the United States, considerable opposition to out-of-wedlock births has existed, while teen pregnancy occurring within marriage has been readily accepted. Before the second wave of the women's movement, teenage girls tended to marry soon after they were graduated from high school, and many couples had children immediately. In addition, fewer young women attended institutions of higher education. The 1970's ushered in changes to this traditional plan, with more young women attending college and putting off marriage and children. Moreover, the sexual revolution brought more tolerant attitudes regarding sexual activity among adults. While societal proscriptions continue to discourage sexual activity and consequent pregnancy among teenagers, there has been greater acceptance of teen pregnancy when it does occur.

Many factors have been associated with the high incidence of teen pregnancy and the out-of-wedlock birthrate. Perhaps the most significant factor is that the stigma associated with teen pregnancy has drastically declined. There is greater societal acceptance of sexual activity among youths, as reflected in the mass media on television (especially in situation comedies, soap operas, commercials, and music videos), in motion pic-

A bus bench in San Antonio, Texas, urges teenagers to consider the consequences of sexual activity. (James L. Shaffer)

tures, and in the graphic lyrics in popular music. The decision on the part of a growing number of teenagers not to terminate their pregnancies is also responsible for the increase in the teenage out-of-wedlock birthrate, aided by a lack of adequate sex education and the failure of many teenagers to use contraceptives.

Sociological Theories. Several sociological theories attempt to explain teenage pregnancy. According to one theory, adolescent pregnancy occurs primarily because young women perceive that they have limited career choices. Consequently, they do not believe that making their education a top priority will result in a rewarding occupation or profession. Other theorists argue that teenage pregnancy is a function of low self-esteem: A teenager may believe that giving birth will provide her with someone to nurture who will return her affection, thus elevating her self-esteem. Another theory holds that an adolescent may become pregnant in order to establish and maintain a permanent bond with the young man who fathered her child.

Still other theorists suggest that the higher proportion of pregnant teenagers living in poor families is a result of a number of factors that are attributable to their impoverishment. For example, these teenagers, because of scarce financial resources, tend to have most dating experiences within their homes or the houses of male dates. When dating and courtship occur more frequently within the confines of the home and neighborhood, rather than in a variety of more public settings, the opportunities for sexual activity and the corresponding likelihood of unplanned pregnancy are greater. It is also the case that pregnant teenagers generally have mothers who themselves were once pregnant teenagers living in poverty. The intergenerational nature of teen pregnancy reveals its cyclical nature and that of poverty itself, both of which, once entered, are virtually inescapable within the existing social structure of the United States.

Health Implications. Teen pregnancy raises serious health concerns for teenagers as well as for their infants. A lack of adequate prenatal care and the failure to maintain a healthy diet during pregnancy are significant factors that place pregnant teenagers and their infants at risk. More than one-half of pregnant teenagers do not receive prenatal care within their first trimester. Furthermore, one in ten does not receive prenatal care until her third trimester. Often, these problems are associated with being poor and lacking the resources to afford quality health care. In addition, pregnant teenagers frequently require assistance in preparing balanced meals. The resulting health complications that they experience also affect the health of their unborn children. Consequently, the children of pregnant teenagers may require specialized medical care. Their babies are at risk for being born prematurely or having a low birth weight. These conditions are more likely to lead to infant death during the first year, birth injuries, serious childhood illnesses, nerve defects, and developmental problems.

Many programs are sponsored by private organizations and the government in order to educate teenage girls about the risks associated with teen pregnancy. Schools are also involved in providing various forms of education in this area through school-based clinics. Specifically, teen pregnancy prevention programs are offered by the following organizations: the Alan Guttmacher Institute, the Center for Population Options, the Children's Defense Fund (CDF), the National Organization on Adolescent Pregnancy and Parenting, and Planned Parenthood.

Impact on Women's Issues. Many women have contributed to the discussion of teen pregnancy by raising the public awareness of a young woman's right to be educated about sexual functioning, sexual activity, birth control, and various means of addressing unplanned pregnancies, including abortion, adoption, and programs that support pregnant teenagers and teenage parents. Other women have counseled pregnant teenagers and have established and directed programs that educate them regarding nutrition and health care during pregnancy. Margaret Sanger is noted for founding Planned Parenthood in New York City in 1916 to provide women with information regarding birth control.

Such involvement in this issue has resulted in women of all ages becoming more aware of and responsible for their reproductive rights. Women have also assumed a more active role in influencing policies and laws regarding reproductive issues and other gender-related issues and policies. Furthermore, women have become more involved in the selection of health care providers. Accordingly, they are expanding the criteria for selecting physicians, particularly those who specialize in obstetrics and gynecology, to include the ability to relate well with female patients in addition to the knowledge of and ability to practice medicine. —*K. Sue Jewell*

See also Abortion; Adoption; Birth control and family planning; Family planning services; Health and medicine; Motherhood; Parental notification; Planned Parenthood; Pregnancy and childbirth; Prenatal care; Sanger, Margaret; Sexual revolution; Sexuality, women's; Single mothers; Socialization of girls and young women

Bibliography

Berlfein, Judy. *Teen Pregnancy*. San Diego: Lucent Books, 1992.

Bode, Janet. *Kids Still Having Kids: People Talk About Teen Pregnancy*. New York: Franklin Watts, 1992.

Henshaw, Stanley K., et al. *Teenage Pregnancy in the United States: The Scope of the Problem and State Responses*. New York: Alan Guttmacher Institute, 1989.

McCuen, Gary E., ed. *Children Having Children: Global Perspectives on Teenage Pregnancy*. Hudson, Wis.: Gary E. McCuen, 1988.

Meier, Gisela. *Teenage Pregnancy*. North Bellmore, N.Y.: Marshall Cavendish, 1994.

Television, women in

Relevant issues: Arts and entertainment, business and economics

Significance: Women have achieved positions of power in the television industry in far greater numbers than in any other area of American entertainment

Television was introduced in the United States at the 1939 New York World's Fair, but it did not become widely popular until the post-World War II period. After 1946, however, television's growth was rapid, and by 1950 Americans were purchasing more than seven million television sets annually. Four major networks were broadcasting by 1950—the American Broadcasting Companies (ABC), the Columbia Broadcasting System (CBS), the National Broadcasting Company (NBC), and the DuMont Network—most offering a seven-day-a-week schedule of daytime and nighttime programming. From the beginnings of television, women were important as performers, and many of these women went on to careers as powerful and influential executives. Perhaps because of the need for a large amount of programming to fill broadcast days, women also found work as writers and producers in television far in excess of their numbers in film or theater. Since the 1970's, several women have headed networks and achieved other top executive positions in the industry.

History. Network television has always featured women in significant roles as performers, especially as lead actors in situation comedies such as *Mama Rosa*, which made its debut in the 1949-1950 season on ABC. Most did not go on to run studios, but several key performers helped to define the future of television both as performers and as executives. The most significant of these actresses was also one of the most important figures in television history: Lucille Ball. Previously a minor contract actress at RKO Studios, Ball was barely known to American audiences when her landmark series *I Love Lucy* premiered on October 15, 1951, on CBS; it costarred her husband, Desi Arnaz. The show was an instant success and remained near the top of the ratings until the stars voluntarily ended its run on June 24, 1957. Two other successful series followed, *The Lucy Show* (1962-1968) and *Here's Lucy* (1968-1974); these three Lucille Ball series together constitute the most popular block of shows in television history. Her enormous ratings successes translated into executive success for Ball. After her 1960 divorce from Arnaz, she emerged as president of Desilu Productions, one of the largest independent suppliers of programming to the networks; she remained president until Paramount Studios purchased Desilu in 1967. This same route from performer to producer and executive would later be followed by others, most notably Mary Tyler Moore, the star of *The Mary Tyler Moore Show* from 1970 to 1977 and the cofounder of MTM Productions, also a leading supplier of situation comedies. It was Ball's unprecedented achievements in the developing years of television, however, that set the stage for women's acceptance as both performers and behind-the-scenes players in the medium.

In addition to situation comedy, another area in which women enjoyed early success in television was the field of daytime drama, also known as "soap operas," a format carried over from radio. Irna Phillips was the leading developer and writer of television serials from 1949 until 1974, for which she earned the title "Queen of the Soaps." Among the shows that she developed for television were *Guiding Light*, which has also been a radio serial, and *As the World Turns*, one of the first two thirty-minute soap operas and the most successful television serial ever. Phillips continued to write for *As the World Turns* until 1973. After her death, Agnes Nixon, who had been her employee, inherited the "Queen of the Soaps" title. Nixon packaged and wrote for *One Life to Live* and *All My Children*, two long-running shows on ABC. Both Phillips and Nixon helped to define the daytime drama genre, which continues to be a major source of advertising revenue for the three major broadcast networks.

Public Television. Another arena of television production largely defined by women has been public television, and more specifically programming for children. Joan Ganz Cooney served as president of the Children's Television Workshop (CTW) until 1990. In 1966, she designed, along with Lloyd Morrisett, a research project that later became *Sesame Street*. Along with this show, CTW also produced *The Electric Company*, *Ghostwriter*, and several other shows praised for their positive educational values, most of them carried over public television stations throughout the United States. Ethel Winant joined CTW in 1975, after two decades as casting director for CBS, a position that made her the most powerful casting director in the field of children's television. The Children's Television Workshop and their various programs virtually invented positive children's programming on television, winning almost every conceivable award in the process and adding immeasurably to the viability of public broadcast television channels.

Network Executives. Since the late 1970's, several women have risen through the ranks to command entire television networks. Jane Cahill Pfeiffer became chairperson of NBC and a director of its parent company, RCA Corporation, in 1978. This position was the highest ever attained by a woman in the broadcast industry to that time. In April, 1980, Kay Koplovitz became president and chief executive officer (CEO) of the USA cable network, the first woman to head a television network in the United States. USA became, under her direction, one of the most popular basic cable channels, presenting off-network series, sports, and original films. Bridget Potter joined the Home Box Office (HBO) pay cable network in 1982 as senior vice president of original programming, and, under her control, HBO became a highly respected producer of original motion pictures and series, winning multiple Emmy Awards and attracting top directing and performing talent from feature films. In 1986, Ruth Otte became president and CEO of Discovery Networks, the parent of two basic cable services, the Discovery Channel and the Learning Channel, both of which expanded dynamically under her control. Lucie Salhany joined Twentieth Century-Fox Television in July, 1991, as its chairperson and in this capacity oversaw all of Fox Broadcasting's network, syndication, and cable production and distribution. With a strong slate of innovative programming aimed at younger audiences, women, and African Americans, the Fox network increased its market share steadily after 1991 to become a serious contender with the "big three" networks in many markets.

Impact. Throughout its history, television as a medium has been more receptive to women as performers, producers, and executives than any other major entertainment medium. Though often working in specialty markets such as daytime dramas and children's programming, women have shaped the face of television broadcasting from its beginning and have enjoyed unprecedented success. With their increasing influence as executives and network heads since the 1980's, women will continue to shape the future of America's most popular and pervasive entertainment medium.

—Vicki A. Sanders

See also Acting; Business and corporate enterprise, women in; Journalism, women in; National Association of Media Women

Bibliography

Brown, Mary Ellen, ed. *Television and Women's Culture: The Politics of the Popular*. London: Sage, 1990.

Bryant, Jennings, and Dolf Zillman, eds. *Perspectives on Media Effects*. Hillsdale, N.J.: Lawrence Erlbaum Associates, 1986.

Hawes, William. *American Television Drama*. University: University of Alabama Press, 1986.

Kaplan, E. Ann, ed. *Regarding Television: Critical Approaches—An Anthology*. Frederick, Md.: University Publications of America, 1983.

Lowe, Carl, ed. *Television and American Culture*. New York: H. W. Wilson, 1981.

Papazian, Ed. *Medium Rare: The Evolution, Workings, and Impact of Commercial Television*. 2d ed. New York: Media Dynamics, 1991.

Steinberg, Cobbett S. *TV Facts*. New York: Facts on File, 1980.

Van Evra, Judith Page. *Television and Child Development*. Hillsdale, N.J.: Lawrence Erlbaum Associates, 1990.

Temperance movement and women

Relevant issues: Family, politics, social reform

Significance: The temperance movement offered North American women one of their first sustained opportunities to campaign for social reform in a manner that was culturally acceptable

Reform was a leading issue throughout the nineteenth and early twentieth centuries as social critics attacked a variety of problems ranging from slavery to mental health. One of the most significant of these reform efforts was directed against alcohol, and women were among the temperance movement's most active leaders and participants.

Women's Cultural Roles. To understand why many women participated in the temperance movement, one must consider the prevailing nineteenth century social and cultural constraints that they faced. Society mandated that women live within their "sphere." As such, women were expected to be homemakers who managed their households and nurtured their children. They were also expected to live according to a set of cultural standards that scholars have deemed the Cult of True Womanhood. Accordingly, women were thought to be more morally pure than men. They were likewise assumed to be more pious and God-fearing than men. Further, in addition to their role as keepers of the home, women were expected to be submissive to male authority, especially that of their husbands.

Nineteenth century women had few legal rights, and many were victims of alcohol-related spousal abuse. Wives had no legal recourse against drunken, abusive husbands. Likewise, men who squandered their wages on liquor had nothing left for family maintenance. Carry Nation, best remembered as a temperance crusader who single-handedly destroyed saloons with a hatchet, had herself been brutalized by an alcoholic spouse.

Clearly, women believed that liquor threatened their persons and homes, and, as they began to call for an end to alcohol abuse, they were acting within the bounds of the Cult of True Womanhood. As supposedly pure and pious individuals, they could not let their homes be destroyed; indeed, God would be displeased with them if they failed to act. Alcohol abuse had to be curbed, or stopped entirely, if women were to ensure tranquil homes for their families.

Women and Temperance Organizations. The number of nineteenth and early twentieth century temperance organizations was legion. The largest and most successful of these early organizations was the American Society for the Promotion of Temperance, more commonly known as the American Temperance Society. The society admitted women into its membership, but, like many early temperance societies, it was dominated by men. Consequently, women sometimes felt the need to organize their own temperance societies, notably the Daughters of Temperance and the Women's New York State Temperance Society. When a group of men formed the Washington Temperance Society in 1840, named in honor of George Washington, Cornelia Dow organized a sister organization, the Martha Washington Society, for women.

Antebellum temperance advocates generally appealed directly to drinkers' individual consciences to convince them that they had a problem. Women proved to be especially good public lecturers on the evils of alcohol. On the one hand, they could cite mounting medical evidence that demonstrated alcohol's debilitating effects on the body. On the other hand, they could also offer first-hand testimony of alcohol's negative impact on the home.

Early temperance organizations enjoyed modest success, but, by the 1870's, the number of saloons in North America was increasing and liquor appeared to be more available than ever before. Most temperance advocates came to believe that moral suasion was no longer an effective weapon against liquor traffic. It was also clear to female temperance workers that their efforts, while noteworthy, were largely scattered and needed focus.

The Women's Christian Temperance Union (WCTU) helped to refocus temperance efforts. The WCTU was organized in Cleveland, Ohio, in 1874, after numerous women throughout Ohio banded together to confront saloon keepers and petition them to close their businesses for the well-being of the community. These spontaneous, peaceful confrontations proved moderately successful, and the WCTU sought to parlay this success into more meaningful gains.

In its early years, the WCTU remained committed to moral suasion as a means to curbing alcoholic abuse. Frances Willard changed that philosophy when she became president of the organization in 1879. A native of Evanston, Illinois, Willard worked tirelessly to broaden the scope of the WCTU until her death in 1898. She believed that alcohol-related problems were a part of more complicated nineteenth century social and economic problems. She also believed that despite the fact that women could not vote, they should do what they could to secure laws to curb excessive liquor consumption. In 1880, Willard led the WCTU to create "departments" to work with various elements of the working class. Initially, WCTU workers attempted to persuade male laborers to vote along lines established by the relatively new Prohibition Party. Gradually, however, the WCTU became an organization of advocates, speaking out against such evils as prostitution and calling for governmental aid for day care.

In spite of her reform tendencies, Willard made sure that WCTU activities reflected concerns within the "woman's sphere." For example, woman suffrage was a hotly debated reform in the late nineteenth century. Frances Willard supported it, but only because it could be used to relieve the plight of oppressed women and families. Nevertheless, politics ultimately split the WCTU. In 1889, a minority within the organization left because they believed the WCTU had become too political. Led by Willard's longtime friend J. Ellen Foster, this small group formed the Non-Partisan Woman's Christian Temperance Union. This schism notwithstanding, the WCTU was about 150,000 strong in 1890 and was easily the largest mass women's organization in the nineteenth century.

By 1900, the Anti-Saloon League had joined the WCTU in the fight against alcohol. By this time, advocates were calling for a ban on the production and consumption of alcoholic beverages. Their wish came true in 1919 when the Eighteenth Amendment to the United States Constitution prohibited the manufacture, sale, and transportation of liquor. Ironically, twenty-two years after Willard's death, alcohol was no longer a "woman's issue." For some, Prohibition had become a means to control the drinking habits of immigrants. Moreover,

The fight for temperance, led primarily by women who saw the effects of alcoholism on families at first hand, was elevated to a moral issue and portrayed in the press as "Woman's Holy War." (Library of Congress)

the Volstead Act, the legislation that officially launched Prohibition, was a World War I measure designed, among other things, to conserve grain. Yet, perhaps the most ironic twist in the temperance movement came in 1933 when Prohibition was repealed. The reform that its supporters claimed would cure most of society's ills survived only thirteen years on the national level.

Significance of Temperance. The temperance movement proved especially significant for women for several reasons. First, it created organizations whereby women expressed their social concerns and learned organizational skills that would benefit them in the future. Second, it gave women a heightened sense of purpose, potential, and self-awareness. Finally, the temperance movement paved the way for women to enter the political arena. —*Keith Harper*

See also Alcoholism and drug abuse among women; Cult of True Womanhood; Religion; Social reform movements and women; Willard, Frances; Women's Christian Temperance Union (WCTU)

Bibliography

Blocker, Jack S. *American Temperance Movements: Cycles of Reform*. Boston: Twayne, 1989.

Bordin, Ruth. *Frances Willard: A Biography*. Chapel Hill: University of North Carolina Press, 1986.

________. *Woman and Temperance: The Quest for Power and Liberty, 1873-1900*. Philadelphia: Temple University Press, 1981.

Clark, Norman. *Deliver Us from Evil: An Interpretation of American Prohibition*. New York: W. W. Norton, 1976.

Gusfield, Joseph. *Symbolic Crusade*. Urbana: University of Illinois Press, 1963.

Kerr, K. Austin. *Organized for Prohibition: A New History of the Anti-Saloon League*. New Haven, Conn.: Yale University Press, 1985.

Tyrrell, Ian. *Sobering Up: From Temperance to Prohibition in Antebellum America, 1800-1860*. Westport, Conn.: Greenwood Press, 1979.

Tennis, women in

Relevant issue: Sports

Significance: Tennis was the first sport to produce well-known female athletes, one of whom, Billie Jean King, led the battle for equal pay for all women in professional sports

History of the Sport. While modern tennis can trace its roots to a game developed by an Englishman, Major Walter Clopton Wingfield, in 1873, an American woman, Mary Ewing Outerbridge, brought it to New York a year later; the sport quickly caught on among wealthy Easterners who belonged to private clubs. Many students in the Northeast also began playing tennis, and, in 1899, an intercollegiate group accepted an invitation to demonstrate the game in California, where the suitable climate soon made it a popular pastime.

Californian Hazel Hotchkiss made her first appearance in the nationals in 1909. Along with the "California Rocket" Maurice McLoughlin, she was responsible for changing the style of the game, making it more aggressive. They also popularized tennis among the middle classes, and many cities across the country began to build public tennis facilities. This set the stage for promotion of the sport and the emergence of the first well-known female athletes: Americans Helen Wills, Helen Jacobs, and Alice Marble and Frenchwoman Suzanne Lenglen. Lenglen was an important influence on women's tennis; in 1926, when the game was first played professionally, she was paid $50,000 for her part in a tour of the United States.

In 1931, other players turned professional, and the sport began to grow internationally. In 1953, Maureen "Little Mo" Connelly became the first woman to win the Grand Slam of tennis: Wimbledon, the French Open, the U.S. Open, and the Australian Open. Her recognition as the Woman of the Year by the Associated Sportswriters made the public aware of female athletes. In 1968, the All-England Club announced that Wimbledon, the world's most prestigious tournament, would welcome both professionals and amateurs. With better players, television executives were interested in tennis, and the prize money grew.

Struggles and Triumphs. Although women were recognized as professional tennis players, they encountered many problems. Neither World Champion Tennis nor the Grand Prix recognized female professionals, nor were they paid on the same scale as men. In 1971, in order to address these issues, one of the sport's most accomplished players, Billie Jean King, along with Gladys Heldman of *World Tennis Magazine*, organized the Women's International Tennis Association and their own tour, the Virginia Slims Circuit. Women's prize money began to grow and to reach parity with men's. King extended her efforts for equal pay to include not only tennis players but other female athletes as well. King was also responsible for publicizing tennis when, on September 20, 1973, in the Houston Astrodome, she defeated tennis professional Bobby Riggs in the Battle of the Sexes. The match was played in front of large live and television audiences and earned for King a record amount of money.

Since the mid-1970's, many talented women have played professional tennis and, with expanding media coverage, have become highly paid stars. Chris Evert and Martina Navratilova became household names. The return of tennis in 1988 as an Olympic sport after a sixty-four-year absence increased its visibility. German player Steffi Graf cemented her reputation as one of the all-time great female athletes that year by winning the gold medal in the Games as well as the Grand Slam. In 1994, only two of the top twenty most highly paid athletes were women, both tennis players: Graf and Gabriela Sabatini. Yet, such fame has also brought its problems, most clearly shown in the spring of 1993 when Monica Seles was stabbed by a fan of Graf during a changeover; Seles would not return to the court for years.

Pressures and Training. In addition to security, young athletes must deal with other pressures. Tennis organizations have for years debated the young age—fourteen—at which a young woman can turn professional. Many authorities question the strain that intense practice sessions and matches place on a growing adolescent body. Many others debate the emotional toll. Being on the international tennis tour requires a teenager to surround herself with a retinue of coaches and specialists. Her parents may exert other pressures as they give up their own interests to look after her life. She in turn becomes their source of financial support. In such a focused and scheduled environment, she misses out on the normal adolescent activities that allow her to develop friends and a variety of interests. In the early 1990's, Jennifer Capriati, a promising athlete, found the stress overwhelming and became involved with drugs. Stories such as hers reveal the dark side of the spotlight of sports fame.

With such high stakes, however, tennis camps and schools abound. Each year in the United States, promising young women apply for schools in Florida and California that offer high school instruction along with tennis. They spend summers at camps dedicated to improving their game. Some begin before the age of ten, dedicating themselves to a life of practice, exercise, and diet. Even players such as Zina Garrison, a product of the Houston City Parks Department, spent virtually her entire childhood on the tennis courts. Only a very small percentage of tennis players will achieve ranking on even a regional level.

Tennis for Amateurs. For the female athlete whose aims are not as high, tennis is a different story. With the expansion of public courts and summer recreation department instruction, tennis at the recreational level is available to women all over the United States and Canada. Cities such as Washington, D.C., have special programs run by adult leagues or sponsored by the United States Tennis Association (USTA) that are aimed at making the game attractive to inner-city children. Increasing numbers of public and private high schools offer women's tennis as a varsity sport, giving talented players the opportunity to obtain college athletic scholarships. Women's tennis at the college level was formerly associated with California universities such as Stanford or Pepperdine. As promising players emerge and facilities are built, however, more colleges and universities are sponsoring women's teams.

As with other sports, playing tennis at the school team level or the recreational level has a positive effect on women. The sport not only helps young women develop physical skills, such as coordination and strength, but also teaches them valuable skills as they move into careers formerly dominated by men. They learn to take risks and to be aggressive, and they gain self-esteem. In the 1980's, the self-confident, physically fit woman became the role model for young girls. Tennis was the first sport to showcase women as athletes, and female players have helped to pave the way for such a positive image.

—*Louise M. Stone*

See also Association for Intercollegiate Athletics for Women; Battle of the Sexes; Navratilova, Martina; Olympic Games, women in the; Physical fitness for women; Professional sports, women in; Sports, women in; Women's Sports Foundation

BIBLIOGRAPHY

Ashe, Arthur, with Neil Amdur. *Off the Court*. New York: New American Library, 1981.

Clerici, Gianni. *The Ultimate Tennis Book*. Chicago: Follett, 1975.

Collins, Bud, and Zander Hollander, eds. *Bud Collins' Modern Encyclopedia of Tennis*. New York: Doubleday, 1980.

Cummings, Parke. *American Tennis: The Story of a Game and Its People*. Boston: Little, Brown, 1957.

Devereux, Rick. *Net Results: The Complete Tennis Handbook*. Boston: Pathfinder, 1974.

Evans, Richard. *Open Tennis, 1968-1988*. Lexington, Mass.: Stephen Greene Press, 1989.

Grimsley, Will. *Tennis: Its History, People, and Events*. Englewood Cliffs, N.J.: Prentice Hall, 1971.

King, Billie Jean, with Kim Chapin. *Billie Jean*. New York: Harper & Row, 1974.

Mewshaw, Michael. *Ladies of the Court*. New York: Crown, 1993.

Shannon, Bill, ed. *United States Tennis Association Official Encyclopedia of Tennis*. New York: Harper & Row, 1981.

Tenure clock

RELEVANT ISSUES: Education, employment

SIGNIFICANCE: The tenure clock may come into conflict with a woman's biological clock, thus contributing to the lack of women in higher academic ranks

According to one definition, tenure is the "length and conditions of office in civil, judicial, academic, and similar services." In academia, the concept of a tenure clock refers to the length of time remaining for a professor before he or she is considered for tenure. Usually, this length of time is seven years, but it may vary by academic institution and be negotiated according to past accomplishments. Once tenure is granted, sometimes coupled with a promotion to an associate professorship from an assistant professorship, a professor has secured employment that may be terminated only on grounds of serious misconduct.

To be granted tenure, a professor needs to demonstrate accomplishment in research, teaching, and service with different emphasis depending on the institution. Research most often means publishing. As Dean Robert B. Lawton of Georgetown University, Washington, D.C., wrote in a 1991 article in *America*, "The pressures of the so-called tenure clock . . . can cause a scholar's writing to suffer. In the rush to get something published, to teach and design courses, and to meet with students, professors often do not have enough time to let their ideas germinate. The pressures of tenure can also corrupt whatever leisure time a scholar does have."

The problem is worse for women who must balance career and family life. In a study entitled "The Final Disadvantage: Barriers to Women in Academic Science and Engineering," by Henry Etzkowitz of SUNY Purchase, which was coauthored by Carol Kemelgor and Michael Neuschatz and funded by the National Science Foundation, it was found that one factor

PERCENTAGE OF FULL-TIME FACULTY WITH TENURE IN THE U.S.

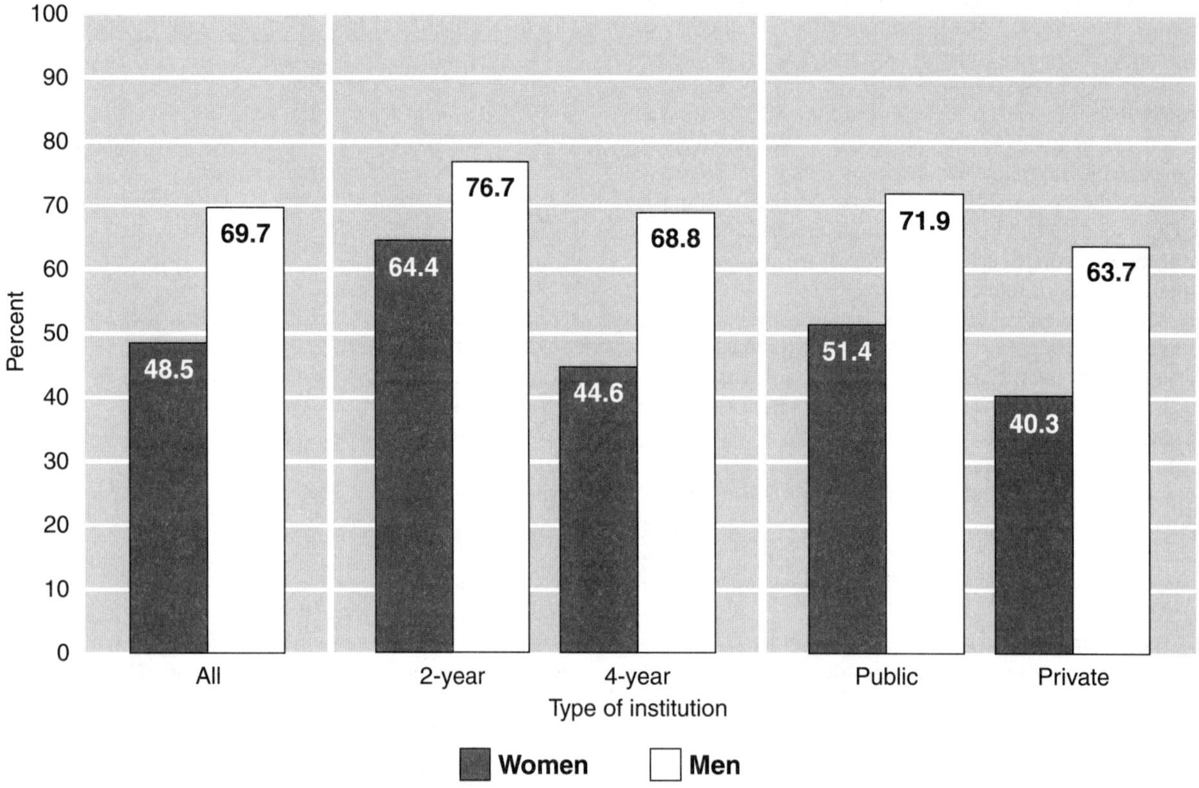

Type of institution	Women	Men
All	48.5	69.7
2-year	64.4	76.7
4-year	44.6	68.8
Public	51.4	71.9
Private	40.3	63.7

Source: U.S. National Center for Education Statistics, *Digest of Education Statistics* (1991)

pushing women from academia to industry is the "tenure clock versus the biological clock." The academic route and tenure were incompatible with having a family. According to the authors, in many disciplines "pregnancy is discouraged and graduate women who have children are encouraged to take leaves of absence that tend to become permanent withdrawals." Once women obtain their degrees, going into academia part-time is not feasible. According to Etzkowitz, these women find they have to choose between two approaches: They can either follow the "male model" for success in academia, which demands driven (if not obsessive) devotion before tenure and involves the publish-or-perish pressures that can lead to exploitation, or they can go into industry, where jobs are more traditional and where it is easier to balance career and family needs. Relatively few women adopt the first model. Etzkowitz proposes to change the tenure structure to allow a more flexible schedule. Indeed, some universities in the United States have begun to examine the problems of maternity and professorship. The University of California and the University of Oregon, for example, adopted a systemwide policy of stopping the tenure clock for the year following childbirth.

See also Academia and scholarship, women in; American Association of University Women; Biological clock; Career vs. homemaker debate; Higher education, women in; Maternity leave; Pregnancy and employment

Thalidomide babies

RELEVANT ISSUES: Health and medicine

SIGNIFICANCE: The birth defects found in thalidomide babies caused the medical community to reevaluate the use of nonessential drugs during pregnancy

Thalidomide is a sedative that also lessens morning sickness during pregnancy. The drug, deemed so safe that it could be sold without a prescription, was first marketed in West Germany in 1958 and was soon widely used in Canada, Great Britain, Australia, and Europe. While the drug produced no ill effects in most people, at least ten thousand pregnant women who took thalidomide during their first trimester gave birth to babies with malformed fingers or toes attached to stunted limbs, making them resemble flippers. Although the link between the drug and the deformities was overlooked at first (the placenta was believed to protect the fetus from harmful substances in the mother's blood), thalidomide usage was identified as the common denominator in 1961. Thalidomide did not always show parallel effects in humans and animals during clinical tests. Even one dose taken early in pregnancy when the limb buds are forming, however, puts the fetus at risk. Although never approved for use by the Food and Drug Administration (FDA), thalidomide was distributed to more than three thousand women in the United States as a marketing promotion disguised as a clinical test, resulting in at least nine deformed infants. This tragedy led to more stringent drug approval laws. Today, new drugs must be tested on at least two species of pregnant animals, and physicians warn pregnant women to avoid use of even seemingly innocuous nonprescription drugs.

See also Diethylstilbestrol (DES); Health and medicine; Pregnancy and childbirth; Prenatal care

Theologians and women's theology

RELEVANT ISSUES: Ecology and the environment, religious beliefs and practices

SIGNIFICANCE: Because religion has often been blamed for women's subordinated position in society, many female theologians have worked to develop a theology that upholds women's basic goodness and value

From the time of the founding of the United States, women were active in religion but generally were blocked from studying theology. Many women studied on their own by listening to sermons and holding discussions in their homes, but they were not encouraged to do this and were sometimes punished for it. For example, in the early seventeenth century, Anne Hutchinson was taught to read and think about the Bible by her father. She invited women to her home to discuss the Sunday sermons, and she gradually concluded that people could be guided by the Holy Spirit rather than by clergy authorities. The ministers passed a resolution prohibiting the meetings and chided her for neglecting her family and encouraging other women to neglect theirs. In 1638, she was excommunicated. When she later bore a badly deformed baby, this was thought to be evidence of her spiritual condition.

Contradictions to the public perception of religion as the source of women's implied inferiority and second-class citizenship probably began in the 1840's with Elizabeth Cady Stanton and Susan B. Anthony. They realized that the Bible was often used to restrict the activities of women. People said, for example, that Eve was at fault for committing the first sin, and therefore women were more gullible and morally weak. Stanton decided to counteract this idea by producing, with Anthony, *The Woman's Bible* (1895-1898). They found and quoted many passages from the Bible that affirmed women, such as those in Paul's letter to the Romans. In these passages, women are seen teaching, leading prayer services, and working with Paul to spread the message of the gospel.

For the most part, theological study was the purview of those studying for the ministry, and because women generally could not be ministers, they were not able to study theology. Not until the 1960's were large numbers of women admitted to theological schools. Since then, however, there has been a veritable explosion in women's theology and in the number of female theologians. The field of theology has changed significantly from what it was before 1970. There is a greater consciousness of women's role in early Christianity and of the misogyny evident in some of the early church fathers. The contributions of female mystics in the Middle Ages have been studied, as well as the bias against women that was shown in the burning, in both Europe and the United States, of thousands of women who were thought to be witches. One topic that is widely discussed by female theologians is the body and its place in religion. Before 1970, if the body had a place in religion, it was only as something to be controlled by the mind. Women, however, have been closely associated with the body throughout history. A landmark article by Sherry B. Ortner, "Is Female to Male as Nature Is to Culture?" (1976), exposed the dualism between mind and body, culture and nature, spirit and matter, male and female, implying that the

The figure of Eve as the temptress and cause of Man's ruin has often provided justification for the persecution of women and restrictions on their religious role. (Library of Congress)

second of the two items in the comparison is of lesser value than the first. Since then, women have shown, for example, that the body as well as the mind can be said to be made in the image and likeness of God. Humans have the power to give birth as well as to nurture human life, which are godlike qualities. Among others, Christine E. Gudorf, in the 1987 essay "The Power to Create: Sacraments and Men's Need to Birth," has pointed out how men have taken over women's roles through religious rites: Whereas a woman bears a child, the man has the privilege of helping it to be "reborn." A woman puts food on the table at home, and a man puts it on the altar in the formal ceremony in church. Female theologians, then, are examining all of theology in many different religious settings throughout the world to expose the gender issues contained in them.

Bible Study. Female theologians have done much to enhance the study of Scripture. They have brought their own experience to the text and have paid particular attention to the experiences of biblical women. Two prominent scholars in this area are Phyllis Trible, a professor of sacred literature at Union Theological Seminary, New York, and Elizabeth Schussler Fiorenza, a professor at Harvard University. Trible wrote *God and the Rhetoric of Sexuality* (1978) and *Texts of Terror: Literary-Feminist Readings of Biblical Narratives* (1984), both of which closely examine texts in which women play an important part in the biblical narratives. The story of Adam and Eve is a pivotal one for women because Adam is thought to have been created first, making the man more important than the woman in the order of Creation. In addition, Eve has often been seen as seducing Adam into eating the forbidden fruit, supposedly proving that women are more gullible and prone to evil than are men. Trible proposed the theory that according to the story, the first man and woman were created at the same time, that the first human creature was not a sexual person at all but an "earth creature," a literal translation of the word "Adam." The man and the woman were differentiated from each other, created simultaneously out of the original earth formation. Trible also pointed out how the serpent spoke to both the man and the woman and that they both ate of the forbidden fruit at the same time. In *Texts of Terror*, Trible told the stories of four women from the Hebrew Scriptures—stories of murder, rape, and rejection.

A well-known scholar of the Christian New Testament is Elizabeth Schussler Fiorenza. *In Memory of Her: A Feminist Theological Reconstruction of Christian Origins* (1984) brings together the language study, archeological findings, historical study, and anthropological conclusions in the understanding and analysis of New Testament writings. She concludes that women's leadership and contributions were central to the early Christian missionary movement. Traditionally, translations of the Bible indicated that women were helpers of Paul; the writing clearly indicates that they were coworkers and apostles. Fiorenza pointed out that often women were present in the biblical narrations but are subsumed by the gender-exclusive language and thus are invisible to the reader.

History. Along with biblical scholarship, female theologians have undertaken the enormous task of examining all of religious history to see where women have been overlooked. In *When God Was a Woman* (1976), Merlin Stone related how, when visiting European museums of prehistoric sites, she realized that many of the gods that were worshiped were female. Since then, much archeological evidence has shown that in many areas before 3,000 B.C., people thought of God as female. These religions are thought to have been earth-centered and body-centered rather than oriented toward the transcendent. The Goddess was the life force, and people looked to her for regeneration and renewal of life in the form of children and nature.

By the time of Jesus, cultures had become patriarchal, and women's behavior was strictly regulated. Their bodily functions were thought to be unclean, and they were valued only for their ability to bear children. They were thought to be less intelligent than men, and often they were not considered to be full human beings. Jesus himself was countercultural: He spoke to women in public, used images of women in his parables of the kingdom, and even had some female friends. By the year A.D. 300, however, women had been forced out of leadership positions in the church and in many writings were thought of as evil. Elaine Pagels told of this era in *Adam, Eve, and the Serpent* (1988). She claimed that writers used the story to justify and establish their belief that sexual intercourse was not for pleasure but only for procreation. Christians of this era took pride in their sexual restraint and rejected extramarital sexual practices. In the process of teaching these beliefs, however, they wrote that women were the cause of sexual license and warned men to stay away from women if they wanted to be saved.

Female theologians have recently discovered the writings of women in the Middle Ages and have found a rich store of information, some of which was previously unknown. An author who has written in this area is Caroline Waker Bynum, a professor of history and comparative religion and women's studies at the University of Washington. In *Holy Feast and Holy Fast: The Religious Significance of Food to Medieval Women* (1987), Bynum examined the lives of many medieval women and proposed that food, rather than poverty or chastity, was central to their lives. She collected a vast amount of information gathered from hagiographies showing how food played an essential part in women's spirituality. Bynum contradicted the notion that medieval asceticism was world-denying or self-hating dualism. Instead, it was motivated by a deep desire to imitate the suffering Christ in their bodies. They saw their own female bodies as symbols of the humanity of God.

Contemporary Feminist Theology. Contemporary female theologians throughout the world are reexamining, from a feminist perspective, every form of contemporary religious life and thought. Perhaps the most outstanding of these is Rosemary Radford Ruether, professor of theology at Garrett-Evangelical Seminary on the campus of Northwestern University in Chicago. Of her two dozen books and more than five hundred articles, the book *Sexism and God-Talk: Toward a Feminist Theology* (1983) has been most influential because it systematically reviews all the major theological topics: God, the Creation, the human person, Christology, Mariology, evil, redemption, and life after death. The chapter "Can a Male Savior Save Women?" has inspired Christians by the realization that the Jesus of the synoptic Gospels is compatible with feminism. He preached that a person's status is not indicative of the favor or disfavor of God and renounced systems of domination. Another volume of this type is Catherine Mowry LaCugna's *Freeing Theology: The Essentials of Theology in Feminist Perspective* (1993), which contains ten articles dealing with various theological topics from a feminist perspective. LaCugna is a professor of theology at Notre Dame University.

Female theologians such as Denise Lardner Carmody and Ursula King have taken on the task of examining world religions. Carmody's book *Women and World Religions* (1989) looks at women in primal societies, as well as women in Hinduism, Buddhism, Taoism, Shintoism, Judaism, Islam, and Christianity. King's book *Women in the World's Religions: Past and Present* (1987) includes African traditional religions and evangelical feminism. Generally, the authors have concluded that women have not been honored in these religions but have been thought of as bearers of children and as belonging to a lower position than that of men. By exposing these attitudes, these authors hope to make women aware of how their status needs to be enhanced. Other interesting authors in this regard are Karen McCarthy Brown, who has studied Haitian voudou in *Mama Lola: A Voudou Priestess in Brooklyn* (1991), and Paula Gunn Allen, who has written about Native American religion in *The Sacred Hoop: Recounting the Feminine in American Indian Traditions* (1986).

A point that plagues women in religion is whether to stay with a sexist religion to try to change it from within or to leave it because of its sexism. Sandra Schneiders, professor of the New Testament and spirituality at the Jesuit School of Theology in Berkeley, California, in her lecture series published as *Beyond Patching: Faith and Feminism in the Catholic Church* (1991), addresses this dilemma. Feminist Catholics, she says, are those who stay within the Catholic Church but who work to change it by using inclusive language in the liturgy and by including all members of the church in its decision making whenever possible. Catholic feminists, however, want to remain Catholic but are not willing to wait for the church to make changes in its hierarchical structures. Some of the women have formed small communities of their own in which they pray and hold liturgical services. Rosemary Radford Ruether's book *Woman-Church: Theology and Practice of Feminist Liturgical Communities* (1986) also reflects on this dilemma and offers suggestions and readings for such woman-centered liturgies.

A Canadian woman who has written much about women in ministry is Ellen Leonard, a professor at the University of Toronto. Two books are *George Tyrrell and the Catholic Tradition* (1982) and *Unresting Transformation: The Theology and Spirituality of Maude Petre* (1991). She has also written dozens of articles, most of which concern the role of women in the church and their contributions to the theological endeavor.

—*Winifred Whelan*

See also Christianity and women; Feminism, spiritual; Goddess, concept of the; Islam and women; Judaism and women; Religion; Spirituality movement, women's; Stanton, Elizabeth Cady; Witchcraft; Womanchurch; *Woman's Bible, The*

Bibliography

Gadon, Elinor W. *The Once and Future Goddess: A Symbol for Our Time*. New York: Harper & Row, 1989. Describes the prehistoric Goddess religions, tells of their demise, and speaks of how the Goddess is being revived in many areas.

Gudorf, Christine E. "The Power to Create: Sacraments and Men's Need to Birth." *Horizons* 14, no. 2 (Fall, 1987): 296-309. Proposes that by taking on the sacramental roles for themselves, men have assumed the duties and privileges of women—for example, giving birth, feeding, and healing.

Loades, Ann, ed. *Feminist Theology: A Reader*. London: SPCK, 1990. Contains excerpts from twenty-two feminist theologians on many different topics concerning biblical tradition and interpretation, Christian history and tradition, and the effects of feminist theology on modern life.

McFague, Sallie. *The Body of God: An Ecological Theology*. Minneapolis: Fortress Press, 1993. McFague invites readers to think of the world as God's body, not pantheistically but metaphorically. This would force people to look at the world ecologically and to realize that all people and all creation are related to one another.

Ortner, Sherry B. "Is Female to Nature as Male Is to Culture?" In *Women, Culture, and Society*, edited by Michelle Z. Rosaldo and Louise Lamphere. Stanford, Calif.: Stanford University Press, 1974. Ortner's landmark article speaks of dualistic attitudes that separate male/female, light/dark, mind/body, and spirit/matter and proposes that women are often connected to the second and inferior half of the duality.

Ruether, Rosemary Radford, and Eleanor McLaughlin, eds. *Women of Spirit: Female Leadership in the Jewish and Christian Traditions*. New York: Simon & Schuster, 1979. This anthology of articles presents insights into women's religious activities from each major period of Jewish and Christian history.

Time Has Come: A Catholic Doctor's Proposals to End the Battle over Birth Control, The

Author: John Rock

Date: 1963

Relevant issues: Health and medicine, religious beliefs and practices, reproductive rights

Significance: This book by a Roman Catholic gynecologist suggested ways to reconcile religious controversies about birth control

Published at a time of increasing concern about overpopulation and the role of the Catholic church in public policy, *The Time Has Come* addressed such issues as the impact of world population growth, the provision of fertility control methods to developing nations, and the role of public agencies regarding birth control for clients. It was influential not only because of the author's scientific reputation—John Rock had pioneered research on women's reproductive processes including treatment of infertility and the development of oral contraceptives—but also because of his religion—he was Roman Catholic. Rock argued that religious differences on family planning could be bridged by a policy of tolerance and set forth principles for setting family planning policy in a democratic society. Finally, he suggested that the use of birth control pills should be acceptable to Roman Catholics because the hormones involved are analogous to natural ones. Population control advocates received the book enthusiastically, while many Roman Catholics criticized Rock for failing to obtain an imprimatur (permission to publish) from the Catholic church for work of this kind and for attempting to minimize the obligation of Catholics to accept official teachings.

See also Birth control and family planning; Christianity and women; Family planning services; Religion; Reproductive rights

Title VII of the Civil Rights Act of 1964

DATE: Enacted on July 25, 1964

RELEVANT ISSUES: Civil rights, employment, politics, sex and gender

SIGNIFICANCE: Even earliest participants in the women's rights movement recognized that employment discrimination based on gender was rampant; this legislation was one of the first attempts to address the issue

Title VII of the Civil Rights Act of 1964 prohibits discrimination based on race, color, religion, national origin, or sex in all terms, conditions, or privileges of employment. Originally, the Civil Rights Act was geared toward easing racial discrimination. The inclusion of the sex prohibition was tacked onto the bill by a Southern member of Congress to make a joke of the bill, divide its supporters, and ultimately lead to its defeat. The enactment of this major piece of antidiscrimination legislation is interesting because no organized women's group spoke on its behalf, although Democrat Martha W. Griffiths and other female legislators solidly supported its passage. It was decided that the best strategy to ensure the success of the initiative was to downplay the gender issue, and the strategy worked.

Title VII included an important exception: Discrimination based on sex, religion, or national origin (but not race) is permissible if it is a "bona fide occupational qualification reasonably necessary to the normal operation of that particular business enterprise." To enforce the act's provisions, the Equal Employment Opportunity Commission (EEOC) was established. From the beginning, EEOC officials refused to take the sex provision seriously. It was the EEOC's nonenforcement of the act that served as the catalyst for the formation of the National Organization for Women (NOW) in 1966.

See also Affirmative action; Antidiscrimination laws; Bona fide occupational qualifications (BFOQs); Civil Rights Act of 1964; Equal Employment Opportunity Commission (EEOC); National Organization for Women (NOW)

Title IX of the Education Amendments of 1972

RELEVANT ISSUES: Civil rights, education, sports

SIGNIFICANCE: This law was the first federal legislation in the United States to prohibit sexual discrimination in educational institutions and agencies

Title IX of the Education Amendments of 1972 states that "No person in the United States shall, on the basis of sex, be excluded from participation in, be denied the benefits of, or be subjected to discrimination under any education program or activity receiving Federal financial assistance." Male and female students must be given equal opportunity and treatment in admissions, curricular and extracurricular programs and activities, student benefits and services, and employment.

Why Title IX? Testimony at congressional hearings before the passage of Title IX documented the pervasiveness of direct and indirect sexual discrimination in educational institutions. For example, secondary vocational schools were often completely segregated on the basis of gender. Financial assistance was distributed unevenly, with women less likely to receive awards. At some colleges, rules required female students to live on campus while male students could live off campus. Discriminatory policies affected hiring and promotions so that women with advanced degrees were not working in jobs that matched their qualifications. Men's and women's athletic programs were not equal in size or quality, availability of coaching, equipment, or facilities.

Objectives. The regulations to implement Title IX, which became effective on July 21, 1975, specified five tasks for educational institutions: first, to state the policy of sexual nondiscrimination in all school and employment documents; second, to appoint an employee to coordinate compliance efforts; third, to develop a grievance procedure for student and employee complaints; fourth, to conduct an institutional self-evaluation to assess current practices and institute new policies; and, fifth, to submit an assurance form of the Office for Civil Rights with all applications for federal financial assistance. Institutions were required to take both remedial and affirmative action if sexual discrimination was determined to exist. Exemptions applied to schools that were traditionally single-sex or that held religious tenets that prevented compliance.

Impact. Title IX has eliminated the most blatant discriminatory practices in education, especially in admissions. Colleges can no longer set higher admission standards for women than for men, and graduate schools cannot use the "equal rejection rate" system that ensured acceptance of equal numbers of men and women even when women might be more highly qualified. Placement in courses in all subjects, including vocational, technical, and advanced courses, cannot be determined by sex, and institutions are required to take reme-

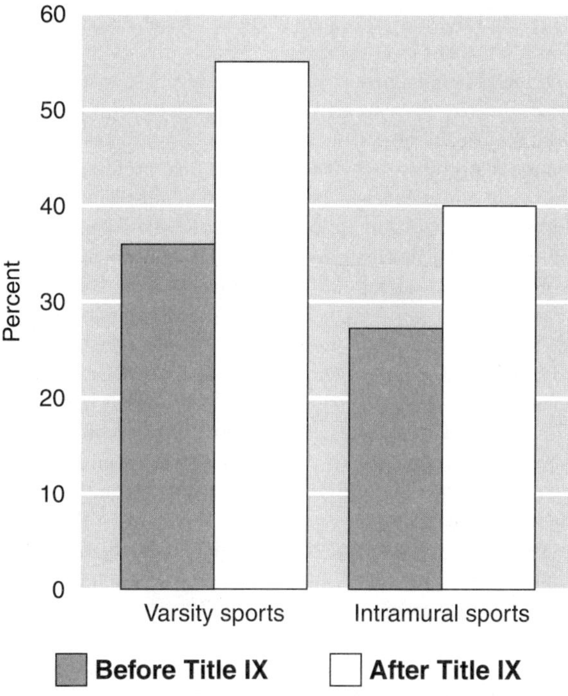

Source: Women's Sports Foundation

dial action through recruiting and course revisions to ensure that access is open.

Title IX was especially felt in athletics. There was a tremendous increase in the number of women participating in school sports. The percentage of female high school athletes increased from 7 percent to 35 percent between 1972 and 1982, and girls' teams were included in local, state, and national high school organizations. In 1971, the Association for Intercollegiate Athletics for Women was formed as an independent organization; eventually, membership grew from 278 to 973 institutions by 1979-1980. Between 1971 and 1980, the percentage of female college athletes increased from 15 percent to 30 percent. Many institutions voluntarily expanded their women's athletic programs prior to the passage of Title IX or following the self-studies required for implementation in 1975-1976. Teams were created, schedules were expanded, and more money was budgeted for travel and equipment. State, regional, and national championships were added. Coaches of female teams began to be compensated at a higher level, although they were usually required to also fill teaching and administrative roles. Perhaps most significant, there was a general change in attitude about the importance of sports activities for girls and young women.

Limited Success. Beyond admissions and athletics, Title IX has had limited impact on other sources of gender bias: curriculum, classroom procedures, the interaction between male and female students, and faculty support. Assumptions that female students are gifted verbally and male students are gifted in science and mathematics prevail, and most young women are not encouraged to take courses that provide entry to scientific and technical fields. Many vocational programs are still segregated by sex, with change stymied by the virtual lack of role models for women or men outside of a narrow range of occupations. Moreover, although sexual harassment is prohibited under Title IX, schools often do little to prevent such behavior.

By the mid-1990's, women still did not have equal opportunity in sports programs and may have actually lost ground. While women generally formed 50 percent of the student body at various institutions, they made up only 33 percent of college athletes. At the high school level, women accounted for 39 percent of athletes. The number of female coaches had declined significantly. With improved salaries, men applied for jobs coaching female teams. In 1972, more than 90 percent of the coaches for women's college teams were women; in 1990, only 47.3 percent were women. Traditional female sports such as volleyball or field hockey were being coached by men or eliminated from the schedule. The two fastest growing sports between 1977 and the 1990's were soccer and cross-country running, but the percentage of female coaches in these sports continued to decline. Women had not moved into jobs coaching male teams; in the 1995, 99 percent of male college teams were coached by men. Women also lost leadership roles: When men's and women's athletic departments were combined, often the head of the men's department became the chief administrator. The same was true for sports officials. As the payment for officiating at an athletic contest increased for women, the number of female officials decreased, especially in women's basketball, softball, and volleyball. In sports media, women have a limited, usually insignificant role. Women are writing about and broadcasting women's sports, but they have made little progress in covering male sports, often because they lack access to the locker room.

The Reaction of Women. Despite the opening of opportunities by Title IX, many women believe that real progress can only be made by changing the practices that limit women and men to traditionally accepted areas of study, work, and play, which requires effective monitoring of programs and strong enforcement of Title IX. Women are calling for a renewed commitment to this law in order to improve the quality of public education for everyone. Schools and teachers need to use methods that promote gender equity and include the experiences of women in the curriculum. National boards and professional organizations should include women as part of reform efforts.

Female athletes must continue to work to overcome the same problems that existed in 1972. Reformers call for compliance with Title IX as a precondition for membership in the

National Collegiate Athletic Association (NCAA). They also seek more scholarships for women and the appointment of female athletic administrators to regulate and evaluate women's athletic programs. —*Jeanne M. McGlinn*

See also Affirmative action; Antidiscrimination laws; Association for Intercollegiate Athletics for Women; Civil Rights Restoration Act of 1987; Education of women; Gymnastics, women in; Higher education, women in; Professional sports, women in; Sexism; Softball, women in; Sports, women in

BIBLIOGRAPHY

Durrant, Sue M. "Title IX: Its Power and Its Limitations." *Journal of Physical Education, Recreation, and Dance* 63 (March, 1992): 60-64.

Hoepner, Barbara J., ed. *Women's Athletics: Coping with Controversy*. Washington, D.C.: American Association for Health, Physical Education, and Recreation, 1974.

National Foundation for the Improvement of Education. *Title IX: Selected Resources*. Washington, D.C.: Government Printing Office, 1977.

Wellesley College. Center for Research on Women. *How Schools Shortchange Girls: A Study of Major Findings on Girls and Education*. Washington, D.C.: AAUW Educational Foundation and National Education Association, 1992.

Westervelt, Esther Manning. *Barriers to Women's Participation in Postsecondary Education: A Review of Research and Commentary as of 1973-74*. Washington, D.C.: Government Printing Office, 1975.

Tokenism

RELEVANT ISSUES: Business and economics, employment

SIGNIFICANCE: Women pursuing careers in male-dominated professions are often judged by male peers on the basis of dubious gender stereotypes rather than on objective assessments of job performance

After passage of the Civil Rights Act of 1964, which made sexual discrimination illegal, career opportunities in professions traditionally associated with white men (such as business management) gradually increased for women. Entry into such professions, however, did not end the sexual discrimination that many professional women faced. Instead, it marked the beginning of a new, subtle form of sexual discrimination: tokenism. Tokenism occurs in situations where small numbers of people from previously excluded groups are brought into the dominant group to satisfy society's demands for their inclusion. Gender-based tokenism refers to situations in which small numbers of women are brought into male-dominated professions to serve as symbolic representatives of the female sex. As tokens, such women are typically viewed by their male colleagues as women first and professionals second. Thus, they are automatically gender-stereotyped as being too passive, too emotional, and not competitive enough to handle the responsibilities of the positions into which they have moved.

Therefore, token women and their work tend to be more closely scrutinized than is normal for the situation. Ironically, when women under scrutiny measure up and perform well, their success tends to be attributed to luck or happen-stance rather than to skill and ability. Tokenism leads not only to excessive scrutiny but also to exclusion. In many cases, token women are never fully embraced by the dominant group. They are excluded from both formal and informal activities that would put them in contact with potential clients and others who might help them succeed in their careers. Consequently, these women are prevented from adequately fulfilling their work responsibilities, a situation that only reinforces the perception that women are not suitable for some professions.

Female professionals may further appear unsuitable if they find themselves playing traditional female roles while on the job. Sociologist Rosabeth Moss Kanter became aware of this problem while studying the experiences of token women in a large American corporation. Her findings, though published in 1978, are still relevant. Kanter noted that a token woman might be miscast in the role of "mother" simply because she is female, and therefore is perceived to be naturally nurturing and caring. Male colleagues then bring their private troubles to her in anticipation of being comforted. A token woman might also be viewed sexually, miscast in the role of "seductress," an object of sexual competition.

Such stereotypical casting clouds the employment picture, minimizing the possibility that a fair assessment of a woman's job performance can be made. Gender stereotyping creates an environment in which female professionals are misjudged in many ways because they are perceived as automatically inferior to male professionals. Some women, however, enjoy success in the male world, which signals other women that career opportunities do not have to be limited by sex.

See also Affirmative action; Employment of women; Glass ceiling; Hiring quotas; Sexism; Stereotypes of women

Toxic shock syndrome

RELEVANT ISSUES: Health and medicine

SIGNIFICANCE: This disease caused by a bacterial infection in particular affects women who are using tampons and may cause serious illness that leads to death

Toxic shock syndrome, a rare form of septic shock, occurs when the immune system mounts an excessive response to a bacterial infection, usually one caused by the *Staphylococcus aureus* bacterium. The symptoms include a high fever, vomiting, diarrhea, a sudden drop in blood pressure, and a rash that causes the skin to peel. The result can be shock, organ failure, and death. In most cases, toxic shock syndrome has occurred in menstruating women. The condition has usually been traced to the use of high-absorbency tampons, but it has also been associated with contraceptive devices such as sponges and diaphragms.

During the 1970's, the occurrence of toxic shock syndrome in menstruating women became dramatically noticeable, and some women died. Research indicated a connection with the use of high-absorbency tampons whose composition included superabsorbent chemicals and synthetic fibers. Tampon manufacturers voluntarily withdrew these products from the market. In 1990, the Food and Drug Administration (FDA) issued a standard for labeling the absorbency rate of tampons. Although these measures have contributed to a decrease in toxic shock syndrome, it still occurs in association with tampon use. Because of the seriousness of this condition, women should be aware of the dangers and risk factors, particularly if they are using tampons, and seek immediate medical attention if they experience symptoms.

See also Health and medicine; Health movement, women's; Menstruation

Track and field, women in

RELEVANT ISSUE: Sports

SIGNIFICANCE: No other sports story reflects the transformation of public attitudes concerning women and sports than the success, despite early resistance, of women in track and field competition

Vassar College in New York was the venue for the first women's track and field contests in 1895, featuring competition in sprints, hurdles, and jumps. In 1888, men's tournaments were sponsored by the new Amateur Athletic Union (AAU), which staged these annual contests until 1980, when The Athletic Congress assumed sponsorship. Despite the promising beginnings at Vassar College, it took society a long time to accept the idea of national competitions for women in track and field sports.

Women had no sporting organization until the Fédération Sportive Féminine Internationale (FSFI) was formed in Paris in 1921; the United States was one of the six founders. In 1927, the AAU began offering indoor national contests for female track and field athletes, and the next year the Olympic Games provided some similar events in Amsterdam. In 1934, women's events were introduced at the British Commonwealth Games. They were included in the Pan American Games from their inception in 1951 and in World Cup competition since 1977.

When the AAU opened women's competition in the 1920's, there was great excitement nationwide, but this interest lagged in the next decade and was not revived until the 1950's. During this era, African American athletes from Tuskegee Institute and Tennessee State College captured most of the AAU medals and later at the Pan American Games as well. Most high schools and colleges provided limited opportunities for women in these sports. The Association for Intercollegiate Athletics for Women sponsored competitions for female track and field athletes at the college and university level after 1969, but the National Collegiate Athletic Association (NCAA) absorbed its operations after 1981.

Among the early heroines of American track and field were eleven-time AAU titleholders Stella Walsh in the 200-meter sprint (1930-1948); Maren Saidler in the shotput (1967-1980); and Dorothy Dodson in the javelin toss (1939-1949). From Canada, there was the heralded J. Haist, winner of both the discus and the javelin toss at the Commonwealth Games in 1974.

Endurance Factor. Aside from social conventions about the "proper" place of women in society, most fears about female athletes centered on the question of endurance. For example, controversy erupted over the 800-meter race for women at the Olympic Games at Amsterdam in 1928, when six of the nine women allegedly finished in a state of exhaustion and sportswriters suggested that the event was too demanding for the female body. The race was eliminated from women's Olympic events and not reinstated until 1960.

By the 1970's, such concerns were almost eliminated when Boston Marathon and New York Marathon officials agreed to allow women in these grueling events. In 1972, the first woman to finish the Boston Marathon, Nina Kuscsik of New York, did so in a time of 3:08:58, which was fifty-three minutes, nineteen seconds behind the top male finisher; in 1994, Uta Pippig of Germany finished with a mark of 2:21:45, a mere fourteen minutes, thirty seconds behind the male leader. The first woman to win the New York Marathon, in 1971, was American Beth Bonner with a time of 2:55:22, which was thirty-three minutes, thirty-two seconds behind the men's winner; in 1993, Pippig won the New York Marathon with a time of 2:26:24, only sixteen minutes, twenty seconds after the men's champion. Such figures indicate that concern about the gender gap in endurance was overrated.

Olympic Games. Baron Pierre de Coubertin, founder of the modern Olympic movement, illustrated popular views about female athletes when he banned them from the first modern Games in 1896 because he considered them physically (and socially) unfit for such endeavors. Although a handful of women did enter the Games before World War I, their restricted participation led women to form their own Olympic-type contests. Some were allowed to enter golf, tennis, and a few swimming events before 1928, but women were excluded from track and field competition, the central attraction of the Olympic Games. Female representatives of the FSFI then organized their own Women's Olympics at Paris in 1922. Their success was sufficient to persuade the world track and field associations to permit women to compete in the Olympic Games in Amsterdam in 1928. The separate women's games were abandoned after 1934.

Canadian women captured the most medals at these first track events at Amsterdam. In the finals of the relay race, the Canadians shattered their own world's record, beating the second-place Americans. The Canadian team won the highly celebrated 400-meter relay, and Ethel Catherwood (the "Saskatoon Lily") won the gold medal in the high jump, setting a record that lasted until 1948. Young Betty Robinson won the first track and field gold medal for the United States in the 100-meter sprint. Although the International Amateur Athletic Federation voted to retain women's track and field events in future Olympic Games, surprisingly, the Canadian representatives voted against continuing them.

North American winners were comparatively few in the next generation. The exception was Mildred "Babe" Didrikson Zaharias, voted the top female athlete of the first half of the twentieth century. The winner of the javelin throw and the 80-meter hurdles at Los Angeles in 1932, she set a world record in the high jump but was placed second because of a questionable style of leap.

A new era opened at Rome in 1960 when Wilma Rudolph won three gold medals in track and field. She was the first great African American female runner and was followed by such stars as Evelyn Ashford, Florence Griffith-Joyner, and Jackie Joyner-Kersee. Ashford's four gold and one silver medal were almost as startling as her participation in four Olympics: in Montreal, Los Angeles, Seoul, and Barcelona. Sprinter Griffith-Joyner won three gold medals at Seoul in 1988; she was also awarded two silver medals. Joyner-Kersee also won three gold medals—for the long jump (1988), the pentathlon (1988), and the heptathlon (1992)—as well as one silver and two bronze medals. Gail Devers won the 100-meter race in the Atlanta Games in 1996. Joan Benoit achieved fame when she won the first Olympic marathon race for women in 1984.

Impact of Women in the Sport. The slow acceptance of women in track and field sports was attributable to a variety of factors. It took many years to shed the Victorian conception that athletic competition was a physical danger to future mothers. Even some women's organizations subscribed to that shibboleth. No doubt women's participation on the home front in World Wars I and II contributed to changing attitudes, as well as economic progress that created the leisure time for more women to participate in sports. The challenge of the Cold War was a significant reason for the expansion of female competitors in track and field: The success of Soviet and other East European women after 1952 threatened to sweep all medals in international competition and was combined with the widespread perception that the accumulation of medals at the World and Olympic Games would promote ideological victory.

—John D. Windhausen

Florence Griffith Joyner hands off the baton to Evelyn Ashford for the final leg of the 4 x 100 relay, as the U.S. team captures the gold medal in the Seoul Games of 1988. (AP/Wide World Photos)

See also Association for Intercollegiate Athletics for Women; Olympic Games, women in; Sports, women in

Bibliography

Meserole, Mike, ed. *The 1995 Information Please Sports Almanac*. Boston: Houghton Mifflin, 1995.

Porter, David L., ed. *Biographical Dictionary of American Sports: Outdoor Sports*. New York: Greenwood Press, 1988.

Runner's World, the editors of. *The Complete Woman Runner*. Mountain View, Calif.: World, 1978.

Watman, Mel, comp. *Encyclopedia of Track and Field Athletics*. 2d ed. New York: St. Martin's Press, 1981.

Triangle Shirtwaist Company fire

Date: March 25, 1911

Place: New York City

Relevant issues: Business and economics, employment, women's history

Significance: This tragic accident that killed 146 people, most of them women, led to tougher laws in New York State to protect women and spurred union organizing among women

On March 25, 1911, a deadly fire broke out in the building that housed the Triangle Shirtwaist Company, located in the Greenwich Village district of New York City. The entire structure was soon consumed by flames. The firm was a notorious sweatshop where a predominantly female force of immigrant workers turned out cheap clothing in wretched, unsanitary, and unsafe conditions. Such establishments were common in the garment district of New York at the beginning of the twentieth century, a time when poor women had to take work where they could find it. As the fire spread from the discarded rags where it had started, the trapped workers sought to escape by jumping out of windows to the pavement; they fell ten stories to their deaths. Others died inside from the effects of the smoke. Those who sought to flee found that exit doors did not open or that faulty fire escapes blocked their route. The death toll reached 146, most of them women. Dramatic pictures filled the New York newspapers the next day, depicting the horrors of the scene. The fire became one of the worst fatal accidents in the history of American industrialism.

Protests about the unsafe conditions followed. A rally was organized by the National Women's Trade Union League (NWTUL) and drew eighty thousand marchers. An outraged public opinion became even more incensed when a jury acquitted the building's owners of wrongdoing. The popular outcry against sweatshops accelerated the campaign of the NWTUL and the International Ladies' Garment Workers' Union (ILGWU) to reform the system in New York City that kept many women in economic serfdom to the clothing trade. The ILGWU, led by Rose Schneiderman and other female activists, joined with middle-class reformers in demands for a state investigating commission to probe the causes of the blaze and to recommend laws to prevent future fires in the garment district.

The New York State Factory Investigating Commission made its report in 1914 and advocated sweeping changes in health and safety regulations. At first, the New York legislature resisted an effort to implement the commission's findings, but leading Democrats, including state senator Robert F. Wagner and future governor Alfred E. Smith, pressed for and secured passage of tougher laws against sweatshops. The Triangle Shirtwaist Company fire became a landmark episode in the effort to improve working conditions for all American women and to safeguard them against the devastating effects of industrial accidents. It represented a turning point in the struggle for decent treatment of women in the workplace during the era of progressive reform from 1900 to 1920 in the United States.

See also Employment of women; Garment industry and women; Immigrant women; International Ladies' Garment Workers' Union (ILGWU); Labor movement and women; National Women's Trade Union League (NWTUL); Protective legislation for women

Truth, Sojourner

(Isabella Baumfree or Isabella Van Wagener; c. 1797, Hurley, Ulster County, N.Y.--Nov. 26, 1883, Battle Creek, Mich.)

Areas of achievement: Civil rights, race and ethnicity, social reform

Significance: Truth escaped slavery as a young adult and spent the rest of her life speaking on spiritual themes and urging abolition, social justice, and woman suffrage

Fleeing slavery, Sojourner Truth eventually settled in New York City. Although illiterate, she believed in the efficacy of law and successfully pursued several lawsuits to free her son Peter. Always deeply religious, Truth was convinced by a series of visions in 1843 that her true calling was truth-speaking to the world. Taking the name "Sojourner Truth," she began forty years of lecturing, preaching, and singing.

Truth traveled the United States with antislavery organizations. Her extemporaneous speeches wove personal experiences, wit, Bible stories, and scripture into persuasive calls for social justice, as did her dictated autobiography, *Narrative of Sojourner Truth* (1850). Truth's most famous speech was "Ain't I a Woman?" It blends religious and women's rights themes: "Then that little man . . . says women can't have as much rights as men, 'cause Christ wasn't a woman! Where did your Christ come from? . . . From God and a woman! Man had nothing to do with Him."

After the Civil War, Elizabeth Cady Stanton recruited Truth for the woman suffrage movement, and Truth continued lecturing for almost twenty years, calling her audiences "chil'n," because "you are somebody's chil'n, and I am old enough to be mother of all that is here."

See also Abolitionist movement and women; African American women; Black feminism; Civil rights and civil liberties for American women; Evangelists and faith healers, women as; Religion; Religious movements founded by women; Slavery; Suffrage movement and suffragists

Tubal ligation

Relevant issues: Health and medicine

Significance: Tubal ligation, which has been performed since 1823, is the method of choice for women desiring nonreversible sterilization in a safe and effective procedure

Tubal ligation produces permanent sterilization by interrupting the Fallopian tubes, the pathways through which eggs travel from the ovaries to the uterus. The procedure has a failure rate of less than 1 percent and takes effect immediately. Three options are commonly available for performing this procedure. First, in laparoscopy, a 2-centimeter incision is made just above the navel and air is pumped into the body to help the physician separate and identify the Fallopian tubes, intestines, and uterus. The laparoscope, a fiber-optic tube, is inserted into the cavity, and the Fallopian tubes are cut, clamped, or cauterized with electrical current in order to disconnect the passageway. The laparoscope is removed, and the incision is closed. This procedure may occur under general or local anesthesia. Second, a laparotomy may be performed, in which the pelvic cavity is opened in order to sever the Fallopian tubes. This more invasive procedure may be performed for many reasons, including difficulty in assessing the position of the tubes or the presence of endometriosis or infection. Laparotomies require a general anesthetic and significant recuperation time. Third, tubal ligation can be performed pursuant to a delivery by cesarean section, when the tubes are readily accessible.

Major complications, such as infection, bleeding, or death, develop in 1.7 percent of cases. Complications may also arise from anesthesia. Research indicates a positive side effect of tubal ligation: The procedure reduces the risk of ovarian cancer. Candidates for the procedure include women who have completed their families, who do not desire children, or who have physical or mental health reasons precluding children. Ethical concerns include the age of the client, the consent of the spouse, payment for the procedure, and informed consent.

See also Birth control and family planning; Cesarean section; Endometriosis; Pregnancy and childbirth; Sterilization of women

Tubman, Harriet

(Araminta Ross; c. 1820, Bucktown, Dorcester County, Md.—Mar. 10, 1913, Auburn, N.Y.)

Areas of achievement: Civil rights, race and ethnicity

Significance: Tubman was one of the creators of the Underground Railroad, which transported slaves to safety in the North and Canada

Harriet Tubman escaped from slavery in 1849 and became a prominent member of the abolitionist movement. As one of the "conductors" on the Underground Railroad, a daring system that helped slaves escape to the North and Canada, she helped more than three hundred slaves travel to freedom. Tubman worked closely with leading abolitionists such as Wendell Phillips and John Brown. She also worked for the Union cause during the Civil War.

See also Abolitionist movement and women; African American women; Black feminism; Civil War and women; Slavery

Turner's syndrome

Relevant issues: Health and medicine; sex and gender

Significance: Turner's syndrome, a genetic condition of human females which was first described by H. Turner in 1938, is believed to be caused by the failure of the sex chromosomes to segregate during early fetal development; the result is the presence of a single X chromosome in either all cells or certain lines of cells.

The incidence of Turner's syndrome in the population ranges from 1 in 2,000 to 1 in 5,000 live-born phenotypic girls. Certain physical, neuropsychological, and temperamental characteristics are found in individuals who have been born with this syndrome. Physical characteristics that are always found among these individuals are infertility and growth retardation that results in small stature. Many women discover that they have Turner's syndrome when they are investigating possible causes of their infertility, and this condition is one of the most common contributing factors because it prevents the ovaries from forming. Other physical characteristics of Turner's syndrome may include a webbed neck, and cubitus valgus, in which the forearm is turned outward from the body.

Neuropsychological function may be impaired in specific ways. The cognitive abilities affected include spatial difficulty called space-form blindness and attentional short-term memory. Individuals with Turner's syndrome may also have trouble with cognitive tasks such as numerical concepts. Despite these problems, these individuals display normal intelligence, and no evidence has been found of disabling psychopathology.

In temperament and personality, individuals with Turner's syndrome tend to be extroverted and emotionally stable. They are accepting of change and variance in their environment, compliant, sensitive, and passive. These patients have been called "ultrafeminine." Considering the personality attributes listed above, a sexist bias can be detected, recalling a time when all women were expected to be compliant, passive, and accepting.

The presence of Turner's syndrome is not always evident in an individual and certainly does not preclude an active life. During the 1992 Olympic Games, the sex-test used to determine the sexual identity of competing athletes was challenged because it disqualified women who had certain medical conditions, including Turner's syndrome. This test, called the buccal smear test, detects the presence of two X chromosomes in cells gathered from the inside of the cheek. This test has probably disqualified Olympic contenders unfairly in the past, and it may be discontinued in favor of means that do not discriminate against women with Turner's syndrome and others who lack a second X chromosome.

Several ongoing studies seek to treat girls with this condition, helping them to overcome their growth retardation. Early detection of Turner's syndrome in girls can help their parents gain valuable information needed to deal with any problems associated with the syndrome, including certain behavioral problems exhibited in early childhood. A support group exists for individuals with Turner's syndrome and their families.

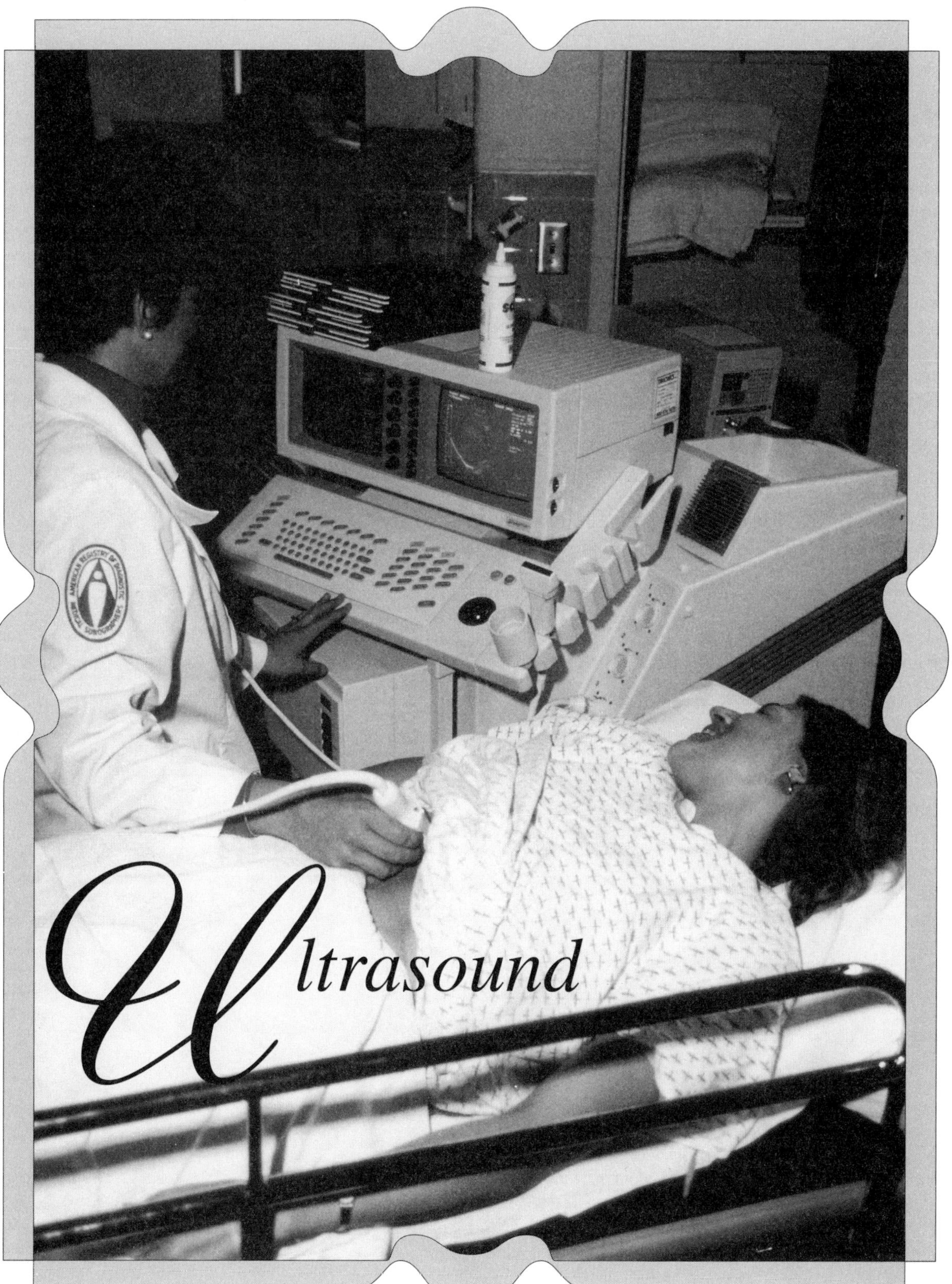

Ultrasound

Ultrasound

Relevant issues: Health and medicine

Significance: This medical procedure is used to assess fetal development during pregnancy and internal soft tissue structures

The first use of ultrasound was in industry, where it was used to detect flaws in metal. Ultrasound has developed into a medical diagnostic procedure during which sound waves are beamed into body tissues. The sound waves create an image of the fetus or internal soft tissue structure by bouncing back from soft tissue, like an echo. They are then converted into electrical energy and seen as bright spots on an oscilloscope.

The age of a fetus and the presence of some birth defects can be determined using ultrasound. The procedure may be used at any time during pregnancy, but birth defects may not be accurately assessed during the first three months. Ultrasound has not been found to have negative side effects.

Ultrasound has many other medical uses. It can detect abnormal pregnancies such as ectopic pregnancy. During ectopic pregnancy, the fertilized egg implants and grows outside the uterus. With ultrasound, the embryo can be detected before any major damage occurs. Ultrasound is also used to monitor ovulation, in order to enhance fertility, and to detect ovarian tumors. Birth defects detected by ultrasound may lead parents to choose a therapeutic abortion. The result is a conflict between a woman's right to have an abortion and value judgments concerning individuals with birth defects.

See also Abortion; Amniocentesis; Family planning services; Pregnancy and childbirth; Prenatal care

United Nations Decade for Women

Also known as: International Women's Decade

Date: 1976-1985

Relevant issues: Civil rights, education, employment, family, politics, poverty, sex and gender, social reform

Significance: Recognizing that discrimination against women is an international problem with cultural variations, the United Nations Commission on the Status of Women declared a Decade for Women

At the United Nations First World Conference on Women, held in Mexico City in 1975, the delegates declared 1976-1985 to be the Decade for Women, with the intention of providing an opportunity to focus on women's development and equality from a global perspective. In this manner, the United Nations succeeded in putting women's issues on the international agenda and provided valuable research data. The Second World Conference on Women, held in Copenhagen, Denmark, in 1980, was intended to provide guidelines and action plans for governments to improve the status of women during the second half of the decade. Instead, the conference agenda was politicized and the delegates were divided by the inclusion of Middle-Eastern issues related to the socioeconomic needs of Palestinian women. At the Third World Conference on Women, held in Nairobi, Kenya, in 1985 at the end of the Decade for Women, the delegates concluded that much of women's inequality is attributable to the economic undervaluation of their roles as wives and mothers.

See also International Women's Year; United Nations First World Conference on Women; United Nations Second World Conference on Women; United Nations Third World Conference on Women

United Nations First World Conference on Women

Also known as: United Nations World Conference of the International Women's Year; Mexico City Conference

Date: June 19-July 2, 1975

Place: Mexico City, Mexico

Relevant issues: Civil rights, education, health and medicine, politics, poverty, sex and gender, social reform

Significance: This conference was an attempt to promote awareness of and action on women's issues at an international level, illustrating that the need for reform extended across borders

As a focal point of the International Women's Year and the start of the United Nations Decade for Women, this United Nations conference set out to establish a ten-year World Plan of Action to improve the status of women. Its goals were to improve health care and education for women and to increase their participation in government; it excluded any position regarding birth control and abortion. The plan was not legally binding and allowed each country to establish its own policies. Many of the conference delegates, having been sent to represent their own governmental agendas, focused on economic and political issues as necessary precursors to gender equality. Across town from the official conference, a separate tribune sponsored by the United Nations was set up that included nongovernmental organizations and special-interest groups participating in an open forum on women's issues. While the conference did not institute any major policy changes regarding the status of women, it was a starting point for raising awareness of gender inequality worldwide.

See also International Women's Year; United Nations Decade for Women

United Nations Second World Conference on Women

Also known as: United Nations World Conference of the Decade for Women; Copenhagen Conference

Date: July 14-July 30, 1980
Place: Copenhagen, Denmark
Relevant issues: Civil rights, family, politics, poverty, sex and gender, social reform
Significance: This international symposium was designed to help women and governments work together to improve conditions for women worldwide

The Second United Nations Conference on Women was held to determine what progress had been made in the United Nations Decade for Women. Although women constituted half of the world's population, data indicated that governments still had little understanding of women's problems. In some countries, conditions had not improved. Women attending were disappointed when representatives used the formal conference for political debates.

On the positive side, attendance was higher at the Copenhagen Conference than at the Mexico City Conference in 1975, and most of the top officials were women. Members adopted a World Plan of Action and forty-eight resolutions, which offered constructive measures for women to create legislation and change attitudes and prejudices. The plan revitalized the energies of women to pressure their governments and agitate for change. A nongovernmental side forum attended by eight thousand participants from 128 countries emphasized practical solutions to common problems of women from countries as diverse as Peru, India, and the United States. New relationships were formed through the exchange of ideas and information on such topics as running a health clinic, setting up a day care center, and working on rural development problems.

See also United Nations Decade for Women; United Nations First World Conference on Women

United Nations Third World Conference on Women

Also known as: The World Conference to Review and Appraise the Achievements of the United Nations Decade for Women; Nairobi Conference
Date: July 15-26, 1985
Place: Nairobi, Kenya
Significance: The purpose of this conference was to review and appraise the progress achieved and obstacles encountered in attaining the goals and objectives of the United Nations Decade for Women and to implement the document *Nairobi Forward-Looking Strategies for the Advancement of Women*

This international conference was attended by delegations from 157 countries, with 2,020 official delegates appointed by governmental organizations. The heads of delegations included Conference President Margaret Kenyatta of Kenya, Maureen Reagan of the United States, Sally Mugabe of Zimbabwe, Margaret Papandreou of Greece, Suzanne Mubarek of Egypt, and more than four hundred male delegates. Reaffirming the World Plan of Action adopted in Mexico City in 1975 and the Programme of Action adopted in Copenhagen in 1980, the third part of the series of world conferences examined

A highlight of the fourth United Nations women's conference, held in Beijing, China, in 1995, was a speech by First Lady Hillary Rodham Clinton. (AP Photo/Doug Mills)

world development from the woman's point of view and outlined long-term plans of action for equality, development, and peace. The goals to be achieved by the year 2000, according to the document *Nairobi Forward-Looking Strategies for the Advancement of Women*, included the eradication of illiteracy, the extension of life expectancy, self-supporting employment, guaranteed equality in all areas, and the elimination of discriminatory practices.

Independent of but concurrent with the conference was Forum '85, held on the University of Nairobi campus from July 10 to July 19. An informal, grassroots gathering of nongovernmental organizations and individuals, Forum '85 attracted fourteen thousand women from 170 nations. More than one thousand seminars, panels, and workshops addressed practical issues regarding the political, economic, social, and cultural life of women around the world.

See also United Nations Decade for Women; United Nations First World Conference on Women; United Nations Second World Conference on Women; United Nations Fourth World Conference on Women

United Nations Fourth World Conference on Women

Also known as: Beijing Conference

Date: September 4-15, 1995

Place: Beijing, China

Significance: Notwithstanding the widespread harassment and surveillance of delegates by Chinese security officers, the conference successfully worked out and adopted a Platform for Action

The previous United Nations conferences on women were held in Mexico City, Mexico (1975); Copenhagen, Denmark (1980); and Nairobi, Kenya (1985). At the four conferences, some four thousand government delegates represented 185 governments. Meeting in tandem with the official conference was the Nongovernmental Organization Forum on Women, which brought together approximately thirty thousand representatives of some two thousand organizations. The decision to convene in China was controversial because of the country's poor record on human rights. Furthermore, China actively sought to limit criticism by denying visas to selected outspoken women, by prohibiting delegations from Tibet and Taiwan, and by moving the site of the forum to Huairou, 30 miles away from Beijing. Although the conference's Platform for Action lacked the force of law, it was considered to be a politically important instrument to bring about changes in the status of women worldwide. The key issues in the platform were raising the economic circumstances of women, protecting women from violence (and affirming their right to say "no" to sex), and improving the status of girls. On September 5, Hillary Rodham Clinton delivered a forceful speech condemning the violation of the human rights of women. Although censored by the Chinese media, her speech energized the conference. She and Prime Minister Benazir Bhutto of Pakistan emphasized the importance of women in politics.

See also United Nations First World Conference on Women; United Nations Second World Conference on Women; United Nations Third World Conference on Women

United Nations Population Conference

Also known as: Cairo Conference

Date: September 5-13, 1994

Place: Cairo, Egypt

Relevant issues: Demographics, family, politics, reproductive rights

Significance: This conference endorsed a new strategy for stabilizing the world's population, mainly by giving women more control over their lives

The United Nations Population Conference brought some twenty thousand delegates from one hundred fifty countries to consider a program to limit the growth of the world's population. In 1994, the world's population was estimated at 5.67 billion. The aim of the conference was to limit population growth to reach an estimated total population of 7.27 billion by the year 2015. The most controversial issues of the conference centered on abortion and the means to promote family planning. Vigorous objections to family planning—especially abortion—came from the Vatican and several Muslim countries. Saudi Arabia and Sudan boycotted the conference. Previous world population conferences had virtually ignored the abortion issue. At the Bucharest conference in 1974, abortion was not mentioned. A world population conference held in Mexico City in 1984 alluded to abortion only once—to exclude it from the catalog of family planning methods.

Differences over abortion, however, did not prevent approval for the first time of a new concept of population policy going beyond traditional family planning to areas such as reproductive health care. The conference approved a 113-page declaration urging education for girls and the provision to women of a range of choices for family planning and health care. The family was affirmed as "the basic unit of society." The document anticipated a three-fold increase in the amount that the world spent in 1994 annually on population stabilization. Although not binding on governments, the final declaration was widely viewed as an important step toward equality between the sexes and the greater empowerment of women.

See also Abortion; Birth control and family planning; Family planning services; Muslim women; Pro-choice; Reproductive rights; United Nations Decade for Women; United Nations First World Conference on Women; United Nations Second World Conference on Women; United Nations Third World Conference on Women; United Nations Fourth World Conference on Women

United Nations Tribunal on Crimes Against Women

Also known as: International Tribunal on Crimes Against Women

Date: March 4-9, 1976

Place: Brussels, Belgium

Relevant issues: Crime, law, sex and gender

Significance: At this first exclusively female conference of the United Nations, crimes against women in the broadest sense were discussed, testimony was heard, and resolutions were agreed upon

The United Nations addressed women's problems such as health and childbearing long before this tribunal, having proclaimed 1975 as the International Women's Year. Feminists, however, were dissatisfied with the goals announced at the Mexico City Conference held in June, 1975—equality of men and women within existing society. The feminist view was that the patriarchal society itself must be restructured to elevate women from an inevitable second place. With this background, a coordinating committee hastily set up the Brussels tribunal, allowing only female delegates and press representatives, to shed light on crimes against women, defined as "all man-made forms of women's oppression." More than forty nations were represented, and the crimes addressed included forced motherhood, compulsory heterosexuality and the persecution of lesbians, economic oppression, oppression of Third World and immigrant women, and many types of physical violence such as rape, battering, assault, clitoridectomy, excision and infibulation, and forced prostitution. Specific proposals and resolutions were passed for further action by the United Nations, but the real accomplishment of the tribunal appears to have been the solidarity that was generated among women of all countries. This solidarity served as a foundation for the United Nations Decade for Women (1976-1985) and the ever more effective and well-publicized conferences that have followed since 1976.

See also Genital mutilation; Hate crimes against women; International Women's Year; Rape; United Nations Decade for Women; United Nations First World Conference on Women; United Nations Second World Conference on Women; United Nations Third World Conference on Women; United Nations Fourth World Conference on Women; Violence against women

United States Commission on Civil Rights

DATE: Founded on September 9, 1957

RELEVANT ISSUES: Civil rights, politics

SIGNIFICANCE: This civil rights agency has lobbied effectively for legislation and increased enforcement relating to the civil rights of minorities and women

When the U.S. Supreme Court ruled in *Brown v. Board of Education* (1954) that schools could no longer refuse admission to students on the basis of race, members of Congress realized that segregation was to end in due course and that an enormous civil rights agenda loomed. Unable to pass comprehensive legislation because of filibusters from Southern senators, a bipartisan congressional majority managed to pass the mildly worded Civil Rights Act of 1957, which included a provision for the establishment of a federal Commission on Civil Rights with six commissioners, a full-time staff director, and other staff positions.

The commission's main charge is to investigate denials of voting rights and to present studies of problems of civil rights to Congress and the president for action. An important power of the commission is to hold public hearings and to subpoena witnesses regarding alleged denials of these rights. In addition, the Commission on Civil Rights has established state advisory committees to carry out studies at the state level.

Although the commission was set up to provide an arena in which to formulate broad bipartisan policy in regard to minority rights, the concerns of women had more visibility when Frankie Freeman was appointed as the first female commissioner in 1964. In 1974, Congress amended the scope of the commission's work to include the civil rights of women.

Initially, there were six commissioners, nominated by the president and confirmed by the Senate, consisting of three Democrats and three Republicans. In 1981, President Ronald Reagan nearly abolished the commission. As a compromise, the United States Commission on Civil Rights Act of 1983 authorized four members to be appointed by the president, two members by the present pro tempore of the Senate, and two members by the Speaker of the House of Representatives, for a total of four Democrats and four Republicans.

Today, the Commission on Civil Rights has seven divisions. The Office of General Counsel handles proposed legislation, executive actions, and commission hearings. The Office of Program and Policy develops new programs, projects, and policies. The Office of Management looks after personnel, publications, and the library. The Office of Federal Civil Rights Evaluation monitors, evaluates, and reports on civil rights enforcement efforts. The Office of Research conducts studies and prepares monographs. The Office of Congressional and Public Affairs handles liaison with various agencies and outreach to newsmedia. The Office of Regional Programs oversees the fifty state advisory committees.

A controversial report by Mary Frances Berry on constitutional aspects of childbearing for the commission during the late 1970's prompted Congress to remove the subject of abortion from the scope of concerns of the commission during the early years of Reagan's presidency. With Berry's elevation to the position of chair of the commission in 1993, the agency regained its vitality. The Commission on Civil Rights held public hearings on affirmative action in the fall of 1995 in order to sort out facts from fiction on the subject.

See also Civil rights and civil liberties for American women; Politics

Vietnam
Women's
Memorial

Vassar College

Also known as: Vassar Female College

Date: Chartered in 1861, opened in 1865

Relevant issues: Education, women's history

Significance: Vassar was the first adequately financed women's college offering a liberal arts education comparable to the best men's colleges

Matthew Vassar, a childless brewer, decided to found an institution memorializing himself. Milo Parker Jewett, an educator, gradually persuaded Vassar to endow a women's college, which he conceived and organized and which was chartered in 1861 with Jewett as president. Jewett offended Vassar, however, and resigned in 1864, a year before the college opened. His successor, John H. Raymond, selected the faculty and organized the curriculum. In 1878, Samuel Lunt Caldwell became president but was forced to resign in 1885. James Ryland Kendrick served for one year, securing significant donations that alleviated the college's financial distress. In 1886, the word "Female" was dropped from the college's name. In 1898, during James Monroe Taylor's presidency, the college received the first Phi Beta Kappa chapter granted to a women's college. Henry Noble MacCracken, who served from 1915 to 1946, was the first president to be neither a Baptist nor a minister. Sarah Gibson Blanding was the first female president, serving from 1946 to 1964. Beginning in 1963, merger with Yale University was seriously entertained and by 1967 agreement had largely been reached, but alumnae and faculty opposition frustrated the move. In 1969, Vassar was the first prestigious women's college to become fully coeducational, during Alan Simpson's presidency.

Vassar's original faculty was dominantly male and remains so. Astronomer Maria Mitchell, the only original faculty member with an international reputation, insisted upon high academic standards and upon payment equaling that of male faculty.

Under Hannah Lyman, the first "lady principal," the college rigidly controlled student religious and social life. By the beginning of the twentieth century, student advocacy for woman suffrage and personal rights became notable. Defying President Taylor, students organized suffrage meetings in a graveyard in 1908 and supported the Consumers' League, a prolabor organization. Later, in the 1930's, students joined picket lines. They also opposed loyalty oaths, supported academic freedom, and participated in pacifistic and antifascist activity. In the 1950's, students opposed the harassment of American Communists but aided Eastern European anti- Communists. Later, students became involved in the Civil Rights movement.

Graduates have included Ruth Benedict, an anthropologist and a professor at Columbia University from 1924 to 1928; Elizabeth Bishop, a Pulitzer Prize-winning poet; Mary Bunting, a president of Radcliffe College; Lucinda Franks, a Pulitzer Prize-winning reporter; Mildred McAfee Horton, a president of Wellesley College and the director of the Women Accepted for Voluntary Emergency Service (WAVES) during World War II; Margaret Leech, a Pulitzer Prize-winning historian; Mary McCarthy, the author of *The Group* (1954); Anne MacKay, the author of *Wolf Girls at Vassar: Lesbian and Gay Experiences, 1930-1990* (1993); Inez Milholland, who rode a white horse down Fifth Avenue in New York City in a suffrage parade; Edna St. Vincent Millay, Pulitzer Prize-winning poet; Barbara Newell, a president of Wellesley College; and poet Muriel Ruykeyser. First Lady Jacqueline Kennedy spent two years at Vassar.

See also Academies, female; Barnard College; Bryn Mawr College; Colleges, women's; Education of women; Mills College; Mount Holyoke College; Radcliffe College; Smith College; Wellesley College

Veterans and reservists, women as

Relevant issues: Health and medicine, war and the military

Significance: Women have battled for the right to equal benefits as veterans and reservists and have realized many of these goals

Although equally entitled to veteran's advantages, retired women of the armed forces were not always given full benefits following their military service. Although the Veterans Administration (VA) hospitals were intended to meet the health care of all veterans, women's needs were often neglected.

Prior to World War II, a lack of military status while in the service prevented women from obtaining benefits. Congresswoman Edith Nourse Rogers introduced a bill, passed in 1942, that granted women financial relief from injuries and illnesses sustained during war service. It also established the Women's Army Auxiliary Corps (WAAC), which was considered a civilian unit. In 1943, women were made eligible for military status when the WAAC became part of the regular U.S. Army as the Women's Army Corps (WAC). Women in the WAAC and Women's Airforce Service Pilots (WASPs) were never militarized during the war and received veteran status much later.

Although provisions in the federal law were made for men and women to receive equal benefits under the GI Bill, such as housing and education, inequities continued after the Korean War. Married male veterans were granted additional monies for dependent wives, while married female veterans generally were considered dependents themselves and could receive benefits only if they were their family's main support. A 1972 bill passed to change this status. In 1986, Congress enacted the

Economic Equity Act, which granted pension rights for military spouses.

Since only a small contingent of women remained in the services following World War II, President Harry S Truman signed a bill in 1948 that established a women's reserve force, which was not to exceed 2 percent of the total military. Reserve training for officers began in 1969 when the Air Force allowed women to join the Reserve Officers Training Corps (ROTC) on a test basis. The program was a success: It ended the separate women's commissioning program and enabled women to enter service academies.

Women composed less than 2 percent of the veteran population between 1940 and 1960. Because of low numbers and a feeling that women would not avail themselves of VA facilities, women's health care needs were never included in any veteran study or future projection. Hospitals operated in makeshift fashion where women were concerned and offered them no separate facilities.

As the numbers of women serving in the military increased during the 1960's and 1970's, the percentage of female veterans rose to 3.8 percent by 1983, a total of 1,218,000 women. Female veterans returning from Vietnam experienced the same disorders as men, and many had been exposed to the defoliant Agent Orange. Eventually, Army psychiatrists recognized that women suffered from greater trauma because their experiences had been a more radical departure from their normal lives. In 1982, the Working Group on Women Vietnam Veterans was established to help these veterans.

See also Medical units in the armed forces, women's; Military, women in the; Vietnam War, women in the; War and women

Vietnam War, women in the

RELEVANT ISSUES: War and the military

SIGNIFICANCE: American military and civilian women served in a wide variety of primarily sex-specific roles during the Vietnam War and shared the same danger as male support personnel with whom they worked

Between April, 1956, when the first U.S. Army nurses arrived in South Vietnam to train Vietnamese nurses, and April, 1975, when Americans fled South Vietnam as the North Vietnamese army rapidly advanced on the capital city of Saigon, an estimated 33,000 to 55,000 American civilian and military women served in a variety of roles in the war. There is no reliable count of these women because few organizations recorded personnel by sex. The Department of Defense does not even know exactly how many military women served. Most of the estimated 7,500 servicewomen in Vietnam were members of the Army, Air Force, or Navy nurse corps. Only 1,300 women in the line and staff corps of the armed forces (the nonmedical components of the female military) served in Vietnam. Civilians account for the remainder of the 33,000 to 55,000 women.

Servicewomen. About 6,000 military nurses served in more than thirty hospitals throughout the country. Army nurses worked in field, surgical, and evacuation hospitals. Navy nurses staffed two hospital ships, the USS *Repose* and the USS *Sanctuary*, and naval hospitals in Danang and Saigon. Air Force nurses served at casualty staging facilities or evacuation hospitals and as flight nurses on evacuation flights. These women experienced the worst of the war as they cared for a constant stream of badly injured young servicemen.

The thirteen hundred servicewomen of the line and staff included about seven hundred members of the Women's Army Corps (WAC), five hundred to six hundred Women in the Air Force (WAF), thirty-nine members of the Women's Reserve in the Marine Corps, and nine Women Accepted for Voluntary Emergency Service (WAVES). Members of the WAC, WAF, WAVES, and the Women's Reserve volunteered for the Vietnam War in far larger numbers than were accepted; cultural attitudes toward women kept a majority of them from serving. Military leaders expressed concern about the need to provide guards to protect women in Vietnam. Some women feared that deploying women to a war zone would detract from the feminine image that they wished to maintain. Therefore, servicewomen were requested for duty in Vietnam in a narrow range of sex-specific specialties.

Civilians. Civilian women who served in the Vietnam War can be roughly divided into three groups: those who provided humanitarian aid to the Vietnamese people; those who provided recreation, entertainment, or social services to the troops; and those who provided secretarial and administrative support. A few groups of women—journalists, flight attendants, and wives who came to Vietnam with their husbands—do not fit neatly into any one of these categories.

Women provided humanitarian aid to the Vietnamese as part of what became known as "the other war in Vietnam," the battle to win the hearts and minds of the people. Aware that military force alone could not win the war, some sought to increase the quality of life for the Vietnamese people to help them resist communism. More than forty nonprofit voluntary organizations worked in Vietnam and cooperated with the United States Agency for International Development (USAID), which was sponsored by the State Department. Many of these organizations recruited women to work as doctors, nurses, teachers, social workers, and home economists in a vast number of projects. USAID and organizations such as Catholic Relief Services, the American Friends Service Committee, and International Voluntary Services helped the Vietnamese establish hospitals, orphanages, day care centers, recreation programs, rehabilitation centers, agricultural projects, refugee centers, and training programs of all kinds.

The American Red Cross, Army Special Services, and United Services Organization (USO) hired women to work as social workers, librarians, entertainers, and craft and recreation specialists. They recruited primarily young, single, college-educated women, though supervisors were often older and sometimes male. The Red Cross provided both social services and recreation programs through Service to Military Installations (SMI), Service to Military Hospitals (SMH), and

Nurses played a vital role in Vietnam, treating both combat and civilian patients. (AP/Wide World Photos)

Supplemental Recreation Activities Overseas (SRAO). SMI, which employed both men and women, received and delivered emergency messages for military personnel and provided emergency loans. SMH women worked as hospital case workers or recreation specialists. SRAO women (nicknamed "donut dollies" after the Red Cross women who served during World War II) provided recreation for able-bodied enlisted men through the club mobile program or at recreation centers. Recreation centers, found at most military bases and operated by SRAO, Army Special Services, or USO women, provided a place where soldiers could relax, listen to music, write letters, play pool, or talk to an American woman. Army Special Services also provided libraries and craft shops at many of the bases. USO-sponsored shows, often featuring female entertainers, regularly toured the military bases for a month or two at a time to entertain the troops.

Women in secretarial or administrative positions worked for the Department of Defense serving under the Army, Navy, or Air Force; for the State Department in the American Embassy or consulates, with United States Information Services, or Joint U.S. Public Affairs Office; or with the Central Intelligence Agency (CIA). They also worked for private companies under contract to the government. Some were well-seasoned civil service career women, while others were young women with little experience.

Risks and Aftermath. Although most men treated these women with respect, some men believed that the real reason for the presence of women in Vietnam was to provide sexual favors. This misperception led to sexual harassment, innuendoes, propositions, sexual assault, and rape. One young Red Cross woman was murdered by an American serviceman.

Most women who came to Vietnam expected to work "behind the lines" in areas of safety. In Vietnam, however, no area was impervious to rocket and mortar attacks, sniper fire, and terrorist bombings. Sixty-five American women are known to have died in Vietnam: eight military women, whose names are inscribed on the Vietnam Veterans Memorial, and fifty-seven civilian women.

Women came home to a nation bitterly divided by the war and experienced the same feelings of alienation as male veterans. No one could understand what they had seen and done, and no one wanted to hear about their experiences. Some women repressed their emotions, only to have them surface later as post-traumatic stress disorder. By the 1980's, some female veterans began to talk and search for others like themselves. Reunions and the dedication of the Vietnam Veterans Memorial and the Vietnam Women's Memorial began to unite many of the women who had for so long been silent and isolated. Talking about their experiences with others who had served in Vietnam began the process of healing.

—*Lenna H. Allred*

See also Army Nurse Corps; Medical units in the armed forces, women's; Military, women in the; Nurses, women as; Red Cross and women; Veterans and reservists, women as; Vietnam Women's Memorial; War and women; Women Accepted for Voluntary Emergency Service (WAVES); Women's Army Corps (WAC)

Bibliography

Freedman, Dan, and Jacqueline Rhoads. *Nurses in Vietnam: The Forgotten Veterans*. Austin: Texas Monthly Press, 1987.

Holm, Jeanne. *Women in the Military: An Unfinished Revolution*. Novato, Calif.: Presidio Press, 1982.

Marshall, Kathryn. *In the Combat Zone: An Oral History of American Women in Vietnam, 1966-1975*. Boston: Little, Brown, 1987.

Morden, Bettie J. *The Women's Army Corps, 1945-1978*. Washington, D.C.: Center of Military History, 1990.

Norman, Elizabeth. *Women at War: The Story of Fifty Military Nurses Who Served in Vietnam*. Philadelphia: University of Pennsylvania Press, 1990.

Walker, Keith. *A Piece of My Heart: The Stories of Twenty-Six American Women Who Served in Vietnam*. New York: Ballantine Books, 1985.

Vietnam Women's Memorial

Date: Dedicated on November 11, 1993
Place: Washington, D.C.
Relevant issues: War and the military
Significance: This first national memorial to female veterans recognizes the contributions of women who served during the Vietnam War

On November 11, 1993, the unveiling of a bronze sculpture-in-the-round by Glenna Goodacre, depicting three servicewomen tending a wounded soldier, marked the culmination of a ten-year effort by Diane Carlson Evans and the Vietnam Women's Memorial Project (VWMP) to place a statue honoring female veterans near the Vietnam Veterans Memorial in Washington, D.C. In 1983, Evans, a former Army nurse, conceived the idea of creating a memorial to women who had served in Vietnam. In order to realize her dream, she founded the VWMP, a nonprofit organization dedicated to educating the public about the participation of American women in the war, to locating the women who had served, and to placing a woman's statue in the vicinity of the Vietnam Veterans Memorial. The VWMP established a sister search program to find female veterans. Many of these women, once contacted, became volunteers for the project, helping to recruit supporters and raise the funds that eventually made the monument a reality. Both houses of Congress passed bills approving the construction of the monument; they were signed into law by President Ronald Reagan on November 15, 1988. The memorial has become a place of healing for many of the estimated 55,000 American women who served in Vietnam during the war.

See also Army Nurse Corps; Military, women in the; Nurses, women as; Veterans and reservists, women as; Vietnam War, women in the; War and women

Vindication of the Rights of Woman, A

Author: Mary Wollstonecraft (1759-1797)
Date: 1792
Relevant issues: Civil rights, education, social reform
Significance: This book adapted revolutionary ideals to gender relations, challenging the male "divine right" to dominate women as lesser, irrational creatures and demanding sociopolitical changes

Mary Wollstonecraft's *A Vindication of the Rights of Woman*, subtitled *With Strictures on Political and Moral Subjects*, followed fast on her work *Vindication of the Rights of Man* (1790), the earliest radical rebuttal to Edmund Burke's conservative *Reflections on the French Revolution* (1790). In the second book, dedicated to Talleyrand, the French minister of education, Wollstonecraft agitated for "a revolution in female manners." She argued that complete and genuine social reform depended on validation of women as rational, moral beings fully capable of attaining virtue and knowledge and of contributing to civic welfare. Disputing the traditional view of women as naturally flawed, inferior creatures, Wollstonecraft instead blamed patriarchal socialization for stunting female identity. Prominent among the misogynist authorities whom she denounced for propaganda against women were John Milton, Jean-Jacques Rousseau, Dr. John Gregory, and James Fordyce. Learnedly and often acerbically, she defended women's need and right to be educated into adult independence; to pursue social, bodily, intellectual, and professional fulfillments; and ultimately to share "in those duties which dignify the human character."

In its extensive analysis of female oppression by, and collusion with, a sexist status quo, *A Vindication of the Rights of Woman* anticipated most key concerns of subsequent women's movements. Wollstonecraft's thirteen chapters closely examined such crucial feminist issues as women's debarment from formal education, institutions of power, and suffrage; their misrepresentation in images under male control; their confinement to the domestic sphere; their overvaluation of romance and sexual partnership; their mental, emotional, and (especially) economic dependence on men; their pursuit of an artificial and harmful feminine ideal that simultaneously infantilizes and oversexualizes them; their importance as mentors and role models for their children; their duty to struggle for a restructured society in which they could reconcile motherhood and career; their mistaken reliance on the ambiguous powers of the oppressed—in short, all the interlocking aspects of women's second-class citizenship.

Wollstonecraft's forceful treatise received little serious response. Her critics contented themselves with vicious attacks on her nonconformist life, particularly her cohabitation with Gilbert Imlay and her illegitimate daughter from this union. Moreover, her feminist contemporaries and nineteenth century successors tended to dissociate themselves from Wollstonecraft's uncompromising assault on male privilege and the social superstructure. Despite the work's imperfections—diffuseness, an exclusive focus on middle-class women, severity toward conventional women, and Enlightenment reverence for reason and distrust of passion—late twentieth century feminists hark back to *A Vindication of the Rights of Woman* as a cornerstone of feminist philosophy. In *Sexual Politics* (1971), Kate Millett paid tribute to Wollstonecraft's work as "the first document asserting the full humanity of women and insisting on its recognition."

See also Cult of True Womanhood; Feminism; Feminism, radical; Patriarchy; *Sexual Politics*; Socialization of girls and young women; Stereotypes of women; Women's movement

Violence against women

RELEVANT ISSUES: Civil rights, crime, psychology

SIGNIFICANCE: Violence against women has been a focus of the women's rights movement since the mid-nineteenth century in the belief that women will never be free until such physical, sexual, and emotional abuse is eliminated

Violence against women appears in many forms and involves emotional, physical, and sexual abuse. The areas featured in the current article include rape, domestic violence, child sexual abuse, and elder abuse. Although these forms of violence are not limited to female victims, women are primarily targeted. Each has its own distinct features; however, all have several characteristics in common. In addition, different forms of violence commonly occur together. For example, some battered women are raped by their husbands, and some occurrences of elder abuse are a product of domestic violence. Thus, several generalities can be drawn with regard to violence against women.

Generalities. In spite of a common stereotype that women are at most risk for danger with strangers in public places, research on violence against women suggests that they are at greatest risk in close relationships and in their own homes. Women are most likely to be sexually, physically, and emotionally abused by relatives, partners, friends, and acquaintances. Thus, they are most vulnerable to victimization from people whom they care about. This causes many problems for abuse victims. For example, women often blame themselves for the abuse, and others, especially the perpetrator, blame the victim. This causes the victim to experience embarrassment, shame, and guilt, whereas the abuser often feels himself to be the victim. Both victim and abuser engage in minimalization and denial. Thus, victims may inadvertently invite repeated victimization, which fosters even greater minimalization and denial and is associated with further embarrassment, shame, and guilt.

Acts of violence against women often involve an enormous betrayal of trust because they are perpetrated in close relationships. Survivors may have a difficult time trusting anyone, even people who are trustworthy. This further isolates the individual and makes it less likely that she will report the abuse and seek help. For this reason, most violence against women goes unreported. Moreover, because of minimalization and denial, many victims of violence may not know they are victims. In addition, many perpetrators do not know they are aggressors. Of those who do know they are aggressors, many are secure in the knowledge that they will never be reported. Therefore, it is difficult to estimate the incidence and prevalence of violence against women. This causes much controversy in the field as people debate the worth of different measures of violence and the appropriateness of different definitions of abuse. It also makes it difficult for researchers and social service agencies to get needed funds from the government and other sources.

The most obvious forms of violence against women are the more severe acts of physical and sexual abuse. Less obvious are milder acts of physical and sexual abuse. Even less obvious are acts of emotional abuse, which include oral and symbolic aggression. Nevertheless, many in the field believe that emotional abuse is an important precursor to and accompaniment of physical and sexual abuse. Some even suggest that the assault on self-esteem is more harmful than the assault on the body.

Verbal aggression includes belittling, derogating, and swearing at the victim. Symbolic aggression includes punching walls, punishing loved ones (including pets), and destroying treasured possessions. Emotional abuse is at the core of violence against women. Whether it is intended or unintentional, emotional abuse has serious consequences for the victim, often leaving her unable to fight back or leave.

There are several theories about the causes of emotional, physical, and sexual abuse. Feminists blame a patriarchal society that objectifies and marginalizes women; they see violence as a product of exaggerated sex-role socialization. Some psychologists view this type of violence as an aberration and believe it is caused by a mental defect or personality flaw in the perpetrator. Sociologists view violence against women as attributable to structural causes such as social and economic stress, a culture that supports this type of violence, and a criminal justice system that ignores family violence. Finally, social learning theorists believe that witnessing violence as a child can create violent behavior in the future.

The Extent of Violence Against Women. It is difficult to obtain reliable statistics about the amount of emotional, physical, and sexual abuse of women, in part because researchers sometimes vary in their definitions of abuse. For example, some researchers may see threats to do physical harm as physical abuse, whereas others may see this as symbolic or oral abuse. One of the most controversial debates is whether to measure aggression in terms of specific acts, the injuries that result, or the perceptions of the individuals involved. In addition, different subject populations may yield different estimates. For example, estimates of the incidence of rape obtained from high school and college women are often higher than those from older or younger women. Therefore, extrapolating from these estimates to the general population may result in overestimates. Estimates that come from government statistics or police reports often underestimate incidence rates. For example, until 1993, the National Crime Victim Survey estimates of rape and assault were obtained by a random telephone survey of adults who were asked whether they had ever been a victim of a crime and then were asked to elaborate on its description. If the respondent did not define the event as a crime or if she chose not to talk about it with a stranger, the rape or assault would not be included in the resulting estimates.

Rape. In 1991, the National Crime Victim Survey estimated an incidence rate of 0.6 in 1,000 rapes and 0.8 in 1,000 attempted rapes for females over the age of twelve. According to the same survey, approximately 155,000 women were raped every year between 1973 and 1987, or one in every 600 women. In contrast, Mary Koss, a prominent expert in the field, estimated a lifetime prevalence rate of approximately 15 to 25 percent of women for rape and a similar range for attempted rape. Even when one takes into account the difference in incidence versus prevalence (incidents in a limited period), it is still difficult to reconcile these estimates. Most believe that the survey data of Koss and her colleagues provide a more accurate estimate than do the National Crime Victim Surveys because Koss's survey is completely anonymous and does not require the victim to self-label the event as rape. Koss and her colleagues found that, in many instances, women would say that something happened to them that fit the legal definition of rape, but they would not call it rape. Nevertheless, these women knew the behavior was wrong, and they showed many of the same symptoms as self-labeled rape victims.

An International Crime Survey conducted by Alvassi del Frate and others asked respondents about sexual victimization, including unwanted sexual touching as well as sexual assault. Results showed that Canada was ranked second and the United States was ranked third, with 4.1 percent and 3.7 percent of the respondents reporting sexual victimization, respectively. In addition, in 1993, Health Canada sponsored a telephone survey that specifically addressed violence against women. Results showed that 24 percent of the women reported experienc-

AMERICAN WOMEN AS VICTIMS OF CRIME, BY RACE

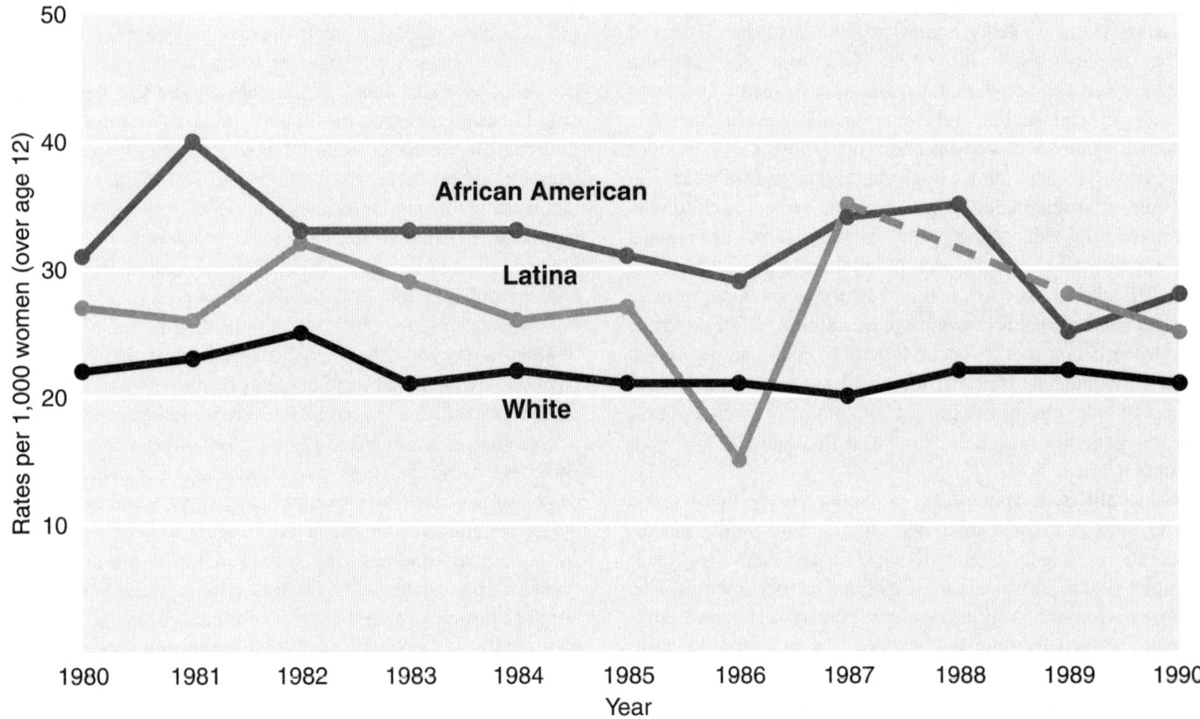

Source: U.S. Bureau of Justice Statistics
Note: 1988 data not available for Latinas

The members of the National Organization for Women (NOW) have been an outspoken army in the war on violence against women. (Sally Ann Rogers)

ing a sexual attack and 8 percent of the married women said they were sexually assaulted. Walter S. DeKeseredy and his colleagues reported incidence rates among female college students in Canada to be similiar to those found by Koss and her colleagues in the United States.

Domestic Violence. Family violence is not estimated separately in the National Crime Victim Survey, but respondents are asked about characteristics of the perpetrators of crimes. Family violence accounted for 7 percent of all crimes in 1991. In National Crime Victim Surveys from 1979 to 1987, women were less likely than men to report being assaulted by a stranger (for women, 11.4 in 1,000; for men, 29.4 in 1,000). Women were more likely than men, however, to report being assaulted by an intimate (for women, 6.3 in 1,000; for men, 1.8 in 1,000). The most common perpetrators who were intimates of the victims were former spouses, boyfriends, and spouses. Among violent crime victims, 25 percent of women and only 4 percent of men were victimized by a family member. In addition, more than half the victims of intimate offenders were injured, compared with less than one quarter of victims of strangers.

The most popular survey measure of domestic violence is the Conflict Tactics Scale, which was developed by Murray A. Straus. This survey asks respondents to reflect on their and/or their spouse's behavior during "spats or fights." The scale begins with innocuous behaviors such as discussing the issue calmly and sulking. It later asks about verbal aggression, symbolic aggression (for example, throwing objects), and physical aggression. Sometimes researchers discriminate between minor and severe aggression (the latter are more likely to result in serious injury), and sometimes they do not. Because the Conflict Tactics Scale does not measure context (for example, who started the fight), motives, or injury, and because it does not measure every type of aggression (for example, hair pulling, pinching, restraining, and arm twisting are not present), the resulting statistics are sometimes hard to interpret. Nevertheless, the Conflict Tactics Scale does provide a standardized measure of relationship violence.

A National Family Violence Survey conducted by Straus and his colleagues in 1985 yielded a slightly higher estimate for wife-to-husband violence (121 in 1,000) than for husband-to-wife violence (118 in 1,000). Straus and others, however, have noted that this may be attributable to husbands' underreporting their violence and to wives' defending themselves against their husbands' violence. In addition, Straus cites a 3.0 percent injury rate for female victims of domestic violence, as opposed to a 0.5 percent injury rate for male victims of domestic violence.

According to Walter DeKeseredy and Ronald Hinch, research in Canada has shown a pattern similar to that found in the United States. The Canadian Urban Victimization Survey consistently underestimates the amount of wife abuse to be less than 1 percent. In contrast, work with the Conflict Tactics Scale provides much higher estimates of wife abuse in Canada (11 to 24 percent). Furthermore, Statistics Canada reported in 1993 that 29 percent of the women in their telephone survey experienced a physical assault and an additional 5 percent experienced the threat of an assault. Most assaults (including both physical and sexual assaults) were by husbands, boyfriends, and other men known to the victim.

Child Abuse. According to the National Center on Child Abuse and Neglect, more than 800,000 instances of substantiated child abuse occurred each year between 1990 and 1992. Girls made up slightly more than half of all abuse victims, and sexual abuse accounted for between 14 and 16 percent of all types of abuse. David Finkelhor studied retrospective accounts of childhood sexual victimization in a sample of U.S. college students in 1979 and found that 19 percent of the women and 9 percent of the men reported experiencing childhood sexual victimization. The National Research Council reported that population surveys find child sexual abuse lifetime prevalence rates for females of between 6 percent and 62 percent and for males of between 3 percent and 31 percent.

Elder Abuse. According to the U.S. Center for Health Statistics, injuries requiring medical attention are more common among people over sixty-five (21 percent) than among people from forty-five to sixty-four years of age (15 percent). Nevertheless, it is difficult to determine how these injuries were sustained. Survey research has found estimates of between 1 and 10 percent of the older population who are abused by relatives. The House Select Committee on Aging estimated that about 4 percent of the older population are abused by relatives. The lack of a standardized measure of abuse and neglect and differences in definitions of abuse make it difficult to compare estimates of elder abuse.

Characteristics of the Abuser. Most is known about perpetrators of rape and domestic violence, and least is known about perpetrators of elder abuse. Most abusers are men. There are several types of rapists and batterers, and there may also be different types of child molesters and elder abusers. Nevertheless, abusers share several common characteristics.

The two most common motives for rape and wife battery are the need for power and control and the expression of hostility and aggression. The need for power and control can explain rape, battery, and child sexual abuse, and it also may explain some forms of elder abuse, especially those with regard to the financial exploitation of the older adult. It is ironic that the abuser often feels powerless and is overly dependent on the victim. He uses emotional, physical, and sexual abuse to control family members and partners and he does not recognize the destructive nature of his own behavior. The power batterer sometimes feels guilt and remorse for his behavior. Lenore Walker has noted how this can produce a "honeymoon period" in the cycle of violence in which the wife abuser treats his wife especially well after a beating, at least initially. (Honeymoon periods seem to diminish and eventually disappear as the relationship progresses.) The power rapist uses just enough aggression to subdue his victim. Power abusers are better at hiding the abuse from others, their victims, and themselves. Hostility and aggression are also involved in rape and domestic violence, and they may also be a factor in some elder abuse and child sexual abuse. Research on rape and wife abuse shows that hostile abusers tend to use much more aggression than power abusers. In addition, they also tend to be more generally aggressive. This also may be the case with child molesters and elder abusers. In research by Irene H. Frieze, David Finkelhor, and others, hostile batterers were shown to be more likely than power batterers to also rape their partner.

Men's attitudes may be more important than their personalities in predicting violence against women. Feminists assume that a belief system including the notion that men are better than women encourages the physical, sexual, and emotional abuse of women. Research shows that men who are traditional in their sex role ideology are more likely to be abusers. Moreover, those who are hostile toward women, view women as seducers responsible for their victimization, and view relations between the sexes as basically adversarial are more likely to batter and rape. They also may be more likely to abuse children sexually and to abuse elderly relatives, especially their mothers.

Characteristics of the Survivor. Low self-esteem may be one of the few common features of victims of violence against women. Emotional, physical, and sexual abuse can violate the victim's core identity and her relation to the world. It can destroy her belief in a fair, predictable, and just world. It can also change her view of herself. She may lose the illusion of invulnerability that tends to protect people. She may dramatically alter her behavior, such as becoming withdrawn and fearful, cold and numb, self-destructive and promiscuous, or even aggressive. As previously noted, victims often minimize or deny the abuse. Many researchers and therapists believe that some survivors of rape, battery, and child sexual abuse show a severe and sometimes prolonged reaction to the trauma. This reaction has been called rape trauma syndrome, the battered woman syndrome, and post-traumatic stress disorder. Post-traumatic stress disorder involves reliving the experience through nightmares and flashbacks, a prolonged hypervigilant state and subsequent emotional and physical problems, persistent avoidance, and an inability to "connect" with other people and enjoy life. Even survivors who do not realize that they were victims of abuse can commit suicide and, in the case of domestic violence, homicide. Experts such as Angela Browne and Lenore Walker believe that continuous battering and humiliation can lead the victim to murder her abuser out of extreme fear of imminent danger and the belief that there is no other way out.

Historical Trends. The sexual, physical, and emotional abuse of women is as old as humankind. Religious and historical examples of rape, wife abuse, and child sexual abuse abound. Legal approval of domestic violence was evident in "the rule of thumb" that no man could beat his wife with a stick wider than his thumb. Nevertheless, many believe that these issues were recently invented. According to Elizabeth Pleck, in *Domestic Tyranny* (1987), the United States has seen several periods of legislative and social reform with regard to family violence. These periods include 1640 to 1680, 1874 to 1890, and the 1960's and 1970's. The issues of wife abuse and cruelty to children were addressed by separate political movements, though both were influenced by society's unwillingness to question the belief in the perfect family and to violate the sanctity of the home. Even when laws were written to protect women and children from family violence, they were rarely enforced except in extreme cases.

Historically, the worst period for women and children was under Roman law in the seventh through fifth centuries B.C., when the husband and father had the absolute right to sell his wife and children into slavery and even put them to death. The best period for women and children occurred in the last part of the twentieth century in both the United States and Canada. The roots of efforts against child abuse lie in the gradual liberalization of beliefs about corporal punishment in Western society and the mid-nineteenth century anticruelty movements, first against cruelty to animals and later against cruelty to children. Participants in this movement were often wealthy middle-class men and women addressing their concerns about lower-class immigrant families. Twentieth century advocates include medical, educational, and social welfare professionals. Both the United States and Canada enacted child welfare legislation in the 1970's, the United States preceding Canada by a very short time.

The roots of efforts against wife abuse lie in the mid-nineteenth century temperance and women's rights movements. Participants in these movements were men and women who believed that the causes of domestic violence were alcohol abuse and the absence of legal rights for married women. They fought long and hard for a woman's right to divorce an alcoholic or cruel husband, her right to own property (including her own earnings), and her right to be with her children

Take Back the Night marches have given many women a new sense of power as they unite against the fear that night brings for women. (Bettye Lane)

after a divorce. Many of these people were also involved in the woman suffrage movement, such as Elizabeth Cady Stanton, Lucy Stone, and Amelia Bloomer. It is interesting to note that wife beating was prominent in the English reform movement earlier than it was in the U.S. reform movement. In fact, as late as 1910, stopping assaults on wives was still part of the legislative platform of American suffragists.

The fight against rape and domestic violence was again made an issue by the women's rights movement in the 1960's and 1970's. Many of the most dramatic social and legal changes have occurred since 1975. Advocates have included shelter and hot line workers, survivors, and other feminists. Educational forums include "speak outs," Take Back the Night rallies, and other consciousness-raising efforts in North America that took place in the 1970's. Thus, the antirape movement is a grassroots organization stimulated by sexist rape laws and trials in which women commonly were revictimized. This movement has led to many changes in the social construction of rape and its legal adjudication, including the 1992 Canadian Supreme Court decision that pornography may violate women's civil rights and therefore can be restricted, a position championed by Andrea Dworkin and Catharine A. MacKinnon.

In the 1970's, the antirape movement inspired a movement against domestic violence. Rape crisis hot lines and battered women's shelters arose in most cities in the 1970's. In 1976, the National Organization for Women (NOW) established a National Task Force on Battered Women, chaired by Del Martin and Nancy Kirk-Gormley. In 1978, Greta Rideout unsuccessfully brought a charge of rape against her husband. In 1985, however, the New York Court of Appeals revoked the state's marital exemption from the rape laws. On October 8, 1990, the Clothesline Project was begun, an effort for women to air their "dirty laundry" and demonstrate the extent of violence against women by creating shirts that represent victimization and survival. The shirts were color-coded for murder victims and battery, rape, and gay-bashing survivors. Many of the shirts were displayed in a rally protesting violence against women on April 5, 1995, sponsored by NOW.

The U.S. Senate enacted the Violence Against Women Act of 1994 as a response to "the underlying attitude that this violence is somehow less serious than other crimes and the resulting failure of our criminal justice system to address such violence." It states that "the Nation's misconceptions that crimes against women are second-class crimes needs to change. Americans need to brand these attacks as brutal and wrong; we need to prosecute and punish those who perpetrate these acts." The Violence Against Women Act created a National Task Force on Violence Against Women and the Domestic Violence Resource Network, which includes the Resources Center on Domestic Violence. Canadians can obtain information on violence against women from the National Clearinghouse on Family Violence, Family Violence Prevention Division, Health and Welfare Canada. —*Kathryn M. Ryan*

See also *Against Our Will*; Antioch College Sexual Consent Code; Battered woman syndrome; Bobbitt case; Criminals, women as; Date rape; Domestic violence; Hate crimes against women; Incest; Machismo; Marital rape; Misogyny; National Coalition Against Domestic Violence; Patriarchy; Pornography; Prison, women in; Rape; Rape crisis centers; Rape trauma syndrome; Rape victims, treatment of; Sexual harassment; Take Back the Night; Violence Against Women Act of 1994

Bibliography

Bart, Pauline B., and Eileen G. Moran, eds. *Violence Against Women: The Bloody Footprints*. Newbury Park, Calif.: Sage Publications, 1993. Articles are easy to read and of interest to a general audience. Covers a wide variety of acts of violence against women, including murder, sexual harassment, fraternity rape, and obscene phone calls.

Browne, Angela. *When Battered Women Kill*. New York: Free Press, 1987. A thorough overview of research on battered women. Answers the important question of why victims of domestic violence stay in their relationships and the legal system's inability to deal with spouse abuse.

DeKeseredy, Walter S., and Ronald Hinch. *Woman Abuse: Sociological Perspectives*. Toronto: Thompson Educational, 1991. This is a "leftist realist" perspective on violence against women, focusing on wife abuse, courtship violence, rape, and corporate violence. A good overview of violence against women in Canada.

Funk, Rus E. *Stopping Rape: A Challenge for Men*. Philadelphia: New Society, 1993. Challenges men to change the way they think, talk, and act about women and sex. An excellent example of the feminist perspective. Also tries to convince men to change their behavior without burdening them with excessive blame.

Gelles, Richard J., and Donileen R. Loseke, eds. *Current Controversies on Family Violence*. Newbury Park, Calif.: Sage Publications, 1993. Provides a much-needed overview of several ongoing debates between researchers and theorists interested in violence against women. Includes articles on rape, battery, child sexual abuse, and elder abuse. Structures the discussion of theory and research around several controversies, which are then debated in the articles that follow.

Gondolf, Edward W. *Man Against Woman: What Every Woman Should Know About Violent Men*. Blue Ridge Summit, Pa.: TAB Books, 1989. A practical review of research on wife batterers written for a general audience, including potential victims.

Jones, Ann, and Susan Schechter. *When Love Goes Wrong: What to Do When You Can't Do Anything Right*. New York: HarperCollins, 1992. A guide for women, written by two experts on domestic violence, to help them to determine whether their partners are excessively controlling and likely to become abusive.

Koss, Mary P., et al. *No Safe Haven: Male Violence Against Women at Home, at Work, and in the Community*. Washington, D.C.: American Psychological Association, 1994. Concentrates on domestic violence, sexual harassment, and rape but may apply to other forms of violence against women.

One very strong point is the effort to include information on ethnic minority and low-income women.

Searles, Patricia, and Ronald J. Berger, eds. *Rape and Society*. Boulder, Colo.: Westview Press, 1995. Includes essays by many prominent experts on rape and deals with a variety of important rape-related issues.

Walker, Lenore E. *Terrifying Love: Why Battered Women Kill and How Society Responds*. New York: Harper & Row, 1989. Written by a noted specialist on domestic violence, this book reviews theories presented in earlier books and documents the problems women have with violent partners and the criminal justice system.

Violence Against Women Act of 1994

Also known as: Title IV of the Violent Crime Control and Law Enforcement Act of 1994

Date: Passed on September 13, 1994

Relevant issues: Crime, social reform

Significance: First introduced in 1990, this act is a comprehensive, multifaceted attack on all forms of violence against women in the United States

This act's many provisions include restitution to victims, money for rape prevention education, significant funding for battered women's shelters, a national toll-free domestic violence hot line, and grants to educate judges and court personnel about rape and sexual assault. The act also declares that gender-motivated violent acts are federal civil rights violations for which victims can seek damages; this controversial tenet caused the judicial community to fear that civil rights counts in divorce and domestic violence cases would clog the courts. Some commentators speculated that because of stiffer penalties for rapists and remuneration for victims, innocent men would be falsely accused. Still others argued that rape and battering are not gender-based crimes; rather, they are sexual outlets or reflections of generalized anger and aggression. Nevertheless, many legal scholars hailed the act's strong message that violence against women, which subordinates women as a class, will not be tolerated. Nevertheless, they worried that the requirement of intentionality would be difficult to comply with because intentionality is rare: Most perpetrators are not aware or do not believe that they are motivated by sexism.

See also Battered woman syndrome; Domestic violence; Hate crimes against women; Misogyny; Rape; Sexism; Violence against women

Visual art

Relevant issues: Arts and entertainment

Significance: Women as well as men have created art throughout history. Certain factors, such as documentation, obstacles, and criticism, have prevented women's assimilation into the mainstream of art history.

Twenty years after the feminist art movement, female artists were still poorly represented in all aspects of the profession. According to the 1995 U.S. study, *Gender Discrimination in the Artfield*, although women held 53.1 percent of the degrees in art, only 50.7 percent of all visual artists and 20.0 percent of the nation's art faculty were women. Female artists earned 31.4 percent of the total art income and received 27.0 percent of all art grants and fellowships.

According to the group Guerrilla Girls, the work of female artists represents 15 percent of curated museum exhibits, and the work of minority women stands at only 0.003 percent. In addition, works created by female artists represent a mere 4 percent of all museum acquisitions. In all editions published before 1986 of H. W. Janson's *History of Art*, the standard text used in college introductory art history classes, three thousand male artists were covered but not one female artist. In the 1995 version of this textbook, thirty-eight women were represented.

Documentation. When discussing the representation of female artists in any period, it is important to consider that, unlike the hard sciences, art history is an ideological practice, not the outcome of objective, neutral research. According to scholars Rozsika Parker and Griselda Pollock in *Old Mistresses* (1981), art history "is a particular way of seeing and interpreting in which the beliefs and assumptions of art historians . . . shape and limit the very picture of the history of art." Several recognized early art historical sources illuminate how female artists have been documented throughout early art history. *Historia Naturalis* by Pliny the Elder (A.D. 23?-79) discussed the origins of painting and sculpture in the classical world and mentioned the names of six female artists of antiquity. Three were Greek female painters who lived before Pliny's time—Timarete, Aristarete, and Olympia—about whom he provided no information, either biographical or historical. Of the remaining three Hellenistic artists, two were identified as the daughters of painters. Pliny related nothing about the artist Kalypso and told readers only that Helen of Egypt was known for a painting of the Battle of Issus that included Darius and Alexander. This painting was thought to be the basis for the composition for the Alexander Mosaic, a spectacular masterpiece of antiquity. Unlike his treatment of the male artists, Pliny neither analyzed nor described these women's works of art or their daily lives and personalities.

In Boccaccio's *De Claris Mulieribus* (1355-1359), a collection of 104 biographies of real and mythical women drawn from Greek and Roman sources, three ancient painters were mentioned: Thamyris, Irene, and Marcia. Boccaccio stated, "I thought that these achievements were worthy of some praise, for art is very much alien to the mind of woman, and these things cannot be accomplished without a great deal of talent, which in women is usually very scarce." In 1405, Boccaccio's remarks provoked a rebuttal from Christine de Pizan; scholar Susan Groag Bell claims that she could not "understand why men write so scathingly about women when they owe their very existence to them." And she asks in a question rephrased throughout history, "how can women's lives be known when men write all the books?"

Giorgio Vasari documented the artists of the sixteenth century by tracing the development of Renaissance culture from the thirteenth century to the sixteenth century, using artists' biographies to establish the artistic greatness he considered to have culminated in the work of Michelangelo. Although the second edition of Vasari's *Vite* mentions thirteen women, none of the artists he considered inspired by genius were women. Vasari's praise of women is genuine but qualified. He stated that "to the woman artist belongs diligence rather than invention, the locus of genius. Should women apply themselves too diligently . . . they risk appearing to wrest from us the palm of supremacy. While men can achieve nobility through their art, women may practice art only because they are of noble birth and/or deportment." In this way, Vasari created a double-edged sword. Although he did provide several female artists a place in art history, scholar Whitney Chadwick has pointed out that "women artists appear in Vasari's *Vite* in ways which would come to characterize their relationship to painting and sculpture in the literature of art from the sixteenth to the twentieth centuries: as exceptions."

Obstacles. The obstacles confronted by female artists throughout history manifested themselves in art historical documentation and societal impediments. Obstacles regarding their accurate documentation through history include problems related to attribution, authentication of authorship, and agreement regarding the size and significance of their oeuvre. With regard to this last point, Chadwick has noted that "attempts to juggle domestic responsibilities with artistic production have often resulted in smaller bodies of work and smaller works than those produced by male contemporaries."

Socially imposed obstacles that have hindered the advancement of women with artistic ambitions include educational limitations, ranging from deficient training in mathematics and perspective drawing to the reluctance of art schools to admit women for training; lack of familiarity with basic anatomy and little access to drawing the nude model; and lack of admission into the apprenticeship system and the academic salon system. (Women were not allowed to participate in the salon system until the end of the nineteenth century, by which time its importance had diminished.) An examination of the plight of female artists in nineteenth century France shows that there were a third as many female as male artists. None of these women had been educated at the important École des Beaux-Arts, only 7 percent had received a salon medal, and none had been awarded the prestigious Medal of the Legion of Honor. Mathematics was essential in understanding the principle of vanishing point perspective, which revolutionized pictorial space. Because women were excluded from studying mathematics and sciences, their participation in the long history of multifigured historical and religious paintings was impossible.

As artistic training progressed, artists' apprentices, who usually worked for seven years, were expected to have a liberal arts education with special emphasis on mathematics and the laws of perspective and to have considerable knowledge of ancient art. It became understood that the training of every serious artist would include the study of the human body, usually from male nude models, as well as travel to major art centers to study contemporary work. The average fifteenth or sixteenth century woman had a slim chance of obtaining this level of experience and education.

The structure of the artistic programs of the times involved the young artist's learning first to copy from drawings and casts of famous sculptures, then to draw from the nude model. Yet, the nude model was unavailable to female artists from the Renaissance until the nineteenth century. To be denied this path was to be denied the opportunity to be counted among the "great" artists as defined during this period. Women were thus reduced to the category of "minor" artists and were destined to be restricted to the less highly regarded fields of portraiture, landscape, still life, and genre.

Most women who did achieve artistic success either had artistic fathers or had a close relationship with a strong or dominant male artist. Many daughters, wives, and sisters worked in the studios and shops of their male relatives, who often taught these women and were proud of their talents. This was especially true for the artists in the Renaissance. Because of the high demand for works wanted by the courts, family members had to be brought in to help speed the production of the family business. Many of these women's works were signed by their male relatives because the worth of their works increased when thought to be produced by a man.

The Twelfth through Fifteenth Centuries. Most art by women during the Middle Ages was produced in monasteries. There were secular female artists, though convents provided the best working conditions, training, material, and support for the talented and educated women of the times. In these early days, nuns were among the first women to learn to read, write, teach, practice medicine, and develop skills in the visual arts. Nuns were the female professional class. Recent scholarship has discovered playwrights, calligraphers, illuminators, embroiderers, laceworkers, printers, scholars, and writers in the ranks of female medieval monastics. Access to the convent was often determined by noble birth.

When a monastery gained special distinction as a religious or educational center, it was run by an abbess of superior talents. Two abbesses who led their nuns to great intellectual, artistic, and spiritual heights were Hildegard of Bingen (1098-1179) and Herrad of Landsberg (1125-1195). These women produced literary and artistic works that exemplified the highest quality of education available to monastic women of medieval Europe. The two most famous medieval illuminated manuscripts associated with these women, *Scivias* and *Hortus Deliciarium*, were not actually painted by the women concerned, nor do their manuscripts survive. They are, however, two of the most remarkable religious compilations developed by women in Western history.

In general, men sculpted, painted, carved, and worked in metal and stained glass, whereas women wove, sewed, and embroidered the square miles of precious cloth used in the thousands of churches and castles throughout Europe. Most of the larger needlework pieces and tapestries were created collectively in tightly organized, male-controlled guild workshops, particularly in London. This ecclesiastical embroidery, known as *Opus Anglicanum*, was in such demand that women had little opportunity to compete with men in other art forms. Medieval embroiderers were the more likely forerunners of the female painters of the late Renaissance and Baroque than were the nuns who illuminated manuscripts, given the scale and intrinsic value of the former's lavish productions.

During the mid-fifteenth century, the "male" art of painting was elevated above the "female" art of embroidery. Redefined as a domestic art requiring manual labor and collective activity rather than individual genius, mathematical reasoning, and divine inspiration, embroidery and needlework came to signify domesticity and femininity.

The Fifteenth and Sixteenth Centuries. During the Renaissance, a revolutionary change occurred when artists who had identified themselves as craftspeople began to achieve the status and rewards formerly reserved for those engaged in pursuits known for intellectual prowess and individual achievement. The educational and practical experience necessary to become an artist consequently became more involved than before. A result of this shift in status appears to be an absence of female artists during the fourteenth and fifteenth centuries. During the Renaissance, some female artists began to achieve recognition as individuals. The artistic careers of some women were made possible because they were born into artistic families and received the necessary training. Others were born into the upper class, where the spread of Renaissance ideas about the desirability of an education included training in the visual arts. Two examples of artists active in the Renaissance are Sofonisba Anguissola, court painter to Spain, and Artemisia Gentileschi, a peer of Michaelangelo Caravaggio during the Baroque period.

The Seventeenth Century. Learned women were becoming increasingly visible during the beginning of the century as leaders of salons, a social institution that began in the seventeenth century. It was in this unique social space that certain women were greatly respected and spoke in support of the new Enlightenment literature, science, and philosophy. For female artists, the salons provided a context with relaxed class distinctions and, therefore, an opportunity to meet upper-class patrons on more equal ground.

Women in Northern Europe seem to have enjoyed greater freedom and mobility in the professions that did their Italian contemporaries. The spread of humanism and the educational and domestic ideology of the Protestant Reformation increased literacy and participation in the visual arts for women. Judith Leyster, painter of portraits, genre, and still lifes, was active in seventeenth century Holland, along with her contemporary Frans Hals.

The Eighteenth Century. During this century, academies were founded to distinguish the artist from the artisan, and membership became essential to obtaining commissions. The academies limited their memberships and accepted only a token number of women. Although only 3 percent of artists at this time were women, there was an increasing representation of women in salon exhibitions: By 1835, 22.2 percent of the artists exhibiting in the salon were women. Because only members of the upper class and aristocracy could achieve distinction, it was impossible for a working woman to be an artist. Artists active during this period include Marie-Elisabeth-Louise Vigee-Lebrun and Adelaide Labille-Guiard.

The Nineteenth Century. This century was the period of greatest female social progress in history. The feminist campaigns of the twentieth century had their roots in the nineteenth century reform movements started in Western Europe and America. This reform sentiment grew out of middle-class reactions to the social and economic changes that occurred after the Industrial Revolution. The middle class emerged as the dominant political and social force. Novels, plays, paintings, sculpture, and prints produced at the time helped form a middle-class identity out of the diverse incomes, occupations, and values that made up the class in actuality. Female artists came to the profession in droves, displaying their talent in every medium, genre, and style.

Art by Women in Early America. Centuries before European settlers came to the New World, American Indian women were working within the fine arts of basketry, pottery, quillwork, weaving, and painting on leather. Once stored and exhibited only in indigenous culture museums, such artwork eventually began to find its way into the mainstream and influenced much of the modern art of the twentieth century.

Needlework and painting were also modes of expression for early American female settlers, with folk art being the best represented. Little formal training was available, and therefore, most female artists in the first half of the century were self-taught. Class and geography were also major factors shaping the identity of the nineteenth century female American artists. Most of these women came from wealthy and educated East Coast families. Notable early American female artists include Mary Ann Willson, Jane Stuart, Lily Martin Spencer, and Ellen and Rolinda Sharples.

Victorian England. During Queen Victoria's reign from 1837 to 1901, female artists found themselves in a contradictory position. The very qualities that were attributed to successful artists, such as independence, self-reliance, and competitiveness, were considered to be exclusive to the male sphere. Women who rejected the accepted art forms, such as needlework, china painting, watercolor, and flower painting, were seen as sexual aberrations. Critics during this period frequently described aspiring female artists as unsexing themselves; at the same time, they placed exceptional female artists, such as Rosa Bonheur, in high esteem because they could "paint like a man." Opportunities for female artists were increasing with the establishment of academies and art societies for women only, but considerable pressure remained on women to lead traditional, domestic lives.

Impressionism. One of the most radical movements in nineteenth century art was Impressionism, which challenged the current ideas with a new way of seeing and portraying the world. Many women were drawn to Impressionism because it legitimized the themes of domestic social life, of which they had intimate knowledge, considering that their subject matter had to evolve within the boundaries of their sex and class. Examples of Impressionist female artists include Berthe Morisot, Mary Cassatt, Cecilia Beaux, and Marie Braquemond.

The Early Twentieth Century: Modernism. The early twentieth century opened with an eruption of scientific and technological discoveries. The philosophical and scientific changes affected the art world with such new artistic movements as fauvism, expressionism, cubism, Dadaism, and surrealism. Female artists were actively involved in these new movements; a significant number of new countries emerged as sources for women's art, including Russia, Sweden, Canada, and Portugal. Paris was still considered the dominant force in Western art during the first half of the century. Women finally were allowed to study from the nude model and compete for major prizes alongside their male counterparts. The principles of abstract art were applied less commonly in early twentieth century American art than in Europe and Russia; however, a core group of artists were exploring its potential, including Georgia O'Keeffe.

During the late 1920's and 1930's, surrealism became a powerful movement throughout Europe and the United States. During the 1930's, female artists were attracted to surrealism in large numbers, drawn by the group's antiacademic position and the interest in an art that comes from personal experience. These women, however, soon found themselves working within a movement that was sexist and in which male artists portrayed women through violent and erotic themes. Consequently, many women who had come to the movement through personal relationships with the male artists made significant contributions, asserted their independence, and left. Female artists actively involved in this movement include Remedios Varo, Frida Kahlo, Leonora Carrington, and Dorothea Tanning.

The Mid-Twentieth Century: Abstract Expressionism. In the 1940's and 1950's, New York City became the new center for the international art world. This shift coincided with the emergence of postwar United States as a world power. The evolution of the abstract expressionist movement was related to the psychological impact of World War II. Previous art forms were seen as too cold, so abstract expressionism grew out of the collective need for emotion and expression. The

Judy Chicago stands in front of her controversial multimedia exhibit The Dinner Party, *which honors the accomplishments of notable women and celebrates women's crafts.* (Bettye Lane)

process of the abstract expressionist artist was automatic, often without drawing or studies, usually emerging from the subconscious. Several women emerged from this traditional male group of painters who had the reputation of hard drinking, chain-smoking, and violently throwing paint onto canvases. They include Lee Krasner, Grace Hartigan, Miriam Schapiro, and Elaine De Kooning.

The Late Twentieth Century: The Feminist Art Movement. The feminist movement, defined as art that reflects women's political and social consciousness, took seed in the early 1970's. This movement transformed the art world in the United States by the constant questioning and challenging of the patriarchal assumptions, definitions, and idealogies of "art" and "artists." The issues that came into the forefront were reclaiming past histories of female artists, exhibition opportunities, space to work, and various political, theoretical, and aesthetic issues. Women active in the feminist art movement include Judy Chicago, Suzanne Lacy, Judy Baca, and Faith Ringgold.

Performance Art. Performance art began in the late 1960's concurrent with the women's movement. Used as a vehicle to explore private and personal experience drawn from the feminist movement, performance art reflected women's reexamination of their lives and redefinition of the models on which they had placed their self-images. This fresh and passionate investigation of self and of identification with other women created the first female performers and their supportive audiences. Carolle Schneeman, Ana Mendieta, Hannah Wilke, Betsy Damon, and Eleanor Antin were among the women active in this movement.

Trends Since the 1970's. By the late 1970's, women and minority artists began to experience an adverse reaction from the art world. A new crop of neoexpressionist figurative male artists came into prominence by portraying women in violent and erotic themes. Exhibitions boasting of the "return" to painting focused on this new generation of artists and virtually excluded women. In 1984, women again picketed New York City's Museum of Modern Art to protest an exhibition, which was entitled "An International Survey of Recent Painting and Sculpture." It included 14 female artists of the total of 165. The Guerrilla Girls, an anonymous group of female artist-activists, placed posters near galleries citing these statistics.

Postmodernism. During the 1970's and 1980's, a number of artists, male and female, worked with language as a new medium. According to Whitney Chadwick, they were "decenter[ing] language within the patriarchal order, exposing the ways that images are culturally coded, and renegotiating the position of women and minorities as 'other' in patriarchal culture." Some of the themes were feminist, others assumed a more generalized postmodernist discourse. Women active in the postmodern movement include Barbara Kruger, Cindy Sherman, Sherrie Levine, and Jenny Holzer.

Conclusion. In 1976, when Linda Nochlin and Ann Sutherland Harris published a catalog of their exhibition, *Women Artists, 1550-1950*, they wrote, "neither one of us believes that this catalog is the last word on the subject. On the contrary, we both look forward to reading the many articles, monographs, and critical responses that we hope this exhibition will generate." This has not been the case. An excellent point stated by Thalia Gouma-Peterson and Patricia Matthews in the article "The Feminist Critique of Art History," in *The Art Bulletin* (September, 1987), suggests that "most monographs on female artists are still very few . . . since many of the same female artists have been repeatedly discussed, feminist art history has come dangerously close to creating its own canon of white female artists (primarily painters), a canon that is almost as restrictive and exclusionary as its male counterparts." When suggesting a means for changing the structure and basis for women's representation in art history, Chadwick offers, "the gradual integration of women's historical production with recent theoretical developments can be achieved only through a reexamination of the woman artist's relationship to dominant modes of production and representation in the light of a growing literature concerned with the production and intersection of gender, class, race, and representation."

According to Mary D. Garrard, in *Feminism: Has It Changed Art History?* (1980), there are two ways of studying the prevailing historical attitudes of female artists:

> One . . . is to compensate for the lack of scholarly attention to women artists' achievements by writing as apologists . . . . All of this is perfectly true, but it is a lament from the ghetto, and it will not get us out because it is defensive. The other way is to approach the historic fact of discrimination against women from the other end—what has this politics of exclusion meant for male art?

Finally, in Lucy Lippard's view, in *From the Center: Feminist Essays on Women's Art* (1976),

> perhaps the greatest challenge to the feminist movement in the visual arts, then, is the establishment of new criteria by which to evaluate not only the esthetic effect, but the communicative effectiveness of art attempting to avoid becoming a new establishment in itself, or, god forbid, a new stylistic "movement," to be rapidly superseded by some other one.

There have been thousands of female artists throughout history. The danger of concentrating on those who are sufficiently documented is that a canon of great female artists will soon become formed (if it has not already). Once that canon is established, historians will have taken care of the problem, documented the artists, mentioned them in the appropriate capacity, and then moved on. It is probable that there are many more artists to discover who may have skills and talent greater than those already discovered. —*Robin Masi*

See also Art, images of women in; Crafts and home arts; Feminist art movement; Painting and painters; Photography and photographers; Printmaking and printmakers; Sculpting and sculptors

BIBLIOGRAPHY

Chadwick, Whitney. *Women, Art, and Society*. New York: Thames and Hudson, 1990. A comprehensive text that covers art history from the Middle Ages to the 1980's. Offers more in-depth analysis than most general reference books.

Fine, Elsa Honig. *Women and Art*. Montclair, N.J.: Allanheld & Schram/Prior, 1978. Presents solid background information on prominent female artists in history.

Greer, Germaine. *The Obstacle Race: The Fortunes of Women Painters and Their Work*. New York: Farrar, Straus & Giroux, 1979. Greer, a noted feminist, provides a politicized and analytical view, combined with factual information, of female artists up to the 1970's.

Hedges, Elaine, and Ingrid Wendt, comps. *In Her Own Image: Women Working in the Arts*. Old Westbury, N.Y.: Feminist Press, 1980. This interdisciplinary text focuses on female writers and artists in various historical periods.

Heller, Nancy G. *Women Artists: An Illustrated History*. New York: Abbeville Press, 1987. An excellent introduction about women in art is followed by brief biographical material and beautiful color reproductions.

Loeb, Judy, ed. *Feminist Collage: Educating Women in the Visual Arts*. New York: Teachers College Press, Columbia University, 1979. Focuses on art education, especially the integration of female artists into mainstream curricula.

Munro, Eleanor. *Originals: American Women Artists*. New York: Simon & Schuster, 1979. This text provides comprehensive biographical material on hundreds of female American artists.

Rosen, Randy, and Catherine C. Brawer, comps. *Making Their Mark: Women Artists Move into the Mainstream, 1970-85*. New York: Abbeville, 1989. This text, originally an exhibition catalog, provides excellent analyses of contemporary women in art, with references to female artists throughout history. Offers comprehensive statistics on female artists in the modern art world.

Rubinstein, Charlotte Streifer. *American Women Artists*. New York: Avon Books, 1982. An excellent reference book on hundreds of female American artists from pre-Colonial times to the early 1980's.

Slatkin, Wendy. *Women Artists in History: From Antiquity to the Twentieth Century*. Englewood Cliffs, N.J.: Prentice Hall, 1985. A good reference book for general information on women in art.

Waller, Susan. *Women Artists in the Modern Era: A Documentary History*. Metuchen, N.J.: Scarecrow Press, 1991. Contains biographies of female artists throughout history, as well as a bibliography.

Volleyball, women in

RELEVANT ISSUE: Sports

SIGNIFICANCE: Significant gains in women's volleyball have been made in player participation, school support, fan popularity, media coverage, and international competitiveness

Invented in 1895, volleyball is one of the four most popular women's sports. It is a complex reaction game requiring superb concentration and is adaptable to many levels of participation. Little equipment is required: a net, a ball, and a relatively smooth playing surface. A team usually consists of six players. The official court measures 60 feet by 30 feet for indoor and outdoor play; the height of the net for women is 88.25 inches. The official U.S. volleyball rules and summary of rule changes, as well as techniques and mechanics of officiating the game, can be found in the regularly updated National Association for Girls and Women in Sport *Volleyball Guide*.

The growth of women's volleyball has paralleled the development of opportunities for women in sports generally. Prior to the enactment of Title IX of the Education Amendments of 1972, these opportunities were extremely limited. Title IX forced educational institutions to offer equal athletic opportunities to young women. Public school participation increased from 7.0 percent in 1971 to 35.7 percent in 1991. At the collegiate level, women's participation increased to approximately 30 percent of the athletic population.

Little progress occurred in the 1980's, when Title IX was not enforced by the government. The agency responsible for monitoring and enforcing Title IX compliance is the Office for Civil Rights within the Department of Education. A 1992 gender-equity lawsuit blocked the attempt of California State University at Fullerton to drop its women's volleyball program. The volleyball coach who instigated the action was subsequently fired. In 1994, jurors awarded the coach $1.35 million in damages for wrongful termination.

As the sport's governing body, the United States Volleyball Association conducts national championships, including the Women's Open, Women's YWCA, and Senior Women (over thirty). The National Collegiate Athletic Association (NCAA) designates three women's volleyball divisions, which compete in conferences across the United States. The best players from nationally ranked Division I teams are invited to try out for the national team.

In 1962, the International Olympic Committee specified that a women's volleyball division be included in the Tokyo Olympic program, and, in 1964, women's volleyball became an Olympic sport. The U.S. National Volleyball Team won a silver medal in 1984 and a bronze medal in 1992. The International Olympic Committee added women's beach volleyball to the medals sport roster for the 1996 Olympic Games in Atlanta.

The Women's Professional Volleyball Association organizes national and international tournaments. Professional beach volleyball has become highly popular and is an expanding multimillion-dollar sport backed by large sponsors. NBC Sports covered beach volleyball live for the first time in 1993 at the Association of Volleyball Professionals' Seal Beach Open. Coverage has grown to include other networks. In 1993, coed volleyball began to be played in adult sports leagues in New York.

See also Olympic Games, women in the; Professional sports, women in; Sports, women in; Title IX of the Education Amendments of 1972

Voting patterns among women

RELEVANT ISSUES: Politics, sex and gender

SIGNIFICANCE: Women differ from men in both their rate of participation and the issues they consider to be important

More than two thousand years ago, the Greek poet Aristophanes, in his play *Lysistrata*, stirred the imagination and aroused the concern of men about what might happen if women banded together for their own benefit. Such images remained purely fictional throughout most of history. Although some women voted and were active in politics, not until the twentieth century did women emerge as a powerful force in the political arena.

History. Political rights in England and the American colonies were based on custom and usage. The right to participate was restricted on the basis of property, wealth, age, race, and sex. In Colonial America, suffrage was limited to white property owners. A few female landholders voted, and several were appointed to public positions.

The American Revolution resulted in a loss of political rights for women. Constitutions of the thirteen states began specifically to limit the franchise to men. Even propertyless men could vote as part of the newly adopted policy of universal manhood suffrage, whereas wealthy female property holders were denied the vote. Sexual discrimination in politics and voting characterized the new nation.

In the nineteenth century, several states began to extend political rights to women. Kentucky was the first to do so in 1838 when widows were given the right to vote in school board elections. Although partial suffrage was restored in some states, the passage of the Nineteenth Amendment in 1920 theoretically restored suffrage rights to all American women. In fact, black women were denied the franchise in most parts of the American South, and their suffrage rights were not restored until the Civil Rights movement of the 1950's and 1960's.

The reasons for extending suffrage rights to women were both moral and political. Morally, it was hard to justify denying the right to vote to half the population in a nation that prided itself on its democratic heritage. Politically, many reform organizations supported woman suffrage because they believed female voters would support their political agenda. Women were viewed as key allies in the struggle to eliminate corruption at all levels of government.

Turnout. The initial impact of the Nineteenth Amendment was limited. Groups that have been denied the right to participate in the political process cannot be expected to vote at the same rate as those who have never been denied the franchise. Because voter turnout by women was so low, one female suffragist of the 1920's observed: "I know of no politician who is afraid of the woman vote on any question under the sun."

From the passage of the Nineteenth Amendment in 1920 through the presidential election of 1976, women turned out at lower rates than men. The 1980 presidential race found identical turnout rates for men and women, and from the 1984 election, women voted at a higher rate than men. Not only is female voter participation greater than male participation, there are also more female voters. In the 1992 presidential election, women constituted 51.3 percent of the electorate, which means there are approximately six million more female

1992 VOTER TURNOUT IN THE U.S., BY RACE AND SEX

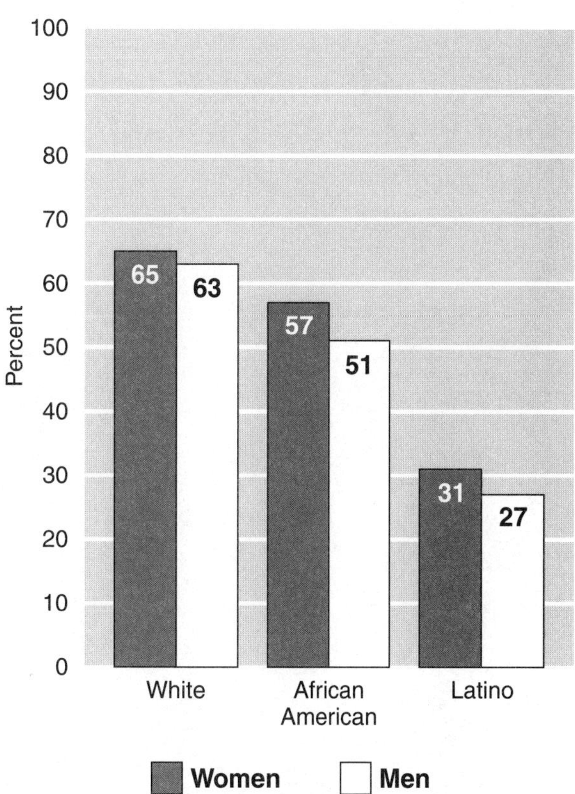

Source: Center for the American Woman and Politics, Eagleton Institute of Politics, Rutgers University

voters than male voters. In 1993, the Democratic majority in Congress passed the so-called motor voter bill, which was quickly signed into law by the newly elected Democratic president Bill Clinton. The bill allows individuals to register to vote at driver's license offices and other governmental agencies. Democrats believe that many unregistered voters, some of whom are poor and female, are likely supporters of the Democratic Party.

Presidential Elections. Ever since the 1980 presidential election, attention has focused on the so-called gender gap. Although both men and women supported Republican Ronald Reagan over Democrat Jimmy Carter, women were less supportive of Reagan and Republican congressional candidates. Fifty-three percent of men voted for Reagan, 38 percent for Carter, and 7 percent for Independent candidate John Anderson. Women gave Reagan 49 percent of their vote, Carter 44 percent, and Anderson 6 percent. The concern and controversy over the gender gap caused both parties to pay more attention to female voters and women's issues.

As a direct result of the gender gap, the Democratic Party

Evidence of the gender gap in presidential elections in the United States has caused many politicians, both male and female, to consider the women's vote more carefully. (Jim West/Impact Visuals)

presidential nominee in 1984, Walter Mondale, selected New York congresswoman Geraldine Ferraro as his vice presidential running mate. Democrats hoped that Ferraro, the first female vice presidential nominee of a major party, would help the party win the White House. Most studies concluded that Ferraro's nomination had little impact on the outcome of the election. Voters generally cast their ballots for president, not vice president. Many women were concerned about the motivations behind the Ferraro nomination. According to a CBS/*New York Times* poll, 60 percent of women believed Ferraro was selected "because of pressure from women's groups," whereas only 22 percent believed she was chosen "because she was the best candidate." Columnist George Will argued in *Newsweek* that Mondale had painted himself into a corner with the Ferraro nomination. By nominating Ferraro, Mondale became "the wimp who was bullied by the National Organization for Women." If he did not select a female running mate, Will claimed, "he will have got half the population up upon its tiptoes, and then not kissed it." The Mondale- Ferraro ticket captured only 41 percent of the national vote. Although it did better among women (45 percent) than men (36 percent), women still gave Reagan 55 percent of their vote.

The 1988 presidential election pitted Republican George Bush against Democrat Michael Dukakis. Early in the campaign, Dukakis held a sizable lead among female voters, and six months before the election, women preferred Dukakis over Bush (53 percent to 33 percent). By election day, however, Bush not only won the election but did so with a majority of women's votes (52 percent). As the campaign developed, Bush and his staff were able to persuade men to like him more and women to dislike him less. The Bush campaign team divided women into sixty-four subcategories and targeted specific messages to these subgroups. For example, advertisements dealing with economic issues were targeted to single working women, married working women, and elderly or widowed working women. This careful targeting and mobilization of groups of female voters worked well for Bush and the Republican Party. Bush was able to divert attention away from the economy, which was a strong issue for the Democrats, and instead focus attention on Dukakis as someone who was weak on crime.

The 1992 presidential campaign was a three-way contest among incumbent president George Bush, Democratic challenger Bill Clinton, and Independent candidate Ross Perot. There was no substantial gender gap in the 1992 campaign. Although women supported Clinton over Bush (46 percent to 37 percent), so did men (41 percent to 38 percent). Perot received 17 percent of the vote from women and 21 percent of the male vote. Clinton, like most Democrats, did much better with unmarried as opposed to married women. Married women cast 42 percent of their votes for Clinton and 39 percent for Bush, whereas unmarried women voted 51 percent for Clinton and 34 percent for Bush. Also, Clinton did extraordinarily well among black female voters. Although white women split their votes evenly between Clinton and Bush (41 percent to each candidate), black women gave more than 80 percent of their vote to Clinton. Clinton won the votes of working women by ten points and of younger women by fifteen points. One of the few segments that Bush was able to win was the homemaker vote, which he carried by nine points.

Year of the Woman. In 1992, designated the "Year of the Woman," 61 percent of the electorate said government would be better if more women held political office. Women did well in the 1992 elections. A record number of women, 150, ran for the House of Representatives, and forty-seven were elected, an increase of nineteen. Four more women were elected to the Senate, increasing the total number of female senators from two to six. In 1992, California became the first state to elect women for both U.S. Senate positions when Democrats Barbara Boxer and Dianne Feinstein won. Joining them were Democrats Patty Murray of Washington, the self-styled "mom in tennis shoes," and Carol Moseley-Braun of Illinois. Moseley-Braun had run after being dismayed at the treatment of Anita Hill during the Clarence Thomas confirmation hearings; she became only the third African American and the first African American woman to serve in the Senate.

Although 1992 was the Year of the Woman, only 13 percent of all contestants for major party nominations to Congress were female. Women continue to be one of the most underrepresented segments of the American population. In 1973, women made up 53 percent of the U.S. population but only 4 percent of the House of Representatives; there were no women in the Senate that year. After the 1994 elections, women made up 11 percent of the House and 8 percent of the Senate. For women to have congressional representation equal to their proportion of the population, voters would have to elect 175 more women to the House and 43 more to the Senate.

If women are a majority of the electorate and vote at higher rates than men, why are so few women elected to office, particularly to the U.S. Congress? Women continue to have primary responsibility for child rearing, which makes it virtually impossible to devote the long hours needed in a successful campaign. Only in the last several decades have substantial numbers of women entered the fields of business and law, professions that have served as launching pads for political careers. The tremendous increase in the number of women holding positions at the city, county, and state levels provides a pool of potential candidates for Congress. In addition, the lack of adequate funding for female candidates has proved to be an impediment. With the emergence of groups such as Early Money Is Like Yeast (EMILY's List), which provides financial support for female Democratic candidates, and Women in the Senate and House (WISH List), which supports Republican women, the financial problems confronting female candidates will be reduced.

Studies show that once women decide to run, gender does not affect their chance of success. Women are as likely as men to advance from primary candidate to party nominee. Lower-level offices provide a stepping-stone to higher offices. With women filling these lower-level offices in increasing numbers, growth in the number of women elected to Congress and other high office can be expected.

Political Issues. Explanations for the gender gap often focus on how the issue positions of women differ from those of men. Studies have shown that women in the House vote in a more liberal direction, even when party affiliation has been taken into account. Opinion surveys have found the same to be true among women in general. A 1992 national election study found that women were much less likely to favor decreasing government services. Another study found that women were less likely than men to cast egocentric economic votes (voting in terms of their own economic interests). Instead, women are more likely to vote in terms of their perceptions of the nation's best interest rather than their own or their family's economic well-being.

Female members of the House were more likely to support feminist concerns than were male legislators. In state legislatures and the U.S. Congress, women supported the Equal Rights Amendment (ERA) more than did men. Women have also been more supportive of equal pay for equal work, family leave legislation, day care funding, and guaranteed health care.

On foreign policy and military issues, female members in Congress have been less supportive of military intervention and increases in defense spending. For example, women were far less supportive than men of U.S. intervention in the Persian Gulf during the Bush Administration.

Do female politicians have a different operational style than men? One who believes this to be true is Madeleine Kunin, former governor of Vermont. Kunin argues that women have different life experiences, particularly child rearing, that they bring with them to their political careers. "I learned my negotiating skills early," said Kunin, "with four children at the dinner table."

Implications. With women composing more than 51 percent of the electorate and voting in greater numbers than men, what are the implications for society? Legislative bodies have given more serious attention to what used to be perceived as "women's issues." Issues such as health care, family leave and child care, and workplace equality have received more attention. Male candidates running against women have attempted to defuse gender issues by advocating vigorous child support enforcement or other legislation that typically was supported by women. Another tactic taken by male candidates is to argue that "all issues are women's issues." This strategy was successfully employed by Pete Wilson in his victory over Dianne Feinstein in the 1990 California gubernatorial race.

Fostering a feminist agenda will be easier if more women hold positions of political influence. There has been substantial growth in the number of female officeholders at all levels of government, but women are still drastically underrepresented at the higher levels of politics, such as governors and members of the U.S. Congress. Until women are elected to public office in numbers approximate to their strength in the general population, issues of concern to women will remain on the back burner of the political agenda. —*Darryl Paulson*

See also Candidacy and political campaigns, women's; Congressional Caucus for Women's Issues; Early Money Is Like Yeast (EMILY's List); Gender gap; Politics; Stereotypes of women; Women in the Senate and House (WISH List); Year of the Woman

Bibliography

Baxter, Sandra, and Marjorie Lansing. *Women and Politics: The Invisible Majority*. Ann Arbor: University of Michigan Press, 1980. One of the significant works focusing on the neglect of women's issues in politics.

Carroll, Susan J. *Women as Candidates in American Politics*. Bloomington: Indiana University Press, 1985. Focuses on the difficulties confronting women seeking political office.

Darcy, R., Susan Welch, and Janet Clark. *Women, Elections, and Representation*. New York: Longman, 1987. From colonial to contemporary America, the authors examine the barriers to female candidates and their contributions to the political system.

Deckard, Barbara Sinclair. *The Women's Movement*. 3d ed. New York: Harper & Row, 1983. An overview of the women's movement through the early 1980's.

Gelb, Joyce, and Marian Lief Palley. *Women and Public Policies*. Princeton, N.J.: Princeton University Press, 1982. One of the few books that attempt to examine the role that women voters and politicians have played in influencing public policy.

Paget, Karen M. "The Gender Gap Mystique." *The American Prospect* no. 15 (1993): 93-101. An analysis of how politicians and political parties have responded to female candidates and voters.

Pivan, Frances Fox, and Richard A. Cloward. *Why Americans Don't Vote*. New York: Pantheon, 1988. An exploration of nonvoting by various social groups, including women, and what can be done to increase voter registration and voting.

Alice
Walker

Wages, women's

Relevant issues: Business and economics, employment

Significance: Women's wages have lagged behind men's since the American Revolution; more recently, structural changes in the economy and in labor force participation rates have begun to reduce the wage disparity

History. From the end of World War II to approximately 1980, the ratio of women's to men's wages in the United States remained remarkably constant at approximately sixty cents to one dollar. Since 1980, however, the wage gap, though still significant, has begun to narrow. Factors in greater wage equity include a changing workforce, structural changes in the U.S. economy, and wage parity legislation.

Since 1975, sea changes in the composition of the U.S. labor force and in the apportionment of national income between the sexes have been the rule rather than the exception. For example, in 1995, 65 percent of women with children under age sixteen participated in the workforce compared with 32 percent in 1948. Women in the mid-1990's earned a higher percentage of advanced degrees than in prior years. Women's total income has increased substantially since 1960, largely because of higher labor force participation rates by women and because of higher relative women's wages. Women's wage gains, however, have been partly undermined by changes in the American social fabric that place greater economic burdens on women. Specifically, as the American divorce rate doubled to 50 percent of all marriages, women's financial responsibility for dependent children grew exponentially. When joint residential custody of children is not court-mandated, women gain custody of dependent children in 90 percent of cases. Furthermore, as more women choose not to marry, they must rely more on themselves to generate income.

Nevertheless, after a quarter-century of social, legislative, and economic change, a sizable differential remains between men's and women's earnings. The persistence of the wage gap provides fertile ground for continuing economic analysis of why it occurs. A large part of the gap is attributable to differences in personal attributes such as education and training, but 30 percent or more cannot be so attributed, which opens the door to the possibility of gender discrimination.

Labor Market Experience. On average, women work fewer hours and leave the labor force more often than men. General work skills of those out of the labor force deteriorate; job-specific skills (which also fade) are beneficial only when a person returns to the same employer. Therefore, one might expect a lower wage on reentering the workforce than was received before exit. For women, family obligations may dictate both shorter hours (a greater preference for part-time work as compared with men) and more frequent exits from the labor force. Although a woman might quickly regain her former wage level after reentering the workforce, she will not achieve the same wage level at the end of ten years of work as will a man with ten years of continuous service. An employer may be less likely to invest in female worker training; this may result in lower productivity and, inevitably, a lower wage.

Preferences for Children. Marriage and children act to lower women's wages relative to men's. First, bearing children can require repeated exits from the job market. Second, rearing children increases the preferences for part-time over full-time work and reduces a woman's ability to accept a higher-paying job that might require more travel, distanced training, or a new location. Some social scientists hypothesize that women have a greater need for children than do men and obtain more satisfaction from having children. They cite, as evidence, the high rate of unintended births that do not result in adoption. Given fertility factors, the demand for children tends to be concentrated in the years before thirty-five or forty, which is also the primary time for skill acquisition, whether self- or employer-financed.

Segregation by Occupation. Occupational segregation by race has markedly declined since the 1960's, but segregation by sex among whites persists. Males still dominate those occupations with higher skill and pay characteristics; women are concentrated in lower-skill career fields. As competent women are unable to enter predominantly male occupations, supply is restricted and the wage is higher in the absence of women. Consequently, the supply of women in female-dominated occupations increases, lowering the wage and widening the male-female wage gap. Studies show that 74 percent of white men and women are working in occupations in which the wage ratio is 0.5 to 0.69. This leads to speculation as to why employers prefer to hire one sex over another.

According to the crowding model of occupational segregation, employers may choose to hire only men because the interactions between men and women may cause workplace problems and reduce productivity and profits. Furthermore, employers may decide that job characteristics (dangerous environment, heavy lifting, repetitive movements) dictate preferential hiring of one gender. Indeed, jobs with the highest compensating wage differentials (wage premiums to compensate the worker for danger, noise, harsh working conditions, and so on) tend to be dominated by males, a fact that widens the gender wage gap. Conversely, employers may act rationally in believing (based on statistical evidence) that one sex would be more productive than the other. In this instance of statistical discrimination, the female job applicant is treated as if she were endowed with the average characteristics of the group (for example, women, on average, quit more frequently). Therefore, the employer will hire only men and fail to hire women who will quit less frequently than the average male.

Comparable Worth. The idea of comparable worth or pay equity evolved from the reality of occupational segregation and the persistence of the gender pay gap. Comparable worth broadens the doctrine of equal pay for equal work to "equal value to the firm/equal pay." Under the concept of comparable worth, people holding different jobs should be paid equally if the skills, knowledge, effort, and overall value of the job to the firm or government agency are equal. Points are assigned to different job characteristics and summed in order to determine the pay (and worth) of a job to a firm or agency. Therefore, if a secretarial and a delivery position merit the same number of points, the pay for the two jobs will be the same. Various states have passed comparable worth legislation, but its venue has been restricted to the public rather than the private sector in the United States.

Antidiscrimination Legislation. Direct government intervention in the labor market has been one means of remedying discrimination against minorities and women. Legislation has made it illegal for firms and agencies to engage in discriminatory wage, hiring, and promotion policies.

In amending the Fair Labor Standards Act of 1938, the Equal Pay Act of 1963 mandated equal pay for men and women for work that requires equal skills and responsibility and that is performed under similar working conditions. The Equal Pay Act does not, however, address the question of occupational segregation, in which access to a particular labor market is restricted by sex. The Equal Pay Act is enforced through routine monitoring and complaints about perceived violations.

Title VII of the Civil Rights Act of 1964 has evolved as the cornerstone of the government's antidiscrimination policy. Title VII made it illegal for an employer to refuse to hire, discharge, or pay a different wage on the basis of race, color, origin, or sex. In 1967, Executive Order 11375 formally extended affirmative action to women. In 1972, the Equal Employment Act required federal contractors to maintain written affirmative action plans for women.

Women and Labor Unions. Many of the barriers that constrained women's participation in the labor (union) movement have crumbled. The decline of the so-called smokestack industry and the structural shift to a services-oriented economy, in addition to increase labor force participation rates, have placed women at the forefront rather than the rearguard of the labor movement. As a result, women have become increasingly aware of the benefits attendant on collective action and have become more active in the labor movement. The unionization in the 1960's and 1970's of female-dominated occupations (teaching, health care, and federal, state, and local government) has dramatically changed the sexual composition of organized labor. In 1954, women constituted 17 percent of unionized labor; by 1988, this number had increased to 37 percent. By 1990, women made up an equal part or a majority of the membership of newer unions that rose to prominence in the 1960's: the American Federation of State, County, and Municipal Employees; the Service Employees International Union; and teachers' unions. Women were also in the majority in established unions such as the Communications Workers of America, the United Food and Commercial Workers, and various garment unions.

Gradually, women are beginning to attain union leadership positions at local and national council levels. It is inevitable that women's growing proportion of organized labor will slowly translate into top executive positions in the labor movement.

The Canadian Experience. Though demographically similar, labor force characteristics in Canada differ markedly from those in the United States. The degree of unionization and the unemployment rate are approximately twice as high in Canada as in the United States. The latter may be explained in part by a more generous social welfare net that operates in Canada. Unionized women (67 percent) are more likely to work in the public sector in Canada than is the case in the United States (51 percent); as a result, unionization is concentrated among higher-skilled women in Canada and, to a lesser degree, also in the United States. Generally speaking, a higher degree of unionization is associated with a higher standardization (lower variance) of wages and greater wage equality.

Reinforcing the trend toward greater wage equality in Canada relative to the United States has been a more activist government stance against wage discrimination. Although government is decentralized in Canada, with much of the relevant legislation initiated at the provincial rather than the federal level, Canada's provinces have taken the lead in passing comparable worth legislation. In 1951, Ontario passed the first piece of equal pay legislation, followed by Quebec in 1976 and the federal government in 1978.

More recently (1987), Ontario took equal pay for equal value one step further by mandating comparable worth adjustments in both public (1990) and private (1991) sectors of the economy. Rather than rely on traditional complaint-generated enforcement, Ontario requires all employers in public and private sector firms with 100 or more workers to initiate formal evaluation procedures and to make necessary wage adjustments. Provided that the provincial government actively enforces the new laws, this will be the first significant attempt to implement comparable worth in the private sector.

The Inevitable Closing of the Male-Female Wage Gap. From 1980 to 1986, women's wages rose to 65 percent of men's wages, an increase of 5 percentage points in six years. Nondiscriminatory factors, such as labor force experience and education, which once justified a higher male wage, are becoming more similar between the sexes.

In the 1960's and 1970's, while some women were successfully entering formerly all-male arenas, their efforts were more than offset by an influx of undertrained, underskilled women into the labor force. This huge influx of new female entrants and reentrants, with lower levels of self-investment and human capital, earned lower wages, which suppressed any gains of the minority. This flood of new entrants has essen-

MEDIAN SALARIES IN THE U.S. IN 1993

	Women	*Men*
Accountants	$ 26,936	$ 36,816
Computer programmers	31,616	37,596
Engineers	48,555	59,750
Financial managers	31,876	51,064
General surgeons	150,108	190,269
Insurance salespeople	23,504	35,308
Lawyers	47,684	61,100
Nurses	34,476	32,916
Obstetricians/gynecologists	180,800	202,956
Personnel, training, and labor specialists	29,120	39,572
Physical therapists (staff)	25,895	28,221
Pharmacists (independent)	44,000	45,600
Professors—public institutions	52,905	59,240
Psychiatrists	110,270	117,879
Public relations supervisors	41,707	59,627
Real estate salespeople	24,908	34,632
Teachers, elementary school	28,548	34,216

Source: Working Woman (January, 1994)

tially run its course. Given current high labor force participation rates for women, population characteristics are fully reflected in labor force characteristics; no longer are those with the highest levels of human capital development more likely to be sitting on the sidelines.

One harbinger of greater future intergender wage equality is the fact that recent wage gains have been highest among the youngest element of the female workforce—that element with the longest working life. In 1980, women age twenty to twenty-four earned 78 percent of the wage earned by men in that age range. This percentage increased to 86 percent by 1986.

Furthermore, as female entrants of the 1970's gained job experience, the learning curve shifted and productivity rose, as did wages relative to men's wages. Working women are opting for longer, more contiguous careers. The educational levels of women in the labor force has risen faster than have male levels. Moreover, the most highly educated elements of the female labor force are more likely to participate in the workforce than ever before.

Projecting ongoing trends into the future, it appears that labor market skills of the average female worker will increase faster than those for the average male through the year 2000. As women's rate of college enrollment accelerates faster than men's (particularly in advanced degrees), their relative educational levels will rise. In addition, the job experience levels of the average working woman will also rise significantly. It has been estimated that by the year 2000, the typical forty-five-year-old woman will have worked 5.5 more years than her predecessor had worked in 1980. Conservative simulations indicate that by 2000, the female-male wage ratio will have risen to eighty cents to one dollar. —*John A. Sondey*

See also Antidiscrimination laws; Civil Rights Act of 1964; Comparable worth; Employment of women; Equal Pay Act of 1963; Equal pay for equal work; Labor movement and women; Pay equity; Poverty, feminization of; Pregnancy and employment; Title VII of the Civil Rights Act of 1964

BIBLIOGRAPHY

Card, David, and Richard B. Freeman, eds. *Small Differences that Matter*. Chicago: University of Chicago Press, 1993. An incisive, statistically intense look at the U.S. and Canadian labor markets which considers their similarities and wide divergences from different perspectives.

Cobble, Dorothy Sue, ed. *Women and Unions*. Ithaca, N.Y.: ILR Press, 1993. Forty authors discuss virtually every aspect of the contemporary women's labor movement, from organizing clerical and home workers to cracking the "glass ceiling" in achieving top union jobs.

Flanagan, Robert J., Lawrence M. Kahn, Robert S. Smith, and Ronald G. Ehrenberg. *Economics of the Employment Relationship*. Glenview, Ill.: Scott, Foresman, 1989. Essentially a business student's guide to labor markets with a minimum of technical analysis and a strong section on collective bargaining.

Fuchs, Victor R. "Women's Quest for Economic Equality." *Journal of Economic Perspectives* 3, no. 1 (1989): 25-42. An excellent, nontechnical article that looks at why women earn less than men.

Gunderson, Morley. "Male-Female Wage Differentials and Policy Responses." *Journal of Economic Literature* 27, no. 1 (1989): 46-72. A survey of the wage gap literature, with supporting empirical evidence. A bit technical for the non-economist.

Hamermesh, Daniel S., and Albert Rees. *The Economics of Work and Pay*. 5th ed. New York: HarperCollins College, 1993. One of the standard texts on labor economics, replete with strong diagrammatics.

McConnell, Campbell R., and Stanley L. Brue. *Contemporary Labor Economics*. 3d ed. New York: McGraw Hill, 1992. An easy-to-read labor text, with less emphasis on micro-economic diagrammatics.

Smith, James P., and Michael War. "Women in the Labor Market and in the Family." *Journal of Economic Perspectives* 3, no. 1 (1989): 9-23. The authors provide an insightful, nontechnical dual focus on the ongoing progress of women in the labor force and the feminization of poverty.

Walker, Alice (b. Feb. 9, 1944, Eatonton, Ga.)

Areas of achievement: Literature and communications, race and ethnicity

Significance: Walker's prize-winning poems, essays, and novels document the oppression faced by African American women, as well as their great strengths

While Alice Walker's focus is African American women, her works are calls for universal human dignity. In her poetry and essay collections—such as *Revolutionary Petunias and Other Poems* (1973), *In Search of Our Mothers' Gardens: Womanist Prose* (1983), and *Living by the Word* (1988)—she also expresses concern for the environment, animal rights, and world peace. A strong spiritual element can be found in her work, as well as an enduring message of hope.

Walker's involvement in the Civil Rights movement is reflected in her fiction, especially the novel *Meridian* (1976), but national prominence came with her Pulitzer Prize-winning novel *The Color Purple* (1982), an exploration of racism and violence against women. She worked with Steven Spielberg on the 1985 film version, which some critics accused of watering down the novel's feminist stance.

Walker's focus on violence against women has been criticized by some African American men for repeatedly presenting black men as abusive and insensitive to black women. Often cited are such short stories as "Coming Apart" and "Porn" from *You Can't Keep a Good Woman Down* (1981), which portray self-absorbed husbands and lovers unaware of the pain that their use of pornography causes the women in their lives. Walker's novel *Possessing the Secret of Joy* (1992), dedicated "with tenderness and respect to the blameless Vulva," deals with the individual, social, and political costs of female genital mutilation.

See also African American women; Black feminism; Civil Rights movement and women; Clitoridectomy; Fiction writers; Genital mutilation; Poetry and poets; Pornography; Racism; Violence against women; Womanist

War and women

Relevant issues: Peace advocacy, war and the military

Significance: The debate among historians and political scientists over whether participation in or opposition to war is natural for women is one aspect of the argument over whether any intrinsic differences between the sexes truly exist

History. Since the time of ancient Greece, when Aristophanes wrote a play about women putting an end to their husbands' wars by withholding their affections, the view of women as essentially opposed to war because of their role as nurturers has been expressed again and again. A more modern version was put forward in the 1990's, when a theorist of strategy, Edward Luttwak, argued that the trend toward smaller families in modern states was making war less and less likely by making the emotional investment of mothers in their sons more intense. Yet, throughout history, women, though not usually participants in combat, have provided the support services necessary to keep their countries' war efforts going. They have also extended moral support and exhortations to battle to the men doing the fighting. Male soldiers have, in turn, seen themselves as fighting to protect their country's women and children from the enemy. Wars have sometimes offered women the chance to gain opportunities in the workforce that would have been closed to them in peacetime. Military service, which is a more open career in wartime than in peacetime, can offer both men and women a chance to travel abroad and opportunities for advancement that they might not enjoy in civilian life. The dual image of woman as peacemaker and supporter of war can be seen in the history of the United States.

Women as War Victims. In many wars throughout history, civilian women have not only seen husbands, brothers, and sons killed or maimed but have also been themselves attacked. They have been killed or raped by enemy armies, have seen their homes destroyed by aerial bombing or mortar shelling, have been forced to become refugees, and have suffered from sickness or hunger directly attributable to the war. Such sufferings endured personally by civilian women, so noticeable in Europe in World War II and in the post-1992 conflict in the former Yugoslavia, tend to make women's antipathy toward war considerably sharper than that of men. These particular types of suffering, however, have not been part of America's twentieth century wars. White women were occasionally killed by American Indian warriors in the frontier wars that lasted throughout the nineteenth century; U.S. soldiers sometimes retaliated by killing American Indian women and children. Women and men who chose the Loyalist side in the

American Revolution (1775-1783) often found themselves refugees in British-held Canada after 1783. Union armies committed depredations against the homes of Southern whites during the last stages of the American Civil War (1861-1865). Canada has not seen its cities attacked, or its soil occupied by a foreign enemy, since the War of 1812; hence, twentieth century Canadian women, like their American sisters, had (unless they were immigrants from Europe) no memory of war-induced destruction and deprivation.

Throughout American history, women typically have not engaged in combat, but they have served as nurses, cooks, launderers, or sewers. In the American Revolution and the American Civil War some women served in the regular armies disguised as men. During the American Revolution, with all able-bodied male patriots in the army, wives on the frontier sometimes had to defend against marauding Indians; when the United States was independent, however, the male troops of the Federal Army were usually relied on when the local frontiersmen could not manage the Indian "threat"; among American Indians, being a warrior was an exclusively male calling. Clara Barton, who founded the Red Cross during the Civil War to tend to the wounded, exemplified the notion of woman as provider of support rather than as fighter. It was not until World War I (1914-1918) that women began to join the U.S. military as auxiliaries to make it possible for more military men to engage in combat. Thirteen thousand women served as yeomen in the naval reserve and the Marine Corps reserve (the Army did not accept women).

Women in the Military: World War II as a Watershed. The range of jobs women could perform for the military was broadened somewhat during World War II (1939-1945). The women admitted into the Women's Army Corps (WAC) and the women's naval reserve, the Women Accepted for Voluntary Emergency Service (WAVES), generally performed clerical or nursing duties; they were not authorized to kill anyone. Because servicewomen were inducted in order to free men for combat, some enlisted men resented them. Military nurses who were taken as prisoners of war by the Japanese in the Philippines, however, probably suffered as much as their male counterparts. A handful of American women won the right, as members of the Women's Airforce Service Pilots (WASPs) but without the status of members of the military, to fly military airplanes across the United States; a few of them died while performing their duties. Some American women of upper-class backgrounds, who had enjoyed the privilege of foreign travel in childhood or adolescence, were smuggled into France to aid the resistance in sabotage and to help rescue downed Allied airmen. During World War II, the proportion of U.S. military personnel that were women was much smaller than their percentage of the American population as a whole, and the proportion of young women in the military was much smaller than the proportion of young men who served.

In Canada, during World War II about fifty thousand women served in the armed forces, where they were allowed to perform, for the first time, other jobs besides that of nurse: driver, mechanic, and radio operator. Other countries went significantly beyond the United States and Canada in their use of women as a military resource. In Great Britain and the Soviet Union, women were subject to the draft. In the resistance movements in continental European countries against the German occupation, women played an important role, often accepting tasks as dangerous as those performed by the men (including that of killing the enemy). The Polish resistance made especially extensive use of women in its ranks.

Women in the Military in the Vietnam War. Although Americans of both sexes were protesting the Vietnam War (1965-1975) in the United States, young American women contributed to the American military effort in that country by serving as nurses. All the women who served in Vietnam had volunteered to be in the military; a high proportion of the fighting men in Vietnam after 1965 were draftees. It is ironic that the female nurses in Vietnam were sometimes in as much danger as the male soldiers. (Canada did not send military forces, male or female, to Vietnam.) It was not until the 1980's, when former military nurses began publishing their reminiscences of Vietnam, that the general public realized to what traumatic experiences these women had been subjected.

The Struggle over Combat Roles for Women. The effort by women to gain access to combat specialties in the American military became more intense after the end of the Vietnam War in 1975. With the draft abolished since 1973, the military tried harder to recruit women. The post-1970 feminist movement, which attacked the traditional gender stereotyping of occupations, was a powerful force for greater equality of treatment of women in the military. At the same time, the economic difficulties that the United States experienced in the decades after 1973, and the constantly rising cost of higher education, made military service a more attractive post-high-school option for both men and women. Access to combat specialties was necessary if women were to be promoted at the same rate as men.

Beginning in the 1980's, the Navy gradually allowed more female naval personnel to work on the same ships as male Navy personnel. In the Persian Gulf War of February, 1991, in which female soldiers were far more visible than in previous American wars, three American servicewomen were killed in a missile attack on the Dhahran barracks; eleven servicewomen died in Operation Desert Storm, five of them in action; and two American servicewomen (Rhonda Cornum and Melissa Rathbun-Nealy) were taken prisoner by the Iraqis. The fact that none of these women was technically in a combat specialty made the argument for eliminating combat exclusion seem more persuasive. In 1991, the U.S. Congress passed a law permitting, but not requiring, the Air Force to utilize women as combat pilots.

In the military forces of Canada, Belgium, Denmark, Norway, Great Britain, and The Netherlands, women were legally allowed the chance to apply for combat positions. By the early 1990's, however, not many women had been assigned to such positions, and these countries did not seem as likely to engage in war as the United States. Although Israeli women had en-

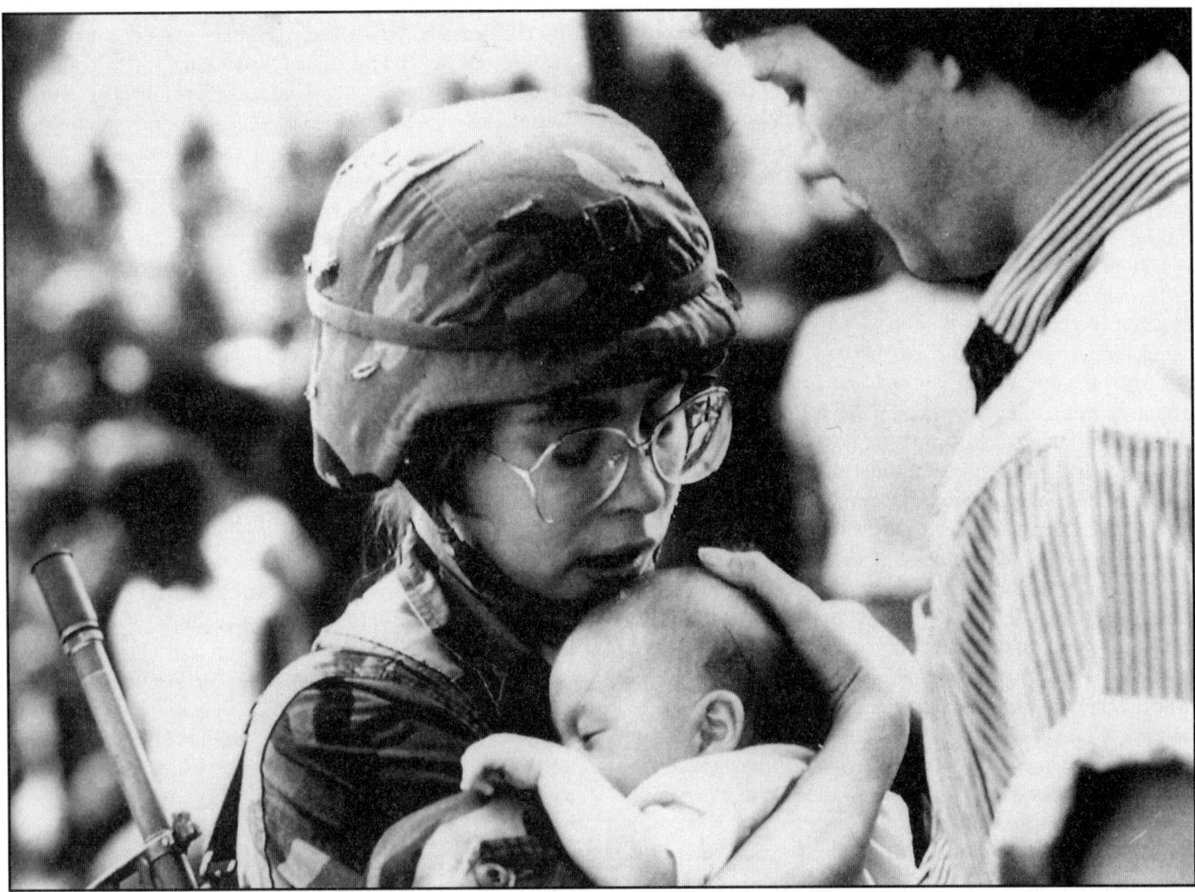

Images such as this one, of a mother saying good-bye to her baby as she leaves for war, have encouraged feminists who seek equal opportunities for women but have troubled others. (AP LaserPhoto)

gaged in combat during the struggle for independence in the 1940's, the Israeli military in the 1990's kept them in support rather than combat positions; Israeli women were, in theory at least, subject to the country's draft.

Women in War Industries. In World War I, some American women entered the munitions industries, leaving their jobs after the war. In World War II, the inflow of women (both married and single) into the workforce was much more substantial, though it never amounted to a majority of adult women. American women helped to build the ships, airplanes, and bombs necessary to defeat the Germans and the Japanese. Because many of the working women had children, some employers, such as the shipbuilder Henry Kaiser, provided day care services; finding child care, however, was still a problem for many female wartime workers. The influx of women into industry was reversed with the end of World War II, when returning servicemen reclaimed their old jobs. The female defense workers either left the workforce entirely or accepted lower-paid jobs outside the defense industry. In Canada, about 900,000 women entered the defense industries as factory workers during World War II; in Canada, as in the United States, most women were laid off from such jobs when the war ended.

Female American historians have often stressed the independence and self-reliance that female defense workers gained during World War II from holding down paying jobs in a man's world; they stress the precedent the war set for the massive entry of women into the workforce in the 1970's. Yet, the experience of the United States during World War II also indicates that most women have no scruples against helping to manufacture weapons or war material (even though these help kill people), given sufficient economic incentives and social supports and sufficiently widespread patriotic sentiment. Women, even if inherently pacific, are not all doctrinaire pacifists.

Pacifist Feminism Versus Equal Rights Feminism. There is, as the political scientists Jean Bethke Elshtain and Cynthia Enloe have pointed out, at least a potential conflict between the type of feminism that insists on equal access of women to jobs in defense plants and to combat duty in the military, on the one hand, and the kind of feminism that sees greater female participation in politics as a path to a more peaceful world, on the other. The two views may be expressed by the same person at different times: Congressperson Patricia Schroeder, in the 1990's the leading advocate of ending the ban on combat specialties for women in the armed services, had been an opponent of the Vietnam War in the 1970's.

The conflict would be sharper were it not for the differences among those who consider themselves pacifist. Absolute pacifists reject war under any circumstances; a woman with such beliefs, for example, would avoid combat service in the military even if it were open to women and would disapprove of her daughter's entering a combat arm. More moderate pacifists, while working to pressure governments to eliminate the causes of armed conflict between nations, concede that peace might sometimes have to be sacrificed to protect other human values. The title of one long-lived American women's peace organization, the Women's International League for Peace and Freedom (WILPF), illustrates the dilemma of which such moderate pacifists are acutely aware: Preserving peace and preserving (or extending) freedom can sometimes be incompatible goals in the short run. Not all female peace activists are feminists; and an advocate of peace, whether a man or a woman, might not necessarily believe in such other laudable values as racial and ethnic tolerance or the protection of women's rights and human rights in general.

Women's Peace Movements in the United States. The United States has a long tradition of peace advocacy by women. Women played a role in the peace movement that arose before the Civil War; considering that most antebellum pacifists also opposed slavery, neither male nor female peace activists were able to either prevent the outbreak of the Civil War or stop it once it had started. Julia Ward Howe, who had written the stirring "Battle Hymn of the Republic" during the Civil War, issued in 1870, in response to the suffering wrought by the Franco-German War of 1870-1871, a call for cooperation for peace among the women of the world. Between 1870 and 1914, world peace was a favorite cause for many women of sufficient freedom from financial or family cares and of sufficiently strong religious background or reformist persuasion. One such woman was Lucia Ames Mead, a lecturer who urged international peace through arbitration and disarmament.

In 1915, after the outbreak of general war in Europe, Carrie Chapman Catt, a long-time advocate of woman suffrage, helped to found, together with other women social reformers, the Women's Peace Party. Yet, she supported the American war effort once war was declared on Germany in April, 1917, with the hope that such support would be rewarded by the right of American women to vote; Lucia Ames Mead also supported the war effort. Among those female peace advocates who refused to support the war effort after the war had started were suffragist Alice Paul, social reformer Jane Addams, and teacher Emily Greene Balch.

In the immediate aftermath of World War I, feminists helped to found the WILPF, which condemned the Treaty of Versailles (1919) as excessively harsh to a defeated Germany. The adoption by the United States of the Nineteenth Amendment to the Constitution in 1920 seemed to promise greater political power for America's women. In the period between World Wars I and II, the U.S. section of the WILPF, thanks to the efforts of the gifted lobbyist Dorothy Detzer, achieved at least some of its goals. In the early 1930's, the U.S. government was pressured into ending its military intervention in Nicaragua (this was a low-intensity operation, fought by a strictly volunteer army); and a congressional committee headed by Senator Gerald Nye was prodded, in 1934, into investigating the alleged warmongering of the American munitions manufacturers in the years prior to America's entry into World War I in 1917. Other American women's peace groups of the interwar period included the Women's Peace Union and the Women's Peace Society, both of which went into sharp decline in the early 1930's, and the National Committee on the Cause and Cure of War. Female college students also played a role in the active student peace movement of the 1930's, which tried to be both in favor of peace and antifascist.

After World War II broke out in Europe with Germany's invasion of Poland in 1939, the women's peace movement was thrown into disarray. Following the sudden defeat of France by Nazi Germany in May-June, 1940, many female peace activists joined those American men, inside and outside the peace movement, who urged all aid short of war to Great Britain and other foes of Nazi Germany. On the other side of the debate, relatively obscure middle-aged women, marching into Washington, D.C., and using the rhetoric of nurturing motherhood, constituted the placard-carrying shock troops of those politicians (the so-called isolationists, most of whom were men) who argued in September, 1940, against the introduction of peacetime conscription and in January-March 1941 against lend-lease aid to Great Britain. These female activists were discredited among later generations of scholars for several reasons: the extreme right-wing political views (often tainted with anti-Semitism) that many of these women held; the surprise Japanese attack on Pearl Harbor (December 7, 1941), which seemed to show that American entry into World War II was inevitable; and the uncovering in 1945 of German attempts to exterminate Europe's Jews, which showed that America's entry into World War II against Nazi Germany was justifiable. Once the United States was in the war, the National Committee on the Cause and Cure of War was transformed into the Women's Committee for Victory and Lasting Peace.

The coming of the Soviet-American Cold War in the late 1940's stifled peace activism among both women and men; in 1950, one peace organization, the Congress of American Women, was forced to dissolve after the government harassed it for its expression of pro-Soviet opinions. WILPF continued into the 1950's and 1960's, though with much less influence than it had had between the two world wars.

The peace movement in the United States began to revive with the struggle for a nuclear test ban in the late 1950's and early 1960's. It was during this struggle, in 1961, that Women Strike for Peace (WSP) was formed. WSP, an organization consisting predominantly of relatively well educated, middle-class homemakers (often of left-wing backgrounds), used some of the motherhood rhetoric utilized in 1940-1941 by female advocates of isolationism, though in the service of a different cause. The 1963 test ban agreement between the Soviet Union and the United States could be seen as a partial triumph of this women's organization's efforts.

In the early and middle years of the twentieth century, some women stuck to pacifist principles fairly courageously over a long period. One such woman was the Roman Catholic peace activist Dorothy Day, founder of the Catholic Worker movement (it was devoted to acts of charity as well as witness against war). In her movement newspaper, she opposed American involvement in World War II, the Korean War, and the Vietnam War. Another scrupulous adherent to principle was Jeannette Rankin. Elected from Montana as the first female member of the House of Representatives, she was one of the few representatives to vote against the declaration of war on Germany in 1917; once again, in Congress in 1941, as one of a handful of female representatives, she alone voted against declaring war on Japan. As an eighty-seven-year-old woman no longer in Congress, she would also stand in opposition to a less popular war, the American intervention in Vietnam: A coalition of women active in the peace, feminist, and Civil Rights movements, led by Rankin, marched in protest against the Vietnam War in Washington, D.C., on January 15, 1969, calling themselves the Jeannette Rankin Brigade.

Women's Peace Activism and the Vietnam War. The success of the movement to end U.S. involvement in the Vietnam War cannot be attributed solely to American women as a group. Many of the major antiwar organizations were male dominated; some young American women served in the military in Vietnam as nurses; and some politically active women (such as Senator Margaret Chase Smith of Maine and the Republican pamphleteer and future antifeminist activist Phyllis Schlafly) stood apart from the antiwar struggle. Nevertheless, a significant minority of women did play a prominent (and historically unprecedented) role in the antiwar movement, departing dramatically from the traditional female pattern of supporting (or at least not opposing) the nation in its battles with its enemies. Female college students took part in large numbers in antiwar demonstrations; WSP, having moved from antinuclear activism to antidraft work and antiwar demonstrations, went so far as to send a delegation to the enemy state of North Vietnam. The threat to the survival of the United States posed by Vietnamese communism, unlike the menace arising from Japan and Germany during World War II, seemed remote to many American women; the threat of the Vietnam War to the lives and limbs of their sons, husbands, and boyfriends, and the immediate harm being done to Vietnamese women and children, seemed all too real.

WSP was a political proving ground for the New York City-bred lawyer Bella Abzug, who, during her years in Congress after her election to that body in 1970, helped to push for a speedy end to the Vietnam War. In her combination of staunch opposition to war and passionate advocacy of feminism, Abzug differed, at least initially, from most WSP members. She resembled, however, many of the younger women who were drawn into the antiwar movement from college campuses. The pre-1920 feminist movement (for woman suffrage) had sown the seeds for such interwar women's peace organizations as the WILPF. The lack of respect that many younger female college-educated peace activists suffered from their male colleagues in the anti-Vietnam War movement helped to hasten the creation of the post-1970 feminist movement.

Two female entertainers probably became better known to the general American public as crusaders against the Vietnam war than anyone associated with WSP. Motion-picture actress Jane Fonda made highly publicized visits to North Vietnam and tried to spread antiwar propaganda among soldiers stationed in the United States. Folk and protest singer Joan Baez sang antiwar ballads to antiwar demonstrators and also made a symbolic trip to North Vietnam. The presence of female entertainers in the antiwar movement shows how much opportunity had opened up for female dissent by the unpopularity of one specific war: In World War II, the sole role played by America's female entertainers had been that of raising the morale of American troops overseas and encouraging American civilians to buy war bonds.

Some African American women also joined the movement against the Vietnam war, including Coretta Scott King (after the murder of her husband, civil rights leader Martin Luther King, Jr.). Although most women in WSP were white, the group did have some African American members. Some African American women who opposed the war used the rhetoric

Actress Jane Fonda was a prominent and controversial activist against the Vietnam War. (AP/Wide World Photos)

of motherhood, as did white female dissenters; some believed that the war was wasting money that could have helped poor African Americans; and some younger African American women radicals (such as those associated with the Black Panther Party) saw an analogy between the communist struggle to expel Americans from Vietnam and the African American struggle for liberation in the United States. The more precarious socioeconomic status of many African American women (compared with that of white women) might have deterred some from carrying their opposition beyond anonymous answers to public opinion polls. African American singer Eartha Kitt saw her career in the United states destroyed after she openly denounced the war at a White House party in January, 1968; she had to go to Europe to get work.

Post-Vietnam Women's Peace Activism. After 1975, the efforts of both male and female peace activists were diffused over different areas. In the following two decades, the wars in which the United States became involved (Grenada in 1983; Panama in 1989; the Persian Gulf War in 1991) tended to be extremely short and decisive; the one long-lasting (1980-1992) military effort, intervention in Central America (for the government in El Salvador, against the government in Nicaragua) cost only a handful of lives of U.S. soldiers.

The early 1980's were a time of sharp tensions between the United States and the Soviet Union; those tensions did not end until the withdrawal of the Soviet Union from its Eastern European satellites in 1989 and the breakup of the Soviet Union itself in 1991. In the early 1980's, Betty Bumpers, the wife of Arkansas Senator Dale Bumpers, organized Peace Links, a group designed to help individuals from the United States and the Soviet Union get to know one another across the ideological divide. Another major area of women's peace activism was the movement to limit the manufacture of nuclear weapons (the so-called nuclear freeze movement), in order to make a nuclear war between the Soviet Union and the United States impossible. The Canadian-born physician Helen Caldicott was one of the chief spokespersons of the freeze movement in the United States, which embraced both men and women; she founded the organization Women's Action for Nuclear Disarmament (WAND) to give women a special role in the movement for a nuclear freeze. The movement's goal of peace through disarmament was rendered irrelevant by the warming of relations between the Soviet Union and the United States after 1985 and the end of the Cold War from 1989 to 1991; peace was finally achieved through the renunciation of communism by the other side rather than by the limitation of armaments.

The early 1990's were hard times for peace activists, whether male or female. Opposition voiced by some women's peace groups to the U.S. intervention in the Persian Gulf War against Iraq (February, 1991) was not popular. Yolanda Huett-Vaughn, a female Army physician who unsuccessfully pleaded for conscientious objector status, was almost completely ignored by the American public in general and was deprived of her career. Another female Army physician, Rhonda Cornum, received much applause in the United States for withstanding several days of prisoner-of-war status in the hands of the Iraqi army. As of 1995, various peace groups, both exclusively female and those under male leadership, continued to struggle on, often facing financial difficulty. One of the more successful was WAND, the organization that Caldicott had founded. The new name of this Boston-based group, Women's Action for New Directions, indicated the new task, in a post-Cold War era, of lobbying for lower military budgets.

After Bosnia, in the former Yugoslavia, was dragged into a bloody war in 1992, American feminists began to note with anguish a terrifying strategy allegedly used by one side in that conflict: the systematic rape of the enemy's women. The occurrence of such atrocities, if confirmed, illustrated the classic dilemma often faced by all peace movements, whether feminist or not: the potential conflict between peace and other human values. Whatever the U.S. government did to stop atrocities in Bosnia, either alone or in cooperation with others, ran the risk of war.

Female peace activists have not worked for peace simply by pressuring the governments of their own countries to do something or to stop doing something. Another task of the female peace activist is to maintain relationships with like-minded activists in other countries. Such people-to-people diplomacy can, at least theoretically, build bridges between nations beyond what governments can do. During the period between the two world wars, the Women's International League for Peace and Freedom sent delegates to attend conferences where they would meet other women with similar aims. The rise of fascism in Europe in the 1930's, and the world war that resulted, may have disrupted international ties of friendship among women at a time when they were beginning to be woven. A good example of such people-to-people diplomacy in the 1990's was the international conference of female heads of nongovernmental organizations, held in Beijing, China, in August and September, 1995. There, delegates from the United States (such as Bella Abzug) rubbed shoulders with delegates from Third World and other countries, talking about issues common to women of all countries as well as issues common to both men and women.

Women as Combat Journalists. The phenomenon of the female combat journalist offers a seeming challenge to the notion of women's inherent aversion to war. Yet, war reporters, although they risk their lives, do not try to kill anyone. Moreover, honest war reporting, by exposing the horrors that wars inflict on civilians as well as on soldiers, can help to bring the pressure of public opinion to bear on governments that are quick to resort to force rather than rely on diplomacy.

One of the earliest female war correspondents, who covered the American involvement in World War I, was Peggy Hull. Hull had the advantage of having met the commander of the American Expeditionary Force when he was waging war against Mexican guerrillas. Martha Gellhorn, who married novelist Ernest Hemingway, first made a name for herself by her coverage of the Spanish Civil War (1936-1939); she later reported on World War II. Marguerite Higgins covered World

War II, the Korean War, and the beginnings of the Vietnam War; she died in the mid-1960's of a mysterious tropical disease. Dickey Chapelle, who had become a war correspondent to be with her combat photographer husband during World War II, later divorced him and began an independent career as war journalist and combat photographer; she was killed in Vietnam in 1965. Although some female American journalists in Vietnam (such as television combat reporter Liz Trotta) supported U.S. government policy to the end, those journalists in Vietnam who criticized the American intervention, such as Frances Fitzgerald, did much through their writings to turn the American public against continuing U.S. involvement.

In the 1990's, Christiane Amanpour, a reporter for the Cable News Network (CNN), exemplified the good that a competent war correspondent can do. Beginning in 1992, she gave televised reports again and again on the suffering inflicted on civilians in the war in Bosnia. In 1995, the United States and several European countries finally intervened to impose a peace settlement in that troubled part of the world.

—Paul D. Mageli

See also Abzug, Bella; American Revolution and women; Army Nurse Corps; Baez, Joan; Barton, Clara; Catt, Carrie Chapman; Civil War and women; Combat, women in; Day, Dorothy; Gulf War, women in the; Howe, Julia Ward; Jeannette Rankin Brigade; Journalism, women in; Military, women in the; Nurses, women as; Pacifism and nonviolence; Peace movement and women; Rankin, Jeannette; SPAR; Vietnam War, women in the; Women Accepted for Voluntary Emergency Service (WAVES); Women's Airforce Service Pilots (WASPs); Women's Army Corps (WAC); Women's International League for Peace and Freedom (WILPF); Women's Peace Party; Women's Reserve in the Marine Corps; World War I and women; World War II, women's military roles in

BIBLIOGRAPHY

Adams, Michael C. C. *The Best War Ever: America and World War II*. Baltimore: The Johns Hopkins University Press, 1994. Examines, among other things, the myths surrounding American women's participation in both the military and the defense industry labor force during World War II. Illustrations; abbreviated references in text. The full references, in the back, are a mine of information for scholars.

Alonso, Harriet Hyman. *Peace as a Women's Issue: A History of the U.S. Movement for World Peace and Women's Rights*. Syracuse, N.Y.: Syracuse University Press, 1993. In this well-written history of women's peace activism in the United States, from the pre-Civil War period to the Persian Gulf War, the author, a historian, provides particularly good coverage of both WILPF and WSP. By including only those activists who were conscious believers in women's rights, the author excludes the female isolationist protesters of 1940 and 1941, and the possibility of feminist militarism is not fully explored. Photographs; list of feminist peace organizations existing between 1820 and 1985; chronology of the New York City branch of the WILPF; endnotes; bibliography; and index.

Elshtain, Jean Bethke. *Women and War*. New York: Basic Books, 1987. In this all-encompassing work, arranged topically rather than chronologically, the author, a political scientist, cites examples from all eras of American history and analyzes the thought of political philosophers from ancient Greece to late twentieth-century United States. Elshtain disputes the common view of man as essentially warlike and of women as essentially peaceful. Endnotes; photographic and other illustrations; index. For college students.

Enloe, Cynthia. *The Morning After: Sexual Politics at the End of the Cold War*. Berkeley: University of California Press, 1993. The author, a political scientist who applies gender analysis to international politics, provides interesting insights into the significance of the Persian Gulf War as a milestone in the growth of an ethos of professionalism among female American soldiers and of the breakdown of the traditional association of soldierly bravery with masculinity. Photographs; endnotes; index.

Hartmann, Susan M. *The Home Front and Beyond: American Women in the 1940s*. Boston: Twayne, 1982. Provides, among other things, a good introduction to the topics of women's participation in the defense industry labor force during World War II and of women in military uniform during World War II. Photographs; essay on sources; chapter notes; index.

Jeffreys-Jones, Rhodri. *Changing Differences: Women and the Shaping of American Foreign Policy, 1917-1994*. New Brunswick, N.J.: Rutgers University Press, 1995. The author tries to shed light on American women's attitudes toward the question of intervention in World War II; to measure the width of the gender gap in attitudes toward issues of war and peace; and to provide comparisons with countries outside the United States (such as Canada). Some pre-1917 background is also provided. Photographs; endnotes; bibliography; index.

McEnaney, Laura. "He-Men and Christian Mothers: The America First Movement and the Gendered Meanings of Patriotism and Isolationism." *Diplomatic History* 18, no. 1 (Winter, 1994): 47-57. The only available scholarly study, as of 1995, of the female isolationist protesters of 1940 and 1941.

Rupp, Leila. "Constructing Internationalism: The Case of Transnational Women's Organizations, 1888-1945." *American Historical Review* (December, 1994): 1571-1600. In her study of three international-minded American women's organizations of the period from c. 1900 to the outbreak of World War II, the author shows how logistical problems, travel costs, and language barriers posed obstacles to efforts to create an international community among women. Illustrations; footnotes.

Stanley, Sandra Carson. *Women in the Military*. New York: Julian Messner, 1993. The best short history of women in the U.S. military forces from the American Revolution to the Persian Gulf War. Illustrations (including photographs); time line; glossary; bibliography; tables; index.

Swerdlow, Amy. *Women Strike for Peace: Traditional Motherhood and Radical Politics in the 1960s*. Chicago: University of Chicago Press, 1993. A history of a major American women's peace organization of the 1960's by a female historian who was also a member of that organization. Based on private papers, organization newsletters, and FBI reports. Photographic illustrations; endnotes; bibliography; index.

War Brides Act

Date: Passed on December 28, 1945

Relevant issues: Family, war and the military

Significance: This law set aside previous immigration policies, making it possible for families established overseas during World War II to be reunited in the United States after the war

During and immediately after World War II, nearly one million members of the U.S. armed forces (and civilian employees of the military) married citizens of other nations in ceremonies overseas. Overwhelmingly, these marriages were between American men and foreign women, and the spouses came to be known as war brides. Many war brides were widowed or deserted; many couples set up housekeeping abroad because of restrictive U.S. immigration and marriage laws. By 1945, however, hundreds of thousands of people—mostly women, many with children—from fifty countries wanted to come to the United States to live with their legal spouses. At the time, U.S. law permitted only 150,000 immigrants per year, and from specific areas only. When three thousand British wives of American soldiers demonstrated outside the American embassy, thousands of GIs demanded to be reunited with their wives, and foreign governments demanded that the United States accept responsibility for these women and children, Congress finally had to act. The War Brides Act was passed on December 28, 1945, and was to remain in effect for three years. By setting aside immigration quotas, the act made it easier for war brides (and husbands) and their children to enter the United States. The act applied only to spouses of members of the armed forces, excluding spouses of civilian employees of the armed services and of members of the merchant marine. It also excluded widows of servicemen.

Within six months, some sixty thousand British war brides made highly publicized trips to the United States on military ships. Others arrived in similar fashion from Australia, New Zealand, and Europe. German spouses had to wait longer. Officially, American servicemen were not allowed to "fraternize" with Germans during or just after the war. Couples could not marry, and an American man could not give financial support to the German mother of his children. In December, 1946, the marriage ban was lifted, and a few months later the first German war brides arrived in the United States. Asian spouses had the hardest time. Immigration laws based on race, including the Chinese Exclusion Act of 1882 and the Immigration Act of 1924, made it impossible for most Asian immigrants to become citizens, married or not. The War Brides Act temporarily allowed entry to Chinese spouses, because China had been an ally during the war. It was not until 1952, however, that Japanese spouses were allowed to immigrate.

The War Brides Act, although enacted somewhat unwillingly, was the first formal acknowledgment by the U.S. government that the men and women affected by a war are indeed men and women, with family feeling and responsibility. For the first time, women who formed relationships with American soldiers abroad were treated with respect, instead of being viewed only as necessary "recreation."

See also Immigrant women; Marriage and marital status; War and women

War Labor Board and women

Relevant issues: Employment, law

Significance: The principles of this board recognized that a female worker should be paid a wage equal to her male counterpart for the same job

In the twentieth century, the rapid expansion of industry as a result of the wartime demand for arms and munitions gave women new opportunities to enter the workforce. Continuing the flow of production became essential, and millions of middle-class homemakers and unskilled female workers were trained to fill the jobs of men who had joined the military. As more women replaced men, employers had to focus on issues of health and safety, maximum daily hours, a woman's physical capabilities, and, most important, equal pay. The War Labor Board (WLB) was formed to resolve these issues. The board established principles that aided all workers, male or female, and brought many new members into labor unions. Although WLB policies never completely eliminated wage discrimination, the pay gap narrowed.

World War I History. The WLB was created by President Woodrow Wilson in March, 1918. Its purpose was to combat the problems associated with mobilization and to increase industrial war production. This increase had brought nearly one and a half million women into the industrial workplace during World War I. Because most people viewed these women primarily as mothers and as only temporary members of the workforce, women's wages totaled only one-half to two-thirds that of men's wages. Many women, however, were not working to earn extra money and needed the income to support their families. Wilson specifically asked the WLB to investigate the pay equity of women as compared to men.

The WLB addressed disputes apart from the cantonment construction, shipbuilding, and railroad industries, which had established their own boards. A set of principles were developed by the WLB, including collective bargaining, the right of workers to belong to a union, and a basic eight-hour day where required by law, but no decisions were made in any cases until June, 1918. Members of the board consisted of five industrial workers, five union members, and two chairs, Frank P. Walsh and William Howard Taft. During the sixteen months that it was in operation, the WLB had success in prohibiting blacklisting, "yellow-dog" contracts, and lockouts. Under its established principles, the WLB achieved better conditions for working women, such as shorter workdays and the right for women to join unions. It did not, however, make any permanent policy changes giving women "basic equality" in industry and business, nor did it prepare women for the return of veterans into the workforce.

World War II History. Following the Japanese attack on Pearl Harbor on December 7, 1941, when large numbers of the male labor force suddenly entered the armed services, opposition to women as replacement workers lessened. Military production became an essential component to winning the war, and government action became necessary to ensure that no work stoppage occurred. The formation of the War Manpower Commission met the demand for workers, and a new War Labor Board was ordered by President Franklin D. Roosevelt to arbitrate labor-management disputes, stabilize wages, and prevent work stoppages. The WLB consisted of four members each from the general public, labor, and industry, and it oversaw twelve regional boards.

Inflation made it necessary to pass the Economic Stabilization Act of 1942, which regulated prices and limited pay increases. The WLB argued that the nation was obligated to protect women from wage discrimination. In November, 1942, the WLB issued a general order which stipulated that equal wages were to be paid to women who performed work that was equal in quality and quantity to that of male workers. A companion bill prohibiting wage differences based on sex did not pass through Congress.

Pay Disputes. The WLB had mixed results in equal pay disputes. In the fall of 1942, when a wage differential was discovered at General Motors, the WLB ruled against the company and granted women equal pay plus back pay for those women who had been paid lower rates. It took months, however, before the company accepted the ruling. The United Electrical Workers' Union, which had a large membership of female workers, aggressively supported the rights of women. The union petitioned the WLB to eliminate the pay gap and won, but when the war ended, some companies refused to comply with the board's order. The data from these companies would aid women in the 1970's who filed lawsuits to fight against continuing discrimination.

Enforcement of the principle of equal pay depended largely on the type of company. Where women replaced men, the wage equity was more readily followed in order to keep wages intact for returning soldiers. Government agencies likewise promoted equal pay principles. Some manufacturers failed to enforce the principle. When companies found loopholes to place women in different job classifications so that they could be paid less, women wanted the wording for an equal wage to read "equal pay for equal work."

Impact. The WLB ceased operations on December 31, 1945, ending its jurisdiction over labor disputes. While the problem of unequal pay for equal work continued after the war, the attempts of the WLB should not be overlooked. Many women made advances in numerous industries and in the newer businesses that adhered to WLB standards. Many war industries had "pay for job" policies or increased the pay rate of certain male-specified jobs to make them more attractive to women. Although wage inequity was not eliminated, wage differences shrunk. Workers also received other forms of compensation in vacations, benefits, and health care when wage stabilization went into effect. War mobilization had removed certain aspects of women's protective labor laws, such as provisions against night shifts and longer hours, but with the establishment of the WLB and its connection to the National Labor Relations Board (NLRB), these protections returned. By 1945, women made up 36 percent of the industrial workforce. Many enjoyed full union membership as a result of the provision set up by the WLB requiring that plant employees automatically become union members. Women entered into union leadership roles and had a voice in the conditions of their workplaces. Addressing gender-specific issues and developing a working-class unity, many women took the initiative to become labor activists.

The WLB's association as a federal government agency and the provisions of the Economic Stabilization Act of 1942 hindered the board's capabilities, but it remained a strong protective agency for all workers during both world wars. The principles of equal pay continued, and legislation began in earnest following World War II. The underlying principles of the WLB eventually were acted on when Congress passed the Equal Pay Act of 1963.

—Marilyn Elizabeth Perry

See also Breadwinner ethic; Employment of women; Equal Pay Act of 1963; Equal pay for equal work; Labor movement and women; Pay equity; Protective legislation for women; Wages, women's; War and women

Bibliography

Bureau of National Affairs. *Equal Pay for Equal Work: Federal Equal Pay Law of 1963*. Washington, D.C.: Author, 1963.

Chafe, William Henry. *The American Woman: Her Changing Social, Economic, and Political Roles, 1920-1970*. New York: Oxford University Press, 1972.

Hartmann, Susan M. *The Home Front and Beyond: American Women in the 1940's*. Boston: Twayne, 1982.

Milkman, Ruth. *Gender at Work: The Dynamics of Job Segregation by Sex During World War II*. Urbana: University of Illinois Press, 1987.

Miller, Glenn W. *American Labor and the Government*. New York: Prentice Hall, 1948.

Riley, Glenda. *Inventing the American Woman: An Inclusive History*. 2d ed. 2 vols. Wheeling, Ill.: Harlan Davidson, 1995.

Wards Cove Packing Company v. Atonio

Date: Decided on June 5, 1989

Relevant issues: Employment, law, race and ethnicity

Significance: This case increased the burden of proof for plaintiffs, often women, seeking judicial redress for inequality in employment

Appealing to Title VII of the Civil Rights Act of 1964, employees of a salmon cannery in Alaska filed a lawsuit claiming employment discrimination. In their so-called disparate impact case, the plaintiffs argued that nonwhite employees held a high percentage of unskilled, low-paying cannery jobs and only a small percentage of skilled, higher-paid "noncannery" jobs. The Supreme Court held that the plaintiffs had failed to make their case because the statistical evidence was flawed. More important, the Court shifted the burden of proof in Title VII employment discrimination cases from defendants to plaintiffs, holding that plaintiffs must show that a company's practices actually caused any statistical disparity demonstrated. *Wards Cove Packing Company v. Atonio* had a profound impact not only on racial minorities attempting to rectify longstanding employment discrimination but also on female workers, with their continuing history of inequities in hiring, promotion, and wages. Congress reacted to the decision by passing the Civil Rights Act of 1991, which eliminated the "business necessity" defense to intentional discrimination validated by the decision. By once more reversing the burden of proof in employment discrimination cases, the act made it easier for women and minorities to prevail in employment discrimination suits.

See also Affirmative action; Antidiscrimination laws; Civil Rights Act of 1991; Supreme Court rulings on discrimination against women; Title VII of the Civil Rights Act of 1964

Weddings

RELEVANT ISSUES: Family, law

SIGNIFICANCE: Wedding planning and financing have traditionally been the responsibility of women and their families

A wedding is the ceremony that marks the beginning of a marriage. Before the ceremony, the wedding can be called off without legal consequence. After the ceremony, the marriage can be dissolved only by death, divorce, or annulment.

In a traditional wedding in the United States, the bride often wears a white dress and veil, which were originally meant to symbolize purity and a desire to be faithful to her husband. The groom often wears a dark suit or tuxedo. Friends and relatives of the couple are chosen as attendants, the bridesmaids wearing matching outfits in colors of the bride's choice and the groomsmen wearing suits or tuxedos.

Religious ceremonies are often held in churches or temples, while secular services may take place in a family home or at another location important to the couple. Music, flowers, and candles may set the mood of the event. Most ceremonies begin with a procession of bridesmaids, followed by the bride and her father. In a Christian religious service, for example, the minister or priest conducts a series of events that may include vows, a blessing of rings, prayers, and a benediction. Secular services may be performed by a judge and feature vows written by the couple. Most vows include promises to remain faithful, and the exchange of rings symbolizes a new life together. The ceremony usually ends with the bride and groom sharing a first kiss as a married couple and walking down the aisle together. A reception often follows.

Receptions may include a receiving line made up of the bride, the groom, and their immediate families. Friends and relatives walk down the line offering their blessings and congratulations. Food and dancing are also a part of the celebration. There may be a formal meal, a buffet, or cake and punch. The new couple may participate in a ceremonial cutting of the cake, a bride's dance, and the throwing of the bouquet and garter. The people who catch the garter and bouquet are sometimes thought to be the next to marry. The couple usually leaves the reception to begin a honeymoon trip under a shower of rice or birdseed for good luck.

The cost of a wedding can be very high. Traditionally, the bride and her family plan and finance the ceremony and reception, the groom provides the engagement ring and honeymoon, and his parents arrange the rehearsal dinner. These expectations began when couples married at a young age and were still living at home. They usually had small incomes and could not afford to help with wedding expenses. Now, couples often have well-established careers and their own living arrangements. They are usually able, and willing, to pay for the event. The couple and their families may choose to meet and plan the division of expenses. Invitations, flowers, musicians, photographers, reception halls, and caterers can be discussed and budgeted.

Couples may also decide to break with tradition and hold their ceremonies in unusual locations. Those who have been previously married may have a less formal ceremony and may elect to invite their children to be a part of the ceremony.

See also Dowry; Marriage and marital status

A traditional Protestant wedding. (Dale Gehman/Photo Agora)

Weeks v. Southern Bell

DATE: Rendered March 4, 1969

RELEVANT ISSUES: Civil rights, employment, sex and gender

SIGNIFICANCE: This opinion by the U.S. Court of Appeals Fifth Circuit strictly interpreted the Civil Rights Act of 1964 with regard to the prohibition of discrimination in employment based on sex, thus opening many jobs to women

In 1966, Lorena W. Weeks, an employee of Southern Bell for nineteen years, applied for the job of switchman. Her employer refused to consider her application, stating that the decision had been made that women would not be employed as switchmen. Weeks responded by filing a complaint with the Equal Employment Opportunity Commission (EEOC) stating that the refusal to hire women as switchmen violated the Civil Rights Act of 1964. An investigation by the EEOC indicated that Weeks might have a valid claim of discrimination based on sex.

Southern Bell argued that the job of switchman was an exception to the law because it required the lifting of heavy objects and emergency work. The Court responded that Southern Bell had not proven the position to be an exception to the law. While "men are stronger on average than women," the court stated, "it is not clear that any conclusions about relative lifting ability would follow." The Court ruled that many women are capable of performing the duties of a switchman.

See also Civil Rights Act of 1964; Employment of women; Equal Employment Opportunity Commission (EEOC); Supreme Court rulings on discrimination against women; Title VII of the Civil Rights Act of 1964

Wellesley College

ALSO KNOWN AS: Wellesley Female Seminary

DATE: Founded in 1870; opened on September 8, 1875

RELEVANT ISSUES: Education, sex and gender, women's history

SIGNIFICANCE: Wellesley was one of the first colleges founded to provide advanced education for women

After his son died, Henry Durant gave up his law practice and became a revivalist preacher. He decided to found a college to "offer to young women opportunities for education equivalent to that usually provided in colleges for young men." In 1870, he and his wife Pauline founded Wellesley Female Seminary, changing its name to Wellesley College on March 7, 1873. The college opened in 1875 after Durant constructed College Hall, which housed all students and faculty, classrooms, library, and offices. He specified the curriculum and appointed the faculty, including the world's first female college president, Ada Lydia Howard, who served from 1875 to 1882. At that time, the college had a classical curriculum and an evangelical environment not intended for preprofessional training.

Alice Elvira Freeman, president of the college from 1882 to 1887, began modernizing the curriculum and replacing the "old guard" faculty. She supervised the construction of new buildings and placed the college on a sound financial footing. After resigning to marry George Herbert Palmer, she remained active, selecting the next three presidents: Helen Almira Shafer (1888-1894); Julia Irvine (1894-1898), who completed the reformation of the faculty and curriculum; and Caroline Hazard (1899-1910), who doubled enrollment and supervised the construction of additional buildings.

College Hall burned on March 17, 1914, disrupting Wellesley's close-knit community. Ellen Fitz Pendelton, president from 1911 to 1936, led the fund-raising to finance reconstruction and to build an adequate endowment; the present college is essentially her creation. Mildred McAfee (1937-1949) went on leave from 1942 to 1946 to direct Women Accepted for Voluntary Emergency Service (WAVES) during World War II. Margaret A. Clapp, the president from 1950 to 1966, supervised the building of four large dormitories, restoring the residential campus.

Wellesley's liberal arts program now prepares women for any career. College organizations, faculty members, and students were active in the suffrage movement and have continued the work to expand women's rights. Through 1880, the faculty of Wellesley was entirely female. In the early 1970's, when many single-sex colleges became coeducational, Wellesley resolutely remained a women's college.

Notable graduates have included Meiling Soong, also known as Madame Chiang Kai-Shek; Sophonisba Preston Breckinridge, the first female lawyer in Kentucky; Annie Jump Cannon, a distinguished astronomer; Diane Sawyer, a television journalist; novelist Judith Krantz; and First Ladies Barbara Bush and Hillary Rodham Clinton. Notable female faculty have included Mary Whiton Calkins, a psychological theorist; novelist May Sarton; Katherine Lee Bates, who wrote the poem "America the Beautiful" after climbing Pikes Peak; and Emily Greene Balch, an activist dismissed from the college for opposing the U.S. entry into World War I who later helped found the Women's International League for Peace and Freedom (WILPF) and shared the 1946 Nobel Peace Prize.

See also Academia and scholarship, women in; Balch, Emily Greene; Barnard College; Bryn Mawr College; Colleges, women's; Education of women; Higher education, women in; Mills College; Mount Holyoke College; Radcliffe College; Smith College; Vassar College

Wicca

RELEVANT ISSUES: Religious beliefs and practices

SIGNIFICANCE: This spiritual path, with roots in ancient European Goddess-revering traditions, offers women the potential for unfettered participation in spiritual practices and experiences

Wicca refers to female practitioners (wicce to male practitioners) of what is known as the Old Religion and is commonly used interchangeably with the word "witch." The word "witchcraft" is said to come from the Anglo-Saxon *wiccecraft*, which has been interpreted to mean "craft of the wise," "the art of divination or magic," or "the art of bending or shaping reality."

Followers of this spiritual path, which predates Christianity, see their traditions as descending from ancient European shamanistic nature religions that center heavily on notions of the Goddess and her consort, the God. In some Wiccan traditions (particularly all-female Dianic covens), the Goddess is given precedence or celebrated without reference to a male god. Immanence, or the notion that all of creation is alive, connected, and of Spirit, is central to this tradition. As with other earth-based spiritualities, Wiccans believe there is a direct relationship between the individual and the Divine. Ritual and magic are therefore simply acts or gestures used to direct or manifest that which is already available. "Do what you will, and harm none," is the guiding principle in Wiccan ideology.

Although women participate in all the traditions associated with Wicca, it is the Dianic tradition that actually encourages women in those practices long associated with feminism and/or the women's spirituality movement—that is, fully participatory, nonhierarchical structures wherein leadership is shared. In these circles, the Mother, Maiden, and Crone are celebrated, as are the changing seasons, giving women a spiritual context for their own cycles and experiences.

See also Goddess, concept of the; Spirituality movement, women's; Witchcraft

Widowhood

RELEVANT ISSUES: Aging, demographics, family, poverty

SIGNIFICANCE: In the 1990's, it was estimated that three of every four women in the United States and Canada would eventually be widowed

In 1991, the United States had 13.7 million widowed people, 11.4 million of them women. This gender disparity is not surprising. The average age at which men marry in the United States and Canada is about twenty-six; the average woman marries around the age of twenty-four. In 1993, the average life expectancy for men in these two countries was about seventy-two years, for women about eighty years.

Most American and Canadian women face years of widowhood. In the 1990's, the average widow in the United States survived for approximately eighteen years following the death of her spouse. Throughout the twentieth century, men have been older than the women whom they marry, and women have had greater life expectancies than men.

Living Alone. In 1993, more than nine million women over the age of fifty-five lived alone. A breakdown of these statistics reveals that slightly less than two million of these women fell into the fifty-five to sixty-four age group, whereas more than three million were between sixty-five and seventy-four and more than four million were seventy-five or older.

Clearly, the steady increases that occur in the number of women who live alone as they age is accounted for by their having lost their spouses. Many women face two decades or more of widowhood, with its attendant problems and adjustments. Psychologists verify that the loss of a spouse is the most traumatic event that most people endure.

Psychology and Widowhood. Most widows encounter disheartening realities after their husbands die. A widow's first startling realization may be that her identity is linked inextricably to that of her husband. Even though professional women are not the rarities that they once were, a woman may still view herself as someone's wife rather than as a person in her own right.

Many widows quickly discover that most of their social interactions had been based on pairs of people rather than on singles. Despite the efforts of solicitous friends to include a widow in activities immediately after the death of her spouse, most widows begin to feel like "fifth wheels." Many gradually find themselves excluded from the invitations and activities that they once took for granted.

This exclusion often leads to reclusiveness and increased depression, with its attendant problems, often resulting in ill health. Many widows begin to neglect their diets, considering it unrewarding to cook for one person and difficult to find people to share meals with them. Some neglect their appearances and lapse into a pattern of unstructured days empty of purpose.

Economic Concerns. Economists verify that many widows in the United States and Canada experience not only a significant loss of income when their spouses die but also the added responsibility of managing their finances, which many of them had previously left to their husbands.

For most, income from private pension funds either ceases or is reduced by one-third to one-half on the death of a retired spouse. Some widows lose the health insurance that was a part of their spouse's retirement package. This is a devastating blow because the death of a spouse often leaves the survivor vulnerable to disease and illness caused by the depression accompanying such a loss.

Although retired working women usually have their own pension benefits, most of their husbands also had pensions. These women find their overall income substantially reduced when their spouses die, making it difficult for them to maintain their accustomed lifestyles. The lifetime earning power of women has characteristically been less than that of men, as has their number of years in the workplace, resulting in significantly smaller pensions for them when they retire.

Women widowed early in life often must manage a household that contains dependent children. Even a woman who has been a wage earner through most of the marriage faces the reduction in income that accompanies the death of her husband, forcing her to find more financially rewarding work or a second job.

Those widows who have been well provided for usually have to make long-term financial decisions that will inalterably affect their future lives and those of their dependents. They are forced to make these decisions, often on their own, at the time when the pain of their loss is greatest.

Looking Ahead. The most fundamental advice for any widow is to go on living. This means creating activities that add purpose to her life and impose a structure. A widow's new activities might be unrelated to her former life as someone's wife. Widows who have not already established their selfhood must work strenuously toward doing so, perhaps returning to school or finding work, either remunerative or volunteer.

For widows over the age of fifty-five, although remarriage is possible, the prospects are not encouraging. Three of every four men over fifty-five are married, and because women live longer than men, this statistic is unlikely to change dramatically. One in three such women is married. Most men who have lost their spouses eventually remarry, but most widows do not.

Younger widows face unique problems when they consider remarrying. Many of them find it difficult to meet eligible men, and when they do meet them, they find courtship difficult because of family and work demands. Support groups for widows of all ages exist in most communities and provide the most reasonable possibilities for meeting people in situations and with interests similar to theirs.

When they consider marrying, widows with dependent children must deal with the resentment that their children may feel toward the new spouse. If that husband brings his own children into the household, the merging of two families requires unique patience and unflagging diplomacy, tempered by the genuine concern, understanding, and love of all concerned.

Facing Widowhood Realistically. The worst thing that a widow can do is to give up hope. Life must go on, and, regardless of a widow's age and family situation, the only reasonable solution for her is to maintain an optimistic outlook. Such optimism is best achieved by widows who are involved in support groups to which other widows and widowers belong.

The bane of most widows is loneliness. People who are not cheerful, who refuse to reach out to others, and who cease to care about life and appearance will be lonely. In order to combat such isolation, widows should plan each day, structuring it around work or activities that involve other people, require one to attend to personal appearance, and, if necessity demands, offer remuneration to compensate for the loss of income that widowhood usually brings. *—R. Baird Shuman*

See also Aging; Aid to Families with Dependent Children (AFDC); Demographics, women's; Depression and women; Elderly women; Insurance eligibility; Life expectancy of women; Marriage and marital status; Self-esteem, women's; Single mothers; Single women

BIBLIOGRAPHY

Boston Women's Health Book Collective. *The New Our Bodies, Ourselves: A Book by and for Women*. Rev. ed. New York: Simon & Schuster, 1992.

Brothers, Joyce. *Widowed*. New York: Simon & Schuster, 1990.

Gates, Philomene. *Suddenly Alone: A Woman's Guide to Widowhood*. New York: Harper & Row, 1990.

Hyman, Herbert H. *Of Time and Widowhood: Nationwide Studies of Enduring Effects*. Durham, N.C.: Duke University Press, 1983.

Lopata, Helena. *Widowhood in an American City*. Cambridge, Mass.: Schenkman, 1973.

________. *Women as Widows: Support Systems*. New York: Elsevier, 1979.

Scadron, Arlene, ed. *On Their Own: Widows and Widowhood in the American Southwest, 1848-1939*. Urbana: University of Illinois Press, 1988.

Willard, Frances (Sept. 28, 1839, Churchville, N.Y.—Feb. 17, 1898, New York, N.Y.)

AREA OF ACHIEVEMENT: Social reform

SIGNIFICANCE: One of the great nineteenth century social reformers, Willard combined her work on temperance (the prohibition of liquor) and suffrage, urging women to have a role in changing society

Beginning as an educator, Frances Willard soon joined the temperance movement, serving as president of the Women's Christian Temperance Union (WCTU) from 1879 to 1898 and becoming a major influence in the Prohibition Party. In 1888, she was elected president of the National Council of Women, which advocated woman suffrage. Willard's organizations involved more women in social reform work than any others. She wrote *Women and Temperance* (1883) and *Glimpses of Fifty Years* (1889).

See also Social reform movements and women; Suffrage movement and suffragists; Temperance movement and women; Women's Christian Temperance Union (WCTU)

Willmar 8

RELEVANT ISSUES: Employment, law

SIGNIFICANCE: This bank strike in Minnesota by underpaid female employees produced some publicity but only minimal changes in employment practices

In November, 1976, the female employees of the Citizens National Bank (CNB) of Willmar, Minnesota, commenced a series of actions against the bank that produced a partial victory but ultimate defeat. Spurred by the hiring of a male management trainee at a salary substantially greater than those of nearly all the female tellers and receptionists ($700 per month versus $400 per month), they filed charges of wage and job opportunity discrimination with the Equal Employment Opportunity Commission (EEOC). The following spring, they formed a union and pushed unsuccessfully for a labor contract.

In December, 1977, the women filed further charges of unfair labor practices with the National Labor Relations Board (NLRB). On December 16, eight of the women—the "Willmar 8"—went on strike, picketing the bank. CNB responded to these activities by hiring high-priced legal counsel to contest, appeal, and delay action and by threatening or cajoling the employees, who had originally numbered eleven. In June, 1978, the EEOC complaint resulted in a cash settlement of $11,750 to the eleven women, together with some slightly hollow promises about equal opportunity hiring.

The NLRB case was a disaster: Findings at the local level were appealed to the NLRB in Washington, D.C., which for technical reasons denied back pay or reinstatement to the Willmar 8. On April 2, 1981, the U.S. Circuit Court of Appeals refused to review this decision, and the matter was finished. The only thing that the Willmar 8 gained was some favorable publicity in the form of magazine articles and a television documentary. *The Willmar 8* (1980), directed by Oscar-winning actress Lee Grant, depicted the heroism of the women and the homeyness of their lives aside from their struggle.

See also Affirmative Action; Civil Rights Act of 1964; Comparable worth; Equal Employment Opportunity Commission (EEOC); Pay equity; Wages, women's

Witchcraft

RELEVANT ISSUES: Religious beliefs and practices

SIGNIFICANCE: Modern witchcraft differs significantly from past epochs, in which women accused of being witches were persecuted and sometimes killed

The term "witchcraft" conjures up images of old hags using evil spells and charms from secret books to bewitch innocent young men. It was thought that their incantations could raise fearful storms, cause accidents, and wreck homes and crops. They could dry up a neighbor's cow, stealing its milk by milking the corners of a tablecloth. At night, they flew through the air and attended sex orgies served up by their familiars—black cats or dogs. They were considered particularly dangerous to unbaptized children, finding them tasty morsels. They made pacts with the Devil, written in their own blood, exchanging their souls for magical powers.

History. By 1054, the western branch of the Catholic church became powerful enough to ban pagan religions and magical demonstrations. Although the Church dismissed witchcraft as mere illusion, peasants and some clergy firmly believed in its existence and of both good witches (wise women) and bad witches (Satan's handmaidens).

During the thirteenth century, the witchcraft mythos was deliberately cultivated by Dominican friars who believed that Satan's climactic battle against God had begun. To combat Satan's diabolical plans, the Inquisition was founded in Europe. It sought out heretics and witches, interrogated them through torture, and executed them to win back their souls.

Catholics and Protestants, with equal zeal, vigorously persecuted heretics and witches from 1450 to 1700. Most of the victims were women. Men of the times often viewed women as inferiors and considered them extremely dangerous in unsexing men, killing children through menstruation, and feigning virginity to disguise pregnancy.

The persecutions focused primarily on unmarried women or widows, who often worked in spinning and weaving occupations, on prostitutes, and on aged, lonely spinsters. As the witch-hunt mania increased, the persecutions broadened to encompass married women and young girls. Even midwives and wet nurses were suspected of witchery because they knew about birth control and had the ability to kill babies. They too paid the price.

The mania spread to the American colonies, which suffered from high taxes, bad crops, pirates, virulent smallpox, and hostile American Indians. Rumors spread that witches were at work. Salem, Massachusetts, the stronghold of Puritanism, became the site of the most famous witch-hunt in 1692. A group of young, unmarried women fell under the spell of Tituba, a slave who told tales of the West Indies and black magic. They went into convulsions, becoming the center of attention of the community. A special court presided over the cases of 150 suspected witches, resulting in twenty executions. The witch-hunt mania lasted about one year before the hysteria ran its course.

Experts estimate that between 1450 and 1700, more than half a million accused witches were tortured to death by burning, drowning, or hanging. An estimated 85 to 95 percent of the victims were women. The worst witch crazes occurred in Germany, Switzerland, and France; the mildest, in Spain and Portugal. The last execution for witchcraft took place in Scotland in 1722.

Women as Victims. Anthropologists and sociologists offer a variety of reasons that women were singled out for persecution and accused of witchcraft during these early centuries. The most basic was that women were safe, easy targets because of their inferior status. In addition, the Black Death (1347-1351) and other major epidemics caused massive deaths because of ignorance and unsanitary conditions in growing cities; witches were blamed for these calamities because no better explanation existed.

Because of industrial development and growth in cities during these centuries, women's role and status within the traditional family structure changed markedly. Many poor women remained unmarried or were forced into the job market. The increased number of spinsters and late marriages and the stigma of being single may have also given impetus to charges that these women practiced witchcraft. So-called female crimes, such as widespread use of contraception and increased infanticide, may have fueled increased hatred toward women.

Modern medicine sometimes views the persecution of witches as part of the prescientific revolution wherein science, magic, and witchcraft questioned traditional religious dogma. Insanity and mass hysteria might also explain the persecutions. Medical authorities also speculate about witch fantasies; for example, the wild dancing at the Sabbath orgies may have been the result of the taking of jimson weed. Ointments and hallucinogenic drugs, such as deadly nightshade, may have induced fancies of flight and the bizarre behavior of some so-called witches.

Modern Witchcraft. Belief in witchcraft was supposedly destroyed forever by the eighteenth century and the Age of Reason. Yet, two centuries later, especially during the 1970's, witchcraft flourished in the United States, along with exorcism, poltergeists, astral projections, reincarnation, and occult activities.

Social scientists believe that the 1970's revival was caused by publicity in the media and the entertainment world, such as witches' weddings and sabbats, attracting mainly white-collar workers, highly educated, urban middle-class women who wanted a changed lifestyle. Especially vulnerable were those in their twenties to late thirties with no religious affiliation, who joined satanic cults and covens.

When some feminists discovered witches worshipping female deities as part of a Dianic cult, they organized a political activist and protest group in 1968 called Women's International Terrorist Conspiracy from Hell (WITCH). By using

Modern witch Selena Fox uses a feather and incense in her ceremony. (Mary Langenfeld)

exotic costumes, chants and herbs, and witchcraft paraphernalia, WITCH attracted attention to their cause, satirizing male domination and a repressive establishment. Many feminists, however, disapproved of such tactics because they trivialized the movement.

Most witches, however, resent being used by feminists or any other group to make political statements. They reject a monolithic organizational structure; some prefer covens that include both women and men, some exclude men, and others act as exclusive lesbian sanctuaries. Modern witches tend to reject patriarchal religion, especially the Judeo-Christian system.

Modern witches are a diverse group. An estimated 15 percent are considered "neopagans," venerating nature and glorifying human powers; others are family traditionalists, following ideas passed down through the generations. Then there are hereditary "genetic" witches and those who draw on the Cabala, Sufism, or Eastern religions for their practices.

Modern witches tend to accentuate the positive about themselves and their magic. They consider themselves to be charitable, seldom using their powers for retaliation. They stress the sheer joy of their religion, which promises a happier and more constructive attitude toward life. Although they cultivate strong wills, they try to avoid extremes and keep a balanced outlook through such practices as meditation, astrology, divination, herbology, and incantation.

The consequence of being labeled a witch in contemporary society is not the serious matter it was three centuries ago. Modern witches are often viewed as glamorous personages or, at worst, as "freaks" who appear on talk shows rather than being burned at the stake. Popular culture, especially television, has transferred the ominous witches of old into svelte sprites. For example, in the television series *Bewitched*, modern-day witches Samantha and Esmeralda used their powers to solve mainly domestic problems, as well as to punch holes in male pride. In such films as *The Witches of Eastwick* (1987) and *Hocus Pocus* (1993), witches are used for comic effect, forming sisterhoods to assist each other in a "man's world."

—*Richard Whitworth*

See also Christianity and women; Folklore, women's; Lilith; Religion; Sisterhood; Wicca

Bibliography

Ben-Yehuda, Nachman. *Deviance and Moral Boundaries: Witchcraft, the Occult, Science Fiction, Deviant Sciences and Scientists*. Chicago: University of Chicago Press, 1985.

Faber, M. D. *Modern Witchcraft and Psychoanalysis*. London: Associated University Presses, 1993.

Parker, John. *At the Heart of Darkness: Witchcraft, Black Magic, and Satanism Today*. New York: Carol, 1993.

Rosenthal, Bernard. *Salem Story: Reading the Witch Trials of 1692*. New York: Cambridge University Press, 1993.

Russell, Jeffrey. *A History of Witchcraft*. London: Thames and Hudson, 1980.

Woman question, the

Relevant issues: Family, law, social reform, women's history

Significance: The woman question was a nineteenth century phrase to describe the discourse on women's issues, discussions that paved the way for later waves of the women's movement; Marxists later adopted the phrase, using it as their principal term to refer to women's concerns

The phrase "the woman question" can be traced to nineteenth century debates on women's proper roles in the family and society in the United States and England. In both countries, the discussion was conducted by middle-class women. In the United States, women had played significant roles in the Colonial era and the American Revolution. As the American republic evolved, middle-class women were told to focus their lives on the home. To be a lady at home was the epitome of one's existence. As women became better educated, they questioned this assumption. The debate on women's roles evolved into political action groups closely identified with gaining the right to vote and abolishing slavery. In so doing, they expanded women's horizons. As women gained sophistication and maturity as political activists, they gradually organized, creating the women's movement.

Parallel developments occurred in Victorian England, where womanhood was placed on a pedestal. The "true" woman was little more than an ornament, despite the presence of a powerful female monarch on the English throne. Under the general rubric of the woman question, the Victorians debated women's proper roles in society. As in the United States, the discussion evolved into social action movements. Concerns were wide-ranging, from infant mortality to working conditions in factories.

In the late nineteenth century, the phrase was adopted by socialist thinkers to refer to women's issues. August Bebel (1840-1914) regarded the woman question as the focus for discussion on how women could "best develop their abilities." Bebel influenced late nineteenth century socialist thinking on women. When Marxist socialist governments were established in the twentieth century, problems concerning women were classified as the woman question. The phrase, which originated in Anglo-American discourse, in fact became better known as the Marxist description for women's concerns.

In the United States and Great Britain, the phrase "the woman question" was superseded by terms such as "feminism" or "the women's movement." Its significance has all but disappeared and is principally historical. It is still associated with women's concerns in Eastern Europe.

See also Cult of True Womanhood; Feminism; Feminism, Marxist; History of women; Social reform movements and women; Suffrage movement and suffragists; Women's movement

Womanchurch

RELEVANT ISSUES: Religious beliefs and practices, sex and gender

SIGNIFICANCE: Founded to address the issue of discrimination in institutional religions, this Christian religious movement provides women with an alternative to patriarchal churches

Womanchurch arose out of the women's movement of the 1960's, which recognized the discrimination against women caused by the patriarchal ecclesiastics. Female linguists pointed out the male-centered nature of the language in Christian religious literature, hymns, and rituals, while biblical scholars noted the marginality of women in sacred Scripture. Rosemary Radford Ruether has compared the Womanchurch movement, in which some women left the patriarchy of institutional churches, to the biblical Exodus, in which the Jews left the oppression of Egypt.

When rituals are always performed by men and address male experience, hierarchical structures emerge. When women plan rituals emerging from their own experience, the structures remain egalitarian and the language inclusive. The experiences of women are emphasized in the rituals created by Diann Neu in the publication *Waterwheel*, a newsletter of the group Women's Alliance for Theology, Ethics, and Ritual. These rituals contain words, religious images, gestures, music, dance, and readings that include women.

Some of the ideas regarding women's liberation from the religious structures that oppress them emerged from the liberation theology of South America. Liberation theologians stress scriptures, traditions, and religious practices that support the idea of a God who is concerned with the liberation and freedom of the poor and oppressed. Womanchurch theologians desire to extend this image of God to concern for the plight of women who have been oppressed by the sin of sexism. They look to Jesus, whose concern for the poor and marginal in his society always extended to women. Female theologians especially concern themselves with the injustices directed toward women that are justified by religious laws, scriptures, and practices. Members of Womanchurch are concerned that the movement not restrict itself to middle-class North American women, so they extend themselves in solidarity to all women of the Third World. Some of the women associated with Womanchurch are Ruether, Elizabeth Schussler Fiorenza, Phyllis Trible, and Carol P. Christ.

The women's ordination movements in both the Roman Catholic and Anglican churches have associated themselves with the Womanchurch movement because it welcomes the full participation of women in its rituals and decision-making structures. The movement for inclusive language in church hymnals, scriptures, and catechisms has benefited from Womanchurch's attempts to recognize the talents and experiences of all people, using Paul's formula "There is no difference between Jews and Gentiles, slaves and free, men and women" (Galatians 3:28).

Scholars from Womanchurch have earned the respect of academics in women's theology and scriptural studies because of their dedication and serious research. Their writings have been published and incorporated into college classes that deal with women's issues in the field of religious studies. Womanchurch has helped to raise the esteem of women who try to achieve recognition and decision-making status in their institutional churches and has prepared them better to counter the influences of ecclesiastical patriarchy.

See also Christianity and women; Feminism, spiritual; Inclusive language; Language and sexism; Religion; Religious movements founded by women; Spirituality movement, women's; Theologians and women's theology

Womanist

RELEVANT ISSUES: Literature and communications, race and ethnicity

SIGNIFICANCE: This term is used by Alice Walker to identify feminists of color

African American novelist Alice Walker's definition of "womanist" appears in a traditional dictionary format as a preface to her collection of essays *In Search of Our Mothers' Gardens: Womanist Prose* (1983). Just as feminists urge women to embrace a self-view that is "woman-identified" rather than "male-identified"—that is, to take their identities and senses of self-worth from their own womanness rather than from their "otherness" according to male attributes and values—Walker presents women of color with a self-identification that emphasizes their identities in terms of what both their sex and their ethnicities have given them.

Walker's definition, derived from the black folk expression "womanish," states that a womanist is "Responsible. In charge. *Serious*." A womanist wants "to know more and in greater depth than is considered 'good' for one." She may engage in "outrageous, audacious, courageous or *willful* behavior." The definition goes on to say that a womanist "loves other women, sexually and/or nonsexually. Appreciates and prefers women's culture, . . . emotional flexibility, and women's strength." This reflects Walker's solidarity with the struggle of lesbians for recognition within the women's movement. Yet Walker's definition also says that a womanist is "Committed to survival and wholeness of entire people, male *and* female. . . . Loves struggle. *Loves* the Folk." African American literary critic Barbara Smith has stated that Walker's "focus on the struggle of Black people, especially Black women, to claim their own lives, and the contention that this struggle emanates from a deepening self-knowledge and love . . . are characteristics of Walker's work. Walker's "womanist" is, above all, one who loves life, "*Loves* the Spirit. . . . Loves herself. *Regardless*."

See also African American women; Black feminism; Ethnic identity; Sisterhood; Walker, Alice; Women-identified women; Women of color

Woman's Bible, The

Author: Elizabeth Cady Stanton (1815-1902)

Date: 1895, 1898

Relevant issues: Religious beliefs and practices, women's history

Significance: This pioneering commentary on biblical texts relating to women, documenting sexism in Western religion, deeply divided the woman suffrage movement

Although it was intended to be a product of a committee of women, on the order of the all-male boards that produced Bible translations, *The Woman's Bible* was written mostly by Elizabeth Cady Stanton; she assembled a revising committee of women to lend the project legitimacy. Stanton, a leader of the women's movement in the nineteenth century, originally envisioned the text as a feminist translation of the Bible but could find no female scholar of Greek or Hebrew willing to risk her reputation on such a controversial project. In her preface, Stanton states her object as "to revise only those texts and chapters directly referring to women, and those also in which women are made prominent by exclusion." Such passages comprised one-tenth of the entire Scriptures.

An appendix in part 1 describes the life and work of Julia Smith, whose translation of the biblical text was, at the time, the only one made by a woman. Stanton used Smith's translation, as well as the 1881 revised version of the Bible. It was likely the failure of this version to take sexism into account that prodded Stanton to undertake a feminist Bible.

Much of *The Woman's Bible* reiterates feminist creeds that Stanton had long preached, stressing that the Scriptures "bear the impress of fallible man, and not of our ideal great first cause." She believed that "the chief obstacle in the way of woman's elevation today is the degrading position assigned her" in the Bible and Western religions: "an afterthought in creation, the origin of sin, cursed by God." She took the opportunity to point out that women in the Scriptures were little more than chattel of fathers and husbands, drawing parallels to the position of women in the nineteenth century. Stanton emphasized the patriarchal nature of biblical society, in which polygamy and prostitution flourished, and she admonished contemporary social reformers who sought to abolish these ills while espousing the Scriptures for teaching morality.

The Woman's Bible failed to be accepted as a major work of biblical scholarship, though it became a best-seller. It also outraged churchgoing feminists and caused a rift in the woman suffrage movement. At its 1896 convention, the National American Woman Suffrage Association (NAWSA), led by a contingent of younger members who focused on practical politics, officially disowned the part of *The Woman's Bible* then published. This action marked a shift in power within the movement away from the old leadership of radical dissent, embodied by Stanton. Undaunted, Stanton included the NAWSA resolution in the second part of the work, published in 1898.

See also Christianity and women; Clergy, women as; Patriarchy; Religion; Stanton, Elizabeth Cady; Suffrage movement and suffragists; Theologians and women's theology

Women Accepted for Voluntary Emergency Service (WAVES)

Date: Founded on July 30, 1942

Relevant issues: War and the military

Significance: The acceptance of women into the U.S. Navy during World War II freed many men for fighting and established women in the workforce

On July 30, 1942, President Franklin Delano Roosevelt signed the bill creating a Navy women's reserve. The bill allowed women to serve in certain noncombat jobs and areas.

The first director of Women Accepted for Voluntary Emergency Service (WAVES) was Mildred McAfee, the president of Wellesley College. McAfee became the first permanent female officer of the armed forces, with the rank of lieutenant commander. Ten days later, Elizabeth Reynard of Barnard College was sworn in as lieutenant and became the second permanent officer.

Officer training began in August of 1942 at Smith College in Northampton, Massachusetts, to fill 1,200 officer positions with women. Several colleges offered their campuses as training facilities for enlisted personnel. Colleges could readily provide housing, dining, classroom, and recreation space for the large numbers of trainees being inducted.

The first "boot camp" for women was opened at Iowa State Teachers College in Cedar Falls, Iowa, in December of 1942. In February of 1943, Hunter College in New York City was commissioned as a U.S. naval training station to handle between six thousand and seven thousand female recruits at one

In 1944, African American women were finally permitted to serve in the WAVES. (National Archives)

time. More than eighty thousand recruits trained there between February, 1943, and October, 1945. Some of the ratings available at naval training schools were control tower operator, cryptologist, electrician, storekeeper, operating room technician, and pharmacist mate. Thirty-four specialist ratings were available to women by the end of the war.

More than one hundred thousand women served as WAVES during World War II at nine hundred shore facilities. Eight thousand WAVES officers and seventy-eight thousand enlisted WAVES were on active duty, with another eight thousand in training, at the end of the war. More than twenty thousand WAVES served in the Navy Department in Washington, D.C., and made up more than 55 percent of the uniformed personnel at Navy headquarters. Women constituted 18 percent of the total Navy shore duty in the United States and released an estimated fifty thousand men for overseas duty. In the summer of 1944, African American women were permitted to serve in the WAVES. By July of 1945, seventy-two black WAVES had been trained in a fully integrated and racially progressive program.

The end of the war saw cutbacks for women in the Navy. Only 2,054 WAVES officers and enlisted personnel were permitted to reenlist, and the remainder were quickly demobilized. On June 12, 1948, the Women's Armed Services Integration Act was signed by President Harry S Truman. It permitted women between the ages of twenty and thirty-one to enter the regular Navy, to a maximum of five hundred officers and six thousand enlisted personnel. On November 8, 1967, President Lyndon Johnson signed a law granting basic equality rights with men. During World War II, female enlistees and officers did not receive pay equal to that of their male counterparts. They were also not allowed to give men orders. In 1967, after women had served their country for twenty-five years, WAVES gained equality in the male-dominated Navy.

In the 1990's, women were serving in the Navy on shore and at sea throughout the world. They served in all areas of specialization and were permitted to attain the rank of admiral. The WAVES of World War II paved the way for women to progress from household and domestic duties to working equally with men in the traditional male workforce.

See also Army Nurse Corps; Military, women in the; Smith College; SPAR; Women's Airforce Service Pilots (WASPs); Women's Army Corps (WAC); Women's Reserve in the Marine Corps; World War II, women's military roles in

Women-identified women

Relevant issues: Psychology, sex and gender

Significance: This term, an essential change in women's self-understanding and their presence to one another, has empowered women's affirmation of themselves and one another and fostered the recognition of women's experience as a basis of real knowledge

Explained by feminist scholar Mary Daly as "an immeasurable qualitative leap," the term "women-identified" builds on Simone de Beauvoir's insight in *Le Deuxième Sexe* (1949; *The Second Sex*, 1953): "She is defined and differentiated with reference to man and not he with reference to her." "Women-identified" signifies the presence of women to one another and recognizes women as having primary interest for other women. Women-identified women take their self-understanding from women's grounded experience rather than from its description in patriarchal culture's terms. The term describes self-identified, enspirited women who are comfortable with themselves, their bodies, their knowing, and their self-awareness. This "self-centering" makes possible female bonding based on women's integrity as self-defined rather than as defined by male-constructed laws and customs. The opposite of women-identified women would be men-identified women—those who identify with patriarchal descriptions, prescriptions, and expectations. The term "women-identified" has led to women-centered terminology and concepts, those which consider women as deserving of primary focus. All these terms are interrelated and consider "woman" as normative to humanness rather than as derivative from and related to "man."

See also Daly, Mary; Empowerment; Patriarchy; *Second, Sex, The*; Self-esteem, women's; Sisterhood

Women in the Senate and House (WISH List)

Date: Founded in March, 1992

Relevant issues: Politics

Significance: The WISH List endorses and funds pro-choice Republican women's campaigns for federal and state offices

Women in the Senate and House (WISH List) makes direct cash and in-kind contributions to candidates, generally early in the campaign cycle when women's candidacies are likely to be jump-started by an infusion of funds. The organization also funnels contributions of members to candidates. The funds collected from yearly membership dues of $100 are the source of direct cash contributions made to viable candidates identified by WISH List or who approach the organization for support. This support, financial and otherwise, is credited by both the organization and candidates as helping to win races and maintain candidacies that would otherwise have fallen apart.

WISH List is modeled on Early Money Is Like Yeast (EMILY's List), which funds Democratic pro-choice women, and was created as a direct response to it. It was founded in March, 1992, in Red Bank, New Jersey, by a group of twenty-four individuals. Glenda Greenwald served as president until the organization moved to Washington, D.C., in May, 1995, when Patricia Goldman took over the helm of the expanded office operations.

In 1992, $150,000, out of a total of approximately $230,000 contributed, was donated to congressional candidates. Overall that year, WISH List supported twenty-two candidates, three of whom—Jennifer Dunn of Washington, Deborah Pryce of Ohio, and Tillie Fowler of Florida—were elected to the House of Representatives.

In 1993, WISH List contributed $40,000 to Christine Todd Whitman's successful campaign for the New Jersey governorship. In 1994, it supported Kay Bailey Hutchison of Texas and Olympia Snowe of Maine in their races for the Senate and Sue Kelly in her race for the seat in the 19th congressional district in New York.

As of March, 1996, WISH List had indicated support for six candidates for the House, four for the Senate, and one gubernatorial candidate, Lieutenant Governor Barbara Snelling of Vermont. It also planned to support a number of state legislative incumbents who no longer had the support of their state party organizations because of their pro-choice position.

See also Candidacies and political campaigns, women's; Early Money Is Like Yeast (EMILY's List); Politics; Pro-choice; Republican Party and women

Women of All Red Nations (WARN)

Also known as: Dakota Women of All Red Nations (DWARN)

Date: Founded in 1978

Relevant issues: Civil rights, community affairs, family, politics, race and ethnicity

Significance: This grassroots organization has provided American Indian women with a voice in their future and a forum in which to address community concerns

In the 1970's, when the American Indian Movement (AIM) brought American Indian problems to the forefront, American Indian women gained some recognition, made strides in control over schools, and began to attend college. Nevertheless, they still did not have control over their own destinies. Women of All Red Nations (WARN) enabled them to regain leadership status and become spokeswomen on American Indian issues. The establishment of WARN brought American Indian women together to challenge forced sterilization, political imprisonment, the decline of Indian family life and culture, and the loss of land. Lorelei Means and Madonna (Thunder Hawk) Gilbert, from the Lakota Nation, formed WARN in 1978. In 1985, WARN became Dakota Women of All Red Nations (DWARN). The same year, the Indigenous Women's Network gave support to DWARN's programs. DWARN established local chapters by networking. The organization has aided battered women, sought to preserve the rights of women's health, and fought against foster-care abuse and political imprisonment. University members have been influential in instituting American Indian courses and programs.

See also American Indian women; Americans for Indian Opportunity (AIO); Ethnic identity; Mentoring and networking by women; Politics; Prisons, women in; Sterilization of women; Women of color

Women of color

RELEVANT ISSUES: Race and ethnicity

SIGNIFICANCE: As a reaction to the second wave of the American women's movement, which was initially led by middle-class white women, many women of color sought to emphasize the diversity of race in feminism, as well as of class, gender, and sexuality

"Women of color" as a name for a representative coalition has only been in use since the late 1960's. From that time, women of color groups, such as the Combahee River Collective and the Women of Color Association, have challenged race and class blindness in the women's movement and sexist practices in male-centered antiracist groups. The descriptive term "woman of color," however, has been in use at least since the nineteenth century. The *Oxford English Dictionary* records the use of "women of color" in Sir Charles Lyell's *Second Visit to the United States of North America* (1849). The more inclusive term "people of color" has been used at least since the eighteenth century, initially in reference to people of African descent.

In the United States, women of color typically include four racial/ethnic groups—African Americans, Asian Americans, American Indians, and Latinas—defined by discriminatory racial laws in which the racial universe is demarcated by the five "color" categories of black, yellow, red, brown, and white. Although "women of color" can be used as a purely descriptive term, this label, in the context of feminism, is typically applied to women of color coalitions. As an organized group, women of color are products of the Civil Rights and women's movements, highlighting the complexity of the intersecting issues of both race/ethnicity and gender.

Oppression and Identity. Although constituting a diverse group, women of color are united by two major issues: a history of oppression and exclusion and a shared desire to combat racist and sexist domination. Members of each of these racially defined minorities have faced a history of oppression: American Indians were massacred, African Americans were enslaved, Mexican Americans suffered under colonialization, and Asian Americans were systematically excluded by immigration laws. Nevertheless, as scholars have noted, these racial and color categories are ambiguous and problematic. What about individuals who are multiracial? What about those nationalities or ethnic and cultural groups—such as Arabs and South Asians—that do not "fit" neatly into any of these categories? Despite the ambiguity of their name and the diversity of their numbers, women of color activists perceive themselves as a coalition committed to challenging oppressive dominant ideologies. For them, the term carries social and political significance.

Although many groups arising from the modern Civil Rights movement—such as the Black Power movement, La Raza, the American Indian Movement (AIM), and the Asian American Political Alliance—have emphasized cultural nationalism, even separatism, women of color have found unity in the very issue of diversity. Initially, women of color activists such as the Combahee River Collective (composed of black feminists) and Asian Women United worked to help fight against social discrimination within the specific context of their own racial and ethnic groups, but these organizations also recognized their ties with other women of color.

Influence and Commitments. In the late 1960's and early 1970's, women of color groups formed as a reaction against the second wave of the women's movement, which had been led by such white women as Betty Friedan and Gloria Steinem and which had emphasized the needs of the middle-class (generally white) homemaker. As the women's movement sought to challenge the white man as a universal norm, the women of color groups sought to dislodge any myth that the white, middle-class woman represented all women. Recognizing the multiple inequities in their society, women of color challenged white feminists to rethink the relationship among race, gender, class, and sexuality. For them, gender is one factor in a complex system of socially structured oppression. Aware of the discrimination faced by men of color, women of color try to avoid privileging gender over race. At the same time, however, recognizing that as a group they often find themselves at the bottom of the socioeconomic ladder, women of color also vigorously attack the gender inequities found in patriarchal societies.

Early on, women of color activists, often working in both women's and nationalist liberation movements, acknowledged their multiple commitments and the ways in which these commitments affected their identity. Women such as Audre Lorde, Bell Hooks, Gloria Anzaldúa, and Cherríe Moraga believed that discussions of their identity should not exclude their diverse experiences. Acknowledging their hybrid existence, some women of color constructed theories that accounted for the multiplicity of their identity. Anzaldúa's *Borderlands: The New Mestiza-La Frontera* (1987) offers a key reading of this theory of multiplicity, which the author calls a borderland or *mestiza* consciousness. Her new *mestiza* finds that she straddles two or more cultures. Rather than demanding that women of color choose one identity, Anzaldúa understands that she can affirm her multiple "differences." For Anzaldúa, the borderland/*frontera* provides a space that accommodates multiple discourses of race/ethnicity, class, gender, and sexuality.

While women of color may find this multiplicity liberating, it can also cause fragmentation. In fact, their very strength—their diversity—can be the point that divides women of color. In order to further specific political goals, these individuals may need to form other coalitional groups, highlighting different aspects of their multiple identities.

As women of color gain a greater voice, an increasing number are engaging in coalition projects. In 1980, a group predominantly composed of African American women and led by such activists as Barbara Smith organized the Kitchen Table: Women of Color Press, a publishing company for women of color. In 1981, Anzaldúa and Moraga edited *This Bridge Called My Back: Writings by Radical Women of Color*, a groundbreaking anthology that signaled a shift in feminist studies. During the 1980's and 1990's, growing interest in women of color was demonstrated by the creation of the Women of Color Association, the organization of an annual Women of Color Conference, and the publication of works by and about women of color.

As women of color in the United States create bridges between women from different ethnic and racial groups, they are also encouraging ties with Third World women. In the 1970's and 1980's, the United Nations World Conferences on Women brought together women from both Third World and First World countries. Encouraging women to consider the impact of a global feminism, the conferences further solidified the commitment of American women of color groups to become instruments for global social change for all oppressed peoples. —*Sandra K. Stanley*

See also African American women; American Indian women; Asian American women; Black feminism; Civil Rights movement and women; Combahee River Collective; Ethnic identity; Hooks, Bell; Latinas; Multiculturalism; Racism; Second wave of the women's movement; United Nations First World Conference on Women; United Nations Second World Conference on Women; United Nations Third World Conference on Women; United Nations Fourth World Conference on Women; Women's movement

Bibliography

Anzaldúa, Gloria. *Borderlands: The New Mestiza-La Frontera*. San Francisco: Spinsters/Aunt Lute, 1987.

________, ed. *Making Face, Making Soul: Haciendo Caras*. San Francisco: Aunt Lute, 1990.

Madison, D. Soyini, ed. *The Woman That I Am: The Literature and Culture of Contemporary Women of Color*. New York: St. Martin's Press, 1994.

Mohanty, Chandra Talpade, Ann Russo, and Lourdes Torres, eds. *Third World Women and the Politics of Feminism*. Bloomington: Indiana University Press, 1991.

Moraga, Cherríe, and Gloria Anzaldúa, eds. *This Bridge Called My Back: Writings by Radical Women of Color*. 2d ed. New York: Kitchen Table: Women of Color Press, 1983.

Zinn, Maxine Baca, and Bonnie Thornton Dill, eds. *Women of Color in U.S. Society*. Philadelphia: Temple University Press, 1994.

Women's Airforce Service Pilots (WASPs)

Date: Established in 1942

Relevant issues: War and the military

Significance: This military branch gave women the opportunity to prove that they could pilot a plane under conditions that would have taxed the ability of any pilot, male or female

In 1941, more than 2,700 American women were licensed pilots, but General Henry Harley "Hap" Arnold, chief of the Air Corps (subsequently renamed the Army Air Forces), rejected plans to use female pilots in noncombat jobs such as flying transport planes or in ferrying planes from one air base to another within the United States. After the United States entered World War II in December, 1941, Arnold conceded that the Air Corps was in dire need of flyers. He turned to two women, both prominent aviators, to organize women to serve as pilots. Jacqueline Cochran was selected to head the Women's Flying Training Detachment, and in September of 1942, Nancy Harkness Love was placed in charge of the Women's Auxiliary Ferrying Squadron (WAFS). Arnold came to realize, however, that maintaining two separate organizations, one for women who required significant amounts of training and the other composed of women who were already experienced in the air, would not work. In August of 1943, the two groups were merged into the Women's Airforce Service Pilots (WASPs), with Cochran becoming director of female pilots.

The new organization proved so popular that some 25,000 women volunteered for duty. Fewer than 10 percent were accepted, about half of whom completed the basic training program. The percentage compared favorably with that of men who entered pilot training. In addition to ferrying planes of many types, including multiengined transports and bombers and single-engine pursuit planes, female pilots performed other duties, including utility flying and operating tracking and searchlight missions to relieve men for combat duty.

Throughout their service, members of the WASPs worked with and for the Air Force even though they legally remained civilians and had civil service status. Cochran had not thought it wise to seek military status for her pilots until sufficient women had completed training and qualified for operational duties. In 1943, she and Arnold both requested the necessary legislation to bring Women's Airforce Service Pilots into the military. The War Department, which had authority over the Air Force (which was still part of the Army), demurred, arguing that female pilots should be commissioned in the Women's Army Corps (WAC) rather than in their own organization. In any event, the Air Force had a surplus of pilots by 1944 and planned to transfer some personnel into the infantry. Congress began to receive letters protesting that women should not take men's jobs in the air. As a result of the protests and progress in the course of the war, the WASPs were deactivated in December, 1944.

At the time the WASPs were deactivated, there were 916 women serving as pilots for the Air Force. Each averaged more than thirty hours of flying time per month, performing every type of mission assigned to members of the WASPs well enough to persuade at least some men that women could carry out the noncombat duties of a pilot as ably as men. More than three decades later, Congress passed legislation that made former members of the WASPs eligible to participate in the various programs directed by the Veterans Administration.

See also Army Nurse Corps; Military, women in the; Pilots, women as; SPAR; Veterans and reservists, women as; Women Accepted for Voluntary Emergency Services (WAVES); Women's Army Corps (WAC); Women's Reserve in the Marine Corps; World War II, women's military roles in

Women's Army Corps (WAC)

Date: 1942-1978

Relevant issues: Politics, war and the military

Significance: This separate branch of the United States Army, established during World War II, evolved over three and a half decades into an impressive avenue for fuller participation of women in the armed services

The Women's Army Corps (WAC) began when Congress created the Women's Army Auxiliary Corps (WAAC) in May, 1942, at the start of U.S. involvement in World War II. Led by Oveta Culp Hobby, the WAAC reached sixty thousand members by 1943. Since it treated women as auxiliary personnel for the Army, it proved cumbersome and inefficient. Congress approved a change from auxiliary status to incorporation into the United States Army in July, 1943. Hobby became the first director of the corps, with the rank of colonel. Nearly one hundred thousand women had joined by the time that the war ended in Europe in May, 1945. Women served as drivers, stenographers, mechanics, and mail officers. More than six hundred WACs had been decorated, including sixteen who received the Purple Heart.

A U.S. Army recruitment poster encourages women to join the WAC by appealing to a sense of adventure. (National Archives)

After the fighting ended, the size of the peacetime WAC declined to under five thousand by 1948. With the increased demand for military forces during the Cold War, however, the Pentagon, with the endorsement of General Dwight David Eisenhower, pushed for the creation of a permanent women's army corps. Congress, after much debate, passed the Women's Armed Services Integration Act in June, 1948. The legislation barred women from combat, did not allow female officers to command men, and prevented WAC officers from rising above the rank of colonel.

The strength of the corps fluctuated with the military conflicts of the next two decades. Twelve thousand women was the highest number of women who served during the Korean War, and the corps attained the same total during the Vietnam War. In the 1970's, the size of the WAC grew steadily, reaching a total of fifty-three thousand by 1978. Over the years, the separate functions of WACs became absorbed into the Army, and, by 1978, the high command decided that women should serve in the Army on the same footing as men. The Women's Army Corps ceased to exist as a separate institution in October, 1978.

While it existed, the WAC provided a means by which talented and motivated women could serve in the United States Army with distinction and make an important contribution to the mission of their units. It was a measure of its overall success that as time passed, the reason for a separate female branch of the Army disappeared. The women who serve in the U.S. Army today are the spiritual descendants of the women who participated in this important and far-reaching social experiment in the military. The impact of the WAC experience on American women has not yet been fully measured, but by all accounts it was significant.

See also Combat, women in; Military, women in the; Vietnam War, women in the; War and women; World War II, women's military roles in

Women's Bureau of the Department of Labor

Date: Founded on June 5, 1920

Relevant issue: Employment

Significance: Founded to formulate standards and policies to promote the welfare of employed women and improve their working conditions and opportunities, the bureau remains an important source of statistics and employment-related publications

In July, 1918, the Committee on Women in Industry was created in the United States Council of National Defense to facilitate women's entry into wartime production while protecting their health and welfare. Mary Van Kleek was named director, with Mary Anderson as her assistant. The Armistice ended World War I shortly after the first standards were formulated, but pressure from women's organizations turned the service into a permanent women's bureau under the Department of Labor with the passage of the 1920 Kenyon-Campbell Bill. President Woodrow Wilson named Anderson as director. Anderson, a largely self-educated Swedish immigrant and former factory worker and labor organizer, remained director until 1944. Her long and active tenure make her the best-known woman to have held that position.

While the bureau was given no enforcement powers, its studies of women's working conditions gained, under Anderson, a lasting reputation for reliability. In 1920, bureau publications included "The New Position of Women in American Industry" and "Industrial Opportunities and Training for Women and Girls." Other publications, such as "Night-Work Laws in the U.S., 1919" (1920), favored protective legislation for women, an issue opposed by many feminists. The Women's Bureau examined issues concerning minorities with "Negro Women in Industry" (1922) and "Negro Women in Industry in Fifteen States" (1929). Equal pay was addressed in "Women in the Federal Government" (1920), which exposed hiring and wage discrimination in government jobs and led to the Federal Government Classification Act of 1923; this act ensures that government salaries are based on duties, not sex. The bureau pointed to occupational hazards in studies such as "Women Workers and Industrial Poisons" (1926).

During World War II, when industrial employment of women was first resisted, then demanded, bureau publications encouraged the employment of women, examining their roles and recommending equal pay and postwar economic opportunity. After the war, the bureau issued publications on job opportunities in fields such as police work (1949), health and medicine (1950), and the physical sciences (1959), while also studying maternity protection for employed women, problems of older women in the workplace, and child care. In 1974, the Women's Bureau and the Department of Labor helped finance the first Trade Union Women's Conference in New York, and the bureau was influential in the formulation of the 1977-1978 Department of Labor affirmative action guidelines. Through the Job Training Partnership Act of 1983, the Women's Bureau developed programs for displaced homemakers, disadvantaged teenagers, and dislocated and chronically unemployed workers, while conducting research on employment needs of female veterans, immigrant women, older workers, and those in career transition; it also has examined the influence of technology on office workers and the persistence of poverty among working women despite changes in the economy. The bureau has regularly issued statistical handbooks on women in business and industry.

See also Business and corporate enterprise, women in; Clerical work; Employment of women; Equal pay for equal work; Federal government, women in; Gender-neutral legislation and gender-based laws; Pay equity; Protective legislation for women; Wages, women's

Women's Christian Temperance Union (WCTU)

DATE: Founded on December 15, 1873

RELEVANT ISSUES: Politics, social reform

SIGNIFICANCE: The WCTU was one of the first female-led organizations to wield substantial political power

The impetus for the formation of the Women's Christian Temperance Union (WCTU) was Diocletian Lewis' lecture "The Duty of Christian Women in the Cause of Temperance," delivered in Fredonia, New York, on December 13, 1873. The WCTU was founded in Fredonia just two days after Lewis' speech, and the first convention was held on October 14, 1874, in Syracuse, New York. The press referred to the events occurring during the winter of 1874 as the "Woman's War." While women were effectively barred from formal politics, they created an alternative political culture found in women's clubs and voluntary associations. By the close of the century, the WCTU was a major force in forming the national political agenda. When Frances Willard was elected national president of the union in 1879, she expanded the organization's goals from temperance to the championing of woman suffrage. Her slogan was "Do Everything," and the WCTU of the 1880's and 1890's appears to have taken on most of the social issues of the day. Willard's union espoused such causes as dress reform for women, health reform, prison reform, alcohol and tobacco reform, the free kindergarten movement, labor reform, education for women, and animal rights. The WCTU of the nineteenth century paved the way for the women's movement of the twentieth century.

See also Politics; Social reform movements and women; Suffrage movement and suffragists; Temperance movement and women; Willard, Frances

Women's Educational Equity Act

DATE: Established on November 1, 1978

RELEVANT ISSUES: Education, science and technology, sex and gender

SIGNIFICANCE: This program was established by Congress to combat sexual discrimination and to develop a curriculum that does not perpetuate sex-role stereotyping in education, in so doing recognizing that excellence in education cannot be achieved without gender equity

The purpose of the Women's Educational Equity Act (WEEA) is to provide educational equity for women and girls in the United States and financial assistance to enable educational agencies and institutions to meet the requirements of Title IX of the Education Amendments of 1972. At first, the effort to purge sexism from curricular materials was enthusiastically embraced by educators and publishers. When President Ronald Reagan took office in 1981, however, the WEEA was immediately targeted for funding cuts. The program continues to struggle against hostile opponents.

The program funds programs to open mathematics, science, and technology courses and careers to girls and women; helps female students gain access to nontraditional vocational education; funds projects to eliminate bias against girls and women in school and the workplace; funds major programs to improve educational opportunities and career choices for women who do not earn incomes; and targets resources toward the educational needs of disabled women.

See also Biased classrooms; Disabilities, women with physical; Education of women; Math anxiety; Nontraditional Employment for Women Act of 1992; Perkins Act; Science, women in; Sexism; Title IX of the Education Amendments of 1972

Women's International League for Peace and Freedom (WILPF)

DATE: Founded in 1915

RELEVANT ISSUES: Peace advocacy, social reform

SIGNIFICANCE: This international peace organization, founded during World War I, linked permanent peace to equality between men and women

The Women's International League for Peace and Freedom (WILPF) was established during World War I at The Hague International Congress of Women to promote what many saw as women's special connection to the issue of peace. Organized by Dutch physician Aletta Jacobs and Chrystal Macmillan, a Scottish lawyer, the congress was attended by prominent women from twelve neutral and belligerent countries who met in The Netherlands in April, 1915, to discuss the war. Their principal goals were to end the European conflict and to establish a postwar society that resolved international disputes without bloodshed. These women asserted that permanent peace must be based on national independence, justice between nations, and equal rights for all men and women.

The WILPF became an effective means through which women organized to address both pacifist and feminist concerns. Its members constantly strove to subordinate national issues to international ideals, favored international cooperation over special interests, advocated fundamental economic and social changes that they believed would lead to the abolition of war, and attempted to demonstrate the importance of women's work and values in achieving these goals. One indication of the success of the organization was the awarding of the Nobel Peace Prize to both Jane Addams and Emily Greene Balch, leading members of the U.S. section of the WILPF.

See also Addams, Jane; Balch, Emily Greene; Hague Women's Peace Conference, The; Pacifism and nonviolence; Peace movement and women; War and women; Women's Peace Party; World War I and women

Women's movement

RELEVANT ISSUES: Civil rights, education, employment, law, politics, social reform, women's history

SIGNIFICANCE: Conscientious women, seeking equal treatment for all citizens of the United States since the nation's founding, inaugurated the women's movement following the Seneca Falls Women's Rights Convention of 1848; most historians consider that year the beginning of an organized women's movement in the United States

On July 19 and 20, 1848, heeding a call issued by four prominent feminists, about one hundred male and female crusaders for women's rights convened at Seneca Falls, New York, to assess the status of women in their country. Although this historic convention marked an official beginning for a movement aimed at obtaining social, economic, and political equality for women, questions regarding women's rights had been raised many years before that in many quarters. As early as 1647, Margaret Brent, executor of the estate of the late Leonard Calvert, former governor of Maryland, went before Maryland's State Assembly to demand her rights as a citizen. Her demands were refused.

Early Voting Rights of Women. Women could vote in the American colonies from 1691 to 1780. Like all citizens of that period, the only requirement was ownership of property. Shortly after the revolutionary war, women were granted suffrage in New Jersey, which prevailed from 1790 to 1807, when the wording of the state's electoral law was changed by the omission of the second pronoun from the term "he or she." In 1838, Kentucky granted widows the right to vote in matters relating to schools. It was not until 1890, however, that the state of Wyoming, on entering the union, included woman suffrage in its constitution. Colorado followed suit in 1893; Idaho and Utah in 1896. The next state to grant woman suffrage was Washington in 1910, followed by twenty-three other states and the Territory of Alaska by 1919. These initial steps toward woman suffrage were not all-inclusive. Women could vote only in state and local elections. In Arkansas and Texas, they could vote only in primary elections at the state and local levels.

The Seneca Falls Convention. Between 1830 and 1840, feminists such as Pauline Wright Davis, Abigail Kelley Foster, Angelina and Sarah Grimké, Lucretia Mott, and Ernestine Rose were making speeches about women's rights wherever audiences would gather. These women, also outspoken abolitionists and, in some cases, prohibitionists, drew crowds. Their public presentations, touching on the emotion-laden issues of abolition, prohibition, and woman suffrage, sparked controversy that gained them celebrity.

When the call was issued for concerned men and women to attend a convention on women's rights in Seneca Falls in late July, 1848, the response was heartening. The conveners of the conference knew where to look for support, especially among men sympathetic to their cause. The main accomplishment of the convention was the issuing of its historic Declaration of Sentiments, which pointed to the repeated injuries and usurpations that male-dominated societies had inflicted on women throughout history. It demanded equal religious, educational, and vocational opportunities. Although the Declaration of Sentiments did not mention woman suffrage, another resolution passed by the convention addressed this matter. It is significant that of the one hundred people who signed the declaration, thirty-two were men. This gave renewed hope to the women attending the conference.

Worcester and Syracuse. The Seneca Falls Convention was more regional than national. As a tentative step toward

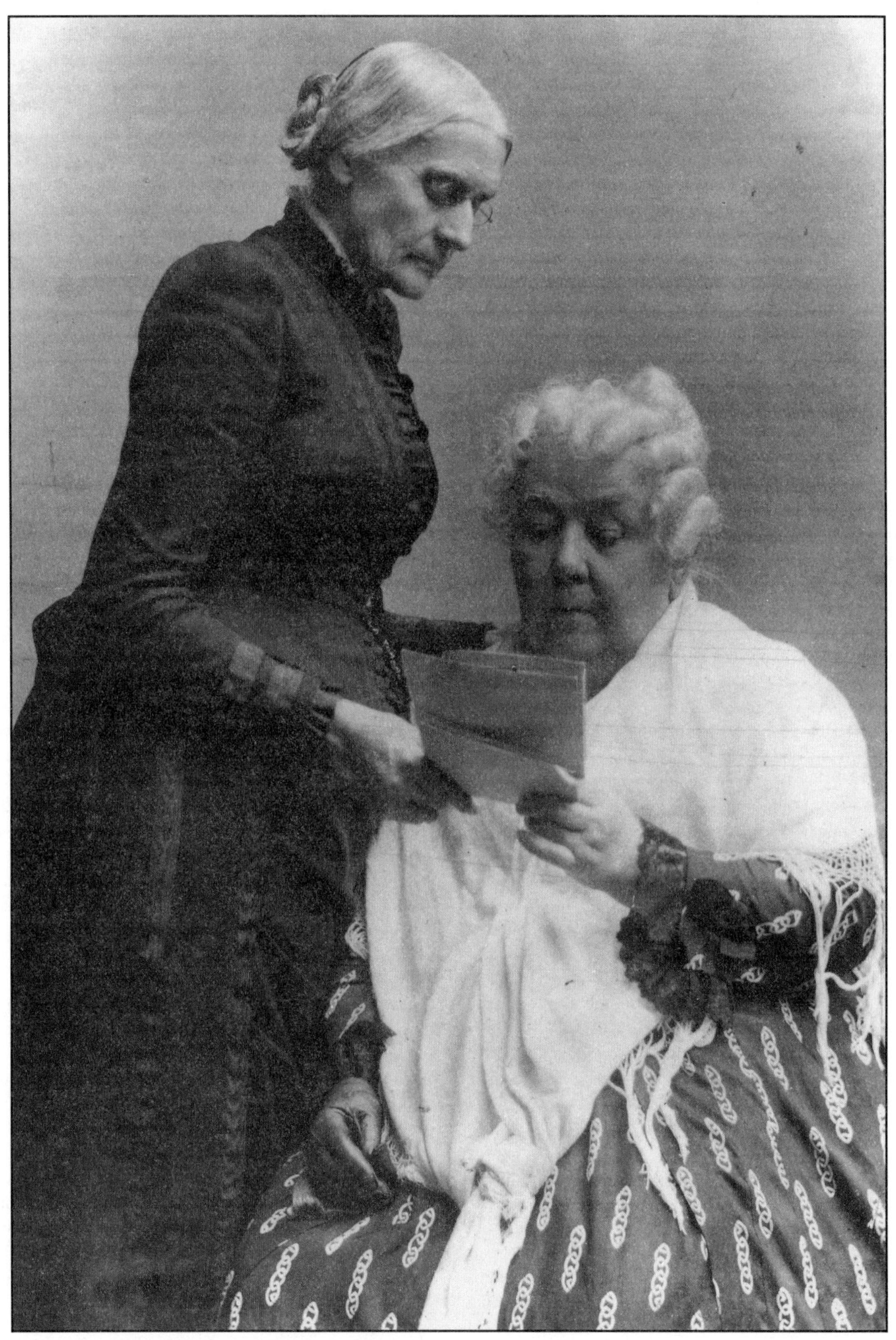

Susan B. Anthony (left) and Elizabeth Cady Stanton's friendship of more than fifty years served as the foundation of the early women's movement. (Library of Congress)

securing women's rights, it was a resounding success. The Declaration of Sentiments and other resolutions were widely distributed and discussed, spurring like-minded people to hold local or regional meetings that would focus on women's roles in American society. The first national convention of women's rights advocates was called for 1850 in Worcester, Massachusetts. This meeting drew feminists from many parts of the country but most notably from the Northeast. Its success was repeated in 1852, when a second national meeting was convened in Syracuse, New York. Sharing the responsibility for organizing this meeting were Susan B. Anthony and Elizabeth Cady Stanton, who emerged as giants in the women's movement. They worked relentlessly on women's rights for the next half century.

The Worcester and Syracuse meetings turned feminists who felt powerless in the past into activists who put pressure on state legislatures to alter their voting rights laws. The wives of many prominent men exerted significant pressure on their husbands to reexamine the status of women in a rapidly changing society. These conventions caused regional and local organizations to play a more visible role in advancing women's rights and led to annual national conventions that promoted feminist causes. Certainly from 1848 to 1869, the inevitability of drastic change in the status of women grew clearly apparent.

The women's movement, presenting a united front, remained a reasonably cohesive group until shortly after the Civil War. At that time, partly because the unifying cause of abolition was no longer an issue, and partly because the passage of the Fifteenth Amendment gave black men but neither black nor white women the franchise, dissension arose within the organization over whether the movement's aims could best be attained through changes in state constitutions or through amending the U.S. Constitution to enfranchise all citizens.

The National Woman Suffrage Association. In 1869, Anthony and Stanton cast their lot with those who favored an amendment to the Constitution to extend women the right to vote in national elections. They reasoned that until they achieved the vote nationally, women could work only indirectly to effect change, as they had done with great effort but quite successfully. With the franchise, women could influence legislation at all levels and seek national office. Anthony and Stanton formed the National Woman Suffrage Association (NWSA) on May 15, 1869. Stanton was president of the organization until 1890, when it merged with the American Woman Suffrage Association (AWSA) to form the National American Woman Suffrage Association (NAWSA); she served as NAWSA president from 1890 until 1892. Between 1880 and 1886, Stanton, Anthony, and Matilda Joslyn Gage published their landmark *History of Woman Suffrage* in three volumes.

The American Woman Suffrage Association. Feminists who favored achieving women's rights through state legislatures formed the AWSA in 1869. This grassroots group, led by Lucy Stone and Julia Ward Howe, gained a substantial following. Its activities forced state legislators to think about women's rights and caused Wyoming to write woman suffrage into its constitution when it gained statehood. After a twenty-one-year split in the women's movement, the 1890 merger of the AWSA and the NWSA formed the National American Woman Suffrage Association (NAWSA); under Stanton's leadership for its first two years, the NAWSA worked strenuously to influence both state and national legislative bodies. Anthony assumed the presidency in 1892, serving in that capacity for eight crucial years in the organization's history.

An Early Woman Suffrage Amendment. The first official congressional effort to amend the U.S. Constitution to provide for woman suffrage was launched by Senator Aaron A. Sargent of California, a close friend of Susan B. Anthony, in 1878. The NWSA orchestrated this early attempt to amend the Constitution. When the vote on this amendment, with wording identical to that of the Nineteenth Amendment, which became law in 1920, reached the Senate floor on January 17, 1887, nine years after Sargent first proposed it, the amendment was defeated by a vote of sixteen to thirty-four. This so-called Anthony Amendment was presented to the Senate during every session until 1914, but it never received a favorable report in committee and so was not voted on. The NAWSA, headquartered in remote Warren, Ohio, the home of its treasurer, fell into disarray partly because its president from 1904 to 1915, Anna Shaw, despite her favorable public impression, was hard to work with. Grassroots support evaporated.

Nevertheless, around 1910, Alva Smith Belmont, former wife of William K. Vanderbilt, helped to rescue the women's movement by buying property on New York City's Fifth Avenue near Forty-Second Street, which she allowed NAWSA and its New York state affiliate to use virtually rent free. Belmont was a close friend of Alice Paul, the staunch suffragist and leader of the National Woman's Party who was jailed for seven months as a result of her demonstrations and was later forcibly placed in a psychiatric ward when judges unsympathetic to her cause declared her insane.

In 1914, Woodrow Wilson could not ignore a petition signed by a half million citizens calling for a reconsideration of the woman suffrage amendment. Wilson and the NAWSA, assisted by the National Woman's Party, benefiting from Belmont's money and influence, pressured Congress to bring the amendment to a vote, which it did on March 19, 1914. The Senate voted thirty-four to thirty-five against passage, a great advance from the 1887 vote of sixteen to thirty-four. The amendment reached the House of Representatives on January 12, 1915, failing 174 to 204.

Although the two-thirds majority vote needed for eventual passage was far off, the margin by which the amendment lost encouraged its supporters. This change reflected a softening attitude among many legislators, who presumably reflected the will of their constituencies.

World War I and the Nineteenth Amendment. Carrie Chapman Catt, president of NAWSA from 1900 until 1904, returned to that post in 1915 and served during the half-decade that preceded the eventual passage of the Nineteenth Amendment. When Catt assumed office, war raged in Europe, and the United States seemed certain to become involved.

NAWSA prospered under Catt's leadership. As president, she recalled the militant suffragists picketing in Washington for NAWSA, admonishing them to serve their country as effectively as possible during this crisis. The nation appreciated its women for their enormous contributions to the war effort. On January 10, 1918, the House of Representatives passed the Nineteenth Amendment by a vote of 274 to 136. On June 4, 1919, the Senate voted sixty-six in favor and thirty opposed, giving the amendment its two-thirds majority in the House and Senate. The amendment now went to the states, two-thirds of which had to ratify it. On August 18, 1920, Tennessee became the thirty-sixth state to ratify the amendment, which became effective on August 26.

Woman Suffrage in Canada. While women in the United States agitated to obtain the franchise, Canadian women were equally involved in their suffrage movement. The Canadian National Suffrage Association was similar to its counterparts in the United States. The course of suffrage for Canadian women closely parallels that of American women, although Canada enfranchised women at the national level two years earlier than the United States. Appreciative of women's contributions to the war effort, Canadian parliamentarians had permitted women on active military duty to vote in provincial elections in 1917. In 1916, the provinces of Alberta, Manitoba, and Saskatchewan had given women the right to vote in provincial elections. Nova Scotia followed suit in 1918, but women in New Brunswick and Ontario, though enfranchised nationally, were not enfranchised at the provincial level until 1919, nor were they permitted to vote at that level in British Columbia until 1920, in Newfoundland until 1922, and in Quebec until 1940.

Woman Suffrage in Other Countries. Woman suffrage swept most of the world in the fifteen years before World War I. Strides were made in the first decade of the twentieth century to extend the franchise to women in Australia, following the earlier example of New Zealand, which granted equal suffrage in 1893. Sweden and Finland enfranchised women in 1863 and 1865, respectively, but with limitations not applied to male citizens. Norway, Denmark, and Iceland allowed women to vote in national elections in the second decade of the twentieth century. The International Council of Women and the International Woman Suffrage Alliance made effective cases internationally for women's voting rights.

By the end of World War I, Luxembourg, Germany, and The Netherlands permitted women to vote; Belgium followed suit, with limitations, in 1921. Spain enfranchised women in 1931. Austria, Czechoslovakia, and Poland granted woman suffrage in 1919, and Hungary followed, with stipulations, a year later. Greece and Romania extended the vote to women in 1929. In several of these instances, the permissible voting age for women was higher than that for men.

The Equal Rights Amendment (ERA). Having overcome the greatest obstacle to women's participation in government through the enactment of the Nineteenth Amendment, women's organizations now supported the passage of an equal rights amendment stating simply, "Equality of rights under the law shall not be denied or abridged by the United States or any state on account of sex." This amendment, drafted by feminist Alice Paul and, through pressure from the National Woman's Party, brought before Congress in 1923, languished in committee for many years but was finally passed by both houses of Congress in 1972. The Senate vote was eighty-four to eight. Once approved by the needed two-thirds majority of both houses, the ERA required ratification by two-thirds, or thirty-eight, of the states. ERA proponents had seven years to achieve ratification. When, by the deadline of March 22, 1979, the two-thirds majority had not been obtained, Congress allowed an extension to June 30, 1982. By that day, however, only thirty-five of the needed thirty-eight states had voted for ratification. Since 1982, the ERA has regularly been reintroduced in Congress but has not passed. Many opponents who support equal rights for women argue that existing laws guarantee such rights and are strictly enforced, and therefore a constitutional amendment would be redundant. Others fear that passage of the amendment might work to the detriment of women in marriage and in the workplace, where its provisions would override various labor laws designed to protect women. Many believe the ERA defeat reflects women's lack of political clout.

Working Women. In the 1920's, the number of women employed outside the home did not rise much. Women received less pay than men for equal work, and their chances of promotion to top managerial positions was severely limited. In the 1940's, when World War II created both a manpower shortage and a need for increased production, women came into their own. During the war, most women between twenty and fifty worked, and many continued working after the war.

In 1950, women comprised about 28 percent of the workforce; this percentage increased by 1960 to twenty-three million, one-third of the workforce. In 1984, about fifty million women worked outside the home, which was 53 percent of all women over the age of sixteen. The percentage of working women increased throughout the late twentieth century. Equal pay for equal work has been achieved, as have comparable worth and equal opportunity. The Civil Rights Act of 1964, proposed by President John F. Kennedy in 1963 and passed by Congress the following year, prohibits employment discrimination based on gender. In 1957, the Commission on Civil Rights was established, originally with six members and, since 1983, with eight members serving six-year terms. Complainants suffering gender discrimination can appeal directly to the commission for redress, eliminating the expense of hiring attorneys.

In 1960, the Canadian Parliament passed the Canadian Bill of Rights, which became part of its constitution in 1962. It guarantees men and women equal treatment in employment and other aspects of life and contains many of the guarantees of the Civil Rights Act of 1964.

Women have made strides in the workplace, although a glass ceiling still keeps many of them from securing top positions. Employers have, in many cases, sought to accommodate women's family responsibilities by allowing them to work on flexible schedules and/or to do much of their work at home, which modern technology has made increasingly feasible. Many large employers provide free or low-cost day care facilities within the workplace.

Women and Education. The gains achieved in the education of women involve not only equal access to education but also curricular changes that women's groups have sought. Most U.S. colleges and universities offer women's studies programs. Many institutions have devised programs that enable women with families to attend school. Higher institutions have substantially increased their hiring of women as faculty members, assuring them opportunities for advancement comparable to those available to men. Faculty members have become aware of the contemporary roles and status of women sometimes through formal school-sponsored programs. They have been made especially aware of the implications of using sexist language in their writing and speaking. Sexual harassment by faculty members is severely punished and, in schools at all levels, is grounds for revocation of tenure and even dismissal. Some schools have passed rules that prohibit faculty-student dating, though the constitutionality of these rules has continued to be tested in the courts.

Although most female students in higher institutions still major in nontechnical, nonquantitative subjects—notably art, music, literature, sociology, anthropology, and foreign languages—increasing numbers are gravitating to prelaw, predental, and premedical programs, as well as to colleges of agriculture, business administration, and engineering. Professions such as library science, teaching, and social work continue to attract larger numbers of female students than other professions, even though admissions policies barring discrimination against women are strictly enforced in most higher institutions.

The 1960's and Beyond. The social upheavals of the 1960's, though fueled largely by efforts to redress racial inequalities, gave impetus to other minority groups that sought equal rights. The women's liberation movement burgeoned during this period. The National Organization for Women (NOW) was formed in 1966, followed by the Women's Equity Action League (WEAL) and the Coalition of Labor Union Women (CLUW) in the early 1970's. Members of these groups focused attention on the physical and psychological abuse of women, women's rights to decisions regarding their own bodies, abortion, and rape. The courts established that

Participants in a women's rights march in 1970 parody traditional roles and question the actual progress that women have made. (Washington Post; reprinted by permission of the D.C. Public Library)

rape occurs in marriage if a woman's husband forces her into unwilling sex, a wholly new concept in male-dominated environments. Newly established groups pressed for and won strict enforcement of the Civil Rights Act of 1964.

American and Canadian women made more gains in the early 1970's than they ever had before. They shed titles that revealed their marital status—"Miss" and "Mrs." in favor of "Ms."; Ms. also became the title of a successful magazine for women founded by Gloria Steinem, perhaps the preeminent feminist of the period. Women began to establish their own businesses, and at least one women's bank was opened and succeeded. Female stockbrokers specialized in handling women's investments, ferreting out investment opportunities in corporations that supported ERA and that endorsed women's rights.

Sexist Language. Society quickly became aware of the implications of sexist usage. Phrases such as "The typical cardiologist advises his patients to exercise" led to the impression that all cardiologists are men. "The second grade teacher . . . she" and "The astronaut . . . he" built and reinforced stereotypes in people's minds, particularly in the minds of children. In the late 1960's, the National Council of Teachers of English announced that it would summarily reject submissions to any of its publications that used sexist language. Other professional organizations made similar pronouncements or at least strongly encouraged nonsexist writing.

Some elements of the language debate, however, seemed to reach absurd levels and harm the feminist cause. Some, for example, called for a change from the word "history" to "herstory," which had symbolic meaning but reflected an ignorance of etymology. Nonsexist language, nevertheless, has remained a policy of many publishers and is formally encouraged in writing and grammar courses at all instructional levels. It is firmly entrenched as preferred usage.

Progress in Women's Rights. Although women's status has changed remarkably since the Seneca Falls convention, women still have not achieved parity with men. They comprise more than half the population, but they are not equally represented in the workplace, especially in its higher echelons.

Having won the franchise and participated in elections much more fully than has the male population, women still find that the political power brokers are men. Progress, nevertheless, is apparent. Women have been elected to high office and are present in both houses of Congress in record (if still disappointing) numbers. President Franklin Delano Roosevelt in 1933 appointed Frances Perkins as secretary of labor, making her the first female cabinet member. Since then, few cabinets have failed to include women. President Ronald Reagan appointed Sandra Day O'Connor as the first female Supreme Court justice in 1981, and President Bill Clinton followed suit in 1993 with the appointment of Ruth Bader Ginsburg. In 1984, Democrat Geraldine Ferraro became the first vice-presidential candidate in U.S. history. Some feminists view these developments as little more than tokenism, but they are significant steps toward the equality women have long desired.

Feminism has as many faces as any long-entrenched social movement. There are pro-life and pro-choice feminists, Marxist feminists, separatists (often representing a lesbian constituency), and conservative and liberal feminists. Women do not represent a single voting bloc, but their economic and political impacts are stronger than ever before. The war for equality has not yet been won, but many of its major battles have been decided in favor of women.

—*R. Baird Shuman*

See also Abortion; Civil rights and civil liberties for American women; Civil rights and civil liberties for Canadian women; Education of women; Equal Rights Amendment (ERA); Feminism; History of women; Language and sexism; Lesbian rights movement; Politics; Rape; Reproductive rights; Second wave of the women's movement; Sexism; Social reform movements and women; Suffrage movement and suffragists; Violence against women

BIBLIOGRAPHY

Becker, Susan. *The Origins of the Equal Rights Amendment.* Westport, Conn.: Greenwood Press, 1981. Published a year before the failure of thirty-eight states to ratify the ERA, first presented to Congress in 1923, this book recounts its whole grueling history.

Boxer, Marilyn, and Jean H. Quataert, eds. *Connecting Spheres: Women in the Western World, 1500 to the Present.* New York: Oxford University Press, 1987. The essays in this book view the women's movement from a broadly international and philosophical perspective. A unique collection.

Buechler, Steven M. *Women's Movements in the United States: Woman Suffrage, Equal Rights, and Beyond.* New Brunswick, N.J.: Rutgers University Press, 1990. A clear and penetrating view of various aspects of the women's movement, at times becoming quite specialized. Not for beginners.

Buhle, Mari Jo, and Paul Buhle, eds. *The Concise History of Woman Suffrage: Selections from the Classic Work of Stanton, Anthony, Gage, and Harper.* Urbana: University of Illinois Press, 1978. Although the focus of this collection on Elizabeth Cady Stanton's most significant writing is limited, the selections provide excellent overviews of the women's movement from the Seneca Falls Convention to the turn of the twentieth century.

Flexner, Eleanor. *Century of Struggle: The Woman's Rights Movement in the United States.* New York: Atheneum, 1973. A comprehensive, compact history of the women's movement, this volume is an excellent starting point.

Fuchs, Victor R. *Women's Quest for Economic Equality.* Cambridge, Mass.: Harvard University Press, 1988. Fuchs addresses a crucial issue of the women's movement, presenting the economic status of women in sharp and accurate perspective.

Katzenstein, Mary F., and Carol M. Mueller, eds. *The Women's Movements of the United States and Western Europe: Consciousness, Political Opportunity, and Public Policy.* Philadelphia: Temple University Press, 1987. The strength of this book is its comparative view of women's movements in various venues. The presentation is intellectually demanding.

Simon, Rita J., and Gloria Danziger. *Women's Movements in America: Their Successes, Disappointments, and Aspirations*. New York: Praeger, 1991. Written at a level nonspecialists can understand, this book presents a balanced view of a complex social movement.

Stasz, Clarice. *The Vanderbilt Women: Dynasty of Wealth, Glamour, and Tragedy*. New York: St. Martin's Press, 1991. Stasz provides valuable insights into Alva Smith Vanderbilt Belmont's work for woman suffrage and the equal rights amendment drawn up by her friend, suffragist Alice Paul.

Women's Peace Party

Date: 1915-1919

Relevant issues: Peace advocacy, social reform

Significance: This organization was founded during World War I to promote women's special connection to the issue of peace and to urge that women's values be integrated with men's in the political sphere

When World War I broke out in Europe in 1914, many peace activists were shocked and dismayed by the slaughter. The idea that civilized nations such as France, Germany, and Great Britain could so ignore the ideals of internationalism paralyzed many traditional peace organizations. The idleness of male-dominated peace groups reinforced the views of many women who believed that the conflict in Europe demonstrated more clearly then ever before the dichotomy between peaceful women and belligerent men. Holding that women's values had to be integrated into the public sphere before international harmony would prevail, they concluded that it was time for women to form a gender-specific peace society to promote women's special moral and social values.

In January, 1915, at the urging of Jane Addams and Carrie Chapman Catt, a group of respectable and elite peace activists and club women met in Washington, D.C., to form the Women's Peace Party (WPP). They asked for democratic control of foreign policy, the nationalization of arms manufactures, and, most important, suffrage for women. These women were asserting that their views deserved to be integrated equally with male views in the political sphere. In the spring of 1915, the WPP sent a delegation to The Hague International Congress of Women. This congress initiated an international pacifist movement that reinforced the idea that women had a special ability to change the course of civilization. The American delegation took a leading role at the conference and became affiliated with the international organization that later became the Women's International League for Peace and Freedom (WILPF).

The United States broke off diplomatic relations with Germany in April, 1917, and entered the war. It was a critical time for the WPP, which needed to keep the ideal of internationalism before the American people. Despite its pacifist stance, the WPP did not want to criticize the government or obstruct the war effort. Since the executive board of the WPP did not come out with any official policy, the state branches were left to decide on their own what course to take. Many followed Addams' example and participated in humanitarian and civic relief efforts. Others followed the radical Crystal Eastman, a leader of the New York branch of the WPP, and actively protested the war and attempts by the government to mobilize women into relief work. The Massachusetts branch of the WPP, under Lucia Ames Mead's direction, was the most conservative. Its relief efforts differed little from those of war supporters. Despite the discretion exhibited by most members of the WPP, the movement lost many supporters. Those who remained found themselves harassed by the government, vilified by the press, and ostracized by society. At the end of the war, WPP leaders attended the second meeting of the International Congress of Women and at this time officially changed its name to the U.S. Section of the WILPF.

See also Addams, Jane; Catt, Carrie Chapman; Hague Women's Peace Conference, The; Pacifism and nonviolence; Peace movement and women; War and women; Women's International League for Peace and Freedom (WILPF); World War I and women

Women's Reserve in the Marine Corps

Date: Founded on July 30, 1942

Relevant issues: War and the military

Significance: This agency provided qualified women for duty at shore establishments during World War II, releasing men for combat duty

On July 30, 1942, President Franklin Delano Roosevelt signed a bill creating the U.S. Marine Corps Women's Reserve as part of the Marine Corps Reserve. The mission of the Women's Reserve was to provide qualified women for duty at shore establishments, releasing men for combat duty.

The first director of the Marine Corps Women's Reserve was Colonel Ruth Cheney Streeter from Morristown, New Jersey. The first female Marine commissioned officer was Captain Anne Lentz, a civilian clothing designer who designed the women's uniform. The first enlisted woman in the Marine Corps Women's Reserve was Lucille McClarren from Nemahcolin, Pennsylvania. The first commissioned officer class of 71 women reported to Mount Holyoke College in South Hadley, Massachusetts. The first enlisted class of 722 women reported to Hunter College in New York City in March of 1943. The specialty training provided to the female Marines prepared them for more than two hundred jobs, including radio operator, driver, parachute rigger, aerial gunnery instructor, baker, cook, auto mechanic, control tower operator, post exchange manager, stenographer, agriculturist, and motion-picture operator.

The last of the service branches to open its doors to women, the Marine Corps saw more than twenty-three thousand women serve in its Women's Reserve during World War II. Women commanded twenty-eight units and made up another seventeen. Of the 17,640 enlistees and 820 officers on active duty at the end of World War II, only one thousand were permitted to remain on active duty. At the end of the war, female Marines were working in 225 specialties in sixteen out of twenty-one functional fields, filling 85 percent of the enlisted jobs at headquarters Marine Corps and constituting one-half to two-thirds of the permanent personnel at all large Marine Corps posts and stations. Complete disbandment of the Marine Corps Women's Reserve was to be completed by September 1, 1946.

In August, 1946, the commandant authorized keeping one hundred female Marines on active duty at Marine Corps headquarters. This number was later increased to two hundred and finally to three hundred. The 12 officers and 286 enlisted women were designated Company E, 1st Headquarters Battalion, Headquarters, U.S. Marine Corps, and commanded by First Lieutenant Regina M. Durant.

The Marine Corps was the toughest challenge of all the service branches for women. The traditional fighting role of the Marine Corps caused prejudice among many men in the Corps, and female Marines were subject to criticism and some harassment. No African American women were allowed in the Marine Corps Women's Reserve.

The recruiting slogan "Free a Marine to Fight" attracted many women to the uniformed war effort. Although women were ready to serve their country, their country was not yet ready to grant them the same privileges as their male counterparts. More than twenty years would pass before President Lyndon Johnson, on November 9, 1967, signed the bill creating a law that would grant basic equality rights to women in the armed forces. It would be the 1990's before women were permitted to become pilots and serve in rear areas of combat zones.

See also Army Nurse Corps; Military, women in the; SPAR; Women Accepted for Voluntary Emergency Service (WAVES); Women's Airforce Service Pilots (WASPs); Women's Army Corps (WAC); World War II, women's military roles in

Women's Review of Books, The

Date: Founded in October, 1983; published monthly except August

Relevant issues: Education, literature and communications

Significance: This large, tabloid-format journal publishes lengthy, analytical feminist reviews of primarily academic books by women or about women's issues

Founded and edited by Linda Gardiner and sponsored by the Wellesley College Center for Research on Women, *The Women's Review of Books* was established because female writers and scholars were discontented with mainstream review media. The journal aims, in its choice of books and in the reviews themselves, to represent the broadest possible range of feminism. Each issue averages twenty-seven pages and reviews approximately twenty-three books. Its paid circulation is around 13,500. Good coverage is given to literary works by and about women, as well as criticism and collections of women's writings. The February issue features a series of articles on some aspect of women in academia, and the summer double issue focuses on a current topic. Most issues contain one or two poems. Advertisements are for women's books and journals from both large and small publishers or for academic positions and degree programs. The letters column has been praised for its thoughtful, often impassioned debate.

A regular feature is the selective, one-page list of woman-related books published that month. The list is informative, not evaluative; a brief annotation is included, if necessary, to elaborate the book's subject. The books chosen for longer review reflect a global perspective and a wide range of issues affecting women, such as sustainable development, Aphra Behn, black feminism, women's college basketball, and gender and the Civil War. Detailed and evaluative, a review regularly includes substantial quotations from the book and is often accompanied by a photograph of the author or an illustration from the book. Occasionally, combined reviews cover three or four books on the same topic. These essays always represent the reviewer's opinion; the journal takes no official editorial stance. Each issue lists that month's reviewers and their credentials; they are usually college and university faculty or professional writers. The journal strives to enlist accomplished writers for its signed reviews—a group that has included Carolyn Heilbrun, Catharine Stinson, and Adrienne Rich.

The journal held a conference, "Women Reviewing/Reviewing Women," in November, 1993, to celebrate its tenth anniversary and published several of the insightful presentations in its issues of 1994 and 1995. During the conference, a women's studies librarian remarked that if a book was reviewed in *The Women's Review of Books*, she could expect women's studies faculty or students to request it. An editor of women-identified books noted that she uses a positive review in the journal as ammunition to persuade her marketing manager to give the book more exposure. The journal is indexed in *Book Review Index*, *Women's Studies Index*, *Alternative Press Index*, and *Left Index*. Its tables of contents are reprinted in *Feminist Periodicals*, published quarterly by the Office of the University of Wisconsin System's women's studies librarian.

See also Academia and scholarship, women in; Feminist literary criticism; Periodicals, feminist; Women's studies journals

Women's Sports Foundation

Date: Founded in 1974

Relevant issue: Sports

Significance: This organization promotes equal opportunities for female athletes

Some of the world's top female athletes, led by tennis star Billie Jean King and Olympic swimmer Donna de Varona, founded the Women's Sports Foundation (WSF) in 1974. The nonprofit foundation, which acts as an umbrella organization for those interested in the development of women's sports, is supported by donations from members and grants from foundations and corporations. More than 2,300 people representing female athletes, sports organizations, sports-related services, and public supporters of women's sports act as trustees/

members. The main purpose of the WSF is to educate the public about the value of women's sports and the need for equal sports opportunities for women. The foundation provides free information, maintains a speakers bureau, sponsors the National All-Star High School Awards program, and runs the annual WSF Awards program. It also publishes annual scholarship, camp, and organization guides; provides camp scholarships for needy girls; offers guidance for the development of local women's sports associations; and compiles statistics on women's sports. The WSF actively supports the enforcement of Title IX of the Education Amendments of 1972, which prohibits sexual discrimination in educational institutions that receive federal funding, and the Amateur Sports Act. In the late 1970's, many feminists became more vocal in their support of equality in sports. Since then, the Women's Sports Foundation has flourished.

See also Physical fitness for women; Professional sports, women in; Sports, women in; Title IX of the Education Amendments of 1972

Women's studies journals

RELEVANT ISSUES: Education, literature and communications

SIGNIFICANCE: These journals have provided a publishing outlet for scholarship on women, gender, and feminism; consolidated the academic field of women's studies; and offered a public forum of debate for activists and scholars

The women's studies journals founded in the 1970's emerged because of the marginal position of feminist scholarship within academia. The journals serve different audiences: feminists inside academia but also outside it, women's studies scholars in their discipline or within the interdisciplinary women's studies community, or other scholars within their own disciplines. Since the 1970's, however, the target audience for these journals has changed as new editors, editorial boards, and editorial collectives wrestle with the significance of changes within the women's movement and the growing importance of women's studies within academia.

The first journals, *Feminist Studies* (University of Maryland) and *Women's Studies* (Queens College), began in 1972. *Frontiers* and *Signs*, the most self-consciously academic publications, began in 1975. Journals such as *Feminist Teacher* and *Women's Studies Quarterly*, as well as the *National Women's Studies Association Journal*, addressed feminist pedagogy. Law schools have been the site for enormous growth in such journals, beginning with the *Women's Rights Law Reporter* in 1978; by the mid-1990's, more than eleven feminist law reviews existed. The explosion in feminist law journals reflects the growth of scholarship within separate disciplines. Consequently, women's studies scholars now speak to more focused and specialized audiences. Other journals, such as *Gender and Society*, grew out of a concern that interdisciplinary women's studies journals did not give sufficient attention to social science and quantitative work—in this case, sociology. Such journals as *Women and Politics*, *Journal of Women's History*, *Psychology of Women Quarterly*, *Women and Therapy*, and *Camera Obscura* (covering film studies) illustrate the growth and breadth of these specialized journals. *Hypatia*, a journal of feminist philosophy, grew out of dissatisfaction with both mainstream philosophy journals and women's studies journals. *Quest* and *Sinister Wisdom* published feminist theory geared to a nonacademic audience. Other journals reflect the growing importance of issues of race (*Sage: A Journal of Scholarship on Black Women*), sexuality and queer theory (*Genders*), and cultural studies (*differences*). *Women's Studies International Forum* and *International Journal of Women's Studies* have been in existence since 1978, and journals are springing up in Canada, India, Europe, and Australia.

Patrice McDermott published a book-length study of women's studies journals entitled *Politics and Scholarship: Feminist Academic Journals and the Production of Knowledge* (1994). At least three commercial abstracts of women's studies journals exist: *Women's Studies Abstracts* (56 journals), *Studies on Women Abstracts* (309 journals), and *Women's Studies Index* (92 journals). *The Women's Review of Books* evaluates scholarly works, popular books, and fiction, and it includes articles of ongoing debates in women's studies. The University of Wisconsin produces the reference works *Feminist Collections*, *New Books on Women and Feminism*, and *Feminist Periodicals* (122 journals). Feminist publishing entered cyberspace with the WMST-L list at the University of Maryland and a specific list for feminist editors (FEM-EDIT).

See also Academia and scholarship, women in; National Women's Studies Association (NWSA); Periodicals, feminist; *Women's Review of Books, The*; Women's studies programs

Women's studies programs

RELEVANT ISSUES: Education, sex and gender, women's history

SIGNIFICANCE: Women's studies program have both challenged and made important contributions to higher education by generating the study of, by, and for women and incorporating it into traditional curricula, as well as transforming academic knowledge to reflect interdisciplinary scholarship and the diverse perspectives of women

In the traditional higher education curriculum, women are typically omitted, excluded, or made invisible. When they are included, they often are presented in stereotyped ways, as exceptional women, or as appendages to powerful men. Such inclusion not only represents a male point of view but also promotes unexamined assumptions about who and what women are, which controls knowledge about women and, therefore, women themselves. Academic institutions, originally created by and for men, have mediated and interpreted women's experience and, in so doing, have ensured women's acquiescence to a male view of the world (in the West, that of white, elite men) that has asserted itself as the only reality. Since the late 1960's, women's studies scholars in the United States and Canada, and more recently in other countries, have challenged the validity of knowledge based on a male hegemonic world view. In questioning the way knowledge is organized and taught, and by developing new theories and methods, those involved in women's studies have offered an alternative model of academic knowledge. The growth and development of women's studies programs in North America and around the world has had a significant effect on traditional academic thought and practice by forging links between the disciplines, incorporating heretofore excluded perspectives into research and curricula, and transforming classrooms into collaborative learning laboratories.

History. Women's studies as a distinct academic field emerged in the 1969-1970 academic year, when the first program was established at San Diego State University in California. At that time, there were only seventeen courses about women taught in the United States. By 1982, there were more than three hundred programs and twenty thousand courses; by 1990, the number of programs had grown to more than nine hundred. In Canada, the first women's studies course was offered in 1971 at Concordia University in Montreal. By the mid-1990's, thirty-one Canadian universities had women's studies programs.

Women's studies appeared in the United States and Canada as a response to growing criticism of academia and the role of women in society. At the time, there was widespread dissatisfaction with universities, the disciplines they encompassed, and so-called value-neutral knowledge. Challenged to meet the educational needs of women and ethnic minorities, universities and colleges were also the targets of student and antiwar movements, whose leaders saw institutions of higher education as bastions of the all-powerful Establishment. Many female college students of the late 1960's and early 1970's, raised by mothers subjected to the consequences of what Betty Friedan termed "the feminine mystique" in a book of the same name published in 1963, had been exposed to powerful examples of the limitations and risks of an exclusively domestic role for women. At the same time, they were partaking of an androcentric education, one that, for the most part, excluded them both as producers of knowledge and subjects of study. A number of these female students, as well as some of their female professors (of whom there were few), had participated in one or more of the social movements that were active in the 1960's, discovering that, as women, they were neither able to assume leadership roles nor express women's concerns. These contradictions, along with the fledgling women's movement of the time (consisting largely of small consciousness-raising groups), provided some university and college women an impetus to start offering and taking courses on women and to find other ways to challenge the status quo.

The early stage in the development of women's studies programs focused on creating a new discipline. While the study of women as a specific focus emerged within established academic fields (most notably literature, history, sociology, and psychology), women's studies scholars soon discovered the limitations of any single discipline to a full understanding of women's lives. Introductory women's studies courses began to combine information and methods from many disciplines and apply them to the study of women. Women's studies scholars began to develop a critique of existing scholarly fields and traditions and to identify the omissions associated with these traditions. Throughout the 1970's, women's studies programs also typically maintained links with activist women's groups in the communities within which their universities and colleges functioned, and organized activities to raise the consciousness of people on their campuses to women's issues. All of this activity did not receive much institutional support. Typically, a few female junior faculty and graduate students administered women's studies on a voluntary basis, without an officially recognized program, coordinator, or adequate funding. For example, at the University of New Mexico, where women's studies began in 1972, in 1973-1974, there was $50 for supplies, and a part-time work-study student was supported with a $100 donation.

The second phase in women's studies development, beginning in the early 1980's, focused on mainstreaming women's studies or bringing about a gender-based curriculum by incorporating the new scholarship on women within all the disciplines. This objective was to be accomplished by initiating curriculum transformation projects in diverse academic settings, usually with the support of external funding. The earliest and best known of these projects took place in 1980 at Wheaton College in Massachusetts, where new scholarship on women was integrated into all of the college's introductory-level courses. In 1983, Wheaton convened the first national conference on curriculum integration and shared its experience with representatives of close to one hundred institutions of higher learning in the United States and Canada. While the mainstreaming of women's studies projects took many forms, generally they consisted of a group or a committee of women's studies faculty who, sometimes with the help of a consultant, conducted seminars or workshops for faculty in traditional fields. Feminist theory and pedagogy were discussed, along with ways to balance the curriculum to include knowledge about women and women's perspectives. The traditional faculty then would work on revising their courses for inclusion of content by and about women. By the mid-1980's, almost four hundred institutions had initiated some form of curricular revision to integrate women's studies. Although some feminist scholars have argued that mainstreaming efforts would eventually eliminate the need for separate women's studies programs, most women's studies advocates support a dual strategy, consisting of specialized programs existing alongside gender-balanced courses within the disciplines, for transforming academic knowledge.

During the 1980's, women's studies became institutionalized. Programs and courses proliferated, and greater resources were allocated to such programs. Universities were now likely to hire faculty who spanned traditional disciplines and women's studies and, in many cases, created full-time positions for program directors.

Despite significant contributions and growing institutionalization of women's studies in the academy, throughout the

Anne Hannaman leads a class entitled "The Psychology of Gender" at UCLA; such courses have become part of women's studies programs. (Bob Myers)

1970's and 1980's, many advocates, particularly women of color and lesbians, found themselves increasingly discontented with the continual assumption of an essential similarity among all women. In the late 1970's, African American women began to critique both women's studies and curriculum integration projects for their lack of attention to racial, ethnic, and class differences in conceptualizing womanhood. This led to the establishment in some institutions of black women's studies concentrations and closer links with African American studies programs. Lesbian feminists criticized women's studies for their proponents' heterosexism and the omission of lesbian experience from the new scholarship on women. In the 1980's, Asian and American Indian women and Latinas also began to challenge women's studies to incorporate work by and about women of color. As a result, the subsequent phase in the development of women's studies focused on understanding and conceptualizing differences among women, especially those of race or ethnicity, sexuality, and class. Beginning in the mid-1980's, there was growing scholarship in women's studies focusing on the intersection of gender, race, and class; new courses were developed that addressed the interaction of these factors; and differences among women were incorporated into most women's studies courses. This development has posed a troubling challenge for women's studies to retain both a commitment to full recognition of the diversity of women's experience and the acceptance of a common core of shared experience that defines all women.

Since the early 1990's, women's studies programs increasingly have focused on internationalization. This approach has included both the establishment of infrastructures for women's studies globally and greater emphasis on international women's issues on the part of the U.S.- and Canadian-based institutions and programs. The growth of women's studies scholarship and programs in Western Europe, Third World countries, and Eastern and Central Europe has led to numerous initiatives among women's studies scholars to exchange information, share experiences and resources, and build linkages. Institutes, international conferences, and seminars have proliferated since the late 1980's. Examples include the pioneering International Cross-Cultural Black Women's Studies Summer Institute, which has met in England, New Zealand, Zimbabwe, and the United States; Third World Women's Policy Research Conferences sponsored by the Women's Policy Research in Washington, D.C.; the international interdisciplinary congresses on women that convene every three years in different parts of the world; and numerous women's nongovernmental organizations that have sponsored women's studies seminars at United Nations conferences for women. Women's studies, which was more Eurocentric in orientation in its earlier days, by the 1990's, had responded to the new Third World and international scholarship on women (both in North America and elsewhere), not only in specialized courses on women of color but also in its core curriculum.

The disciplines that have been most affected by women's

studies and by curriculum integration and reform have been in the humanities (particularly literature, history, religion, and philosophy) and the social sciences (especially sociology, anthropology, and psychology). By the early 1990's, the sciences and professional fields such as medicine, law, and business also had started to incorporate the new scholarship on women and gender. Graduate study in women's studies increased greatly; by 1991, one hundred universities in the United States offered graduate-level work in women's studies, most of these through traditional departments, although a few institutions had free-standing master's and doctoral programs. By 1995, the number of graduate offerings had grown to 130. At that time, several women's studies programs had attained the status of autonomous departments. In Canada, since the mid-1980's, the federal government has funded endowed chairs in women's studies, and five such chairs were in existence by the mid-1990's.

Issues and Challenges. Since their emergence, women's studies programs have been credited with transforming some of the traditional disciplines by challenging curricular and pedagogical practice, changing or blurring disciplinary boundaries, and introducing the social construction of gender as a major focus of academic inquiry. The field of women's studies has experienced tremendous growth, become institutionalized on many college and university campuses, added graduate courses and degrees, generated a large body of knowledge and resources, and facilitated the establishment of feminist research centers.

Nevertheless, women's studies in the mid-1990's faced a critical juncture in its continued development. Women's studies, feminism, and the women's movement have come under increasing attack by neoconservatives and the New Right, both within and outside the academy. On university and college campuses, claims have been made that exposure to feminist scholarship undermines the core curriculum, that faculty and students in women's and ethnic studies programs are imposing a standard of political correctness when they object to sexist or racist comments and sexual or racial harassment, that women's studies programs are taking over campuses, and that their members are policing the thoughts of others. Such claims are difficult to substantiate, given the fact that, despite their growth, most women's studies programs remain small and without the type of departmental power held by traditional disciplines. Moreover, because criticism and openness to new ideas are central to women's studies, it is hard to imagine how this field could become the core of ideological imposition. At the same time, women's studies has had to define itself as a field and thus to develop some criteria for what should be included under its name.

Academic developments such as gay and lesbian studies, new ethnic studies programs, cultural studies, gender studies (including men's studies), and peace studies have raised questions about the future of women's studies programs. What will be the relationship of women's studies programs to other interdisciplinary concentrations? Will women's studies become absorbed into the multicultural movement that has been under way on many campuses since the early 1990's, or will women's studies programs hold their own and become strengthened by addressing categories of difference in more fundamental ways?

As women's studies nears the end of its third decade of existence, it faces several important challenges. One of these is the need to provide, both theoretically and institutionally, a center of unity for women, while simultaneously recognizing the differences among them, without fostering unbridgeable divisions. Another problem is the need to increase and retain academic acceptance and influence without compromising the goals of transforming the academy intellectually, pedagogically, and structurally. Still another involves finding ways of working with other interdisciplinary programs, to strengthen curricular reform and avoid duplication, without losing integrity and distinctiveness. Finally, as institutions of higher learning move to streamline their programs as a result of limited budgets, women's studies programs need to seek more support for their efforts outside the academy (as in gaining the backing of private foundations and other organizations and groups) while simultaneously retaining their scholarly and reformist commitments. While these issues are not entirely new to women's studies programs in North America, they became more apparent during the 1990's. Women's studies will have to maintain a fine balance between a number of cross-pressures in order to survive and prosper into the future.

—Jill M. Bystydzienski

See also Academia and scholarship, women in; Feminism; Higher education, women in; Mainstreaming; Men's studies programs; Women's movement

BIBLIOGRAPHY

Butler, Johnnella, and John Walter. *Transforming the Curriculum: Ethnic Studies and Women's Studies*. Albany: State University of New York Press, 1991. A foremost source on integrating the new scholarship on women, race and ethnicity within traditional disciplines.

Hull, Gloria T., Patricia Bell Scott, and Barbara Smith, eds. *All the Women Are White, All the Blacks Are Men, but Some of Us Are Brave: Black Women's Studies*. Old Westbury, N.Y.: Feminist Press, 1982. The first major text on African American women's studies.

Hunter College Women's Studies Collective. *Women's Realities, Women's Choices*. 2d ed. New York: Oxford University Press, 1995. An introduction to the field of women's studies.

Rao, Aruna, ed. *Women's Studies International: Nairobi and Beyond*. New York: Feminist Press, 1991. A collection of articles on development on women's studies in several countries, including the United States.

Richardson, Diane, and Victoria Robinson, eds. *Thinking Feminist: Key Concepts in Women's Studies*. New York: Guilford Press, 1993. A collection of articles that seek to define women's studies.

Ruth, Sheila. *Issues in Feminism*. 3d ed. Mountain View, Calif.: Mayfield, 1995. An overview of the field of women's studies, which includes both essays and original documents.

Womyn

Relevant issues: Literature and communications, sex and gender

Significance: The invention of words such as "womyn" represents an attempt by some feminists to distance themselves symbolically from men and male oppression

One of the efforts of the women's movement of the late twentieth century was to create gender-neutral language. The English language has many terms that unthinkingly incorporate the root "man" or "men." Many words that employ this root, even though they refer to both sexes, are basically masculine (such as "chairman" and "fireman"). For some words, the process of degenderization is simple (such as the use of "chair" or "firefighter"), while others require cumbersome locutions. Laws, religious rituals and hymns, and the like are gradually being degenderized, usually by substitution of such terms as "he/she" or "s/he." The invention of the term "womon" (plural "womyn" or "wimmin") takes this trend one step further by trying to remove the masculine syllable from "woman" and "women" altogether. Such alteration attempts to reform the English language so that it incorporates and reflects women's experiences. Within feminism (particularly radical feminism), terms such as "womyn" often act as a form of separatism from men and from any association with patriarchal society. Although the use of "womyn" or "wimmin" has become popular among many feminists and within women studies programs, there has been little indication that such terms will be embraced as standard English.

See also Biased language; Feminism, radical; Generics, false; Inclusive language; Language and sexism; Marginalization of women; Patriarchy; Separatism; Women's studies programs

World War I and women

Relevant issues: Sex and gender, war and the military

Significance: More educated and more independent than ever before, women found World War I both a challenge to pacifist beliefs and an opportunity to advance their cause as full equals in society

Background. The early years of the twentieth century presented a dichotomy in terms of society's view of the role of women. The traditional or Victorian view held that women's role centered on motherhood, household, and caregiving—a role well distanced from the economic mainstream. A second, emerging perspective was one of militant but pacifist feminism. This view centered on a violent, flawed world guided by male posturing and blundering, one that could be improved by full incorporation of a feminist perspective.

A synthesis between the two viewpoints was eventually forged by female activists, correlating the more gentle, feminine nature with pacifist, antiwar tendencies. Military pacifism grew as an important plank supporting the woman suffrage movement, in Europe as well as America. Implicitly, it held that allowing women the vote would reduce the possibilities for war. Pacifist women became strident in their espousal of antiwar views. Emmeline Pankhurst, leader of British suffragists, drew a distinction between destruction of property (for which she was jailed) and destruction of human life, which could never be condoned.

The onset of World War I, however, created a dilemma for pacifist feminists. Should women continue in blind opposition to the reality of another war, or should they use the war to forward women's causes by enlisting underutilized feminine resources in the process of war? They did both.

Women Against War. The declaration of war in 1914 inspired greater fervency within the global peace movement, in which women held leadership positions. In part because of the close association between woman suffrage and peace, in part because many women regarded civilization as having progressed beyond war as a means of settling disputes, and in part because women were widely held as morally superior to men, women banded together to find ways of ending the war. In the United States, many women's organizations, from the Young Women's Christian Association (YWCA) to the Daughters of the American Revolution, went on record as seeking an early resolution to the conflict. To coordinate national efforts toward peace, Carrie Chapman Catt founded the Women's Peace Party (WPP). In turn, the WPP made plans for an international peace conference. In 1915, the International Congress of Women, presided over by Jane Addams, social reformer, pacifist, and ultimate cowinner of the 1931 Nobel Peace Prize, met at The Hague to discuss conditions for a permanent state of peace. The neutrality of the meeting was underlined by the full participation of a German women's contingent. Heckled by the press but unawed by the seemingly impossible task facing them, the congress attendees established a set of principles as cornerstones of a lasting peace. President Woodrow Wilson is said to have borrowed the WPP conference principles in establishing his Fourteen Points as the foundation for a League of Nations.

Women in Uniform. Drawing on the immense contributions of nurses to the recovery and welfare of military patients during both the Civil War and the Spanish-American War, Congress authorized an Army Nurse Corps in 1901 and Navy Nurse Corps in 1908. Both nurse corps, however, existed outside the regular military establishment. Nurses did not receive military rank, pay, or retirement benefits. Yet, the permanency of the congressionally mandated nurse corps illustrated their integrity to the military mission. By the end of World War I, the Army Nurse Corps had expanded to twenty thousand and the Navy Nurse Corps to more than one thousand women.

In 1917, while mobilizing U.S. forces for entry into the war, both Secretary of War Newton Baker and Secretary of the Navy Josephus Daniels found the Army and Navy short on skilled administrative clerks. Their solutions to the problem, however, were markedly different. Finding no legal requirement that a Navy clerk (yeoman) be a man, Daniels ordered that sufficient clerically skilled women be enlisted as yeomen in the naval reserve, with the same pay and rank as men. Thus,

Women served as U.S. Marines during World War I but were discharged soon after the conflict was over. (National Archives)

12,500 female yeomen were enlisted and ultimately came to function as draftsmen, fingerprint experts, intelligence experts, and clerks. Despite the stated demand for female enlisted skills by many Army officers, including General John Pershing, Baker was uncomfortable with any formal military status for women and hired female clerical workers on a civilian contractual basis.

By war's end, more than 34,000 uniformed women had served in the Army and Navy nurse corps, Navy, Marines, and Coast Guard. With the exception of the two nurse corps, however, all the female military personnel were discharged.

Women's Contribution to the Civilian War Effort. More than 25,000 American women served overseas during World War I under a host of civilian war relief organizations. All told, fifty-two American organizations and forty-five foreign organizations made up the war relief effort in Europe. The women who volunteered were in their thirties or older, with above-average levels of education and socioeconomic status. The "new" American woman was perceived by foreigners as skilled, independent, and, most of all, determined.

The plethora of organizations made for some duplication of effort and complexities in distribution. General John Pershing, commander of the American Expeditionary Forces, commented about the difficulties of coordinating military and civilian efforts among the multitude of agencies. Nevertheless, the immense civilian (and largely female) war relief effort was vital from both a humanitarian and a military perspective. While many of the U.S. organizations operated under the umbrella (and impressive financial resources) of the American Red Cross, others functioned independently. American civilian women wishing to serve abroad could select among a host of quasi-government agencies, church organizations such as the Quakers, the Young Men's Christian Association (YMCA), the YWCA, the Red Cross, and the Salvation Army. They might opt to serve in private charities established by the rich and famous, such as Edith Wharton. They might enlist in foreign relief and medical agencies (as ambulance drivers, among other hazardous occupations) or the relief agencies sponsored by women's universities in the United States, such as Smith, Vassar, Wellesley, and Pembroke colleges. In all, more than 300 American women in service would perish by the end of World War I.

The Canadian Experience. The Canadians anticipated putting 500,000 men in uniform (from a national population of eight million). Therefore, women were substituted for men in "men's jobs" to a greater degree than in the United States. For example, the chief armament supplier, the Imperial Munitions Board, eventually employed 250,000 Canadians, of whom 40,000 were women. As in the United States, a strong feminist movement reinforced the substitution effect in changing the way society regarded women's roles.

Impact of Women's Involvement in World War I. In the aftermath of World War I, women's role in society had irrevocably changed. The war would act as a propellant of women's interests such as suffrage and greater equality in the workplace. The war allowed women a unique opportunity for responsible, fulfilling action independent of men. Moreover, it proved to society that women were completely capable in "men's occupations" such as factories, shipyards, and aircraft construction. The Victorian perception of women as retiring, frail ancillaries to men was eclipsed. *—John A. Sondey*

See also Addams, Jane; Army Nurse Corps; Pacifism and nonviolence; Peace movement and women; Suffrage movement and suffragists; War and women; Young Women's Christian Association (YWCA)

BIBLIOGRAPHY

Binkin, Martin, and Shirley L. Bach. *Women and the Military.* Washington, D.C.: Brookings Institution, 1977.

Devilbiss, M. C. *Women and Military Service.* Maxwell Air Force Base, Ala.: Air University Press, 1990.

Holm, Jeanne. *Women in the Military.* Novato, Calif.: Presidio Press, 1992.

Macdonald, Sharon, Pat Holden, and Shirley Ardener, eds. *Images of Women in Peace and War.* Madison: University of Wisconsin Press, 1988.

Morton, Desmond. *A Military History of Canada.* Edmonton, Alberta: Hurtig, 1985.

Schneider, Dorothy, and Carl Schneider. *Into the Breach.* New York: Viking Press, 1991.

World War II, women's military roles in

RELEVANT ISSUES: War and the military

SIGNIFICANCE: World War II provided American women with their first major opportunity to serve their country in a military capacity, paving the way for expanded roles in succeeding decades

Although military service traditionally had been limited to men, the personnel demands of World War II spurred the U.S. military leadership to accept women in significant numbers. By 1943, women's military branches had been established in all the services. A total of 350,000 women served in the U.S. Armed Forces during World War II. Although women were not permitted to serve in combat, many served with distinction, and some were counted among American war casualties. Women's military service during the war altered perceptions about the capabilities of female soldiers and helped bring some specific women's issues to the fore.

The Women's Corps. The impetus for women's corps in the United States began with the extension of the vote to women in 1920. Fearing extreme pacifism among the new female voters, the War Department (the forerunner of the Department of Defense) established a director of women's relations, whose job was to bolster support for the U.S. military among women's groups. Anita Phipps held the position throughout the 1920's, during which time she developed a plan to create a women's corps within the Army. The War Department was not amenable, and it was not until World War II was underway, and with the support of First Lady Eleanor Roosevelt, that such a corps was finally authorized. Edith Nourse Rogers, a member of Congress and a longtime advocate of women's military service, introduced a bill in 1941 to create a women's Army auxiliary corps. The Japanese attack at Pearl Harbor on December 7, 1941, which brought the United States into the war, virtually ensured passage of the bill.

In 1942, the Women's Army Auxiliary Corps (WAAC) was established. The following year, its auxiliary status was dropped, and it was placed under the direction of Oveta Culp Hobby. Members of the Women's Army Corps (WAC) were uniformed servicewomen with full military status. The Navy established a women's reserve and placed as its head Mildred McAfee, the president of Wellesley College; members of the Navy women's reserve would be known as Women Accepted for Voluntary Emergency Service (WAVES). The Coast Guard also established a women's reserve, based on the acronym SPAR, from the Coast Guard motto "Semper Paratus—Always Ready." The Marine Corps was less eager to take on women, but in 1943 it finally established a reserve for women, headed by Ruth Cheney Streeter; members of the Marine Corps Women's Reserve were not given an official acronym, and thus were simply "marines."

Although the women's corps represented a major advancement in the removal of barriers to women's service, most jobs within the corps were clerical and secretarial. In effect, women in the military were taking office jobs from men, who thus were released to serve in combat assignments. Many women also were placed in nursing jobs or other traditional occupations for women.

The most dramatic exception to the tendency of relegating women to office jobs were Women's Airforce Service Pilots (WASPs). A severe shortage of pilots during the war spurred the Air Force to use female pilots in noncombat assignments. Between 1942 and 1944, more than a thousand women ferried warplanes, tested aircraft, and towed practice targets. By all accounts, these women performed exceptionally. Although never involved in battle, thirty-eight WASPs died in the line of duty. The leader of the WASPs, Jacqueline Cochran, resisted integration of her unit with the Women's Army Corps, and thus her pilots retained civilian status. In an example of the changing attitudes that followed the military performance of women during the war, military status was retroactively granted to the WASPs in 1977.

Impact. The employment of women in the U.S. military during World War II was largely driven by need. This situation was not unique to the United States; other countries, notably Great Britain, Japan, and the Soviet Union, pressed women into more integral military assignments. Although women's military assignments in the United States during the war generally were limited to support roles, the very entrance of women into military service had far-reaching effects on the military and society in general.

The widespread inclusion of women forced a number of unspoken gender issues. In many ways, the U.S. military leadership—including its female officers—continued to impose a traditional cultural value system on women, expecting chastity, temperance, and otherwise "ladylike" language and behavior. Meanwhile, women in the military often were subjected to sexual harassment and intimidation. Double standards were evident throughout the armed forces. Pregnancy was frowned on and, if it occurred outside of wedlock, could lead to various official sanctions. At the same time, abortion was discouraged, and an illegal abortion could lead to a dishonorable discharge.

Although the military contributions of women during the war were significant and recognized within the military leadership and society, some people disapproved of, and even actively opposed, women serving in military roles. Among the complaints were that women "feminized" the military, that military service "masculinized" women, and that the presence of women caused morale problems. Some people believed that any woman who would volunteer to serve in the military was a lesbian. These and similar charges reached a peak in a slander campaign against the WAC in late 1943 and early 1944. Charges (later to be deemed unfounded) surfaced that women's official role in the military was primarily to improve troop morale, that the War Department was providing them with contraceptives, and that a high rate of lesbianism existed among female personnel. Many of these stories were traced to servicemen who resented the presence of women in the military.

The friction, double standards, and clashing social conventions caused by the introduction of women into the military were addressed in a variety of ways, including compromises on an individual basis and some policy changes in the services. In the long run, these incidents created an awareness that various social customs were biased and outmoded, eventually leading to their demise. Most directly, women's military service during World War II caused changes in the military itself. Women had proved that they have the strength, courage, and commitment to make tremendous sacrifices in defense of their country, and therefore that the military excluded their contributions to its own detriment. Indeed, by 1945, President Franklin D. Roosevelt was prepared to draft women as nurses, but the war ended before such an action could take place. These developments started a long process of accepting women into all areas of military service. In 1948, the U.S. Congress passed the Women's Armed Services Integration Act, which permanently opened all branches to women. For the next several decades, advancements in women's military service would occur until women were even accepted in some combat roles. *—Steve D. Boilard*

See also Military, women in the; Nurses, women as; SPAR; War and women; Women Accepted for Voluntary Emergency Service (WAVES); Women's Airforce Service Pilots (WASPs); Women's Army Corps (WAC); Women's Reserve in the Marine Corps

Bibliography

Chrisman, Catherine Bell. *My War: WW II, As Experienced by One Woman Soldier*. Denver, Colo.: Maverick, 1989.

Cole, Jean Hascall. *Women Pilots of World War II*. Salt Lake City: University of Utah Press, 1992.

Lyne, Mary C., and Kay Arthur. *Three Years Behind the Mast: The Story of the United States Coast Guard, SPARS*. Washington, D.C.: U.S. Coast Guard, 1946.

Soderbergh, Peter A. *Women Marines: The World War II Era*. Westport, Conn.: Praeger, 1992.

Treadwell, Mattie E. *The Women's Army Corps*. Washington, D.C.: Office of the Chief of Military History, Department of the Army, 1954.

Year of
the Woman

Year of the Woman

Date: 1992

Relevant issues: Arts and entertainment, politics

Significance: The Year of the Woman in politics and entertainment was a concept largely unrealized in terms of women's advancement

The media declared 1992 to be the "Year of the Woman" in U.S. politics largely because of the public reaction to the Senate confirmation hearings of Supreme Court Justice Clarence Thomas; many women were frustrated at the treatment of Anita Hill by the all-male panel when she testified about Thomas' alleged sexual harassment of her. Some gains were made by women in the 1992 elections: The number of women in the United States Senate tripled from two to six, and the number of women in the House of Representatives rose from twenty-three to forty-seven. After 1993, however, the mood of the country turned sharply more conservative, and most of the goals of female legislators concerning such women's issues as child care and health insurance remained unfulfilled.

In Hollywood, 1992 was envisioned as a year in which women's power at the box office, demonstrated by the success of *Thelma and Louise* and *Fried Green Tomatoes* in 1991, would spark a new wave of important woman-themed films. These ambitions were also largely unrealized: The most successful woman that year was director Penelope Spheeris, whose film *Wayne's World*, one of the highest-grossing motion pictures of 1992, focused not on women's issues but on adolescent male fantasies. The Year of the Woman in Hollywood saw no women nominated for Academy Awards in major categories behind the cameras.

See also Acting; Candidacy and political campaigns, women's; Filmmaking; Films, women's; Hill, Anita Faye; Politics; Sexual harassment

Yeast infections

Relevant issues: Health and medicine

Significance: Yeast infections, also called candidiasis or moniliasis, affect approximately 75 percent of all women at some time in their lives, most frequently between the ages of sixteen and thirty-five

An overgrowth of *Candida*, a single-celled fungus naturally present in certain parts of the body, causes candidiasis (a yeast

Percentage of Women Elected to the U.S. Congress in 1992

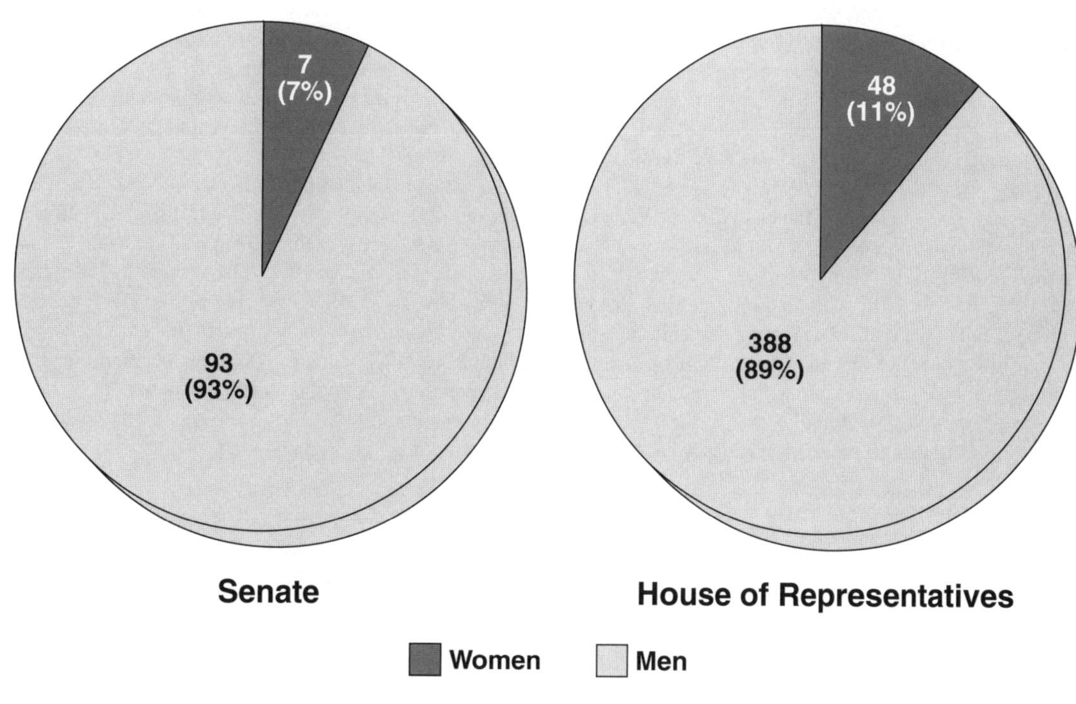

infection), which may affect the vagina, skin, or mouth (thrush). Yeast infections result from an imbalance in the body's system caused by illness or infection, certain medications (broad-spectrum antibiotics or birth control pills), or physical or mental stress. Studies have linked some chronic or difficult-to-treat yeast infections to the human immunodeficiency virus (HIV) that causes acquired immunodeficiency syndrome (AIDS). The fungus can be passed between sexual partners. Common symptoms of vaginal candidiasis are an irritating itch, soreness, and a thick, white discharge. Other possible symptoms include discomfort during intercourse, abdominal pain, and burning during urination. Treatment is usually with one of two antifungal medications, available in cream or suppository form: clotrimazole or miconazole nitrate. These medications, once available only by prescription in the United States, were approved for over-the-counter use in 1990. The Food and Drug Administration (FDA) has also approved fluconazole, an oral antifungal medication that can cure a yeast infection in a single dose, available only by prescription. Because *Candida* organisms thrive in warm, moist places, prevention includes keeping the vaginal area dry and cool. Wearing loose, natural-fiber clothing and cotton-crotch underwear is recommended, as is limiting the use of deodorant tampons and feminine hygiene products.

See also AIDS epidemic and women; Health and medicine; Health movement, women's; Sexually transmitted diseases

Young Women's Christian Association (YWCA)

Date: Founded in 1855

Relevant issues: Community affairs, race and ethnicity, religious beliefs and practices, social reform

Significance: Open to women and girls worldwide, the YWCA is the oldest and largest multiracial women's organization

The Young Women's Christian Association (YWCA) originated in London in 1855 as two separate groups. One group, led by Emma Roberts, organized to find adequate housing for nurses returning from the Crimean War (1853-1856). The other, the Prayer Union, organized prayer circles. Since both aimed to better the condition of women in industrial society, the two united in 1877 as the Young Women's Christian Association. In 1858, in New York City, a group similar to the London groups, called the Ladies' Christian Association, was founded, and, in Boston in 1866, the first YWCA opened to provide housing for single working women. In the United States, the two groups united in 1906. Thereafter, the organization spread rapidly throughout the United States, Canada, and other industrialized countries. With headquarters in Geneva, Switzerland, the World YWCA is active in more than eighty countries and by the 1980's had more than two and a half million members— including men and boys, who may join as YWCA associates.

Continuing its tradition of bringing women together to work on common problems, the philosophy of the YWCA states that the group

> is a women's membership movement nourished by its roots in the Christian faith and sustained by the richness of many beliefs and values. Strengthened by diversity, the association draws together members who strive to create opportunities for women's growth, leadership and power in order to attain a common vision: peace, justice, freedom and dignity of all people.

Its expressed imperative is "to thrust our collective power toward the elimination of racism wherever it exists, and by any means necessary."

To achieve its purposes, the YWCA provides activities and services for groups of all ages and interests in cities, towns, and rural areas and on college campuses. Local YWCAs offer recreation, education, citizenship training, service projects, and opportunities to develop social relationships. They serve an increasing number of families by providing day care centers, health education, job training, and hobby facilities. Groups such as the Y-Teens help teenage girls develop self-esteem. YWCA residences continue to help young women begin their work experiences in new surroundings by providing support services. In many urban areas, the YWCA sponsors programs to fight crime and delinquency. Its campus groups provide leadership training, and its international service programs extend its mission into developing countries.

As the largest worldwide women's association, the YWCA is a leader in improving the status of women. Not only does it meet the needs of its members with specific programs that combine service and social action, but it cooperates with other organizations engaged in similar services, such as the United Services Organization (USO). The National Travelers Aid Society and day care centers and women's exchanges that originally were part of the YWCA now stand as independent organizations. The YWCA concept of group work has become a standard concern of social workers. Its services and training continue to help women of all ages become equal partners with men in developing their respective nations.

See also Family life; Mentoring and networking by women; Multiculturalism; Socialization of girls and young women

Educational Institutions with Programs in Women's Studies

Compiled by Victoria Price

A by-product of the women's movement, the field of women's studies grew out of a perception that women were being given too little attention in educational courses or that they were being viewed with a bias or described in stereotypical terms. As a result of discussions at the Conference on Women at Cornell University in 1969, the first multidisciplinary college course on women was developed. The first women's studies program to receive official sanction on a college campus was the one at California State University, San Diego, in 1970. The first graduate course of study in women's history was at Sarah Lawrence University in Bronxville, New York. By 1972, thirty-two women's studies programs existed, although what constituted a bona fide women's studies "program" was still somewhat problematic. Since that time, degrees at the graduate and undergraduate levels have been developed, in addition to numerous programs offering a minor or less. Another large group of schools offer one or more women's studies courses. Some programs are a single discipline; others are interdisciplinary. Courses and formal programs are provided by both private and public institutions of higher learning.

In general, fields of women's studies can be defined by three kinds of activities: learning more about women, developing new ways to approach existing bodies of knowledge from a feminist point of view, and sharing women's works with both male and female students in the hope of effecting changes in attitudes.

U.S. Colleges and Universities Offering Graduate Degrees in Women's Studies

Institution	Type	Degree
Alabama		
University of Alabama Tuscaloosa	Public	M.A.
Arizona		
Arizona State University Tempe	Public	Certificate
California		
Institute of Integral Studies San Francisco	Independent	M.A.
New College of California San Francisco	Independent	M.A.
San Jose State University San Jose	Public	M.A.
District of Columbia		
George Washington University Washington	Independent	M.A.
Georgia		
Atlanta University Atlanta	Independent	M.A., Ph.D.
Clark College Atlanta	Independent	Ph.D.
Emory University Decatur	Independent	M.A., Ph.D.
Illinois		
De Paul University Chicago	Independent	M.A.
Southern Illinois University Edwardsville	Public	M.A.
Massachusetts		
Brandeis University Waltham	Independent	M.A.
Clark University Worcester	Independent	Ph.D.
Michigan		
East Michigan University Ypslanti	Independent	M.L.S.
Minnesota		
Mankato State University Mankato	Independent	M.A.
New Jersey		
Rutgers—The State University of New Jersey Camden	Public	M.A.
Rutgers—The State University of New Jersey New Brunswick	Public	Ph.D.
New York		
Cornell University Ithaca	Independent	M.A., Ph.D.
Graduate School and University Center of the City College of New York New York City	Public	M.S., Ph.D.
New School for Social Research New York City	Independent	M.A.
New York University New York City	Public	M.A., Ph.D.
Sarah Lawrence University Bronxville	Independent	M.A.
State University of New York Buffalo	Public	M.A.

Ohio

Institution	Type	Degree
Ohio State University, Columbus	Public	M.A.
University of Cincinnati, Cincinnati	Public	M.A.

Oklahoma

Institution	Type	Degree
University of Oklahoma, Norman	Public	M.A.

U.S. Colleges and Universities Offering a Four-Year Degree or a Major in Women's Studies (Disciplinary or Interdisciplinary)

Arizona

Institution	Type
Arizona State University, Tempe	Public
Arizona State University West, Phoenix	Public
Prescott College, Prescott	Independent
University of Arizona, Tucson	Public

California

Institution	Type
California State University, Bakersfield	Public
California State University, Northridge	Public
California State University, Sacramento	Public
California State University, Stanislaus	Public
Chapman University, Orange	Independent
Christian Heritage College, El Cajon	Independent
Claremont McKenna College, Claremont	Independent
Mills College, Oakland	Independent
Occidental College, Los Angeles	Independent
Pitzer College, Claremont	Independent
Pomona College, Claremont	Independent
San Diego State University, San Diego	Public
San Francisco State University, San Francisco	Public
Scripps College, Claremont	Independent
Sonoma State University, Rohnert Park	Public
Stanford University, Stanford	Independent
University of California, Berkeley	Public
University of California, Davis	Public
University of California, Los Angeles	Public
University of California, Riverside	Public
University of California, San Diego	Public
University of California, Santa Barbara	Public
University of California, Santa Cruz	Public
University of Redlands, Redlands	Independent
University of Southern California, Los Angeles	Independent

Colorado

Institution	Type
Colorado College, Colorado Springs	Independent
Metropolitan State College, Denver	Independent
University of Colorado, Boulder	Public
University of Denver, Denver	Independent

Connecticut

Institution	Type
Hartford College for Women, Hartford	Independent
Sacred Heart University, Fairfield	Independent
Trinity College, Hartford	Independent
University of Connecticut, Hartford	Independent
University of Connecticut, Storrs	Public
University of Hartford, West Hartford	Independent
Wesleyan University, Middletown	Independent
Yale University, New Haven	Independent

Delaware

University of Delaware Newark	Public

Florida

Eckerd College St. Petersburg	Independent
University of Miami Coral Gables	Independent
University of South Florida Tampa	Public

Georgia

Emory University Decatur	Independent

Illinois

De Paul University Chicago	Independent
Knox College Galesburg	Independent
Lake Forest College Lake Forest	Independent
Northwestern University Evanston	Independent
Roosevelt University Chicago	Independent

Indiana

DePauw University Greencastle	Independent
Earlham College Richmond	Independent
Indiana State University Terre Haute	Public
Purdue University-Calumet Hammond	Public

Iowa

Cornell College Mount Vernon	Independent
Drake University Des Moines	Independent
Grinnell College Grinnell	Independent
University of Iowa Iowa City	Public

Kansas

University of Kansas Lawrence	Public
Wichita State University Wichita	Public

Louisiana

Tulane University New Orleans	Independent

Maine

Bates College Lewiston	Independent
University of Southern Maine Gorham	Public
University of Southern Maine Lewiston	Public
University of Southern Maine Portland	Public

Maryland

Goucher College Towson	Independent
Towson State University Towson	Public

Massachusetts

Amherst College Amherst	Independent
Atlantic Union College South Lancaster	Independent
College of the Holy Cross Worcester	Independent
Curry College Milton	Independent
Hampshire College Amherst	Independent
Harvard University Cambridge	Independent
Massachusetts Institute of Technology Cambridge	Independent
Mount Holyoke College South Hadley	Independent
Simmons College Boston	Independent
Simon's Rock of Bard College Great Barrington	Independent
Smith College Northampton	Independent
Suffolk University Boston	Independent
Tufts University Medford	Independent
University of Massachusetts Amherst	Public
University of Massachusetts Boston	Public
Wellesley College Wellesley	Independent

Michigan

Alma College Alma	Independent
Aquinas College Grand Rapids	Independent

Grand Valley State College
Allendale — Public

Kalamazoo College
Kalamazoo — Independent

Michigan State University
East Lansing — Public

University of Michigan
Ann Arbor — Public

University of Michigan
Dearborn — Public

Wayne State University
Detroit — Public

Western Michigan University
Kalamazoo — Public

Minnesota

Augsburg College
Minneapolis — Independent

Carleton College
Northfield — Independent

College of St. Catherine
St. Paul — Independent

Hamline University
St. Paul — Independent

Macalester College
St. Paul — Independent

Saint Cloud State University
St. Cloud — Public

Saint Olaf College
Northfield — Independent

University of Minnesota at Duluth
Duluth — Public

University of Minnesota at Minneapolis St. Paul
Minneapolis — Public

University of St. Thomas
St. Paul — Independent

Missouri

Central Missouri State University
Warrensburg — Public

Washington University
St. Louis — Independent

Webster University
St. Louis — Independent

Montana

University of Montana
Missoula — Public

Nebraska

University of Nebraska
Lincoln — Public

Nevada

University of Nevada
Las Vegas — Public

New Hampshire

Dartmouth College
Hanover — Independent

University of New Hampshire
Durham — Public

New Jersey

Princeton University
Princeton — Independent

Rutgers—The State University of New Jersey, Camden
Camden — Public

Rutgers—The State University of New Jersey, Douglass College
New Brunswick — Public

Rutgers—The State University of New Jersey, Livingston
New Brunswick — Public

Rutgers—The State University of New Jersey, Newark College
Newark — Public

Rutgers—The State University of New Jersey, University College
New Brunswick — Public

Thomas A. Edison State College
Trenton — Independent

New York

Barnard College of Columbia University
New York City — Independent

Brooklyn College of the City University of New York
New York City — Public

City College of the City University of New York
New York City — Public

Colgate University
Hamilton — Independent

College of New Rochelle
New Rochelle — Independent

College of Staten Island of the City University of New York
Staten Island — Public

Columbia College
New York City — Independent

Columbia University
New York City — Independent

Cornell University
Ithaca — Independent

Eugene Lang College of the New School for Social Research
New York City — Independent

Fordham University, Lincoln Center
New York City — Independent

Hamilton College
Clinton — Independent

Hobart College
Geneva — Independent

Hunter College of the City University of New York
New York City — Public

Manhattanville College Purchase	Independent
Nazareth College of Rochester Rochester	Independent
Sarah Lawrence College Bronxville	Independent
State University of New York Albany	Public
State University of New York Buffalo	Public
State University of New York College Brockport	Public
State University of New York College New Paltz	Public
State University of New York College Potsdam	Public
Syracuse University Syracuse	Independent
Union College Schenectady	Independent
University of Rochester Rochester	Independent
Vassar College Poughkeepsie	Independent
Wells College Aurora	Independent
William Smith College Geneva	Independent

North Carolina

Duke University Durham	Independent
University of North Carolina Chapel Hill	Public
University of North Carolina Greensboro	Public

Ohio

Antioch University Yellow Springs	Independent
Bowling Green State University Bowling Green	Public
College of Mount St. Joseph on-the-Ohio Mount St. Joseph	Independent
College of Wooster Wooster	Independent
Denison University Granville	Independent
Kenyon College Gambier	Independent
Lake Erie College Painesville	Independent
Oberlin College Oberlin	Independent
Ohio State University Columbia	Public
Ohio University Athens	Public
Ohio Wesleyan University Delaware	Independent
Union Institute Cincinnati	Independent
University of Toledo Toledo	Public

Oklahoma

University of Oklahoma Norman	Public

Oregon

Portland State University Portland	Public
University of Oregon Eugene	Public

Pennsylvania

Allegheny College Meadville	Independent
Bryn Mawr College Bryn Mawr	Independent
Bucknell University Lewisburg	Independent
Chatham College Pittsburgh	Independent
Gettysburg College Gettysburg	Independent
La Salle University Philadelphia	Independent
Lehigh University Bethlehem	Independent
Penn State University University Park	Public
Rosemont College Rosemont	Independent
Swarthmore College Swarthmore	Independent
Temple University Philadelphia	Public
University of Pennsylvania Philadelphia	Independent
Villanova University Villanova	Independent

Rhode Island

Brown University Providence	Independent
Rhode Island College Providence	Public
University of Rhode Island Kingston	Public

Tennessee

Middle Tennessee State University Murfreesboro	Public
University of Memphis Memphis	Public
University of Tennessee Knoxville	Public
Vanderbilt University Nashville	Independent

Texas

Southwestern University Georgetown	Independent

Vermont

Burlington College Burlington	Independent
Goddard College Plainfield	Independent
Marlboro College Marlboro	Independent
Middlebury College Middlebury	Independent

Virginia

Old Dominion University Norfolk	Public
Randolph-Macon College Ashland	Independent
University of Richmond Richmond	Independent
Virginia Polytechnical Institute and State University Blacksburg	Public

Washington

Evergreen State College Olympia	Public
Washington State University Pullman	Public
Western Washington University Bellingham	Public

Wisconsin

Beloit College Beloit	Independent
Carroll College Waukesha	Independent
University of Wisconsin Green Bay	Public
University of Wisconsin Madison	Public
University of Wisconsin Milwaukee	Public
University of Wisconsin Whitewater	Public

Wyoming

University of Wyoming Laramie	Public

U.S. Colleges and Universities Offering an Associate Degree in Women's Studies

California

Chabot College Hayward	Independent
City College of San Francisco San Francisco	Public
Cosumnes River College Sacramento	Public
Diablo Valley College Pleasant Hill	Independent
Fresno City College Fresno	Public
Monterey Peninsula College Monterey	Public
Rancho Santiago College Santa Ana	Public
Sacramento City College Sacramento	Public
Saddleback College Mission Viejo	Independent
West Valley Community College Saratoga	Public
Yuba College Marysville	Public

Massachusetts

North Essex Community College Haverhill	Public

New Hampshire

University of New Hampshire Durham	Public

New Jersey

Bergen Community College Paramus	Public

New York

Suffolk County Community College, Ammerman campus Selden	Public
Tompkins-Cortland Community College Dryden	Public

Pennsylvania

West Chester State College
West Chester — Independent

Wisconsin

Lakeshore Technical College
Cleveland — Public

University of Wisconsin
Green Bay — Public

U.S. Colleges and Universities Offering a Minor or Concentration in Women's Studies

California

California Lutheran College
Thousand Oaks — Independent

California State University
Chico — Public

Santa Clara University
Santa Clara — Independent

University of California
Fullerton — Public

Connecticut

Sacred Heart College
Fairfield — Independent

Florida

Florida State University
Tallahassee — Public

Stetson University
De Land — Independent

Georgia

Agnes Scott College
Decatur — Independent

Emory University
Decatur — Independent

Mercer University
Macon — Independent

Idaho

Idaho State University
Pocatello — Public

University of Idaho
Moscow — Public

Illinois

Barat College
Lake Forest — Independent

Knox College
Galesburg — Independent

Loyola University
Chicago — Independent

Wheaton College
Wheaton — Independent

Indiana

Indiana University
Bloomington — Public

St. Mary's College
Notre Dame — Independent

University of Notre Dame
Notre Dame — Independent

Maine

Colby College
Waterville — Independent

Massachusetts

Clark University
Worcester — Independent

Emmanuel College
Boston — Independent

Hampshire College
Amherst — Independent

Northeastern University
Boston — Public

Williams College
Williamstown — Independent

Michigan

Alma College
Alma — Independent

Kalamazoo College
Kalamazoo — Independent

New Jersey

Rutgers—The State University of New Jersey,
Camden College of Arts and Sciences
Camden — Public

Rutgers—The State University of New Jersey,
University College
New Brunswick — Public

New York

Bard College
Annandale-on-Hudson — Independent

Hamilton College
Clinton — Independent

State University of New York
Stony Brook — Public

North Carolina

Duke University
Durham — Independent

Ohio

Institution	Type
College of Wooster Wooster	Independent
Otterbein College Westerville	Independent
Youngstown State University Youngstown	Public

Pennsylvania

Institution	Type
Albright College Reading	Independent
University of Pittsburgh Pittsburgh	Independent

Wisconsin

Institution	Type
Ripon College Ripon	Independent

U.S. COLLEGES AND UNIVERSITIES OFFERING A PROGRAM OR CERTIFICATE IN WOMEN'S STUDIES FOR FEWER THAN FIFTEEN HOURS OR OFFERING ONE OR MORE WOMEN'S STUDIES COURSES

A number of schools offer a few courses for which a student may or may not be awarded a certificate. In other schools, one or more courses are offered in women's studies but are taken to fulfill requirements for other degrees. An exhaustive list of schools is not available, but the following are representative of colleges and universities providing courses such as Gender, Culture, and Society; Classics of Feminist Thought; Gender Issues in Communication; The American Heroine: Fiction and Fact; Women in American History; African Women in History; The Psychology of Women; Women Writers; and Women's History.

Institution	Type
Alabama State University Montgomery, Alabama	Public
Albright College Reading, Pennsylvania	Independent
Angelo State University San Angelo, Texas	Public
Barry College Miami, Florida	Independent
Baylor University Waco, Texas	Independent
Bowdoin College Brunswick, Maine	Independent
College of Notre Dame Belmont, California	Independent
College of Wooster Wooster, Ohio	Independent
Concordia Lutheran College Austin, Texas	Independent
Dartmouth College Hanover, New Hampshire	Independent
Dominican College Orangeburg, New York	Independent
Emmanuel College Boston, Massachusetts	Independent
Emory University Decatur, Georgia	Independent
Hampshire College Amherst, Massachusetts	Independent
Haverford College Haverford, Pennsylvania	Independent
Howard University Washington, D.C.	Independent
Huntingdon College Montgomery, Alabama	Independent
Indiana University Bloomington, Indiana	Public
La Salle University Philadelphia, Pennsylvania	Independent
Lamar University Beaumont, Texas	Public
Mercy College Dobbs Ferry, New York	Independent
Montclair State University Upper Montclair, New Jersey	Public
Northern Arizona University Flagstaff, Arizona	Public
Pasadena City College Pasadena, California	Public
Post College Waterbury, Connecticut	Independent
St. Louis University St. Louis, Missouri	Independent
Santa Clara University Santa Clara, California	Independent
State University of New York Stony Brook, New York	Public
Trinity College Burlington, Vermont	Independent
Trinity College Washington, D.C.	Independent
Troy State University Troy, Alabama	Public
University of Alabama Huntsville, Alabama	Public
University of Maine Augusta, Maine	Public
University of North Alabama Florence, Alabama	Public

University of Oregon Eugene, Oregon	Public
University of Pittsburgh Pittsburgh, Pennsylvania	Independent
University of San Francisco San Francisco, California	Independent
University of South Carolina Columbia, South Carolina	Public
Whittier College Whittier, California	Independent

CANADIAN UNIVERSITIES OFFERING DEGREES IN WOMEN'S STUDIES

Alberta

Athabasca University Athabasca	B.A.
University of Calgary Calgary	B.A.
University of Lethbridge Lethbridge	B.A.

British Columbia

Simon Fraser University Burnaby	B.A., M.A.
University of British Columbia Vancouver	B.A.
University of Victoria Victoria	B.A.

Manitoba

University of Manitoba Winnipeg	B.A.
University of Winnipeg Winnipeg	B.A.

Nova Scotia

Dalhousie University Halifax	B.S., M.A., Ph.D.
Mount St. Vincent University Halifax	B.A.
Saint Mary's University Halifax	B.A.
University of King's College Halifax	B.A.

Ontario

Brock University St. Catharines	B.A.
Carleton University Ottawa	B.A.
Laurentian University of Sudbury Sudbury	B.A.
McMaster University Hamilton	B.A.
Queen's University at Kingston Kingston	B.A.
Trent University Peterborough	B.A.
Université d'Ottawa Ottawa	B.A.
University of Guelph Guelph	B.A.
University of Toronto Toronto	B.A.
University of Waterloo Waterloo	B.A.
University of Western Ontario London	B.A.
Wilfrid Laurier University Waterloo	B.A.
York University Toronto	B.A., M.A., Ph.D.

Quebec

Bishop's University Lennoxville	B.A.
Concordia University Montreal	B.A.
McGill University Montreal	B.A.

Landmarks, Monuments, and Historic Sites

Compiled by Barbara Bair

Alaska

Rika Roadhouse
Mile 252
Old Richardson Highway
The site of a shelter for wilderness travelers was maintained from the 1920's to 1947 by Swedish immigrant Erika Wallen, known locally as Rika. It is now a state historic park.

California

Asilomar Conference Center
800 Asilomar Boulevard
Pacific Grove
Designed by architect Julia Morgan in 1913, this retreatlike 102-acre facility was operated as a training center for women leaders by the Young Women's Christian Association (YWCA) until 1955. Still a meeting place for women's groups, it is now part of the California State Park system.

Biddy Mason Homestead and Public Art Project
3d Street (between Spring Street and Broadway)
Los Angeles
Mason came to Los Angeles as a slave in 1851 and successfully sued for her freedom in the California courts. A midwife and benefactor, she became a mainstay of the Angeleno community. The Power of Place Project commissioned artists Sheila de Brettville and Betye Saar to create public art installations honoring Mason that have been incorporated into a parking garage and office complex erected on the site of her 1866 homestead, where Mason lived and where she helped found Los Angeles' first African Methodist Episcopal Church in 1872.

Coit Memorial Tower
Telegraph Hill
San Francisco
The interior of Coit Tower was decorated with murals of city and regional life by artists commissioned by the Civil Works Administration Public Works of Art project in 1934. The tower is itself a memorial to city benefactor Lillie Hitchcock Coit. The art represents women in various occupations, including factory and agricultural workers, waitresses, musicians, sports enthusiasts, library patrons, consumers, and urban pedestrians. Artists Jane Berlandina, Maxine Albro, Edith Hamlin, Julia Rogers, and Shirley Staschen Triest were among the creators of the murals. The downstairs murals are open to public viewing.

Donner Party Memorial
Route 80
Truckee
This huge grouping of a man, woman, and child is set on a stone base that illustrates the height of the snow (22 feet) that trapped the Donner Party as they emigrated across the Sierra mountains in 1846. Twenty-five of the thirty-five women in the original group survived the winter of suffering, as did all five of the women who participated in the rescue party that hiked out of the mountains in search of help. A nearby museum contains exhibits that tell the history of the travail and the women's part in it.

Connecticut

Home of Harriet Beecher Stowe
73 Forest Street
Hartford
This home where the abolitionist author of *Uncle Tom's Cabin* (1852) lived in the 1870's was based on the design ideas of domestic feminists Catharine Beecher and Andrew Jackson Downing, as detailed in their guide *The American Woman's Home*. It is open for tours.

Prudence Crandall House
Routes 14 and 169
Canterbury
This site of the first academy for African American girls, opened in 1832, is now the Prudence Crandall Museum maintained by the Connecticut Historical Commission. Crandall and her students were subjected to such severe harassment, including vandalism of the school and the arrest of Crandall on charges that her schooling of African Americans was illegal, that the school was forced to close in 1834. The museum contains exhibits on women's, African American, and Canterbury history.

Florida

Home of Zora Neale Hurston
1734 School Court Street
Fort Pierce
The author of *Their Eyes Were Watching God* (1937), a story of a black woman's liberation, lived in a simple concrete block house in the 1950's at the end of her life.

The Zora Neale Hurston Memorial Park
11 People Street
Eatonville

This memorial park commemorates the place where African American author Hurston was born circa 1901.

Hawaii

Queen Liliuokalani Statue
State Capitol entrance
Honolulu
This statue of Hawaii's last monarch is the only public sculpture of a woman in the state of Hawaii and is illustrative of women in public office and leadership roles. It was created by sculptor Marianne Pineda and dedicated in 1982.

Illinois

Grave of Emma Goldman
Dissenter's Row of Forest Home Cemetery
863 South Desplaines Avenue
Forest Park
The grave of this radical activist is located near a monument to the victims of the Haymarket massacre of 1887.

Grave of Mother Jones
Union Miners' Cemetery
Mount Olive
Mother Jones is buried near the graves of miners killed in the 1898 massacre at Virden, Illinois. A bas relief monument depicting the union organizer is flanked by two statues of miners.

Home of Frances Willard
1730 Chicago Avenue
Evanston
The residence of Willard, a temperance movement leader and an advocate of dress reform, women's rights, economic reform, and woman suffrage, this two-story cottage was also the headquarters for the Woman's Christian Temperance Union (WCTU). It is now a museum housing exhibits about wctu history.

Hull-House
800 South Halstead Street
Chicago
Jane Addams' settlement house, founded to help immigrant families, has been designated as a National Historic Landmark.

Indiana

Walker Building
617 Indiana Avenue
Indianapolis
This four-story brick building was the site of black entrepreneur Madam C. J. Walker's beauty supply business in the early twentieth century, a center for black female employment and entertainment that featured offices, a manufacturing and packaging plant, a theater and ballroom, and other facilities. It has been restored.

Kentucky

Mary Breckinridge Frontier Nursing Service and Hospital
Hospital Drive
Hyden
The Wendover Big House, a large log building, was built in 1925 for use by Breckinridge's Frontier Nursing Service and Graduate School of Midwifery, which brought health and childbirth services to rural women in eastern Kentucky by horseback, significantly lowering maternal mortality rates in the region. The center is still operating as a hospital.

The Shaker Village at Pleasant Hill
3500 Lexington Road
Harrodsburg
This site honoring the religious sect founded by Mother Ann Lee is a National Historic Landmark. Operated as a living museum, it features thirty buildings and demonstrations of women's contributions to Shaker religious services, arts and crafts, farming, and foodways.

Louisiana

Home of Kate Chopin
Route 1
Cloutierville
The residence of feminist writer Chopin and her family from 1880 to 1883, this two-story house is now the Bayou Folk Museum. Chopin captured the Creole culture of the Bayou region in her work and is best known for her 1899 novel *The Awakening*, a feminist story of a young wife's growing self-knowledge and independence from the traditional norms of middle-class womanhood.

Melrose Plantation
Route 119
Melrose
This 13,000-acre estate is the site of the home of freedwoman Marie Therese Coincoin, who was born a slave in 1742. Her lover purchased her freedom and deeded land to her, which she managed as a successful plantation. She used the profits from the fields to purchase the freedom of her children and grandchildren.

Maryland

Clara Barton Historic Site
5801 Oxford Road
Glen Echo
The supply center, headquarters, and home of the founder of the American branch of the International Red Cross from 1897 to 1912, this site is now maintained by the National Park Service.

Massachusetts

Lowell National Historic Park
169 Merrimack Street
Lowell
Now operated by the National Park Service, these restored textile mill yards and interpretive exhibits show where and how young unmarried rural women who came to Lowell as mill workers participated in the Industrial Revolution. Mill buildings, a boardinghouse, and the lyceum are among the restored sites where 75 percent of the workers were women.

Mount Auburn Cemetery
580 Mount Auburn Street
Cambridge
This famed cemetery includes memorials to Transcendentalist and women's rights theorist Margaret Fuller and Christian Science church founder Mary Baker Eddy. Many prominent women are buried at Mount Auburn, including mental health champion Dorothea Dix, black women's club leader Josephine St. Pierre Ruffin, former slave and writer Harriet Jacobs, and poet Amy Lowell.

Statue of Anne Hutchinson
State House grounds
Boston
Outspoken Massachusetts Bay Colony exile Hutchinson is here depicted as a national symbol of religious freedom and civil liberties.

Witchcraft Victims' Memorial
176 Hobart Street
Danvers
This large granite sculpture depicts a pulpit smashing through broken shackles. It is dedicated to the innocent people accused of witchcraft and killed in the Salem witch hunts of the 1690's.

Montana

Jeannette Rankin Park
Madison Street
Missoula
This park is named for the first congresswoman in the United States and located near her childhood home. Rankin, a woman suffrage supporter, was elected to Congress two years after women's right to vote was approved in her state. She was a staunch pacifist in both world wars and the Vietnam War, and, in 1968, she led the Jeannette Rankin Brigade march to the Capitol.

Nebraska

Home of Willa Cather
3d and Cedar Streets
Red Cloud
Cather's childhood home is open to the public. Historical markers identify sites that were significant in Cather's life or that she used as settings for *My Ántonia* and other novels and short stories about women's lives on the plains.

Willa Cather Historical Center
338 North Webster Street
Red Cloud
The Cather center museum offers displays of the writer's letters, memorabilia, and first editions of her works. The center is maintained with interpretive programs by the Nebraska State Historical Society.

Nevada

Julia Bulette Memorial
Union and D Streets
Virginia City
This plaque embedded in stone commemorates Bulette, a madame whose establishment was once patronized by firefighters and men who worked in the local mines. Bulette's life illustrates the importance of prostitution and the sex trade as women's issues in the history of the West.

Sarah Winnemucca Birthplace Site
Humboldt Sink
Lovelock
Winnemucca was displaced along with other Paiute Indians from her birthplace at Lovelock when the Paiutes were removed by federal mandate. She spent much of her life trying to regain rights to their homeland for her people. Winnemucca traveled widely on lecture tours to educate white people about the repressive operations of the Bureau of Indian Affairs.

New Hampshire

Christa McAuliffe Planetarium
3 Institute Drive
Concord

This multimedia planetarium is a living memorial to the schoolteacher who became the first private citizen and one of few women to be accepted by NASA for space flight. McAuliffe died in the January, 1986, explosion of the space shuttle *Challenger*.

New Mexico

Home of Mabel Dodge Luhan
Luhan Lane
Taos
This southwestern style adobe house was the residence of Luhan, a writer and patron of the arts who supported the work of many American writers and artists of the 1920's. Luhan also was a champion of Pueblo culture and used her influence to bring about revisions in federal Indian policies during the New Deal, shifting their emphasis from assimilation to the recognition of cultural pluralism. The house is now operated as a bed and breakfast inn.

New York

Harriet Tubman Home for the Aged
180-182 South Street
Auburn
This is the death place of the famed Underground Railroad leader and abolitionist Harriet Tubman, who operated the house toward the end of her life as a home for African American aged. It is now a museum open to visitors on a part-time schedule and maintained by the Auburn African Methodist Episcopal Church.

Henry Street Settlement House
Lower East Side
New York City
Lillian D. Wald's settlement house, which was founded in the late nineteenth century to offer visiting nursing and health education services to poor families, has been designated as a National Historic Landmark.

Home of Emma Goldman
210 East 13th Street
New York City
This New York tenement building is where radical thinker and orator Goldman lived, edited the *Mother Earth* newspaper, and offered refuge to fellow anarchist intellectuals and activists.

Home of Margaret Sanger
17 West 16th Street
New York City
The residence of family planning activist Sanger, a central leader in the movement to make birth control education and devices legally available to women of all walks of life, was used as her research bureau for decades.

The Margaret Sanger Birth Control Clinic
46 Aboy Street
New York City
Family planning activist Sanger offered her services at this clinic in Brooklyn.

Site of the Triangle Shirtwaist Company Fire
Brown Building
Washington Place and Greene Street
New York City
Now a New York University classroom building, this is the site where hundreds of female workers were trapped and almost a third died on March 25, 1911, when a fire swept through the factory. The owners had locked the exit doors, and the workers were unable to escape. The tragedy caused Progressive reformer Frances Perkins and others to spearhead labor legislation to regulate safety conditions in American workplaces.

The Statue of Liberty
Liberty Island
New York City
This colossal sculpture of a female Liberty was given to the United States by the French government in 1886 and serves as a beacon and tourist destination in New York Harbor. It represents the epitome of the tradition in landmark and memorial design to use the female form in an emblematic way to depict abstract values such as virtue, victory, and liberty. The statue is also the nation's primary symbol of the contributions of immigrants of many cultural heritages to North American society.

Susan B. Anthony House
17 Madison Street
Rochester
This former residence of the suffrage leader and historian of the women's rights movement is open to the public as a museum.

Women's Rights National Historic Park
Seneca Falls
The site of the 1848 Seneca Falls Women's Rights Convention, which spawned the nineteenth century women's movement, this park has a visitors' center and nineteen life-size bronze statues of the leaders who attended the conference, including Elizabeth Cady Stanton. Stanton's home is also part of the park, as is the Wesleyan Chapel where the historic meeting took place. It is administered by the National Park Service.

North Carolina

Loray Mill
1101 West 2d Avenue
Gastonia
This abandoned mill was the site where labor activist, ballad writer, and mother Ella May Wiggins was killed during violence stemming from owners' repression of a textile workers' strike of 1929. Wiggins' death made her a symbol of the efforts of Southern workers to gain union representation, safety protections, and collective bargaining rights.

North Dakota

Sacajawea Statue
State Capitol
Bismarck
Sacajawea was a Shoshoni woman who guided Lewis and Clark on their westward expedition. This memorial was designed by Leonard Crunelle and erected in 1910.

Ohio

Kent State University Memorial
Kent
A plaque commemorates Allison Krause, Jeffrey Miller, Sandra Scheur, and William Schroder, the four student protestors who were killed when Ohio National Guardsmen opened fire on a group of anti-Vietnam War demonstrators on May 4, 1970. The memorial is emblematic of women's activism in the movement against the war, and, by extension, other social protest movements, as well as of the right of women to public dissent.

Oregon

Sacajawea Statue
Washington Park
Portland
This statue depicts the Shoshoni woman who guided Lewis and Clark on their westward expedition. Sculpted by Alice Cooper Hubbard, it was dedicated in 1905 with a speech by Susan B. Anthony.

Pennsylvania

Medical College of Pennsylvania
3300 Henry Avenue
Philadelphia
A bas-relief by sculptor Clara Hill commemorates the female physicians who graduated from the first medical school for women established in the United States. Founded in 1850, the school represents the right of women to enter the medical profession and commemorates the history of separatist education for women. The college became coeducational in 1970.

Rachel Carson Homestead
613 Marion Avenue
Springdale
This farmhouse birthplace of scientist and writer Carson, one of the founders of the environmental movement, is preserved by the Rachel Carson Foundation.

Tennessee

Monument to Women of the Confederacy
War Memorial Building
Nashville
Sculptor Belle Kinney caused an uproar in 1909 when she was selected to design this monument in competition with dozens of male competitors. It was one of the first state-commissioned monuments to a group of women and one of many U.S. memorials dedicated to the women of the Confederacy.

Texas

National Cowgirl Hall of Fame and Western Heritage Center
515 Avenue B
Hereford
This museum honors more than one hundred outstanding women who broke into the male-dominated world of cattle ranching and professional rodeo. This group includes Lucille Mulhall, the "first cowgirl" whose outstanding career in roping contests and Wild West Shows represents the way in which women excelled in this traditionally male domain.

Virginia

Maggie Lena Walker National Historic Site
110 1/2 East Leigh Street
Richmond
This two-story brick home was the residence of African American businesswoman Walker, who was the first woman to establish a successful banking organization in the United States and an important figure in Richmond history. It has been maintained with original furnishings by the National Park Service since 1978.

Washington, D.C.

The Bethune Museum and Archives
1319 Vermont Avenue, NW
The Bethune museum features exhibits on black women's history and is located in the Victorian house that once was Bethune's residence.

Mary McLeod Bethune Memorial
Lincoln Park
13th and East Capitol Streets
This memorial to Bethune, a leading educator and founder of the National Council of Negro Women, was the first statue of an African American woman to be erected in a public park in Washington, D.C.

National Cathedral Association Bay
Washington Cathedral
Wisconsin and Massachusetts Avenues, NW
This bay pays tribute to the role of women in American society. Social reformers and activists Helen Keller and Jane Addams are among those featured through various genres of art, including stained-glass windows, statues, and effigies in the cathedral's vaulted ceiling.

National Woman's Party Headquarters
144 Constitution Avenue, NE
The historic home of the militant wing of the women's movement, this three-story brick house was headquarters to the association begun by Alice Paul in 1913. It was from this building that Paul organized the massive woman suffrage demonstration and parade that took place in Washington, D.C., on March 3, 1913.

Statue of Alice Cogswell
Gallaudet University
800 Florida Avenue, NE
This tribute to women's access to education and the rights of disabled people to educational opportunity depicts Alice Cogswell, a female student admitted to the nation's first school for the deaf. She is portrayed in this sculpture with Thomas Hopkins Gallaudet, the educator for whom the school was named.

Vietnam Women's Memorial
West Potomac Park
This sculpture of four figures by Glenna Goodacre is a tribute to the 265,000 women who served during the Vietnam War, particularly the army nurses who cared for the wounded. The nearby Vietnam Veterans Memorial, designed by Maya Ying Lin, includes among the inscriptions of the names of the dead those of eight women who served as medical personnel in the war.

WEST VIRGINIA

Mother Jones Prison
Center Street
Pratt
This former military prison where labor leader Mother Jones was incarcerated for three months in 1913 is now a private home. Each year, residents of Pratt perform a pageant about the life of Mother Jones using the building as their backdrop.

FOR MORE INFORMATION

Cantor, George. *Historic Landmarks of Black America.* Detroit: Gale Research, 1991. Includes landmarks and sites of significance to African American women.

Dubrow, Gail Lee. "Restoring a Female Presence: New Goals in Historic Preservation." In *Architecture: A Place for Women*, edited by Ellen Perry Berkeley and Matilda McQuaid. Washington, D.C.: Smithsonian Institution Press, 1989. A scholarly discussion of the meaning of women's memorials and landmarks within the context of American women's history and their traditional exclusion from historic preservation.

Hayden, Dolores, Gail Lee Dubrow, and Carolyn Flynn. *The Power of Place.* Los Angeles: Power of Place, 1995. Establishes links between women's issues, ethnic history, public art, and historical preservation in the urban environment.

Huyck, Heather. "Beyond John Wayne: Using Historic Sites to Interpret Women's History." In *Western Women: Their Land, Their Lives*, edited by Lillian Schlissel, Vicki L. Ruiz, and Janice Monk. Albuquerque: University of New Mexico Press, 1988.

Miller, Page Putnam, ed. *Reclaiming the Past: Landmarks of Women's History.* Bloomington: Indiana University Press, 1992. Includes a title essay by Page Putnam Miller and thematic chapters by Barbara J. Howe, Barbara Melosh, Gail Lee Dubrow, Helen Lefkowitz Horowitz, Joan Hoff, Jean R. Soderlund, and Lynn Y. Weiner.

Sherr, Lynn, and Jurate Kazickas. *Susan B. Anthony Slept Here: A Guide to American Women's Landmarks.* New York: Random House/Times Books, 1994. A comprehensive state-by-state guide with excellent background information and anecdotes about the places, statues, and landmarks listed.

Tinling, Marion. *Women Remembered: A Guide to Landmarks of Women's History in the United States.* New York: Greenwood Press, 1986. A comprehensive guide arranged biographically within regions, with an emphasis on the significance of the lives of the women to whom the landmarks pay tribute.

Museums, Archives, and Research Centers

Compiled by Robin Masi

Activist Organizations

National Organization for Women (NOW) Action Center Library
425 13th St., NW, # 1048
Washington, DC 20004
ph.: (202) 347-2279
Subject: Women's issues
Special Collections: The history of NOW; the history of the women's movement
Holdings: 650 books and bound periodical volumes; 18 vertical file drawers of clippings, reports, statistics; 40 videotapes
Subscriptions: 130 journals and other serials; 7 newspapers

African American Women

Bennett College
Thomas F. Holgate Library
Special Collections
Greensboro, NC 27420
ph.: (919) 273-4431
Holdings: 386 books; 2 vertical file drawers

Bethune Museum and Archives for Black Women's History
1318 Vermont Ave., NW
Washington, DC 20005
ph.: (202) 332-1233
Subject: Black women's history

Prudence Crandall Museum
P.O. Box 47
Rtes 14 and 169
Canterbury, CT 06331
ph.: (203) 546-9916
Special Collections: Permanent and changing exhibits about African Americans in pre-Civil War Connecticut
Remarks: The museum is built on the site of New England's first black female academy. The research library is open to the public.

Aging

National Center for Women and Retirement Research
Long Island University
Southampton Campus
Southampton, NY 11968
Subject: Aging

Southwest Institute for Research on Women (SIROW)
University of Arizona
102 Douglass Building
Tucson, AZ 85721
ph.: (602) 621-7338
Subjects: Elderly women; women in the Southwest

Canadian Women

Canadian Advisory Council on the Status of Women
Documentation Centre
Sta. B, Box 1541
Ottawa, ON
Canada K1P 5R5
ph.: (613) 995-8284
Subject: Women
Special Collections: Newsletters of Canadian women's groups; briefs and reports on status of women's issues
Holdings: 500 books; 1,000 reports and briefs; 15 drawers of clippings, manuscripts, and dissertations
Subscriptions: 100 journals and other serials

Employment

Alverno College Research Center on Women
3401 S. 39th St.
Milwaukee, WI 53215
ph.: (414) 671-5400
Subjects: Careers and professions; education; lifestyles; employment; religion; the women's movement
Holdings: 2,300 books; 50 bound periodical volumes; 113 microfiche; 12 vertical file drawers of clippings and pamphlets; 80 audiovisual items
Subscriptions: 104 journals and other serials

Business and Professional Women's Foundation
Marguerite Rawalt Resource Center
2012 Massachusetts Ave., NW
Washington, DC 20036
ph.: (202) 293-1200
Subjects: Careers; comparable worth; displaced homemakers; jobs; the legal status of women; occupational segregation; sexual harassment
Holdings: 5,000 books; 650 dissertations on microfilm; 12,000 vertical file items; archival material
Subscriptions: 113 journals and other serials

Coal Employment Project (CEP) Archives
P.O. Box 3403
Oak Ridge, TN 37830
ph.: (615) 482-3428
Subject: Women in coal mining
Holdings: 100 clippings (1978 to the present); 15 videotapes; 3 audiotapes; 20 photographs

Equal Employment Opportunity Commission (EEOC) Library
2401 E. St., NW
Washington, DC 20506
ph.: (202) 634-6990
Subject: Women

International Archive of Women in Architecture
Virginia Polytechnic Institute and State University
University Libraries
Special Collections Department
P.O. Box 90001
Blacksburg, VA 24062-9001
ph.: (703) 231-9215
Subject: Women in architecture
Special Collections: 107 collections of architectural drawings, photographs, specifications, brochures, and articles, including those of the Association for Women in Architecture, Sena Sekulic, Elsa Leviseur, Susana Torre, and Diana Lee-Smith

Ninety-nines, Inc., Library
Will Rogers World Airport
P.O. Box 59965
Oklahoma City, OK 73159
ph.: (405) 685-7969
Subject: Women in aviation
Special Collections: Archives of the Ninety-nines; records from the Powder Puff Derby
Holdings: 300 books

Ontario Ministry of Labour Library
400 University Ave.
Toronto, ON
Canada M7A 1T7
ph.: (416) 965-1641
Subject: Women

FEMINISM

Contemporary Culture Collection
Temple University
Central Library System
13th and Berks Sts.
Philadelphia, PA 19122
ph.: (215) 787-8667
Subject: Feminism
Special Collections: Early second-wave feminist publications; literary chapbooks

Southern California Library for Social Studies and Research
6120 S. Vermont Ave.
Los Angeles, CA 90044
ph.: (213) 759-6063
Subject: The women's movement

Washington Area Women's Center Feminist Library and Archives
1519 P St., NW
Washington, DC 20005
ph.: (202) 347-5078
Subjects: Feminism; lesbianism; sexism
Special Collection: Lesbian Heritage Archives (1960 to the present)
Holdings: 1,123 books; oral histories and Feminist Radio Network tapes

Women's Center
California State University, Northridge
18111 Nordhoff
Northridge, CA 91330
ph.: (818) 885-2780
Subjects: Child development; employment and career development for women; feminism; parenting; psychology; sociology; women in history
Holdings: 1,000 books; 700 bound periodical volumes; 500 reports and clippings

Women's Center of Southeastern Connecticut
120 Broad St.
P.O. Box 572
New London, CT 06320
ph.: (203) 447-0366
Subjects: Feminism; health; violence against women; women's issues
Holdings: 500 books; 25 bound periodical volumes; vertical files
Subscriptions: 15 journals and other serials

Women's Movement Archives
Women's Educational Center, Inc.
46 Pleasant St.
Cambridge, MA 02139
ph.: (617) 354-8807
Special Collections: Houses archives on the following Boston-area women's organizations: Bread & Roses (1969-1971), Female Liberation (1970-1974), Cell 16 (1968-1975), and The Women's Center (1971 to the present)

Women's Resource and Action Center
Sojourner Truth Women's Resource Library
130 N. Madison
Iowa City, IA 52242
ph.: (319) 353-6265
Subject: Feminism
Special Collection: Complete holdings of *Ain't I a Woman*, a feminist periodical published from 1970 to 1973
Holdings: 700 books
Subscriptions: 25 journals and other serials

Women's Studies Pamphlet Collection
University of Maryland, College Park
McKeldin Library
Reference Department
College Park, MD 20742
ph.: (301) 454-5704
Subjects: Feminism; the women's movement; women's studies
Holdings: 100 items

GENERAL ISSUES

American Association of University Women Educational Foundation
Library and Archives
111 16th St., NW
Washington, DC 20036
ph.: (202) 785-7763

Subjects: Education; the status of women; women's activities and achievements

Holdings: Archival material relating to the history and formation of the AAUW; work done on research education topics; biennial reports for the association (1933 to the present) and the foundation (1958 to the present); 158 microfilm reels of archival materials (1881-1976)

Birdie Goldsmith Ast Resource Collection
Barnard College Women's Center
100 Barnard Hall
3001 Broadway
New York, NY 10027
ph.: (212) 280-2067

Subjects: Education; employment; health; the legal status of women; sex roles and sex differences; violence and sexual exploitation; the women's movement

Holdings: 1,000 volumes; 5,000 journal articles, reports, clippings, fact sheets, pamphlets, conference proceedings, handbooks, directories, and special issues of journals

Subscriptions: 80 periodicals, newspapers, and newsletters

Birmingham Southern College
Charles Andrew Ruth Learning Center and Library
Special Collections
800 8th Ave., W
Birmingham, AL 35254
ph.: (205) 328-5250

Special Collection: The Branscomb Collection for, by, and About Women (189 volumes)

Boston University's Women's Center
775 Commonwealth Ave., North Tower
Boston, MA 02216
ph.: (617) 353-4240

Subjects: Fiction; health; poetry; sociology; women's studies

Holdings: 150 books; 300 unbound periodicals; 200 issues of *Ms.* magazine from the 1970's; clippings and archives

Subscriptions: 16 journals and other serials

Centennial College of Applied Arts and Technology
Warden Woods Campus Resource Centre
Sta. A, P.O. Box 631
Scarborough, ON
Canada M1K 5E9
ph.: (416) 694-3241

Subject: Women's studies

Center for Women's Studies and Services Library
908 E St.
San Diego, CA 92101
ph.: (714) 233-8984

Subjects: Biographies; fiction; nonsexist children's literature; radical movements; the women's movement

Special Collection: Feminist newspapers (1969 to the present)

Holdings: 200 books

Chicago Public Library
Central Library
400 N. Franklin St.
Chicago, IL 60602
ph.: (312) 269-2900

Subjects: Women; women's organizations

Special Collection: Mrs. Harlan Ward Cooley Papers

Duke-UNC Center for Research on Women
University of North Carolina
03 Caldwell Hall
CB 3135
Chapel Hill, NC 27599-3135
ph.: (919) 684-6641

Subject: Women's studies

Duke University
Special Collections Department and Library
344 Perkins Library
Durham, NC 27706
ph.: (919) 684-3372

Subject: Women's studies

Ella Strong Denison Library
Scripps College
Claremont, CA 91711
ph.: (909) 621-8000

Subject: Women

Hartford Feminist Library
350 Farmington Ave.
Hartford, CT 06105
ph.: (203) 232-7393

Subjects: Fiction; health; literature; politics

Holdings: 900 books

Helen Keller Archives
American Foundation for the Blind
15 W. 16th St.
New York, NY 10011
ph.: (212) 620-2157

Subjects: Factory work by women and children; labor movements; Planned Parenthood; pacifism; the suffrage movement; visual- and hearing-impaired persons

Special Collections: The Helen Keller, Anne Sullivan Macy, John Albert Macy, and Polly Thomson Collections

Know, Inc.
P.O. Box 86031
Pittsburgh, PA 15221
ph.: (412) 241-4844

Subject: Feminist literature

Holdings: 40 file drawers of feminist publications

Los Angeles Public Library
Social Science Department
630 W. Fifth St.
Los Angeles, CA 90071
ph.: (213) 626-7461

Subject: The women's movement

Massachusetts Institute of Technology (MIT)
Humanities Library
Room 14S-200
Cambridge, MA 02139
ph.: (617) 253-5683

Subject: Women's studies

May Bonfils Stanton Library
Loretto Heights College
3001 S. Federal Blvd.
Denver, CO 80236
ph.: (303) 936-8441
Subject: The role of women in today's world

Montreal Young Women's Christian Association Library
1355 Dorchester Blvd., W
Montreal, PQ
Canada H3G 1T3
ph.: (514) 866-9941
Subjects: The roles of women in society (with an emphasis on education and employment); social group work

National Women's Christian Temperance Union
Frances E. Willard Memorial Library
1730 Chicago Ave.
Evanston, IL 60201
ph.: (312) 864-1396
Subject: The history of the women's movement

Newark Public Library
Social Science Division
5 Washington St.
P.O. Box 630
Newark, NJ 07101-0630
ph.: (201) 733-7782
Subject: Women's studies

Northeast Minnesota Historical Center
Library 375
University of Minnesota, Duluth
Duluth, MN 55812
ph.: (218) 726-8526
Subject: Women's studies

Southern Illinois University at Carbondale
Morris Library
Carbondale, IL 62901
ph.: (618) 453-2818
Subject: Women's studies

Swarthmore College Friends Historical Library
500 College Ave.
Swarthmore, PA 19081-1399
ph.: (215) 328-8496
Subjects: Quakers; women's rights
Special Collection: Lucretia Mott manuscripts

Wesleyan Women's Coalition Library
281 High St.
Wesleyan Station, Box WW
Middletown, CT 06457
ph.: (203) 347-9411
Subjects: Fiction; health; history; poetry; sports
Holdings: 300 books; 3 drawers of subject files; directories
Subscriptions: 15 journals and other serials

Western Historical Manuscript Collection/State Historical Society of Missouri
University of Missouri
23 Ellis Library
Columbia, MO 65201
ph.: (314) 882-6028
Subject: Women

Women's Action Alliance, Inc., Library
370 Lexington Ave.
New York, NY 10017
ph.: (212) 532-8330
Subjects: Child care; divorce; family; marriage; sex discrimination; women
Special Collection: A card file of women's organizations and their programs
Holdings: 1,500 books; 40 vertical file drawers
Subscriptions: 250 journals and other serials

Women's Center
University of California, Davis
Women's Resources and Research Center Library
Davis, CA 95616
ph.: (916) 752-3372
Subjects: Women's issues, concerns, and research
Special Collection: Native and pioneer women in Yolo and Solano counties, California, containing oral history collections (28 tapes and 2 photograph albums)
Holdings: 1,600 books; 4,800 vertical file materials; 375 tapes
Subscriptions: 65 journals and other serials

Women's Center
University of Missouri, St. Louis
107A Benton Hall
8001 Natural Bridge Rd.
St. Louis, MO 63121
ph.: (314) 553-5380
Subject: Medicine; politics; psychology; sex roles
Holdings: 450 books; 500 unbound periodicals; 8 vertical file drawers of clippings and reports

Women's Center Library
Montclair State College
Upper Montclair, NJ 07043
ph.: (201) 893-5106
Subjects: Career information; health; the legal rights of women; literature
Holdings: 550 books; 5 vertical file drawers of clippings

Women's Center Library
Western Michigan University
A-331 Ellsworth Hall
Kalamazoo, MI 49008
ph.: (616) 387-2990
Subjects: Careers; discrimination; displaced homemakers; equal pay for equal work; the financial status of women; health; nontraditional jobs
Special Collections: A local history of women's groups and causes; a local history of women in education

Women's Studies Library
Ohio State University
220 Main Library
1858 Neil Ave. Mall
Columbus, OH 43210
ph.: (614) 292-3035
Subject: Women's studies
Holdings: 15,000 volumes; 2,500 pamphlets and newsletters; and 50 microform collections

Working Women's Institute
593 Park Ave.
New York, NY 10003
ph.: (212) 838-4420
Subjects: Sexual discrimination; sexual harassment; unions; violence against women; the women's movement; working women
Holdings: 100 books; 15 bound periodical volumes; 50 newsletters; clippings and reprints; legal papers
Subscriptions: 21 journals and other serials

Young Women's Christian Association
National Board Library
135 W. 50th St.
New York, NY 10020
ph.: (212) 753-4700
Subjects: Civil rights; health; racism; sexism; women
Special Collection: Woman's Press publications from 1918 to 1952 (2,500 volumes)
Holdings: 10,000 books; 25 vertical file drawers of subject files, clippings, pamphlets, reports, and catalogs
Subscriptions: 175 journals and other serials

GOVERNMENT

Center for the American Woman and Politics Library
Eagleton Institute, Rutgers University
Wood Lawn, Neilson Campus
New Brunswick, NJ 08901
ph.: (201) 932-9384
Subjects: Women in American politics and government
Holdings: 500 books; 2,000 papers, pamphlets, and clippings
Subscriptions: 50 journals and other serials

Ellis County Historical Society Archives
100 W. 7th St.
Hays, KS 67601
ph.: (913) 628-2624
Special Collection: Miscellaneous papers of former U.S. Congresswoman Kathryn O'Loughlin McCarthy

HEALTH

Alliant Health System Library/Media Services
P.O. Box 35070
Louisville, KY 40232
ph.: (502) 629-8125
Subject: Health

Ann May School of Nursing Library and Media Center
Jersey Shore Medical Center
1945 Rte. 33
Neptune, NJ 07754
ph.: (201) 776-4195
Subject: Health
Special Collection: National League for Nurses' and American Nursing Association publications

Boston Women's Health Book Collective
240 S. Elm St., 3d Floor
Somerville, MA 02144
ph.: (617) 625-0271
Subject: Health
Holdings: Books, periodicals, and clippings

Cornell Medical Center, Medical Archives
New York Hospital
1300 York Ave.
New York, NY 10021
ph.: (212) 746-6072
Subject: Health
Special Collections: Manhattan Maternity and Dispensary records (1905-1939); Nursery for the Children of Poor Women and Nursery and Child's Hospital records (1854-1910); New York Asylum for Lying-In Women records (1823-1899); Women's Medical Association of New York City records (1902 to the present); American Medical Women's Association archives (1915 to the present)

George Brown School of Social Work
Washington University
Library and Learning Resources Center
Campus Box 1196
St. Louis, MO 63130
ph.: (314) 935-6633
Subject: Women's issues

Henry A. Murray Research Center
Radcliffe College
10 Garden St.
Cambridge, MA 02138
ph.: (617) 495-8140
Subjects: Developmental issues; life patterns; mental and physical health; self-esteem; sex roles; work and family life
Special Collections: Archival materials dealing with data sets of raw and computer-accessible social science research studies
Holdings: 95 data sets; 50 books; 300 boxes of raw data; 35 dissertations; 150 unpublished reports; 100 boxes of computer data cards; 25 computer magnetic tapes

Medical College of Pennsylvania Archives and Special Collections on Women in Medicine
3300 Henry Ave.
Philadelphia, PA 19129
ph.: (215) 842-7124
Subjects: Education; health care for women; women in medicine
Special Collections: Women in Medicine Collection; Black Women Physicians Collection; Asian American Women Physicians Project; Oral History Project; American

Women's Hospitals records; Medical Women's International Association records

HISPANIC WOMEN

National Association of Cuban-American Women of the U.S.A.
2119 S. Webster
Ft. Wayne, IN 46802
ph.: (219) 745-5421
Subjects: Hispanic and minority women
Holdings: 2,000 volumes

HISTORY

Arthur and Elizabeth Schlesinger Library on the History of Women in America
Radcliffe College
10 Garden St.
Cambridge, MA 02138
ph.: (617) 495-8647
Subjects: Education; family; the history of American women; labor; law; medicine; organizations; social service; the suffrage movement
Special Collections: Beecher-Stowe, Blackwell Family, Charlotte Perkins Gilman, Somerville-Howorth, Dr. Martha May Eliot, and Jeannette Rankin Collections; papers on the National Organization for Women (NOW) and women's rights; the Black Women Oral History Project; cookbooks; etiquette books; a picture collection (40,000 items)
Holdings: 23,000 books and bound periodical volumes; 400 major collections of papers on individual American women, families, and women's organizations; 1,800 reels of microfilm; 800 magnetic tapes; 40 vertical file drawers
Subscriptions: 310 journals and other serials

Boston Public Library Rare Books and Manuscripts
Copley Square
P.O. Box 286
Boston, MA 02117
ph.: (617) 536-5400
Special Collection: Galatea Collection of the History of Women (5,200 volumes)

Bowling Green State University Center for Archival Collections
Library, 5th Floor
Bowling Green, OH 43403-0175
ph.: (419) 372-2411
Subject: Women's history

Cheney Cowles Museum
Eastern Washington State Historical Society
Research Library and Special Collections
W. 2316 1st Ave.
Spokane, WA 99204
ph.: (509) 456-3931
Subject: Women's history

Chicago Historical Society Library and Archives
Clark St. at North Ave.
Chicago, IL 60614
ph.: (312) 642-4600
Subjects: Biographies of leading Chicago women; professions and occupations; social service; the suffrage and temperance movements; women's history; women's rights; women's societies and clubs
Special Collections: Papers of the Board of Lady Managers of the World's Columbian Exposition (1893); archives of the Chicago Women's Liberation Union

Christine Dunlap Farnham Archives
Brown University
John Hay Library
Box A
Providence, RI 02912
ph.: (401) 863-2148
Subjects: Higher education; the history of Brown alumnae; the history of women at Brown University and Pembroke College; literature; social history; women in Rhode Island
Holdings: Manuscripts; organizational records; photographs; correspondence, memorabilia, films, and scrapbooks

Dana Porter Arts Library
University of Waterloo
Waterloo, ON
Canada N2L 3G1
ph.: (519) 885-1211
Special Collection: Rare materials from the Lady Aberdeen Library of the History of Women

Emily Taylor Women's Resource Center
University of Kansas
218 Strong Hall
Lawrence, KS 66045
ph.: (913) 841-7611
Subjects: Career planning; education; health; law; literature; minorities; politics; sexuality; women's history
Special Collections: Woman's World Encyclopedia (39 volumes); History of Woman Suffrage (6 volumes)
Holdings: 1,000 books; 900 bound periodical volumes; 152 career planning resources; 144 topical notebooks; 125 film, tape, and sound recordings; 30 financial aid sources
Subscriptions: 43 journals and other serials

Emory University
Woodruff Library
Special Collections Department
Atlanta, GA 30322
ph.: (404) 329-6887
Special Collection: Manuscript Sources for Women's History, a descriptive list of holdings in the special collections department (revised 1978)

Friends Historical Library Peace Collection
Swarthmore College
McCabe Library
Swarthmore, PA 19081
ph.: (215) 447-7557
Subjects: Peace and justice

Special Collections: Women's International League for Peace and Freedom (WILPF); Women's Strike for Peace

Library of Congress Public Service and Collections
Management II
Microform Reading Room
10 First St., SE
Washington, DC 20540
Subjects: Literature; women's history

Lucy Stone Center
University of Wisconsin, Green Bay
Resource Library
LC 750
Green Bay, WI 54302
ph.: (414) 465-2136
Subjects: Biography; resources available to women; women's history; the women's movement
Holdings: 200 books; 50 bound periodical volumes; information files
Subscriptions: 15 journals and other serials

Mills College
F. W. Olin Library
Special Collections Department
5000 MacArthur Blvd.
Oakland, CA 94613
ph.: (510) 430-2047
Subject: Women's history

National Women's History Collection
Smithsonian Institution
Museum of American History
Division of Political History
Washington, DC 20560
ph.: (202) 357-2008
Subject: Women in politics and society
Special Collection: National American Women Suffrage Association (NAWSA) materials
Holdings: Includes material objects and political images of women

National Women's History Project
7738 Bell Rd.
Windsor, CA 95492-8518
ph.: (707) 838-6000
Subjects: Women's history (primarily in the United States)
Holdings: 4,000 books; 12 vertical file drawers of clippings; photographs of individuals and topics
Remarks: This information and referral resource can be visited by appointment only.

New York Public Library
Microforms Division
Fifth Ave. and 42d St.
New York, NY 10018
ph.: (212) 930-0838
Special Collection: A women's history collection

Oberlin College Library Archives
420 Mudd Center
Oberlin, OH 44074-1532
ph.: (216) 775-8014
Subject: Nineteenth century women's history

Pioneer Woman Museum
701 Monument
Ponca City, OK 74604
ph.: (405) 765-6108
Special Collections: Collections of artifacts from pioneer homes

Princeton University Rare Books and Special Collections
Firestone Library
Princeton, NJ 08544
ph.: (609) 258-3184
Subject: Women's history

Rockefeller University
Rockefeller Archive Center
15 Dayton Ave.
Pocantico Hills
North Tarrytown, NY 10591
ph.: (914) 631-4505
Subject: Women's history

Sangamon State University
Oral History Office Library
Brookens Library
Springfield, IL 62708
ph.: (217) 786-6521
Subject: Women's history

Seneca Falls Historical Society Library
55 Cayuga St.
Seneca Falls, NY 13148
ph.: (315) 568-8412
Special Collection: Women's Rights Collection (1848 to the present)

Simmons College Archives
300 The Fenway
Boston, MA 02115
ph.: (617) 738-3141
Subject: Women's history

Sophia Smith Collection
Smith College
Women's History Archive
Northampton, MA 01063
ph.: (413) 584-2700
Subjects: Birth control; intellectual and social history, with a contemporary and worldwide emphasis; professions; social reform; the suffrage movement; women's rights
Special Collections: 149 major collections, including those on Margaret Sanger (200 document boxes); suffragist and artist Blanche Ames (120 document boxes); the Hale Family (150 document boxes); Clara Barton (4 document boxes); the Garrison Family (extensive); and Ellen Gates Starr (19 document boxes)
Holdings: 85,000 books; 2,100 linear feet of document boxes
Subscriptions: 62 journals and other serials

State University of New York at Buffalo University Archives
420 Capen Hall
Buffalo, NY 14260
ph.: (716) 636-2916
Subject: Women's history

Staten Island Institute of Arts and Sciences
Archives and Library
75 Stuyvesant Pl.
Staten Island, NY 10301
ph.: (718) 727-1135
Subject: Women's history

Strong Museum
One Manhattan Square
Rochester, NY 14607
ph.: (716) 263-2700
Subject: Nineteenth century women in the home

Texas Woman's University
Braillcy Memorial Library
Special Collections
TWU Station, Box 23715
Denton, TX 76204
ph.: (817) 566-6415
Subjects: Biography; cookery; history; literature
Special Collections: Woman's Collection (14,200 books and bound periodical volumes, including the Madeleine Henrey and the LaVerne Harrell Clark Collections); Cookbook and Menu Collection (6,500 books and bound periodical items and 1,027 menus, including the Julie Bennell and the Margaret Scruggs Cookbook Collections); a play collection (1,800 books); the Genevieve Dixon Collection (1,051 books); university archives (7,500 items)
Holdings: 35,000 books and bound periodical volumes; 28,400 microforms; 450 media items

University of North Dakota
Chester Fritz Library
Department of Special Collections
Grand Forks, ND 58202
ph.: (701) 777-4625
Subject: Women's history

University of Rochester
Government Documents and Microtext Center
Rush Rhees Library
Rochester, NY 14627
ph.: (716) 275-4484
Subject: Women's history

Western Historical Manuscript Collection/State Historical Society of Missouri
University of Missouri, St. Louis
Thomas Jefferson Library
8001 Natural Bridge Rd.
St. Louis, MO 63121
ph.: (314) 453-5143
Subject: Women
Special Collections: League of Women Voters of Missouri (59 boxes); Women's Historical Collections

Woman's Collection
College of St. Catherine
2004 Randolph Ave.
St. Paul, MN 55105
ph.: (612) 690-6648
Subjects: Education; history; the psychological liberation of women; sociological and economic studies on women published in the early twentieth century; the status of women
Special Collections: Herstory, a microfilm collection of 300 women's journals, newspapers, and newsletters from 1956 to 1971 (23 reels); microfiche of the U.S. Department of Labor, Women's Bureau Bulletin (1918-1954)
Holdings: 3,850 books; 20 bound periodical volumes; 8 vertical file drawers of pamphlets and clippings

Woman's Collection
University of North Carolina, Greensboro
Jackson Library
Special Collections
Greensboro, NC 27412
ph.: (919) 379-5246
Subjects: Authors; child rearing and family life; education; history; manners and morals; suffrage
Special Collections: Women in the Seventeenth Through Nineteenth Centuries
Holdings: 4,000 books; 254 bound periodical volumes

Women's Heritage Museum
1509 Portola Ave.
Palo Alto, CA 94306
ph.: (415) 321-5260
Special Collection: Maintains a "Museum-Without-Walls" to increase awareness of global women's history

Women's History Museum
Box 209
West Liberty, WV 26074
ph.: (304) 335-7159
Special Collection: A mobile museum featuring seven women from U.S. history, with performances about each woman

Women's History Research Center, Inc.
Women's History Library
2325 Oak St.
Berkeley, CA 94708
ph.: (510) 548-1770
Subjects: Artists; black and Third World women; children; films by and/or about women; Soviet women; women's health and mental health
Special Collections: International Women's History Archive (850 titles on microfilm on health and law); 90 reels of microfilm of women's periodicals in Herstory Collection

INTERNATIONAL ISSUES

Library of Social Alternatives
Salem State College
Salem, MA 01970
ph.: (508) 741-6000
Subjects: Alternative lifestyles; ecology; gay men and lesbians; health care; social change; Third World countries; women

Population Council Library
1 Dag Hammarskjold Plaza
New York, NY 10017
ph.: (212) 644-1620
Subjects: Contraception; demographics; economic, social, and agricultural development; family planning; population; public health; statistics

JEWISH WOMEN

Hadassah, the Women's Zionist Organization of America
50 W. 58th St.
New York, NY 10019
ph.: (212) 355-7900
Holdings: 4,000 volumes on Judaism and Zionism

LESBIANISM

Alternative Press Center Library
Box 7229
Baltimore, MD 21218
ph.: (301) 243-2471
Subjects: Homosexuality; women's rights

Library of Social Alternatives
Salem State College
Salem, MA 01970
ph.: (508) 741-6000
Subjects: Alternative lifestyles; ecology; gay men and lesbians; health care; social change; Third World countries; women

LITERATURE

Lambada, Inc.
Barnes Library
516 S. 27th St.
Birmingham, AL 35233
ph.: (205) 326-8600
Subject: Gay and lesbian literature
Special Collections: Alabama Gay Archives; Lady B. J. Memorial Collection (gay and lesbian books and records from the entertainment world)

Library of Congress Public Service and Collections
Management II
Microform Reading Room
10 First St., SE
Washington, DC 20540
Subjects: Literature; women's history

Naiad Press, Inc.
Gay and Lesbian Archives
Box 10543
Tallahassee, FL 32302
ph.: (904) 539-5965
Subject: Lesbian, gay, and feminist literature

National League of American Pen Women
1300 17th St., NW
Washington DC, 20036
ph.: (202) 785-1997
Subjects: Artists; composers; writers
Holdings: 3,000 books; a computerized database

Oakland University Library
Kresge Library
Special Collections and Archives
Rochester, MI 48063
ph.: (313) 377-2492
Special Collection: Hicks Collection of Women in Literature of the Seventeenth and Eighteenth Centuries

Pforzheimer Foundation, Inc.
Carl H. Pforzheimer Library
41 E. 42d St., Room 815
New York, NY 10017
ph.: (212) 697-7217
Subject: Female writers (1790-1840)

Research in Women's Literature
University of Tulsa
600 S. College
Tulsa, OK 74104
ph.: (918) 631-2503
Subject: Literature, with an emphasis on literary history, criticism, and bibliography

Women Detectives Fiction Collection
University of North Carolina, Greensboro
Jackson Library
Special Collections
Greensboro, NC 27412
ph.: (919) 379-5246
Subject: Female detectives in American fiction (1890 to the present)
Holdings: 300 books

Women Writers Archive
Sonoma State University
Ruben Salazar Library
Special Collections
Rohnert Park, CA 94928
ph.: (707) 664-2861
Subject: Female writers
Holdings: Articles, student papers, and clippings on several hundred female writers

MILITARY SERVICE

National Women's Military Museum
c/o Isobel Van Lom
P.O. Box 68687
Portland, OR 97268
ph.: (503) 292-4046
Special Collection: Exhibits honoring women from all branches of the U.S. military

Music

American Women Composers
1690 36th St., NW
Suite 409
Washington, DC 20007
ph.: (202) 342-8179
Subjects: Composers; musicologists; performers
Holdings: 3,000 scores of women's music and biological archives

Library of Congress Public Service and Collections
Management I
Music Division
10 First St., SE
Washington, DC 20540
Subject: Female composers

Women's Music Archives
208 Wildflower Lane
Fairfield, CT 06430
ph.: (203) 255-1348
Subject: Women's music
Special Collections: Collects, preserves, and shares materials relating to women's music (records, tapes, songbooks, periodicals, concert programs, and posters); also maintains and collects all varieties of women's music memorabilia

Regional Issues

California Historical Society
Schubert Hall Library
2099 Pacific Ave.
San Francisco, CA 94109
ph.: (415) 567-1848
Subject: Women in California

Emory University
Woodruff Library
Special Collections Department
Atlanta, GA 30322
ph.: (404) 329-6887
Subject: Southern Women

Kentucky Women's Heritage Museum
108 Paddock Dr.
Nicholasville, KY 40356
Special Collection: A permanent, visible display honoring and recognizing the achievements of Kentucky women

Linn-Henley Library for Southern Historical Research
Birmingham Public and Jefferson County Free Library
Department of Archives and Manuscripts
2100 Park Pl.
Birmingham, AL 35203
ph.: (205) 226-3645
Subject: Women's history
Special Collection: Southern Women's Archives

Memphis State University Center for Research on Women
Clement Hall 339
Memphis, TN 38152
ph.: (901) 678-2770
Subjects: Southern women; women of color; working class women in the South

Midwest Women's Historical Collection
University of Illinois at Chicago
University Library
Box 8198
801 N. Morgan
Chicago, IL 60680
ph.: (312) 996-2742
Subject: Nineteenth and twentieth century Chicago and Midwestern women active in literature, education, social welfare and social work, design, the arts, health sciences, politics and social reform
Special Collections: The papers of Emma Goldman; records of the Young Women's Christian Association (YWCA) of Metropolitan Chicago, the League of Women Voters of Chicago, the Chicago Urban League, and the Women's Advertising Club of Chicago; the Jane Addams Memorial Collection; the Gutter Collection of Chiganoana; Swallow Press Archives; the Society of Midland Authors Collection

University of Nevada, Reno
University Library
Special Collections Department and University Archives
Reno, NV 89557
ph.: (702) 784-6538
Subjects: Women in the trans-Mississippi West; women in the West

Religion

Lutheran Deaconess Association
Deaconess Hall Library
Deaconess Hall, E. Union St.
Valparaiso, IN 46383
ph.: (219) 464-5033
Subject: Women in the Lutheran church

Mount St. Mary Research Center
Sisters of St. Mary of Namur
3756 Delaware Ave.
Kenmore, NY 14217
ph.: (716) 875-4705
Subject: The history of the Sisters of St. Mary

Multnomah School of the Bible
John and Mary Mitchell Library
8435 NE Glisan St.
Portland, OR 97220
ph.: (503) 255-0332
Subject: Women's ministries

National Sisters Vocation Conference Library
1307 S. Wabash Ave.
Chicago, IL 60605
ph.: (312) 939-6180
Subject: Church-related careers for women

Special Collections: Brochures that are specific to the various religious communities of women in the United States
Holdings: 8 vertical file drawers of pamphlets; 50 statistical and research studies
Subscriptions: 13 journals and other serials

St. Walburg Convent of Benedictine Sisters of Covington, Kentucky, Archives
2500 Amsterdam Rd.
Covington, KY 41016
ph.: (606) 331-6771
Subject: The history of the Benedictine Sisters of Covington
Holdings: 150 square feet of archival material, peculiar to religious women
Subscriptions: 12 newspapers

SUFFRAGE

Austin-Travis County Collection
Austin Public Library
810 Guadalupe
Austin, TX 78701
ph.: (512) 472-5433
Subject: The suffrage movement

Dayton and Montgomery County Public Library
215 E. Third St.
Dayton, OH 45402-2103
ph.: (513) 227-9500
Subject: The suffrage movement

Frederick Douglass National Historic Site Library
1411 W. St., SE
Washington, DC 20020
ph.: (202) 426-5962
Subject: The suffrage movement
Special Collections: A History of Women's Suffrage; Executive Documents, 1820-1895

Missouri Historical Society
Archives and Manuscripts
Jefferson Memorial Building
Forest Park
St. Louis, MO 63112
ph.: (314) 361-1424
Subject: The suffrage movement

Southern Regional Council, Inc.
Reference Library
60 Walton St., NW, 2d Floor
Atlanta, GA 30303-2199
ph.: (404) 522-8764
Subject: The suffrage movement

Stowe-Day Foundation Library
77 Forest St.
Hartford, CT 06105
ph.: (203) 728-5507
Subject: The suffrage movement
Special Collections: The suffrage papers of Isabella Beecher Hooker; the Katharine S. Day Collection; the literary manuscripts of Harriet Beecher Stowe

Western Historical Manuscript Collection/State Historical Society of Missouri
University of Missouri, St. Louis
Thomas Jefferson Library
8001 Natural Bridge Rd.
St. Louis, MO 63121
ph.: (314) 453-5143
Special Collections: League of Women Voters of Missouri (59 boxes); Women's Historical Collections

THIRD WORLD WOMEN

New Transcentury Foundation
Secretariat for Women in Development
Documentation Center
1789 Columbia Rd., NW
Washington, DC 20009
ph.: (202) 328-4400
Subject: Culture and society; developing countries; law; politics; rural development; socioeconomics
Holdings: 1,300 documents
Subscriptions: 100 journals and other serials

VIOLENCE AGAINST WOMEN

Center for Women Policy Studies
Family Violence Project Library
2000 P St., NW
Suite 508
Washington, DC 20036
ph.: (202) 872-1770
Subjects: Battered women; child sexual abuse; family violence; spouse abuse

VISUAL ART

Ade Bethune Collection
College of St. Catherine Library
2004 Randolph Ave.
St. Paul, MN 55105
ph.: (612) 690-6650
Subjects: Ade Bethune and other female artists

California Institute of the Arts Library
24700 McBean Pkwy.
Valencia, CA 91355
ph.: (805) 255-1050
Special Collection: Slide Collection of Women Artists

National Museum of Women in the Arts
Museum, Library, and Research Center
1250 New York Ave.
Washington, DC 20037
ph.: (202) 783-5000
Subject: Female artists
Special Collections: The personal library of Irene Rice Pereira; Archives of the International Conference of Women Artists in Copenhagen

Holdings: 6,500 books and exhibition catalogues; 50 subscription periodicals; more than 13,000 files on female artists of all periods and nationalities

Rutgers University Special Collections and Archives
Alexander Library
College Ave. and Huntington St.
New Brunswick, NJ 08903
ph.: (908) 932-7006
Subject: Visual arts
Special Collections: The records of *SIGNS* and the Women's Caucus for Art

Southwestern University Center for Texas Women in the Arts
Georgetown, TX 78626
ph.: (512) 863-6511
Subject: Texas women in the visual and performing arts

Women Artists Archive
Sonoma State University
Ruben Salazar Library
Special Collections
Rohnert Park, CA 94928
ph.: (707) 664-2861
Subject: Female artists from Middle Ages to the present
Holdings: 15 vertical file drawers; 5,000 slides; 6 slide sets; a visual image database of research collection

Women Artists Library
Fulham Palace, Bishops Ave.
London, England SW6 6EA
ph.: (071) 731-7618
Subject: Female artists
Special Collections: A Women of Colour/Black Women Artists index; the Society of Women Artists archive; the Women's International Art Club (1900-1978); archival photographs from Dame Laura Knight's private collection
Holdings: 24,000 slides; black and white print section; audiovisual collection; cuttings

Women Artists News Archives
Grand Central Station
New York, NY 10163
ph.: (212) 666-6990
Holdings: 24 vertical file drawers of archival material on women in the arts, primarily from the 1970's to present
Subscriptions: 25 journals and other serials
Remarks: Publishes *Women Artists News* (bimonthly), *Guide to Women's Art Organizations* (biennial), and *Voices of Women* (criticism, poetry, graphics)

WITCHCRAFT

University of Nevada, Reno
University Library
Special Collections Department and University Archives
Reno, NV 89557
ph.: (702) 784-6538
Subject: Witchcraft

WOMEN OF COLOR

Memphis State University Center for Research on Women
Clement Hall 339
Memphis, TN 38152
ph.: (901) 678-2770
Subjects: Southern women; women of color; working class women in the South

Significant Organizations and Societies

Compiled by Glenn Ellen Starr

This list describes some of the most important women's organizations. Government agencies are not included. The following abbreviations denote directories and handbooks in which fuller descriptions of each organization can be found:

EA	*Encyclopedia of Associations*. Detroit: Gale Research, 1995.
EWAW	*Encyclopedia of Women's Associations Worldwide*. Edited by Jacqueline K. Barrett. London: Gale Research International, 1993.
RRWI	*Ready Reference: Women's Issues*
RW	*Resourceful Woman*. By Shawn Brennan. Detroit: Visible Ink, 1994.
WDR	*The Women's Desk Reference*. By Irene Franck. New York: Viking Press, 1993.
WID	*Women's Information Directory*. Edited by Shawn Brennan. Detroit: Gale Research, 1993.

Aging

American Association of Retired Persons (AARP)
601 E St., NW
Washington, DC 20049
ph.: (202) 434-2277
Date founded: 1958
Works for programs and policies that enhance conditions for midlife and older women. Concerns include health care, consumer decisions, pension benefits, and Social Security.
EA RW WDR WID

Gray Panthers
2025 Pennsylvania Ave., NW
Suite 821
Washington, DC 20006
ph.: (202) 466-3132
Date founded: around 1970
Nonprofit group with members of all ages who combat ageism and work for universal health care, justice, and world peace. Has opposed forced retirement, nursing home abuse, and increased military spending at the expense of Medicare and Medicaid.
EA RRWI RW

Older Women's League (OWL)
666 11th St., NW
Suite 700
Washington, DC 20001
ph.: (202) 783-6686
Date founded: 1980
Strives to enhance the status and image of women midlife or older. Concerns include workplace discrimination, Social Security, universal health care, support of family caregivers, and individual control of quality-of-life decisions.
EA EWAW RRWI WDR WID

Arts

National Museum of Women in the Arts
1250 New York Ave.
Washington, DC 20037
ph.: (202) 783-5000
Date founded: 1981
Owns more than 1,500 works, from the Renaissance to the twentieth century, by female artists, including prints, drawings, paintings, and sculptures. Library contains more than 6,000 volumes and an extensive vertical file on female artists.
EA RW WID

Women in Film
6464 Sunset Blvd.
Suite 530
Hollywood, CA 90028
ph.: (213) 463-6040
Date founded: 1973
Fosters women working in film and television and finances women's education, internship, or film projects through its foundation.
EA EWAW RW WID

Women in the Arts Foundation
1175 York Ave., Apt. 2G
New York, NY 10021
ph.: (212) 751-1915
Date founded: 1971
Opposes bias toward female artists, especially their omission from galleries and museums. Handles exhibitions of female artists and arranges competitions.
EA EWAW RW

Business, Economics, and Occupations

Catalyst
250 Park Avenue South
New York, NY 10003
ph.: (212) 777-8900
Date founded: 1962
Provides corporate consultation services and sponsors research on issues concerning female employees. Manages an information center.
EA EWAW RRWI RW WDR WID

Families and Work Institute
330 Seventh Ave.
New York, NY 10001
ph.: (212) 465-2044
Date founded: 1989
Helps people maintain harmony between work and family through research, public policy work, and educational programs. Offers management training and maintains a clearinghouse on work and the family.
EA WDR

National Association of Female Executives (NAFE)
127 West 24th St., 4th Floor
New York, NY 10011-1914
ph.: (212) 645-0770 or (800) 669-1002
Date founded: 1972
Assists women in business careers through career development seminars, loans by mail, résumé assistance, and support of their interests in public policy discussions. Provides a venture capital fund for members starting their own businesses.
EA RRWI RW WDR WID

National Association of Women Business Owners (NAWBO)
600 South Federal St.
Suite 400
Chicago, IL 60605
ph.: (312) 922-0465
Date founded: 1974
Represents female entrepreneurs in all types of businesses with day-to-day management responsibility. Services include public policy representation, internships, training, a clearinghouse, and a database of women-owned businesses.
EA EWAW RW WDR WID

National Committee on Pay Equity
1126 16th St., NW
Suite 411
Washington, DC 20036
ph.: (202) 331-7343
Date founded: 1979
Organizations and individuals working together to educate the public on pay inequities based on sex or color. Maintains a clearinghouse and publishes reports.
EA EWAW RW WID

National Displaced Homemakers Network
1625 K St., NW
Suite 300
Washington, DC 20006
ph.: (202) 467-6346
Date founded: 1979
Links displaced homemakers with more than 1,100 support groups and training programs. Functions as a clearinghouse and catalyst for the development of programs and services.
EA RW WDR WID

National Federation of Business and Professional Women's Clubs
2012 Massachusetts Ave., NW
Washington, DC 20036
ph.: (202) 293-1100
Date founded: 1919
Also known as: Business and Professional Women/USA (BPW/USA)
Works to provide equal opportunities and economic independence for individual women from three hundred occupations. Monitors legislation and endorses female and pro-woman candidates.
EA EWAW RW WDR WID

9 to 5, National Association of Working Women
614 Superior Ave., NW
Cleveland, OH 44113
ph.: (216) 566-1699
Date founded: 1973
Provides advocacy for working women, especially office workers. Conducts research on related topics, such as office automation, and on job sharing. Offers basic legal assistance and counseling through the Job Survival Hotline.
EA RRWI RW WDR WID

Wider Opportunities for Women (WOW)
815 15th St., NW
Suite 916
Washington, DC 20005
ph.: (202) 638-3143
Date founded: 1974
Strives to increase opportunities for, and surmount barriers to, employment and financial equity for women. Coordinates a network of women's employment programs that monitors sensitivity to women's employment needs.
EA EWAW RW WID

CHILDREN, YOUTH, AND FAMILY

American Adoption Congress
1000 Connecticut Ave., NW
Suite 9
Washington, DC 20036
ph.: (800) 274-6736
Date founded: 1978
Composed of adoptive parents, biological parents, and adopted persons. Functions as a clearinghouse and publishes materials.
EA WDR

Children's Defense Fund
25 E St., NW
Washington, DC 20001
ph.: (800) 233-1200
Date founded: 1973
A national charity, founded by Marian Wright Edelman, offering a voice for children, who are unable to vote, lobby, or speak out for themselves. Conducts the Child Watch Visitation Program and sponsors a national observance of Children's Sabbath.
EA RW WID

Committee for Mother and Child Rights
210 Old Orchard Dr.

Clear Brook, VA 22624
ph.: (703) 722-3652

Date founded: 1980

Provides guidance and emotional support for mothers who have lost custody of their children or who are involved in custody disputes.

EA RW WDR WID

Foundation for Grandparenting
P.O. Box 31
Lake Placid, NY 12946

Date founded: 1982

Asserts the importance of the grandparent-grandchild bond, protects grandparents' rights, and develops policy.

EA

Girl Scouts of the U.S.A.
420 Fifth Ave.
New York, NY 10018
ph.: (212) 852-6548

Date founded: 1912

Works for the development of girls into well-adjusted, resourceful citizens. Offers programs dealing with values, service, and interpersonal skills. Teaches a code of ethics and promotes the study of career options and the development of skills and interests.

EA RRWI RW WID

Girls Incorporated
30 E. 33d St.
New York, NY 10016
ph.: (212) 689-3700

Date founded: 1945

Provides daily programs concerning leadership, career planning, sports, communication, health, and sexuality for girls between the ages of six and eighteen.

EA RW WID

National Committee for Fair Divorce and Alimony Laws
11 Park Pl.
Suite 1116
New York, NY 10007
ph.: (212) 766-4030

Date founded: 1965

Advocates a uniform divorce code for all states, limits on alimony, and equal child support, responsibility, and visitation for both parents.

EA RW WID

Organization for the Enforcement of Child Support
1712 Deer Park
Finksburg, MD 21048
ph.: (410) 876-1826

Date founded: 1979

Works with all levels of government to ensure the enforcement of child support laws.

EA

Parents Without Partners
8807 Colesville Rd.
Silver Spring, MD 20910
ph.: (301) 588-9354

Date founded: 1957

Addresses the problems of single parents (custodial and non-custodial) regarding child welfare.

EA EWAW WDR

Young Women's Christian Association of the United States of America (YWCA-USA)
726 Broadway
New York, NY 10003
ph.: (212) 614-2700

Date founded: 1858

Offers clubs and classes to girls and women over the age of twelve, who receive assistance and information concerning self-improvement, citizenship, human sexuality, and employment.

EA EWAW RRWI RW WID

COMPREHENSIVE ORGANIZATIONS

Center for Women Policy Studies
2000 P Street, NW
Suite 508
Washington, DC 20036
ph.: (202) 872-1770

Date founded: 1972

Independent policy research institution focusing on issues of women's equality, such as women and AIDS, law and pregnancy, barriers to equal education for women, and leadership development.

EA EWAW RRWI RW WDR WID

Clearinghouse on Women's Issues
P.O. Box 70603
Friendship Heights, MD 20813
ph.: (301) 871-6016 or (202) 363-9795

Date founded: 1972

Women's organizations united to gather and disseminate information on issues such as women's health, discrimination, low-income women, civil and human rights, workplace problems, and homemakers' status.

EA RRWI RW WDR WID

Fund for the Feminist Majority (FFM)
186 South St.
Boston, MA 02111
ph.: (617) 695-9688

Date founded: 1987

Promotes a national feminist agenda. Through its Feminization of Power campaign, urges women to seek leadership positions. Its Feminist Media Center analyzes media reporting of feminist issues.

EA RRWI RW WDR WID

General Federation of Women's Clubs
1734 N St., NW
Washington, DC 20036
ph.: (202) 347-3168

Date founded: 1890

Coordinates volunteer service clubs in which women engage in home life, education, conservation, arts, and public affairs projects. Maintains the Women's History and Resource Center.
EA EWAW RRWI RW WID

Ms. Foundation for Women
141 Fifth Ave.
Suite 6-S
New York, NY 10010
ph.: (212) 353-8580
Date founded: 1972
Provides grants for activist, grassroots, and self-help women's efforts in the areas of job training and creation, microbusinesses, leadership development, empowerment, AIDS and reproductive rights, and violence against women.
EA EWAW RRWI RW WDR WID

National Organization for Women (NOW)
1000 16th St., NW
Suite 700
Washington, DC 20036
ph.: (202) 331-0066
Date founded: 1966
A key organization with more than 250,000 members. Worked for passage of the Equal Rights Amendment (ERA) and continues litigation and lobbying for the elimination of sex discrimination in all arenas.
EA EWAW RRWI RW WDR WID

EDUCATION

American Association of University Women
1111 Sixteenth St., NW
Washington, DC 20036
ph.: (202) 785-7722
Date founded: 1881
A national organization of college graduates that works to promote education and equity for all girls and women. Funds community action projects, pioneering research on girls and education, and grants for outstanding women.
EA EWAW RRWI RW WID

Educational Equity Concepts
114 E. 32d St.
Suite 710
New York, NY 10016
ph.: (212) 725-1803
Date founded: 1982
Develops educational materials, workshops, training programs, and consulting services on disability awareness that are free of sex, race, or disability bias.
EA RW WID

ETHNIC WOMEN

National Black Women's Political Leadership Caucus
3005 Bladensburg Rd., NE, #217
Washington, DC 20018
ph.: (202) 529-2806
Date founded: 1971
Seeks to integrate African American women into all levels of politics and urges women to work for equality. Conducts research on economics, politics, and the black family.
EA EWAW RRWI RW WDR WID

National Council of Negro Women
633 Pennsylvania Ave., NW
Washington, DC 20004
ph.: (202) 463-6680
Date founded: 1935
A coalition of organizations striving to develop women's leadership. Maintains a museum and archives and operates a center for minority women pursuing nontraditional careers.
EA EWAW RRWI RW WID

National Institute for Women of Color
1301 20th St., NW
Suite 702
Washington, DC 20036
ph.: (202) 296-2661
Date founded: 1981
Works for economic and educational equality for all women of color. Concerns include cooperation between women of color and broader women's organizations and the placement of women of color on boards and commissions.
EA EWAW RW WID

Organization of Chinese American Women
P.O. Box 6207
Washington, DC 20015
ph.: (202) 638-0330
Date founded: 1977
Works for the advancement and networking of Chinese American women. Areas of concern are equal employment, the combating of sexual and racial stereotypes, and aid of recent immigrants.
EA EWAW RW WID

GLOBAL ISSUES

International Center for Research on Women (ICRW)
1717 Massachusetts Ave., NW
Suite 302
Washington, DC 20036
ph.: (202) 797-0007
Date founded: 1977
Works with policy makers concerning the status of women in developing countries. Especially interested in female microentrepreneurs and subsistence farmers.
EA EWAW RW WDR WID

International Women's Tribune Centre
777 United Nations Plaza, 3d Floor
New York, NY 10017
ph.: (212) 687-8633
Date founded: 1976
Unites groups and individuals around the world working on

women's issues, especially women's development projects in the Third World. Disseminates information and technical assistance from women's organizations.
EA EWAW WDR WID

Women's International League for Peace and Freedom (WILPF)
1213 Race St.
Philadelphia, PA 19107-1691
ph.: (215) 563-7110
Date founded: 1915
A multinational peace organization whose members are women working to end sexism, racism, and other forms of oppression.
EA WDR RRWI

Women's International Resource Exchange (WIRE)
122 West 27th St., 10th Floor
New York, NY 10001-6202
ph.: (212) 741-2955
Date founded: 1981
A collective that opposes discrimination based on sex, class, or race and provides inexpensive materials on Third World women.
EA EWAW WDR WID

HEALTH

Anorexia Nervosa and Related Eating Disorders
P.O. Box 5102
Eugene, OR 97405
ph.: (541) 344-1144
Date founded: 1979
Provides support for anorectics and bulimics, their friends and family, professionals, and community workers through medical referrals, workshops, and the dissemination of information.
EA RW WID

Boston Women's Health Collective
240A Elm St.
Somerville, MA 02144
ph.: (617) 625-0271
Date founded: 1969
Prepares, publishes, and distributes books related to women's issues and health—most notably *Our Bodies, Ourselves* (1971; 1973) and *The New Our Bodies, Ourselves* (1984). Maintains a library, the Women's Health Information Center.
RRWI RW WID

National Women's Health Network
1325 G St., NW
Washington, DC 20005
ph.: (202) 347-1140
Date founded: 1976
A coalition of health centers, organizations, and individuals working to monitor health policies affecting women and to promote feminist health projects. Operates the Women's Health Clearinghouse.
EA EWAW RW WDR WID

Society for the Advancement of Women's Health Research
1920 L St., NW
Suite 510
Washington, DC 20036
ph.: (202) 223-8224
Date founded: 1990
A society composed of women in the medical sciences combatting bias in medical research. Concerns are omission of women from clinical trials, lack of attention to gender differences, and insufficient funding for research on conditions mainly affecting women.
EWAW WDR WID

Y-ME National Breast Cancer Organization (Y-ME)
18220 Harwood Ave.
Homewood, IL 60430
ph.: (708) 799-8228 or (800) 221-2141
Date founded: 1978
Offers peer support and information to women with breast cancer—including hot-line counseling, counseling and referral prior to surgery, and self-help groups.
EA EWAW RW WDR WID

HISTORY AND RESEARCH

Daughters of the American Revolution (DAR), National Society
1776 D St., NW
Washington, DC 20006-5392
ph.: (202) 628-1776
Date founded: 1890
A society for women descended from revolutionary war patriots. Focuses on educational, historical, and patriotic works. Operates a genealogical library and established American History Month.
EA EWAW RRWI WID

National Council for Research on Women
Sara Delano Roosevelt Memorial House
47-49 East 65th St.
New York, NY 10021
ph.: (212) 570-5001
Date founded: 1988
Connects more than one hundred committees and associations that supply resources for feminist research. Serves as a clearinghouse and maintains a national database of work in progress.
EA EWAW RW WDR WID

National Women's History Project
7738 Bell Rd.
Windsor, CA 95492
ph.: (707) 838-6000
Date founded: 1977
Promotes the multicultural study of women's contributions by sponsoring the annual National Women's History Month and operating the Women's History Network.
EA EWAW RW WID

National Women's Studies Association
University of Maryland
College Park, MD 20742
ph.: (301) 403-0525
Date founded: 1977
An association of more than four thousand members, including both students and teachers. Seeks to enhance women's studies programs and supports feminist causes.
EA EWAW RRWI RW WID

POLITICS, PUBLIC POLICY, AND WOMEN'S RIGHTS

ASTRAEA National Lesbian Action Foundation
666 Broadway
Suite 520
New York, NY 10012
ph.: (212) 529-8021
Date founded: 1977
A grassroots organization opposing sexism, homophobia, and heterosexism. Seeks to end all forms of oppression of lesbians.
EWAW RW WDR WID

Center for Policy Alternatives
1875 Connecticut Ave., NW
Suite 710
Washington, DC 20009
ph.: (202) 387-6030
Date founded: 1975
Also known as: National Center for Policy Alternatives
Works with state officials and legislators to develop progressive policies and legislation to assist economically disadvantaged women. Concerns include family and medical leave, child care, and a balance between work and family.
EA EWAW RW WDR WID

Center for the American Woman and Politics
Eagleton Institute of Politics
Rutgers, State University of New Jersey
New Brunswick, NJ 08901
ph.: (908) 828-2210
Date founded: 1971
Observes the status of women in politics and government and maintains a database on women in public office.
EA EWAW RW WDR WID

Institute on Women and Technology
P.O. Box 338
North Amherst, MA 01059
ph.: (413) 367-9725
Date founded: 1987
Studies areas in which technology and accompanying public policy affect women, including reproductive, office, and household technologies.
WDR

League of Women Voters
1730 M St., Nw
Washington, DC 20036
ph.: (202) 429-1965
Date founded: 1920
A nonpartisan organization that strives to empower voters, urging citizens to be informed, active participants in government. Maintains an education fund that studies key community issues at all levels of government in an unbiased manner.
EA EWAW RRWI WDR WID

National Gay and Lesbian Task Force
1734 14th St., NW
Washington, DC 20009-4309
ph.: (202) 332-6483
Date founded: 1973
A civil rights advocacy organization that seeks to end prejudice based on sexual orientation. Concerned with national AIDS policy, the reform of sodomy laws, and military policies on homosexuality.
EA EWAW RW WDR WID

National Woman's Party
Sewall-Belmont House
144 Constitution Ave., NE
Washington, DC 20002
ph.: (202) 546-1210
Date founded: 1913
Created by activist Alice Paul to work for passage of the Nineteenth Amendment and continues to advocate the ratification of the ERA. Other concerns include pay equity, political and government participation, and violence against women. Advocates the ratification of the International Bill of Rights for Women.
EA EWAW RRWI RW WDR WID

NOW Legal Defense and Education Fund (NOW LDEF)
99 Hudson St.
New York, NY 10013
ph.: (212) 925-6635
Date founded: 1970
Provides public education on gender discrimination and equal rights, offers legal aid to women, and sponsors educational and community projects. Maintains the Project on Equal Education Rights (PEER), which works for better enforcement of sex discrimination laws regarding girls and women in education.
EA RRWI RW WDR WID

PREGNANCY AND REPRODUCTIVE RIGHTS

American Life League (ALL)
P.O. Box 1350
Stafford, VA 22555
ph.: (540) 659-4171
Date founded: 1979
A pro-life group that seeks a Human Life Amendment to the Constitution protecting a fetus from the moment of fertilization.
EA WID

Cesarean Prevention Movement
1118 Ct. St.
Syracuse, NY 13208
Date founded: 1982

Also known as: International Cesarean Awareness Network (ICAN); Cesarean Prevention Inc.

Encourages vaginal births for new parents, as well as for women wanting vaginal births after having had a cesarean section. Promotes Birth Works, a holistic birth education program.

EA EWAW RRWI WID

Healthy Mothers, Healthy Babies

409 12th St., SW
Room 523
Washington, DC 20004
ph.: (202) 638-5577

Date founded: 1980

A coalition of organizations focusing on infant and maternal health. Distributes information concerning infant mortality, low birth weight, and prenatal and infant care and nutrition.

EA EWAW RW WID

Hysterectomy Educational Resources and Services (HERS) Foundation

422 Bryn Mawr Ave.
Bala Cynwyd, PA 19004
ph.: (215) 667-7757

Date founded: 1982

Helps improve women's decision making about hysterectomy through education, medical and legal referrals, and the sharing of experiences among women.

EA RRWI RW WDR WID

La Leche League International

9616 Minneapolis
P.O. Box 1209
Franklin Park, IL 60131
ph.: (708) 455-7730 or (800) 525-3243

Date founded: 1956

Provides support, information, and encouragement for women who choose to breast-feed. Offers continuing education and current information for health care professionals.

EA RRWI RW WDR WID

National Abortion and Reproductive Rights Action League (NARAL)

1101 14th St., NW
Washington, DC 20005
ph.: (202) 408-4600

Date founded: 1969

Protects the rights of women to several options for reproduction, such as legal abortion, contraception, or childbearing. Monitors legislation, backs pro-choice candidates, and funds research and education.

EA EWAW RRWI RW WDR WID

National Organization of Adolescent Pregnancy and Parenting

4421A East-West Hwy.
Bethesda, MD 20814
ph.: (301) 913-0378

Date founded: 1979

Unites policy makers, professionals, and others to offer services regarding teenage pregnancy issues. Works to improve family life, provides advocacy services, and plans conferences and workshops.

EA EWAW RW WID

Planned Parenthood

810 Seventh Ave.
New York, NY 10019
ph.: (212) 541-7800 or (800) 829-7732

Date founded: 1916

Also known as: Planned Parenthood Federation of America (PPFA)

Supports the principle that each individual has the right to choose when or whether to have a child. Operates family planning centers in all states.

EA EWAW RRWI RW WDR WID

Religious Coalition for Abortion Rights

100 Maryland Ave., NE
Washington, DC 20002
ph.: (202) 543-7032

Date founded: 1973

Links religious organizations seeking to protect legal abortion. Monitors legislative efforts to curtail abortion rights.

EA EWAW WDR WID

Social Reform

Mothers Against Drunk Driving (MADD)

100 N. Main
Corsicana, TX 75110
ph.: (817) 595-0192

Date founded: 1980

Works to stop drunk driving and to support victims of this violent crime. Activities include public awareness community programs (such as the use of designated drivers), a victim hot line, and lobbying to strengthen existing laws and adopt new ones.

EA RRWI

Women Against Pornography

P.O. Box 845
Times Square Station
New York, NY 10108-0845
ph.: (212) 307-5055

Date founded: 1979

Strives to alter public opinions on pornography so that it will be viewed as degrading and neither sexually liberating nor socially acceptable. Collects statistics and publishes a newsletter.

EA EWAW RW WID

Women's Christian Temperance Union (WCTU)

1730 Chicago Ave.
Evanston, IL 60201
ph.: (708) 864-1396 or (800) 755-1321

Date founded: 1873

Also known as: National Woman's Christian Temperance Union

A group for Christian women advocating total abstinence who educate young people on the harmful effects of drugs, alcohol,

and tobacco. Produces films and research materials and holds abstinence training camps.
EA EWAW RRWI RW WDR WID

SPIRITUALITY

Church Women United
475 Riverside Dr.
New York, NY 10115
ph.: (212) 870-2347
Date founded: 1941
A coalition of groups striving to increase the impact of church women. Concerned with global peace and justice, human rights, and women's poverty. Holds the World Day of Prayer.
EA EWAW RW WDR WID

Hadassah, the Women's Zionist Organization of America
50 W. 58th St.
New York, NY 10019
ph.: (212) 355-7900
Date founded: 1912
A service organization that plans programs in leadership development, Jewish education, and Zionist affairs. Maintains a hospital in Israel and a career counseling institute for young adults and new immigrants.
EA EWAW RW WID

SPORTS AND RECREATION

Women's Sports Foundation
342 Madison Ave.
Suite 728
New York, NY 10173-0728
ph.: (212) 972-9170
Date founded: 1974
A educational organization that seeks to improve sports and fitness for girls and women and to alter policies and social patterns that discourage their participation. Operates the international Women's Sports Hall of Fame.
EA EWAW RRWI RW WDR WID

VIOLENCE

American Humane Association, Children's Division
63 Inverness Dr. East
Englewood, CO 80112
ph.: (303) 792-9900
Date founded: 1877
Protects children from child neglect and abuse. Responsibilities include in-service training of professionals, research, policy advocacy, and operation of the National Resource Center on Child Abuse and Neglect.
EA RW WID

Child Welfare League of America
440 First St., NW
Washington, DC 20001
ph.: (202) 639-2952
Date founded: 1920
A coalition of child welfare agencies that strives to improve services for dependent, neglected, or abused children and youths. Conducts research, develops standards, accredits child welfare services, and publishes materials.
EA RW WDR WID

National Coalition Against Domestic Violence
P.O. Box 18749
Denver, CO 80218-0749
ph.: (303) 839-1852
Date founded: 1978
A network of shelters and service organizations for battered women. Services include advocacy on funding and public policy at all levels, training and assistance for member agencies, and the publication of materials.
EA EWAW RRWI RW WDR WID

Significant Supreme Court Decisions Affecting Women

Compiled by Timothy L. Hall

Date	Case name	Citation	Decision
1873	*Bradwell v. Illinois*	83 U.S. 130	Held that the state's refusal to permit women to practice law did not violate equal protection.
1875	*Minor v. Happersett*	88 U.S. 162	Held that a state constitutional provision denying women the right to vote did not violate equal protection.
1879	*Reynolds v. United States*	98 U.S. 145	Held that the prosecution of a Mormon under federal law prohibiting bigamy in United States territory did not violate religious freedom.
1908	*Muller v. Oregon*	208 U.S. 412	Held that the state law prohibiting women (but not men) from working more than ten hours a day in a laundry did not violate freedom of contract.
1912	*Quong Wing v. Kirkendall*	223 U.S. 59	Held that a state law exempting women (but not men) from license fee for operating a laundry did not violate equal protection.
1923	*Adkins v. Children's Hospital*	261 U.S. 525	Held that a federal minimum-wage law for women working in the District of Columbia violated liberty of contract.
1924	*Radice v. New York*	264 U.S. 292	Held that the state law prohibiting women from employment in certain restaurants late at night did not violate liberty of contract.
1927	*Buck v. Bell*	274 U.S. 200	Held that forced sterilization of mentally impaired men and women by a state did not violate due process or equal protection.
1937	*West Coast Hotel v. Parrish*	300 U.S. 379	Held that a state minimum-wage law for women and children did not violate liberty of contract.
1937	*Breedlove v. Suttles*	302 U.S. 277	Held that a state poll tax requirement applying generally to all adult males but only to females registered to vote did not violate equal protection.
1942	*Skinner v. Oklahoma*	316 U.S. 535	Held that the state law requiring forced sterilization of certain repeat criminal offenders violated equal protection.
1946	*Ballard v. United States*	329 U.S. 187	Dismissed criminal indictment when a state did not summon eligible females for federal grand jury duty, holding that this practice violated equal protection.
1948	*Goesaert v. Cleary*	335 U.S. 464	Held that a state law prohibiting most females from being employed as bartenders did not violate equal protection.
1961	*Hoyt v. Florida*	368 U.S. 57	Upheld the criminal conviction of a woman by an all-male jury even though the state law granted women (but not men) an absolute exemption from jury duty and though not all eligible females were included in the list of potential jurors.
1965	*Griswold v. Connecticut*	381 U.S. 479	Held that the state law preventing the use of contraceptives by married couples violated their right of privacy.
1971	*Phillips v. Martin Marietta Corp.*	400 U.S. 542	Found that a federal antidiscrimination law prevented private employers from refusing to hire women (but not men) with preschool-age children without first showing that different familial obligations made parenting responsibilities more relevant to job performance for females than for males.
1971	*Reed v. Reed*	404 U.S. 71	Held that a state law preferring men over equally qualified women as administrators of wills violated equal protection.

DATE	CASE NAME	CITATION	DECISION
1972	*Eisenstadt v. Baird*	405 U.S. 438	Held that a state law prohibiting the distribution of contraceptives to unmarried individuals violated equal protection.
1972	*Stanley v. Illinois*	405 U.S. 645	Held that the state law automatically denying child custody to the only surviving male parent of an illegitimate child while automatically granting custody to the only surviving female parent of the illegitimate child violated equal protection.
1973	*Roe v. Wade*	410 U.S. 113	Held unconstitutional laws that prohibit or restrict abortion, except for the prohibition of abortions performed during the last trimester of pregnancy or after fetal viability where there is no danger to the life or health of the woman or for laws restricting aspects of abortion after the first trimester for the purpose of safeguarding a woman's health.
1973	*Doe v. Bolton*	410 U.S. 179	Held unconstitutional state requirements that abortions be performed in hospitals, that the abortion decision be reviewed by a panel of physicians, and that abortions only be performed on state residents.
1973	*Frontiero v. Richardson*	411 U.S. 677	Held that a law automatically allowing male members of the armed forces to claim their spouses as dependants and thus receive greater housing allowances and medical benefits but allowing female personnel to claim their spouses as dependants only if they can demonstrate that their spouses are in fact dependent upon them for more than half of the spouses' support violated equal protection.
1973	*Pittsburgh Press v. Human Relations Commission*	413 U.S. 376	Upheld from a First Amendment challenge a municipal ordinance prohibiting sex-specific "Help Wanted" advertisements.
1974	*Cleveland Board of Education v. LaFleur*	414 U.S. 632	Held that school board policies requiring schoolteachers to leave their jobs when they became four or five months pregnant and preventing them from returning to work until three months after childbirth violated equal protection.
1974	*Kahn v. Shevin*	416 U.S. 351	Held that a law granting automatic property tax exemption to widows but denying exemption to widowers did not violate equal protection.
1974	*Corning Glass v. Brennan*	417 U.S. 188	Held that a company policy paying night inspectors (positions historically held by males) substantially more than day inspectors (positions historically held by females) in terms of the normal company shift differential violated federal law.
1974	*Geduldig v. Aiello*	417 U.S. 484	Held that a state law denying disability benefits to pregnant workers did not violate equal protection.
1975	*Schlesinger v. Ballard*	419 U.S. 498	Held that a federal law permitting female members of the armed forces more time than males to attain promotion as officers did not violate equal protection.
1975	*Taylor v. Louisiana*	419 U.S. 522	Held that the state practice of systematically excluding women from jury duty in state courts violated equal protection.
1975	*Weinberger v. Wiesenfeld*	420 U.S. 636	Held that a law providing Social Security benefits to sole surviving female parents of dependent children in some circumstances but denying benefits to sole surviving male parents in similar circumstances violated equal protection.
1975	*Stanton v. Stanton*	421 U.S. 7	Held that a state law establishing the age of female adulthood at 18 years and male adulthood at 21 years for the purpose of determining how long to continue child support payments from a divorced parent violated equal protection.

Date	Case name	Citation	Decision
1975	*Turner v. Department of Employment Security*	423 U.S. 44	Held that a law denying unemployment compensation to any woman in her last three months of pregnancy violated equal protection.
1976	*Planned Parenthood v. Danforth*	428 U.S. 52	Held unconstitutional a state law prohibiting saline amniocentesis abortions and abortions without written consent of the woman's husband or, for an unmarried minor, a parent; held unconstitutional a state requirement that the physician attempt to save the life of the aborted fetus; upheld state laws requiring record-keeping rules relating to abortions, requiring the written consent of a pregnant woman seeking an abortion, and forbidding abortions of viable fetuses.
1976	*General Electric v. Gilbert*	429 U.S. 125	Held that private employers' denial of medical disability benefits to workers absent from the job for maternity-related reasons did not violate federal law.
1976	*Craig v. Boren*	429 U.S. 190	Held that a state law prohibiting males from purchasing nonalcoholic "3.2%" beer while allowing females in the same age group to purchase such beer violated equal protection.
1977	*Califano v. Goldfard*	430 U.S. 199	Held that a federal law providing Social Security benefits to surviving female spouses of males who paid Social Security taxes but denying benefits to surviving male spouses unless they could prove "actual dependency" on their spouses violated equal protection.
1977	*Califano v. Webster*	430 U.S. 313	Held that a federal law providing females a more advantageous technique than males for calculating Social Security benefits in relation to earnings did not violate equal protection.
1977	*Fiallo v. Bell*	430 U.S. 787	Held that a federal law providing preferred immigrant status to illegitimate children of American females and to mothers of illegitimate American children but denying such status to illegitimate children of American males and to fathers of illegitimate American children did not violate equal protection.
1977	*Carey v. Population Services*	431 U.S. 678	Held unconstitutional a state law prohibiting the distribution of contraceptives to individuals under the age of sixteen.
1977	*Beal v. Doe*	432 U.S. 438	Held that a state law denying Medicaid benefits for "unnecessary" abortions did not violate federal law.
1977	*Maher v. Roe*	432 U.S. 464	Held that a state law denying Medicaid benefits for "unnecessary" abortions did not violate the right to obtain an abortion.
1977	*Poelker v. Doe*	432 U.S. 519	Upheld a law forbidding the performance of "unnecessary" abortions in publicly funded hospitals.
1977	*Dothard v. Rawlinson*	433 U.S. 321	Held that minimum height and weight requirements for employment as a prison guard violated federal law, but that the "males only" requirement for contact positions within maximum-security male penitentiaries characterized by "violence and disorganization" and in which sex offenders were mixed with other prisoners did not violate federal law.
1977	*Nashville Gas v. Satty*	434 U.S. 136	Held that denying accumulated seniority benefits to women returning from maternity leave while granting such benefits to employees returning from other disability leaves violated federal law.
1978	*Quilloin v. Walcott*	434 U.S. 246	Upheld a state law permitting a divorced father to block the adoption of a natural child by the child's stepfather but not allowing an unwed father to block such proceedings.

DATE	CASE NAME	CITATION	DECISION
1978	*Los Angeles Department of Water and Power v. Manhart*	435 U.S. 702	Held that an employer's deduction of greater amounts from the wages of female employees than of male employees for pension did not violate federal law.
1979	*Colautti v. Franklin*	439 U.S. 379	Held unconstitutionally vague a state law requiring physicians to exercise life- saving efforts on fetuses that "may be viable."
1979	*Orr v. Orr*	440 U.S. 268	Held that a state law authorizing courts to impose alimony obligations on husbands but not on wives violated equal protection.
1979	*Parham v. Hughes*	441 U.S. 347	Held that a state law allowing mothers but not fathers of illegitimate children to sue for wrongful death of a child did not violate equal protection.
1979	*Caban v. Mohammed*	441 U.S. 380	Held that a state law requiring the permission of the mother but not of the father to offer an illegitimate child for adoption violated equal protection.
1979	*Personnel Administration of Massachusetts v. Feeney*	442 U.S. 256	Held that a state law granting preference for veterans for civil service positions did not violate equal protection even though most veterans were male.
1979	*Califano v. Westcott*	443 U.S. 76	Held that a federal law awarding welfare benefits to families with an unemployed father (but not an unemployed mother) violated equal protection.
1979	*Bellotti v. Baird*	443 U.S. 622	Held unconstitutional a state law requiring a minor seeking an abortion to obtain either the written consent of both parents or permission from a judge after a showing of "good cause."
1980	*Wengler v. Druggists Mutual Insurance*	446 U.S. 142	Held that a state workers' compensation law providing death benefits to widows but not to widowers violated equal protection.
1980	*Harris v. McRae*	448 U.S. 297	Upheld a federal law restricting federal funding of medically necessary abortions.
1981	*H. L. v. Mattheson*	450 U.S. 398	Upheld the constitutionality of a state law requiring a minor seeking an abortion to notify parents "if possible" prior to the abortion.
1981	*Kirchberg v. Feenstra*	450 U.S. 455	Held that a state law giving husbands complete control over the disposition of marital property violated equal protection.
1981	*Michael M. v. Sonoma County*	450 U.S. 464	Held that a state statutory rape law punishing males 14-17 years old for acts of consensual sex with females 14-17 years old but not punishing the females did not violate equal protection.
1981	*Washington County v. Gunther*	452 U.S. 161	Held that the practice of paying female prison guards less than state officials believed would have to be paid to male guards if they served in the same positions violated federal law.
1981	*Rostker v. Goldberg*	453 U.S. 57	Held that the exclusion of women from the draft did not violate equal protection.
1982	*Mississippi University for Women v. Hogan*	458 U.S. 718	Held that a state law denying males the ability to gain admission to nursing school violated equal protection.
1983	*Akron v. Akron Center for Reproductive Health*	462 U.S. 416	Held unconstitutional state requirements that abortions after the first trimester be performed in a hospital, that the consent of the parents be obtained for an abortion performed on a minor, that physicians give women various information, and that a 24-hour waiting period must be imposed.

Date	Case name	Citation	Decision
1983	*Planned Parenthood v. Ashcroft*	462 U.S. 476	Upheld the constitutionality of a state law requiring the presence of second physician to attempt to save the life of fetuses in abortions performed after viability and requiring a pathology report for all abortions.
1983	*Simopoulos v. Virginia*	462 U.S. 506	Upheld the constitutionality of the state law requiring that abortions after the first trimester be performed in either a full-service hospital or a licensed clinic.
1983	*Newport News Shipbuilding v. EEOC*	462 U.S. 669	Held that an employer's refusal to pay the medical costs associated with pregnancy for the spouses of male employees but paying all medical costs for the spouses of female employees violated federal law.
1983	*Lehr v. Robertson*	463 U.S. 248	Held that a state law allowing the adoption of an unmarried father's child without notice to him did not violate due process or equal protection.
1983	*Arizona Governing Committee v. Norris*	463 U.S. 1073	Held that an employer's practice of having employees choose from between several pension companies, each of which provided lower retirement benefits to females than to males, violated federal law.
1984	*Hishon v. King Spaulding*	467 U.S. 69	Held that federal law prohibited a law firm from denying partnership to a female associate on the basis of her gender.
1984	*Roberts v. Jaycees*	468 U.S. 609	Held that the application of a state antidiscrimination law to a male-only private association did not violate freedom of association.
1986	*Hudnut v. American Booksellers Assoc.*	475 U.S. 1001	Summarily affirmed a lower court's finding that a local antipornography ordinance attempting to prohibit the sale of pornography on the grounds of sex discrimination violated freedom of speech.
1986	*Thornburgh v. American Counsel of Obstetricians and Gynecologists*	476 U.S. 747	Held unconstitutional a state abortion law imposing informed consent and reporting requirements and requiring that the physician attempt to preserve the life of the fetus.
1986	*Meritor Savings Bank v. Vinson*	477 U.S. 57	Held violative of federal antidiscrimination law the sexual harassment of employees by an employer or supervisor.
1987	*California Federal Savings and Loan v. Guerra*	479 U.S. 272	Held that a state law requiring up to four months leave for pregnant women did not violate federal law.
1987	*Wimberly v. Labor and Industrial Relation Commission*	479 U.S. 511	Held that a state law denying unemployment benefits to all employees who left work voluntarily, including women who left work to have a baby, and were not subsequently rehired did not violate federal law.
1987	*Johnson v. Transportation Agency*	480 U.S. 616	Held that an affirmative action plan designed to increase the number of women in the traditionally male-dominated state transit system did not violate federal antidiscrimination law.
1989	*Price Waterhouse v. Hopkins*	490 U.S. 228	Held that federal law required that once an employer is shown to have considered an employee's gender in making an employment decision, the employer can avoid liability for sex discrimination only by showing that it would have made the same decision even if it had not considered the employee's gender.
1989	*Webster v. Reproductive Health Services*	109 S.Ct. 3040	Upheld a ban on abortions performed by state employees or in public facilities and a requirement that physicians perform a test to determine the viability of a fetus.

DATE	CASE NAME	CITATION	DECISION
1989	*Michael H. v. Gerald D.*	491 U.S. 110	Held that a state law creating the presumption that a child born to a married woman living with her husband was the child of the marriage did not violate due process or equal protection.
1990	*University of Pennsylvania v. EEOC*	493 U.S. 182	Held that a university charged with sex and race discrimination in connection with the denial of tenure to a female applicant could not refuse to disclose confidential peer review materials relevant to such a charge.
1991	*International Union, UAW v. Johnson Controls, Inc.*	499 U.S. 187	Held that an employer's policy of excluding fertile women (but not fertile men) from certain positions because of concern for the health of the fetus a woman might conceive violated federal law.
1991	*Rust v. Sullivan*	500 U.S. 173	Upheld federal regulations prohibiting abortion counseling or referrals in federal-funded clinics.
1991	*Farrey v. Sanderfoot*	500 U.S. 291	Held that a lien on a homestead granted to a former wife in divorce proceedings in order to secure the value of her interest in this portion of the marital estate was not avoidable in bankruptcy.
1991	*Barnes v. Glen Theatre, Inc.*	501 U.S. 560	Held that a state public indecency law applied to prohibit nude dancing did not violate freedom of speech.
1992	*Ankenbrandt v. Richards*	504 U.S. 689	Held that the domestic relations exception to the diversity jurisdiction of federal courts, preventing federal courts from issuing divorce, alimony, and child custody decrees, did not apply to a woman's child abuse claim against her former husband and his female companion.
1992	*R. A. V. v. St. Paul*	112 S.Ct. 2538	Held that a hate speech ordinance punishing speech likely to arouse anger, alarm, or resentment in others on the basis of race, color, creed, religion, or gender violated freedom of speech.
1992	*Planned Parenthood v. Casey*	112 S.Ct. 2791	Upheld a 24-hour waiting requirement and an informed consent statute relating to abortions but held unconstitutional a provision requiring notification of the spouse of intent to obtain an abortion.
1993	*Bray v. Alexandria Women's Health Clinic*	113 S.Ct. 753	Held that a federal civil rights statute making unlawful actions that represent a class-based animus toward women did not apply to abortion protest groups.
1993	*Harris v. Forklift Systems, Inc.*	114 S.Ct. 367	Held that federal law prohibits employers from sexual harassment in the form of allowing a sexually abusive workplace even if abuse does not seriously affect employee's psychological well-being or cause employees to suffer injury.
1994	*National Organization for Women, Inc. v. Scheidler*	114 S.Ct. 798	Held that a federal antiracketeering law did not require proof of an economic purpose and thus, under a proper showing, might be used in an action against antiabortion groups claimed to be engaged in a nationwide conspiracy to shut down abortion clinics through a pattern of racketeering activities.
1994	*J. E. B. v. Alabama*	114 S.Ct. 1419	Held that a state attorney's use of peremptory challenges to exclude males from jury in a paternity suit violated equal protection.
1994	*Madsen v. Women's Health Center, Inc.*	114 S.Ct. 2516	Upheld against a First Amendment challenge parts of an injunction against abortion protests, those prohibiting protests in a 36-foot buffer zone around clinic entrances and driveways and restricting noise in the vicinity of a clinic, but invalidated other attempts to limit abortion protests.

Time Line

Compiled by Lewis L. Gould

1614 Pocahontas, an American Indian princess in Virginia, marries John Rolfe; she moves to England in 1616 and dies in 1617. The legend that she saved the life of Captain John Smith becomes an enduring American folktale.

1619 A Dutch ship brings African slaves to Virginia, with one woman among them.

1620 The *Mayflower* lands in Massachusetts, with eighteen women and eleven girls among its passengers.

1637 Anne Hutchinson is tried for heresy in the Massachusetts Bay Colony and expelled from the community; she becomes a symbol for religious liberty in Colonial America.

1641 The Massachusetts Bay Colony enacts a law forbidding a husband to abuse his wife, except in the case of self-defense.

1662 A Virginia law states that a person will be deemed slave or free depending on the status of his or her mother; another law prohibits whites from having sexual relations with blacks.

1692-1693 The Salem witchcraft trials convict twenty women of these practices and put them to death; the episode becomes a symbol of religious bigotry and intolerance in Colonial America.

1764 The Pennsylvania Supreme Court rules in *Davey v. Turner* that a married woman must give her legal consent to the sale or transfer of property held with her husband.

1775-1783 Women participate in the American Revolution in varied ways; a few fight, while others raise money and supplies for the Patriot cause. The upheaval does not produce expanded rights for women in the new United States.

1776 Women gain the right to vote in some parts of New Jersey if they own $250 worth of property.

1777 New York's constitution prevents even women who own property from voting.

1780 The Ladies' Association of Philadelphia is formed to collect money to support the American rebels against the British.

1787 The Philadelphia Young Ladies' Association is started to provide educational instruction for young women.

1792 English writer Mary Wollstonecraft publishes *A Vindication of the Rights of Woman*, arguing for expanded opportunities and rights for women; knowledge of the volume circulates among upper-class women in the new United States.

1797 The Society for Relief of Poor Widows with Small Children is founded by Isabella Graham in New York City.

1805 Mercy Otis Warren publishes *History of the Rise, Progress, and Termination of the American Revolution*, a lengthy interpretation of the revolt against the British.

1807 New Jersey ends the right of women to vote in elections, which had been granted in the 1776 constitution, because many women have been voting for the political enemies of the legislators.

1809 Elizabeth Ann Seton forms what becomes the Sisters of Charity, a Roman Catholic religious order for women; Mother Seton will be canonized as the first American saint in 1975.

1818 The Colored Female Religious and Moral Reform Society is set up in Salem, Massachusetts, to work for the betterment of black women.

Hanna Barnard publishes *Dialogues on Domestic and Rural Economy*, regarded as probably the first housekeeping manual.

A boarding school for African American girls opens in Washington, D.C.

1821 Emma Willard founds the Troy Female Seminary, the first school to offer a high school education for white women.

Francis Cabot Lowell of Massachusetts introduces the boardinghouse system, in which young single women are hired as employees in mills and provided with lodgings.

Working-class women in Philadelphia found the Daughters of Africa, a society for their mutual benefit.

1823 Catherine Beecher starts the Hartford Academy for women.

1824 Weavers in Pawtucket, Rhode Island, strike in the first work stoppage by both men and women.

1828 Female employees at a Dover, New Hampshire, cotton mill stage a brief strike to protest new work rules.

The Coloured Female Roman Catholic Beneficial Society is started in Washington, D.C., to help black women.

Ladies' Magazine is published in Boston to instruct middle-class women about their duties in the home.

1830's Many women become active participants in growing reform movements to abolish slavery and other ills of society.

1830 Congress makes abortion a crime.

1832 The Afric-American Female Intelligence Society begins in Boston to further education for free women of color.

1833 Oberlin College is established in Ohio and admits students regardless of gender or race.

1834 The Factory Girls Association is organized in Lowell, Massachusetts, to oppose blacklists and lower wages in cotton mills; the organization disappears during the Panic of 1837.

1835 Harriot K. Hunt begins practicing as an unlicensed physician in Boston.

The Boston Female Moral Reform Society is begun to help needy women and to curb prostitution.

The Mount Pleasant Female Prison of New York is opened as the first woman's prison in the United States.

1836 The American Antislavery Society proposes that women be employed to spread the antislavery message.

1837 The first permanent women's college is founded as Mount Holyoke Seminary by Mary Lyon.

1838 Sarah and Angelina Grimké publish *Letters on the Equality of the Sexes and the Condition of Women.*

1839 Margaret Fuller issues "The Great Lawsuit: Man Versus Men, Woman Versus Women."

Mississippi legislators pass the first Married Women's Property Act; women can own property, including slaves.

1840 The American Female Reform Society becomes a national organization.

1841 The first college degree to a woman is awarded.

Catherine Beecher publishes *Treatise on Domestic Economy*, an influential book on homemaking and housekeeping that will be reprinted frequently.

1845 The Lowell Female Labor Reform Association is set up in Massachusetts as the first women's labor union.

Margaret Fuller's *Women in the Nineteenth Century* considers the position of women in American society.

1848 The Seneca Falls Women's Rights Convention is held in New York. Three hundred delegates, including Elizabeth Cady Stanton and Lucretia Mott, attend and pass resolutions favoring woman suffrage in this important milestone in the evolution of the women's movement.

1849 Elizabeth Blackwell graduates from Geneva Medical College in Syracuse, New York; after two years of training in Europe, she will practice medicine in the United States.

The Canadian government passes a law barring women from voting in both Upper and Lower Canada.

1850 The first national women's rights convention is held in Worcester, Massachusetts, under the leadership of Lucy Stone.

The Women's Medical College of Philadelphia is established.

1851 Isabella van Wegener begins preaching against slavery and for women's rights as Sojourner Truth; she gives her famous "Ain't I a Woman" speech at a suffrage convention in Akron, Ohio.

1852 The Women's Temperance Convention meets in New York City to address the evils of alcohol use in society as the State Women's Temperance Association is begun.

Harriet Beecher Stowe publishes *Uncle Tom's Cabin: Or, Life Among the Lowly*, which achieves wide popularity for its attack on slavery.

1852 cont. Antioch College opens in Ohio to provide fully coeducational instruction for men and women with "absolutely equal opportunities" to all students.

1853 Antoinette Brown Blackwell is ordained by the Congregational Church in South Butler, New York, as the first female minister in the United States.

1855 Woman's Hospital opens in New York City to treat "diseases peculiar to women."

1857 Drs. Elizabeth and Emily Blackwell launch the New York Infirmary for Indigent Women and Children.

The English Matrimonial Causes Act becomes the foundation of divorce proceedings in most Canadian provinces.

Seamstresses hold a demonstration in New York for improved wages and working conditions.

1860's Married women are allowed to own property and keep their wages throughout the United States.

1861 The New York Women's Central Association for Relief is formed to buy supplies and equipment for the Union Army during the Civil War.

1862 The Morrill Act funds land-grant colleges in the Midwest and West that in the 1860's and 1870's will follow coeducational policies and admit women as students.

1863 The National Women's Loyal League is organized to collect a million signatures for a thirteenth amendment to the Constitution to abolish slavery.

1864 Lady Cigar Makers organizes as a union in Providence, Rhode Island.

The Collar Laundry Union organizes women in Troy, New York.

1865 Vassar College is founded.

1866 Elizabeth Cady Stanton runs for Congress as an independent but is defeated.

The American Equal Rights Association is started; it will be the forerunner of woman suffrage organizations.

The U.S. Equal Rights Convention is chaired by Lucretia Coffin Mott.

1867 The Young Women's Christian Association (YWCA) is founded in Boston to meet the needs of single women who are seeking work in cities.

Caroline Wells Dall publishes *The College, the Market, and the Court: Or, Women's Relation to Education, Politics, and Law*, in which she criticizes middle-class women for taking little account of women who work in impoverished conditions.

Susan B. Anthony and Elizabeth Cady Stanton campaign for the adoption of a woman suffrage amendment in Kansas, but voters defeat the proposal.

1868 The New England Woman's Club is established to give its members a chance to influence society.

Sorosis is founded by women in the newspaper business and other professions in New York City.

Susan B. Anthony and Elizabeth Cady Stanton begin publishing the women's rights periodical *The Revolution*.

The Working Women's Association attempts to unite women of all classes.

1868-1869 Louisa May Alcott publishes *Little Women*, a novel that follows the adventures of four sisters into womanhood.

1869 The Daughters of St. Crispin is launched as the first national labor union for women; it lasts only until 1876.

Some female abolitionists oppose the Fifteenth Amendment granting black men the right to vote because it does not include votes for white and black women.

The St. Louis Law School admits women.

Female lawyers are licensed in the United States.

Woman suffrage is adopted in Wyoming Territory merely as an effort to advertise and attract settlers, but it becomes established as part of the political culture of the future state.

PEO Society, a secret women's organization, is founded at Iowa Wesleyan College.

The women's movement splits with the founding of two suffrage organizations, the American Woman Suffrage Association (AWSA) and the National Woman Suffrage Association (NWSA).

1870 Utah Territory institutes woman suffrage.

Kappa Alpha Theta, the first sorority named with Greek letters, starts at Indiana Asbury University (now DePauw University).

1870-1890 The Knights of Labor becomes the first national union to welcome and recruit women as members.

1871 Julia Ward Howe becomes president of the Women's International Peace Association.

1872 Victoria Woodhull runs for president of the United States.

A group of women that includes Susan B. Anthony is arrested for voting in the presidential election.

1873 The Woman's Christian Temperance Union (WCTU) is founded in Chicago; it emerges as a significant reform organization throughout the remainder of the nineteenth century under the leadership of Frances Willard.

Congress enacts the Comstock law, named for Anthony Comstock, head of the New York Society for the Suppression of Vice, which bans contraceptive devices from being distributed.

Female property owners in British Columbia receive the right to vote, the first women in Canada to do so.

1874 The first Canadian local chapter of the WCTU is founded in Picton, Ontario.

1875 On March 9, the U.S. Supreme Court rules in *Minor v. Happersett* that women are citizens but that they do not have the right to vote.

Mount Allison University in New Brunswick grants a Bachelor of Science degree to Grace Annie Lockhart and becomes the first institution of higher learning in the British Empire from which a woman has been graduated.

Wellesley College is established.

1876 Women are denied exhibit space at the Centennial Exposition in Philadelphia, but some collect money to open their own pavilion.

The Ancient Order of the Eastern Star is started by wives of members of the Masonic Order, an all-male organization.

Elizabeth Cady Stanton and Matilda Joslyn Gage issue their Declaration of the Rights of Women during the celebration of the centennial of United States independence.

The Toronto Women's Literary Club is started as a means of lobbying for expanded rights for women in Canada.

1878 The first woman suffrage amendment to the U.S. Constitution (often called the Anthony Amendment) is introduced in Congress but defeated in 1887.

1879 Belvah Lockwood becomes the first female attorney to be admitted to practice before the U.S. Supreme Court.

1880 Bryn Mawr College opens.

The Women's Auxiliary Conference of the Unitarian Church begins, based on the ideas of Fanny Baker Ames.

1881 Clara Barton founds the American Red Cross.

The New England Divorce Reform League is organized.

Helen Hunt Jackson publishes *A Century of Dishonor*, which details the poor treatment that American Indians have received.

1882 Emily Talbot and her daughter Marion form the Association of Collegiate Alumni.

The Women's National Press Association is created.

1883 The Canadian Woman Suffrage Association is formed out of the Toronto Women's Literary Club.

The Women's Relief Crops is initiated by the wives of members of the Grand Army of the Republic, the major organization of Union Civil War veterans.

1885 Bryn Mawr College offers the first graduate programs for women in the United States.

Mills College is started.

The Women's Anthropological Society of America is created to advance the careers of women in that field.

1885 cont. The Women's Teachers Association is founded in Toronto; female teachers in other Canadian cities and provinces also organize.

1886 Susan B. Anthony, Elizabeth Cady Stanton, and Matilda Joslyn Gage complete the first three books in the six-volume study *History of Woman Suffrage*.

1887 The Massachusetts legislature enacts a law limiting the working day for women to ten hours.

1888 The International Council of Women is founded.

The Ladies' Federal Labor Union is created.

1889 Hull-House begins operations in Chicago under Jane Addams and Ellen Starr; the settlement house becomes a model for other women-led reform efforts in a nation undergoing rapid urbanization.

Reporter Elizabeth Seamen, writing under the name Nellie Bly, travels around the world in seventy-two days to prove that it can be done faster than Phileas Fogg's journey in *Around the World in Eighty Days* (1873), a novel by Jules Verne.

The Dominion Women's Enfranchisement Association revitalizes the struggle for woman suffrage in Canada.

1890 The Daughters of the American Revolution is established; First Lady Caroline Harrison serves as the organization's first president.

The schism in the women's movement is healed with the creation of the National American Woman Suffrage Association (NAWSA) out of the NWSA and the AWSA.

Mary Elizabeth Lease campaigns for an agrarian People's Party in Kansas by urging farmers to "raise less corn and more hell."

The General Federation of Women's Clubs is formed to serve as a vehicle for reform among middle-class women.

Wyoming is admitted into the Union and becomes the first state in which women have the right to vote in all elections.

1891 The Women's Athletic Association is established by students at Bryn Mawr College to formalize sports competition among college women.

1892 Congress gives belated formal recognition to Civil War nurses in the form of a $12-a-month pension.

Elizabeth Cady Stanton issues "The Solitude of the Self."

1893 The National Council of Jewish Women is founded by Hannah Greenbaum Solomon.

Woman suffrage is achieved in Colorado.

The National Council of Women of Canada is established as an umbrella organization for women from various groups across the nation.

The Colored Women's League of Washington, D.C., is started by Hallie Quinn Brown.

1895 The Henry Street Settlement House is established by Lillian Wald in New York City.

The National Association of Colored Women is founded by Mary Church Terrell.

Elizabeth Cady Stanton publishes *The Woman's Bible* to argue the role of religion in oppressing women.

1896 Utah and Idaho adopt woman suffrage.

Eleanor Gilmer, using the pen name Dorothy Dix, writes her first advice to the "lovelorn" column in the *New Orleans Picayune*.

Stanford University and University of California play the first women's intercollegiate basketball game.

1897 The National Conference of Mothers is established.

The American Nurses Association is founded by Isabel Robb, its first president.

1898 Charlotte Perkins Gilman publishes her influential work *Women and Economics.*

1899 Florence Kelley, an important female reformer, becomes the general secretary of the National Consumers League.

Edith Griswold and other female attorneys form the Women Lawyer's Guild, which later evolves into the Women's National Bar Association.

1900 The International Ladies' Garment Workers' Union (ILGWU) is founded.

The College Equal Suffrage League is begun by Maud Wood and Inez Haynes.

1900-1920 The Progressive Era of social and political reform produces wide-ranging gains for women in the United States through protective legislation in the workplace and suffrage at the ballot box.

1901 The Junior League is founded.

The U.S. Army Nurse Corps is formed.

The Canadian Nursing Service is established as part of the Army Medical Corps.

Jessie Field Shambaugh begins organizations that will evolve into 4-H Clubs.

1903 The Catholic Daughters of the Americas is launched.

The Southern Association of College Women is created.

Charlotte Perkins Gilman publishes *The Home: Its Work and Influence*.

The Women's Trade Union League is established.

The Oregon legislature passes a law barring the employment of women for more than ten hours a day in a laundry or factory, which leads to the case *Muller v. Oregon* in 1908.

1904 The International Woman Suffrage Alliance is created.

The National Child Labor Committee is organized to press for reform at state and national levels.

1906 Women's groups write letters to Congress in support of the federal Pure Food and Drug Act, helping to secure its passage.

1907 The Chicago School of Civics and Philanthropy is started by Sophonisba Breckinridge and Julia Lathrop.

The National Progressive Women's Suffrage Union is formed in New York City, mainly among Jewish garment workers.

The Equality League of Self-Supporting Women is established by Harriet Stanton Blatch, the daughter of Elizabeth Cady Stanton; it is open to women who earn their own living.

The Dominion Women's Enfranchisement Association changes its name to the Canadian Suffrage Association.

1908 The U.S. Navy Nurse Corps is created.

In *Muller v. Oregon*, the U.S. Supreme Court rules that protective legislation for women may be regarded as a reasonable exercise of state power; in his famous brief submitted on behalf of the law's defenders, attorney Louis D. Brandeis convinced the Court that the law was in accord with other workplace conditions allowing for the differential treatment of women.

The American Home Economics Association is established by Ellen Richards and others.

1909 Charlotte Perkins Gilman begins publication of the periodical *The Forerunner.*

Bessie Locke founds the National Kindergarten Association to spread the idea of schools for young children.

President Theodore Roosevelt convenes the White House Conference on the Care of Dependent Children in an important step toward the creation of the Children's Bureau in 1912.

1910 Jane Addams publishes her memoir *Twenty Years at Hull-House*.

Congress passes the Mann Act, barring the transportation of women across state lines for immoral purposes.

Women's Wear Daily begins publication in New York City.

Charlotte Vetter Gulick, Luther H. Gulick, and William C. Langdon establish the Camp Fire Girls.

1910-1920 Japanese "picture brides" arrive in the United States.

1911 The National Association Opposed to Woman Suffrage is founded.

1911 cont. Charlotte Perkins Gilman publishes *The Man-Made World: Or, Our Androcentric Culture.*

The Triangle Shirtwaist Company fire in New York City kills more than a hundred female workers. The event stimulates growth in the labor movement and inspires the passage of protective legislation, especially in New York State.

The Political Equality Association is founded by Alvah Belmont.

Missouri becomes the first state to supply aid to mothers of dependent children from state funds. The idea spreads to eighteen other states by 1913, but the standards for participation are restrictive and the coverage for needy mothers is limited.

The Wage Earners' League is started in New York City by the Woman Suffrage Party.

1912 Textile workers in Lawrence, Massachusetts, launch a strike in which female strikers display banners stating "We want bread and roses too." The three-month walkout, dubbed the Bread and Roses Strike, leads to wage increases.

Heterodoxy, an important feminist group, is formed in New York City.

Juliette Low founds the Girl Guides, an organization that becomes the Girl Scouts of America the following year.

The Children's Bureau is set up within the U.S. Department of Labor.

The National Organization of Public Health Nurses is started.

1913 A suffrage parade is held in Washington, D.C., the day before Woodrow Wilson's inauguration as president. Eight thousand marchers are watched by half a million spectators, and police allow rioters to disrupt the march.

Alice Paul founds the Congressional Union for Woman Suffrage to pursue a more militant strategy for obtaining the vote; it becomes a radical alternative to the more mainstream NAWSA.

1914 Margaret Sanger founds the National Birth Control League, coining the term "birth control."

President Woodrow Wilson announces the first national Mother's Day.

The National Women's Trade Union League (NWTUL) holds the first organized protest of unemployed women and girls in New York City.

Suffragists stage a march on Washington, D.C., to ask for voting rights.

Woman suffrage is achieved in Montana.

1915 Carrie Chapman Catt becomes president of the NAWSA and reenergizes this mainstream suffrage group.

Charlotte Perkins Gilman publishes the utopian novel *Herland.*

The International Congress of Women is held at The Hague.

The Medical Women's National Association is started.

The International Association of Policewomen is established.

1916 Alice Paul and Lucy Burns found the National Woman's Party, which has grown out of the Congressional Union for Woman Suffrage.

The Federation of Teachers is organized.

The National Association of Deans of Women is created.

Montana elects the first female member of Congress, Jeannette Pickering Rankin.

Canadian women in Manitoba, Alberta, and Saskatchewan win the right to vote; several other provinces extend franchise to women during the next several years.

Elizabeth Burchenal founds the American Folk Dance Society.

1917 The Stenographers Union is organized in Boston by Mabel Gillespie.

Voters in New York State adopt woman suffrage in an important referendum signaling national approval of the reform.

1917-1918 Alice Paul and other advocates of woman suffrage picket the White House to advance their cause during World War I; some are jailed amid growing controversy over tactics.

1918 The Maternity Care Association of New York offers prenatal care to poor women.

Women in Industry Service is set up within the U.S. Department of Labor.

Euro-American women in Canada gain the right to vote when Women's Franchise Act grants suffrage to all women over the age of twenty-one who are British subjects.

1919 The National Federation of Business and Professional Women's Clubs is founded to seek equal rights for professional women.

The Women's International League for Peace and Freedom (WILPF) is founded.

The International Congress of Working Women is started in Washington, D.C.

The Voluntary Parenthood League is begun by Mary Ware Dennett.

1920 The Nineteenth Amendment, establishing the right of women to vote in the United States, is ratified when the Tennessee legislature votes for its adoption.

Members of the National American Woman Suffrage Association (NAWSA) form a new organization called the League of Women Voters.

The Women's Bureau is created within the U.S. Department of Labor.

A group of Tlingit women found Alaska Native Sisterhood, lobbying for Alaskan statehood and the protection of cultural identity.

The National Council of Catholic Women is organized.

1921 Edith Wharton wins the Pulitzer Prize in fiction for *The Age of Innocence.*

The American Association of Social Workers is set up to enhance professionalism and rationality in the field.

The American Birth Control League (the predecessor of Planned Parenthood) is founded by Margaret Sanger.

The Miss America Contest is held in Atlantic City and becomes an annual national ritual.

Congress passes the Sheppard-Towner Act, providing states with federal matching funds to establish prenatal and child care centers.

M. Carey Thomas, the president of Bryn Mawr College, and Hilda Smith start Summer Schools for Women Workers, a program that lasts until the mid-1930's.

The Lucy Stone League is launched to promote the right of women to keep their own names after marriage.

The Women's Overseas Service League is founded.

1922 The International Council of Women of Darker Races is established by members of the National Association of Colored Women.

The Cable Act establishes individual citizenship for women.

Margaret Sanger publishes *Women, Morality, and Birth Control.*

Mary B. Talbert organizes the Anti-Lynching Crusade.

1923 In *Adkins v. Children's Hospital*, the U.S. Supreme Court rules that federal minimum wage law for women is unconstitutional violation of the due process clause of the Fourteenth Amendment; the decision is a major setback for protective legislation for women.

Alice Paul proposes the Equal Rights Amendment (ERA): "Equality of rights under the law shall not be denied or abridged by the United States or by any State on account of sex."

The Women's Division of the National Amateur Athletic Federation is formed by Lou Henry Hoover and others active in athletics to promote sports for women at the school and college level.

Edna St. Vincent Millay wins the Pulitzer Prize in poetry.

1924 Congress passes a child labor amendment, but it is not ratified by a sufficient number of states.

1924 cont. American Indian women gain the right to vote in the United States.

Nellie Tayloe Ross of Wyoming and Miriam Amanda Ferguson of Texas are elected as the first female governors of American states.

1925 Carrie Chapman Catt organizes the National Conference on the Cause and Cure of War.

Vassar College launches the School of Euthenics, emphasizing care and promotion of the family.

Smith College offers the Institute to Coordinate Women's Interests as means to explore ways for women to combine family and career.

1926 The Association of American Women composers is founded by Amy March Cheney Beach.

Gertrude Ederle becomes first woman to swim the English Channel.

Gertrude Bonnin founds the National Council of American Indians.

1927 The first female member of New York Stock Exchange is seated.

1928 Jane Addams and other notable female pacifists lobby for acceptance of the Kellogg-Briand Pact, an international agreement outlawing war.

The Canadian Supreme Court rules that the term "qualified persons" in the Constitution does not apply to women seeking to be appointed to the Senate or other offices; the judgment is reversed a year later in England by the Judicial Committee of the Privy Council, and women are no longer excluded from these appointive offices.

Amelia Earhart, accompanied by two male pilots, becomes the first woman to fly across the Atlantic Ocean.

1929 Under pressure from the American Medical Association (AMA), Congress terminates the Sheppard-Towner Act.

Virginia Woolf, an English author, publishes *A Room of One's Own*, in which she writes of the ways in which women have been denied their proper place in society; the work becomes important among feminists throughout the remainder of the century.

Amelia Earhart helps found the Ninety-Nines, an international group of women pilots.

The Women's Organization for National Prohibition Repeal (WONPR) is launched and becomes the largest antiprohibition organization in the United States.

1930 Two million women work in offices and constitute one-fifth of employed women.

Jessie Daniel Ames starts the Association of Southern Women for the Prevention of Lynching.

The Canadian Federation of Business and Professional Women's Club is begun.

The White House Conference on Child Health and Protection is held.

1931 Jane Addams wins the Nobel Peace Prize.

1932 Hattie Caraway of Arkansas is the first woman elected to the U.S. Senate; she serves two terms.

Amelia Earhart becomes the first woman to fly solo across the Atlantic Ocean.

1933 Frances Perkins becomes secretary of labor and the first female cabinet member in the United States.

Section 213 of the National Economy Act prohibits more than one member of a family from working for the federal government, substantially reducing the number of government jobs for women.

Eleanor Roosevelt becomes First Lady and holds press conferences with female press corps; during the next twelve years, she will emerge as an activist on behalf of numerous social causes.

1934 The Grandmothers Clubs of America is founded.

1935 Congress establishes Aid to Dependent Children (ADC), a program designed to assist low-income families.

Mary McLeod Bethune founds the National Council of Negro Women, uniting major national black women's organizations.

Eleanor Roosevelt starts her "My Day" column, which gives her a national forum for her views.

1936 The right of doctors to prescribe birth control devices becomes legal in *United States v. One Package Containing 120, More or Less, Rubber Pessaries to Prevent Conception.*

Mary McLeod Bethune is appointed Director of Negro Affairs within the National Youth Administration of the New Deal.

Margaret Mitchell publishes *Gone with the Wind*, for which she will win the Pulitzer Prize in fiction.

In *Morehead v. New York ex rel. Tipaldo*, the U.S. Supreme Court decides that a New York law establishing a minimum wage for women is unconstitutional, but the Court will change its position within a year.

1937 In *West Coast Hotel v. Parrish*, the U.S. Supreme Court upholds a minimum wage for women.

1938 The Fair Labor Standards Act mandates maximum hours and minimum wages, achieving goals that female reformers had long sought.

1939 Marian Anderson is denied the right to sing in Constitution Hall in Washington by the Daughters of the American Revolution (DAR) because she is African American; after protests led by Eleanor Roosevelt and others, she sings at the Lincoln Memorial on Easter Sunday.

1940 The Canadian province of Quebec grants women the right to vote.

1941 The American Women's Voluntary Service is created by Alice Throckmorton McLean to prepare women for support duty in the military in the event of American entry into World War II.

The Canadian Women's Army Corps is established.

1942 The Planned Parenthood Federation of America evolves out of activities begun by Margaret Sanger's American Birth Control League.

The Lanham Act sets up child care centers in forty-one states.

The U.S. Navy creates Women Accepted for Volunteer Emergency Service (WAVES).

The Committee on Women in World Affairs is initiated to lobby for women appointees to international organizations in the United States.

The U.S. Coast Guard creates a women's auxiliary called SPAR.

1943 Women's Airforce Service Pilots (WASPs) is formed to ease the shortage of male pilots during World War II; once enough men are available, the WASPs are disbanded and do not receive credit or benefits.

The U.S. Marine Corps Women's Reserve is started.

The All American Girls Professional Baseball League is founded by Philip K. Wrigley.

The White House Conference on Women in Policy-Making is held.

1944 President Franklin Delano Roosevelt orders the Navy to accept African American women into the WAVES.

1945 After her husband's death, Eleanor Roosevelt is named a delegate to the United Nations by President Harry S Truman.

1946 Benjamin Spock publishes *The Common Sense Book of Baby and Child Care*, which influences several generations of parents.

The first U.S. Women's Open Golf Tournament is played in Spokane, Washington.

The Congress of American Women is founded to represent the views of "left feminists" in the United States.

The United Nations Commission on the Status of Women is formed.

Congress passes the War Brides Act to allow for the immigration of foreign wives.

1947 The Women's Trade Union League (WTUL) disbands.

1948 Under Eleanor Roosevelt's guidance, the United Nations Commission on Human Rights issues the Universal Declaration of Human Rights.

Congress passes the Women's Armed Forces Integration Act, giving women official status within the military; all-female units continue to exist.

1950 With the encouragement of historian Mary Beard, Radcliffe College establishes the Woman's Archives.

1950 cont. Aid to Dependent Children (ADC) becomes Aid to Families with Dependent Children (AFDC), the cornerstone of the modern welfare system.

The U.S. Justice Department orders the Congress of American Women to register as an agent of a foreign government, the Soviet Union.

1952 Ontario becomes the first Canadian province to implement legislation providing equal pay for men and women for comparable work.

1953 Simone de Beauvoir's *The Second Sex* is published in the United States; it has a great impact on the attitudes and lives of women during the 1950's.

The second report by Alfred C. Kinsey, *Sexual Behavior in the Human Female*, is published.

1955 Rosa Parks refuses to sit in the "colored" section of a bus in Montgomery, Alabama; her action starts a bus boycott.

Esther Pauline Friedman Lederer begins her "Ann Landers Says" advice column in the *Chicago Sun-Times*.

The Daughters of Bilitis (DOB), the first lesbian organization, is created in San Francisco; its publication *The Ladder* becomes a way for lesbians to communicate and share common concerns.

Margaret Mead publishes *Male and Female: A Study of the Sexes in a Changing World*; it offers a more conservative interpretation of American sexual attitudes and the role of women than Mead herself will adopt in the 1960's.

The Women's Bureau sponsors a White House conference on "Effective Uses of Womanpower."

The Whirly-Girls is formed as the first association of female helicopter pilots.

1956 The Canadian government institutes equal pay legislation for all women working under the jurisdiction of the federal government.

La Leche League International starts in a Chicago suburb to promote knowledge about the benefits of breast-feeding infants.

1957 Althea Gibson becomes the first African American to win the Wimbledon and U.S. Open tennis tournaments.

1958 The National Defense Education Act expands funding for higher education, enabling more women to attend college during the 1960's.

1959 Lorraine Hansberry's *A Raisin in the Sun* wins the New York Drama Critics' Best Play of the Year award for its portrayal of African American life.

Eleanor Flexner's pioneering study *Century of Struggle: The Women's Rights Movement in the United States* is published.

1960 American Indian women gain the right to vote in Canada.

Association of American Foreign Service Women begins to obtain greater recognition and training for wives of diplomats overseas.

Sex discrimination is banned in the Canadian Bill of Rights.

Voice of Women is established in Canada to protest nuclear weapons.

The National Conference on Day Care is held in Washington, D.C., and sponsored by several federal government agencies.

The Student Nonviolent Coordinating Committee (SNCC) is launched to pursue civil rights in the South; it owes much to ideas of longtime activist Ella Baker.

The introduction of "the Pill" encourages greater sexual activity.

1961 Jacqueline Kennedy becomes First Lady, investing the position with a high degree of glamour and a public allure that carries the wives of presidents to new levels of international celebrity.

Women Strike for Peace is founded to oppose nuclear weapons and the arms race.

Planned Parenthood of Canada is organized by Barbara and George Cadbury.

President John F. Kennedy creates the President's Commission on the Status of Women, with Eleanor Roosevelt as chair.

1962 Rachel Carson publishes *Silent Spring*, which deals with environmental pollution and helps spark national concern about ecology.

United Farm Workers is founded in California by César Chávez and Dolores Huerta, but Huerta's role is rarely recognized.

The group Catalyst starts the first of many offices to assist women who are moving in and out of the workforce with finding jobs.

Helen Gurley Brown publishes *Sex and the Single Girl*, which champions sexual liberation for single women.

Ursula Le Guin publishes her first science-fiction story; she will become a major figure in the genre.

Marilyn Monroe takes an overdose of sleeping pills, and her death becomes the subject of unending speculation because of an alleged affair with President John F. Kennedy.

Eleanor Roosevelt dies at the age of seventy-eight.

1963 Betty Friedan publishes *The Feminine Mystique*, articulating grievances of middle-class women of the 1950's and launching a renewed women's movement.

Congress passes the Equal Pay Act, which requires employers to offer equal pay for equal work.

Gloria Steinem publishes the exposé "I Was a Playboy Bunny,," in which she reports on the male attitude that "all women are bunnies." The article begins her career as a celebrated feminist writer.

Sylvia Plath, a gifted poet, commits suicide; her novel *The Bell Jar* (1963), gains importance as a fictional work that defines the role of women in the early 1960's.

1964 Congress enacts the Head Start program to provide preschool education for impoverished children.

Title VII of the Civil Rights Act prohibits sex discrimination in employment.

1965 The Voting Rights Act improves voting rights for African American women.

In *Griswold v. Connecticut*, the U.S. Supreme Court strikes down a ban on contraception and affirms couples' right to privacy.

Lady Bird Johnson launches a movement to beautify the American landscape, which becomes an important forerunner of the environmental movement of the next two decades.

Activists Casey Hayden and Mary King circulate a memorandum that attacks how women were being treated within the Civil Rights movement to abolish racial discrimination.

The National Association of Media Women is established to encourage networking among women in mass communications.

Daniel Patrick Moynihan's report *The Negro Family: The Case for National Action* argues that the African American family is threatened by the growing absence of black men and the dominant role of black women; controversy ensues about whether the report is accurate and whether it reflects racist and sexist views.

1966 The National Organization for Women (NOW) is formed by Betty Friedan and others; it becomes a major lobbying group for feminist issues.

Constance Baker Motley is named to the U.S. District Court, the first African American woman named to the federal bench.

The New York Philharmonic Orchestra hires its first female musician.

Fédération des Femmes du Québec, the first major organization of women in that Canadian province since the suffrage campaigns of the 1920's, is founded.

The Committee on Equality for Women formed in Canada.

The publication of William Masters and Virginia Johnson's *Human Sexual Response* brings new attention to the issue of female sexuality.

Patricia Maginnis creates the Association to Repeal Abortion Laws in California.

1967 Another Mother for Peace is founded in California by Barbara Avedon to protest the Vietnam War.

President Lyndon Johnson issues an executive order barring federal contractors from engaging in gender discrimination.

Shulamith Firestone and Pam Allen found Radical Women, which later becomes the Redstockings; the group will dissolve in 1970.

Rita Mae Brown founds the first Student Homophile League to advance gay causes.

The Royal Commission on the Status of Women is named in Canada to examine the problems facing women and to recommend national responses.

1968 The Jeannette Rankin Brigade brings five thousand women to Washington, D.C., for a peace march.

Shirley Chisholm becomes the first African American woman elected to Congress.

Students at McGill University in Quebec publish the *Birth Control Handbook* illegally.

Federally Employed Women is started to battle discrimination against women within the federal government.

Human Rights for Women, Inc., is chartered in Washington by Mary Eastwood, Ti-Grace Atkinson, and others to provide legal assistance to further women's rights.

Radical feminists demonstrate against the Miss America Pageant in Atlantic City; they suggest throwing away bras, which the press describes as "bra burning."

University of Toronto students establish Toronto Women's Liberation, the first such group in Canada.

Mary Daly criticizes the Roman Catholic church's attitude toward women in *The Church and the Second Sex.*

The radical organization Women's International Terrorist Conspiracy from Hell (WITCH) is formed.

The National Conference for Repeal of Abortion Laws is established and becomes the National Abortion Rights Action League (NARAL).

The National Women's Hall of Fame is opened.

1969 The group New York Radical Feminists is founded.

In *Weeks v. Southern Bell*, the U.S. Court of Appeals for the Fifth Circuit holds that the Civil Rights Act of 1964 has opened many jobs to women that had previously been barred to them—including, in the case of Lorena Weeks, the post of telephone "switchman."

International Women's Day is revived by feminist Laura X, who also starts the Women's History Center Research Library.

The Canadian government liberalizes abortion laws.

The NOW chapter in New York forms New Yorkers for Abortion Law Repeal.

The Boston Women's Health Collective is established to address women's issues and to provide advice about the health concerns of women.

The Coordinating Committee on Women in the Historical Profession is set up to advance the interests of female historians.

A police raid at a gay bar at Stonewall Inn in Greenwich Village, New York, sparks violent protests and leads to the gay liberation movement.

1970 Women's Strike for Equality stages a demonstration to mark the fiftieth anniversary of the ratification of the Nineteenth Amendment granting woman suffrage in the United States.

The White House Conference on Children is held to address issues involving children and working mothers.

New York Radical Feminists hold the first Rape Speak Out.

Germaine Greer, an Australian feminist, publishes *The Female Eunuch.*

Anne Koedt publishes "The Myth of the Vaginal Orgasm,," which has great influence on how the women's movement views sexual responses and female needs.

The first Virginia Slims tournament is held in Houston, beginning the long and sometimes controversial relationship between the Philip Morris tobacco company and the women's professional tennis tour.

Kate Millett publishes *Sexual Politics*, a major reevaluation of the male literary canon and one of the founding works of contemporary feminist criticism.

Shulamith Firestone publishes *The Dialectic of Sex: The Case for Feminist Revolution*, in which men are identified as major oppressors of women.

The Professional Women's Caucus is created.

Robin Morgan publishes *Sisterhood Is Powerful*, an important and influential anthology of feminist writings.

The United Nations Tribunal on Crimes Against Women is held.

The North American Indian Women's Association is initiated by representatives from forty-three tribes.

The NOW Legal Defense and Education Fund (NOW LDEF) is begun to supply legal assistance to women facing gender discrimination and other women's rights abuses.

1971 The Ontario Committee on the Status of Women sets a pattern for other Canadian provinces.

Rita Mae Brown publishes *Rubyfruit Jungle*, a semiautobiographical novel about her lesbian experiences that becomes a best-seller and launches her literary career.

The first National Chicana Conference held in Houston, Texas.

Happiness of Womanhood (HOW) started by Jacquie Davison to oppose the ERA.

The Boston Women's Health Collective publishes *Our Bodies, Ourselves*, a guide to women's health issues and concerns that has a significant impact on the attitudes of American women.

Bay Area Women Against Rape organizes in Berkeley, California, and becomes a model for other groups across the United States.

Gloria Stein founds *Ms.* magazine; regular issues begin appearing in July, 1972.

The National Women's Political Caucus is founded.

The Association for Intercollegiate Athletics for Women is launched to replace the dormant Woman's Division of the National Collegiate Athletics Association.

In *Reed v. Reed*, the U.S. Supreme Court decides that an Idaho law preferring men over women in administering estates violates the equal protection clause of the Fourteenth Amendment.

The National Black Women's Political Leadership Caucus is started to enhance the role of African American women in political and economic processes.

1972 Congress passes the Equal Rights Amendment; supporters of the amendment begin their campaign to secure the necessary ratification by thirty-eight states.

The journal *Feminist Studies* is founded.

The National Action Committee on the Status of Women is started by Canadian feminists.

Women's Lobby, Inc., is founded by Carol Burns and Flora Crater to promote women's issues.

The National Conference of Puerto Rican Women is organized to encourage equal participation of Puerto Rican women and other Latinas in political and economic life.

The Center for Women Policy Studies is started in Washington, D.C.

William H. Chafe publishes *The American Woman*, an influential history of women in the twentieth century.

The first Berkshire Conference on the History of Women is held.

The U.S. Supreme Court decides in *Eisenstadt v. Baird* that unmarried people have the right to use contraceptives as part of privacy rights.

Phyllis Schlafly, a conservative Republican activist, sets up a group to block the Equal Rights Amendment called Stop E.R.A.

1972 cont. Congress passes the Equal Employment Opportunity Act.

Rape crisis centers are founded in Washington, D.C., Los Angeles, and Ann Arbor, Michigan.

The Ms. Foundation for Women is begun to help women organize and to change public attitudes toward women.

Title IX of the Education Amendments prohibits sexual discrimination in higher education institutions receiving public funds; among its other results, the legislation produces a large expansion in women's athletics.

Congress passes the Child Development Act, but President Richard Nixon vetoes it.

The National Association of Female Executives (NAFE) is started to help women pursue successful business careers.

Shirley Chisholm seeks the Democratic presidential nomination, and Texas feminist Frances "Sissy" Farenthold receives more than four hundred votes for the vice presidential nomination at the Democratic National Convention.

1973 The U.S. Supreme Court decides in *Frontiero v. Richardson* that the dependents of female military personnel are eligible to receive the same monetary benefits as the dependents of male personnel.

The Canadian government creates a federal Advisory Council on the Status of Women.

In *Roe v. Wade*, the U.S. Supreme Court rules on state antiabortion laws and strikes down Texas statute outlawing abortions; the decision generates intense political controversy over women's reproductive rights.

Call Off Your Old Tired Ethics (COYOTE) forms to protect prostitutes and former prostitutes from violence and intimidation.

Billie Jean King and other female tennis players found the Women's Tennis Association to pursue more equitable policies toward women in the sport.

The National Black Feminist Organization is created.

Billie Jean King defeats Bobby Riggs in the Battle of the Sexes, a tennis match in the Houston Astrodome.

The YWCA sponsors the first national lesbian conference in Toronto, Canada; a newsletter called *Long Time Coming* is started.

9 to 5 creates a network of office workers to achieve better pay and working conditions for women; the organization will merge with Working Women, National Association of Officeworkers in 1977 to form 9 to 5, National Association of Working Women.

The Comprehensive Employment and Training Act (CETA) is passed in Congress; it provides grants to local agencies to train displaced homemakers and prepare them for future jobs.

1974 The Women's Sports Foundation is started to expand opportunities for women in athletic pursuits.

Catholic Women for the ERA is established.

The Coalition of Labor Union Women is founded to pursue equity in the labor movement.

The Women's Campaign Fund begins to raise money for female candidates.

Betty Ford becomes First Lady; her announcement that she has breast cancer alerts American women to the dangers of this disease.

The Mexican American Women's National Association (MANA) is begun to promote educational and economic development among Mexican American women and other Latinas.

Little League Baseball is opened to women by congressional action.

The Canadian Association for the Appeal of the Abortion Laws (CARAL) forms; it becomes the Canadian Abortion Rights League in 1980.

1975 The Office of Child Support Enforcement is established in Title IV-D of the Social Security Act.

The U.S. Supreme Court, in *Taylor v. Louisiana*, allows women to serve on juries.

NOW sets up a Task Force on Battered Women/Household Violence.

Susan Brownmiller publishes *Against Our Will: Men, Women, and Rape*, a best-selling study of rape as a tool of intimidation wielded by men.

The United Nations First World Conference on Women is held in Mexico City, Mexico.

The Public Health Service Act is passed, creating the National Center for the Prevention and Control of Rape.

Phyllis Schlafly founds Eagle Forum to oppose the ERA and abortion.

The National Women's Health Network is started to improve women's health at all levels of society.

1976 The Republican Women's Task Force fights for a pro-ERA plank at the Republican National Convention.

In *General Electric v. Gilbert*, the U.S. Supreme Court holds that a company insurance plan is not discriminatory by virtue of excluding disabilities related to pregnancy; the impact of this case leads to passage of the Pregnancy Discrimination Act of 1978.

Les Têtes de Pioche, a feminist newsletter, is founded in Montreal.

The first Take Back the Night march occurs after a meeting of the International Tribunal on Crimes Against Women in Brussels, Belgium; it becomes a tradition for spreading awareness about violence against women.

U.S. Army Academy at West Point and the U.S. Naval Academy at Annapolis admit women into their programs.

Congress passes the Equal Credit Opportunity Act, making it unlawful for a creditor to discriminate against an applicant on the basis of race, age, sex, or marital status.

Shere D. Hite publishes *The Hite Report: A Nationwide Study of Female Sexuality*, which creates controversy because of its methodology and its interpretation of women's ambivalence toward the sexual revolution.

The U.S. Supreme Court, in *Planned Parenthood v. Danforth*, strikes down a Missouri law requiring a woman to obtain her husband's consent in order to obtain an abortion.

Asian Women United is started in the San Francisco Bay area to address the status and treatment of Asian American women; the organization publishes books and videotapes about its agenda.

1977 The U.S. Supreme Court decides that minors have a right to use contraceptives in *Carey v. Population Services*.

The Lesbian Rights Project is founded in San Francisco by Donna Hitchens to end discrimination against lesbians; it later becomes the National Center for Lesbian Rights (NCLR).

Feminists in Quebec establish *Pluri-elles*, a newsletter that is renamed *Des Luttes et des Rires des Femmes* in October, 1978.

The U.S. Supreme Court, in *Beal v. Doe*, rules that states do not have to use public funds to pay for abortions.

Carol Ochs publishes *Behind the Sex of God: Toward A New Consciousness-Transcending Matriarchy and Patriarchy*, which attempts to show "the matriarchal alternative to the patriarchal mode of thought."

Women Against Violence Against Women is started in Canada to protest pornography and other examples of violent attitudes or behavior toward women.

Canada's Human Rights Act protects women and minorities.

Women are permitted to hold Rhodes Scholarships.

The National Coalition for Women in Defense is formed; composed of representatives from various feminist groups, it pushes to open up military jobs for women and to win veteran status for WASP servicewomen from World War II.

Rosalynn Carter becomes First Lady and pursues an activist agenda on behalf of mental health and other causes; critics call her "The Steel Magnolia."

The National Women's Conference brings twenty thousand women to Houston in a federally sponsored meeting to address women's issues; many political points of view are represented.

1978 Judy Chicago exhibits her multimedia piece *The Dinner Party*.

1978 cont. In *Los Angeles Department of Water and Power v. Manhart*, the U.S. Supreme Court rules that female employees must be given retirement benefits equal to those of men.

The Toronto International Women's Day Committee is formed.

First Lady Rosalynn Carter testifies before a congressional committee on mental health; the only previous appearance by a First Lady before Congress was Eleanor Roosevelt in 1940.

Congress passes the Pregnancy Discrimination Act to protect pregnant workers.

American Indian women establish Women of All Red Nations (WARN) to protect Indian culture.

1979 In *Bellotti v. Baird*, the U.S. Supreme Court rules that teenagers do need parental consent to obtain abortions.

In *Personnel Administrator of Massachusetts v. Feeney*, the U.S. Supreme Court upholds a state law providing veterans with a preference in civil service hiring; the Court formulates a new guideline which states that laws that adversely affect women but do not specifically classify workers on the basis of sex cannot be challenged on the basis of equal protection under the law.

The Department of Health, Education, and Welfare establishes the Office on Domestic Violence.

The Feminist Party of Canada is founded.

The U.S. Supreme Court, in *Duren v. Missouri*, rules that laws pertaining to jury service must treat men and women equally.

United Nations Convention on the Elimination of All Forms of Discrimination Against Women is held.

With the introduction of the Family Protection Act, Congress hopes to provide incentives that shift the public burden of family support away from the federal government and toward state agencies and private industry.

Sandra M. Gilbert and Susan Gubar publish *The Madwoman in the Attic: The Woman Writer and the Nineteenth-Century Literary Imagination*, a landmark study in the field of feminist literary criticism.

Catharine A. MacKinnon publishes *Sexual Harassment of Working Women*, which argues that sexual harassment in the workplace is a kind of sex discrimination.

Beverly LaHaye forms Concerned Women for America to oppose the feminist agenda in national politics.

1980 Medicaid cannot be used to pay for abortions, according to the U.S. Supreme Court decision *Harris v. McRae*.

The Older Women's League (OWL) is founded to address the concerns of middle-aged and older women.

The United Nations Second World Conference on Women is held in Copenhagen, Denmark.

The National Asian Pacific American Women's Conference on Educational Equity meets in Washington, D.C.

1981 In *County of Washington v. Gunther*, the U.S. Supreme Court rules that women can seek remedies for sex-based wage discrimination under the provisions of Title VII of the Civil Rights Act of 1964.

Sandra Day O'Connor becomes the first woman appointed to the U.S. Supreme Court.

The Equal Rights Amendment fails to meet the deadline for state ratification.

The Congresswomen's Caucus reorganizes as the Congressional Caucus for Women's Issues and admits male members.

Congress adopts a National Woman's History Week.

The National Council for Research on Women organizes, with twenty-one research units.

The Reagan Administration closes down the Office of Domestic Violence.

1982 To remedy her sagging popularity, First Lady Nancy Reagan becomes identified with the "Just Say No" campaign against drug abuse.

The Hysterectomy Educational Resources and Services (HERS) Foundation is formed by Nora Coffey to provide information about alternatives to this frequently performed surgical procedure.

The ERA dies after failing to achieve the necessary thirty-eighth state ratification; the amendment is reintroduced annually in Congress thereafter.

1983 In *City of Akron v. Akron Center for Reproductive Health*, the U.S. Supreme Court strikes down a state law requiring a twenty-four-hour waiting period before abortion and mandating that the physician must tell the patient that a fetus is a "human life from moment of conception."

The Coalition Against Media Pornography is founded in Canada to protest cable television showings of soft-core pornography.

1984 Congress passes the Child Support Enforcement Amendments to give women the means of collecting late child support payments.

Jeanne Sauvé becomes the first female governor-general of Canada; she serves until 1990.

Antiabortion women in Canada create Real, Equal, Active, for Life (REAL) and claim to speak for "real" women of the nation.

Congress passes the Retirement Equity Act.

In *Grove City v. Bell*, the U.S. Supreme Court rules that Title IX of the Education Amendments of 1972 applies only to college programs receiving direct federal support; nonfederally funded programs such as women's athletics are affected.

Geraldine Ferraro is nominated for vice president by the Democrats as the first female candidate of a major party in the United States; despite the appeal of her candidacy and the gender gap in voting between men and women, Ronald Reagan defeats her running mate, Walter Mondale.

The Reagan Administration ends U.S. financial contributions to international birth control programs.

1985 The United Nations Third World Conference on Women is held in Nairobi, Kenya.

EMILY's List is established to raise funds for Democratic women's campaigns; the acronym EMILY stands for "Early Money Is Like Yeast"—"it makes the dough rise."

Feminists Andrea Dworkin and Catharine A. MacKinnon draft an antipornography ordinance for Indianapolis, Indiana, that calls such works an infringement on women's rights; the Feminist Anti-Censorship Task Force (FACT) is founded to oppose the ordinance.

1986 In *Meritor Savings Bank v. Vinson*, the U.S. Supreme Court unanimously recognizes that sexual harassment in the workplace represents a violation of Title VII of the Civil Rights Act of 1964.

The U.S. Supreme Court strikes down an antipornography ordinance as a violation of the First Amendment in *American Booksellers Association v. Hudnut*.

Randall Terry creates Operation Rescue to close down abortion clinics.

1987 The National Museum of Women in the Arts opens in Washington, D.C.

Canada passes the Pay Equity Act.

Fund for the Feminist Majority (FFM) is launched to place women in positions of leadership in business, education, government, law, and other fields.

1988 Congress passes the Civil Rights Restoration Act, restoring the ability to enforce provisions of Title IX of the Education Amendments of 1972.

The Canadian Supreme Court strikes down a federal abortion law as unconstitutional.

Congress passes the Women's Business Ownership Act.

Congress passes the Family Support Act, which is designed to enforce child support orders and to promote self-sufficiency among large numbers of female welfare recipients.

1989 In *Wards Cove Packing Company v. Atonio*, the U.S. Supreme Court shifts the burden of proof in Title VII employment discrimination cases to the plaintiffs, requiring them to show that the employment practices they challenge actually cause the discrimination they claim to have suffered.

The U.S. Supreme Court, in *Lorance v. AT&T Technologies*, rules that an employee filing a complaint about unfair employment practices must do so within 180 days of the alleged violation; the case is regarded as a setback for female employees who cannot anticipate the deadlines that they confront in filing charges.

1989 cont. Antonia Novello is appointed U.S. surgeon general, the first woman and first Latino to fill that position.

Ms. magazine suspends publication because of difficulty attracting national advertisers.

The U.S. Supreme Court rules in *Webster v. Reproductive Health Services* that states have the authority to limit a woman's ability to obtain an abortion.

1990 The Displaced Homemakers Self-Sufficiency Assistance Act is passed by Congress.

The U.S. Supreme Court requires teenagers to notify one parent before obtaining an abortion in *Ohio v. Akron Center for Reproductive Health.*

Boys Clubs of America changes its name to Boys and Girls Clubs of America to reflect the increasing number of girls and young women participating in club activities.

First Lady Barbara Bush delivers the commencement address at Wellesley College following public controversy arising from student protests that she was chosen because of her husband's fame; Bush brings Raisa Gorbachev, the wife of Soviet president Mikhail Gorbachev, and the First Lady's speech is a success.

The Women's Health Equity Act is introduced by the Congressional Caucus for Women's Issues as a group of measures aimed at addressing women's health concerns.

Ms. magazine resumes publication without advertising under the editorship of Robin Morgan.

The Office of Research on Women's Health is created at the National Institutes of Health.

1991 Thirty-five thousand women in the U.S. military serve in the Persian Gulf War; eleven lose their lives, five of them killed in action.

In Senate Judiciary Committee confirmation hearings, Anita Hill testifies that U.S. Supreme Court nominee Clarence Thomas had sexually harassed her; despite the testimony, Thomas is confirmed to a seat on the high court. The case sets off national debates about sexual harassment in the workplace.

In *UAW v. Johnson Controls*, the U.S. Supreme Court rules that an employer cannot use gender to bar women from specific jobs.

Congress passes the Civil Rights Act of 1991.

Congress passes the Nontraditional Employment for Women Act.

The National Breast Cancer Foundation is founded to obtain more funding for breast cancer research.

The U.S. Supreme Court issues a ruling in *Rust v. Sullivan* upholding the constitutionality of federal guidelines forbidding government-funded family planning agencies from providing abortion information or counseling; President George Bush vetoes legislation allowing such agencies to discuss abortion in their counseling.

Deborah Tannen's *You Just Don't Understand: Women and Men in Conversation* (1990) reaches the top of the best-seller list; it argues that women emphasize intimacy and connection while men stress status and dependence in talking to one another.

The Tailhook Convention of naval aviators in Las Vegas leads to numerous complaints of sexual harassment and assault; Lieutenant Paula Coughlin files an official complaint about her treatment at the event.

Susan Faludi's best-selling book *Backlash: The Undeclared War Against American Women* argues that government, media, and other forces have sought to roll back feminist gains during the 1980's.

1992 In *Planned Parenthood v. Casey*, the U.S. Supreme Court upholds most of the restrictions that the Pennsylvania legislature has imposed on women seeking abortions, including a twenty-four-hour waiting period and parental consent; the case is regarded as a significant setback for abortion rights, although it reaffirms the principle of the 1973 *Roe v. Wade* decision.

In *R. A. V. v. St. Paul*, the U.S. Supreme Court overturns a Minnesota law criminalizing hate speech.

The U.S. Supreme Court allows sexually harassed students to collect damages from school districts in *Franklin v. Gwinnet County Public Schools.*

The Tailhook scandal involving sexual harassment at convention of fighter pilots rocks the U.S. Navy; Secretary of the Navy Lawrence Garrett resigns.

The Twenty-first Century Party founded with a feminist agenda.

NOW stages a pro-choice rally in Washington, D.C., that draws a crowd of 760,000.

The U.S. Supreme Court bars personal use of RU-486, the abortion pill developed in France.

Antioch College develops rules requiring that students secure clear verbal consent before any romantic gestures or actions are initiated.

Swarthmore College becomes the first institution of higher education to launch a date-rape prevention program.

The Year of the Woman brings many female senators and representatives to Congress, including Carol Moseley-Braun, the first African American woman elected to the Senate.

1993 Hillary Rodham Clinton becomes First Lady and is placed in charge of the health care reform initiative of her husband's administration; she becomes a highly controversial figure because of her role in policy and questions about her performance as an attorney before coming to the White House.

Women who are prospective cabinet appointees in the new Clinton Administration encounter difficulties that prevent their service because they have employed undocumented immigrants to provide domestic help and have not paid Social Security taxes on these wages; a national debate ensues about the role of women in public life and the special demands made upon them when they have young children.

President Bill Clinton signs the Family and Medical Leave Act.

Janet Reno becomes the first woman to serve as attorney general of the United States; her unmarried and childless status again raises the issue of the disadvantages facing women who try to combine marriage and children with public careers.

Restrictions on women in aerial combat roles are removed by the U.S. secretary of defense.

The first Take Our Daughters to Work Day is organized by the Ms. Foundation for Women.

Ruth Bader Ginsburg takes the oath as the second female U.S. Supreme Court justice.

Kim Campbell becomes the first female prime minister of Canada as the leader of the Progressive Conservative government; her party loses a general election later in the year, however, and her own bid for reelection is defeated.

Following an alleged sexual assault by her husband, Lorena L. Bobbitt cuts off his penis, which is later successfully reattached; she is acquitted of malicious wounding by reason of temporary insanity in 1994, after he is aquitted of spousal battery.

Paul Hill murders a physician who performs abortions at a Florida clinic; the episode symbolizes rising reliance on violence by some participants in the antiabortion movement.

In a unanimous decision, the U.S. Supreme Court rules in *Harris v. Forklift Systems* that plaintiffs in sexual harassment cases need only show that their workplace environment would "reasonably be perceived" as hostile.

The Vietnam Women's Memorial is dedicated in Washington, D.C., to honor women who served in the Vietnam War.

1994 Figure skater Nancy Kerrigan is attacked and injured during a practice session; rival skater Tonya Harding is implicated but skates in the Olympics anyway. Harding is later banned from professional skating.

Lieutenant Paula Coughlin, the naval officer who exposed the Tailhook scandal, resigns from the military because of harassment.

The United Nations Population Conference is held in Cairo, Egypt.

Congress passes the Violence Against Women Act, which declares that gender-motivated acts of violence can be prosecuted as federal civil rights violations.

Paula Jones files a lawsuit alleging that President Bill Clinton sexually harassed her while he was governor of Arkansas in 1991 and she was working for the state. A court rules that trial of the suit should be postponed until after Clinton no longer holds the presidency; Jones's attorneys appeal the decision.

1994 cont. The murder of Nicole Brown Simpson and Ronald Goldman in Los Angeles and the subsequent sensational televised trial of her former husband, football hero O. J. Simpson, brings national attention to the issue of sexual abuse in marriage and the plight of battered women.

A federal judge rules that the Citadel, an all-male military college in Charleston, South Carolina, must admit Shannon Faulkner, a female applicant.

The election of a Republican House and Senate changes the political landscape for women and calls into question the future of feminist initiatives on Capitol Hill.

1995 Christine Todd Whitman, the governor of New Jersey, gives the Republican response to President Clinton's State of the Union address, the first woman to do so.

The United Nations Fourth World Conference on Women is held in Beijing, China; First Lady Hillary Rodham Clinton makes an important address attacking elements of the Chinese government's policies toward women.

After gaining admission to the Citadel on August 14, Shannon Faulkner resigns from the military college amid extreme harassment; another plaintiff takes up the suit to admit women to the all-male institution.

The acquittal of O. J. Simpson on murder charges renews the debate about women as objects of violence.

Ruth Simmons is inaugurated as the president of Smith College, the first African American woman to serve as head of one of the prestigious women's colleges in the United States.

Robert Packwood, a Republican from Oregon, resigns from the Senate because of charges that he has harassed female employees for more than two decades; he would have faced probable expulsion from the Senate if he had not resigned.

Longtime feminist advocate in Congress Patricia Schroeder, a Colorado Democrat, announces her retirement at the end of her term in 1996; Senator Nancy Kassebaum, a Kansas Republican, also declares that she will not run for a fourth term in 1996.

The number of female applicants to medical schools reaches an all-time high of nearly twenty thousand; women comprise more than 42 percent of all applicants to medical programs.

Congresswoman Enid Greene Waldholtz, a Utah Republican, comes under fire for financial irregularities in her 1994 campaign that are attributed to her husband; her defense that she was blinded by love raises the issue of female responsibility in politics.

The Republican House and Senate debate welfare reform; proposals involve ending entitlement provisions for the poor and unemployed and transferring control of the programs to the states.

1996 The Whitewater scandal and other issues raise questions about the role and character of First Lady Hillary Rodham Clinton; she becomes the target of two congressional probes and sets off renewed national debate about the proper role of the wife of a president.

The American Bar Association's Commission on Women in the Profession reports that prejudice against female lawyers remains strong within the legal community and that inequities persist in pay, advancement, and overall opportunity for female attorneys.

A federal appeals court rules that Paula Jones's sexual harassment suit against President Bill Clinton can go forward while the president is in office; the president's lawyers vow to appeal the case to the U.S. Supreme Court.

In Florida high schools, a debate about whether female students should be allowed to wear tight uniforms in track and field events raises issues of female autonomy in athletic competition.

U.S. women capture gold medals in gymnastics, basketball, swimming, track and field, soccer, and softball at the Olympic Games in Atlanta.

Bibliography

Compiled by Robin Sakina Mama

Academia and Education

Bernard, Jessie. *Academic Women*. University Park: Pennsylvania State University Press, 1964.

Clifford, Geraldine Joncich, ed. *Lone Voyagers: Academic Women in Coeducational Universities, 1870-1937*. New York: Feminist Press at the City University of New York, 1989.

Gordon, Lynn D. *Gender and Higher Education in the Progressive Era*. New Haven, Conn.: Yale University Press, 1990.

Kaufman, Polly W. *Women Teachers on the Frontier*. New Haven, Conn.: Yale University Press, 1984.

Parezo, Nancy J., ed. *Hidden Scholars: Women Anthropologists and the Native American Southwest*. Albuquerque: University of New Mexico Press, 1993.

Thibault, Gisele Marie. *The Dissenting Feminist Academy: A History of the Barriers to Feminist Scholarship*. New York: Peter Lang, 1987.

Tryon, Ruth W. *Investment in Creative Scholarship: A History of the Fellowship Program of the American Association of University Women, 1890-1956*. Washington, D.C.: American Association of University Women, 1957.

Woody, Thomas. *A History of Women's Education in the United States*. New York: Octagon Books, 1966.

Affirmative Action

Clayton, Susan D., and Faye J. Crosby. *Justice, Gender, and Affirmative Action*. Ann Arbor: University of Michigan Press, 1992.

Ezorsky, Gertrude. *Racism and Justice: The Case for Affirmative Action*. Ithaca, N.Y.: Cornell University Press, 1991.

Greene, Kathanne W. *Affirmative Action and Principles of Justice*. New York: Greenwood Press, 1989.

Paul, Ellen Frankel. *Equity and Gender: The Comparable Worth Debate*. New Brunswick, N.J.: Transaction Books, 1989.

Rosenfeld, Michel. *Affirmative Action and Justice: A Philosophical and Constitutional Inquiry*. New Haven, Conn.: Yale University Press, 1991.

Aging

Banner, Lois W. *In Full Flower: Aging Women, Power, and Sexuality*. New York: Alfred A. Knopf, 1992.

Barusch, Amanda S. *Older Women in Poverty: Private Lives and Public Policies*. New York: Springer, 1994.

Butler, Robert N. *Why Survive?: Being Old in America*. New York: Harper & Row, 1975.

Copper, Baba. *Over the Hill: Reflections on Ageism Between Women*. Freedom, Calif.: Crossing Press, 1988.

Doress-Worters, Paula Brown, et al. *Ourselves, Growing Older*. New York: Simon & Schuster, 1987.

Friedan, Betty. *The Fountain of Age*. New York: Simon & Schuster, 1993.

Keith, Jennie, et al. *The Aging Experience: Diversity and Commonality Across Cultures*. Thousand Oaks, Calif.: Sage Publications, 1994.

Kerns, Virginia, and Judith K. Brown. *In Her Prime: New Views of Middle-Aged Women*. 2d ed. Urbana: University of Illinois Press, 1992.

Kuhn, Maggie. *No Stone Unturned: The Life and Times of Maggie Kuhn*. New York: Ballantine Books, 1991.

Macdonald, Barbara, with Cynthia Rich. *Look Me in the Eye: Old Women, Aging, and Ageism*. San Francisco: Spinsters Ink, 1983.

Porcino, Jane. *Growing Older, Getting Better: A Handbook for Women in the Second Half of Life*. Reading, Mass.: Addison-Wesley, 1983.

Art

Broude, Norma, and Mary D. Garrard, eds. *The Expanding Discourse: Feminism and Art History*. New York: Icon Editions, 1992.

________. *The Power of Feminist Art*. New York: Harry N. Abrams, 1994.

Felstiner, Mary Lowenthal. *To Paint Her Life: Charlotte Salomon in the Nazi Era*. New York: HarperCollins, 1994.

Greer, Germaine. *The Obstacle Race: The Fortunes of Women Painters and Their Work*. New York: Farrar, Straus & Giroux, 1979.

Heller, Nancy G. *Women Artists: An Illustrated History*. Rev. ed. New York: Abbeville Press, 1987.

Herrera, Hayden. *Frida Kahlo: The Paintings*. New York: HarperCollins, 1991.

Lippard, Lucy. *From the Center: Feminist Essays on Women's Art*. New York: E. P. Dutton, 1976.

Nochlin, Linda. *Women, Art, and Power and Other Essays*. New York: Harper & Row, 1988.

Raven, Arlene, Cassandra Langer, and Joanna Frueh, eds. *Feminist Art Criticism: An Anthology*. Ann Arbor, Mich.: UMI Research Press, 1988.

Robinson, Roxana. *Georgia O'Keeffe*. New York: Harper & Row, 1989.

Rubinstein, Charlotte Streifer. *American Women Artists from Early Indian Times to the Present*. New York: Avon Books, 1982.

Slatkin, Wendy. *Women Artists in History: From Antiquity to the Twentieth Century*. 2d ed. Englewood Cliffs, N.J.: Prentice Hall, 1990.

Aviation

Bell, Elizabeth S. *Sisters of the Wind*. Pasadena, Calif.: Trilogy Books, 1994.

Boase, Wendy. *The Sky's the Limit: Women Pioneers in Aviation*. New York: Macmillan, 1979.

Cole, Jean Hascall. *Women Pilots of World War II*. Salt Lake City: University of Utah Press, 1992.

Hodgman, Ann, and Rudy Djabbaroff. *Skystars: The History of Women in Aviation*. New York: Atheneum, 1981.

Holden, Henry M., and Lori Griffith. *Ladybirds: The Untold Story of Women Pilots in America*. Freedom, N.J.: Black Hawk, 1991.

Lomax, Judy. *Women of the Air*. New York: Dodd, Mead, 1987.

Moolman, Valerie. *Women Aloft*. Alexandria, Va.: Time-Life Books, 1981.

Beauty and Fashion

Banner, Lois. *American Beauty*. Chicago: University of Chicago Press, 1983.

Boucher, François. *Twenty Thousand Years of Fashion: The History of Costume and Personal Adornment*. Rev. ed. New York: Harry N. Abrams, 1987.

Brownmiller, Susan. *Femininity*. New York: Fawcett, 1985.

Callaghan, Karen, ed. *Ideals of Feminine Beauty*. Westport, Conn.: Greenwood Press, 1994.

Chapkis, Wendy. *Beauty Secrets: Women and the Politics of Appearance*. Boston: South End Press, 1986.

Chorlton, Penny. *Coverup: Taking the Lid off the Cosmetics Industry*. Wellingborough, England: Grapevine, 1988.

Ewen, Stuart, and Elizabeth Ewen. *Channels of Desire: Mass Images and the Shaping of American Consciousness*. New York: McGraw-Hill, 1982.

Freedman, Rita. *Beauty Bound*. Lexington, Mass.: Lexington Books, 1986.

Frings, Gini Stephens. *Fashion: From Concept to Consumer*. 4th ed. Englewood Cliffs, N.J.: Prentice Hall, 1994.

Hatfield, Elaine, and Susan Sprecher. *Mirror, Mirror: The Importance of Looks in Everyday Life*. Albany: State University of New York Press, 1986.

Kaiser, Susan B. *The Social Psychology of Clothing: Symbolic Appearances in Context*. 2d ed. New York: Macmillan, 1990.

Potter, Eliza. *A Hairdresser's Experience in High Life*. New York: Oxford University Press, 1991.

Seid, Roberta Pollack. *Never Too Thin: Why Women Are at War with Their Bodies*. New York: Prentice Hall, 1989.

Wolf, Naomi. *The Beauty Myth: How Images of Beauty Are Used Against Women*. New York: William Morrow, 1991.

Black Feminism

Collins, Patricia Hill. *Black Feminist Thought: Knowledge, Consciousness, and the Politics of Empowerment*. Boston: Unwin Hyman, 1990.

Davis, Angela. *Women, Culture, and Politics*. New York: Random House, 1989.

________. *Women, Race, and Class*. New York: Random House, 1981.

Jewell, K. Sue. *From Mammy to Miss America and Beyond: Cultural Images and the Shaping of U.S. Social Policy*. New York: Routledge, 1993.

Sterling, Dorothy. *We Are Your Sisters: Black Women in the Nineteenth Century*. New York: W. W. Norton, 1984.

Communications and Film

Beasley, Maurine H., and Sheila J. Gibbons. *Taking Their Place*. Washington, D.C.: American University Press, 1993.

Brown, Mary Ellen, ed. *Television and Women's Culture: The Politics of the Popular*. London: Sage Publications, 1990.

Carson, Diane, and Lester Friedman, eds. *Shared Differences: Multicultural Media and Practical Pedagogy*. Urbana: University of Illinois Press, 1995.

Creedon, Pamela J., ed. *Women in Mass Communication*. Newbury Park, Calif.: Sage Publications, 1989.

Doane, Mary Ann. *Femmes Fatales: Feminism, Film Theory, Psychoanalysis*. New York: Routledge, 1991.

Doane, Mary Ann, Patricia Mellencamp, and Linda Williams, eds. *Re-Vision: Essays in Feminist Film Criticism*. Frederick, Md.: University Press of America, 1984.

Hosley, David H., and Gayle K. Yamada. *Hard News*. New York: Greenwood Press, 1987.

Kaplan, E. Ann. *Women and Film: Both Sides of the Camera*. New York: Methuen, 1983.

Mills, Kay. *A Place in the News*. New York: Dodd, Mead, 1988.

Penley, Constance. *Feminism and Film Theory*. New York: Routledge, 1988.

Ricchiardi, Sherry, and Virginia Young. *Women on Deadline*. Ames: Iowa State University Press, 1991.

Sanders, Marlene, and Marcia Rock. *Waiting for Prime Time: The Women of Television News*. Urbana: University of Illinois Press, 1994.

Schilpp, Madelon Golden, and Sharon M. Murphy. *Great Women of the Press*. Carbondale: Southern Illinois University Press, 1983.

Stacey, Jackie. *Star Gazing: Hollywood Cinema and Female Spectatorship*. New York: Routledge, 1994.

ETHNIC IDENTITY

Abalos, David T. *The Latino Family and the Politics of Transformation*. Westport, Conn.: Praeger, 1993.

Asian Women United of California, ed. *Making Waves: An Anthology of Writings by and About Asian American Women*. Boston: Beacon Press, 1989.

Daniels, Roger. *Coming to America: A History of Immigration and Ethnicity in American Life*. New York: HarperCollins, 1990.

Dill, Bonnic Thornton, and Maxine Baca Zinn, eds. *Women of Color in U.S. Society*. Philadelphia: Temple University Press, 1994.

Foerstel, Lenora, ed. *Women's Voices on the Pacific*. Washington, D.C.: Maisonneuve Press, 1991.

Haizlip, Shirlee Taylor. *The Sweeter the Juice*. New York: Simon & Schuster, 1994.

Kim, Ai Ra. *Women Struggling for a New Life: The Role of Religion in the Cultural Passage from Korea to America*. Albany: State University of New York Press, 1995.

Kitano, Harry H. L., and Roger Daniels. *Asian Americans: Emerging Minorities*. Englewood Cliffs, N.J.: Prentice Hall, 1988.

Knoll, Tricia. *Becoming Americans: Asian Sojourners, Immigrants, and Refugees in the Western United States*. Portland, Oreg.: Coast to Coast Books, 1983.

Lagerquist, L. DeAne. *In America the Men Milk the Cows: Factors of Gender, Ethnicity, and Religion in the Americanization of Norwegian American Women*. Brooklyn, N.Y.: Carlson, 1991.

Mihesuah, Devon A. *Cultivating the Rosebuds: The Education of Women at the Cherokee Female Seminary, 1851-1909*. Urbana: University of Illinois Press, 1993.

Minatoya, Lydia. *Talking to High Monks in the Snow: An Asian-American Odyssey*. New York: HarperCollins, 1992.

Moraga, Cherríe, and Gloria Anzaldua, eds. *This Bridge Called My Back: Writings by Radical Women of Color*. New York: Kitchen Table/Women of Color Press, 1983.

Neidle, Cecyle S. *America's Immigrant Women*. Boston: Twayne, 1975.

Rodriguez de Laguna, Asela, ed. *Images and Identities: The Puerto Rican in Two World Contexts*. New Brunswick, N.J.: Transaction Books, 1987.

Swyripa, Frances. *Wedded to the Cause: Ukrainian-Canadian Women and Ethnic Identity, 1891-1991*. Toronto: University of Toronto Press, 1993.

Takaki, Ronald. *Strangers from a Different Shore: A History of Asian Americans*. New York: Little, Brown, 1989.

Tamura, Linda. *The Hood River Issei: An Oral History of Japanese Settlers in Oregon's Hood River Valley*. Urbana: University of Illinois Press, 1993.

Waters, Mary. *Ethnic Options: Choosing Identities in America*. Berkeley: University of California Press, 1990.

Wei, William. *The Asian American Movement*. Philadelphia: Temple University Press, 1993.

Weyr, Thomas. *Hispanic U.S.A.: Breaking the Melting Pot*. New York: Harper & Row, 1988.

FAMILY AND RELATIONSHIPS

Bellah, Robert N., et al. *Habits of the Heart: Individualism and Commitment in American Life*. Berkeley: University of California Press, 1985.

________, et al. *Individualism and Commitment in American Life: Readings on the Themes of Habits of the Heart*. New York: Perennial Library, 1987.

Bird, Gloria, and Keith Melville. *Families and Intimate Relationships*. New York: McGraw-Hill, 1994.

Degler, Carl. *At Odds: Women and the Family in America from the Revolution to the Present*. New York: Oxford University Press, 1981.

Edelman, Marian Wright. *Measure of Our Success: A Letter to My Children and Yours*. Boston: Beacon Press, 1992.

Ehrenreich, Barbara. *Fear of Falling: The Inner Life of the Middle Class*. New York: Pantheon Books, 1989.

Fisher, Helen. *Anatomy of Love: A Natural History of Mating, Marriage, and Why We Stray*. New York: Fawcett, 1994.

Gerson, Kathleen. *No Man's Land: Men's Changing Commitments to Family and Work*. New York: HarperCollins, 1994.

Liebow, Elliot. *Tell Them Who I Am: The Lives of Homeless Women*. New York: Penguin Books, 1993.

Parke, Ross D., and Sheppard G. Kellam. *Exploring Family Relationships with Other Social Contexts*. Hillsdale, N.J.: Lawrence Erlbaum Associates, 1994.

Rubin, Lillian B. *Families on the Fault Line: America's Working Class Speaks About the Family, the Economy, Race, and Ethnicity*. New York: HarperCollins, 1994.

________. *Just Friends: The Role of Friendship in Our Lives*. New York: Harper & Row, 1985.

________. *Worlds of Pain: Life in the Working-Class Family*. New York: Basic Books, 1976.

Skolnick, Arlene, and Jerome Skolnick, eds. *Family in Transition*. 8th ed. New York: HarperCollins, 1994.

Zinn, Maxine Baca, and Stanley Eitzen. *Diversity in Families*. 3d ed. New York: HarperCollins, 1993.

FEMINISM

Adamson, Nancy, Linda Briskin, and Margaret McPhail. *Feminist Organizing for Change: The Contemporary Women's Movement in Canada*. Toronto: Oxford University Press, 1988.

Alpern, Sara, et al. *The Challenge of Feminist Biography: Writing the Lives of Modern American Women*. Urbana: University of Illinois Press, 1992.

Daly, Mary. *Gyn/Ecology: The Metaethics of Radical Feminism*. Boston: Beacon Press, 1978.

Durham, Carolyn. *The Contexture of Feminism: Marie Cardinal and Multicultural Literacy*. Urbana: University of Illinois Press, 1992.

Echols, Alice. *Daring to Be Bad: Radical Feminism in America, 1967-1975*. Minneapolis: University of Minnesota Press, 1989.

Foucault, Michel. *The History of Sexuality, Vol. 1: An Introduction*. Translated by R. Hurley. New York: Vintage Books, 1978.

Freeman, Jo. *The Politics of Women's Liberation: A Case Study of an Emerging Social Movement and Its Relation to the Policy Process*. New York: McKay, 1975.

French, Marilyn. *Beyond Power: On Women, Men, and Morals*. New York: Ballantine Books, 1986.

________. *The War Against Women*. New York: Ballantine Books, 1993.

Hewitt, Nancy A., and Suzanne Lebsock. *Visible Women: New Essays on American Activism*. Urbana: University of Illinois Press, 1993.

Hooks, Bell. *Feminist Theory: From Margin to Center*. Boston: South End Press, 1984.

Kinnard, Cynthia D. *Antifeminism in American Thought: An Annotated Bibliography*. Boston: G. K. Hall, 1986.

Loeffelholz, Mary. *Dickinson and the Boundaries of Feminist Theory*. Urbana: University of Illinois Press, 1991.

McDermott, Patrice. *Politics and Scholarship: Feminist Academic Journals and the Production of Knowledge*. Urbana: University of Illinois Press, 1994.

Maher, Frances A., and Mary Kay Thompson Tetrault. *The Feminist Classroom*. New York: BasicBooks, 1994.

Marks, Elaine, and Isabelle De Courtivron, eds. *New French Feminisms: An Anthology*. New York: Schocken Books, 1980.

Merchant, Carolyn. *The Death of Nature: Women, Ecology, and the Scientific Revolution*. San Francisco: Harper & Row, 1980.

Morgan, Robin. *Sisterhood Is Powerful: An Anthology of Writings from the Women's Liberation Movement*. New York: Random House, 1970.

Moses, Claire Goldbert, and Heidi Hartmann. *U.S. Women in Struggle: A Feminist Studies Anthology*. Urbana: University of Illinois Press, 1995.

Patai, Daphne, and Noretta Koertge. *Professing Feminism: Cautionary Tales from the Strange World of Women's Studies*. New York: BasicBooks, 1994.

Radl, Shirley R. *The Invisible Woman: Target of the Religious New Right*. New York: Dell, 1983.

Ryan, Barbara. *Feminism and the Women's Movement: Dynamics of Change in Social Movement Ideology and Activism*. New York: Routledge, 1992.

Smith, Hilda L. *Reason's Disciples: Seventeenth-Century English Feminists*. Urbana: University of Illinois Press, 1982.

Weisman, Leslie Kanes. *Discrimination by Design: A Feminist Critique of the Man-Made Environment*. Urbana: University of Illinois Press, 1994.

Wolf, Naomi. *Fire with Fire: The New Female Power and How to Use It*. New York: Fawcett, 1994.

Woolf, Virginia. *A Room of One's Own*. New York: Harcourt Brace Jovanovich, 1929.

Folklore

Coffin, Tristram Potter. *The Female Hero in Folklore and Legend*. New York: Seabury Press, 1975.

Farrer, Claire, ed. *Women and Folklore: Images and Genres*. Prospect Heights, Ill.: Waveland Press, 1986.

Hollis, Susan Tower, Linda Pershing, and M. Jane Young. *Feminist Theory and the Study of Folklore*. Urbana: University of Illinois Press, 1994.

Radner, Joan Newlon. *Feminist Messages: Coding in Women's Folk Culture*. Urbana: University of Illinois Press, 1993.

Rich, Adrienne. *Of Woman Born*. 10th ed. New York: W. W. Norton, 1986.

Rolodny, Annette. *The Land Before Her: Fantasy and Experience of the American Frontiers, 1630-1860*. Chapel Hill: University of North Carolina Press, 1984.

Gender Issues and Stereotypes

Basow, S. A. *Gender Stereotypes: Traditions and Alternatives*. 2d ed. Monterey, Calif.: Brooks/Cole, 1986.

Deats, Sara Munson, and Lagretta Tallent Lenker, eds. *Gender and Academe: Feminist Pedagogy and Politics*. Lanham, Md.: Rowman & Littlefield, 1994.

Edwards, Susan. *Gender, Sex, and the Law*. Dover, N.H.: Croon Helm, 1985.

Ellmann, Mary. *Thinking About Women*. New York: Harcourt Brace Jovanovich, 1968.

Epstein, Cynthia. *Deceptive Distinctions: Sex, Gender, and the Social Order*. New Haven, Conn.: Yale University Press, 1988.

Fuchs, Victor R. *Women's Quest for Economic Equality*. Cambridge, Mass.: Harvard University Press, 1988.

Gardiner, Judith Kegan, ed. *Provoking Agents: Gender and Agency in Theory and Practice*. Urbana: University of Illinois Press, 1995.

McLean, Sheila, and Noreen Burrows, eds. *The Legal Relevance of Gender: Some Aspects of Sex-Based Discrimination*. Basingstoke, Hampshire, England: Macmillan, 1988.

Mann, Judy. *The Difference: Growing Up Female in America*. New York: Warner, 1995.

Millett, Kate. *Sexual Politics*. New York: Avon Books, 1971.

Moldow, Gloria. *Women Doctors in Gilded-Age Washington: Race, Gender, and Professionalization*. Urbana: University of Illinois Press, 1987.

Nielsen, Joyce McCarl. *Sex and Gender in Society: Perspectives on Stratification*. Prospect Heights, Ill.: Waveland Press, 1990.

Rakow, Lana F. *Gender on the Line: Women, the Telephone, and Community Life*. Urbana: University of Illinois Press, 1992.

Stansell, Christine. *City of Women: Sex and Class in New York: 1789-1860*. Urbana: University of Illinois Press, 1987.

Whitehead, Tony L., and Barbara Reid, eds. *Gender Constructs and Social Issues*. Urbana: University of Illinois Press, 1992.

HEALTH ISSUES

Childbirth

Abrams, Richard. *Will It Hurt the Baby?: The Safe Use of Medications During Pregnancy and Breastfeeding*. Reading, Mass.: Addison-Wesley, 1990.

American College of Obstetricians and Gynecologists. *ACOG Guide to Planning for Pregnancy, Birth, and Beyond*. Washington, D.C.: Author, 1990.

Arms, Suzanne. *Immaculate Deception: A New Look at Women and Childbirth*. Boston: Houghton Mifflin, 1975.

________. *Immaculate Deception II: A Fresh Look at Childbirth*. Berkeley, Calif.: Celestial Arts, 1994.

Baldwin, Rahima. *Special Delivery*. Berkeley, Calif.: Celestial Arts, 1986.

Boston Women's Health Book Collective. *The New Our Bodies, Ourselves: A Book by and for Women*. New York: Simon & Schuster, 1992.

Edwards, Margot, and Mary Waldorf. *Reclaiming Birth: History and Heroines of American Childbirth Reform*. Trumansburg, N.Y.: Crossing Press, 1984.

Eisenberg, Arlene, Heidi E. Murkoff, and Sandee E. Hathaway. *What to Expect When You're Expecting*. 2d ed. New York: Workman, 1991.

Harrison, Michelle. *A Woman in Residence*. New York: Ballantine Books, 1982.

Jacobs, Sandra, and the American College of Nurse-Midwives. *Having Your Baby with a Nurse-Midwife: Everything You Need to Know to Make an Informed Decision*. New York: Hyperion, 1993.

Kahn, Robbie Pfeufer. *Bearing Meaning: The Language of Birth*. Urbana: University of Illinois Press, 1995.

Kitzinger, Sheila. *Birth at Home*. New York: Oxford University Press, 1979.

________. *The Complete Book of Pregnancy and Childbirth*. 2d ed. New York: Alfred A. Knopf, 1989.

________. *The Experience of Childbirth*. New York: Taplinger, 1972.

________. *Homebirth: The Essential Guide to Giving Birth Outside of the Hospital*. New York: Dorling Kindersley, 1991.

La Leche League International. *The Womanly Art of Breastfeeding*. 5th ed. Franklin Park, Ill.: Author, 1991.

Leavitt, Judith Walzer. *Brought to Bed: Childbearing in America 1750-1950*. New York: Oxford University Press, 1986.

Michaelson, Karen, et al. *Childbirth in America: Anthropological Perspectives*. South Hadley, Mass.: Bergin & Garvey, 1988.

Mitford, Jessica. *The American Way of Birth*. New York: E. P. Dutton, 1992.

Odent, Michel. *Birth Reborn*. New York: Pantheon Books, 1984.

Rogers, Judith, and Molleen Matsumura. *Mother-to-Be: A Guide to Pregnancy and Birth for Women with Disabilities*. New York: Demos, 1991.

Rothman, Barbara Katz. *In Labor: Women and Power in the Birthplace*. New York: W. W. Norton, 1982.

Simkin, Penny. *The Birth Partner: Everything You Need to Know to Help a Woman Through Childbirth*. Boston: Harvard Common Press, 1989.

Wertz, Richard, and Dorothy Wertz. *Lying-In: A History of Childbirth in America*. Rev. ed. New Haven, Conn.: Yale University Press, 1989.

Child rearing

Badinter, Elisabeth. *Mother Love, Myth, and Reality: Motherhood in Modern History*. New York: Macmillan, 1981.

Berry, Mary Frances. *The Politics of Parenthood: Child Care, Women's Rights, and the Myth of the Good Mother*. New York: Viking Press, 1993.

Birns, Beverly, and Dale Hay. *The Different Faces of Motherhood*. New York: Plenum Press, 1988.

Boston Women's Health Book Collective. *Ourselves and Our Children: A Book by and for Parents*. New York: Random House, 1978.

Caron, Ann F. *Strong Mothers, Strong Sons: Raising the Next Generation of Men*. New York: HarperPerennial, 1995.

Chodorow, Nancy J. *The Reproduction of Mothering: Psychoanalysis and the Sociology of Gender*. Berkeley: University of California Press, 1978.

Cowan, Ruth Schwartz. *More Work for Mother: The Ironies of Household Technology from the Open Hearth to the Microwave*. New York: Basic Books, 1983.

Crouch, Mira, and Lenore Manderson. *New Motherhood: Cultural and Personal Transitions in the 1980's*. New York: Gordon & Breach Science Publishers, 1993.

Hayes, Cheryl, John Palmer, and Martha Zaslow. *Who Cares for America's Children?: Child Care Policy for the 1990's*. Washington, D.C.: National Academy Press, 1990.

Kitzinger, Sheila. *Ourselves as Mothers: The Universal Experience of Motherhood*. Reading, Mass.: Addison-Wesley, 1995.

________. *Women as Mothers*. New York: Random House, 1978.

Mahony, Rhona. *Kidding Ourselves: Breadwinning, Babies, and Bargaining Power*. New York: BasicBooks, 1995.

Margolis, Maxine. *Mothers and Such: Views of American Women and Why They Changed*. Berkeley: University of California Press, 1984.

Smith, Dayle. *Kin Care and the American Corporation: Solving the Work/Family Dilemma*. Homewood, Ill.: Richard C. Irwin, 1991.

Family planning

Baruch, Elaine Hoffman, Amadeo F. D'Adamo, Jr., and Joni Seager, eds. *Embryos, Ethics, and Women's Rights: Exploring the New Reproductive Technologies*. New York: Harrington Park Press, 1988.

Callahan, Sidney, and Daniel Callahan, eds. *Abortion: Understanding Differences*. New York: Plenum Press, 1984.

Chesler, Ellen. *Woman of Valor: Margaret Sanger and the Birth Control Movement in America*. New York: Simon & Schuster, 1992.

Chesler, Phyllis. *Sacred Bond: The Legacy of Baby M*. New York: Times Books, 1988.

Condit, Celeste Michelle. *Decoding Abortion Rhetoric: Communicating Social Change*. Urbana: University of Illinois Press, 1994.

Craig, Barbara Hinkson, and David O'Brien. *Abortion and American Politics*. Chatham, N.J.: Chatham House, 1993.

Fleming, Anne Taylor. *Motherhood Deferred: A Woman's Journey*. New York: Fawcett, 1995.

Garrow, David J. *Liberty and Sexuality: The Right to Privacy and the Making of Roe v. Wade*. New York: Macmillian, 1994.

Harrison, Beverly Wildung. *Our Right to Choose: Toward a New Ethic of Abortion*. Boston: Beacon Press, 1983.

Kane, Elizabeth. *Birth Mother: The Story of America's First Legal Surrogate Mother*. San Diego: Harcourt Brace Jovanovich, 1988.

McCorvey, Norma, with Andy Meisler. *I Am Roe: My Life, Roe v. Wade, and Freedom of Choice*. New York: HarperCollins, 1994.

May, Elaine Tyler. *Barren in the Promised Land: Childless Couples and the Pursuit of Happiness*. New York: BasicBooks, 1995.

Rae, Scott B. *The Ethics of Commercial Surrogate Motherhood: Brave New Families?* Westport, Conn.: Praeger, 1994.

Reed, James. *From Private Vice to Public Virtue: The Birth Control Movement and American Society Since 1830*. New York: Basic Books, 1978.

Weschler, Toni. *Taking Charge of Your Fertility: The Definitive Guide to Natural Birth Control and Pregnancy Achievement*. New York: HarperCollins, 1995.

Whitehead, Mary Beth, with Loretta Schwartz-Nobel. *A Mother's Story: The Truth About the Baby M Case*. New York: St. Martin's Press, 1989.

Menopause

Andrews, Lynn V. *Woman at the Edge of Two Worlds: The Spiritual Journey Through Menopause*. New York: HarperCollins, 1993.

________. *Woman at the Edge of Two Worlds Workbook: A Guide to Menopause as Transformation*. New York: HarperCollins, 1994.

Barbach, Lonnie. *The Pause: Positive Approaches to Menopause*. New York: E. P. Dutton, 1993.

Greer, Germaine. *The Change: Women, Aging, and Menopause*. New York: Alfred A. Knopf, 1991.

McCain, Marian Van Eyk. *Transformation Through Menopause*. New York: Bergin & Garvey, 1991.

Sand, Gayle. *Is It Hot in Here or Is It Me?: A Personal Look at the Facts, Fallacies, and Feelings of Menopause*. New York: HarperCollins, 1993.

Sheehy, Gail. *The Silent Passage*. New York: Random House, 1991.

Menstruation

Buckley, Thomas, and Alma Gottlieb, eds. *Blood Magic: The Anthropology of Menstruation*. Berkeley: University of California Press, 1988.

Dan, Alice J., and Linda L. Lewis, eds. *Menstrual Health in Women's Lives*. Urbana: University of Illinois Press, 1992.

Delany, Janice, Mary Jane Lupton, and Emily Toth. *The Curse: A Cultural History of Menstruation*. Urbana: University of Illinois Press, 1988.

Gardner-Loulan, J., B. Lopes, and M. Quackenbush. *Period*. Volcano, Calif.: Volcano Press, 1991.

Grahn, Judy. *Blood, Bread, and Roses: How Menstruation Created the World*. Boston: Beacon Press, 1993.

Knight, Chris. *Blood Relations: Menstruation and the Origins of Culture*. New Haven, Conn.: Yale University Press, 1991.

Lupton, Mary Jane. *Menstruation and Psychoanalysis*. Urbana: University of Illinois Press, 1993.

Madaras, Lynda. *The "What's Happening to My Body?" Book for Girls*. New York: Newmarket Press, 1988.

Pregnancy and employment

Chavkin, Wendy, ed. *Double Exposure: Women's Health Hazards on the Job and at Home*. New York: Monthly Review Press, 1984.

Davies, Margaret Llewelyn, ed. *Maternity: Letters from Working Women*. New York: W. W. Norton, 1978.

Kammerman, Sheila, Alfred Kahn, and Paul Kingston. *Maternity Policies and Working Women*. 2d ed. New York: Columbia University Press, 1993.

Kenen, Regina. *Reproductive Hazards in the Workplace: Mending Jobs, Managing Pregnancies*. New York: Haworth Press, 1993.

Levy, Barry S., and David Wegman. *Occupational Health: Recognizing and Preventing Work-Related Disease*. Boston: Little, Brown, 1983.

Vogel, Lise. *Mothers on the Job: Maternity Policy in the U.S. Workplace*. New Brunswick, N.J.: Rutgers University Press, 1993.

Sexuality

Barbach, Lonnie Garfield. *For Yourself: The Fulfillment of Female Sexuality*. Garden City, N.Y.: Doubleday, 1975.

Bepko, Claudia, and Jo-Ann Krestan. *Singing at the Top of Our Lungs: Women, Love, and Creativity*. New York: HarperPerennial, 1994.

________. *Too Good for Her Own Good: Searching for Self and Intimacy in Important Relationships*. New York: HarperPerennial, 1991.

Caputi, Mary. *Voluptuous Yearnings: A Feminist Theory of the Obscene*. Lanham, Md.: Rowman & Littlefield, 1994.

Dinnerstein, Dorothy. *The Mermaid and the Minotaur: Sexual Arrangements and Human Malaise*. New York: Harper & Row, 1976.

Freedman, Estelle, and John D'Emilio. *Intimate Matters: A History of Sexuality in America*. New York: Harper & Row, 1988.

Friday, Nancy. *Women on Top: How Real Life Has Changed Women's Sexual Fantasies*. New York: Pocket Books, 1991.

Grant, Gwendolyn Goldsby. *The Best Kind of Loving: A Black Woman's Guide to Finding Intimacy*. New York: HarperCollins, 1995.

Janus, Samuel S., and Cynthia L. Janus. *The Janus Report on Sexual Behavior*. New York: John Wiley & Sons, 1993.

Kasl, Charlotte Davis. *Finding Joy: One Hundred and One Ways to Free Your Spirit and Dance with Life*. New York: HarperPerennial, 1994.

Kinsey, Alfred, et al. *Sexual Behavior in the Human Female*. Philadelphia: W. B. Saunders, 1953.

Kitzinger, Sheila. *A Woman's Experience of Sex*. New York; Putnam, 1983.

Reiss, Ira. *An End to Shame: Shaping Our Next Sexual Revolution*. Buffalo, N.Y.: Prometheus Books, 1990.

Rubin, Lillian B. *Erotic Wars: What Happened to the Sexual Revolution?* New York: Farrar, Straus & Giroux, 1990.

Walker, Alice. *Possessing the Secret of Joy*. New York: Harcourt Brace Jovanovich, 1992.

Walker, Alice, and Pratibha Parmar. *Warrior Marks: Female Genital Mutilation and the Sexual Blinding of Women*. New York: Harcourt Brace Jovanovich, 1993.

Other health issues

Corea, Gena. *The Invisible Epidemic: The Story of Women and AIDS*. New York: HarperCollins, 1992.

Costello, C., and A. J. Stone, eds. *The American Woman, 1994-95: Where We Stand, Women and Health*. New York: W. W. Norton, 1994.

Diethrich, Edward B., and Carol Cohan. *Women and Heart Disease*. New York: Ballantine Books, 1994.

Douglas, Pamela. *Cardiovascular Health and Disease in Women*. Philadelphia: W. B. Saunders, 1993.

Fisher, Sue. *In the Patient's Best Interest: Women and the Politics of Medical Decisions*. New Brunswick, N.J.: Rutgers University Press, 1986.

Helfant, Richard. *Women, Take Heart*. New York: G. P. Putnam's Sons, 1993.

Laurence, Leslie, and Beth Weinhouse. *Outrageous Practices: The Alarming Truth About How Medicine Mistreats Women*. New York: Fawcett Columbine, 1994.

McPherson, Ann, ed. *Women's Problems in General Practice*. 3d ed. New York: Oxford University Press, 1993.

Semler, Tracy C. *All About Eve: The Complete Guide to Women's Health and Well-Being*. New York: HarperCollins, 1995.

Swirsky, Joan, and Barbara Balaban. *The Breast Cancer Handbook: A Step-By-Step Guide Taking Control After You've Found a Lump*. New York: HarperPerennial, 1994.

Vasey, Frank B., and Josh Feldstein. *The Silicone Breast Implant Controversy: What Women Need to Know*. Freedom, Calif.: Crossing Press, 1993.

Villarosa, Linda, ed. *Body and Soul: The Black Women's Guide to Physical Health and Emotional Well-Being*. New York: HarperPerennial, 1994.

Lesbian Issues

Barrett, Martha Barron. *Invisible Lives: The Truth About Millions of Women-Loving Women*. New York: HarperCollins, 1990.

Boston Lesbian Psychologies Collective, eds. *Lesbian Psychologies: Explorations and Challenges*. Urbana: University of Illinois Press, 1987.

Burch, Beverly. *On Intimate Terms: The Psychology of Difference in Lesbian Relationships*. Urbana: University of Illinois Press, 1994.

Foster, Jeanette. *Sex Variant Women in Literature*. 2d ed. Baltimore: Diana Press, 1975.

Grier, Barbara, and Coletta Reid, eds. *Lesbian Lives: Biographies of Women from "The Ladder."* Baltimore: Diana Press, 1976.

Hamer, Diane, and Belinda Budge, eds. *The Good, the Bad, and the Gorgeous: Popular Culture's Romance with Lesbianism*. San Francisco: Pandora Press, 1994.

Katz, Jonathan. *Gay American History: Lesbians and Gay Men in the U.S.A.* New York: Avon Books, 1976.

Kennedy, Elizabeth Lapovksy, and Madeline D. Davis. *Boots of Leather, Slippers of Gold: The History of a Lesbian Community*. New York: Routledge, 1993.

Lewin, Ellen. *Lesbian Mothers: Accounts of Gender in American Culture*. Ithaca, N.Y.: Cornell University Press, 1993.

McDaniel, Judith. *The Lesbian Couples Guide: Finding the Right Woman and Creating a Life Together*. New York: HarperCollins, 1995.

Malinowski, Sharon, and Christa Brelin. *The Gay and Lesbian Literary Companion*. Detroit: Visible Ink Press, 1995.

Marcus, Eric. *Making History: The Struggle for Gay and Lesbian Civil Rights, 1945-1990*. New York: HarperCollins, 1992.

Martin, April. *The Lesbian and Gay Parenting Handbook: Creating and Raising Our Families*. New York: HarperPerennial, 1993.

Nestle, Joan, and John Preston. *Sister and Brother: Lesbians and Gay Men Write About Their Lives Together*. New York: HarperCollins, 1995.

Penelope, Julia, and Susan Wolfe. *Lesbian Culture: An Anthology—The Lives, Work, Art, and Visions of Lesbians Past and Present*. Freedom, Calif.: Crossing Press, 1993.

Wysor, Bettie. *The Lesbian Myth: Insights and Conversations*. New York: Random House, 1974.

Midwifery

Davis, Elizabeth. *Heart and Hands: A Midwife's Guide to Pregnancy and Birth*. Berkeley, Calif.: Celestial Arts, 1992.

Donegan, Jane B. *Women and Men Midwives: Medicine, Morality, and Misogyny in Early America*. Westport, Conn.: Greenwood Press, 1978.

Ehrenreich, Barbara, and Diedre English. *Witches, Midwives, and Nurses: A History of Women Healers*. Old Westbury, N.Y.: Feminist Press, 1972.

Jacobs, Sandra, and the American College of Nurse-Midwives. *Having Your Baby with a Nurse-Midwife: Everything You Need to Know to Make an Informed Decision*. New York: Hyperion, 1993

Kitzinger, Sheila, ed. *The Midwife Challenge*. London: Pandora Press, 1988.

Logan, Onnie Lee, as told to Katherine Clark. *Motherwit: An Alabama Midwife's Story*. New York: Penguin Books, 1991.

Ulrich, Laurel Thatcher. *A Midwife's Tale: The Life of Martha Ballard, Based on Her Diary, 1785-1812*. New York: Vintage Books, 1992.

Military Service

Addis, Elisabetta, Valeria E. Russo, and Lorenza Sebesta, eds. *Women Soldiers: Images and Realities*. New York: St. Martin's Press, 1994.

Anderson, Madelyn Klein. *So Proudly They Served: American Military Women in World War II*. New York: Franklin Watts, 1995.

Binkin, Martin, and Shirley J. Bach. *Women and the Military*. Washington, D.C.: Brookings Institution, 1977.

Chrisman, Catherine Bell. *My War: W.W. II, As Experienced by One Woman Soldier*. Denver, Colo.: Maverick, 1989.

Cole, Jean Hascall. *Women Pilots of World War II*. Salt Lake City: University of Utah Press, 1992.

Cornum, Rhonda, as told to Peter Copeland. *She Went to War: The Rhonda Cornum Story*. Novato, Calif.: Presidio Press, 1992.

Dever, John P., and Maria C. Dever. *Women and the Military: Over One Hundred Notable Contributors, Historic to Contemporary*. Jefferson, N.C.: McFarland, 1995.

Devilbiss, M. C. *Women and Military Service*. Maxwell Air Force Base, Ala.: Air University Press, 1990.

Freedman, Dan, and Jacqueline Rhoads. *Nurses in Vietnam: The Forgotten Veterans*. Austin: Texas Monthly Press, 1987.

Goldman, Nancy Loring, ed. *Female Soldiers—Combatants or Noncombatants?: Historical and Contemporary Perspectives*. Westport, Conn.: Greenwood Press, 1982.

Holm, Jeanne. *Women in the Military: An Unfinished Revolution*. Novato, Calif.: Presidio Press, 1982.

Lyne, Mary C., and Kay Arthur. *Three Years Behind the Mast: The Story of the United States Coast Guard, SPARS*. Washington, D.C.: U.S. Coast Guard, 1946.

Marshall, Kathryn. *In the Combat Zone: An Oral History of American Women in Vietnam, 1966-1975*. Boston: Little, Brown, 1987.

Moore, Molly. *A Woman at War: Storming Kuwait with the U.S. Marines*. New York: Charles Scribner's Sons, 1993.

Morden, Bettie J. *The Women's Army Corps, 1945-1978*. Washington, D.C.: Center of Military History, 1990.

Norman, Elizabeth. *Women at War: The Story of Fifty Military Nurses Who Served in Vietnam*. Philadelphia: University of Pennsylvania Press, 1990.

Soderbergh, Peter A. *Women Marines: The World War II Era*. Westport, Conn.: Praeger, 1992.

Treadwell, Mattie E. *The Women's Army Corps*. Washington, D.C.: Department of the Army, 1953.

Walker, Keith. *A Piece of My Heart: The Stories of Twenty-six American Women Who Served in Vietnam*. New York: Ballantine Books, 1985.

Music

Bowers, Jane, and Judith Tick, eds. *Women Making Music: The Western Art Tradition*. Urbana: University of Illinois Press, 1986.

Cook, Susan C., and Judy S. Tsou, eds. *Cecilia Reclaimed: Feminist Perspectives on Gender and Music*. Urbana: University of Illinois Press, 1994.

Gourse, Leslie. *Madame Jazz: Contemporary Women Instrumentalists*. New York: Oxford University Press, 1995.

Hitchcock, H. Wiley, and Stanley Sadie, eds. *New Grove Dictionary of American Music*. 4 vols. London: Macmillan, 1986.

LePage, Jane W. *Women Composers, Conductors, and Musicians of the Twentieth Century*. 3 vols. Metuchen, N.J.: Scarecrow Press, 1980-1988.

Loesser, Arthur. *Men, Women, and Pianos: A Social History*. New York: Simon & Schuster, 1954.

McClary, Susan. *Feminine Endings: Music, Gender, and Sexuality*. Minneapolis: University of Minnesota Press, 1991.

Newman, Katharine D. *Never Without a Song: The Years and Songs of Jennie Devlin, 1865-1952*. Urbana: University of Illinois Press, 1995.

Pendle, Karin, ed. *Women and Music: A History*. Bloomington: Indiana University Press, 1991.

Shelemay, Kay Kaufman. *A Song of Longing: An Ethiopian Journey*. Urbana: University of Illinois Press, 1994.

Solie, Ruth A., ed. *Musicology and Difference: Gender and Sexuality in Music Scholarship*. Berkeley: University of California Press, 1993.

Story, Rosalyn. *And So I Sing: African-American Divas of Opera and Concert*. New York: Amistad Press, 1990.

POETRY AND FICTION

Allen, Mary. *The Necessary Blankness: Women in Major American Fiction of the Sixties*. Urbana: University of Illinois Press, 1976.

Baym, Nina. *Woman's Fiction: A Guide to Novels by and About Women in America, 1820-70*. 2d ed. Urbana: University of Illinois Press, 1993.

Bell-Scott, Patricia, et al., eds. *Double Stitch: Black Women Write About Mothers and Daughters*. Boston: Beacon Press, 1993.

Cahill, Susan, ed. *Writing Women's Lives: An Anthology of Autobiographical Narratives by Twentieth-Century Women Writers*. New York: HarperPerennial, 1994.

Coles, Nicholas, and Peter Oresick, eds. *For a Living: The Poetry of Work*. Urbana: University of Illinois Press, 1995.

Doan, Laura L., ed. *Old Maids to Radical Spinsters: Unmarried Women in the Twentieth-Century Novel*. Urbana: University of Illinois Press, 1991.

Gallagher, Bernice E. *Illinois Women Novelists in the Nineteenth Century: An Analysis and Annotated Bibliography*. Urbana: University of Illinois Press, 1993.

George, Diana Hume. *Oedipus Anne: The Poetry of Anne Sexton*. Urbana: University of Illinois Press, 1987.

Gilbert, Sandra M., and Susan Gubar, eds. *Shakespeare's Sisters: Feminist Essays on Women Poets*. Bloomington: Indiana University Press, 1979.

Gray, Nancy. *Language Unbound: On Experimental Writing by Women*. Urbana: University of Illinois Press, 1992.

Hale, Janet Campbell. *Bloodlines: Odyssey of a Native Daughter*. New York: Random House, 1993.

Hemenway, Robert E. *Zora Neale Hurston: A Literary Biography*. Urbana: University of Illinois Press, 1980.

Higonnet, Margaret R., ed. *The Sense of Sex: Feminist Perspectives on Hardy*. Urbana: University of Illinois Press, 1993.

Hirshfield, Jane, ed. *Women in Praise of the Sacred: Forty-three Centuries of Spiritual Poetry by Women*. New York: HarperCollins, 1995.

Howe, Florence, ed. *No More Masks!: An Anthology of Twentieth-Century American Women Poets*. New York: HarperPerennial, 1993.

Hurston, Zora Neale. *Their Eyes Were Watching God*. Urbana: University of Illinois Press, 1991.

Lifshitz, Leatrice H., ed. *Her Soul Beneath the Bone: Women's Poetry on Breast Cancer*. Urbana: University of Illinois Press, 1988.

Manning, Carol S., ed. *The Female Tradition in Southern Literature*. Urbana: University of Illinois Press, 1994.

Montefiore, Jan. *Feminism and Poetry: Language, Experience, Identity in Women's Writing*. London: Pandora Press, 1987.

Morris, Timothy. *Becoming Canonical in American Poetry*. Urbana: University of Illinois Press, 1995.

Novy, Marianne, ed. *Cross-Cultural Performances: Differences in Women's Re-Visions of Shakespeare*. Urbana: University of Illinois Press, 1993.

________, ed. *Women's Re-Visions of Shakespeare: On the Responses of Dickinson, Woolf, Rich, H. D., George Eliot, and Others*. Urbana: University of Illinois Press, 1990.

Ostriker, Alica Suskin. *Stealing the Language: The Emergence of Women's Poetry in America*. Boston: Beacon Press, 1986.

Plant, Deborah G. *Every Tub Must Sit on Its Own Bottom: The Philosophy and Politics of Zora Neale Hurston*. Urbana: University of Illinois Press, 1995.

Pope, Deborah. *A Separate Vision: Isolation in Contemporary Women's Poetry*. Baton Rouge: Louisiana University Press, 1984.

Roberts, Robin. *A New Species: Gender and Science in Science Fiction*. Urbana: University of Illinois Press, 1993.

Robinson, Lou, and Camille Norton, eds. *Resurgent: New Writing by Women*. Urbana: University of Illinois Press, 1992.

Sherman, Charlotte Watson. *Sisterfire: Black Womanist Fiction and Poetry*. New York: HarperPerennial, 1994.

Showalter, Elaine. *A Literature of Their Own*. Princeton, N.J.: Princeton University Press, 1977.

Silverman, Willa Z. *The Notorious Life of Gyp: Right-Wing Anarchist in Fin de Siecle France*. New York: Oxford University Press, 1995.

Simmons, Thomas. *Erotic Reckonings: Mastery and Apprenticeship in the Work of Poets and Lovers*. Urbana: University of Illinois Press, 1994.

Walker, Cheryl. *Masks Outrageous and Austere: Culture, Psyche, and Persona in Modern Women Poets*. Bloomington: Indiana University Press, 1991.

________. *The Nightingale's Burden: Women Poets and American Culture Before 1800*. Bloomington: Indiana University Press, 1982.

Wallis, Velma. *Two Old Women: An Alaska Legend of Betrayal, Courage, and Survival*. New York: HarperPerennial, 1994.

Watts, Emily Stipes. *The Poetry of American Women from 1632-1945*. Austin: University of Texas Press, 1977.

Wyatt, Edith. *True Love: A Comedy of the Affections*. Urbana: University of Illinois Press, 1994.

POLITICS

Baxter, Sandra, and Marjorie Lansing. *Women and Politics: The Invisible Majority*. Ann Arbor: University of Michigan Press, 1980.

Bystydzienski, Jill M., ed. *Women Transforming Politics: Worldwide Strategies for Empowerment*. Bloomington: Indiana University Press, 1992.

Carroll, Susan J. *Women as Candidates in American Politics*. Bloomington: Indiana University Press, 1985.

Cook, Elizabeth Adell, Sue Thomas, and Clyde Wilcox, eds. *The Year of the Woman*. Boulder, Colo.: Westview Press, 1994.

Darcy, R., Susan Welch, and Janet Clark. *Women, Elections, and Representation*. 2d ed. Lincoln: University of Nebraska Press, 1994.

Golb, Joyce, and Marian Lief Palley. *Women and Public Policies*. Princeton, N.J.: Princeton University Press, 1982.

Hartmann, Susan M. *From Margin to Mainstream: American Women and Politics Since 1960*. New York: Alfred A. Knopf, 1989.

Lovenduski, Joni, and Pippa Norris, eds. *Gender and Party Politics*. London: Sage Publications, 1993.

Piven, Francis Fox, and Richard A. Cloward. *Why Americans Don't Vote*. New York: Pantheon, 1988.

Rajoppi, Joanne. *Women in Office: Getting There and Staying There*. Westport, Conn.: Bergin & Garvey, 1993.

Smeal, Eleanor. *Why and How Women Will Elect the Next President*. New York: Harper & Row, 1984.

Witt, Linda, Karen M. Paget, and Glenna Matthews. *Running as a Woman*. New York: Free Press, 1994.

POVERTY AND SOCIAL WELFARE

Abramovitz, Mimi. *Regulating the Lives of Women: Social Welfare Policy from Colonial Times to the Present*. Boston: South End Press, 1988.

Berrick, Jill Duerr. *Faces of Poverty: Portraits of Women and Children on Welfare*. New York: Oxford University Press, 1995.

Caputo, Richard K. *Welfare and Freedom American Style II: The Role of the Federal Government, 1941-1980*. Lanham, Md.: University Press of America, 1994.

Gelpi, Barbara C., Nancy Hartsock, Clare C. Novak, and Myra Stober, eds. *Women and Poverty*. Chicago: University of Chicago Press, 1986.

Gordon, Linda. *Pitied but Not Entitled: Single Mothers and the History of Welfare, 1890-1935*. New York: Free Press, 1994.

Ladd-Taylor, Molly. *Mother-Work: Women, Child Welfare, and the State, 1890-1930*. Urbana: University of Illinois Press, 1994.

Lord, Shirley A. *Social Welfare and the Feminization of Poverty*. New York: Garland, 1993.

Miller, D. C. *Women and Social Welfare: A Feminist Analysis*. New York: Praeger, 1990.

Polakow, Valerie. *Lives on the Edge: Single Mothers and Their Children in the Other America*. Chicago: University of Chicago Press, 1993.

Rogers, Harrell R. *Poor Women, Poor Families: The Economic Plight of America's Female-Headed Households*. Armonk, N.Y.: M. E. Sharpe, 1990.

Sidel, Ruth. *Women and Children Last: The Plight of Poor Women in Affluent America*. 2d ed. New York: Penguin Books, 1992.

Tarantino, Thomas Howard, and Dismas Becker, eds. *Welfare Mothers Speak Out: We Ain't Gonna Shuffle Anymore*. New York: W. W. Norton, 1972.

Zoef, Paul E. *American Women in Poverty*. New York: Greenwood Press, 1989.

PSYCHOLOGICAL PERSPECTIVES

Bass, Ellen, and Laura Davis. *The Courage to Heal: A Guide for Women Survivors of Child Sexual Abuse*. 3d ed. New York: HarperCollins, 1992.

Bolen, Jean Shinoda. *Goddesses in Everywoman: A New Psychology of Women*. San Francisco: Harper & Row, 1985.

Brown, Lyn Mikel, and Carol Gilligan. *Meeting at the Crossroads: Women's Psychology and Girls' Development*. New York: Ballantine Books, 1993.

Caplan, Paula J. *Don't Blame Mother: Mending the Mother-Daughter Relationship*. New York: HarperCollins, 1990.

Carosella, Cynthia, ed. *Who's Afraid of the Dark? A Forum of Truth, Support, and Assurance for Those Affected by Rape*. New York: HarperCollins, 1994.

Chodorow, Nancy J. *Feminism and Psychoanalytic Theory*. New Haven, Conn.: Yale University Press, 1989.

Chrisler, Joan C., and Alyce Huston Hemstreet, eds. *Variations on a Theme: Diversity and the Psychology of Women*. Albany: State University of New York Press, 1995.

Davis, Laura. *Allies In Healing: When the Person You Love Is a Survivor of Child Sexual Abuse*. New York, HarperCollins, 1991.

Dinsmore, Christine. *From Surviving to Thriving: Incest, Feminism, and Recovery*. Albany: State University of New York Press, 1991.

Estes, Clarissa Pinkola. *Women Who Run with the Wolves: Myths and Stories of the Wild Woman Archetype*. New York: Ballantine Books, 1992.

Frieze, I. H., et al. *Women and Sex Roles: A Social Psychological Perspective*. New York: W. W. Norton, 1978.

Gilligan, Carol. *In a Different Voice: Psychological Theory and Women's Development*. Cambridge, Mass.: Harvard University Press, 1982.

Griffin, Susan. *Woman and Nature: The Roaring Inside Her*. New York: Harper & Row, 1978.

Hall, Nor. *The Moon and the Virgin: Reflections on the Archetypal Feminine*. New York: Harper & Row, 1980.

Hancock, Emily. *The Girl Within*. New York: Fawcett, 1990.

Jack, Dana Crowley. *Silencing the Self: Women and Depression*. New York: HarperPerennial, 1993.

Johnson, Robert A. *She: Understanding Feminine Psychology*. Rev. ed. New York: Perennial Library, 1989.

Maccoby, Eleanor Emmons, and Carol Nagy Jacklin. *The Psychology of Sex Differences*. Stanford, Calif.: Stanford University Press, 1974.

Maltz, Wendy. *The Sexual Healing Journey: A Guide for Survivors of Sexual Abuse*. New York: HarperCollins, 1991.

Miller, Dusty. *Women Who Hurt Themselves: A Book of Hope and Understanding*. New York: Basic Books, 1995.

Mitchell, Juliet. *Psychoanalysis and Feminism: Freud, Reich, Laing, and Women*. New York: Vintage Books, 1974.

Murdock, Maureen. *The Hero's Daughter*. New York: Fawcett, 1994.

Noble, Kathleen. *The Sound of a Silver Horn: Reclaiming the Heroism in Contemporary Women's Lives*. New York: Fawcett, 1994.

Nolen-Hoeksema, Susan. *Sex Differences in Depression*. Stanford, Calif.: Stanford University Press, 1990.

Oksana, Chrystine. *Safe Passage to Healing: A Guide for Survivors of Ritual Abuse*. New York: HarperPerennial, 1994.

Paludi, Michele A. *Exploring/Teaching the Psychology of Women: A Manual of Resources*. Albany: State University of New York Press, 1990.

Pipher, Mary. *Reviving Ophelia: Saving the Selves of Adolescent Girls*. New York: Ballantine Books, 1995.

RELIGION AND SPIRITUALITY

Barboza, Steven, ed. *American Jihad*. New York: Doubleday, 1994.

Baskin, Judith. *Jewish Women in Historical Perspective*. Detroit: Wayne State University Press, 1991.

Beecher, Maureen Ursenbach, and Lavina Fielding Anderson. *Sisters in Spirit: Mormon Women in Historical and Cultural Perspective*. Urbana: University of Illinois Press, 1992.

Brouwer, Ruth Compton. *New Women for God: Canadian Presbyterian Women and India Missions, 1876-1914*. Toronto: University of Toronto Press, 1990.

Carson, Anne. *Goddesses and Wise Women: The Literature of Feminist Spirituality, 1980-1992*. Freedom, Calif.: Crossing Press, 1992.

Clark, Elizabeth, and Herbert Richardson. *Women and Religion: A Feminist Sourcebook of Christian Thought*. New York: Harper & Row, 1977.

Coll, Regina A. *Christianity and Feminism in Conversation*. Mystic, Conn.: Twenty-Third, 1994.

Daly, Mary. *The Church and the Second Sex*. New York: Harper & Row, 1968.

Donovan, Mary Ann. *Sisterhood as Power: The Past and Passion of Ecclesial Women*. New York: Crossroad, 1989.

Eller, Cynthia. *Living in the Lap of the Goddess: The Feminist Spirituality Movement in America*. New York: Crossroad, 1993.

Ellsworth, Maria, ed. *Mormon Odyssey: The Story of Ida Hunt Udall, Plural Wife*. Urbana: University of Illinois Press, 1992.

Ferguson, Marianne. *Women and Religion*. Englewood Cliffs, N.J.: Prentice Hall, 1995.

Goldenberg, Naomi R. *Changing of the Gods: Feminism and the End of Traditional Religions*. Boston: Beacon Press, 1979.

Grimshaw, Patricia. *Paths of Duty: American Missionary Wives in Nineteenth-Century Hawaii*. Honolulu: University of Hawaii Press, 1989.

Haddad, Yvonne Yazbeck, and Adair T. Lummis, eds. *Islamic Values in the United States: A Comparative Study*. New York: Oxford University Press, 1987.

Haddad, Yvonne Yazbeck, and Jane Idleman Smith, eds. *Muslim Communities in North America*. Albany: State University of New York Press, 1994.

Heschel, Susannah. *On Being a Jewish Feminist*. New York: Schocken Books, 1983.

Higginbotham, Evelyn Brooks. *Righteous Discontent: The Women's Movement in the Black Baptist Church, 1880-1920*. Cambridge, Mass.: Harvard University Press, 1993.

Hill, Patricia R. *The World Their Household: The American Woman's Foreign Mission Movement and Cultural Transformation, 1870-1920*. Ann Arbor: University of Michigan Press, 1985.

Johnson, Elizabeth. *She Who Is: The Mystery of God in Feminist Theological Discourse*. New York: Crossroad, 1992.

King, Ursula. *Women and Spirituality: Voices of Protest and Promise*. 2d ed. University Park: Pennsylvania State University Press, 1993.

Leeming, David, and Jake Page. *Goddess: Myths of the Feminine Divine*. New York: Oxford University Press, 1994.

Lerner, Gerda. *The Creation of Patriarchy*. New York: Oxford University Press, 1986.

Loades, Ann, ed. *Feminist Theology: A Reader*. London: SPCK, 1990.

Macy, Joanna Rogers. *World as Lover, World as Self*. Berkeley, Calif.: Parallax Press, 1991.

Marcus, Jacob. *The American Jewish Woman, 1654-1980*. New York: KTAN, 1981.

Plaskow, Judith, and Carol P. Christ, eds. *Weaving the Visions: New Patterns in Feminist Spirituality*. San Francisco: Harper & Row, 1989.

Pogrebin, Letty Cottin. *Deborah, Golda, and Me: Being Female and Jewish in America*. New York: Crown, 1991.

Puleo, Mev. *The Struggle Is One: Voices and Visions of Liberation*. Albany: State University of New York Press, 1994.

Ruether, Rosemary Radford. *Gaia and God: An Ecofeminist Theology of Earth Healing*. San Francisco: HarperSanFrancisco, 1992.

Ruether, Rosemary Radford, and Rosemary Keller. *Women and Religion in America*. 3 vols. San Francisco: Harper & Row, 1981-1986.

Ruether, Rosemary Radford, and Eleanor McLaughlin, eds. *Women of Spirit: Female Leadership in the Jewish and Christian Traditions*. New York: Simon & Schuster, 1979.

Sacks, Maurie. *Active Voices: Women in Jewish Culture*. Urbana: University of Illinois Press, 1995.

Sexson, Lynda. *Ordinarily Sacred*. 2d ed. Charlottesville: University Press of Virginia, 1992.

Sharma, Arvind, ed. *Religion and Women*. Albany: State University of New York Press, 1993.

________, ed. *Today's Woman in World Religions*. Albany: State University of New York Press, 1993.

Stanton, Elizabeth Cady. *The Woman's Bible*. 1895. Reprint. Boston: Northeastern University Press, 1993.

Starhawk. *Dreaming the Dark: Magic, Sex, and Politics*. 2d ed. Boston: Beacon Press, 1988.

Stewart, M. W., J. Lee, J. A. Foote, and V. W. Broughton. *Spiritual Narratives*. In *The Schomburg Library of Nineteenth-Century Black Women Writers*, edited by Henry Louis Gates, Jr. 25 vols. New York: Oxford University Press, 1988.

Umansky, Ellen, and Diane Ashton, eds. *Four Centuries of Jewish Spirituality*. Boston: Beacon Press, 1992.

Wallace, Ruth A. *They Call Her Pastor*. New York: State University of New York Press, 1992.

Welch, Sharon D. *Communities of Resistance and Solidarity: A Feminist Theology of Liberation*. Maryknoll, N.Y.: Orbis Books, 1985.

Wessinger, Catherine, ed. *Women's Leadership in Marginal Religions: Explorations Outside the Mainstream*. Urbana: University of Illinois Press, 1993.

Science

Abel, Elizabeth, and Emily K. Abel. *The Signs Reader: Women, Gender, and Scholarship*. Chicago: University of Chicago Press, 1983.

Alic, Margaret. *Hypatia's Heritage: A History of Women in Science from Antiquity Through the Nineteenth Century*. Boston: Beacon Press, 1986.

Harding, Sandra. *The Science Question in Feminism*. Ithaca, N.Y.: Cornell University Press, 1986.

Kass-Simon, G., Patricia Farnes, and Deborah Nash, eds. *Women in Science: Righting the Record*. Bloomington: Indiana University Press, 1990.

Keller, Evelyn Fox. *Reflections on Gender and Science*. New Haven, Conn.: Yale University Press, 1985.

McGrayne, Sharon Bertsch. *Nobel Prize Women in Science: Their Lives, Struggles, and Momentous Discoveries*. Secaucus, N.J.: Carol, 1992.

Mozans, H. J. *Woman in Science*. New York: D. Appleton, 1913. Reprint. Cambridge, Mass.: MIT Press, 1974.

Phillips, Patricia. *The Scientific Lady: A Social History of Women's Scientific Interests, 1520-1918*. New York: St. Martin's Press, 1990.

Rossiter, Margaret W. *Women Scientists in America: Before Affirmative Action, 1940-1972*. Baltimore: The Johns Hopkins University Press, 1995.

________. *Women Scientists in America: Struggles and Strategies to 1940*. Baltimore: The Johns Hopkins University Press, 1982.

Schiebinger, Londa. *The Mind Has No Sex?: Women in the Origins of Modern Science*. Cambridge, Mass.: Harvard University Press, 1989.

Sonnert, Gerhard, with Gerald Holton. *Gender Differences in Science Careers: The Project Access Study*. New Brunswick, N.J.: Rutgers University Press, 1995.

Yentsch, Clarice M., and Carl J. Sindermann. *The Woman Scientist: Meeting the Challenges for a Successful Career*. New York: Plenum Press, 1992.

Social Reform Movements

Abolitionist movement

Blackett, R. J. *Building an Antislavery Wall: Black Americans in the Atlantic Abolitionist Movement, 1830-1860*. Ithaca, N.Y.: Cornell University Press, 1989.

Hansen, Debra Gold. *Strained Sisterhood: Gender and Class in the Boston Female Anti-Slavery Society*. Amherst: University of Massachusetts Press, 1993.

Hersh, Blanche. *The Slavery of Sex: Feminist-Abolitionists in America*. Chicago: University of Illinois Press, 1978.

Tyler, Alice Felt. *Freedom's Ferment*. Freeport, N.Y.: Books for Libraries Press, 1950.

Yee, Shirley. *Black Women Abolitionists: A Study in Activism, 1828-1860*. Knoxville: University of Tennessee Press, 1992.

Yellin, Jean Fagan. *Women and Sisters: The Antislavery Feminists In American Culture*. New Haven, Conn.: Yale University Press, 1989.

Civil Rights movement

Brown, Elaine. *A Taste of Power: A Black Woman's Story*. Garden City, N.Y.: Anchor Press, 1992.

Carson, Clayborne. *In Struggle: SNCC and the Black Awakening of the 1960's*. Cambridge, Mass.: Harvard University Press, 1981.

Clark, Septima. *Echo in My Soul*. New York: E. P. Dutton, 1962.

Crawford, Vicki L., Jacqueline Anne Rouse, and Barbara Woods, eds. *Women in the Civil Rights Movement: Trailblazers and Torchbearers, 1941-1965*. Bloomington: Indiana University Press, 1993.

Evans, Sara. *Personal Politics: The Roots of Women's Liberation in the Civil Rights Movement and the New Left*. New York: Vintage Books, 1979.

McFadden, Grace Jordan. *Oral Recollections of Septima Poinsette Clark*. Columbia: University of South Carolina Instructional Services Center, 1980.

Mills, Kay. *This Little Light of Mine: The Life of Fannie Lou Hamer*. New York: Plume/Penguin Books, 1993.

Robinson, Jo Ann Gibson. *The Montgomery Bus Boycott and the Women Who Started It: The Memoir of Jo Ann Gibson Robinson*. Edited by David J. Garrow. Knoxville: University of Tennessee Press, 1987.

Simon, Rita James, and Gloria Danziger. *Women's Movements in America: Their Successes, Disappointments, and Aspirations*. New York: Praeger, 1991.

Williams, Juan. *Eyes on the Prize: America's Civil Rights Years, 1954-1965*. New York: Viking Press, 1987.

Labor movement

Blewett, Mary H. *Men, Women, and Work: Class, Gender, and Protest in the New England Shoe Industry, 1780-1910*. Urbana: University of Illinois Press, 1990.

Boris, Eileen, and Cynthia R. Daniels, eds. *Homework: Historical and Contemporary Perspectives on Paid Labor at Home*. Urbana: University of Illinois Press, 1989.

Briskin, Linda, and Patricia McDermott, eds. *Women Challenging Unions: Feminism, Democracy, Militancy*. Toronto: University of Toronto Press, 1993.

Briskin, Linda, and Lynda Yanz, eds. *Union Sisters: Women in the Labour Movement*. Toronto: Women's Press, 1983.

Cameron, Ardis. *Radicals of the Worst Sort: Laboring Women in Lawrence, Massachusetts, 1860-1912*. Urbana: University of Illinois Press, 1995.

Cobble, Dorothy Sue. *Dishing It Out: Waitresses and Their Unions in the Twentieth Century*. Urbana: University of Illinois Press, 1992.

________, ed. *Women and Unions: Forging a Partnership*. Ithaca, N.Y.: ILR Press, 1993.

Cooper, Patricia A. *Once a Cigar Maker: Men, Women, and Work Culture in American Cigar Factories, 1900-1919*. Urbana: University of Illinois Press, 1992.

Costello, Cynthia B. *"We're Worth It!": Women and Collective Action in the Insurance Workplace*. Urbana: University of Illinois Press, 1992.

Fink, Leon, and Brian Greenberg. *Upheaval in the Quiet Zone: A History of Hospital Workers' Union, Local 1199*. Urbana: University of Illinois Press, 1989.

Foner, Philip S. *Women and the American Labor Movement*. 2 vols. New York: Free Press, 1979, 1980.

Gilpin, Toni, Gary Isaac, Dan Lewin, and Jack McKivigan. *On Strike for Respect: The Clerical and Technical Workers' Strike at Yale University, 1984-85*. Urbana: University of Illinois Press, 1995.

Roby, Pamela. *Women in the Workplace: Proposals for Research and Policy Concerning the Conditions of Women in Industrial and Service Jobs*. Cambridge, Mass.: Schenkman, 1981.

Sacks, Karen Brodkin. *Caring by the Hour: Women, Work, and Organizing at Duke Medical Center*. Urbana: University of Illinois Press, 1988.

Strom, Sharon Hartman. *Beyond the Typewriter: Gender, Class, and the Origins of Modern American Office Work, 1900-1930*. Urbana: University of Illinois Press, 1994.

Wikander, Ulla, Alice Kessler-Harris, and Jane Lewis. *Protecting Women: Labor Legislation in Europe, the United States, and Australia, 1880-1920*. Urbana: University of Illinois Press, 1995.

Peace movement

Alonso, Harriet H. *Peace as a Women's Issue: A History of the U.S. Movement for World Peace and Women's Rights*. Syracuse, N.Y.: Syracuse University Press, 1993.

Brock-Utne, Birgit. *Educating for Peace: A Feminist Perspective*. New York: Pergamon Press, 1985.

Bussey, Gertrude, and Margaret Tims. *Pioneers for Peace: Women's International League for Peace and Freedom, 1915-1965*. 2d ed. London: WILPF, British Section, 1980.

Cromwell, Otelia. *Lucretia Mott*. Cambridge, Mass.: Harvard University Press, 1958.

Kunze, Bonnelyn Young. *Margaret Fell and the Rise of Quakerism*. Stanford, Calif.: Stanford University Press, 1994.

McAllister, P., ed. *Reweaving the Web of Life: Feminism and Nonviolence*. Philadelphia: New Society, 1982.

Settlement house movement

Addams, Jane. *Twenty Years at Hull-House*. New York: Macmillan, 1910.

Bryan, Mary L., and Allen F. Davis, eds. *One Hundred Years at Hull-House*. Bloomington: Indiana University Press, 1990.

Carson, Mina. *Settlement Folk: Social Thought and the American Settlement Movement, 1885-1930*. Chicago: University of Chicago Press, 1990.

Crocker, Ruth Hutchinson. *Social Work and Social Order: The Settlement Movement in Two Industrial Cities, 1889-1930*. Urbana: University of Illinois Press, 1992.

Davis, Allen F. *Spearheads for Reform: The Social Settlements and the Progressive Movement, 1890-1914*. New Brunswick, N.J.: Rutgers University Press, 1984.

Lissak, Rivka Shpak. *Pluralism and Progressives: Hull House and the New Immigrants, 1890-1919*. Chicago: University of Chicago Press, 1989.

Polacheck, Hilda Satt. *I Came A Stranger: The Story of a Hull-House Girl*. Edited by Dena J. Polachek Epstein. Urbana: University of Illinois Press, 1991.

Trolander, Judith Ann. *Settlement Houses and the Great Depression*. Detroit: Wayne State University Press, 1975.

Temperance movement

Blocker, Jack S. *American Temperance Movements: Cycles of Reform*. Boston: Twayne, 1989.

Bordin, Ruth. *Woman and Temperance: The Quest for Power and Liberty 1873-1900*. Philadelphia: Temple University Press, 1981.

Gifford, Carolyn De Swarte. *Writing out My Heart: Selections from the Journal of Frances E. Willard, 1855-96*. Urbana: University of Illinois Press, 1995.

Kerr, K. Austin. *Organized for Prohibition: A New History of the Anti-Saloon League*. New Haven, Conn.: Yale University Press, 1985.

Women's movement

Becker, Susan D. *The Origins of the Equal Rights Amendment: American Feminism Between the Wars*. Westport, Conn.: Greenwood Press, 1981.

Buhle, Mari Jo, and Paul Buhle, eds. *The Concise History of Woman Suffrage: Selections from the Classic Work of Stanton*. Urbana: University of Illinois Press, 1978.

Davis, Flora. *Moving the Mountain: The Women's Movement in America Since 1960*. New York: Simon & Schuster, 1991.

Deckard, Barbara Sinclair. *The Women's Movement*. 3d ed. New York: Harper & Row, 1983.

DuBois, Ellen Carol. *Feminism and Suffrage: The Emergence of an Independent Women's Movement in America, 1848-1869*. Ithaca, N.Y.: Cornell University Press, 1978.

Faludi, Susan. *Backlash: The Undeclared War Against American Women*. New York: Crown, 1991.

Ferree, Myra Marx, and Beth B. Hess. *Controversy and Coalition: The New Feminist Movement Across Three Decades of Change*. New York: Twayne, 1994.

Flexner, Eleanor. *Century of Struggle: The Woman's Rights Movement in the United States*. New York: Atheneum, 1973.

Katzenstein, Mary F., and Carol Mueller. *The Women's Movements in the United States and Western Europe: Consciousness, Political Opportunity, and Public Policy*. Philadelphia: Temple University Press, 1987.

McGlen, Nancy E., and Karen O'Connor. *Women's Rights: The Struggle for Equality in the Nineteenth and Twentieth Centuries*. New York: Praeger, 1983.

Nicholas, Susan C., Alice M. Price, and Rachael Rubin. *Rights and Wrongs: Women's Struggle for Legal Equality*. 2d ed. New York: Feminist Press at the City University of New York, 1986.

Scott, Anne Firor, and Andrew MacKay Scott. *One Half the People: The Fight for Woman Suffrage*. Urbana: University of Illinois Press, 1982.

Steiner, Gilbert Yale. *Constitutional Inequality: The Political Fortunes of the Equal Rights Amendment*. Washington, D.C.: Brookings Institution, 1985.

Strong-Boag, Veronica, and Anita Clair Fellman, eds. *Re-Thinking Canada: The Promise of Women's History*. 2d ed. Toronto: Copp Clark Pitman, 1991.

SPORTS

Beecham, Justin. *Olga*. New York: Paddington Press, 1974.

Carruth, Gordon, and Eugene Ehrlich, eds. *Facts and Dates of American Sports from Colonial Days to the Present*. New York: Harper & Row, 1980.

Cayleff, Susan E. *Babe: The Life and Legend of Babe Didrikson Zaharias*. Urbana: University of Illinois Press, 1995.

Cohen, Greta L., ed. *Women in Sport: Issues and Controversies*. Newbury Park, Calif.: Sage Publications, 1993.

Cummings, Parke. *American Tennis: The Story of a Game and Its People*. Boston: Little, Brown, 1957.

Grumeza, Ion. *Nadia*. New York: Hawthorn Books, 1977.

Killanin, Lord. *My Olympic Years*. New York: William Morrow, 1983.

Mewshaw, Michael. *Ladies of the Court*. New York: Crown, 1993.

Moran, Lyn. *The Young Gymnasts*. New York: Grosset & Dunlap, 1978.

Woolum, Janet. *Outstanding Women Athletes*. Phoenix: Oryx Press, 1992.

VIOLENCE AGAINST WOMEN

Domestic violence and abuse

Bart, Pauline B., and Erin G. Moran, eds. *Violence Against Women: The Bloody Footprints*. Newbury Park, Calif.: Sage Publications, 1993.

Browne, Angela. *When Battered Women Kill*. New York: Free Press, 1987.

Burstow, B. *Radical Feminist Therapy: Working in the Context of Violence*. Newbury Park, Calif.: Sage Publications, 1992.

Buzawa, Eve S., and Carl G. Buzawa, eds. *Domestic Violence: The Changing Criminal Justice Response*. Westport, Conn.: Auburn House, 1992.

DeKeseredy, Walter S., and Ronald Hinch. *Woman Abuse: Sociological Perspectives*. Toronto: Thompson Educational, 1991.

Gelles, Richard J., and Donileen R. Loseke, eds. *Current Controversies on Family Violence*. Newbury Park, Calif.: Sage Publications, 1993.

Gillespie, Cynthia K. *Justifiable Homicide*. Columbus: Ohio State University Press, 1989.

Gondolf, Edward W. *Man Against Woman: What Every Woman Should Know About Violent Men*. Blue Ridge Summit, Pa.: TAB Books, 1989.

Gordon, Linda. *Heroes of Their Own Lives: The Politics and History of Family Violence*. New York: Viking Press, 1988.

Jones, Ann, and Susan Schechter. *When Love Goes Wrong: What to Do When You Can't Do Anything Right*. New York: HarperCollins, 1992.

Kirkwood, Catherine. *Leaving Abusive Partners*. London: Sage Publications, 1993.

Koss, Mary P., et al. *No Safe Haven: Male Violence Against Women at Home, at Work, and in the Community*. Washington, D.C.: American Psychological Association, 1994.

Roberts, Albert R., ed. *Helping Battered Women: New Perspectives and Remedies*. New York: Oxford University Press, 1996.

Schechter, Susan. *Women and Male Violence: The Visions and Struggles of the Battered Women's Movement*. Boston: South End Press, 1982.

Straus, Murray A., Richard J. Gelles, and Suzanne K. Steinmetz. *Behind Closed Doors: Violence in the American Family*. Garden City, N.Y.: Anchor Press/Doubleday, 1980.

Walker, Lenore E. *Terrifying Love: Why Battered Women Kill and How Society Responds*. New York: Harper & Row, 1989.

White, Evelyn C. *Chain, Chain, Change: For Black Women Dealing with Physical and Emotional Abuse*. Seattle: Seal Press, 1985.

Rape

Brownmiller, Susan. *Against Our Will: Men, Women, and Rape*. New York: Bantam Books, 1976.

Buchwald, Emilie, Pamela Fletcher, and Martha Roth. *Transforming a Rape Culture*. Minneapolis: Milkweed Editions, 1993.

Funk, Rus E. *Stopping Rape: A Challenge for Men*. Philadelphia: New Society, 1993.

Gordon, Margaret T., and Stephanie Riger. *The Female Fear: The Social Cost of Rape*. Urbana: University of Illinois Press, 1991.

Russell, Diana E. H. *The Politics of Rape*. New York: Stein & Day, 1975.

Warshaw, Robin. *I Never Called It Rape*. New York: Harper & Row, 1988.

Sexual harassment

Dziech, Billie Wright, and Linda Weiner. *The Lecherous Professor: Sexual Harassment on Campus*. 2d ed. Urbana: University of Illinois Press, 1990.

Paludi, Michele A., ed. *Ivory Power: Sexual Harassment on Campus*. Albany: State University of New York Press, 1990.

________, ed. *Sexual Harassment on College Campuses: Abusing the Ivory Power*. Albany: State University of New York Press, 1996.

Paludi, Michele A., and Richard Barickman. *Academic and Workplace Sexual Harassment: A Resource Manual*. Albany: State University of New York Press, 1991.

WOMEN IN HISTORY

General history

Anderson, Bonnie S., and Judith P. Zinsser. *A History of Their Own: Women in Europe from Prehistory to the Present*. 2 vols. New York: HarperCollins, 1988.

Belfrage, Sally. *Un-American Activities: A Memoir of the Fifties*. New York: HarperCollins, 1994.

Berkin, Carol Ruth, and Mary Beth Norton. *Women of America: A History*. Boston: Houghton Mifflin, 1979.

Carroll, Berenice A., ed. *Liberating Women's History: Theoretical and Critical Essays*. Urbana: University of Illinois Press, 1976.

Chafe, William Henry. *The American Woman: Her Changing Social, Economic, and Political Roles, 1920-1970*. New York: Oxford University Press, 1972.

DuBois, Ellen Carol, and Vicki Ruiz. *Unequal Sisters: A Multicultural Reader in U.S. Women's History*. New York: Routledge, 1990.

Fantham, Elaine, et al. *Women in the Classical World*. New York: Oxford University Press, 1994.

Franck, Irene M., and David Brownstone. *Women's World: A Timeline of Women In History*. New York: HarperCollins, 1995.

Ginzberg, Lori D. *Women and the Work of Benevolence: Morality, Politics, and Class in the Nineteenth-Century United States*. New Haven, Conn.: Yale University Press, 1990.

Goodrich, Norma Lorre. *Heroines*. New York: HarperCollins, 1993.

Hartmann, Susan M. *The Home Front and Beyond: American Women in the 1940's*. Boston: Twayne, 1982.

Harvey, Brett. *The Fifties: A Women's Oral History*. New York: HarperPerennial, 1994.

Hewitt, Nancy A., ed. *Women, Families, and Communities: Readings in American History*. Glenview, Ill.: Scott, Foresman, 1990.

Hymowitz, Carol, and Michaele Weissman. *A History of Women in America*. New York: Bantam Books, 1978.

Kerber, Linda K., and Jane Sherron Dehart. *Women's America: Refocusing the Past*. 4th ed. New York: Oxford University Press, 1995.

Lerner, Gerda. *The Majority Finds Its Past: Placing Women in History*. New York: Oxford University Press, 1979.

Miles, Rosalind. *The Women's History of the World*. New York: Harper & Row, 1990.

Mills, Kay. *From Pocahontas to Power Suits: Everything You Need to Know About Women's History in America*. New York: Plume, 1995.

Morris, Celia. *Fanny Wright: Rebel in America*. Urbana: University of Illinois Press, 1992.

Norton, Mary Beth, ed. *Major Problems in American Women's History*. Lexington, Mass.: D. C. Heath, 1989.

Riley, Glenda. *Inventing the American Woman: An Inclusive History*. 2d ed. 2 vols. Wheeling, Ill.: Harlan Davidson, 1995.

Scott, Anne Firor. *Natural Allies: Women's Associations in American History*. Urbana: University of Illinois Press, 1993.

Woloch, Nancy. *Women and the American Experience*. 2d ed. New York: McGraw-Hill, 1994.

The American Revolution

Evans, Sara. *Born for Liberty: A History of Women in America*. New York: Free Press, 1989.

Kerber, Linda K. *Women of the Republic: Intellect and Ideology in Revolutionary America*. New York: W. W. Norton, 1986.

Norton, Mary Beth. *Liberty's Daughters: The Revolutionary Experience of American Women, 1750-1800*. Boston: Little, Brown, 1980.

Young, Philip. *Revolutionary Ladies*. New York: Alfred A. Knopf, 1977.

The Great Depression and the New Deal

Hoff-Wilson, Joan, and Marjorie Lightman, eds. *Without Precedent: The Life and Career of Eleanor Roosevelt*. Bloomington: Indiana University Press, 1984.

Scharf, Lois. *To Work and to Wed: Female Employment, Feminism, and the Great Depression*. Westport, Conn.: Greenwood Press, 1980.

Sternsher, Bernard, and Judith Sealander. *Women of Valor: The Struggle Against the Great Depression as Told in Their Own Life Stories*. Chicago: Ivan R. Dee, 1990.

Ware, Susan. *Holding Their Own: American Women in the 1930's*. Boston: Twayne, 1982.

Women's Studies

Butler, Jonella, and John Walter. *Transforming the Curriculum: Ethnic Studies and Women's Studies*. Albany: State University of New York Press, 1991.

Hull, Gloria T., Patricia Bell Scott, and Barbara Smith, eds. *All the Women Are White, All the Blacks Are Men, but Some of Us Are Brave: Black Women's Studies*. Old Westbury, N.Y.: Feminist Press, 1982.

Hunter College Women's Studies Collective. *Women's Realities, Women's Choices*. 2d ed. New York: Oxford University Press, 1995.

Rao, Anna, ed. *Women's Studies International: Nairobi and Beyond*. New York: Feminist Press, 1991.

Richardson, Diane, and Victoria Robinson, eds. *Thinking Feminist: Key Concepts in Women's Studies*. New York: Guilford Press, 1993.

Ruth, Sheila. *Issues in Feminism*. 3d ed. Mountain View, Calif.: Mayfield, 1995.

Work and Employment

Briggs, Carole S. *Women in Space, Reaching the Last Frontier*. Minneapolis: Lerner, 1988.

Davies, Margery W. *Woman's Place Is at the Typewriter: Office Work and Office Workers, 1870-1930*. Philadelphia: Temple University Press, 1982.

Dublin, Thomas, ed. *Farm to Factory: Women's Letters, 1830-1860*. New York: Columbia University Press, 1981.

Green, James, ed. *Workers' Struggles, Past and Present: A "Radical America" Reader*. Philadelphia: Temple University Press, 1983.

Jensen, Joan M., and Sue Davidson, eds. *A Needle, a Bobbin, a Strike: Women Needleworkers in America*. Philadelphia: Temple University Press, 1984.

Kessler-Harris, Alice. *Out to Work: A History of Wage-Earning Women in the United States*. New York: Oxford University Press, 1982.

Lamphere, Louise. *From Working Daughters to Working Mothers: Immigrant Women in a New England Industrial Community*. Ithaca, N.Y.: Cornell University Press, 1987.

Levin, Beatrice. *Women and Medicine*. 2d ed. Lincoln, Nebr.: Media, 1988.

Levine, Louis. *The Women Garment Workers: A History of the International Ladies' Garment Workers' Union*. New York: B. W. Huebsch, 1924.

Rosen, Ellen Israel. *Bitter Choices: Blue-Collar Women in and out of Work*. Chicago: University of Chicago Press, 1987.

Weiner, Lynn Y. *From Working Girl to Working Mother: The Female Labor Force in the United States, 1820-1980*. Chapel Hill: University of North Carolina Press, 1985.

Filmography

Compiled by Erik Rasmussen

The Accused (1988)
Jodie Foster received her first Academy Award for best actress for her portrayal of a strong young woman who fights to put her attackers on trial after she is gang-raped.

Adam's Rib (1949)
Katharine Hepburn and Judy Holliday star in this film that deals with women's rights and the justice system. Hepburn and Spencer Tracy are husband-and-wife attorneys on opposite sides of a court case involving attempted murder. Holliday plays a woman accused of shooting her two-timing husband.

Agatha (1979)
Vanessa Redgrave stars as Agatha Christie in this fictional account of what happened when the famous mystery writer disappeared for eleven days during 1926. Dustin Hoffman portrays an American journalist who finds Christie hiding out at a health spa.

Agnes of God (1985)
This film adaptation of John Pielmeier's 1982 Broadway play is about a young nun (played by Meg Tilly) who is accused of killing her own baby. Jane Fonda portrays a psychiatrist who analyzes Tilly and deals with the convent's stern mother superior (played by Anne Bancroft).

Alice Adams (1935)
Katharine Hepburn plays a social-climbing young woman living in a small town who seeks romance while trying to downplay her family's lack of money and ambition.

Alice Doesn't Live Here Anymore (1974)
Ellen Burstyn won an Academy Award for her portrayal of an impoverished widow who rears a son on her own while fulfilling her aspirations to become a singer.

Aliens (1986)
In this sequel to *Alien* (1979), Sigourney Weaver returns as Ripley, the sole survivor of a spacecraft crew killed by a malevolent alien from a remote planet. After drifting through space asleep for fifty years, she is found and returned to the same planet with a new crew. There she leads the successful human struggle against a colony of the aliens.

All About Eve (1950)
In this realistic insight into theater, Bette Davis gives an engaging performance as an aging Broadway star in competition with an ambitious young actress (played by Anne Baxter).

Amy (1981)
This sentimental film focuses on a woman (played by Jenny Agutter) who leaves her husband (played by Barry Newman) in order to teach deaf children how to speak.

Anastasia (1956)
Set in Paris in the late 1920's, this film features Ingrid Bergman playing a young woman suffering from amnesia who is chosen by exiled Russians to impersonate the daughter of the murdered czar.

Angie (1994)
Geena Davis stars in this romantic comedy about a young working woman who becomes pregnant. Instead of marrying her boyfriend (played by James Gandolfini), she leaves him and begins a relationship with a charming stranger (played by Stephen Rea).

Ann Vickers (1933)
After being abandoned by her lover (played by Bruce Cabot), a young woman played by Irene Dunne begins a new life as the superintendent of a model women's detention home. This is an example of a story in which the strong female character is not a victimized inmate.

Anna and the King of Siam (1946)
An English governess (played by Irene Dunne) working as the teacher of the Siamese king's many children during the mid-nineteenth century gradually wins the respect and love of the autocratic Asian ruler (played by Rex Harrison). Based on a true story, this tale is best known in its musical version, *The King and I*, which was adapted to film in 1956 starring Deborah Kerr and Yul Brynner.

Anna Karenina (1935)
Based on Leo Tolstoy's novel *Anna Karénina* (1875-1877), this film stars Greta Garbo as the wife of a Russian aristocrat who is having an affair with a cavalry officer (played by Frederic March).

Anne of Green Gables (1985)
Set in 1908 on Canada's Prince Edward Island, this film tells the story of Anne (played by Megan Follows), a foster child taken in by a farmer and his wife (played by Richard Farnsworth and Colleen Dewhurst). Her new parents expect her to behave as a boy by helping with their farm work, but her spirit, intelligence, and mischievous antics produce much different results. Based on L. M. Montgomery's 1909 novel.

Anne of the Thousand Days (1969)
Genevieve Bujold plays Anne Boleyn in this tragic tale about the mother of Queen Elizabeth I. After being forced into marriage with King Henry VIII (played by Richard Burton), Anne eventually falls in love with him, only to be beheaded for failing to produce a son.

Annie Get Your Gun (1950)
Based on a hit Broadway musical, this lavish film stars Betty Hutton as the celebrated sharpshooter Annie Oakley, who toured with Buffalo Bill's Wild West show.

Annie Hall (1977)
Often called Woody Allen's finest film, this story examines the often-neurotic relationship of a young couple living in New York City (played by Woody Allen and Diane Keaton). Keaton won an Academy Award for Best Actress.

Another Time, Another Place (1958)
Lana Turner stars as an American newspaper woman who has an affair with a British war correspondent (played by Sean Connery) during World War II. After tragedy strikes, the couple's relationship falls apart.

Auntie Mame (1958)
Adapted from Patrick Dennis' 1955 novel, this film is about an eccentric aunt (played by Rosalind Russell) who becomes the guardian of her young orphaned nephew. Russell was nominated for an Academy Award.

Bachelor Mother (1939)
Ginger Rogers stars as a working woman who finds an infant on a doorstep. Mistaken for the baby's mother, the woman is in danger of losing her job during the confusion that follows her discovery.

Bad Girls (1994)
This Western tells the story of four prostitutes (played by Drew Barrymore, Andie MacDowell, Mary Stuart Masterson, and Madeleine Stowe) who must start new lives after one of them gets in trouble with the law. Their plans for freedom are altered when the only money they have is stolen.

Basic Instinct (1992)
This controversial film focuses on a psychological game played by a bisexual mystery writer (played by Sharon Stone) whose novels mirror real-life crimes and a San Francisco homicide detective (played by Michael Douglas) who suspects her of murder.

Becky Sharp (1935)
Miriam Hopkins plays a hardened young woman whose only care in the world is the advancement of her social status. Based on William Makepeace Thackeray's novel *Vanity Fair* (1847-1848), this was one of the earliest motion pictures to be filmed in Technicolor.

The Best Little Whorehouse in Texas (1982)
Based on a Broadway musical, this comedy is about a brothel known as the Chicken Ranch, the people that frequent it, and the community that must deal with it. Dolly Parton stars as the amiable madam.

Black Girl (1972)
Directed by Ossie Davis, this intense drama explores the relationship between Mama Rose (played by Louise Stubbs), who feels she is a failure as a mother, and her children. Alienation and isolation are two themes prominent in the film.

Black Narcissus (1946)
In this film based on Rumer Godden's 1939 novel, Deborah Kerr stars as a nun trying to maintain a mission in the isolation of the harsh and inclement Himalaya Mountains.

Blonde Venus (1932)
Marlene Dietrich plays a woman who must deal with a husband afflicted with radium poisoning, a wealthy playboy with whom she has an affair, and a son she almost loses.

Bloody Mama (1970)
Shelley Winters stars as the famous real-life gangster Ma Baker who, with her four sons, terrorized victims during the Depression. Directed by Roger Corman.

Bob & Carol & Ted & Alice (1969)
Directed by Paul Mazursky, this odd romantic comedy is about a couple who, envious of their friends' marriage, almost swap partners. Natalie Wood and Robert Culp and Elliott Gould and Dyan Cannon play the couples in the film. Cannon received an Academy Award nomination for Best Supporting Actress.

Bombshell (1933)
Jean Harlow plays a film star who is shamelessly manipulated by her studio's press agent (played by Lee Tracy). This unusual film has been retrospectively seen as a parody of Harlow's own tragic life as a sex symbol during the 1930's.

Bonnie and Clyde (1967)
Faye Dunaway and Warren Beatty costar as the historical bank robbers who terrorized the Midwest during the Great Depression. Estelle Parsons won an Academy Award in a supporting role.

Boxcar Bertha (1972)
Similar to *Bonnie and Clyde*, this action film stars Barbara Hershey as a small-town woman who joins a group of train robbers, whose leader is played by David Carradine. Directed by Martin Scorsese.

Boys on the Side (1995)
Three young women (played by Drew Barrymore, Whoopi Goldberg, and Mary Louise Parker) with different backgrounds head for Southern California. The trip abruptly stops in Arizona when one woman becomes ill with AIDS, drawing the women closer to one another.

Breakfast at Tiffany's (1961)
Audrey Hepburn stars as Holly Golightly, a free-spirited woman who must change her ways after falling in love with a writer (played by George Peppard) who lives in the same building. Hepburn was nominated for an Academy Award.

Broken Blossoms (1919)
This silent film is a harsh melodrama set in London about a Chinese man (played by Richard Barthelmess) who falls in love with a young white woman (played by Lillian Gish) who is terrified by her father, a boxer. After the father loses a match and beats his daughter to death, the Chinese man avenges her.

Bus Stop (1956)
Based on William Inge's 1955 play, this film stars Marilyn Monroe as a small-time café singer who entices a modern cowboy (played by Don Murray) so strongly that he kidnaps her.

Butterfield 8 (1960)
Elizabeth Taylor won an Academy Award for her performance as a prostitute who wants to leave her profession. The film is based on the 1935 novel by John O'Hara.

Cabaret (1972)
Liza Minnelli received an Academy Award for her powerful portrayal of Sally Bowles, an American cabaret singer in Berlin on the eve of World War II.

Camille (1936)
A dying courtesan (played by Greta Garbo) falls in love with an innocent young man (played by Robert Taylor). The film is an adaptation of Alexandre Dumas' 1852 novel. Garbo received an Academy Award nomination.

Carmen Jones (1954)
Otto Preminger's adaptation of George Bizet's opera *Carmen* (1875) tells a modern story of a beautiful factory worker who seduces a soldier, then leaves him for a prizefighter. Dorothy Dandridge's Academy Award nomination was the first made to an African American for Best Acting.

Carrie (1976)
Based on Stephen King's 1974 novel, this horror film is about a strange and repressed teenager (played by Sissy Spacek) who wishes only to lead a normal life. After her high school classmates play cruel tricks on her at the school prom, she uses her telekinetic powers to exact a devastating revenge. Both Spacek and Piper Laurie, who played her mother, received Academy Award nominations for their performances.

Catherine the Great (1934)
Elisabeth Bergner stars in this story of the famed czarina of Russia and the Grand Duke Peter (played by Douglas Fairbanks, Jr.), who is not happy with his marriage to Catherine. Flora Robson costars.

Cattle Queen of Montana (1954)
Barbara Stanwyck plays a young woman struggling to protect her farm from land barons who murder her father and from unfriendly American Indians. Ronald Reagan costars in this Western directed by Allan Dwan.

The Cemetery Club (1993)
The relationship among three close friends struggling with the difficulties of aging and loneliness is tested when one of the friends (played by Ellen Burstyn) becomes romantically involved with a fellow widower (played by Danny Aiello). Olympia Dukakis and Diane Ladd costar.

Children of a Lesser God (1986)
Adapted from Mark Medoff's award-winning 1980 play, this drama focuses on the romantic relationship between a teacher (played by William Hurt) and one of his deaf students (played by Marlee Matlin), who refuses to learn how to use her voice to communicate. Matlin, who is deaf in real life, won an Academy Award for her performance.

The Children's Hour (1962)
Based on Lillian Hellman's 1934 play, this film tells the story of a mischievous schoolgirl (played by Karen Balkin) who accuses two teachers (played by Audrey Hepburn and Shirley MacLaine) of being lesbians. Fay Bainter, who plays the child's influential grandmother, received an Academy Award nomination.

Choose Me (1984)
Alan Rudolph directed this unconventional film about two women who become unlikely roommates. One is a radio sex therapist (played by Genevieve Bujold) who seeks sexual liberation; the other is a former prostitute (played by Lesley Ann Warren) who falls in love with a man (played by Keith Carradine) who claims to be a pathological liar.

Cimarron (1931)
Irene Dunne received her first Academy Award nomination for her portrayal of a young woman who settles in the Oklahoma Territory with her new husband (played by Richard Dix). After watching the prairie around them develop into a city, the husband moves farther west, leaving the woman behind to establish herself as a town leader.

Cinderella (1949)
An animated version of the classic fairy tale in which a beautiful young woman is mistreated by her stepmother and stepsisters until she is rescued by a prince. Iline Woods, Eleanor Audley, Verna Felton, and Claire Dubrey provide the women's voices in this classic Walt Disney film.

Claudine (1974)
A thirty-six-year-old single mother (played by Diahann Carroll) tries to keep her family of six children together. James Earl Jones plays a garbage collector who is her boyfriend. Directed by John Berry.

Cleopatra (1963)
Elizabeth Taylor plays the Egyptian beauty who beguiled both Julius Caesar (played by Rex Harrison) and Marc Antony (played by Richard Burton) during the Roman occupation of Egypt. Directed by Joseph L. Mankiewicz.

Coal Miner's Daughter (1980)
Sissy Spacek won an Oscar for her role as country singer Loretta Lynn in this film, which documents the singer's rise from poverty in Appalachia to immense fame. Tommy Lee Jones plays Lynn's husband and manager.

The Color Purple (1985)
Adapted from Alice Walker's 1982 novel, director Steven Spielberg's dramatic film is about the enduring love between two African American sisters who are separated as teenagers. Whoopi Goldberg, who later won an Academy Award for Best Supporting Actress for *Ghost* (1990), was nominated for Best Actress, and Oprah Winfrey was nominated for Best Supporting Actress.

Come Back, Little Sheba (1952)
A housewife (played by Shirley Booth) tries to salvage her marriage to an alcoholic (played by Burt Lancaster). The film is based on the 1950 play by William Inge. Booth won an Academy Award for Best Actress.

Come Back to the 5 & Dime Jimmy Dean, Jimmy Dean (1982)
Robert Altman directed this adaptation of a Broadway play about a group of women who hold a twentieth reunion of their James Dean fan club. Sandy Dennis, Cher, Kathy Bates, and Karen Black star in the film.

The Country Girl (1954)
Based on a Clifford Odets 1950 play, this powerful drama centers on an alcoholic singer (played by Bing Crosby) who tries to make a comeback. Grace Kelly won an Academy Award for her performance as the singer's supportive wife.

Cover Girl (1944)
A chorus girl (played by Rita Hayworth) leaves her chorus line in order to become a model in this Charles Vidor musical.

Craig's Wife (1936)
Harriet Craig (played by Rosalind Russell) is a married woman who finds more independence and pleasure in taking care of her home than in being with her husband. Only after everyone she knows dies or deserts her does she realize that marriage should be for love, not money.

Dancing in the Dark (1986)
A dedicated wife's perfect world is decimated when she discovers that her husband is having an affair. Martha Henry plays the unfortunate woman who resorts to drastic actions when faced with her husband's infidelity.

A Dangerous Woman (1993)
In a small California town an ostracized woman (played by Debra Winger) living next door to her aunt (played by Barbara Hershey) experiences a sexual awakening when an alcoholic drifter (played by Gabriel Byrne) comes into their lives.

Dark Victory (1939)
Edmund Golding directed this classic tearjerker about a Long Island socialite (played by Bette Davis) who slowly goes blind until she dies from a brain tumor. George Brent plays the surgeon who falls in love with her while treating her.

Desert Hearts (1985)
Set in the 1950's, this unusual film is about a woman (played by Helen Shaver) who travels to Nevada in order to file for divorce and falls in love with a woman (played by Patricia Charbonneau) on the trip.

Designing Woman (1957)
Two New Yorkers (played by Gregory Peck and Lauren Bacall) meet in Southern California, fall in love, and marry. When they return to Manhattan, they find that the man's life as a sportswriter and the woman's life as a fashion designer do not blend well; however, the strength of their love helps them face the challenges of marriage.

Desperately Seeking Susan (1985)
Rosanna Arquette plays a bored housewife who switches identities with a mysterious woman named Susan (played by Madonna), whose personal ads she has been reading. Laurie Metcalf has a small role in the film, which is directed by Susan Siedelman.

Diary of a Mad Housewife (1970)
Set in Manhattan, this film chronicles the life of a middle-aged woman (played by Carrie Snodgrass) who believes that she is married to the worst husband (played by Richard Benjamin) in the world.

Driving Miss Daisy (1989)
The winner of an Academy Award for Best Picture, this film examines the gradually developing friendship between a rich Southern Jewish widow (played by Jessica Tandy) and her African American chauffeur (played by Morgan Freeman). Tandy won an Academy Award for her performance.

The Effect of Gamma Rays on Man-in-the-Moon Marigolds (1972)
Paul Newman directed this skillful adaptation of the 1971 Pulitzer Prize-winning play about a luckless woman (played by Joanne Woodward) who never loses hope that she and her daughters will achieve greatness.

Eleni (1985)
Based on Nicholas Gage's best-selling 1983 novel, this drama explores the life of a woman (played by Kate Nelligan) who is tortured and executed by Greek communists after she interferes with their abduction of her children. John Malkovich plays the man who devotes his life to finding her killers.

The Farmer's Daughter (1947)
In this variation of the Cinderella story, a young servant (played by Loretta Young) runs for the congressional seat occupied by her boss. Ethel Barrymore, Joseph Cotten, and Charles Bickford costar.

Fatal Attraction (1987)
A tense thriller centering on a respectable executive (played by Michael Douglas) who has an affair with an emotionally unstable woman (played by Glenn Close) when his wife (played by Anne Archer) is out of town. After the man's wife returns and he tries to end the affair, his scorned lover tries to exact a violent revenge.

Fried Green Tomatoes (1991)
Jessica Tandy plays an elderly woman living in a nursing home in the deep South who inspires a housewife (played by Kathy Bates) with her amazing anecdotes about the adventures of two women (played by Mary Stuart Masterson and Mary Louise Parker) during the Great Depression.

The Fuller Brush Girl (1950)
Lucille Ball plays a Fuller Brush salesperson who is accidentally drawn into a murder case. Directed by Lloyd Bacon.

Fundi: The Story of Ella Baker (1981)
A profile of civil rights leader Ella Baker, former executive director of the Southern Christian Leadership Conference (SCLC) and founder of the Student Nonviolent Coordinating Committee (SNCC).

Funny Girl (1968)
In a film debut that won for her an Academy Award for Best Actress, Barbra Streisand plays comedian Fanny Brice in this lavish musical.

Gentlemen Prefer Blondes (1953)
Adapted from Anita Loos's 1925 novel, this musical comedy features Marilyn Monroe and Jane Russell as entertainers traveling to Paris on an ocean liner. Their performance

of "Diamonds Are a Girl's Best Friend" helped to make the song's title a popular cliché.

Gigi (1958)
Leslie Caron stars in this Alan Jay Lerner and Frederick Loewe musical as a young French woman reared to be a courtesan who falls in love with a handsome rake (played by Louis Jourdan). Maurice Chevalier's rendition of "Thank Heaven for Little Girls" is one of the musical's most enduring songs.

Gone with the Wind (1939)
Hattie McDaniel became the first African American to win an Academy Award for her powerful portrayal of a loyal Southern mammy during the Civil War in this adaptation of Margaret Mitchell's epic 1936 novel. Vivien Leigh also won an Academy Award for her role as Scarlett O'Hara, the Southern beauty so obsessed with another woman's husband that she fails to recognize true love when it is within her grasp.

The Good Mother (1988)
Based on Sue Miller's best-selling 1986 novel, this film focuses on a single mother (played by Diane Keaton) whose lifestyle is not easily accepted by society.

Gorillas in the Mist (1988)
This film chronicles the twenty-year career of Dian Fossey (played by Sigourney Weaver), whose research into African mountain gorillas came into the international spotlight in 1977 after reports of their slaughter by poachers.

Grace Quigley (1985)
Katharine Hepburn plays an elderly woman who hires a hit man (played by Nick Nolte) to murder her aging friends who no longer wish to live. This black comedy was a dark precursor to the notorious career of the real-life Michigan doctor Jack Kevorkian during the 1990's.

The Group (1966)
Sidney Lumet directed this adaptation of Mary McCarthy's 1963 novel about the lives of eight women who graduated from Vassar College in 1933. Candice Bergen, Jessica Walter, Joan Hackett, and Shirley Knight star in the film.

Guess Who's Coming to Dinner (1967)
In one of the most commercially successful films ever made about interracial romance, Sidney Poitier stars as an African American doctor engaged to marry a young white woman (played by Katharine Houghton). His appearance at the home of his fiancée's wealthy parents (played by Spencer Tracy and Katharine Hepburn) challenges their liberal views.

Gypsy (1962)
This musical from Mervyn LeRoy is about stripper Gypsy Rose Lee (played by Natalie Wood) and her stage mother (played by Rosalind Russell). Karl Malden and Parley Baer costar in what was originally a Broadway production featuring Ethel Merman.

The Hand That Rocks the Cradle (1992)
When a doctor commits suicide after being charged with sexually molesting a patient (played by Annabella Sciorra), his pregnant wife (played by Rebecca De Mornay) loses her baby. Mentally unstable following the tragedy, she becomes the nanny of the patient's unsuspecting family and vows revenge.

The Handmaid's Tale (1990)
Adapted from Margaret Atwood's 1985 novel, this futuristic story is about one of the few remaining fertile women (played by Natasha Richardson), who is enslaved by a government leader (played by Robert Duvall) trying to get a baby for himself and his wife (played by Faye Dunaway).

Hannah and Her Sisters (1986)
Mia Farrow, Barbara Hershey, and Dianne Wiest star in Woody Allen's romantic comedy about three sisters, their weaknesses, and the men in their lives. Wiest won an Academy Award for Best Supporting Actress.

Happy Hooker (1975)
This humorous film gives a keen insight into the world of prostitution, focusing on the rise of Xaviera Hollander (played by Lynn Redgrave), whose best-selling book was the basis for the film.

Harold and Maude (1972)
This quirky black comedy is about the unlikely relationship between a young man obsessed with death (played by Bud Cort) who marries an elderly woman obsessed with life (played by Ruth Gordon).

Heart Like a Wheel (1983)
Bonnie Bedelia stars as Shirley "Cha-Cha" Muldowney, a drag-strip racer who becomes a champion on the track while unable to find stability in her family life.

Hedda (1975)
Inspired by the Royal Shakespeare production of Henrik Ibsen's *Hedda Gabler* (1890), this tale features Glenda Jackson in the title role as a bored and impatient woman who wrecks the lives of the men who pursue her.

The Heiress (1949)
Olivia de Havilland won an Academy Award portraying a wealthy but lonely spinster who is courted by a charming fortune hunter (played by Montgomery Clift). Set in turn-of-the-century New York, the film is adapted from Henry James's novel *Washington Square* (1881).

Hello, Dolly! (1969)
Adapted from a hit Broadway musical that was based on Thornton Wilder's play *The Matchmaker* (1955), this lavish musical stars Barbra Streisand as a matchmaker in early twentieth century New York who gets married herself. Although many critics regarded Streisand as too young for the part that Carole Channing made famous on the stage, her singing silenced most of the criticism.

His Girl Friday (1940)
This comedic version of *The Front Page* (1931) stars Rosalind Russell as a prima donna reporter who is about to settle down and marry a businessman (played by Ralph Bellamy) when a murder scoop tempts her to write one last story. Cary Grant costars.

Holiday (1938)
Adapted from Philip Barry's 1928 Broadway play, this comedy stars Cary Grant as a young man who feels that in order to please his fiancée (played by Doris Nolan), he must join her father's banking firm. Only his fiancée's sister (played by Katharine Hepburn) realizes that this is not the kind of life he should lead.

Hollywood Boulevard (1976)
Joe Dante directed this Roger Corman studio spoof of B-movies. Candice Rialson plays an aspiring actress who begins working in Hollywood in low-budget films and gets tangled up in several bizarre murders.

I Remember Mama (1948)
Barbara Bel Geddes plays a novelist who reminisces about her Norwegian family, the American Dream, and growing up in San Francisco. Irene Dunne was nominated for an Academy Award for her role as the devoted mother of Bel Geddes.

I Want to Live! (1958)
Susan Hayward received an Academy Award for her powerful portrayal of a prostitute executed for murder. Based on the case of Barbara Graham, who was one of the most prominent women ever sent to the gas chamber, this filmed help to spark a national debate over capital punishment.

I'll Be Seeing You (1944)
Directed by William Dieterle, this drama is about a convicted killer (played by Ginger Rogers) who falls in love with a soldier (played by Joseph Cotten) while paroled for the Christmas holidays.

I'll Cry Tomorrow (1955)
Susan Hayward portrays 1930's stage and film star Lillian Roth, recounting her marital problems and her battle with alcoholism. Jo Van Fleet plays Roth's depressed mother.

The Incredible Shrinking Woman (1981)
A quasi-feminist takeoff on the science-fiction classic *The Incredible Shrinking Man* (1957), this film is also a satire on American consumerism. In contrast to the "shrinking man" whose diminution is caused by a mysterious fog, Lily Tomlin plays a housewife who shrinks to minute proportions after reacting badly to a home-care product that her husband (played by Charles Grodin) advertises.

Jane Eyre (1944)
Adapted from the classic 1847 novel by Charlotte Brontë, this film is about an orphan (played by Joan Fontaine) who grows up to become the governess for the daughter of a wealthy Englishman and gets involved with mystery and romance. Elizabeth Taylor also stars in the film.

Janis (1974)
A powerful documentary study of the 1960's hard-rock singer Janis Joplin and her tragic fall from grace. The film includes interviews with Joplin and her fellow musicians and friends, as well as film clips from her concerts.

Jezebel (1938)
Bette Davis received an Academy Award for Best Actress playing a spoiled Southern belle who cannot decide whether to marry a banker (played by Henry Fonda) or a dandy (played by George Brent). The film was reportedly made to satisfy Davis after she failed to win the role of Scarlett O'Hara in *Gone with the Wind* (1939).

Johnny Belinda (1948)
Jane Wyman won an Academy Award for her performance as a deaf-mute farm girl who survives several numerous calamities, including a rape that leaves her with a child.

Johnny Guitar (1954)
This odd Western tells the story of a saloon owner (played by Joan Crawford) who becomes romantically involved with an outlaw (played by Scott Brady). The leader of a vigilante group (played by Mercedes McCambridge) accuses her of being a member of his gang. Directed by Nicholas Ray.

The Joy Luck Club (1993)
Told through vignettes and flashbacks, this poignant drama tells the story of the difficult, sometimes strained relationships between four Chinese immigrant mothers and their daughters. Based on Amy Tan's popular 1989 novel.

Julia (1977)
Set on the eve of World War II, this film centers around the relationship between two women (played by Jane Fonda and Vanessa Redgrave). Redgrave won the Academy Award for Best Supporting Actress for the film, which is based on a memoir by playwright Lillian Hellman.

King Kong (1933)
In this classic science-fiction film, Fay Wray defined the archetypal woman-as-screaming-victim. She plays a beautiful young woman down on her luck who is taken to an unchartered island by an adventurous filmmaker (played by Robert Armstrong). After islanders try to sacrifice her to a giant ape, the filmmaker and his men rescue her, capture the ape, and take it to New York. There it escapes and terrorizes the city, carrying the young woman to the top of the Empire State Building.

Kitty Foyle (1940)
Adapted from Christopher Morley's 1939 novel, this dramatic story is about a young working woman (played by Ginger Rogers) who falls in love with a wealthy socialite but does not find true happiness until she connects with a man from her own social class. Rogers won an Academy Award for her performance.

Klute (1971)
A New York city prostitute (played by Jane Fonda) trying to find stability in her life is pursued by a police officer (played by Donald Sutherland) who connects her with a missing friend for whom he is searching. Fonda won an Academy Award for what some critics regard as of her most provocative performance.

Kramer vs. Kramer (1979)
The winner of five Academy Awards, including Best Picture, this drama is about a father (played by Dustin Hoffman) and son (played by Justin Henry) who create a strong

bond when the mother (played by Meryl Streep) leaves them. Jane Alexander costars.

Lady Chatterley's Lover (1982)
This visually gripping love story features Sylvia Kristel as an English noblewoman seeking sexual satisfaction. Adapted from D. H. Lawrence's 1928 novel.

The Lady Eve (1941)
This lively screwball comedy directed by Preston Sturges stars Barbara Stanwyck as a con woman who preys on a rich herpetologist (played by Henry Fonda).

Lady in a Cage (1964)
Olivia de Havilland plays a wealthy invalid who is trapped in her own elevator by young hoodlums who go on a violent rampage in her home.

Lady Sings the Blues (1972)
Former Supremes singer Diana Ross made her acting debut in this film treatment of the troubled, drug-infested life of jazz singer Billie Holliday. Billy Dee Williams, Richard Pryor, and Scatman Crothers costar in the film, which is based on Holliday's 1956 autobiography.

A League of Their Own (1992)
This powerful drama pays tribute to the first women's professional baseball league, which was formed during World War II. Geena Davis, Madonna, Rosie O'Donnell, and Lori Petty star as members of a team called the Rockford Peaches. Directed by Penny Marshall, who earlier costarred in the television sitcom *Laverne and Shirley*.

A Letter to Three Wives (1949)
Three women (played by Jeanne Crain, Linda Darnell, and Ann Sothern) receive a letter from a mutual friend who says that she has stolen one of their husbands, but will not say which one. The women react to the shocking news by recounting their marriages, searching for the answer.

Lianna (1983)
Linda Griffiths plays the title role as a young woman who reluctantly falls in love with another woman as her unhappy marriage disintegrates. Writer-director John Sayles plays the husband of Lianna's best friend.

Lili (1953)
This popular musical, based on a Paul Gallico short story, stars Leslie Caron as a French foundling who joins a carnival. As the young woman falls in love with a magician (played by Jean Pierre Aumont), the carnival's puppeteer (played by Mel Ferrer) falls in love with her.

The Little Drummer Girl (1984)
Adapted from best-selling author John Le Carré's 1983 novel, this spy thriller focuses on a theater actress (played by Diane Keaton) who is selected by Israeli agents to trap a Palestinian terrorist.

The Little Foxes (1941)
Bette Davis plays the ruthless matriarch who heads a greedy Southern family. An adaptation of Lillian Hellman's 1939 play, this film explores the difficulties that aristocratic landowners faced in adjusting to twentieth century social changes.

Little Women (1994)
This third film version of Louisa May Alcott's classic novel (1868-1869) centers on the coming-of-age of the March sisters: Jo (played by Winona Ryder), Meg (played by Trini Alvarado), Beth (played by Claire Danes), and Amy (played by Kirsten Dunst and Samantha Mathis). Susan Sarandon stars as their brave mother, Marmee.

Lolita (1962)
The first film adaptation of Vladimir Nabokov's 1955 novel stars James Mason as a professor so obsessed with a fourteen-year-old girl (played by Sue Lyon) that he marries her mother (played by Shelley Winters) in order to be close to her.

The Long, Hot Summer (1958)
Orson Welles plays the head of a wealthy Southern family who is protective of his daughter (played by Joanne Woodward). When a drifter (played by Paul Newman) arrives in town and has his eye on her, problems arise. The film is based on a short story by William Faulkner.

The Long Walk Home (1990)
Whoopi Goldberg stars in this powerful story about the relationship between an affluent white housewife (played by Sissy Spacek) and her African American maid (played by Goldberg), whom she drives to work during the 1956 bus boycott in Montgomery, Alabama.

Losing Isaiah (1995)
Jessica Lange plays a white woman who adopts an African American baby after his crack-addicted mother (played by Halle Berry) abandons him. Four years later, after the biological mother rehabilitates herself, she fights for custody of her child.

Madame Bovary (1949)
Jennifer Jones portrays Emma Bovary, a young woman whose need for romance and numerous love affairs leads to her downfall. Louis Jourdan and James Mason costar in this adaptation of Gustave Flaubert's 1857 novel.

Madame Curie (1943)
Greer Garson portrays the famous Austrian scientist who discovered radium. The film, which also stars Walter Pidgeon as her husband, tells the story behind the discovery of the element. Garson received an Academy Award nomination, as did Pidgeon.

The Major and the Minor (1942)
In Billy Wilder's directorial debut, a struggling young woman (played by Ginger Rogers) falls in love with the head of a military school (played by Ray Milland) whom she meets on a train while she is disguised as a twelve-year-old.

Marjorie Morningstar (1958)
After an ambitious young Jewish girl (played by Natalie Wood) vows to become successful in New York City, she must adjust to life as a housewife. The film is based on the popular 1955 novel by Herman Wouk.

Marnie (1964)
Tippi Hedren plays a glamorous woman who steals because of a trauma that she experienced in her childhood. Sean Connery plays a rich businessman who attempts to save her from her problem by marrying her. Directed by Alfred Hitchcock.

Mary of Scotland (1936)
Legendary Western director John Ford creates this biography of the sixteenth century queen of Scotland (played by Katharine Hepburn) who was executed for treason by order of England's Queen Elizabeth I (played by Bette Davis). Frederic March plays Mary's lover Bothwell.

Mary Poppins (1964)
This musical from Walt Disney tells the story of two English children who are taken under the care of a nanny with magical powers. Julie Andrews, in her film debut, won an Academy Award for her role as the governess.

Meet Me in St. Louis (1944)
A bright musical set in St. Louis during the year leading up to the 1904 World's Fair in which Judy Garland and Margaret O'Brien play sisters, this film is a nostalgic celebration of traditional family values.

The Member of the Wedding (1953)
A twelve-year-old girl (played by Julie Harris) anxiously awaits her elder brother's wedding, thinking that she herself will play a major role in the occasion. Adapted from Carson McCullers' 1950 play of her 1946 novel, this film was the first Hollywood production to cast all the leads from the stage version.

Men Don't Leave (1990)
A mother (played by Jessica Lange) struggles to keep her family intact when she moves to the city after the death of her husband (played by Tom Mason). She and her sons (played by Chris O'Donnell and Charlie Korsmo) survive after they discover their inner strengths and mutual desire to hold the family together.

Mildred Pierce (1945)
Joan Crawford plays a divorced mother who works her way up from a waitress to the owner of a restaurant chain while struggling to maintain a positive relationship with her thankless daughter (played by Ann Blyth). Crawford won an Academy Award for her performance.

Million Dollar Mermaid (1952)
Esther Williams portrays famous Australian aquatic starlet Annette Kellerman, who was one of the first women to wear one-piece suits and perform in vaudeville swimming acts.

Min and Bill (1930)
Marie Dressler and Wallace Beery costar as a luckless, socially unacceptable couple fighting to maintain custody of their daughter (played by Dorothy Jordan). Dressler won an Academy Award for Best Actress.

The Miracle Worker (1962)
Adapted from a long-running Broadway play based on the childhood of Helen Keller, this often-tense film recreates the struggle of a determined woman (played by Anne Bancroft) to teach an unruly deaf and blind girl (played by Patty Duke) how to communicate. Both Bancroft and Duke won Academy Awards for their performances.

Misery (1990)
Adapted from Stephen King's 1987 horror novel, this film is about a best-selling novelist (played by James Caan) injured in an automobile accident in a remote mountain area, where an insane nurse (played by Kathy Bates) holds him prisoner. Angered by the author's killing off of his fictional heroine, the nurse, who calls herself his "number one fan," forces him to resurrect the character in another novel. Bates won an Academy Award for her role.

The Misfits (1961)
Marilyn Monroe's last film was written for her by her third husband, playwright Arthur Miller. The contemporary Western focuses on a divorcée (played by Monroe) who joins a roundup of wild horses with a middle-aged cowboy (played by Clark Gable) with whom she is romantically involved. The arrival of a rodeo rider (played by Montgomery Clift) creates a love triangle.

Mommie Dearest (1981)
Faye Dunaway plays screen star Joan Crawford in this adaptation of the book by Crawford's adopted daughter, Christina. The film chronicles Christina's troubled life with her cruel foster mother.

Morning Glory (1933)
Katharine Hepburn won her first Academy Award for her portrayal of an aspiring young actress from New England whose strong will carries her to the New York stage. The film was remade in 1958 as *Stage Struck*, starring Susan Strasberg.

Mother Teresa (1986)
Ann and Jeanette Petrie spent five years making this documentary about this Nobel Peace Prize-winning nun, who travels around the world helping the poor and starving and instilling a sense of holiness into lives without hope.

Mrs. Miniver (1942)
Greer Garson stars as Kay Miniver, the embodiment of English motherhood, in this film that follows the courageous woman and the English village in which she and her husband (played by Walter Pidgeon) live while coping with German air raids during World War II.

Mrs. Soffel (1984)
Diane Keaton stars as the moral wife of a prison warden who falls in love with a condemned murderer (played by Mel Gibson) and helps him escape. The film is based on a true incident that occurred in 1901. Directed by Gillian Armstrong.

Ms. .45 (1981)
After an attractive mute woman (played by Zoe Tamerlis) is brutally raped twice in one day, she goes insane and seeks revenge with a gun. A female version of the *Death Wish* films popularized by Charles Bronson.

My Fair Lady (1964)
Adapted from a Broadway musical based on George Ber-

nard Shaw's play *Pygmalion* (1913), this film stars Rex Harrison as a professor who falls in love with the Cockney flower seller (played by Audrey Hepburn) whom he transforms into a "proper" lady.

Myra Breckinridge (1970)
In this adaptation of Gore Vidal's odd 1968 novel, a male film critic undergoes a sex change operation and emerges as a glamorous woman (played by Raquel Welch).

National Velvet (1945)
Based on Enid Bagnold's 1935 novel, this classic children's film is about a girl (played by Elizabeth Taylor) who trains a horse to win a national race.

Nell (1995)
Jodie Foster plays a young woman who lives in complete isolation from society and speaks her own language, thereby intriguing social workers who want to study her. Foster received an Academy Award nomination for her performance.

Nell Gwyn (1934)
When England's King Charles II (played by Cedric Hardwicke) invites a commoner (played by Anna Neagle) to sup with him, the woman arouses the jealous wrath of his mistress (played by Jeanne de Casalis). The king grows fond of the young woman, but after he becomes ill and dies, she is left to grieve at the palace gates.

Neptune's Daughter (1949)
This romantic comedy revolves around the friends of a premier swimsuit designer and manufacturer. Esther Williams, Red Skelton, Ricardo Montalban, and Betty Garrett star.

Nine to Five (1980)
Jane Fonda, Lily Tomlin, and Dolly Parton play secretaries who revolt against their domineering, sexist boss (played by Dabney Coleman). While holding him prisoner in his own home, they take advantage of his absence from the office to reorganize their workplace.

Ninotchka (1939)
In this Ernst Lubitsch comedy, a Soviet commissar (played by Greta Garbo) is sent to Paris to investigate on the lack of production of three trade envoys who are enchanted by capitalism. While in the French capital, Garbo is seduced by a playboy (played by Melvyn Douglas).

Norma Rae (1979)
Sally Field won an Academy Award for her performance as a common textile mill worker and widowed mother who leads the fight to unionize her factory. Her dedication to the cause strains her relationship with her new husband (played by Beau Bridges), adding to the pressures with which she must cope.

Operation Petticoat (1959)
In this madcap World War II comedy, the captain (played by Cary Grant) of a U.S. Navy submarine operating in the South Pacific takes aboard a group of Navy nurses. The success of this film later inspired a television series of the same name.

Orphans of the Storm (1921)
With the French Revolution as a backdrop, Lillian Gish and her sister Dorothy Gish costar in this silent film about two girls who are separated after their father is murdered. One girl is blind and reared by thieves; the other is reared by aristocrats who betray her. Directed by D. W. Griffith.

The Other Side of the Mountain (1972)
This melodramatic film is based on the life of Jill Kinmont, an Olympic-bound skier paralyzed by a fall. Marilyn Hassett plays the indomitable athlete whose determination carries her through, even after she fails to recover as expected. Hassett also played Kinmont in a sequel in 1978.

Passion Fish (1992)
A character study of two women with sharply contrasting backgrounds. Mary McDonnell plays an obnoxious soap opera queen who abuses the nurses who care for her after she is paralyzed. She begins to change, however, after an African American nurse (played by Alfre Woodard) comes to care for her.

Pat and Mike (1952)
The popular screen duo of Spencer Tracy and Katharine Hepburn star in this story about a world-class athlete (played by Hepburn) who finds romance in her trainer and manager (played by Tracy). Athlete Chuck Connors makes a cameo appearance.

A Patch of Blue (1965)
After a blind white woman (played by Elizabeth Hartman) falls in love with a man (played by Sidney Poitier) whom she does not realize is African American, she must deal with her racist mother (played by Shelley Winters) and grandfather (played by Wallace Ford).

Peggy Sue Got Married (1986)
Kathleen Turner stars as a forty-three-year-old mother of two contemplating divorce from her immature husband (played by Nicholas Cage). She gets a chance to reshape her life when she attends her high school reunion and is inexplicably sent back to her high school days. Directed by Francis Coppola.

The Perils of Pauline (1947)
An ode to the days of Hollywood silent films, this musical comedy, adorned with Frank Loessner songs, stars Betty Hutton as Pearl White, the silent film star who became famous as the frantic heroine of cliffhanger serials.

Personal Best (1982)
The lives of two women (played by Mariel Hemingway and Patrice Donnelly) training for the Olympics become vastly more complicated when they fall in love with each other.

Pinky (1949)
In this critically acclaimed film, a young African American woman (played by Jeanne Crain) who is nicknamed "Pinky" because of her light complexion, returns to the home of her grandmother (played by Ethel Waters) in the South, where she encounters the harsh realities of racism.

Places in the Heart (1984)
A young widow (played by Sally Field) living in Texas

during the Great Depression struggles to support her two children and maintain her home. John Malkovich and Danny Glover costar. Field won an Academy Award for her role.

Pocahontas (1995)
This animated Disney film tells the story of the historical Powhatan maiden Pocahontas and her romance with the English settler John Smith. Although clearly romanticized, the film has been celebrated for its strong, positive depiction of American Indians in general and Pocahontas in particular.

Poetic Justice (1993)
In John Singleton's second film, a young poet named Justice (played by Janet Jackson) escapes Los Angeles after witnessing a murder and embarks on a road trip up the coast of California with three others (played by Tupac Shakur, Regina King, and Joe Torry). Maya Angelou wrote the poetry that Jackson recites in the film.

The Poor Little Rich Girl (1917)
Mary Pickford utilizes her unrivaled ability to play younger characters in this silent comedy based on Eleanor Gates's 1912 novel and 1916 play. The story revolves around a delirious young girl who relives all the joys and sorrows of life through dreams.

Pretty Woman (1990)
In this romantic fantasy, Julia Roberts plays a prostitute whom an unimaginably rich businessman (played by Richard Gere) hires to pose as his companion for a week. What begins as a short-term job inevitably blossoms into a serious romance.

The Prime of Miss Jean Brodie (1969)
Maggie Smith won an Academy Award for her convincing portrayal of an ostensibly free-spirited schoolteacher at an upper-class Edinburgh girls' school during the 1930's. Miss Brodie's romantic ideals alarm the school's administrators and confuse her students, leading to her downfall. Based on Muriel Spark's 1961 novel.

Prizzi's Honor (1985)
A Mafia hit man (played by Jack Nicholson) and a hit woman (played by Kathleen Turner) fall in love in this black comedy directed by John Huston. Costar Anjelica Huston (John's daughter) won an Academy Award for Best Supporting Actress.

Pygmalion (1938)
Leslie Howard stars in this film that he codirected with Anthony Asquith. He plays a phonetics professor who coaches an ignorant Cockney flower seller (played by Wendy Hiller) into becoming a cultured lady. George Bernard Shaw wrote the Academy Award-winning screenplay from his own 1913 play, which was later adapted into the musical *My Fair Lady*.

Queen Christina (1933)
Greta Garbo plays a sixteenth century Swedish queen who travels through her country disguised as a man. She meets the Spanish ambassador (played by John Gilbert) and shares lodgings with him. After discovering that Christina is a woman, the ambassador falls in love with her, and she gives up her throne in order to be with him.

Rachel, Rachel (1968)
Joanne Woodward plays a thirty-five-year-old schoolteacher whose life in her small town provides her with no excitement. Her mother is demanding and her job is frustrating. Her effort to climb out of her depression by finding romance works only briefly, but she nevertheless gains renewed self-confidence. When her mother moves to another town, she follows, ready for a fresh start in her life.

Rambling Rose (1991)
Told from the vantage point of a thirteen-year-old boy, this film is the story of the impact that a nineteen-year-old housekeeper (played by Laura Dern) has on the rural Georgia home in which she works. Dern won an Academy Award for Best Supporting Actress for her performance.

Rebecca (1940)
In Alfred Hitchcock's first American-made film, Joan Fontaine plays a naïve woman traveling in Europe who marries a British nobleman (played by Laurence Olivier) and learns that she must live in the shadow of his first wife, Rebecca. Judith Anderson costars as Olivier's housekeeper. Based on Daphne du Maurier's 1938 novel.

Red Dust (1932)
Jean Harlow and Clark Gable costar in this romance about an Indochina plantation overseer and the prostitute whom he admires. Mary Astor plays a married woman who is also interested in him. This film, steamy for 1932, was remade in 1953 as *Mogambo*, with Gable repeating his role.

Remodeling Her Husband (1920)
The only motion picture directed by Lillian Gish, this silent film is a gentle romance is about a young woman, played by her sister Dorothy Gish, who leaves her husband (played by James Rennie) when she discovers his infidelity. After the woman goes to work for her father, her former husband returns, hoping for a reconciliation. She hesitates to go along with him until he threatens to commit suicide.

Rodeo Girl (1980)
When the wife (played by Katharine Ross) of a rodeo champ (played by Bo Hopkins) tries roping and bronco riding herself, she discovers that she has the potential to succeed. She gets so caught up in the rodeo circuit that she does not want to quit even after learning that she is pregnant, thereby causing a conflict with her husband.

Romola (1925)
Lillian Gish plays a young woman who realizes that her beloved husband has been unfaithful to her and that he is the father of a child. Based on George Eliot's 1863 novel. This silent film was critically acclaimed, but Gish never was entirely satisfied with her performance.

The Rose (1979)
Bette Midler makes her film debut as a singer whose life begins coming apart under the pressures of fame and drug

and alcohol abuse. Loosely based on the brief but spectacular career of rock singer Janis Joplin.

Rosemary's Baby (1968)
Based on Ira Levin's 1967 novel, this film tells the story of Rosemary (played by Mia Farrow), a young pregnant wife who believes that she is being controlled by a den of witches and their leaders (played by Ruth Gordon and Sidney Blackmer).

Ryan's Daughter (1970)
Set in Ireland in 1916, this visually stunning film tells the story of a schoolteacher's wife (played by Sarah Miles) who falls in love with a British officer (played by Chris Jones). Robert Mitchum and John Mills costar in this David Lean film.

The Scarlet Letter (1926)
Silent film star Lillian Gish portrays Hester Prynne in this adaptation of Nathaniel Hawthorne's classic 1850 novel about sin. The story concerns Prynne, a young woman accused of adultery in a small Puritan town in Massachusetts, and her relationship with her lover.

She (1925)
Betty Blythe portrays Queen Ayesha in this seventh and final silent version of adventure novelist H. Rider Haggard's fantasy tale about a lost tribe and a flame of eternal life in Africa. Carlyle Blackwell costars.

She Done Him Wrong (1933)
Mae West stars as a beautiful singer in this comedy, which is based on her own play *Diamond Lil* (1928). After her jailbird former boyfriend threatens to kill her if she is unfaithful to him, she becomes romantically involved with a police officer (played by Cary Grant) who protects her.

She's Gotta Have It (1986)
Spike Lee's first feature film is about a liberated young African American woman (played by Tracy Camila Johns) who juggles her free time among three lovers (played by Tommy Redmond Hicks, John Canada Terrel, and Spike Lee). The commercial success of this low-budget film helped launch a renaissance of African American filmmaking.

The Silence of the Lambs (1991)
A female FBI trainee (played by Jodie Foster) is assigned to help capture a serial killer by working with an imprisoned psychiatrist, Dr. Hannibal Lecter (played by Anthony Hopkins), who is criminally insane but brilliant. Foster won her second Academy Award for her portrayal of the young trainee.

Silkwood (1983)
Meryl Streep stars in this biography of Karen Silkwood, an Oklahoma nuclear plant worker who was killed in a car crash under mysterious circumstances just before she was about to expose nuclear safety violations.

Sleeping Beauty (1959)
Based on Charles Perrault's seventeenth century story, this classic fairy tale is one of several Walt Disney animated films about damsels rescued by handsome princes.

Snow White and the Seven Dwarfs (1937)
The first animated feature film produced by Walt Disney, this story is based on a Brothers Grimm fairy tale. A beautiful young princess flees a jealous queen and hides in the forest with seven little men who work in a mine. The queen tricks her into eating a poison apple that puts her to sleep, but she is eventually awakened by the kiss of a handsome prince.

So Proudly We Hail! (1943)
Claudette Colbert, Paulette Goddard, and Veronica Lake star in this patriotic film about army nurses on Bataan during World War II. Goddard received an Academy Award nomination for Best Supporting Actress.

The Song of Bernadette (1943)
Jennifer Jones won an Academy Award for Best Actress for her portrayal of a nineteenth century French peasant who sees a vision of the Virgin Mary in the town of Lourdes.

Sophie's Choice (1982)
Meryl Streep won an Academy Award for her unforgettable performance as a guilt-ridden survivor of a Nazi concentration camp. While a Southern writer (played by Peter MacNicol) observes her affair with a biologist (played by Kevin Kline), he falls in love with her. The film is adapted from William Styron's 1979 novel.

Splendor in the Grass (1961)
Two high school students (played by Natalie Wood and Warren Beatty) fall in love in Kansas during the 1920's and have difficulty controlling their passions. Directed by Elia Kazan.

The Star (1952)
An actress (played by Bette Davis) whose popularity is fading tries to make a comeback against the objections of the man (played by Sterling Hayden) who loves her. After she views her performance in an audition, however, she realizes her mistake and abandons her comeback attempt. Some critics have noted the similarities between the film's theme and Davis' own acting career.

Star 80 (1983)
In this true story, Mariel Hemingway plays Dorothy Stratten, the glamorous *Playboy* model who was brutally killed by her manager-husband (played by Eric Roberts), who could not cope with her growing success.

A Star Is Born (1954)
Based on David O. Selznick's 1937 musical, this film stars Judy Garland as a young actress who is discovered by a screen giant. Her fame grows, while his declines. Garland received an Academy Award nomination. In 1976, a remake starring Barbra Streisand was made.

Steel Magnolias (1989)
This film, based on Robert Harling's 1988 play, focuses on the trials and tribulations of six Southern women who often gather at a local beauty shop to discuss their lives. Olympia Dukakis, Sally Field, Daryl Hannah, Shirley MacLaine, Dolly Parton, and Julia Roberts head the cast.

The Stepford Wives (1975)
Based on Ira Levin's best-selling 1972 novel, this strange film is about a group of Connecticut men who replace their wives with android replicas designed to be beautiful and obedient.

Sunday, Bloody Sunday (1971)
In this unusual tale about a bisexual love triangle, a divorced woman in her thirties (played by Glenda Jackson) and a London doctor (played by Peter Finch) fall in love with the same man (played by Murray Head).

Sunset Boulevard (1950)
A classic indictment of Hollywood's ruthless insistence on youth and beauty, this film features Gloria Swanson as an aging silent film star who destroys an unemployed screenwriter (played by William Holden) in her quest for a comeback.

The Swan (1956)
Based on the play *A hattyú* (1921) by Hungarian playwright Ferenc Molnár, this simple story follows a prince (played by Alec Guinness) in his search for a wife, whom he eventually finds (played by Grace Kelly). Estelle Winwood and Agnes Moorehead costar.

Sweet Dreams (1985)
Jessica Lange has the lead role in this treatment of the life of country singer Patsy Cline, who struggled to build a stable life for her family.

Sweet Rosie O'Grady (1943)
A former burlesque entertainer (played by Betty Grable) is investigated by a reporter (played by Adolphe Menjou) in this musical directed by Irving Cummings.

Swing Shift (1984)
Goldie Hawn stars in this 1940's era romance about a young woman who is left alone when her husband (played by Ed Harris) leaves to fight in World War II. America's labor force is drastically reduced because of the war, so Hawn goes to work on an assembly line, where she meets Lucky Lockhart (played by Kurt Russell).

Terms of Endearment (1983)
This stylish film written, produced, and directed by James L. Brooks covers thirty years of the lives of a Houston mother (played by Shirley MacLaine) and her daughter (played by Debra Winger). Jack Nicholson costars as the mother's neighbor.

Tess (1979)
Nastassia Kinski plays an exploited English peasant girl who resorts to murder in this screen adaptation of Thomas Hardy's novel *Tess of the D'Urbervilles* (1891). Directed by Roman Polanski.

That Hamilton Woman (1941)
Real-life husband and wife Laurence Olivier and Vivien Leigh portray the British naval hero Lord Nelson and Lady Emma Hamilton in this dramatization of one of England's most legendary scandals.

Thelma and Louise (1991)
Two women (played by Susan Sarandon and Geena Davis) go off for a rustic weekend, but their plans change when a stop at a roadside bar turns into a disaster. After they kill a would-be rapist, they begin a chase with the police from several states in pursuit.

The Three Faces of Eve (1957)
Nunnally Johnson directed this compelling story about a troubled woman (played by Joanne Woodward) with three different personalities. Lee J. Cobb plays the psychiatrist who tries to cure her so that she can lead a normal life.

Three Women (1977)
Robert Altman directed this unconventional but critically acclaimed study of two young women who work together in a convalescent home and share a motel apartment in a small Southern California desert community. Shelley Duvall plays a confident physical therapist who tries to model her life on what she reads in *Good Housekeeping* magazine. Sissy Spacek plays her strange roommate, and Janice Rule plays an embittered older woman.

The Trojan Women (1972)
Adapted from Euripides' ancient tragedy about the predicament of women during the Trojan War, this Greek-American film is most noteworthy for its unusually strong female cast: Katharine Hepburn, Irene Pappas, Genevieve Bujold, and Vanessa Redgrave .

The Turning Point (1977)
Anne Bancroft and Shirley MacLaine were both nominated for Academy Awards for their roles as lifelong dance rivals who are reunited in this dramatic look at the world of ballet. The dance scenes are the highlight of the film, which also stars Mikhail Baryshnikov.

Unfaithfully Yours (1948)
A symphony conductor (played by Rex Harrison) thinks that his wife (played by Linda Darnell) is cheating on him, so he fantasizes several solutions to the problem. Barbara Lawrence, Rudy Vallee, and Lionel Stander costar. A remake was made in 1984 by Howard Zieff.

An Unmarried Woman (1978)
Paul Mazursky directed this melodrama about a woman's attempt to put her life back together after her husband (played by Michael Murphy) suddenly leaves her. Jill Clayburgh received an Academy Award nomination as the distraught woman.

The Unsinkable Molly Brown (1964)
Based on the life story of Margaret "Molly" Tobin Brown, famous for her heroism during the sinking of the *Titanic*, this large-scale musical depicts her as a feisty, adventurous country girl who rises to social prominence and wealth. Debbie Reynolds received an Academy Award nomination for Best Actress.

Up the Sandbox (1972)
Barbra Streisand plays a young housewife feeling trapped by her marriage and pregnancy who is trying to make sense

of her life. This light comedy is adapted from Anne Richardson Roiphe's best-selling 1970 novel.

Victor/Victoria (1982)
In this unusual comedy directed by Blake Edwards, his wife Julie Andrews stars as a down-on-her-luck singer in Paris during the Depression who becomes famous by pretending to be a man working as a female impersonator. James Garner plays an American gangster who questions his own sexuality when he is attracted to "Victor." Both Andrews and Lesley Ann Warren, who plays the gangster's girlfriend, received Academy Award nominations.

Wait Until Dark (1967)
Audrey Hepburn stars as a blind woman harassed by a psychotic killer (played by Alan Arkin) in her own Greenwich Village house. The film, based on Frederick Knott's 1967 play, earned for Hepburn an Academy Award nomination.

Way Down East (1920)
In this silent film, a young orphan (played by Lillian Gish) is seduced and gives birth to a baby which then dies. The girl tries to forget about the tragedy by working for a farm family, but when they learn about her past, the father forces her to leave.

What Ever Happened to Baby Jane? (1962)
Bette Davis stars in this unsettling film as a former child star who spends her last years tormenting her sister (played by Joan Crawford) and dreaming of lost fame. This was one the last films for both actresses.

What's Love Got to Do with It (1993)
Laurence Fishburne and Angela Bassett both received Oscar nominations for their portrayals of real-life rock stars Ike and Tina Turner in this film. Beginning with Tina's youth in Tennessee, the film chronicles the duo's successful career, their tumultuous marriage and divorce, Tina's solo return to stardom, and Ike's imprisonment.

Who's Afraid of Virginia Woolf? (1966)
Based on Edward Albee's 1963 play, this intense film explores the troubled relationship of a middle-aged couple (played by Richard Burton and Elizabeth Taylor) who psychologically intimidate a younger couple (played by George Segal and Sandy Dennis). The film set new standards in the presentation of adult material, and Taylor and Dennis both won Academy Awards for their performances.

Widow's Peak (1994)
Set in an Irish community of the 1920's, this comedy centers on a psychological battle between two spinsters (played by Joan Plowright and Mia Farrow) and a widow (played by Natasha Richardson), resulting in an unusual ending.

Wisecracks (1992)
The difficulty of being a woman in the world of standup comedy is the theme of this documentary. Mae West, Lucille Ball, Ellen DeGeneres, Whoopi Goldberg, and Paula Poundstone are among the comedians featured and discussed in this film. Directed by Gail Singer.

The Witches of Eastwick (1987)
Three housewives (played by Cher, Michelle Pfeiffer, and Susan Sarandon) who live in a small New England town summon the Devil (played by Jack Nicholson) to add excitement to their lives. The film is based on John Updike's 1984 novel.

Woman of the Year (1942)
One of nine films in which Spencer Tracy and Katharine Hepburn played opposite each other, this comedy is about a sportswriter who falls in love with a columnist.

A Woman Rebels (1936)
Katharine Hepburn plays a young nineteenth century woman who defies her father (played by Donald Crisp) and lives on her own with her infant daughter. After she is abandoned by her lover, she meets another man (played by Herbert Marshall), with whom she gradually falls in love.

A Woman Under the Influence (1974)
Gena Rowlands received an Academy Award nomination for her role in John Cassavetes' film about a failing marriage. Peter Falk costars as her husband.

The Women (1939)
Adapted from the 1936 Clare Boothe Luce play by Anita Loos and Jane Murfin, this drama has a cast of more than 125 women. The plot centers on the divorce of a socialite. Norma Shearer, Joan Crawford, Rosalind Russell, Paulette Goddard, and Ruth Hussey are among the actresses featured.

Women in Love (1970)
Glenda Jackson won an Academy Award for her role in this adaptation of D. H. Lawrence's 1920 novel. Set in England during the 1920's, the film is about two love affairs occurring simultaneously.

Working Girl (1988)
Melanie Griffith plays an ambitious secretary who is smarter than she appears. Sigourney Weaver plays her heartless boss, and Harrison Ford stars as a colleague romantically involved with both women.

Yentl (1983)
Barbra Streisand directed, produced, cowrote, and starred in this adaptation of Isaac Bashevis Singer's tale set in the early twentieth century, about a rabbi's daughter who dresses up as a boy so that she can attend an all-male religious school.

Women's
Issues

LIST OF ENTRIES BY CATEGORY

FEMINISM

HEALTH, SEXUALITY, AND REPRODUCTIVE RIGHTS

Thalidomide babies
Time Has Come, The
Toxic shock syndrome
Tubal ligation
Turner's syndrome
Ultrasound
Yeast infections

LITERATURE, MEDIA, AND THE ARTS
Acting
Against Our Will
Architecture
Art, images of women in
Autobiographies, diaries, and journals by women
Backlash
Baez, Joan
Barbie dolls
Beauty pageants
Behind the Sex of God
Blues music and women
Brown, Rita Mae
Century of Struggle
Chicago, Judy
Comedy and comedians
Comic strips, women's issues in
Common Sense Book of Baby and Child Care, The
Cosmetics and beauty industry
Crafts and home arts
Dance
Diary of a Mad Housewife
Dinner Party, The
Directors and producers, theater
Drama and dramatists
Dress for success
Dress reform
Fashion, women's
Fashion industry and women
Female Eunuch, The
Feminine Mystique, The
Feminist Anti-Censorship Task Force (FACT)
Feminist art movement
Feminist film theory
Feminist literary criticism
Fiction writers
Filmmaking
Films, women's
Flappers
Folk music and women
Folklore, women's
Food and cooking
Gilman, Charlotte Perkins
Herland
Hite Report, The
Humanae Vitae
Humor, women's
Journalism, women in
Kingston, Maxine Hong
Ladder, The
Lang, K. D.
Lin, Maya Ying
Literature, images of women in
Madwoman in the Attic, The
Magazines, men's
Magazines, women's
Male and Female
Miniskirts
Ms. magazine
Music
Music, women's
Musicians, women as
"Myth of the Vaginal Orgasm, The"
National Association of Media Women
Off Our Backs
O'Keeffe, Georgia
Olivia Records
Our Bodies, Ourselves
Painting and painters
Parker, Dorothy
Periodicals, feminist
Photography and photographers
Plath, Sylvia
Poetry and poets
Printmaking and printmakers
Publishing houses, women's
Quilting bees
Rand, Ayn
Rich, Adrienne
Room of One's Own, A
Rubyfruit Jungle
Science fiction, feminist
Sculpting and sculptors
Second Sex, The
Sexual Politics
Shoes
Silent Scream, The
Sontag, Susan
Stein, Gertrude
Talk shows
Television, women in
Time Has Come, The
Vietnam Women's Memorial
Vindication of the Rights of Woman, A
Visual art
Walker, Alice
Woman's Bible, The
Women's Review of Books, The
Women's studies journals
Year of the Woman

MARRIAGE AND FAMILY
Adoption
Aid to Families with Dependent Children (AFDC)
Alimony
Antimiscegenation laws
Battered woman syndrome
Biological clock
Birth control and family planning
Blended families
Breadwinner ethic
Career vs. homemaker debate
Child care
Child custody and visitation rights
Child rearing
Children's Defense Fund (CDF)
Common-law marriage
Common Sense Book of Baby and Child Care, The
Dating and courtship
Diary of a Mad Housewife
Divorce
Domestic violence
Dowry
Electra and Oedipus complexes
Empty nest
Families, nontraditional
Family and Medical Leave Act of 1993
Family Assistance Plan
Family legislation
Family life
Family planning services
Family Protection Act of 1979
Family Support Act of 1988
Father-daughter relationships
Frontiero v. Richardson
Girlhood
Heads of household, female
Home economics
Homemakers and homemaking
Housework technologies
Hyphenated names
Incest
Infanticide
Lesbian mothers
Lucy Stone League
Maiden names
Mail-order brides
Marital rape
Marriage and marital status
Marriage contract
Miscegenation

MOVEMENTS AND HISTORICAL EVENTS

NOTABLE WOMEN

ORGANIZATIONS

POLITICS AND CIVIL RIGHTS

National Woman Suffrage Association (NWSA)
National Woman's Party
New Deal and women
New Left and women
Nineteenth Amendment
Pacifism and nonviolence
Paul, Alice
Politics
President's Commission on the Status of Women
Prison, women in
Property rights, women's
Rankin, Jeannette
Religious Right and women
Republican Party and women
Reverse discrimination
Right to privacy
Roosevelt, Eleanor
Sauvé, Jeanne
Schlafly, Phyllis
Stanton, Elizabeth Cady
State government, women in
Stone, Lucy
Suffrage movement and suffragists
Supreme Court rulings on discrimination against women
Temperance movement and women
Title VII of the Civil Rights Act of 1964
Truth, Sojourner
United States Commission on Civil Rights
Voting patterns among women
Willard, Frances
Women in the Senate and House (WISH List)
Women's Peace Party
Year of the Woman

PSYCHOLOGY AND VIOLENCE

Against Our Will
Alcoholism and drug abuse among women
Assertiveness training
Battered woman syndrome
Biological clock
Bobbitt case
Brownmiller, Susan
Clitoridectomy
Communication, women's methods of
Consciousness-raising
Criminals, women as
Cross-dressing
Cult of True Womanhood
Date rape
Depression and women
Domestic violence
Eating disorders
Electra and Oedipus complexes
Empowerment
Empty nest
Father-daughter relationships
Feminist ethics
Gender differences
Genital mutilation
Hate crimes against women
Heterosexism
Homophobia
Incest
Infanticide
Insanity and women
Juvenile delinquency among girls
Machismo
Male and Female
Marital rape
Mead, Margaret
Mental health
Misogyny
Mother-child relationships
National Coalition Against Domestic Violence
Phallocentrism
Pornography
Prince Charming syndrome
Prison, women in
Problem that has no name
Psychiatry and women
Psychological theories on women
Racism
Rape
Rape crisis centers
Rape trauma syndrome
Rape victims, treatment of
Self-esteem, women's
Sexism
Sexual stereotypes
Socialization of girls and young women
Son preference
Stereotypes of women
Take Back the Night
Violence against women
Violence Against Women Act of 1994

RACE AND ETHNICITY

Abolitionist movement and women
Affirmative action
African American women
American Indian women
Americans for Indian Opportunity
Amish and Mennonite women
Antimiscegenation laws
Appalachian women
Asian American women
Baez, Joan
Berdache
Bethune, Mary McLeod
Black feminism
Black Panther Party and women
Civil Rights movement and women
Colored Women's League
Combahee River Collective
Curanderas
Davis, Angela Yvonne
Deer, Ada Elizabeth
Demographics, women's
Ethnic identity
Executive Orders 11246 and 11375
Fourteenth and Fifteenth Amendments
French Canadian women
Grimké, Angelina and Sarah
Hawaiian and Pacific Islander women
Hernandez, Aileen Clarke
Hill, Anita Faye
Hooks, Bell
Huerta, Dolores Fernández
Immigrant women
Jewish women
Kingston, Maxine Hong
Latinas
Liliuokalani
Lin, Maya Ying
Machismo
Mankiller, Wilma P.
Martínez, Vilma Socorro
Medicine woman
Mexican American Women's National Association (MANA)
Miscegenation
Moynihan Report
Multiculturalism
Muslim women
Nation of Islam and women
National Black Women's Political Leadership Caucus
National Council of Negro Women
Novello, Antonia Coello
Picture brides
Plantation life and women
Quinceañeras
Racism
Reverse discrimination
Slavery
Truth, Sojourner
Tubman, Harriet
Walker, Alice

Womanist
Women of All Red Nations (WARN)
Women of color

RELIGION AND SPIRITUALITY

Behind the Sex of God
Christianity and women
Clergy, women as
Daly, Mary
Day, Dorothy
Eddy, Mary Baker
Evangelists and faith healers, women as
Eve
Feminism, spiritual
Goddess, concept of the
Humanae Vitae
Islam and women
Judaism and women
Lilith
Missionary societies and women
Mormon women
Mott, Lucretia
Nation of Islam and women
New Age movement and women
Nuns and convent life
Rabbis, women as
Religion
Religious movements founded by women
Religious Right and women
Spirituality movement, women's
Stanton, Elizabeth Cady
Starhawk
Theologians and women's theology
Truth, Sojourner
Wicca
Witchcraft
Womanchurch
Woman's Bible, The

SPORTS

All American Girls Professional Baseball League
Association for Intercollegiate Athletics for Women
Auto racing, women in
Baseball, women in
Basketball, women in
Battle of the Sexes
Golf, women in
Gymnastics, women in
Ice skating, women in
Little League Baseball
Navratilova, Martina
Olympic Games, women in the
Physical fitness for women
Professional sports, women in
Softball, women in
Sports, women in
Swimming, women in
Tennis, women in
Track and field, women in
Volleyball, women in
Women's Sports Foundation

WAR AND THE MILITARY

Addams, Jane
American Revolution and women
Army Nurse Corps
Balch, Emily Greene
Barton, Clara
Civil War and women
Combat, women in
"Don't ask, don't tell" policy
Draft and women
Frontiero v. Richardson
Gulf War, women in the
Hague Women's Peace Conference, The
Howe, Julia Ward
Jeannette Rankin Brigade
Kellogg-Briand Pact
Kent State riots
Lesbians in the military
Medical units in the armed forces, women's
Military, women in the
Military academies, integration of
Military officers, women as
Pacifism and nonviolence
Peace movement and women
Personnel Administrator of Massachusetts v. Feeney
Pilots, women as
Rankin, Jeannette
Red Cross and women
SPAR
Tailhook scandal
Veterans and reservists, women as
Vietnam War, women in the
Vietnam Women's Memorial
War and women
War Brides Act
Women Accepted for Voluntary Emergency Service (WAVES)
Women's Airforce Service Pilots (WASPs)
Women's Army Corps (WAC)
Women's International League for Peace and Freedom (WILPF)
Women's Peace Party
Women's Reserve in the Marine Corps
World War I and women
World War II, women's military roles in

Index of Personages

A page number or range in boldface type indicates a full article devoted to the individual. Page numbers in italic type indicate photographs or other images.

Index

A page number or range in boldface type indicates a full article devoted to that topic. Page numbers in italic type indicate photographs, maps, tables, charts, and graphs.